Understanding Administrative Law

Carolina Academic Press Understanding Series

Understanding Administrative Law, Seventh Edition
Kristin E. Hickman

Understanding Alternative Dispute Resolution
Kristen M. Blankley and Maureen A. Weston

Understanding Animal Law
Adam Karp

Understanding Antitrust and Its Economic Implications, Seventh Edition
E. Thomas Sullivan and Jeffrey L. Harrison

Understanding Bankruptcy, Fourth Edition
Jeffrey Ferriell and Edward J. Janger

Understanding California Community Property Law, Second Edition
Jo Carrillo

Understanding Capital Punishment Law, Fourth Edition
Linda E. Carter, Ellen S. Kreitzberg, and Scott W. Howe

Understanding Civil Procedure, Sixth Edition
Gene R. Shreve, Peter Raven-Hansen, and Charles Gardner Geyh

Understanding Civil Procedure: The California Edition
Walter W. Heiser, Gene R. Shreve, Peter Raven-Hansen, and Charles Geyh

Understanding Civil Rights Litigation, Second Edition
Howard M. Wasserman

Understanding Conflict of Laws, Fourth Edition
William M. Richman, William L. Reynolds, and Chris A. Whytock

Understanding Constitutional Law, Fifth Edition
William D. Araiza

Understanding Contracts, Fourth Edition
Jeffrey Ferriell

Understanding Copyright Law, Seventh Edition
Marshall A. Leaffer

Understanding Corporate Law, Fifth Edition
Arthur R. Pinto and Douglas M. Branson

Understanding Corporate Taxation, Fourth Edition
Leandra Lederman and Michelle Kwon

Understanding Criminal Law, Ninth Edition
Joshua Dressler

Understanding Criminal Procedure: Vol. 1: Investigation, Eighth Edition
Joshua Dressler, Alan C. Michaels, and Ric Simmons

Understanding Criminal Procedure: Vol. 2: Adjudication, Fourth Edition
Joshua Dressler and Alan C. Michaels

Understanding Disability Law, Third Edition
Mark C. Weber

Understanding Election Law and Voting Rights
Michael R. Dimino, Bradley A. Smith, and Michael E. Solimine

Understanding Employee Benefits Law Second Edition
Kathryn L. Moore

Understanding Employment Discrimination Law, Third Edition
Thomas R. Haggard and Bruce N. Cameron

Understanding Employment Law, Third Edition
Paul M. Secunda, Richard A. Bales, and Jeffrey M. Hirsch

Understanding Environmental Law, Fourth Edition
Kevin A. Reilly and Philip Weinberg

Understanding Estate and Gift Taxation, Second Edition
Brant J. Hellwig and Robert T. Danforth

Understanding Evidence, Fifth Edition
Paul C. Giannelli

Understanding Family Law, Fourth Edition
John Gregory, Peter N. Swisher, and Robin Wilson

Understanding Federal and California Evidence
Paul C. Giannelli

Understanding Federal Courts and Jurisdiction, Second Edition
Linda Mullenix, Martin H. Redish, and Georgene Vairo

Understanding Federal Income Taxation, Sixth Edition
J. Martin Burke and Michael K. Friel

Understanding the First Amendment, Seventh Edition
Russell L. Weaver

Understanding Immigration Law, Third Edition
Kevin R. Johnson, Raquel Aldana, Bill Ong Hing, Leticia M. Saucedo, and Enid Trucios-Haynes

Understanding Insurance Law, Sixth Edition
Robert H. Jerry, II and Douglas Richmond

Understanding Intellectual Property Law, Fourth Edition
Tyler T. Ochoa, Shubha Ghosh, and Mary LaFrance

Understanding International Business and Financial Transactions, Fourth Edition
Jerold A. Friedland

Understanding International Criminal Law, Fourth Edition
Ellen S. Podgor, Roger S. Clark, and Lucian E. Dervan

Understanding International Law, Third Edition
Stephen C. McCaffrey

Understanding Jewish Law, Second Edition
Steven H. Resnicoff

Understanding Juvenile Law, Fifth Edition
Martin Gardner

Understanding Labor Law, Fifth Edition
Douglas E. Ray, Calvin William Sharpe, and Robert N. Strassfeld

Understanding the Law of Terrorism, Second Edition
Erik Luna and Wayne McCormack

Understanding the Law of Zoning and Land Use Controls, Third Edition
Barlow Burke

Understanding Lawyers' Ethics, Fifth Edition
Monroe H. Freedman and Abbe Smith

Understanding Local Government, Second Edition
Sandra Stevenson

Understanding Modern Real Estate Transactions, Fourth Edition
Alex M. Johnson, Jr.

Understanding Negotiable Instruments and Payment Systems, Second Edition
William H. Lawrence

Understanding Nonprofit and Tax Exempt Organizations, Third Edition
Nicholas P. Cafardi and Jaclyn Fabean Cherry

Understanding Partnership and LLC Taxation, Fourth Edition
Jerold A. Friedland

Understanding Patent Law, Third Edition
Amy L. Landers

Understanding Products Liability Law, Second Edition
Bruce L. Ottley, Rogelio A. Lasso, and Terrence F. Kiely

Understanding Property Law, Fourth Edition
John G. Sprankling

Understanding Remedies, Fourth Edition
James M. Fischer

Understanding Sales and Leases of Goods, Third Edition
William H. Henning, William H. Lawrence, and Henry Deeb Gabriel

Understanding Secured Transactions, Fifth Edition
William H. Lawrence, William H. Henning, and R. Wilson Freyermuth

Understanding Securities Law, Seventh Edition
Marc I. Steinberg

Understanding Sports Law
Timothy Davis and N. Jeremi Duru

Understanding Taxation of Business Entities, Second Edition
Walter D. Schwidetzky and Fred B. Brown

Understanding Torts, Sixth Edition
John L. Diamond, Lawrence C. Levine, and Anita Bernstein

Understanding Trade Secret Law
John G. Sprankling, Thomas G. Sprankling

Understanding Trademark Law, Fourth Edition
Mary LaFrance

Understanding Trusts and Estates, Seventh Edition
Roger W. Andersen and Susan Gary

Understanding White Collar Crime, Fourth Edition
J. Kelly Strader

Understanding Administrative Law

SEVENTH EDITION

Kristin E. Hickman
McKnight Presidential Professor in Law
Distinguished McKnight University Professor
Harlan Albert Rogers Professor in Law
University of Minnesota Law School

Carolina Academic Press
Durham, North Carolina

ISBN 978-1-5310-0449-1
e-ISBN 978-1-5310-0450-7

Library of Congress Cataloging-in-Publication Data

Names: Hickman, Kristin E., author.
Title: Understanding administrative law / by Kristin E. Hickman.
Description: Seventh edition. | Durham, North Carolina : Carolina Academic Press, LLC, [2022] | Series: Understanding series | Includes index.
Identifiers: LCCN 2022000364 (print) | LCCN 2022000365 (ebook) | ISBN 9781531004491 (paperback) | ISBN 9781531004507 (ebook)
Subjects: LCSH: Administrative law--United States. | Administrative procedure--United States. | LCGFT: Textbooks.
Classification: LCC KF5402 .F68 2022 (print) | LCC KF5402 (ebook) | DDC 342.73/06--dc23/eng/20220325
LC record available at https://lccn.loc.gov/2022000364
LC ebook record available at https://lccn.loc.gov/2022000365

Carolina Academic Press
700 Kent Street
Durham, North Carolina 27701
(919) 489-7486
www.cap-press.com

Printed in the United States of America

Contents

Preface

Students study administrative law for different reasons. Some take the course because they anticipate working for a federal or state administrative agency. Other students study administrative law merely because it is a subject tested on the bar examination they anticipate taking. Still other students have some abstract interest in a course that deals with the manner in which government agencies make policy and decide individual cases. Often, it is not until a student graduates and begins to practice law that the pervasiveness of models of administrative decisionmaking becomes apparent.

Administrative decisionmaking is not limited to federal government agencies like the Department of Health and Human Services, the National Labor Relations Board, or the Environmental Protection Agency. Administrative decisionmaking occurs at the state and regional levels, in municipal governments, and even in many private entities such as corporations and educational institutions. This text includes a certain amount of state-based as well as federal-based material, with the caveat that every state's approach to administrative law is a little different. Students who go into a state administrative practice will encounter concepts and terminology nearly identical with federal practice, even as the procedures, requirements, and standards of judicial review vary somewhat.

Law professors also approach the subject of administrative law from different angles. Many professors focus exclusively on the federal system. Other professors emphasize the administrative system of a single state. Still other professors explore only one or two specific administrative agencies, in the belief that administrative *process* can be understood best in the context of a specific agency carrying out a specific assigned mission.

This book will help the reader grasp the fundamental concepts of administrative law regardless of the approach taken by an instructor and regardless of the reader's personal motivation for taking the course. By and large, the book concentrates on the *process* of administrative decisionmaking and judicial review of the same, rather than the substantive law of any one particular agency. But students move through courses in administrative law and then later enter practice, they will find that substance and procedure become more and more intertwined and, in many instances, are almost inextricable. Understanding that no bright line exists between substance and procedure, particularly in an administrative agency context, is especially helpful for a thorough understanding of administrative law.

This book also contains a number of attempts to sensitize law students to the lawyering operations involved in administrative law—*i.e.*, how client problems move through a typical agency, and how a lawyer copes with the various problems and issues encountered in representing clients before administrative agencies. The relative informality of many administrative processes and the fact that agencies exercise both the authority to adopt legally-binding rules and regulations and the power to adjudicate individual cases mean that an administrative lawyer often must be far more creative and adaptable in dealing with an agency dispute than in handling a piece of civil litigation.

In addition, the book contains a significant amount of material on trends in administrative law. Many governmental entities, including a number of federal agencies, have expanded their repertoire beyond traditional, centralized "command and control" models for exercising governmental power. Federal agencies now pursue different approaches to policymaking that utilize partnerships with state and local governments or private parties, or that take full advantage of the marketplace as regulator. In many cases these trends have enhanced, rather than diminished, the lawyer's role.

A good deal of the material in this book consists of suggestions on ways to identify administrative problems and ways to organize the reader's thinking after the problem is identified. The book does not, of course, ignore the statutory and case law basis of administrative law. Often, however, whether the reader is a student or a practicing lawyer, a guide on how to think through a problem is more helpful than a mere paraphrase of a statute or recitation of a case holding. Since one of the assumptions of the author is that most readers will have access to cases through a casebook or other resources, this book emphasizes summary and synthesis rather than lengthy verbatim quotations.

This book should also prove helpful to practitioners who missed the opportunity to take an administrative law course in law school or who find themselves dealing with topics not covered in their law school course. In those instances, a practicing lawyer might profitably read at least a bit of the full text of any case discussed.

This book may be used with any of the existing commercially published casebooks on administrative law, including but not limited to my own book co-authored with Richard Pierce. Although this book's table of contents and chapter headings may not correspond directly with some of the headings used in the casebooks, there is a generally accepted core of administrative law topics that virtually every casebook covers and for which there is a standard vocabulary. There are two ways for a reader to use this book without reading it from cover to cover. First, if an outline heading in this book corresponds to a similar heading in a casebook (for example, the topics of the *nondelegation doctrine* in Chapter 2 or *rulemaking* in Chapter 7), the reader may move immediately to that topic. If there seems to be no correspondence between this book's outline headings and those headings used in the casebook, the most efficient mechanism for finding relevant discussion is to match the case in the casebook against the table of cases at the end of this book.

This Seventh Edition of *Understanding Administrative Law* owes a debt of gratitude to Prof. William F. Fox, who authored the first six editions of the book. I do not know Prof. Fox and did not collaborate with him in revising and updating the book to reflect my own ideas and understandings of administrative law doctrine and practice. Nevertheless, this Seventh Edition retains not only much of Prof. Fox's organizational structure but also many of his thoughts and suggestions. My own thinking on administrative law and practice has been shaped over the years by too many teachers, mentors, colleagues, co-authors, and students to name. Nevertheless, I must acknowledge and express my appreciation to Prof. Richard J. Pierce, Jr., with whom I co-author the *Administrative Law Treatise* and a casebook on federal administrative law. Although Dick and I have our debates and disagreements, after almost fifteen years of collaborating on these publications, my thoughts on many administrative law topics are inevitably influenced by his, and many of the ideas expressed in this book draw upon our work together. I also want to thank Sean Caldwell, who persuaded me to assume authorship of this book and then waited patiently for the manuscript, as well as Jesse Calo, Tom Grab, Douglas Harman, Mallory Harrington, Scott Lowder, and Lee Silberberg for invaluable research assistance. Finally, always, thank you to my family for their love and support.

Understanding Administrative Law

Chapter 1

Introduction

§ 1.01 Studying and Practicing Administrative Law

[A] An Overview of Administrative Law

In the broadest sense, administrative law involves the study of how those parts of our system of government that are neither legislatures nor courts make decisions. These entities, referred to as administrative agencies, are located mostly in the executive branch of government and generally are charged with the day-to-day details of governing. Agencies are created and assigned specific tasks by the legislature. The agencies then carry out these tasks by making decisions of various sorts and supervising the processes by which those decisions are carried out. For example, Congress has charged the United States Social Security Administration (SSA) with administering the federal government's social security program. Under that mandate, SSA does two things: (1) it makes general social security policy (within the terms of the SSA statute, of course), and (2) it processes individual applications for, and terminations of, social security benefits. Affected persons who disagree with the agency's decisions on either the substance of the social security program or the procedures under which that program is implemented—and whose grievances are not resolved within the agency—are permitted to take their dispute into federal court for resolution. Occasionally, aggrieved persons will attempt to persuade Congress to alter the statute under which the social security program functions.

This brief outline is the basic model for the American administrative process; and whether you are studying federal administrative law, a state administrative system, or even a single administrative agency, the process of decisionmaking is likely to be similar even when the missions of the agencies differ. It is the unifying force of the administrative *process*—in dramatic contrast to the wide variety of substantive problems with which agencies deal—that has persuaded most administrative law professors to concentrate on agency procedure rather than agency substance. Accordingly, most contemporary administrative law courses analyze the manner in which matters move through an agency, rather than the wisdom of the matters themselves. In other words, the manner in which the federal Department of Transportation decided to impose a passive-restraint system on automobile manufacturers is a fascinating case history of the administrative process, irrespective of anyone's personal interest in transportation policy or position on the wisdom of air bags versus seat belts. Recognizing that the focus of most administrative law courses is on how decisions are made (rather than what those decisions are) should help you more readily understand the themes of the typical course in administrative law.[1]

[B] The Study and Practice of Administrative Law

In one sense, administrative law can be approached in much the same fashion as many other law school courses. If you regard the field merely as a collection of discrete legal doctrines, it may make a great deal of sense simply to memorize various general principles, apply those principles to a final examination or a bar examination, and then forget about the topic. This book can be used in that fashion. However, a more profitable approach to truly understanding administrative law—and for practicing administrative law after your admission to the bar—is to recognize that, even as administrative law doctrines can be separated and evaluated into separate and distinct strands, they are simultaneously interwoven, and can be merged or blended successfully to illustrate different points and win cases. The key is to merge or blend doctrines deliberately to achieve your own ends, rather than inadvertently from a posture of misunderstanding.

The administrative law course itself will be less fuzzy if you keep in mind a few other fundamentals. First, under our constitutional system, agencies are creatures of statutes, and thus of legislative action. Agencies do not spring up on their own, and they cannot be created by courts. Agencies function only insofar as a legislature has given them the authority to function. That authority may be exceptionally broad (*e.g.*, telling an agency to regulate railroads by applying the standard of "public convenience and necessity") or incredibly narrow (*e.g.*, when Congress sets the specific income levels and other criteria for those persons who qualify for certain government benefits; or when Congress passes a Coal Mine Safety and Health Act containing provisions that tell mine operators what size of mine roofing bolts to install).

Federal administrative agencies are typically endowed with broad, general powers. By contrast, state legislatures frequently enact far more detailed agency statutes because of a lingering reluctance to give state agencies unfettered power. For example, the Nebraska legislature once enacted a statute prescribing the thickness of the walls of metal milk cans. Addressing this kind of detail by statute may be a sign of particular legislative engagement with the topic at hand. It may also signal a legislature's distrust of a specific agency, or possibly with the administrative process in general. While common in state administrative systems, it is much less frequent in the federal government. Congress rarely involves itself in the minutiae of administering federal regulatory programs.

Irrespective of what form a new administrative agency takes or what mission it is given, the legislature *must* enact a statute to create the agency. This statute, sometimes called an agency's *enabling act or statute*, or alternatively an agency's *organic act or statute*, is the fundamental source of an agency's power. This principle—*that the legislature creates agencies and sets limits on their authority*—should be regarded as the first

1. One respected casebook, now unfortunately out of print, disagrees with this approach and postulates that administrative law can be properly understood only if one studies an individual agency in depth, both substantively and procedurally. Glen O. Robinson, Ernest Gellhorn & Harold H. Bruff, The Administrative Process (4th ed. 1993). Contemporary Supreme Court jurisprudence contradicts this view. *See, e.g.*, *Mayo Foundation for Medical Education & Research v. United States*, 562 U.S. 44, 55 (2011) (emphasizing "the importance of maintaining a uniform approach to judicial review of administrative action"); *Dickinson v. Zurko*, 527 U.S. 150, 154 (1999) (same).

cardinal rule of administrative law. Far too many students in law school, and even far too many experienced practitioners, lose sight of this fundamental principal. A misunderstanding of this basic concept can lead to erroneous assumptions about an agency's ability to deal with a particular issue or problem.

Some organic statutes set out specific agency procedures. More often than not, however, the legislature creates an agency with a particular substantive mission but with procedures that are established in a general procedural statute that controls all or most of the agencies in that jurisdiction. The governing procedural statute at the federal level is the Administrative Procedure Act (APA),[2] in place since 1946 and normally the doctrinal thread that holds most law school administrative law courses together. While state administrative procedure statutes differ considerably, a prototype statute, the Model State Administrative Procedure Act,[3] has been promulgated. Many states have either adopted the Model Act *in toto* or incorporated substantial portions of it into their existing administrative procedure statutes. Thus, you are likely to find a fair amount of procedural uniformity even among the states. Those students whose courses emphasize a single state's administrative system would do well to make constant reference to that state's administrative procedure act as they work through their course and this book. They will probably see many similarities between the state act and the federal APA but with enough differences to make generalizations dangerous.[4]

Some law professors understandably disagree with an exclusively "federal" approach to understanding administrative law. Professor Arthur Bonfield argued that a proper study of the state administrative process would pay large dividends for both students and professors. He contended, among other things, that administrative law is best appreciated through a comparative approach to the topic. State administrative systems have adopted approaches that are both creative and effective (what Bonfield called "state solutions") that stodgier, less innovative federal agencies refuse even to consider. Perhaps most importantly, Bonfield said,

> State administrative processes operate under different circumstances than does the federal administrative process; consequently, some of the problems presented [in the states] differ either in degree or kind from those presented in the federal process. Many of the feasible or effective solutions to federal administrative law problems are not feasible or effective in the state context. Therefore, a study of problems and solutions in the federal administrative process cannot be an adequate vehicle to prepare students for dealing with all of the major problems presented in the state administrative process.[5]

2. 5 U.S.C. §§ 551–808. *See* Appendix A.

3. *See* Appendix B.

4. Florida offers an interesting case study in the evolution of state administrative law, having undergone a series of administrative law reforms since the first edition of this book. *See, e.g.*, William Fox & Leonard Carson, *A Comparison of the Florida and Federal Administrative Procedure Acts*, 11 FLA. B.J. 699 (1980); David M. Greenbaum & Lawrence E. Sellers, Jr., *1999 Amendments to the Florida Administrative Procedure Act: Phantom Menace or Much Ado About Nothing?*, 27 FLA. ST. U. L. REV. 499 (2000); Lawrence E. Sellers, Jr., *The 2003 Amendments to the Florida APA*, 77 FLA. B.J. 74 (2003); Lawrence E. Sellers, *The 2008 Amendments to the APA: The Open Government Act*, 82 FLA. B.J. 43 (2008); Larry Sellers, *The 2010 Amendments To The APA: Legislature Overrides Veto of Law to Require Legislative Ratification of "Million Dollar Rules,"* 85 FLA. B.J. 37 (2011); H. French Brown IV & Larry Sellers, *The 2016 Amendments To The APA: Say Goodbye To United Wisconsin—And More*, 90 FLA. B.J. 46 (2016).

5. Arthur E. Bonfield, *State Law in the Teaching of Administrative Law: A Critical Analysis of the Status Quo*, 61 TEX. L. REV. 95, 103–04 (1982). Professor Peter Strauss relatedly has suggested

But no matter how a legislature at either the federal or state level chooses to set up an agency, as a law student and as a practicing attorney, your first task is simple: *Read the agency's organic statute and that jurisdiction's administrative procedure act.* One way to create a lot of trouble for yourself, even at the beginning of the course, is to be casual about reading the applicable statutes. Reading and trying to understand the statutes should be regarded as a corollary to the first cardinal rule for understanding administrative law.

Agencies make a great deal of policy within the boundaries of their organic statutes. Within the boundaries of their generic administrative procedure act, they also establish procedures for efficient and fair decisionmaking. Remember that organic statutes and administrative procedure acts often establish only *minimum* standards and requirements for individual agencies. These statutes are often so broadly phrased that agencies have enormous leeway to fill in the gaps—both procedural and substantive—of the legislation so long as they keep within the terms of the governing statutes. The areas in which many agencies are free to set their own policies and procedures are quite extensive. We refer to this freedom of action as *agency discretion.* Agency discretion is yet another fundamental concept to keep constantly in mind.

Agency discretion is a phenomenon that both students and practitioners need to appreciate if they are to have a thorough understanding of an agency. You can begin to grasp agency discretion by first realizing that the vast majority of agency decisions are never reviewed by either the courts or the legislature. Other parts of the executive branch, such as the president, a governor, or an attorney general, occasionally get involved with agency action. For the most part, however, agencies function on their own, often with only sporadic outside scrutiny and accountability.

Yet another fundamental principle that should never be forgotten is that courts have a relatively limited role in supervising agency conduct. To a fair extent, the federal courts and many state courts are required to take what amounts to a "hands off" attitude toward the agencies. The days when a free-wheeling court could substitute its judgment for that of the agency are largely over, irrespective of whether the issue before the court is substantive or procedural. The United States Supreme Court has been hammering this message home to the lower federal courts for years.[6] Most if not all state courts have adopted a similar posture.

This is not to say that judicial review of agency action is unimportant. As we will see, it is the tail that wags the dog in many instances, as even the possibility of judicial review under unfavorable precedent may prompt agencies to adjust their polices, practices, and procedures. But the mere fact that a dispute *may* be taken to court is no excuse for sloppy lawyering at the agency level. Too many lawyers make the fatal mistake of thinking that a reviewing court will correct any and all mistakes in the proceedings below, or indeed, that a court has plenary review powers over agency action. That simply is not always the case. The ability of a court to change an agency decision is sufficiently limited these days as to give rise to the second cardinal rule for agency practice: *a lawyer who fails to win a case at the agency runs a substantial risk of not winning it at*

---

that administrative law is one of the "hidden" comparative law courses in law school because it combines and requires comparisons between many other law school courses. Peter L. Strauss, *Administrative Law: The Hidden Comparative Law Course*, 46 J. LEGAL EDUC. 478 (1996).

6. *See, e.g., Securities & Exchange Comm'n v. Chenery Corp.*, 332 U.S. 194 (1947), discussed particularly in Chapter 6, § 6.04; *Vermont Yankee Nuclear Power Corp. v. Natural Resources Defense Council, Inc.*, 435 U.S. 519 (1978), discussed in Chapter 7, § 7.02; *Perez v. Mortgage Bankers Ass'n*, 575 U.S. 92 (2015).

all. Of course, many cases exist in which courts overturned agency action. But whether one considers the deferential posture of, and doctrinal limitations placed on, judicial review of agency action or merely looks at the statistics (*i.e.*, the number of all agency decisions overturned by courts), one will find that the vast majority of agency decisions are either never taken to court or ultimately affirmed when they get there. Thus, the message of cardinal rule number two should not be forgotten: cases usually are won or lost *at the agency.* Courts are rarely the answer.

A legislative solution for your client's problem may be possible theoretically, but you should remain realistic about actually achieving a favorable result as a result of legislative action. Most legislatures are far too busy with more generic issues like taxes and the budget to pay any attention to a particular client's grievance. Legislatures are often reluctant to involve themselves in the details of administrative governance. In studying and practicing administrative law, you should try to avoid wishful thinking. If you have a problem that falls within the jurisdiction of an administrative agency, that problem will likely begin with the agency and conclude with the agency, with your client stuck with whatever result the agency dictates.

§ 1.02 The Nature of Administrative Agencies

[A] Addressing Legal Disputes

Hardly any function of modern government exists that does not involve, in some way, an administrative agency. The reason for this is really very simple: agencies are the only government entities equipped to deal with the day-to-day minutiae of governing. It is one thing for Congress to decide that transportation companies should be regulated, but the last thing that Congress wants or possesses the expertise to decide is how much Company X may charge to carry a package from New York to Chicago. Rigorous protection of the environment is now a matter of national consensus, but a court is unlikely to have the technical expertise necessary to decide precisely which specific air pollution control equipment is best suited for coal-fired power plants. Two themes that continually repeat in administrative law with regard to administrative agencies are (1) the agency is charged with the detail of regulation, and (2) the agency is expected to develop expertise in a particular area of regulation.

Understanding the nature of administrative agencies first requires an analysis of the way in which law develops and legal disputes are addressed by our legal system. Consider, for example, the case of a creative business executive with an idea for an innovative new product. One option for the business executive under our system of government might be simply to start developing, manufacturing, and then selling the product without seeking anyone's permission to do so. It could be that only good things will result from this activity and nothing bad will ever happen. However, a wise entrepreneur always considers the potential legal disputes and resulting liability that might emerge from a business undertaking, and how the law might address those issues.

In our legal system, we frequently leave potential legal disputes in the hands of the *common law*: if some harm does occur, the common law can grapple with any legal dispute that arises through the application of general principles of tort or contract liability. By way of comparison, the nineteenth century British courts had no trouble dealing with a water storage tank that broke and flooded some nearby property, even though Parliament had never spoken on the issue, and even though no previous court had addressed the problem.[7] When an injury to an individual's person or property interests occurs, principles drawn from tort law permit a court to dispose of both the issue of liability and the issue of remedy, even if the case is one of first impression. Common law dispute resolution may be triggered by any injured person who feels strongly enough about his or her injury to file a formal action in court and who has a strong enough case to convince the court that liability exists and that some type of monetary relief ought to be granted. Eventually, the cumulative effect of many reported court decisions will establish a body of legal rules to address virtually any business activity without any other government action.

Concededly, court decisions are not perfect. Judge-made rules may be overly narrow or too sketchy to give comprehensive guidance on how an entrepreneur ought to proceed. Still, many problems in our society are handled precisely in this fashion, and it is not necessarily a bad way to handle disputes. The common law solution is flexible enough to react to changing circumstances and predictable enough to give people at least a little warning before they get into trouble.

Looking at the problem realistically, however, our business executive with the innovative product idea will likely want more predictability and stability than the common law system offers. Courts can take years or even generations to develop a comprehensive body of law on a particular issue. Most businesses cannot wait that long and instead require a certain threshold of legal certainty and stability before they will or even can proceed with a new venture. For example, banks are unlikely to lend money to support a new business activity in the face of a great deal of legal uncertainty, or they may charge a higher rate of interest or demand more collateral to compensate for the higher perceived risk.

One way that business interests seek greater legal certainty than the common law can provide is to ask a legislature for assistance. Armed with enough political clout, our business executive might persuade the legislature simply to address the conditions giving rise to the legal uncertainty. For example, if the business executive is worried about liability and accountability for potential injuries that might be associated with the innovative new product, she might ask the legislature to set a cap on possible liability stemming from any accidents.[8] We can refer to this as a "pure" *legislative* solution—*i.e.*, where the legislature resolves the problem on its own without referring the issue to any other branch of government. Yet, the actions of any given legislature are frequently unpredictable. Rather than adopting the statute our business executive seeks, the legislature could decide that her innovative new product is sufficiently dangerous, with hidden social and economic costs, and that the better path is simply to *prohibit* the manufacture and sale of the product in question and impose civil or even criminal penalties on anyone who does so. Legislative prohibitions of this type do not occur all that often, but they do happen. More commonly, a legislature will impose monitoring, safety, insurance, and other requirements that increase costs, perhaps even to the point of discouraging the development, manufacture, and sale of the innovative new product in the first place.

---

7. *Rylands v. Fletcher*, 3 Eng. Rep. (H.L.) 330 (1823) (extending the doctrine of strict liability for ultrahazardous activities).

8. For example, the Price-Anderson Act, 42 U.S.C. § 2210(c), sets a cap of $560 million on any accident occurring in a civilian nuclear power plant.

[B] Legislative Choices Involving Administrative Agencies

Alternatively, a legislature might decide that the legal issues raised by our business executive should be put in the hands of an executive branch agency. In this instance, the legislature has a broad spectrum of choices. In making a choice, a legislature will typically consider the following:

1. The task to be assigned to the agency (often referred to as the agency's "mission"). Two factors are usually considered in this analysis:
   a. what is the nature of the specific business or industry to be regulated (*e.g.*, firms manufacturing pharmaceuticals, firearms, automobiles, or children's toys); and
   b. in what manner should the regulation be carried out (by licensing, monitoring, or performing the actual work at issue);
2. How the agency itself should be structured (whether, for example, it is to be headed by a single administrator or by a multi-person commission and what its internal organization will be); and
3. The placement of the agency within the existing system of government (*e.g.*, whether it is to be a separate cabinet-level agency, a component of an existing cabinet-level agency, or an independent agency).

The choices are plentiful. The legislature could decide to *prohibit* any private sector activity whatsoever and to establish a government agency to perform the entire task. Congress has taken this approach in a few instances. For example, Congress at one time made private space flight unlawful and gave the task solely to a government agency (initially NASA, the National Aeronautics and Space Administration), although it eventually changed its mind. This approach exemplifies one of the tightest forms of government control.

By contrast, if the legislature decided that only limited control of the business activity was necessary, it could create an administrative mechanism at the other end of the "control" spectrum requiring only that those persons wishing to engage in the activity identify themselves, register with some governmental entity, and report periodically on their activities. We usually refer to this model as a *registration-and-reporting* mechanism. The Lobbying Disclosure Act of 1995[9] is a good example of this kind of minimalist control mechanism.

The legislature might decide that it wants more governmental control over the activity in question than is permitted by a registration-and-reporting statute, but not a categorical prohibition. As it investigates the legal concerns associated with our innovative

9. 2 U.S.C. §§ 1601–14. The 1995 Act, with important 1998, 2007, and 2018 amendments, repealed the older Federal Lobbyist Registration Act. Readers should understand that one of the principal reasons for the relaxed controls on lobbyists springs from the First Amendment right to petition the government. Indeed, the 1995 Act expressly provides: "Nothing in this Act shall be construed to prohibit or interfere with—(1) the right to petition the Government for the redress of grievances; (2) the right to express a personal opinion; or (3) the right of association, protected by the First Amendment to the Constitution." Most other forms of private sector activity, particularly business activity, are not protected nearly as much by the Constitution. There are relatively few registration and reporting statutes on either the federal or state level that pertain to businesses. One of the few such examples is a registration and reporting activity under the Federal Pesticide Act, 7 U.S.C. § 136(2) for farmers who intend to administer pesticides on their own lands.

new product, the legislature might conclude that the only aspect of this activity that requires some control is the credentialing of the engineers responsible for its development and design. In other words, the legislature could decide that this was an activity suitable for the private sector, but was still complicated enough and dangerous enough that only a select group of professionals should be permitted to engage in the activity. Based upon this assumption, the legislature could establish a *professional licensing* process for the engineers in question. All other persons would be expressly forbidden from participating in the development and design of the product. Under this model, certified engineers would have the exclusive right to engage in the activity, and any licensed engineer who committed an error could be sued for professional malpractice. Law students in particular should instantly recognize this model and should be especially sensitive to regulation in the form of professional licensing.

[C] "Command-and-Control Regulation"

Still another alternative for a legislature contemplating legal issues associated with an innovative new product is the administrative model that is characteristic of a great deal of the current regulatory activity of both state and federal governments and whose analysis often constitutes the major portion of the traditional course in administrative law. Under this model, an administrative agency is given powers to regulate a particular industry under a broad statutory mandate (*e.g.*, "in the public interest," or "consistent with public health and safety") by first authorizing individual private sector firms to perform the activity in question and then by policing the day-to-day operations of that industry. We usually refer to this type of mechanism as *command-and-control regulation*. When it created the now-defunct Interstate Commerce Commission (ICC), Congress gave the ICC the authority to license individual firms to carry freight and also the authority to approve the prices those companies charged for the transportation. There are a number of variations on this theme. Some agencies—for example, the Environmental Protection Agency (EPA)—are given regulatory powers that extend to setting standards for pollution control but without the authority to decide which companies should be permitted to perform a particular function. The EPA cannot decide outright whether a particular steel manufacturing plant may be built and operated, but it does have the power to regulate that plant's air emissions once the plant is up and running. The EPA does issue permits in certain instances, but its permitting process does not extend to deciding whether or not that particular firm generally may exist and do business. (That said, no steel company will build a manufacturing plant if it does not believe it can get the permits it needs to operate within regulatory parameters.) The National Labor Relations Board and the Federal Trade Commission perform similar tasks in policing unfair labor and unfair trade practices.

[D] Licensing Agencies

Typical licensing agencies on the federal level are the Federal Communications Commission (broadcast licenses) and the Federal Energy Regulatory Commission (hydroelectric facility licenses, among other things). Licensing agencies frequently also regulate many of the day-to-day activities of individual companies, such as rates that licensed companies may charge their customers. On the state level, licensing agencies, such as state public utility commissions, are sometimes given regulatory powers involving health and safety issues as well as economic issues.

[E] The Structure of an Agency

The legislature never stops with a mere statement of agency powers. It must also decide on the agency's structure and that agency's position within the government. For example, in setting up a new administrative agency, Congress will decide whether to make the agency a new *cabinet-level* department, a mere component of one of the existing cabinet-level departments, or an *independent agency.* One of the newer federal cabinet-level agencies is the Department of Veterans Affairs, an agency that had existed prior to 1988 as the sub-cabinet administrative agency known as the Veterans Administration. The newest cabinet-level agency, the Department of Homeland Security, was formed in 2002 as an amalgam of government entities that previously were either freestanding agencies or existed within other cabinet-level departments. By comparison, in 1979, Congress divided the former cabinet-level Department of Health, Education, and Welfare into two separate cabinet-level agencies: the Department of Education and the Department of Health and Human Services.

With regard to agency organization, on the federal level, a *Secretary* typically presides over a cabinet-level agency.[10] Each of these entities consists of a large bureaucracy, usually including several subordinate agencies, administering many different programs. At least in theory, the president as the chief executive has nearly total control over executive branch agencies. The president normally can appoint and fire the cabinet agency's highest officials. The president can dictate agency policy and a great deal of influence over the agency's budget, once Congress approves that budget.

There are, however, some instances when Congress wants a new agency to have some independence from presidential control. In that case, it can create an *independent agency,* such as the Federal Maritime Commission, the Federal Trade Commission, or the Securities and Exchange Commission. On a few occasions, Congress will establish an agency as an independent agency but place it within an existing cabinet department—*e.g.*, the Federal Energy Regulatory Commission (FERC), an independent agency that exists within the cabinet-level Department of Energy. FERC has exclusive responsibility for certain areas of regulation, such as wholesale electric ratemaking. In other matters, FERC's organic statute permits it to issue orders that constitute final agency action for the Department of Energy.[11] In still other matters, different components of the Department of Energy function completely independently from FERC.[12]

---

10. The attorney general is the head of the Department of Justice. 28 U.S.C. § 503. The head of the EPA, which presidents since George H.W. Bush have elevated to cabinet level status, carries the title of administrator. The director of the Central Intelligence Agency, 50 U.S.C. § 3036, and the Director of National Intelligence, 50 U.S.C. § 3023, are two other examples of nondepartmental agency heads given cabinet-level status.

11. *See* the Department of Energy Organization Act, 42 U.S.C. § 7101.

12. There are occasional attempts towards executive branch reorganization often with the goal of eliminating or minimizing jurisdictional overlap. *See, e.g., Toward a Logical Governing Structure: Restoring Executive Reorganization Authority, Before the Comm. on Gov't Reform*, 108th Cong. (2003).

On the federal level, independent agencies are headed by a multi-person commission and staffed by a bureaucracy that is usually much smaller than a cabinet agency.

An agency's status as an independent agency restricts some of a president's prerogatives in controlling the agency. While the president may appoint the agency's commissioners, they typically serve for fixed terms and may not be removed other than on the specific grounds set out in the agency's organic statute. Many independent agencies, by statute, must have a mixture of commissioners from different political parties (typically, but not necessarily, Republicans and Democrats), so the president may not be free to appoint commissioners solely from within his own political party. These constraints on the appointment and removal process in theory make these agencies "independent" of the president. In practice and over time, however, the president can have a substantial effect on such agencies' policymaking simply by filling commissioner vacancies with like-minded people.

Students will encounter many different examples of agency structures at the federal level and in state and local government. There is no single type of structure or degree of chief executive control that characterizes an administrative agency, be it on the federal, state, or municipal level. Regardless, understanding just how an agency's structure compares with those of other agencies is one of the first steps in fully appreciating that agency's role and function.

§ 1.03 Justifications for Regulation

[A] Economic Justifications

Free markets are one of the basic premises of the American economy. Thus, a decision to create an administrative agency to regulate a particular business activity implies a failure on the part of the marketplace to deal adequately with some problem.

In his now classic work on regulation, Supreme Court Justice Stephen Breyer created a list of possible justifications for regulation.[13] These include, among others:

1. to control monopoly power;
2. to control excess profits;
3. to compensate for externalities;
4. to compensate for inadequate information;
5. to inhibit excessive competition; and
6. to compensate for unequal bargaining power.[14]

A statute need not be based solely on one of these justifications, but can be (and often is) a blend of two or more. Many of Justice Breyer's justifications are self-explanatory, but a few examples may make the others a little clearer. "Externalities," occasionally referred to as "spillovers," occur when the cost of producing something does not reflect the true cost to society for producing the good. One example is manufacturing processes that

---

13. Stephen Breyer, Regulation and its Reform (1982). *See also* Andrew P. Morriss, Bruce Yandle & Andrew Dorchak, *Choosing How to Regulate*, 29 Harv. Env't. L. Rev. 179 (2005).

14. Breyer, *supra* note 13, at 12–35.

create air and water pollution for which society bears the burdens of health complications, cleanup costs, and other environmental impacts. A single firm, however high-minded, cannot take it upon itself to install costly pollution control equipment if no other firm invests in the equipment. To do so would drive up that firm's costs to the point where it cannot compete successfully with lower cost goods manufactured by firms that continue to pollute. Some entity, usually the government, must require all firms to make these investments in order to spread the costs of pollution control over the entire industry. Efforts under the Clean Air Act and the Clean Water Act to establish certain national standards for air and water pollution applicable to all firms within particular industries is a recognition of the concept of spillover.

Compensating for inadequate information is a justification for a great deal of current consumer protection legislation. Laypersons do not have the wherewithal to analyze children's sleepwear for flammability. Purchasers of food cannot analyze the nutritional content or the health hazards of various food products. Buyers of major appliances cannot themselves calculate the energy efficiency of a particular model of refrigerator. The Food and Drug Administration's product approval requirements and the Consumer Product Safety Commission's and Department of Energy's labeling regulations reflect this justification. Similarly, compensating for unequal bargaining power is the justification for many of the "truth in lending" regulations issued by the federal banking regulation agencies.

[B] Political Justifications

Political explanations for regulation that are conceptually distinct from economic justifications also exist. One political justification for regulation is that certain matters within our society ought to be subject to the control of persons who are under some obligation of political accountability. It is doubtful, for example, that we would turn over the voting process to a private sector company. In theory, the most politically accountable branch of government is the legislature, but even the executive branch and the judiciary reflect various concepts of political accountability. Agencies derive their political accountability from the actions of the legislature (in establishing and monitoring the agency) and the executive (through the appointment power), as well as agencies' compliance with processes and procedures designed to facilitate transparency and public participation. Political accountability helps ensure that agencies function in the *public interest*, rather than in the interest of narrow single-issue groups. While there is a lot of debate as to whether agencies, in truth, represent the public interest, this concept is a key element of theorizing about the administrative process.[15] Moreover, there are occasions when terms such as public interest become important as a matter of statutory interpretation. For that reason alone, law students should not disregard the more theoretical aspects of the administrative process.[16]

---

15. For a further discussion on understanding and improving administrative rulemaking, see Cary Coglianese, *Empirical and Experimental Methods of Law: Empirical Analysis and Administrative Law*, 2002 U. Ill. L. Rev. 1111 (2002).

16. For better or for worse, this book endeavors to take a highly practical approach to understanding administrative law. Administrative law is blessed, however, with a rich and varied conceptual and theoretical literature that more enthusiastic students of administrative law may enjoy. Some book-length writings on the theory of our administrative system that a careful student might wish to read are as follows: James Landis, The Administrative Process (1938); Kenneth Culp

[C] Evolution of Regulatory Philosophy

Toward the end of the twentieth century, many Americans seemed to develop a renewed faith in market mechanisms as proper control devices and simultaneously seemed to abandon the idea that command-and-control economic regulation by government agencies is the best way to deal with many problems. This movement, often referred to as *deregulation*,[17] began in the mid-1970s during the Ford and Carter administrations and reached full flower during the Reagan years. That same spirit continued into the Clinton administration as President Bill Clinton declared that the era of big government was over. President George W. Bush expressed similar views. President Barack Obama did not pursue a deregulatory agenda, but President Donald Trump did.

Deregulatory efforts have raised questions about some of the economic justifications for regulation. A number of prominent failures of the regulatory process (for example, in the area of regulation of the interstate transportation of natural gas—a program that for years actually created natural gas shortages) weakened public interest in traditional regulatory mechanisms. As globalization, modern telecommunication and transportation systems, and other technological developments have made life more complex, and as the federal government has sought to address ever more problems and issues,

---

Davis, Discretionary Justice: A Preliminary Inquiry (1969); Robert L. Rabin, Perspectives on the Administrative Process (1979); Jerry L. Mashaw, Bureaucratic Justice: Managing Social Security Disability Claims (1983); Jerry L. Mashaw, Due Process in the Administrative State (1985); James Wilson, Bureaucracy: What Government Agencies Do and Why They Do It (1989); Peter L. Strauss, An Introduction to Administrative Justice in the United States (1989); Cass R. Sunstein, After the Rights Revolution: Reconceiving the Regulatory State (1990); Christopher F. Edley, Jr., Administrative Law: Rethinking Judicial Control of Bureaucracy (1990); Glen O. Robinson, American Bureaucracy: Public Choice and Public Law (1991); Susan Rose-Ackerman, Rethinking the Progressive Agenda: The Reform of the American Regulatory State (1992); Peter H. Schuck, Foundations of Administrative Law (1994); Jerry L. Mashaw, Creating the Administrative Constitution: The Lost 100 Years of American Administrative Law (2012); Philip Hamburger, Is Administrative Law Unlawful? (2014); Joseph Postell, Bureaucracy in America: The Administrative State's Challenge to Constitutional Government (2017). Some frequently cited law review articles on broad themes of administrative law are as follows: Robert B. Stewart, *The Reformation of American Administrative Law*, 88 Harv. L. Rev. 1669 (1975); Robert L. Rabin, *Federal Regulation in Historical Perspective*, 38 Stan. L. Rev. 1189 (1986); Gerald E. Frug, *Administrative Democracy*, 40 U. Toronto L.J. 559 (1990); Mark Seidenfeld, *A Civic Republican Justification for the Bureaucratic State*, 105 Harv. L. Rev. 1511 (1992); Richard H. Pildes & Cass R. Sunstein, *Reinventing the Regulatory State*, 62 U. Chi. L. Rev. 1 (1995); Cynthia R. Farina, *The Consent of the Governed: Against Simple Rules for a Complex World*, 72 Chi.-Kent L. Rev. 987 (1997); Steven P. Croley, *Theories of Regulation: Incorporating the Administrative Process*, 98 Colum. L. Rev. 1 (1998); Elena Kagan, *Presidential Administration*, 114 Harv. L. Rev. 2245 (2001); Lisa Schultz Bressman, Symposium, *Getting Beyond Cynicism: New Theories of the Regulatory State Disciplining Delegation After* Whitman v. American Trucking Ass'ns, 87 Cornell L. Rev. 452 (2002); Orly Lobel, *The Renew Deal: The Fall of Regulation and the Rise of Governance in Contemporary Legal Thought*, 89 Minn. L. Rev. 342 (2004); Evan J. Criddle, *Fiduciary Foundations of Administrative Law*, 54 UCLA L. Rev. 117 (2006); Rachel E. Barkow, *The Ascent of the Administrative State and the Demise of Mercy*, 121 Harv. L. Rev. 1332 (2008); Gillian E. Metzger, *The Supreme Court 2016 Term: Foreword: 1930s Redux: The Administrative State Under Siege*, 131 Harv. L. Rev. 1 (2017); Nicholas Bagley, *The Procedure Fetish*, 118 Mich. L. Rev. 345 (2019); Jeffrey A. Pojanowski, *Neoclassical Administrative Law*, 133 Harv. L. Rev. 852 (2020).

17. The term "deregulation" is a bit of a misnomer. Industries that have experienced deregulation are not totally unregulated. They remain subject to a variety of regulatory requirements, including safety requirements, labor and equal employment laws, antitrust statutes, and the like. Thus, the term typically refers more to the introduction of market forces into the regulatory regime than the total elimination or absence of regulation.

government agencies (and sometimes Congress directly) have turned increasingly to *privatization*—relying on private actors to perform a variety of government functions ranging from prison management to developing health and safety standards.[18] Additionally, recent decades have seen efforts to take regulatory powers away from the federal government and give those powers to the states through the process sometimes referred to as *devolution*.[19] At the same time, it is clear that the American public has not given up its consensus on the need for governmental regulation in various areas, including but not limited to the pursuit of clean air and water and employee and consumer safety. The tensions between a perceived need for some control and monitoring and the tight, often irrational, economically-inhibiting forms of traditional economic regulation have provoked a search for different types of controls and new administrative mechanisms.[20] Cooperation between federal and state governments, or between the public and private sectors, to achieve public goals is hardly new.[21] Nevertheless, modern administrative governance has become a complex web of public and private relationships, with an array of command and cooperative structures, wielding hard rules and soft guidance with real world consequences, and giving rise to the term *new governance*.[22]

In recent years, we have seen more than a little public and legislative interest in what has been called *reregulation*.[23] In various areas, including health care, pharmaceuticals, financial institutions, and the technology sector, public interest in some type of increased regulation has persisted. Since September 11, 2001, and the destruction of the World Trade Center in New York City, many new initiatives in regulation have been sparked by international terrorism—a phenomenon that has created sharp new interest in regulation that relates directly to public safety and which prompted the formation of the Department of Homeland Security.[24] Congress enacted the Sarbanes-Oxley Act of 2002 in response to several large corporate and accounting scandals including Enron and WorldCom, and created the Public Company Accounting Oversight Board to oversee public company audits.[25] These days, many commentators have expressed

18. *See, e.g.*, Jody Freeman, *Private Parties, Public Functions and The New Administrative Law*, 52 ADMIN. L. REV. 813 (2000).

19. There is considerable debate about devolution in the regulatory context. *See, e.g.*, Paul E. Peterson, *Devolution's Price*, 14 YALE J. ON REG. 111 (1996); Edward Rubin, *The Myth of Accountability and The Anti-Administrative Impulse*, 103 MICH. L. REV. 2073 (2005); Gillian E. Metzger, *Federalism Under Obama*, 53 WM. & MARY L. REV. 567 (2011).

20. *See, e.g.*, RICHARD H. THALER & CASS R. SUNSTEIN, NUDGE: IMPROVING DECISIONS ABOUT HEALTH, WEALTH, AND HAPPINESS (2008); Jody Freeman, *Extending Public Law Norms Through Privatization*, 116 HARV. L. REV. 1285 (2003); Susan Rose-Ackerman, Foreword, *Regulatory Reform: Where Are We Going*, 31 WAKE FOREST L. REV. 581 (1996); IAN AYRES & JOHN BRAITHWAITE, RESPONSIVE REGULATION: TRANSCENDING THE DEREGULATION DEBATE (1992); LARRY N. GERSTON ET AL., THE DEREGULATED SOCIETY (1988); Thomas O. McGarity, *Regulatory Reform in the Reagan Era*, 45 MD. L. REV. 253 (1986).

21. *See, e.g.*, Louis Jaffe, *Law Making by Private Groups*, 51 HARV. L. REV. 201 (1937).

22. *See, e.g.*, Orly Lobel, *The Renew Deal: The Fall of Regulation and the Rise of Governance in Contemporary Legal Thought*, 89 MINN. L. REV. 342 (2004).

23. *See, e.g.*, Christopher S. Yoo, *Deregulation vs. Reregulation of Telecommunications: A Clash of Regulatory Paradigms*, 36 J. CORP. L. 847 (2011); Faith Stevelman, *Introduction: The Market Meltdown of 2008 and The Future of Financial Reregulation*, 54 N.Y. L. SCH. L. REV. 635 (2010); Anita Mosar, *DOT's Rulemaking Is a Step Toward Reregulation*, 27 No. 3 AIR & SPACE LAW. 15 (2014); Peter Molk & Arden Rowell, *Reregulation and the Regulatory Timeline*, 101 IOWA L. REV. 1497 (2016).

24. *See* Phillip A. Karber, *Re-Constructing Global Aviation in an Era of the Civil Aircraft as a Weapon of Destruction*, 25 HARV. J.L. & PUB. POL'Y 781 (2002).

25. President George W. Bush signed the Sarbanes-Oxley Act of 2002, 116 Stat. 745 (2002), on July 30, 2002.

interest not in abolishing but merely in "fixing" government regulation, possibly by developing concepts of *regulatory flexibility*.[26] People in and out of government have begun to explore *performance based* regulations as an alternative to classic command and control regulation. Performance based regulation sets certain goals that need to be accomplished while permitting the regulated entity relatively free rein in achieving those goals.[27]

During the administration of President Barack Obama, we saw attempts at regulating of the banking and securities industry through the formation of a new consumer finance protection agency. The Dodd-Frank Wall Street Reform and Consumer Protection Act[28] has been described as the most sweeping change in financial regulation since the New Deal. Among other things, Dodd-Frank created the Bureau of Consumer Financial Protection within the Federal Reserve System. In addition to financial regulation, the off-shore oil platform explosion in the Gulf Coast on a rig owned by BP has triggered some renewed interest in fresh regulation of the off-shore oil industry. The 2010 earthquake in Fukushima, Japan, and the resultant leak of radioactive gases from some nearby nuclear power plants, sparked additional interest and comment on regulation of nuclear power.

No matter what form these new developments take, they are healthy in that they force everyone to re-examine some of the fundamental assumptions of the administrative system of government. Putting agencies' specific regulatory programs and conventional administrative procedures under the microscope will help us develop more creative and effective solutions for the problems of twenty-first century America. But even so, as we enter the third decade of the twenty first century, the federal government and most state and local governments look a lot like they did during Franklin Roosevelt's time.

§ 1.04 The Administrative Process

[A] Generally

Much of the discussion in the first three sections of this chapter has focused on matters that involve the substance of administrative law. The substance of regulation is always the primary concern of clients and of the American public. Limits on the amount of social security benefits, changes in water quality standards for the lead smelting industry and prohibitions on the use of flammable fabrics in children's sleepwear are the things that most directly interest companies and individuals. However, lawyers who practice before agencies are always equally concerned with the way an agency decides these matters. You will be surprised as you begin to practice administrative law how

---

26. *See, e.g.*, Symposium on Regulatory Reform, *supra* note 16; Marshall J. Breger, *Regulatory Flexibility and the Administrative State*, 32 Tulsa L.J. 325 (1996); Douglas C. Michael, *Cooperative Implementation of Federal Regulations*, 13 Yale J. on Reg. 535, 541 (1996) ("The government would rely on the regulated entities to develop specific and individual implementation plans, and would thus restrict its role to assisting in and providing incentives for self-implementation programs, and to maintaining a credible residual program of detection, surveillance and enforcement.").

27. *See, e.g.*, Cary Coglianese, Jennifer Nash & Todd Olmstead, *Performance-Based Regulation: Prospects and Limitations in Health, Safety, and Environmental Protection*, 55 Admin. L. Rev. 705 (2003).

28. Pub. L. No. 111-203, 124 Stat. 1376 (2010).

often the manner in which an agency decision is made affects the substance of that decision.

The administrative *process* is governed mainly by the language of an agency's organic statute, the relevant administrative procedure act[29] and the procedural rules adopted by the agency. Many agencies use specific procedures for individual matters, so it is dangerous to over-generalize on a particular agency's process of decisionmaking. In some instances, courts have required that agencies follow certain specified procedures.[30]

There are essentially two main types of agency decisionmaking: *rulemaking* and *adjudication*. Agency procedures normally vary depending on the type of decisionmaking in which the agency is engaged. Much, perhaps even most, agency action is sufficiently *informal* as to entail little in the way of procedural requirements.

[B] Rulemaking

When an agency exercises its legislative functions by making rules, the process ordinarily used is a conceptually straight-forward approach known as *notice and comment* rulemaking.[31] This process requires the agency to give the general public notification that a rule is being contemplated and the language or a general description of the proposed rule, and to invite any interested person to submit comments on the proposed rule. The agency considers the comments and then promulgates a final rule. There are some limited instances on the federal level when rules may be promulgated only after an agency follows the procedures much like those for adjudication described in Chapter 7, § 7.02[B] (so-called *formal* rulemaking), as well as instances when an agency's enabling act requires procedures somewhere between informal and formal rulemaking.

[C] Adjudication

When the agency exercises its judicial function by engaging in what is sometimes called formal adjudication, it uses a process that is very much like a civil bench trial in court. These proceedings—while subject to some variation depending on whether the agency is at the federal or state level and on the precise identity of the agency and the matter being adjudicated—typically permit an oral hearing with direct- and cross-examination, testimony under oath, the development of a complete and exclusive record on which the decision is to be based, and the presence of a neutral presiding officer (sometimes referred to as an administrative judge or an administrative law judge). However, court and agency procedures are not identical. Unlike civil courts, most agencies do not use formal rules of evidence or permit the comprehensive discovery allowed

29. Students concentrating on the administrative law of a particular state should take care to determine the scope of their state's administrative procedure act. Many state administrative procedure acts apply to specific agencies only if the legislature expressly provides, in the enabling act, that the state APA governs. Other states follow the model of the federal APA and make their administrative procedure acts applicable to all agencies unless a specific agency is expressly exempted.

30. The Supreme Court in *Goldberg v. Kelly*, 397 U.S. 254 (1970), required that state agencies wishing to terminate certain welfare benefits—aid to families with dependent children—adopt an elaborate hearing procedure for termination disputes. *See* the discussion of constitutional due process in Chapter 5.

31. Although notice-and-comment rulemaking is categorized as informal by the provisions of the federal APA, the procedures required for rulemaking are discussed extensively in Chapter 7.

under, for example, the Federal Rules of Civil Procedure. Elaborate pre-trial and post-trial procedures are rare, and juries are unheard of. Nonetheless, the similarities between agency adjudication and civil litigation are still far greater than the differences.

[D] Informal Agency Action

Most agency action is informal. Nonbinding agency guidance (generally falling under the labels of *interpretative rules* or *policy statements* in the parlance of the federal APA) resembles rulemaking in that it typically is more general than the resolution of individual cases. Meanwhile, most agency adjudication of individual cases is procedurally informal.

Procedures used when an agency engages in informal action vary considerably. Minimal procedures may include merely giving reasons for a decision—as, for example, when a federal agency denies certain applications for benefits. Other informal actions may involve the giving of notice and some opportunity to comment or submit orally or in writing. While procedures for notice-and-comment rulemaking and formal adjudication are often tightly controlled by either an enabling act or the relevant administrative procedure act, procedures governing informal agency action are often established by the agency itself.

[E] Alternative Dispute Resolution

Much like the current ferment in the substantive law of administrative agencies, traditional agency procedures are under serious re-examination. For some time, a number of agencies, such as the Environmental Protection Agency and the Federal Aviation Administration, have experimented with a new process known as *regulatory negotiation* to make rules. This procedure, in essence, brings representatives of all the major groups affected by a rulemaking around a table for face-to-face negotiation on the terms of the proposed rule, prior to its being published in the *Federal Register*.[32] In 1990, Congress codified regulatory negotiation by adding the Negotiated Rulemaking Act to the Administrative Procedure Act.[33] In the next several years, agency practitioners will have even more procedural devices at their disposal. After a number of proposals to adapt alternative dispute resolution (ADR) techniques to agency decisionmaking surfaced during the 1980s,[34] Congress acknowledged that ADR could become an important part of agency process by enacting in 1990, and substantially amending in 1996, the Administrative Dispute Resolution Act.[35] In appropriate circumstances, such techniques as arbitration, mediation and mini-trial may now be used as part of the agency dispute resolution process.

---

32. *See, e.g.*, Neil Eisner, *Regulatory Negotiation: A Real World Experience*, 31 Fed. B. News & J. 371 (1984), and the more elaborate description of regulatory negotiation in Chapter 7.

33. 5 U.S.C. §§ 570–81. The Negotiated Rulemaking Act was permanently reauthorized in late 1996. Pub. L. No. 104-320.

34. *See, e.g.*, Philip Harter, *Dispute Resolution and Administrative Law: The History, Needs, and Future of a Complex Relationship*, 29 Vill. L. Rev. 1393 (1984), and the discussion of alternative dispute resolution techniques in Chapter 8.

35. 5 U.S.C. §§ 571–83. The ADR Act was permanently reauthorized in late 1996. Pub. L. No. 104-320.

§ 1.05 Judicial Review of Agency Action

[A] Effect of Judicial Review

Lawyers should never lose sight of the important role that courts play in the development of administrative law. The creation of a new agency by the legislature may trigger an attack on the constitutionality of the agency, a dispute that can be resolved with finality only by the courts. The validity of each new regulatory program and many individual agency decisions can be challenged by persons affected by and dissatisfied with the action. Indeed, in most administrative systems, very few truly consequential agency decisions are exempt from judicial review. It is almost unheard of for Congress to enact a new administrative statute without also providing for some type of judicial review. Reflecting the standard federal practice, state administrative systems also favor judicial review.

For law students and lawyers alike, it is possible to make both too much and too little of judicial review. Some traditional teaching of administrative law over-emphasized judicial review to the point that many students and practitioners were deceived into thinking that the only truly important component in an administrative system is the judiciary. Even now, students may get the wrong idea that courts review everything and correct all errors because so many of the administrative law casebooks use large numbers of written decisions of the Supreme Court and circuit courts of appeals as the primary materials for the course. In actual agency practice, nothing could be further from the truth. The vast majority of agency decisions are never challenged in court, and those that are taken to court more often than not see nothing more than an affirmance of the agency's action.[36] The Supreme Court has sent some extraordinarily strong signals to the lower federal courts (and in particular, to the United States Court of Appeals for the District of Columbia Circuit, which reviews a disproportionate number of federal agency appeals) to leave agency decisions alone unless it is clear that the agency erred.[37] State courts have not been quite so deferential to agencies as the Supreme Court, but a quick review of a number of recent state court decisions suggests that a number of state supreme courts have tightened standards for reversing state agency action.

When analyzing judicial review of agency action, a lawyer typically confronts three types of issues: (1) *whether* judicial review is available at all for a particular case or for the challenging party, (2) the timing of judicial review (*i.e., when* judicial review may take place), and (3) if judicial review is both permissible and timely, *what standard* of review a court should apply to the merits of the case. Since most enabling acts provide

---

36. There has been some criticism of judicial review of agency actions. *See, e.g.*, Alan Charles Raul & Julie Zampa Dwyer, *"Regulatory Daubert": A Proposal to Enhance Judicial Review of Agency Science by Incorporating* Daubert *Principles into Administrative Law*, 66 LAW & CONTEMP. PROBS. 7 (2003); Jerry L. Mashaw, *Small Things Like Reasons Are Put in a Jar: Reason and Legitimacy in the Administrative State*, 70 FORDHAM L. REV. 17 (2001).

37. With regard to judicial review of the substance of agency action, see, *e.g.*, *Chevron U.S.A. Inc. v. Natural Resources Defense Council, Inc.*, 467 U.S. 837 (1984) (counseling judicial deference for administering agency interpretations of ambiguous statutes); *Baltimore Gas & Electric Co. v. Natural Resources Defense Council, Inc.*, 462 U.S. 87 (1983) (holding that courts have no business substituting their judgments for the scientific and technical decisions of the agencies); *Vermont Yankee Nuclear Power Corp. v. Natural Resources Defense Council, Inc.*, 435 U.S. 519 (1978) (reviewing an earlier stage of the *Baltimore Gas* case, and instructing lower federal courts not to impose by judicial fiat more rulemaking procedures on agencies than required by the APA "absent extraordinary circumstances").

for some type of judicial review, and since both the federal Administrative Procedure Act (APA) and most state administrative procedure acts provide for judicial review even if the enabling act is silent, the question of whether or not a court may consider a particular issue at all is almost always answered in the affirmative. On the federal level, because federal courts are courts of limited jurisdiction, you must always identify and cite a specific grant of subject matter jurisdiction. Doing so is rarely difficult.

[B] Preclusion from Judicial Review

But finding a jurisdictional statute is not the end of this inquiry. There are instances when an agency decision may be precluded from judicial review because the legislature has specifically prohibited judicial review or because a matter is deemed totally within the agency's discretion. On occasion, a person seeking judicial review of a particular agency determination may not be able to prove that she is sufficiently affected by the agency's action to have the requisite standing to bring the action on her own behalf. The normal test applied in the federal courts is whether a person can show "personal injury in fact, economic or otherwise" that was caused by the agency's action and can be redressed by judicial review.[38]

[C] Other Barriers to Judicial Review

[1] Statutory and Common Law Barriers

Even if jurisdiction and standing exists and the decision is not precluded from review, a court may not be permitted to act at the time judicial review is sought. The doctrine of primary jurisdiction requires that most disputes within an agency's jurisdiction first go to the agency and not directly into court. If a party starts with the agency, the dispute will have to stay in the agency until the agency has taken final agency action. Exactly which agency actions are final in this regard not always clear. The litigant must exhaust the decisional possibilities within the agency. If a litigant fails to pursue a decisional step within the agency, a court will often decline to consider the matter pending further agency action. Additionally, the doctrine of ripeness, a concept related to but not identical with finality and exhaustion, prohibits judicial review if a dispute is not yet a legal (as opposed to a scientific or technical) issue.[39]

The litigant who survives these threshold barriers still faces difficulty in getting the agency action reversed. The federal APA permits a court to overturn agency action on the following grounds:[40]

1. the action violates a statute (including statutes establishing the agency's jurisdiction and authority) or the Constitution;
2. the action violates some procedure established by law;
3. the action is inadequately supported by evidence;

---

38. These matters are extensively discussed in Chapter 10.

39. These doctrines are discussed in Chapter 11.

40. For convenience, these grounds paraphrase the principal grounds available under 5 U.S.C. § 706. These issues are discussed in much greater length in Chapter 13.

4. the action is arbitrary, capricious, an abuse of discretion, or otherwise not in accordance with law as inadequately explained or justified.

This list may seem comprehensive, but there are comparatively few agency actions that give rise to statutory, procedural, or constitutional violations. In considering most of these challenges, courts are deferential to the agency's determinations and will uphold the agency's decision if it is one that a reasonable person could have made, irrespective of whether the court itself would have made the same decision.

[2] Odds of Judicial Reversal of Agency Decisions

There are few meaningful statistics available on the proportion of agency decisions reversed by courts. Threshold barriers to judicial review sometimes make it difficult even to get into court. Once there, a party may be hard pressed to get a reversal on the merits. Judicial review should never be seen as a safety valve in planning a case strategy before an agency. The prospects of winning in court, having lost before the agency, are too unlikely. In reading the remainder of this book, you should constantly remember the second cardinal rule of agency practice mentioned at the start of this chapter: *A lawyer who fails to win a case at the agency runs a substantial risk of not winning it at all.*

There is yet a third cardinal rule for practicing before administrative agencies that needs to be set out here, even though it may be obvious to anyone who has read this far: *Know your agency.* There is no substitute for having a thorough understanding of the manner in which the agency functions. Many practitioners obtain this knowledge over time; but even if this case marks your first experience with a particular agency, you are not excused from getting a good grip on that agency's behavior. As the following section explains, proper research is vital, and, with so much information available electronically these days, not all that difficult.

§ 1.06 Researching Administrative Law

[A] Student Awareness of Administrative Materials

Most teachers of administrative law are surprised by the lack of attention to administrative materials in most first-year legal writing and research courses. Many students come into their first administrative law course knowing virtually nothing about the primary materials of the course and absolutely nothing of the secondary materials. The following is a brief guide to federal materials available for those who are not already familiar with the sources.

[B] Official Materials

[1] *The United States Code*

The essence of administrative law is to be found primarily in government documents. First and foremost of these is the compilation of federal statutes, the *United States Code* (U.S.C.) and its various sources of legislative history such as committee reports. Floor debates transcribed in the Congressional Record are sometimes useful. These materials contain the language of each agency's enabling act and the pre-enactment comments on that legislation by members of Congress and other persons.

The primary federal procedural statute, the Administrative Procedure Act (APA), was first enacted in 1946 but had been the subject of intense discussion for almost ten years prior to enactment, as lawyers, agency officials and members of Congress adjusted to many of the procedural lessons learned during the Progressive and New Deal eras. One central feature of this debate, on which there was virtually a consensus, was the need for a uniform set of procedures applicable to most if not all federal agencies. At the same time, the APA does not control every aspect of every agency's processes. These days, an agency's enabling act may contain many specific procedures directly applicable to that agency. Some of the enabling act requirements may not be consistent with the APA. For example, practice before some highly proceduralized agencies, such as the National Labor Relations Board, almost never requires reference to the APA, because the agency's statutes and internal procedural rules are so detailed and sophisticated. For most agencies, however, the APA has a strong bearing on the process by which the agency makes decisions.

The APA is contained in 5 U.S.C. §§551 *et seq.*, and its legislative history may be found in Administrative Procedure Act—Legislative History 1944–46, S. Doc. No. 248, 79th Cong., 2d Sess. (1946). A crucial executive branch committee report is also widely regarded as part of the APA's legislative history: Final Report of the Attorney General's Committee on Administrative Procedure, S. Doc. No. 8, 77th Cong., 1st Sess. (1941). Both the House and Senate reports on the APA will be found in the Attorney General's Committee report. Finally, although it was written after the APA was enacted, the Attorney General's Manual on the Administrative Procedure Act, published by the Department of Justice in 1947, is widely considered authoritative as a contemporaneous explanation of the APA's terms.

[2] *The Federal Register*

Agencies announce proposed and final rules and various other information on their day-to-day functioning in the *Federal Register.*[41] This document was established by Congress during the New Deal because, at the time, there was no central repository of important agency pronouncements. Indeed, before the *Federal Register*, many agency rules could only be found in the desk drawers of agency employees. The *Federal Register* is published five days each week.

[3] *The Code of Federal Regulations*

The *Code of Federal Regulations* (CFR) is published annually and contains the agency's current rules in force.[42] Rules and certain other documents, such as agency interpretations and rulings published initially in the *Federal Register*, eventually find their way into CFR. For agencies whose rules change only infrequently, CFR is often the primary research tool used by practitioners. Readers should be warned, however, that there often are substantial delays between publication of a final rule in the *Federal Register*

41. The *Federal Register* is available online at https://www.govinfo.gov/app/collection/fr.
42. The *Code of Federal Regulations* is available at https://www.govinfo.gov/app/collection/cfr.

and codification of that rule in CFR. Because of this delay, most agency practitioners subscribe to various print and online commercial publications that track rule and policy changes on a day-to-day basis for specific agencies, such as *E&E News*, *Tax Notes*, or the *Daily Labor Reporter.* Some agencies maintain their own subscription services for such pronouncements, such as the Internal Revenue Service's *Guidewire* or the Federal Communications Commission's *Daily Digest.*

[4] Agency Decisions

Many federal agencies publish some kind of official reporter that includes the reports of agency adjudications. These compilations, like the *FCC Reports Second Series*, look much like court reporters. Again, most practitioners subscribe to the official agency reporter but depend on proprietary subscription services (*see* § [3] *above*) for up-to-the-minute information. In many circumstances, the value of using reported agency adjudications as controlling authority is questionable because most agencies do not consider themselves wholly bound by judicially developed doctrines such as stare decisis. Nonetheless, careful lawyers pay close attention to these decisions to determine the current trend of agency thinking. Most agencies now publish these decisions on their individual websites.

[5] Other Agency Publications

Agencies always publish a great deal of information outside the *Federal Register* or CFR that can be enormously helpful. Documents such as internal agency newsletters, annual reports, and statistical summaries are useful in developing a comprehensive understanding of the entire agency. The Government Printing Office (GPO) publishes a *Monthly Catalog of United States Government Publications* that lists many of these documents. The GPO also publishes *The United States Government Manual*, a single volume compilation of basic information on virtually all government agencies. And the second edition of the *Sourcebook of United States Executive Agencies*, published in 2018 by the Administrative Conference of the United States, provides a comprehensive overview of the organizational structure of the entire executive branch.

These days, there is a great deal of agency information available over the Internet. Virtually every federal agency has a Web site that may be mined for a great deal of basic information on that particular agency. A good basic source for links to the various agencies is provided by the Library of Congress: http://www.loc.gov/rr/news/fedgov.html. Additionally, the website of the Office of Information and Regulatory Affairs, reginfo.gov, provides ongoing and extensive coverage of federal agency regulatory activity in progress.

[6] Presidential Documents

The president figures importantly in the work of administrative agencies. Accordingly, executive orders and presidential proclamations, along with reorganization plans and executive agreements, must often be closely analyzed. These documents may occasionally be found in the *Federal Register*, but more likely are to be found in the *Daily Compilation of Presidential Documents*, published by the Office of the Federal Register and available at https://www.govinfo.gov/app/collection/cpd.

[7] Opinions of the Office of Legal Counsel

The Office of Legal Counsel (OLC) in the Department of Justice, acting on behalf of the Attorney General of the United States, is often asked to provide interpretations of treaties, statutes, presidential documents, and other official material, as well as to advise on other matters of agency functioning.[43] While the precise legal impact of an OLC opinion has never been conclusively determined, OLC's pronouncements carry great weight both inside and outside the executive branch. Most OLC opinions are available at https://www.justice.gov/olc/opinions and are published in a compilation called the Opinions of the Office of Legal Counsel of the United States Department of Justice, which was formerly known as the Official Opinions of the Attorneys General of the United States.

[C] Unofficial Commercial Services

By definition, government documents are the official source of information on administrative agencies, but there is at least one privately-published service available for virtually every major federal regulatory agency. Most practitioners regard these services as indispensable because they are not subject to many of the publication delays associated with government publications. Published by such companies as Bloomberg BNA and Commerce Clearing House, they are gold mines of information on the agencies, containing a wide range of documents and information from proposed and final rules, to adjudications, to agency gossip. Online legal research databases like Westlaw, Lexis, and HeinOnline also include extensive collections of agency materials.

A vast amount of additional information on administrative law in general and on specific agencies may be found in casebooks, law journal articles like those cited in footnotes throughout this book, and treatises like the *Administrative Law Treatise* co-authored by the author of this book and Richard J. Pierce, Jr. Serious students of administrative law never disregard these sources.

---

43. The attorney general of the United States is authorized by statute to perform this function for the president and heads of departments in the executive branch. *See* 28 U.S.C. §§ 511-12. The attorney general has delegated that responsibility to the Office of Legal Counsel. *See* 28 U.S.C. § 510.

Chapter 2

External Controls on Administrative Agencies—The Legislative Branch

§ 2.01 Introduction

Modern administrative agencies have numerous prerogatives and exercise a great deal of discretion. But they do not create themselves, and they are subject to a substantial number of external controls. Each branch of government has an impact on agencies. Since all agencies are created by the legislature, each agency obviously is subject to the terms of its organic statute, also sometimes referred to as its enabling act. Organic statutes are only one of many ways a legislature can exert influence over agencies. Agencies normally are located within the executive branch of government, so they are constrained by various entities within that branch, such as the president and the attorney general. Components of the cabinet-level agencies are, by definition, under the control of the cabinet officer for that agency. Even the nominally "independent" regulatory commissions are subject to a large number of executive controls, exercised mainly through the presidential appointment power and the president's control of the budgetary process. The judicial branch exerts control over agencies by way of judicial review of agency action on an after-the-fact, case-by-case basis; but the power of the courts is no less significant for coming at the end of the administrative process.

The form of these controls ranges from the obvious to the subtle. Virtually everyone with an elementary understanding of the United States system of government realizes that a legislature may amend an organic statute and that the chief executive may appoint cabinet officers and other agency leaders. Even so, the less-obvious controls can be just as compelling. These include the power of the legislature to conduct investigations, the power of the president to order agencies to do—or refrain from doing—certain things, and the power of the courts to write language in judicial opinions that may gently persuade, if not outright compel, an agency to mend its ways.

This Chapter considers the matter of legislative controls on agency action. Chapter 3 discusses executive controls on agency action. Judicial controls are discussed in several chapters, principally Chapter 5, and Chapters 10 through 13.

§ 2.02 Constitutional Limitations on the Creation of Agencies—The Delegation Issue

[A] Legislative Authority

At both the state and federal levels, the legislative branch is responsible for establishing agencies and endowing those agencies with a great deal of power and discretion. This authority does not, however, give the legislature carte blanche. The United States Constitution and most, if not all, state constitutions impose some limits upon when and under what circumstances a legislature may delegate powers to an agency. Most administrative law casebooks refer to this as the *nondelegation* doctrine. Nondelegation is a principle based on the premise that, although a legislature may entrust a variety of responsibilities and functions to agencies, under our Constitution, a legislature may not delegate its own powers to an agency.

[B] Federal Agencies and Nondelegation Doctrine—The Early Cases

On the federal level, the Supreme Court has tussled with the nondelegation doctrine for decades, even though the general rule—that a legislature may not delegate legislative power to an agency—was established very early in our history. The source of the doctrine is the U.S. Constitution itself.

The Vesting Clause of Article I, § 1 provides that "[a]ll legislative Powers herein granted shall be vested in a Congress of the United States." The Vesting Clause of Article II, § 1 correspondingly vests "[t]he executive Power" in the president. Comparing and contemplating these two provisions suggests some of the tensions that have persisted for nearly two hundred years. Article I, § 1 arguably gives legislative powers *exclusively* to the Congress—*i.e.*, says that Congress may never pass on any of those powers to other components of the government. But it does not say so explicitly. Meanwhile, these Vesting Clauses do not define what constitutes legislative power as compared to executive power, except by considering other language in Article I and Article II. For example, the Necessary and Proper Clause of Article I, § 8 provides that Congress has the power "[t]o make all Laws which shall be necessary and proper for carrying into Execution" the other legislative powers specified in Article I. The Take Care Clause of Article II, § 3 requires the president to "take Care that the Laws be faithfully executed." No one questions that the Constitution permits Congress to rely on the executive branch to resolve statutory details in the process of executing the law. The very nature of executive power anticipates some amount of discretion on the part of executive branch officials. Drawing a clean line between requiring Congress to retain the legislative power and allowing executive branch officials the latitude they need to execute the laws effectively has proven challenging.

The Supreme Court moved very gingerly on this issue in the first few decades following ratification of the Constitution. It could not realistically deny the existence of the earliest executive branch agencies, such as the customs office and the Treasury Department. Many of these offices pre-dated the Constitution and were clearly essential to the functioning of national government. The Constitution itself contemplates executive branch agencies, for example in the Appointments Clause of Article II, § 2 by authorizing the president "to require the Opinion, in writing, of the principal Officer in each of the executive Departments" and by allowing Congress to vest the power to appoint inferior officers in the heads of those departments. Chief Justice Marshall, writing in *Wayman v. Southard*,[1] recognized that Congress could not by itself possibly exercise or even meaningfully supervise on a day-to day basis every detail of the functioning of a national government; thus, some delegation was a compelling necessity. Nonetheless, Chief Justice Marshall set certain boundaries on delegation, the traces of which still can be seen today. He insisted that Congress must establish the general outline of a regulatory program, but may leave to the agency the authority "to fill up the details."[2]

Subsequent cases continued to recognize the nondelegation principle, but generally upheld congressional enactments that gave duties to administrative agencies. In *Marshall Field & Co. v. Clark*,[3] the Court upheld a delegation to the president for suspension of certain favorable tariffs on the goods of countries that did not reciprocate favorable treatment. The saving grace of the organic statute in that case was, in the Court's view, that the agency was limited to making purely factual determinations. Later cases permitted the delegation if the agency was limited to determining a "contingency"[4] or where Congress, by statute, set the "primary standard."[5] In *J.W. Hampton, Jr. & Co. v. United States*,[6] the Court considered another tariff statute, this one authorizing the president to increase tariffs by whatever amount he deemed necessary to "equalize ... differences in costs of production" between manufacturers of goods in the United States and competing countries. The statutory specifications were too open-ended to permit the Court to find that the authorization was limited to contingencies or that the statute established the primary standard. Instead, the Court said that a statute could delegate authority to the executive branch so long as Congress "shall lay down by legislative act an *intelligible principle* to which the person or body authorized [to act] is directed to conform."[7]

The trend of these decisions is obvious. The Supreme Court had little or no interest in overseeing the day-to-day workings of the executive branch. Even before the turn of the twentieth century, the federal government dealt with many complicated matters. The Court clearly determined that Congress could not be expected to resolve every detail of those matters on its own, and that Congress needed agencies to do some of the work. A heavy-handed application of the nondelegation doctrine could have stopped the executive branch in its tracks. At the same time, the Court was unwilling to do away with the nondelegation principle altogether—perhaps from an abundance of caution, and because the doctrine reflects the express language of Article I, § 1. Not for the first or the last time in its history, the Court preserved a theoretical façade, the idea that Congress's legislative power could not be delegated, while deciding individual delegation cases to allow Congress to do just that.

1. 23 U.S. (10 Wheat.) 1 (1825).
2. *Id.* at 16.
3. 143 U.S. 649 (1892).
4. *The Brig Aurora*, 11 U.S. (7 Cranch) 382 (1813).
5. *Buttfield v. Stranahan*, 192 U.S. 470 (1904) (discussing standards of purity and fitness of tea imported into the United States). Students interested in the minutiae of government will be delighted to know that, until 1996, the federal government employed a contingent of tea tasters to carry out the duties at issue in the *Buttfield* case.
6. 276 U.S. 394 (1928).
7. *Id.* at 409 (emphasis added).

[C] Nondelegation Doctrine—The New Deal Cases

The Supreme Court has held congressional delegations of power to the executive branch unconstitutional in only two cases, decided in the same year, and concerning the same statute. The dramatic confrontation came in 1935 when two portions of what was probably the centerpiece of the New Deal, the National Industrial Recovery Act of 1933 (NIRA), reached the Court. In both cases, *Panama Refining Co. v. Ryan*[8] (the "Hot Oil" case), and *A.L.A. Schechter Poultry Corp. v. United States*[9] (the "Sick Chicken" case), the Supreme Court used the nondelegation doctrine to strike down two separate sections of the NIRA. Since these two cases are often used as the take-off point for administrative law courses, they warrant close analysis by students. They are also good vehicles for a discussion of legislative drafting and for an introduction to the administrative process itself.

The two opinions appear murky on first reading but are not that difficult to parse. *Panama Refining* ought to be viewed in context. It was an early attempt to establish a coherent federal energy policy in conjunction with existing state regulation of the oil industry. In states with large oil reserves, the state legislatures established state regulatory commissions (for example, the Texas Railroad Commission) with significant powers to control oil and natural gas production. Among other things, those commissions were authorized to enforce production levels for individual oil wells. These production limits had two purposes: (1) they held down total production, and thus, increased the price per barrel of the oil actually produced, and (2) they functioned as oil conservation measures because it is usually possible to get more oil out of a well that produces its oil slowly than it is to get oil from a well that is permitted to produce at a rapid rate. This is a scientific reality established early in the history of oil production by petroleum geologists, rather than merely a tenet of government regulation. Whatever one might think of regulatory agencies, it is indisputable that the state oil and gas commissions had a great deal of experience in what they were doing and that there was a rational basis for this type of regulation. Moreover, production levels had been set by the state agencies for years and were neither creations of the New Deal nor the federal government.

Section 9 of the NIRA, the only section of the statute under review in *Panama Refining*, did only one thing: it permitted the president, acting through the NIRA's jurisdictional agency, the National Recovery Administration (NRA), to write a regulation prohibiting oil producers from shipping in interstate commerce any oil produced from a well in excess of these state-established production levels. Obviously, Congress hoped that controlling excess oil production would have a beneficial effect on the national economy, but did not want to exercise the Supremacy Clause to interfere with the states' setting of the production levels—an activity that had always been carried out by state oil and gas commissions. Instead, Congress chose to control the one part of the process that was within its jurisdiction: the interstate commerce aspects of oil transportation and sale. Remember that a state's authority to regulate business under our Constitution normally stops at the state's boundaries. The federal government is the only entity that may regulate *interstate* commerce under the Commerce Clause.

Thus, perhaps, there was nothing totally outlandish in what the states had been doing all along or in what Congress attempted to do under the Commerce Clause. However,

8. 293 U.S. 388 (1935).
9. 295 U.S. 495 (1935).

a majority of the Court held § 9 unconstitutional as a violation of the nondelegation principle. The Court majority viewed § 9 as a statute giving the president "unlimited authority" to act, with no boundaries set on his discretion. In the Court's words, § 9 set no conditions, established no criteria, nor required any specific findings before the president could act.[10]

In *Schechter Poultry*, the Court reviewed another section of the NIRA and came to the same conclusion as it did in *Panama Refining*. *Schechter* involved § 3 of the Act, in which Congress authorized private bodies, essentially trade associations, to develop standards (or "codes") of fair competition. When these codes were completed, they were handed to the president, and upon presidential approval, became binding (that is, they had the force of law) on the industry as a whole.[11] As in *Panama Refining*, the Court concluded initially that § 3 lacked an appropriate standard for setting out boundaries for executive branch discretion and was thereby unconstitutional.

Moreover, the *Schechter Poultry* Court was also troubled by the statute's giving governmental decisionmaking powers to private entities, although it did not dwell on this defect in the opinion. One year later, in *Carter v. Carter Coal Co.*,[12] the Court re-emphasized the "no-delegation-to-private-parties" rule when it invalidated a portion of the Bituminous Coal Conservation Act. That statute permitted private sector groups comprised of management and labor representatives to develop binding wage and hour standards for the whole industry. The Court declared this statutory delegation "an intolerable and unconstitutional interference of liberty and private property" in violation of the Due Process Clause.[13] But the Court arguably suggested the statute was unconstitutional under the reasoning of *Schechter Poultry* as well.

The majority opinions in both *Panama Refining* and *Schechter Poultry* may have been politically motivated at least in part, as a majority of the justices were hostile to President Franklin Delano Roosevelt's economic programs. Nevertheless, because *Panama Refining* and *Schechter Poultry* are the only cases to invalidate a statute on nondelegation grounds, many litigants and some administrative law courses have spent considerable time debating what makes the NIRA's text so different from that of other statutes upheld in earlier and later cases. Also worth considering from the New Deal delegation cases are the separate opinions by Justice Benjamin Cardozo, who dissented in *Panama Refining* and merely concurred in *Schechter Poultry*.

Justice Cardozo, unlike the *Panama Refining* majority, was willing to read § 9 in light of the statement of purpose for the NIRA contained in § 1 of the statute. Section 1 set out, among many other purposes for the NIRA, a need to conserve natural resources.

---

10. Congress reacted quickly to the decision in *Panama Refining*. Shortly after the opinion was announced, Congress passed the Connolly Hot Oil Act setting out essentially the same prohibition on the interstate transportation of oil produced in excess of state quotas. The Connolly Hot Oil Act never was successfully challenged and remains on the books to this day at 15 U.S.C. § 715c. This statute required the president to make findings on the effect on interstate commerce of shipments of hot oil before prohibiting those shipments.

11. Students should not conclude that President Franklin Delano Roosevelt personally reviewed these codes. To the extent that they were reviewed by the executive branch, they were reviewed by the National Recovery Administration even though the statute directs the president to perform the review. This is an example, frequently utilized by the executive branch, of so-called *subdelegation:* the handing down of powers within the executive branch from a senior official to an official or office further down the organizational chart.

12. 298 U.S. 238 (1936).

13. *Id.* at 311.

Cardozo accepted this purpose as a sufficient standard for curbing executive discretion, and thereby concluded that the statute set appropriate boundaries for executive branch action. However, he was unwilling to use § 1 in similar fashion in *Schechter Poultry*, pointing out that presidential authority to promulgate the codes of competition was not properly "canalized" and deemed § 3 "delegation run riot."

When a judge as distinguished as Cardozo believes that one part of a statute (§ 9) is constitutional and another part (§ 3) is unconstitutional, a more sophisticated analysis of his opinion ought to be made. Looking closely at Cardozo's two opinions, at least three distinguishing factors are present.

First, the Hot Oil provision (§ 9) was a *prohibition* on business conduct, while the Sick Chicken provision (§ 3) was essentially an *authorization* to industry to act for the common good. Consistent with the traditional view of the manner in which American business ought to be regulated, Cardozo viewed the proper role of government as *prohibiting* bad practices, rather than a somewhat fuzzy encouragement of good behavior.

Second, the Hot Oil provision was directed toward a *single industry* and reflected an understanding of conventional practices in that industry (*i.e.*, the setting of production levels by the state agencies), while the Sick Chicken provision affected virtually all American businesses.

Third, the Sick Chicken provision seemed to permit private parties to make decisions that should be reserved for the government, even though the president had to approve the standards before they went into effect. Cardozo apparently believed that the president's role would be largely a matter of rubber-stamping the private decisions.

Regardless, after the *Carter Coal* decision in 1936 and President Roosevelt's unsuccessful attempt to pack the Supreme Court, there were noticeable changes in the Court's attitude toward New Deal legislation, possibly triggered by changes in the Supreme Court's membership.[14] These changes, combined with more care in drafting legislation on the part of Congress, prompted the Court to stop invalidating congressional legislation, at least on nondelegation grounds. Since *Panama Refining* and *Schechter Poultry*, the Supreme Court has not overturned any statute on the basis of the nondelegation principle.

[D] Nondelegation Doctrine Since the New Deal

Between 1936 and the late 1970s, the Supreme Court repeatedly upheld broad statutory delegations of power to the president and his subordinates. In 1943, in *National Broadcasting Co. v. United States*,[15] the Court upheld a delegation of authority to the Federal Communications Commission to regulate broadcasting to further "public interest, convenience, or necessity." In 1944, in *Yakus v. United States*,[16] the Court said that, as a "war emergency measure," Congress could constitutionally delegate authority to the administrator of the Office of Price Administration to establish price controls for commodities that, "in his judgment," would be "fair and equitable." In 1947, the Court upheld an exceptionally vague statutory standard in *Fahey v. Mallonee*,[17] in part because

14. *See* Louis Jaffe, Judicial Control of Administrative Action 51–62 (1965).
15. 319 U.S. 190 (1943).
16. 321 U.S. 414 (1944).
17. 332 U.S. 245 (1947).

the implementing regulations were detailed and explicit, and in part because the statute did not contain criminal penalties. In 1965, in *Zemel v. Rusk*,[18] the Court upheld a delegation to the Secretary of State to "grant and issue passports... under such rules as the President shall designate and prescribe...," noting that Congress "must of necessity paint with a broad brush" when it legislates on foreign affairs. In 1974, in *National Cable Television Ass'n v. United States*,[19] the Court hinted that a statute setting fees for certain cable television operations might have problems under the nondelegation principle, but remanded the case to the Federal Communications Commission on other grounds. In the same case, two dissenters characterized the nondelegation doctrine as "moribund."

In the early 1980s, the nondelegation doctrine surfaced again. In two separate opinions, Justice William Rehnquist (who subsequently served as Chief Justice until his death in 2005) suggested that the Court resuscitate the nondelegation principle in an attempt to force Congress to be more careful when it drafts enabling legislation. He surprised the legal community with his concurring opinion on this issue in *Industrial Union Department, AFL-CIO v. American Petroleum Institute*,[20] also known as *The Benzene Case*, when he suggested that Congress had invalidly delegated to the Department of Labor virtually unfettered authority to set certain employee safety and health standards in the Occupational Safety and Health Act. More to the point, Justice Rehnquist indicated his respect for *Panama Refining* and his sympathy for the nondelegation doctrine by calling attention to the doctrine's underlying purposes. In his view, a proper application of the doctrine (1) forces the elected representatives of the people—Congress—to make the important choices of social and economic policy; (2) guarantees that any delegation to an agency will be accompanied by an intelligible principle guiding the agency's discretion; and (3) enhances judicial review by giving the courts a standard against which to weigh the exercise of the agency's discretion. The next term, joined by Chief Justice Warren Burger, Justice Rehnquist reiterated his position on nondelegation and the Occupational Safety and Health Act in his dissent in *American Textile Manufacturers Institute, Inc. v. Donovan*,[21] also known as *The Cotton Dust Case*. Justice Rehnquist maintained that the post-New Deal Supreme Court was too quick to consign the nondelegation doctrine to the junk heap.

Of course, it is possible to make both too much and too little of the Rehnquist opinions. On the one hand, he was writing alone in the *Benzene* concurrence and in dissent in *Cotton Dust* when he was only an associate justice. As Chief Justice, he never saw fit (or perhaps never had the occasion) to repeat these views in later cases.

Regardless, a majority of the Court has consistently refused to apply the nondelegation doctrine rigidly because it realizes that Congress cannot legislate with precision in all areas of public policy, and devising a standard that can distinguish impermissible from permissible delegations consistently is very difficult if not outright impossible. Indeed, it may be enough for Congress to identify a problem without prescribing its solution, so long as a competent agency is established to deal with it, and providing that the organic statute contains sufficient detail otherwise to provide *some* standard, however minimal and ambiguous, to curtail executive discretion.

18. 381 U.S. 1 (1965).
19. 415 U.S. 336 (1974).
20. 448 U.S. 607 (1980).
21. 452 U.S. 490 (1981).

This was essentially the message the Supreme Court sent to the American public when, in 1989, it upheld the United States Sentencing Commission and the somewhat flawed criminal sentencing requirements imposed on federal courts under the Commission's hotly debated federal sentencing "guidelines." In *Mistretta v. United States*,[22] the Court noted the statute's prescription of three goals for the Commission to pursue; four purposes of sentencing generally; a "specific tool—the guidelines system" to accomplish those goals and purposes; seven factors for formulating categories of offenses; and eleven factors for establishing categories of defendants.[23] Quoting the phrasing of its 1928 *J.W. Hampton* decision, the Court said, "In light of our approval of [all the earlier] broad delegations, we harbor no doubt that Congress' delegation of authority to the Sentencing Commission is sufficiently specific and detailed to meet constitutional requirements.... We cannot dispute petitioner's contention that the Commission enjoys significant discretion in formulating guidelines.... But our cases do not at all suggest that delegations of this type may not carry with them the need to exercise judgment on matters of policy.... The Act sets forth more than merely an '*intelligible principle*' or minimal standards."[24]

In 2001, the Supreme Court in *Whitman v. American Trucking Ass'ns*[25] also refused to deviate from its past nondelegation jurisprudence. Writing for a unanimous Court, Justice Scalia reiterated that the proper standard of review in a delegation challenge is to determine whether Congress had legislated an "intelligible principle" to which the agency's decisionmaking must conform, or whether the statute was so broad and lacked any standard as to be unconstitutional. Reviewing portions of the Clean Air Act, the Court examined language in the Act that authorized the Environmental Protection Agency to set air quality standards that are "requisite to protect public health from the adverse effects of the pollutant in the ambient air." Justice Scalia invoked a 1991 decision, *Touby v. United States*,[26] in which a similar delegation to the Attorney General to designate certain drugs as controlled substances was upheld. Justice Scalia commented that the delegation in *Whitman* was "in fact well within the outer limits of our nondelegation precedents"[27] and noted that the Court had invalidated only two statutes on

---

22. 488 U.S. 361 (1989).

23. *Id.* at 374-76.

24. *Id.* at 374-79 (emphasis added). Except as an example of judicial application of the nondelegation doctrine, *Mistretta* is probably only of historical interest. In *United States v. Booker*, 543 U.S. 220 (2005), the Supreme Court determined that the federal sentencing guidelines are advisory in nature because they interfere with a defendant's right to be convicted and sentenced only on facts proved beyond a reasonable doubt at trial. The *Booker* court did not revisit any of the delegation discussion set out in *Mistretta*.

25. 531 U.S. 457 (2001).

26. 500 U.S. 160 (1991).

27. *American Trucking Ass'ns*, 531 U.S. at 474. On occasion, lower federal courts have relied on the nondelegation doctrine as a justification for requiring agencies to adopt the narrower option among competing interpretations of statutes, and thus to preserve those statutes against a nondelegation attack. In *International Union v. Occupational Safety & Health Admin.*, 938 F.2d 1310 (D.C. Cir. 1991), Judge Stephen Williams determined that certain interpretations by OSHA were "so broad as to be unreasonable" but went on to conclude that at least one of the OSHA interpretations was "reasonable and consistent with the nondelegation doctrine." *Id.* at 1317; *see also* Richard J. Pierce, Jr., *The Inherent Limits on Judicial Control of Agency Discretion: The D.C. Circuit and the Nondelegation Doctrine*, 52 Admin. L. Rev. 63 (2000). Such was the D.C. Circuit's justification for rejecting the EPA's interpretation of the Clean Air Act in in *American Trucking Ass'ns*, but the Supreme Court rejected that argument as well, with Justice Scalia asserting that an agency cannot cure an otherwise defective delegation by adopting rules that narrow the agency's scope of authority. *American Trucking Ass'ns*, 531 U.S. at 472-73.

nondelegation grounds (*Panama Refining* and *Schechter Poultry*). Justice Thomas concurred, but suggested that there might be "cases in which the principle is intelligible and yet the significance of the delegated decision is simply too great for the decision to be called anything other than 'legislative,'" and that the Court on another occasion ought to reconsider its delegation jurisprudence.[28] Meanwhile, however, Justice Stevens in concurrence contended that "it would be both wiser and more faithful to what we have actually done in delegation cases to admit that agency rulemaking authority is 'legislative power,'" and that "there is nothing inherently unconstitutional about it."[29]

In 2019, in *Gundy v. United States*,[30] the Supreme Court again rejected, but narrowly, a nondelegation challenge to a broad delegation of rulemaking power to an agency. The case concerned a provision of the Sex Offender Registration and Notification Act authorizing the Attorney General to "specify the applicability of" the statute's requirements to individuals convicted of sex offenses prior to the statute's enactment. Relying on a combination of the statute's declaration of purpose and legislative history, as well as other Supreme Court precedent, and writing on behalf of a plurality of four, Justice Elena Kagan interpreted the statute as imposing an implicit feasibility requirement that provided an intelligible principle to cabin executive discretion.

Justice Samuel Alito concurred in the judgment in *Gundy*, purely because of stare decisis and the lack of a majority to reconsider the intelligible principle standard. Justice Neil Gorsuch wrote a dissenting opinion, joined by Chief Justice John Roberts and Justice Clarence Thomas, in which he argued that the intelligible principle standard had gained "a life of its own" unmoored from traditional understandings of the nondelegation doctrine. Admitting the need for some test for evaluating congressional delegations, Gorsuch outlined what he described as three "important guiding principles": (1) Congress may authorize the executive branch to "fill up the details" of a statute but must "make the policy decisions when regulating private conduct"; (2) Congress may make the application of the rules it establishes "depend on executive fact finding"; and (3) Congress may delegate "certain non-legislative responsibilities."

Justice Brett Kavanaugh did not participate in *Gundy*. A few months after the *Gundy* decision, however, Kavanaugh wrote a statement regarding the Court's denial of certiorari in *Paul v. United States*[31] in which he agreed that Justice Gorsuch's alternative approach to evaluating delegations "may warrant future consideration in future cases." Kavanaugh then proceeded to suggest that the Court might adopt "a nondelegation principle for major questions."

Everything discussed so far has involved the issue of delegations' text and scope, and doctrines like the intelligible principle standard used to evaluate the same. Remember, however, that there is another component of nondelegation: an inquiry as *to whom* decisionmaking power is given, as concerned the Supreme Court in *Schechter Poultry* and *Carter Coal*. This other aspect of the nondelegation doctrine figured in a very important decision, *Bowsher v. Synar*,[32] overturning a budget-balancing statute known as the Gramm-Rudman-Hollings Act.[33]

---

28. *American Trucking Ass'ns*, 543 U.S. at 487 (Thomas, J., concurring).
29. *Id.* at 488-90 (Stevens, J., concurring).
30. 139 S. Ct. 2116 (2019).
31. 140 S. Ct. 342 (2019) (Mem.) (Kavanaugh, J., statement respecting the denial of certiorari).
32. 478 U.S. 714 (1986).
33. Gramm-Rudman is formally called the Balanced Budget and Emergency Deficit Control Act of 1985, Pub. L. No. 99-177, 99 Stat. 1037

In *Synar*, the Supreme Court reviewed a statute giving certain powers of review over the federal budget to the comptroller general, who heads the General Accounting Office (now called the Government Accountability Office or GAO). The Court determined that the comptroller general and the GAO are properly considered part of the legislative branch because, although the comptroller general is appointed by the president (from a list of three candidates provided by the Speaker of the House of Representatives and the president pro tempore of the Senate), the comptroller general is removable from that office only by Congress. As part of the legislative branch, the comptroller general could not constitutionally make decisions that constitute the "execution of the law." The budgetary powers Congress gave to the comptroller general "plainly entail[ed] execution of the law in constitutional terms."[34] Although this type of delegation is somewhat different from the delegations to private parties in *Schechter Poultry* and in *Carter Coal*, *Synar* is a landmark decision for the proposition that delegation to whom is still an important matter.

The *to whom* question also featured prominently in the *Mistretta* case, discussed above, but with different results. Again, *Mistretta* concerned the delegation to the United States Sentencing Commission of responsibility for establishing federal sentencing guidelines. After concluding that the statute contained the requisite intelligible principles, the Court went on to examine the nature and composition of the Sentencing Commission itself. Specifically, the statute provided for the Sentencing Commission to be a bipartisan, independent agency located in the judicial branch, with three of the agency's six members to be sitting federal judges. The Court concluded that this structure did not violate separation of powers principles. Dissenting, Justice Antonin Scalia argued that "lawful" delegations are predicated at least partly on the notion that "a certain degree of discretion, and thus of lawmaking, inheres in most executive or judicial action," and all that Congress does by delegating is to provide "how small or large that degree shall be." By contrast, Scalia said the Sentencing Commission's enabling statute represented "a pure delegation of legislative power ... divorced from any responsibility for execution of the law or adjudication of private rights under the law."[35]

Most recently, the Court addressed the *to whom* question in *Department of Transportation v. Ass'n of American Railroads*.[36] The case challenged the assignment of joint rulemaking authority over train service to Amtrak and the Federal Railroad Administration. The Court ultimately concluded that Amtrak was a governmental entity for that purpose, and thus could share rulemaking power with the Federal Railroad Administration. Nevertheless, implicit in the Court's decision was the premise that Congress cannot delegate rulemaking power to nongovernmental actors.

In short, although the nondelegation doctrine clearly has had at least one and one-half feet in the grave for several decades, it is too soon to bury the nondelegation doctrine altogether. The *Gundy*, *Synar*, and *Ass'n of American Railroads* cases, as well as Justice Rehnquist's opinions in *Benzene* and *Cotton Dust* and Justice Thomas's opinion in *American Trucking Ass'ns*, suggest that the nondelegation doctrine is still not completely dead, even on the federal level.

---

34. *Synar*, 478 U.S. at 732–33.

35. As noted above, more recently, the Supreme Court held that the Sentencing Guidelines are merely advisory. *United States v. Booker*, 543 U.S. 220 (2005).

36. 575 U.S. 43 (2015).

[E] Nondelegation Doctrine in State Administrative Systems

While broad generalizations about state administrative law are understandably suspect, most observers believe that the nondelegation doctrine has more force and effect at the state level than it currently enjoys at the federal level. For example, in his seminal book on state administrative law, Professor Frank Cooper listed a number of factors that, in his view, have prompted state courts to be tougher on their legislatures than the Supreme Court has been on Congress.[37] Professor Cooper believed that state courts have a stronger interest in limiting the activities of state agencies because state courts tend to trust state agencies less than Congress and the Supreme Court trust federal agencies.

More recently, Professors Jason Iuliano and Keith Whittington have exhaustively documented a more robust nondelegation doctrine at the state level.[38] They observe that, like the U.S. Constitution, most state constitutions include language limiting the ability of state legislatures to delegate the power to make law. However, the text of state constitutions in this regard is different from, and often more specific than, the Vesting Clause of Article I, § 1 of the U.S. Constitution. Whereas the U.S. Constitution contemplates shared as well as separated powers and vests the legislative power in Congress without specifying whether Congress might be able to share that authority with another branch, some state constitutions expressly forbid any one of the three traditional branches—legislative, executive, or judicial—from exercising powers assigned to either of the other branches.[39] Other state constitutions are even more explicit in instructing the legislature not to delegate its powers to state agencies,[40] or alternatively in authorizing delegation in particular instances.[41]

Against that backdrop, Iuliano and Whittington have observed that state courts often invoke historical practice and rely on flexible standards, much like the federal intelligible principle standard, to justify upholding state legislative delegations to state agencies. Nevertheless, surveying more than 1,000 federal and state nondelegation challenges between 1940 and 2015, Iuliano and Whittington also found that states held statutes unconstitutional in 16% of the cases studied.[42] Comparing pre-New Deal and post-New Deal cases, they found a high degree of consistency between the two periods.[43]

Nevertheless, far more state statutes survive challenges on nondelegation grounds than are declared unconstitutional by state courts. The vast majority of delegations of authority by state legislatures to administrative agencies, whether state or federal, have been upheld. Lawyers wondering what a court might do with a statute should keep in mind a principle of judicial review much more important than the nondelegation

37. Frank Cooper, State Administrative Law 73–91 (1965).

38. *See* Keith E. Whittington & Jason Iuliano, *The Myth of the Nondelegation Doctrine*, 165 U. Pa. L. Rev. 379, 416-17 (2017); Jason Iuliano & Keith E. Whittington, *The Nondelegation Doctrine: Alive and Well*, 93 Notre Dame L. Rev. 619 (2017).

39. *See, e.g.*, Minn. Const. art. III, § 1; Okla. Const. art. IV, § 1.

40. *See, e.g.*, Pa. Const. art. III, § 31

41. *See, e.g.*, Cal. Const. art. IV, § 20 (authorizing delegation to a state Fish and Game Commission "such powers relating to the protection and propagation of fish and game as the Legislature sees fit").

42. Iuliano & Whittington, *The Nondelegation Doctrine: Alive and Well*, *supra* note 38, at 636.

43. *Id.* at 639.

doctrine—*i.e.*, courts are always reluctant to hold statutes unconstitutional regardless of the ground on which the statute is attacked.

[F] Evaluating a Nondelegation Problem

[1] Identifying a Nondelegation Issue

Delegation issues are sometimes difficult to spot, but once spotted, they are rarely difficult to analyze. To spot a delegation issue, first consider:

1. What is the *standard*, or "intelligible principle," set out in the statute, if any?
2. *To whom* is the decisionmaking power given? Each of these questions must be separated for proper discussion.

[2] Identifying a Standards Issue

Spotting and resolving the issue of a proper standard is a matter of searching the organic statute in question for words that appear to set out a standard—an intelligible principle—to cabin executive discretion. At least in theory, this inquiry is to be limited to the face of the statute. Yet, the Supreme Court on more than one occasion has inferred intelligible principles from statutory purposes and legislative history.[44] If absolutely no standard, however loose or ambiguous, can be found, there may be serious problems with the delegation, even on the federal level. The Supreme Court has held that no amount of subsequent agency action, no matter how reasonable, can cure an otherwise defective delegation.[45]

But consider this from the standpoint of common sense. Most, if not all, legislative drafters are at least faintly aware of *Panama Refining* and *Schechter Poultry.* Consequently, they can be expected to put language in the statute that at least appears to be some kind of intelligible principle. One way to work through this issue is simply to review the language of the standards that have passed muster.

---

44. *See, e.g., Gundy v. United States*, 139 S. Ct. 2116 (2019); *Industrial Union Department, AFL-CIO v. American Petroleum Institute*, 448 U.S. 607 (1980).

45. *See Whitman v. American Trucking Ass'ns*, 531 U.S. 457 (2001).

Agency	Standard in Organic Statute
Department of Transportation	"public convenience and necessity"[46]
Federal Trade Commission	"unfair methods of competition" and "unfair or deceptive" trade practices[47]
Occupational Safety & Health Administration	"reasonably necessary or appropriate to provide safe or healthful employment" and protect employee health "to the extent feasible"[48]
Environmental Protection Agency	"allowing an an adequate degree of safety, [as] requisite to protect public health"[49]

If a new statute contains language such as the language in these examples, in all likelihood, it will satisfy the intelligible principle standard. At that point, for so long as the Supreme Court continues to use the intelligible principle standard, your inquiry as to this first aspect of the nondelegation doctrine is concerned is at an end. Note that all of the agencies and statutory delegations listed in the above chart continue in force. If these delegations survived an attack on nondelegation grounds, it is highly likely that similar language in a new organic statute will also survive.

[3] Considering the Delegation *to Whom* Issue

The second part of the delegation inquiry may be a bit more troublesome. To whom has the power been given? The organic statute must be examined to determine precisely who will make the decisions thereunder. Among the various possibilities, three are particularly worthy of review:

1. A delegation to the president or to an agency head, like the Secretary of Transportation or the administrator of the Environmental Protection Agency;
2. A subsequent delegation by the named delegee to another officer within the same agency, or to another agency at the same level of government (also known as *subdelegation*);

46. The Secretary of Transportation is authorized to certify citizens to provide air transportation upon a finding that such transportation "is consistent with the public convenience and necessity." 49 U.S.C. § 41102(b). The Supreme Court upheld a similar delegation to the Interstate Commerce Commission in *Interstate Commerce Comm'n v. Railway Labor Executives Ass'n*, 315 U.S. 373 (1942).

47. 15 U.S.C. § 45(a)(1). The D.C. Circuit recognized the FTC's authority to adopt binding regulations to elaborate the meaning of this language in *National Petroleum Refiners Ass'n v. Federal Trade Comm'n*, 482 F.2d 672 (D.C. Cir. 1975). Congress subsequently limited somewhat the FTC's rulemaking powers in the Magnuson-Moss Warranty-Federal Trade Commission Improvement Act, § 88 Stat. 2183 (1975), but left in place the FTC's authority to define those terms through adjudication.

48. 29 U.S.C. §§ 652(8) & 655(b)(5). These were the standards that gave Justice Rehnquist so much trouble in the *Benzene* and *Cotton Dust* cases, discussed in § 2.02[D]. A majority of the Court had no trouble with them.

49. 42 U.S.C. § 7409(b). The Supreme Court upheld this language in *Whitman v. American Trucking Ass'ns*, discussed in § 2.02[D].

3. A delegation or subdelegation to private entities, or from federal agencies to state agencies.

The first alternative is common and causes no constitutional difficulties. The second possibility, subdelegation within the same agency or to another agency at the same level of government, typically is permissible as well.[50] A number of early Supreme Court decisions[51] suggested that the officer to whom Congress delegated authority must be the person who actually decides. These days, however, it is virtually unquestioned that the federal officer named in the statute may hand over day-to-day decisionmaking to lower echelon officials within the same agency.[52] And courts typically have upheld subdelegations from one federal agency to another,[53] except where Congress clearly intended otherwise.[54] When analyzing a subdelegation scenario within the executive branch, therefore, it is important to ensure the subdelegee is an eligible government official and to consider whether the statute either expressly permits or at least does not preclude the subdelegation.

---

50. For an interesting and unusual contrary example, see *New Process Steel, LP v. National Labor Relations Board*, 560 U.S. 674 (2010). In that case, the Supreme Court rejected agency decisionmaking when a five-member Board found itself with only two members. The statute authorized subdelegation from the five-member body to a three-member panel, and also provided that two members of such a panel could make decisions as a quorum of a three-member panel. The Court held that a quorum of the agency acted lawfully when four members voted to delegate all of the agency's power to a three-member body a few days before the term of office of one of the four members expired. But once the term of the third member expired, taking the agency's membership down to two, the Court held that the remaining two members could no longer exercise any power because the three-member body to which a quorum of the five-member agency had subdelegated its powers no longer existed.

51. *See, e.g., Runkle v. United States*, 122 U.S. 543 (1887) (concerning a statutory delegation to "the President" in cases of officers being dismissed from the military services after court martial requiring the exercise of the president's personal judgment).

52. Congress has resolved this by enacting 5 U.S.C. §§ 301–03 which expressly permit subdelegation, as well as other, agency-specific statutes doing the same. *See, e.g.*, 15 U.S.C. § 78d-1 (concerning the Securities and Exchange Commission); 47 U.S.C. § 155(c) (concerning the Federal Communications Commission); *see also Kobach v. U.S. Election Assistance Comm'n*, 772 F.3d 1183 (10th Cir. 2014) (upholding a subdelegation of power to an agency's executive director); *Indiana Bell Telephone Co. v. McCarty*, 362 F.3d 378 (7th Cir. 2004) (allowing a federal agency to subdelegate its power to a subdivision of the agency); *United States v. Cottman Co.*, 190 F.2d 805 (4th Cir. 1951) (discussing the necessity of subdelegation within an agency). For a contrary example, however, see *New Process Steel, LP v. National Labor Relations Board*, 560 U.S. 674 (2010). In that case, the Supreme Court rejected agency decisionmaking when an agency headed by a five-member Board found itself with only two members. The statute both authorized subdelegation from the five-member body to a three-member panel and also provided that two members of such a panel could make decisions as a quorum of a three-member panel. The Court said that a quorum of the agency acted lawfully when four members voted to delegate all of the agency's power to a three-member body a few days before the term of office of one of the four members expired. But once the term of the third member expired, the Court held that the remaining two members could no longer exercise any power because the three-member body to which a quorum of the five-member agency had subdelegated its powers no longer existed.

53. *See, e.g., Louisiana Forestry Ass'n v. U.S. Department of Labor*, 745 F.3d 653 (3d Cir. 2013) (upholding a subdelegation of responsibilities from the Department of Homeland Security to the Department of Labor).

54. *See, e.g., Halverson v. Slater*, 129 F.3d 180 (D.C. Cir. 1997) (rejecting the Secretary of Transportation's subdelegation of functions to the Saint Lawrence Seaway Development Corp., a subordinate agency within the Department of Transportation, because the relevant statute authorized subdelegation to the Coast Guard instead).

The third possibility requires a bit more analysis. With regard to giving governmental decisionmaking powers to the private sector, the principle would seem at first blush to be straightforward and unambiguous. The general rule grew out of the *Schechter Poultry* and *Carter Coal* cases: it is impermissible under our constitutional system for Congress to give governmental decisionmaking powers to private entities. The Supreme Court implicitly reaffirmed this principle in *Department of Transportation v. Ass'n of American Railroads*,[55] when it concluded that Amtrak was a governmental entity that could share joint rulemaking power with the Federal Railroad Administration, but recognized that the same might not be the case if Amtrak were properly characterized as a private company.

But even a principle as seemingly strong as this has given way somewhat, given both the practical necessities of administration and the desire to avoid the inefficiencies of government management. Government routinely relies quite heavily on private actors to perform a variety of regulatory and other government functions.

To some extent, such has always been the case. At the height of the New Deal, Professor Louis Jaffe lauded the longstanding and substantial involvement of private groups in the regulatory sphere.[56] Nevertheless, the blending of the public and private spheres has grown substantially in recent decades. In the 1990s, President Bill Clinton and Vice President Al Gore worked to "reinvent" government by downsizing federal agencies and outsourcing government functions to private actors thought to be more efficient as a result of their participation in a competitive marketplace. President George W. Bush followed suit, seeking new ways to contract with private vendors to perform functions previously handled by government employees.

Today, private companies run prisons, nursing homes, and managed care organizations, all subject to extensive regulation and oversight by government agencies, but with tremendous discretion in managing the day-to-day activities. Professional and trade groups develop health, safety, and product quality standards for their members that legislatures and agencies, in turn, incorporate by reference into statutes and regulations.

The courts generally have been quite permissive in these arrangements. For example, in a 1982 case, *Schweiker v. McClure*,[57] the Supreme Court reviewed the use of private sector insurance carriers to provide hearings (and decisions) on disputed claims for Medicare payments under the Social Security System. The Court dealt with the case purely in terms of due process considerations and concluded that the company's hearing officers did not have any existing pecuniary bias or prior involvement with the cases that would require them to be disqualified from sitting in the capacity of administrative judges to decide the Medicare claims. There was no discussion whatsoever of the delegation-to-private-parties issue. The Court may have determined, albeit silently, that there was really no government policy being made by these private sector adjudicators—with all of the big policy questions (and many smaller ones) made by the Department of Health and Human Services, and the insurance carrier personnel really just functioning in a kind of fact-gathering or investigative capacity.

Although the Supreme Court has upheld the constitutionality of relying on nongovernmental adjudicators with professional or economic connections to the concerns

55. 575 U.S. 43 (2015).

56. *See* Louis Jaffe, *Law Making by Private Groups*, 51 HARV. L. REV. 201 (1937).

57. 456 U.S. 188 (1982).

being adjudicated,[58] in *North Carolina State Board of Dental Examiners v. Federal Trade Commission*,[59] the Court relied on §1 of the Sherman Antitrust Act in holding that a state agency controlled by professional dentists could not prohibit nondentists from providing teeth whitening services. Although the Court did not mention the nondelegation doctrine, it repeatedly emphasized the risk that an agency controlled by active market participants with conflicts of interest might engage in "private self-dealing" instead of acting to further the public good unless the agency is actively supervised by government officials who are not active market participants.

Because neither of these cases, nor many just like them, explicitly discuss nondelegation and separation of powers principles, it is unclear whether or to what extent they suggest a retreat by the Supreme Court from the basic principle of no delegation to private persons. Nevertheless, a consistent hallmark of cases like these is the comparative degree of discretion afforded to private sector decisionmakers. Recall that in *Schechter Poultry* and *Carter Coal*, the private sector entities were actually setting policy that would bind the industry as a whole. In other words, the private sector was functioning in a rulemaking capacity. The Court unequivocally held that this was constitutionally impermissible, but offered no real standard for evaluating whether other, lesser delegations to private sector actors might cross that line. We may have moved into a private sector policymaking setting without full consideration of the constitutional issues at hand, or perhaps the Court has simply decided to utilize other statutory or doctrinal requirements to police that line.[60]

Finally, we have the question of delegations and subdelegations from the federal government to state agencies, or from agencies to the private sector. Many federal statutes expressly contemplate that federal and state agencies will work together in a particular area of regulation or in the provision of government benefits. In the absence of express authorization, however, the ability of a federal agency to subdelegate power to a state agency is more limited. In landmark decision, *U.S. Telecom Ass'n v. Federal Communications Commission*,[61] the D.C. Circuit held that the FCC's subdelegation of its own regulatory authority over competitor access to telephone service network elements to state regulatory commissions was unconstitutional. The court identified three types of subdelegations to actors outside the federal government that were permissible. First, federal agencies may condition permission to engage in certain activities on the decisions of state, local, or tribal governments, so long as a "reasonable connection" existed between those decisions and the requested permission. Second, agencies may rely on outside parties to collect and transmit factual information. Third, agencies may seek policy recommendations or advice from outside parties, so long as the agency remains the final decisionmaker.

58. *See, e.g.*, *Gibson v. Berryhill*, 411 U.S. 564 (1973).

59. 574 U.S. 494 (2015).

60. For scholarly discussions of the "delegation to whom" issue far beyond the scope of this chapter, see, *e.g.*, Gillian E. Metzger, *Privatization as Delegation*, 103 Colum. L. Rev. 1367 (2003); Jody Freeman, *The Private Role in Public Governance*, 75 N.Y.U. L. Rev. 543 (2000).

61. 395 F.3d 554 (D.C. Cir. 2004).

§ 2.03 Other Legislative Controls

[A] Congressional Devices for Policing Administrative Agencies

Beyond the nondelegation doctrine, Congress has many other devices for policing the activities of administrative agencies and for curbing what the members of Congress might deem excessive agency discretion. First, Congress has the ability to write elaborate organic statutes, prescribing as many standards of and limitations on agency behavior as they wish. The nondelegation cases involved statutes that prescribed only the minimum statutory requirements. Congress may always write with far more detail.

Second, the organic statute can prescribe the credentials of the persons who are to occupy important positions in the agency. For example, the Department of Energy Organization Act requires that the president appoint persons with knowledge of the energy industry to the Federal Energy Regulatory Commission.[62] The Internal Revenue Code requires that the president appoint only individuals who have demonstrated management abilities as commissioner of the Internal Revenue Service.[63]

Third, Congress and state legislatures may specify the lifetime of an agency or certain of its programs through provisions known as sunset legislation.[64] State legislatures have employed sunset legislation even more frequently than the federal government. The process is not complicated. The legislature may simply provide in the organic statute a date certain for closing the agency or ending a particular program.[65] A milder form of sunset legislation requires an agency to submit an extensive report to the legislature on its activities as a condition of its survival. In this second option, the legislature reviews the sunset report and then determines whether the agency should continue in business.

[B] Agency Budgets and Specific Statutory Controls

There are many other instruments of congressional control over agencies. Agencies cannot function without money, and all funds spent by agencies must be appropriated by Congress (or the state legislature in the case of state agencies). The power to set an agency's budget may be as important as all the other controls combined. On numerous

62. 42 U.S.C. § 7101.

63. 26 U.S.C. § 7803.

64. Sunset legislation appears to wax and wane in popularity at both the federal and state levels. For some good discussion of this important legislation drafting and agency control concept, see, *e.g.*, Mark B. Blickle, *The National Sunset Movement*, 9 Seton Hall Legis. J. 209 (1986); Lewis A. Davis, *Review Procedures and Public Accountability in Sunset Legislation: An Analysis and Proposal for Reform*, 33 Admin. L. Rev. 393 (1981). For further discussion on the pros and cons of sunset legislation, compare Jacob E. Gerson, *Temporary Legislation*, 74 U. Chi. L. Rev. 247 (2007), with Rebecca M. Kysar, *Lasting Legislation*, 159 U. Pa. L. Rev. 1007 (2011).

65. For example, many provisions of the Patriot Act were originally set to expire beginning December 31, 2005. Pub. L. No. 107-56, §§ 201-224, 115 Stat. 272, 278-295 (2001). Some of these provisions have lapsed, while others have been extended or reauthorized (with amendments) following lapse. *See, e.g.*, PATRIOT Sunsets Extension Act of 2011, Pub. L. 112-14, 125 Stat. 216 (2011); USA Freedom Act, Pub. L. 114-23, 129 Stat. 268 (2015).

occasions, Congress has expanded or contracted an agency's budget, depending on how much in favor or out of favor that agency happens to be. Congress has on numerous occasions directed agencies to spend or not to spend money on particular activities.

Congress also uses the appropriations process in other ways. A member of a congressional appropriations committee can inform an agency head that the amount of money Congress appropriates for the agency will depend to some extent on whether the agency takes an action that is favored by the member. If the agency head believes that the member has the votes needed to make good on that threat, the agency will experience great pressure to act in accordance with the wishes of the member. Members of congressional appropriations committees also often use appropriations hearings as an opportunity to influence an agency's behavior by embarrassing or threatening to embarrass the agency unless it acts in ways the member prefers.

Congress has also enacted many statutes with a specific purpose that have a substantial impact on agency action, such as the Ethics in Government Act,[66] the Freedom of Information Act (FOIA),[67] the Federal Privacy Act[68] and the Government in the Sunshine Act.[69] Each of these statutes imposes constraints on various agency activities. The list can be lengthened to include the National Environmental Policy Act (NEPA),[70] the Regulatory Flexibility Act,[71] and the Paperwork Reduction Act.[72]

In the past, Congress has been disturbed by the imposition of regulatory obligations on state and local governments and Indian tribes without any attention paid to the costs of carrying out these federal "mandates." The Unfunded Mandates Reform Act,[73] requires an agency to place, in its notice of proposed rulemaking, certain explanations of the costs, benefits and burdens of the anticipated rule, to solicit the views of various entities, including state and local governments, and to explore any less-burdensome alternatives to the proposed rule.

---

66. 5 U.S.C. App. § 401–05. The Ethics in Government Act is discussed in Chapter 3.

67. 5 U.S.C. § 552. FOIA permits persons outside the government to have access to government information. The act, among many other things, presumes that an agency ought to disclose information and permits an agency to refuse to disclose only under a number of tightly controlled circumstances. The FOIA is discussed extensively in Chapter 14.

68. This statute requires agencies to take special care in collecting, storing and disseminating information in its possession pertaining to individuals. It is discussed at length in Chapter 14.

69. 5 U.S.C. § 552b. The Sunshine Act requires an agency to conduct most of its business in the open. It is discussed at greater length in Chapter 14. The Federal Advisory Committee Act, 5 U.S.C. App. 2, is also an attempt to promote more public government decisionmaking when agencies use bodies of private persons to help them formulate policy.

70. 42 U.S.C. §§ 4321 *et seq.* NEPA requires an agency to evaluate the environmental consequences of its activities and to prepare an environmental impact statement when an activity "significantly affects the quality of the human environment."

71. 5 U.S.C. § 601. This statute requires agencies to consider the economic impact of its rulemaking activities on small businesses. The Regulatory Flexibility Act was amended to give it more strength in forcing agencies to consider the impact of their rules on small business by the Small Business Regulatory Enforcement Fairness Act. Pub. L. No. 104-121, 110 Stat. 857 (to be codified at 5 U.S.C. § 611(a)). In an attempt to give certain small businesses and individuals who have relatively small net worth some leverage against the agencies in litigating the validity of agency rules, Congress has passed the Equal Access to Justice Act, 5 U.S.C. § 504(a), which permits, in certain carefully controlled circumstances, a private small business or individual to recover his or her attorney's fees if the private party substantially prevails in litigation that challenges agency rules.

72. 44 U.S.C. §§ 3501 *et seq.* This statute was a reaction to the proliferation of agencies and the consequent proliferation of agency reporting and recordkeeping requirements. It is discussed in Chapter 4.

73. 2 U.S.C. §§ 658, 1501–71.

The point of this recitation is simple: Congress has placed an enormous number of restrictions on agency action that have nothing to do with the nondelegation doctrine. Readers should not lose sight of all the strings Congress has attached to agency functioning.

[C] Allocation of Litigating Authority

Some agencies have the statutory authority to go to court to enforce their statutes and rules, while other agencies do not. Those agencies that lack such authority must rely on the Department of Justice (DOJ) to enforce the statutes for which they are responsible. The efficacy of an agency that lacks the authority to go to court depends critically on the attitudes of the DOJ and local U.S. Attorneys toward the importance of the agency's mission. If the DOJ and/or the U.S Attorneys do not attach great significance to an agency's mission, they will allocate their scarce enforcement and litigation resources elsewhere, and the agency's power to perform its mission will be limited.

Of the agencies that possess the statutory authority to go to court, few have the power to litigate before the Supreme Court. The Supreme Court has held that an agency must have explicit statutory authority to represent the government before it.[74] Congress rarely grants that authority. Agencies lacking the power to litigate before the Supreme Court must rely on the Solicitor General to do it for them. As a result, the Solicitor General often has de facto power to veto a position taken by an agency by refusing to argue in support of that position before the Supreme Court.

[D] The Oversight Process

Congress polices day-to-day agency action through what is known as the *oversight* process. Oversight is simply the monitoring of agency activities by the standing committees of Congress, such as the House Committee on Foreign and Interstate Commerce and the Senate Energy Committee. Both members of Congress and, in particular, persons employed as committee staff members become well versed in the operations of the agencies under each committee's jurisdiction. This familiarity permits them to conduct investigations, hold hearings, and engage in informal contact with agency officials to ensure that the agency is carrying out its mission. Although the effectiveness of the process varies, depending on the make-up and enthusiasm of the committee members, it is now an integral part of the ongoing relationship between Congress and the agencies. Investigations and oversight hearings often result in amendments to the organic statute.[75]

---

74. *See Federal Election Comm'n v. NRA Political Victory Fund*, 513 U.S. 88 (1994).

75. Members of Congress are sometimes criticized for too much interference in the workings of the agencies, particularly as agency action affects their constituents. Some agencies such as the Federal Communications Commission have taken steps to reduce congressional influence over individual licensing cases. For a number of case histories, and some good discussion, see RANDALL L. CALVERT, MARK J. MORAN & BARRY R. WEINGAST, CONGRESSIONAL INFLUENCE OVER POLICY MAKING: THE CASE OF THE FTC, IN CONGRESS, STRUCTURE AND POLICY (1987); Mark Bagnoli & Michael McKee, *Controlling the Game: Political Sponsors and Bureaus*, 7 J.L. ECON. & ORG. 229 (1991). For one member of Congress' view that Congress should be even more aggressive in exerting authority over administrative agencies, see Nick Smith, *Restoration of Congressional Authority and Responsibility over the Regulatory Process*, 33 HARV. J. ON LEGIS. 323 (1996).

§ 2.04 Legislative Vetoes

[A] The Bicameralism and Presentment Problem

Over the past hundred years, Congress has created a large number of administrative agencies to perform an enormous number of tasks. In searching for ways to keep some kind of handle on agency actions, apart from its normal prerogatives of amending either the agency's organic statute or the Administrative Procedure Act and the other control mechanisms described in § 2.03 above, Congress hit on the idea of the legislative veto. Legislative vetoes can be structured in different ways, whether by allowing a resolution adopted by one or both houses of the legislature to preclude a proposed executive action, or by requiring the approval of one or both houses of the legislature before a proposed executive action may go into effect. Beginning in 1932, Congress inserted either unicameral or bicameral legislative vetoes in more than 200 different statutes, although Congress rarely exercised such vetoes.[76]

The congressional interest in the veto is apparent. It's what you might call a last-ditch device for controlling agency action prior to the agency action actually going into effect. Moreover, it can be, at least in theory, less arduous and time-consuming than amending the agency's organic statute—a maneuver that requires not only the agreement of both the House of Representatives and the Senate but also the signature of the president. The unicameral veto dispenses even with the need of one house of Congress to secure the assent of the other.

In 1975, Congress exercised its legislative veto powers in a case that eventually made its way to the Supreme Court. The case arose out of an application for permission to remain in the United States filed by Jagdish Rai Chadha, a man of Indian descent born in Kenya and originally admitted to the United States on a student visa. When his student visa expired, the Immigration and Naturalization Service (INS) took steps to deport Chadha. The attorney general of the United States then used statutory authority conferred by the immigration statutes to suspend Chadha's deportation proceedings.[77]

However, the statute also required that the attorney general's decision be transmitted to Congress and permitted either the House of Representatives or the Senate to veto the attorney general's suspension (recall, this is the so-called "unicameral" legislative veto). For reasons that remain unclear, Representative Joshua Eilberg, a member of Congress from Pennsylvania, introduced a House resolution disapproving six suspension cases including Chadha's.[78] The House approved the Eilberg veto resolution on a voice vote.

---

76. The seminal article on the legislative veto prior to *Chadha* (discussed below) is Harold Bruff & Ernest Gellhorn, *Congressional Control of Administrative Regulation: A Study of Legislative Vetoes*, 90 HARV. L. REV. 1369 (1977). For a more recent discussion of the legislative veto and legislative responses to *Chadha*, see Edward H. Stiglitz, *Unitary Innovations and Political Accountability*, 99 CORNELL L. REV. 1133 (2014).

77. Title 8 U.S.C. § 244(a)(1) provides that the Attorney General "may, in his discretion, suspend deportation and adjust the status" of an alien who applies for suspension and who qualifies under the other terms of the statute (*i.e.*, that he lived in the U.S. continuously for at least seven years, that he is of good moral character and that deportation would work a great hardship on him).

78. Eilberg stated on the floor of the House that his subcommittee had reviewed approximately 340 cases and that these six cases, including Chadha's, did not satisfy the hardship requirement in the statute. There is virtually no other explanation for his actions in the record.

Chadha then took his case into the federal courts, arguing, among other things, that the legislative veto itself was unconstitutional.

The majority opinion in *Immigration and Naturalization Service v. Chadha*,[79] written by Chief Justice Warren Burger, is probably best described as a workmanlike tour through basic provisions in Article I of the U.S. Constitution. There are three clauses in Article I at issue here: (1) the Vesting Clause (Art. I, § 1), which vests the legislative power of the government in both the House of Representatives and the Senate (*i.e.*, bicameralism); (2) the First Presentment Clause (Art. 1, § 7, cl. 2), which requires a bill passed by both houses of Congress to be presented to the president for signature; and (3) the Second, or Residual, Presentment Clause (Art. 1, § 7, cl. 3), which that requires the president either to sign or to veto legislation and then permits Congress to override a presidential veto only by a two-thirds vote of both the House and the Senate.

At the outset, the Court made a threshold determination that essentially disposed of the remainder of the case: a legislative veto is the exercise of legislative power. The Court then held that a one-house legislative veto, such as exercised in *Chadha*, violated the constitutional requirements of bicameralism and presentment by allowing one house of Congress alone to exercise the legislative power and by excluding the president from the process altogether.

Bicameralism, in the Court's view, was of fundamental importance in the framing of the 1787 Constitution. Quoting from the *Federalist Papers* and early commentaries on the Constitution by Joseph Story, the Court determined that bicameralism was a prime necessity to the Framers as a check against "legislative despotism."[80] But on the issue of the Presentment Clauses, the Court took a slightly different tack. These clauses were essential, in the Court's view, to preserve the doctrine of separation of powers. First, they enhance the system of checks and balances that is central to our system of government; and second, they ensure, in the Court's words, "that a 'national' perspective is grafted on the legislative process."

One question that remains after the *Chadha* decision concerns severability—*i.e.*, whether the remainder of the statute survives even if the legislative veto provision is unconstitutional. After the *Chadha* decision was handed down, two hundred statutes contained a legislative veto provision that was presumptively invalid. Does the *Chadha* decision mean that the entire statute is defective? The Court in *Chadha* held that the unconstitutional provision at issue in that case was severable, in part because the statute contained a severability clause. But what of statutes that lack a severability clause? The lower courts are split on this question. In one instance, *Exxon Corp. v. Department of Energy*,[81] the Temporary Emergency Court of Appeals held that *Chadha* should not be given retroactive effect (the organic statute in question had expired prior to *Chadha* even though enforcement actions for violations during the life of the statute continued) and that, in any event, the statute was severable even without an express severability clause. Two other circuits split on the validity of the 1977 Equal Employment

79. 462 U.S. 919 (1983).

80. The Court noted only four express exceptions to the requirement of bicameralism in the Constitution: (1) the initiation of charges of impeachment by the House of Representatives; (2) the trial on impeachment charges vested in the Senate; (3) the power to approve or disapprove certain presidential appointments vested exclusively in the Senate; and (4) the power to ratify treaties was given to the Senate. Unquestionably, the legislative veto fits within none of these exceptions.

81. 744 F.2d 98 (Temp. Emer. Ct. App. 1984).

Opportunity Commission Reorganization Act, another statute without a severability clause.[82]

Chadha is not the only case in which the Supreme Court has declined to allow Congress to establish veto authority over agency action in a legislative body of less than the whole. In 1991, the Supreme Court reviewed a different sort of legislative veto. The legislation in question established the Metropolitan Washington Airports Authority (Authority) to manage two of the three major airports in the Washington, D.C. metropolitan area, National Airport (now Reagan National) and Dulles Airport. Congress also provided for the Authority to create a Board of Review (Board), which was given veto power over many decisions made by the Authority. The Board was to consist of nine members of Congress who served on the various congressional transportation committees, with those members to be selected from a list provided by Congress.

In *Metropolitan Washington Airports Authority v. Citizens for the Abatement of Aircraft Noise, Inc.*,[83] the Court rejected this scheme, again at least partly on grounds of the need for legislative action to comply with bicameralism and presentment. Although the legislation called upon Board members to act "in their individual capacities," the Court recognized that the point of the Board's composition was to retain congressional control over the Authority's actions, and thus the management of the airports. To the extent the Board's power was properly characterized as legislative, the Court said that Congress was required to exercise that power in a manner consistent with bicameralism and presentment. Characterizing the Board's powers instead as executive did not resolve the issue; the Board members, as agents of Congress, could not constitutionally exercise executive power. In a strongly worded dissent, Justice Byron White accused the Court of "striking down yet another innovative and otherwise lawful governmental experiment in the name of separation of powers."

[B] Congressional Review Act

In the years since *Chadha*, a number of people, in and out of Congress, have tried to think up alternatives to the legislative veto that might permit some congressional action to disapprove particular agency regulations without running afoul of Article I of the Constitution. To this end, in 1996, Congress enacted the Congressional Review Act.[84]

Under the Congressional Review Act, no "major rule" can take effect until 60 legislative days after the promulgating agency submits to Congress and the Comptroller General a copy of the rule, a concise general statement relating to the rule, and various other documents related to the rule, including an associated analysis of the benefits and costs of regulatory alternatives. During that 60-day period, Congress can veto the rule by enacting a joint resolution of disapproval, with that joint resolution subject to presentment and potential veto by the president. The Congressional Review Act establishes

---

82. *Equal Employment Opportunity Comm'n v. CBS, Inc.*, 743 F.2d 969 (2d Cir. 1984); *Muller Optical Co. v. Equal Employment Opportunity Comm'n*, 743 F.2d 380 (6th Cir. 1984).

83. 501 U.S. 252 (1991).

84. The Congressional Review Act was adopted as part of the Contract with America Advancement Act of 1996, Pub. L. No. 104-121, 110 Stat. 847, and codified at 5 U.S.C. §§ 801–808. For scholarly analysis of the Congressional Review Act, see, *e.g.*, Michael J. Cole, *Interpreting the Congressional Review Act: Why the Courts Should Assert Judicial Review, Narrowly Construe "Substantially the Same," and Decline to Defer to Agencies Under* Chevron, 70 ADMIN. L. REV. 53 (2018); Daniel Cohen & Peter L. Strauss, *Congressional Review of Agency Regulations*, 49 ADMIN. L. REV. 95 (1997).

a special expedited procedure for enacting a joint resolution of disapproval that eliminates the potential for opponents of the regulation to use tactics like a filibuster or introduction of amendments in an effort to forestall enactment.

The critical term "major rule" is defined broadly as one that (1) has "an annual effect on the U.S. economy of $100 million or more"; (2) results in "a major increase in costs or prices for consumers, individual industries, Federal, State or local government agencies, or geographic regions"; or (3) has "significant adverse effects on competition, employment, investment, productivity, innovation, or on the ability of United States-based enterprises to compete with foreign-based enterprises in domestic and export markets."[85] Compliance with the Congressional Review Act is not subject to judicial review.

The Congressional Review Act initially had a limited effect. Between 1996 and 2017, Congress vetoed only one rule. Issued by the Occupational Safety and Health Administration in the last days of the Clinton Administration, the rule in question imposed extensive new obligations on employers to prevent and compensate employees for workplace ergonomic injuries. The ergonomics rule was potentially quite costly and highly controversial, and Congress rejected it by joint resolution under the Congressional Review Act in the early days of the George W. Bush Administration. Otherwise, although members of Congress occasionally introduced resolutions seeking to reject various agency rules, none of those efforts were successful.

In 2017, in the first days of the Trump Administration, Congress vetoed several rules issued in the last weeks of the Obama Administration. This activity brought new attention to the Congressional Review Act as a mechanism of congressional control over agency action.[86] Subsequently, in 2018, Congress used the Congressional Review Act mechanism to reject a rule adopted by the Consumer Financial Protection Bureau concerning auto lending. In the early months of the Biden Administration, Congress discarded a few Trump Administration regulations.

85. 5 U.S.C. § 804(2).

86. *See, e.g.*, Michael J. Cole, *Interpreting the Congressional Review Act: Why the Courts Should Assert Judicial Review, Narrowly Construe "Substantially the Same," and Decline to Defer to Agencies Under* Chevron, 70 ADMIN. L. REV. 53 (2018); Paul J. Larkin, Jr., *The Trump Administration and the Congressional Review Act*, 16 GEO. J.L. & PUB. POL'Y 505 (2018).

Chapter 3

External Controls on Administrative Agencies—The Executive Branch

§ 3.01 Introduction

The executive branch of government exerts numerous and powerful controls over both nominally "independent" administrative agencies and those squarely within the executive branch. These controls run the gamut, from the power of appointment and the termination of agency officials, to supervision of an agency's rulemaking authority, the rendering of opinions by the Attorney General, and deciding which agency actions to defend in court. Controls such as these along with the crucial question of ethical conduct by agency appointees are the topics discussed in this chapter.

§ 3.02 An Excursus on Agency Organization

[A] Introduction

Before getting into the various methods the president and others in the executive branch use to control the actions of administrative agencies, it is important to recall some fundamentals on agency structure and organization. This inquiry first requires a close look at the actions of Congress, even though this chapter is mainly devoted to executive branch controls. The place to start is with the Administrative Procedure Act (APA).

The APA defines *agency* mainly in terms of what an agency is *not*. Section 551 of the APA states: "*Agency* means each authority of the Government... whether or not it is within or subject to review by another agency," and then goes on to exclude specifically Congress and "the courts of the United States," as well as other governmental entities like courts martial and military commissions and the governments of U.S. territories and the District of Columbia. This broad definition tells us virtually nothing about agency structure and organization. Instead, your analysis of what constitutes an agency should proceed from the basic premise that the agency model that Congress ultimately chooses reflects congressional thinking on at least three issues: (1) the task or mission that Congress assigns to the agency, (2) the type of accountability Congress wishes to impose on the agency and (3) the realities of the political process.[1]

1. For a more detailed explanation of the history and operation of independent federal agencies, see Marshall J. Breger & Gary J. Edles, *Established by Practice: The Theory and Operation of Independent Federal Agencies*, 52 Admin. L. Rev. 1111 (2000).

[B] The Agency's Mission

An agency's task or mission—its reason for being—is always limited to a set of specific functions prescribed by statute. For example, the Federal Aviation Administration (FAA) regulates the safety and efficiency of air travel by, among other things, licensing pilots, setting standards for the construction and maintenance of aircraft, and supervising the operation of airports. The FAA has nothing to do with railroads or with ships. Those functions are dealt with, respectively, by the Federal Railroad Administration, and the Coast Guard and Federal Maritime Commission.

One way to develop a better understanding of any particular administrative agency is to ask why the legislature created a particular agency. Sometimes an agency's regulatory mission will be explained in the early portions of its organic statute or in that statute's legislative history. For example, the first substantive provision of the Endangered Species Act[2] details several findings that prompted Congress to act, including congressional notice of the extinction of various species and threats to others as well as pledges by the United States to the international community to protect species threatened with extinction. The same statutory provision contains a statement of purposes that includes "provid[ing] a program for the conservation of such endangered species and threatened species" and a statement of policy "to conserve" the same. On other occasions, a legislature will not state its justifications expressly, but on close examination of an agency's organic statute and that statute's legislative history, justifications can almost always be discerned. For example, neither the Sarbanes-Oxley Act of 2002[3] nor the Dodd-Frank Wall Street Reform and Consumer Protection Act in 2010[4] contained a provision stating Congress's justifications and goals expressly. Nevertheless, it is apparent from the provisions and legislative history of those statutes that they were adopted in response to economic crises associated with the public accounting and financial services industries, respectively. Both pieces of legislation created new agencies to administer statutory programs and requirements. Understanding an agency's reason for being is often helpful in understanding how the agency functions, which in turn is important to a practicing lawyer.

Many agencies pursue missions and perform functions that overlap with those of other agencies. For example, the Department of Agriculture, through its Food Safety and Inspection Service, and the Food and Drug Administration, which is part of the Department of Health and Human Services, include food safety among their missions. And although those two agencies are the principal regulators in that space, a 2017 study by the U.S. Government Accountability Office identified fully sixteen federal agencies

2. Pub. L. No. 93-205, § 2, 87 Stat. 884 (1973) (codified at 16 U.S.C. § 1531).

3. Pub. L. No. 107-204, 116 Stat. 745. The long title to the Sarbanes-Oxley Act offers at least a hint at the justifications and goals that inspired it: "An Act To protect investors by improving the accuracy and reliability of corporate disclosures made pursuant to the securities laws, and for other purposes."

4. Pub. L. No. 111-203, 124 Stat. 1376. Again, the long title to the Dodd-Frank Act provides some indication of the justifications and goals that inspired it: "An Act to promote the financial stability of the United States by improving accountability and transparency in the financial system, to end 'too big to fail,' to protect the American taxpayer by ending bailouts, to protect consumers from abusive financial services practices, and for other purposes."

with at least some responsibility for administering at least thirty federal laws aimed at ensuring the safety and quality of the U.S. food supply.[5]

A quick glance at *The United States Government Manual*, the *Sourcebook of United States Executive Agencies*, or the *Federal Register* will give anyone not already familiar with agency activities a good idea of the breadth and depth of federal agency operations.

[C] Agency Accountability

An agency's accountability is determined by its enabling act and its designation as either an *executive agency* or an *independent agency.* Although Congress sometimes expressly labels an agency as independent, the term is best understood as referring to an agency that is insulated from presidential control in one or more ways. That insulation can take many forms. In *Collins v. Mnuchin*, the Fifth Circuit offered a helpful list of features imposed by Congress in various combinations that the court described as "independence-promoting," including but not limited to establishing fixed terms of service for the agency's leaders, exempting the agency from the standard appropriations process, and granting the agency its own litigation authority apart from the Department of Justice.[6]

The characteristic that most commonly distinguishes independent agencies from executive agencies is a statutory limitation on the president's power to remove the agency's principal officers. Thus, if an agency's enabling statute includes a *for cause* limitation on the president's authority to remove the agency's leaders (*i.e.*, for negligence or malfeasance in office, as contrasted with totally discretionary, or *at will*, removal typical for cabinet secretaries), the agency will probably be deemed independent.

Most major independent agencies are collegially governed—that is, they are headed by multi-member boards or commissions rather than by a single director or administrator. In fact, structuring an independent agency without a multi-member board or commission as its head may lead to a conclusion that the agency's organizational structure is unconstitutional. In *Seila Law LLC v. Consumer Financial Protection Bureau,*[7] the Supreme Court considered the constitutionality of the CFPB, an independent agency headed by a single director who could only be removed from office for cause. The Court concluded that the CFPB's organizational structure violated separation of powers. Emphasizing the need for executive branch officials to be accountable to the president, the Court severed the removal restriction from the agency's enabling act to resolve the constitutional difficulty. In *Collins v. Yellen*,[8] the Supreme Court reached the same conclusion regarding a second independent agency headed by a single director, the Federal Housing Finance Agency (FHFA). Although the Court acknowledged that the CFPB and the FHFA were different from one another in several ways, the Court said none of those distinctions justified "a different result."

5. U.S. Government Accountability Office, Food Safety: A National Strategy Is Needed to Address Fragmentation in Federal Oversight (2017).

6. 896 F.3d 640, 660 (5th Cir. 2018) (per curiam), *aff'd in part & rev'd in part*, 938 F.3d 553 (2019), *aff'd in part & rev'd in part, Collins v. Yellen*, 141 S. Ct. 1761 (2021); *see also* Kirti Datla & Richard L. Revesz, *Deconstructing Independent Agencies (and Executive Agencies)*, 98 Cornell L. Rev. 769 (2013).

7. 140 S. Ct. 2183 (2020). This decision is discussed at greater length below in § 3.03[B][2].

8. 141 S. Ct. 1761 (2021).

Another important factor in the organization of the multi-member independent agencies is the composition of the members. In virtually all instances, the members who serve collectively as the head of an independent agency sit for staggered terms, often from five to seven years. The members typically will include persons from each of the two major political parties, which ensures that each political party will preserve some influence over the agencies, even when the other party holds the Presidency. The parties accomplish this by requiring in an agency's enabling act that no more than a bare majority of the agency's members can come from any one political party. Most, if not all, independent agency members are nominated by the president but also must be confirmed by the Senate, thereby giving Congress additional control.

There often seems to be little rhyme or reason as to Congress's designation of a particular agency as either an executive agency or an independent agency. The federal government is filled with aberrations. For example, the entity charged with regulation of many of the environmental aspects of the nuclear power industry, the Nuclear Regulatory Commission, is an independent agency. The entity charged with supervision of many other environmental statutes, the Environmental Protection Agency (EPA), is an executive agency, even though it is not a cabinet-level department.[9] Congress's choices in this regard are dictated by the political realities and the legislative give-and-take that occurs when a particular agency is created.

A few of the earliest independent agencies have been abolished in recent decades, as Congress has created new agencies, reorganized functions, and deregulated aspects of some industries. The oldest of the traditional independent regulatory agencies known as the "Big Seven,"[10] the Interstate Commerce Commission (ICC), was created in 1887 to regulate the railroad industry. Over time, Congress first expanded its jurisdiction to include the regulation of other common carriers such as bus lines and telephone companies, and then later transferred some of those tasks to other federal agencies. In 1995, Congress abolished the ICC and transferred the last of its remaining responsibilities to the Surface Transportation Board. Another of the Big Seven independent agencies, the Civil Aeronautics Board (CAB), was established in the 1930s to regulate and subsidize the airline industry. Congress reorganized the agencies responsible for transportation and safety regulation a few times over the succeeding decades, and finally abolished the CAB in 1985 and transferred certain of its remaining authority to the Department of Transportation.

Most executive agencies are part of one of the cabinet-level departments and subject to the control of a departmental secretary who, of course, serves at the pleasure of the president. There are exceptions, however, such as the Federal Energy Regulatory Commission, which is expressly and functionally an independent agency but still a component, for certain purposes, of the cabinet-level Department of Energy. The Environmental Protection Agency, an agency whose administrator is totally subject to presidential control, is what might be called a "free-standing" executive agency and is not

9. Although the EPA is not a cabinet-level department, its administrator reports directly to the president, is removable at will, and typically is given cabinet-level rank.

10. The "Big Seven" were originally: The Civil Aeronautics Board (now abolished), Federal Communications Commission, Federal Power Commission (replaced by the Federal Energy Regulatory Commission, an independent agency located within the Department of Energy), the Federal Trade Commission, the Interstate Commerce Commission (now abolished), the National Labor Relations Board, and the Securities and Exchange Commission.

located within any cabinet-level department. Congress occasionally changes its mind. In 1995, the Social Security Administration was removed from the cabinet-level Department of Health and Human Services and given the same free-standing status as that of the EPA.

[D] Political Considerations

Political considerations have an important impact on the organizational process. When Congress decides to establish an agency, it can create an entirely new entity, as, for example, when the Interstate Commerce Commission was set up; or it can create an agency by reorganizing existing components of the executive branch. The federal Departments of Transportation and Education, and to a certain extent the Department of Energy, were formed by rearranging or combining existing entities into cabinet-level departments. The newest cabinet-level department, the Department of Homeland Security, is mainly an amalgam of pre-existing agencies that were placed within the new organization.

Reorganization of government functions is common. The same legislation that created the Department of Homeland Security also disbanded the Immigration and Naturalization Service, which was part of the Department of Justice, and divided its functions among three new agencies: U.S. Citizenship and Immigration Services, U.S. Immigration and Customs Enforcement, and U.S. Customs and Border Protection, all within the new Department of Homeland Security. By comparison, as part of the Dodd-Frank Act of 2010, Congress created the independent Consumer Financial Protection Bureau and reassigned functions from several existing executive agencies to the new entity.

Political decisions also affect the components that are left out of a new agency. For example, when Congress established the Department of Transportation, it decided to preserve the Civil Aeronautics Board and the Interstate Commerce Commission as independent regulatory agencies, even though these two agencies had a great deal to do with transportation.

There is often little consistency in what Congress does. When the Department of Energy (DOE) was formed, Congress granted President Jimmy Carter's express request that the Environmental Protection Agency (retained as a free-standing executive agency) and the Nuclear Regulatory Commission (which remained an independent agency) be continued as agencies separate from the DOE. President Carter believed that these two agencies should remain separate entities so that their important regulatory duties would not be affected by the energy promotion mission of the DOE. But this is only a partial explanation for the EPA's and NRC's continued independence.

In contrast to Congress' treatment of these agencies, consider its actions in renaming the old Federal Power Commission, an agency with heavy regulatory obligations, as the Federal Energy Regulatory Commission (FERC) and merging it with the Department of Energy, albeit while continuing to designate FERC as independent and retaining for it several independence-preserving characteristics. Or consider the history of the Surface Transportation Board (STB). Congress established the STB within the Department of Transportation on January 1, 1996, as a successor to the independent Interstate Commerce Commission, which Congress then abolished. But in 2015, Congress decided to remove the STB from the Department of Transportation, change its composition, and establish it as an independent agency.

Sometimes, and often without explanation, Congress splits agency jurisdiction over matters that seem to cry out for unified treatment. For example, jurisdiction over national forests is vested in the Forest Service—a component of the Department of Agriculture—while jurisdiction over national parks is given to the Department of Interior.

Once the decisions on agency head and basic organization are made, Congress may legislate more specifically on organization. If it does, it may prescribe internal components of the organization and leave other aspects of organization to be fleshed out by the president or the agency itself. For example, Congress prescribed that the Department of Energy would contain a number of specific components, including the Energy Information Administration and the Economic Regulatory Administration. In other cabinet-level departments, Congress has specified the number and titles of the assistant secretaries, but leaves the organization and make-up of the remainder of the agency up to the secretary. Again, there is little rhyme or reason for the specifics of organization.

Excessive generalization about agency structure can get a lawyer or law student into analytical trouble. For example, the Environmental Protection Agency contains "offices" that report to "assistant administrators." Another agency may contain "divisions" that report to "bureaus" that report to "administrators" who report to "assistant secretaries" who report to a "deputy secretary" who reports to the "secretary."

There are similarities, of course. A typical cabinet-level agency organizational chart will look something like the Department of Transportation:[11]

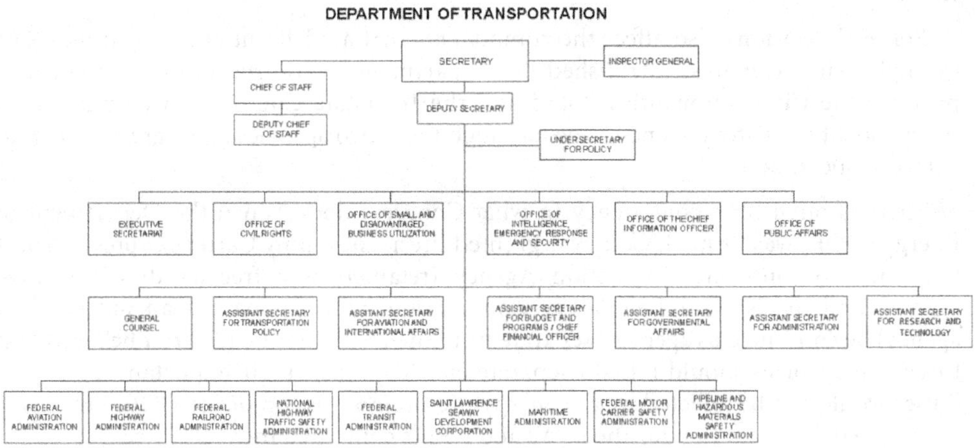

11. Fine sources of such basic information on agencies are the *United States Government Manual* (published annually by the Government Printing Office) and the *Sourcebook of United States Executive Agencies* (published by the Administrative Conference of the United States).

A typical independent agency will look something like the Federal Trade Commission:

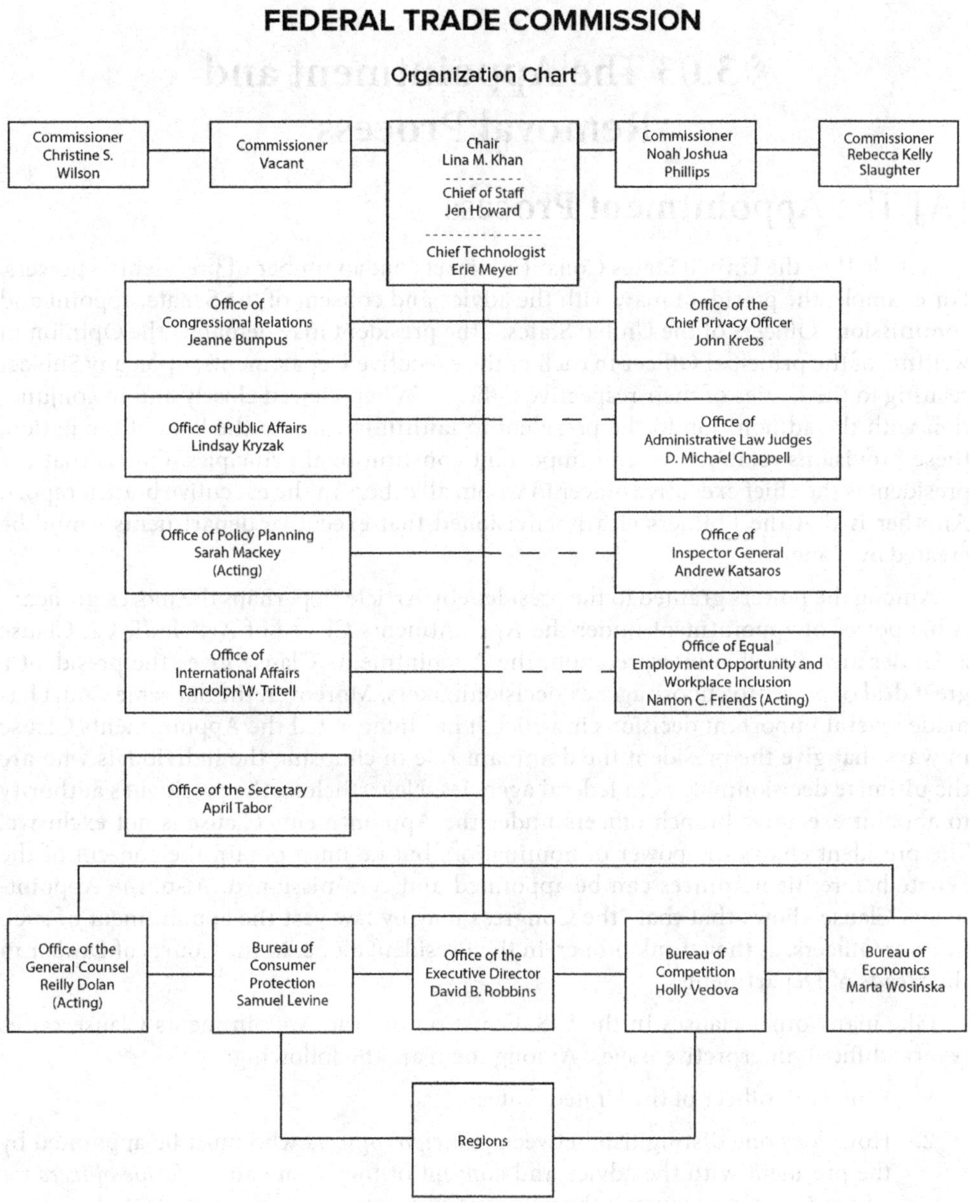

Students with special interest in these matters can work through the congressional floor debates and legislative histories of these agencies usually transcribed in the *Congressional Record* and *U.S. Code Congressional & Administrative News* to garner the precise reasons why congressional and executive branch decisions on agency structure and organization were made. For the purposes of this chapter, it is enough to understand that Congress has a broad spectrum of options and makes myriad choices for many different reasons. The nuances and some of the legal impact of many of these issues are discussed below.

§ 3.03 The Appointment and Removal Process

[A] The Appointment Process

Article II of the United States Constitution sets out a number of presidential powers. For example, the president may, with the advice and consent of the Senate, appoint and commission "Officers of the United States." The president may demand "the Opinion in writing, of the principal Officer in each of the executive Departments, upon any Subject relating to the Duties of their respective Offices." When viewed closely and in conjunction with the admonition to the president to faithfully execute the laws of the nation, these provisions establish several important constitutional principles. One is that the president is the chief executive officer to whom all others in the executive branch report. Another is that the Framers clearly envisioned that executive departments would be created by Congress.

Among the powers granted to the president by Article II, perhaps the most significant is his power of appointment under the Appointments Clause of Article II, § 2, Clause 2. Under any plausible interpretation, the Appointments Clause gives the president a great deal of power to choose agency decisionmakers. Moreover, the Supreme Court has made several important decisions in which it has interpreted the Appointments Clause in ways that give the president the dominant role in choosing the individuals who are the ultimate decisionmakers in federal agencies. Nevertheless, the president's authority to appoint executive branch officers under the Appointments Clause is not exclusive. The president enjoys the power of nomination, but he must obtain the consent of the Senate before his nominees can be appointed and commissioned. Also, the Appointments Clause allows that that "the Congress may by law vest the appointment of such inferior Officers, as they think proper, in the President alone, in the Courts of Law, or in the Heads of Departments."

Like many other clauses in the U.S. Constitution, the Appointments Clause raises several difficult interpretive issues. Among them are the following:

1. Who is an officer of the United States?
2. How does one distinguish between *principal officers* who must be appointed by the president with the advice and consent of the Senate and *inferior officers* for whom Congress may vest the power of appointment in the president alone, in a court of law, or in the head of a department?
3. In appointing inferior officers, what is a court of law, and who is the head of a department?

[1] Who Is an Officer?

Officers of the United States must be appointed in a manner consistent with the Appointments Clause of Article II. Other federal government employees do not. The

Appointments Clause provides explicitly that ambassadors and Supreme Court justices are officers of the United States, but it also makes clear that the category stretches more broadly to include "other public Ministers and Consuls" and "all other Officers" without offering further guidance as to who precisely is included.

In *Buckley v. Valeo*,[12] the Supreme Court unanimously held unconstitutional the congressional decision to confer significant regulatory power upon a Federal Election Commission (FEC) consisting of two appointees each of the president, the House of Representatives, and the Senate. The FEC argued that the Constitution did not prevent the legislative branch from possessing some appointment authority and that the Necessary and Proper Clause of Article I gave Congress sufficient authority to provide an alternative appointment mechanism because the FEC was "performing 'appropriate legislative functions.'"[13] The Court disagreed, holding instead that the appointment of any government official deemed an officer of the United States must comport with the Appointments Clause, which the congressionally-prescribed appointment mechanism for FEC appointees did not.

In evaluating, therefore, whether the members of the FEC were officers of the United States whose appointments must comply with the terms of the Appointments Clause, the Supreme Court reasoned that "any appointee *exercising significant authority* pursuant to the laws of the United States is an 'Officer of the United States.'"[14] FEC members exercised significant authority because they engage in rulemaking and adjudication and because they are free of day-to-day supervision by either Congress or the executive branch. By contrast, the FEC's responsibilities of conducting investigations and preparing reports for Congress alone would not have satisfied that standard. The Court did not need to decide whether the Commissioners were principal officers who had to be appointed by the president with the advice and consent of the Senate or inferior officers the appointment of whom Congress could invest in the president alone, a court of law, or the head of a department, because the appointment of FEC members by the House and the Senate was unconstitutional regardless.

In the many years since *Buckley*, the courts have continued to evaluate claims that particular government officials were officers of the United States by considering whether they exercise significant authority. The Supreme Court has held that special trial judges of the United States Tax Court, who function much like magistrate judges, exercise significant authority because they perform "more than ministerial tasks" and "exercise significant discretion."[15] The Court also has held that administrative law judges working for the Securities and Exchange Commission exercise significant authority and are officers of the United States based on a thorough review of their statutory responsibilities.[16] The D.C. Circuit has held that ex officio members of the FEC who do not vote but nevertheless participate in the deliberative process exercise significant authority through the influence gained by that participation.[17]

12. 424 U.S. 1 (1976).
13. *Id.* at 119.
14. *Id.* at 126 (emphasis added).
15. *Freytag v. Commissioner of Internal Revenue*, 501 U.S. 868, 881–82 (1991).
16. *Lucia v. Securities & Exchange Comm'n*, 138 S. Ct. 2044 (2018).
17. *Federal Election Comm'n v. NRA Political Victory Fund*, 6 F.3d 821 (D.C. Cir. 1993).

[2] Principal Versus Inferior Officers

Establishing that a particular person is an officer of the United States is often only the beginning of the Appointments Clause inquiry. The Appointments Clause provides two different avenues of appointment for officers of the United States. It expressly requires that some officers, commonly referred to as principal officers, be appointed by the president and approved by the Senate. The Appointments Clause also recognizes a separate class of inferior officers who may be appointed, as Congress sees fit, by the president, a court of law, or the head of a department. Yet, the Constitution offers little guidance for distinguishing principal from inferior officers.

In *Morrison v. Olson*, the Supreme Court addressed the constitutionality of the independent counsel provisions of the Ethics in Government Act of 1978. That legislation established a mechanism for the appointment of an independent counsel to investigate and prosecute suspected violations of criminal law by certain high-level executive branch officials, and provided for the removal of an independent counsel by the Attorney General only for good cause. The Court held that independent counsels were inferior officers who could be appointed by a court of law.[18] The Court expressly declined to articulate a particular standard for distinguishing principal from inferior officers, but instead identified four characteristics of independent counsels that it said were relevant to its conclusion that they were inferior officers. First, the authority of an independent counsel was limited to investigating, and potentially prosecuting, only those individuals who participated in some way in the activities the independent counsel was appointed to investigate. Second, an independent counsel was not appointed to serve a fixed term of years, but rather her term would expire upon the completion of her assigned investigatory and prosecutorial duties. Third, an independent counsel had no authority to make policy and instead was required by statute to follow Department of Justice policies. Fourth, an independent counsel could be removed by the Attorney General for "cause."[19]

Justice Antonin Scalia wrote a passionate dissent in *Morrison* in which he criticized the majority for "sweep[ing] into the dustbin" the prior principles used to determine the permissible scope of congressional limits on presidential power without "even attempt[ing] to craft a substitute criterion—a justiciable standard." Justice Scalia also poked holes in the four characteristics on which the Court relied in declaring the independent counsels to be inferior officers. He also argued that independent counsels were not inferior officers because they are not *subordinate* to anyone within the executive branch, although he acknowledged that subordination alone was insufficient for inferior officer status.

Somewhat ironically, ten years later, it was Scalia who authored the opinion for the Court in *Edmond v. United States*,[20] in which he declared Coast Guard Court of Criminal Appeals judges to be inferior officers based on an application of the subordination principle he described in his *Morrison* dissent. "'[I]nferior officers' are officers

18. 487 U.S. 654 (1988). Congress created the independent counsel position to investigate, and potentially to prosecute, criminal wrongdoing by high-ranking members of the executive branch, including the president. If the Attorney General determined, after a preliminary investigation, that there were "reasonable grounds to believe that further investigation or prosecution [was] warranted," she was required to apply to a special three-judge court which, in turn, was required to appoint an independent counsel.

19. Removal power restrictions are discussed at greater length in § 3.03[B].

20. 520 U.S. 651 (1997).

whose work is directed and supervised at some level by others who were appointed by Presidential nomination with the advice and consent of the Senate." The Coast Guard judges in question qualified as inferior officers because their decisions were reviewable by the Court of Appeals for the Armed Forces, whose judges are principal officers, and because the Coast Guard Judge Advocate General had the power to remove the Coast Guard judges, subject only to the qualification that he could not use removal or threat of removal to influence the outcome of any case.

In recent years, the Supreme Court has avoided having to declare that certain officers of the United States were unconstitutionally appointed by severing removal power limitations or other statutory provisions of the governing statutes. In *Free Enterprise Fund v. Public Company Accounting Oversight Board*,[21] the Supreme Court held that members of the Public Company Accounting Oversight Board were inferior officers who were properly appointed by the Securities and Exchange Commission (SEC). The Court reached that conclusion, however, only after it first declared unconstitutional a statutory "double for cause" restriction on the president's authority to remove SEC members and the SEC's authority to remove PCAOB members. Having reached that conclusion, the Court then severed the statutory provision limiting removal of PCAOB members. Once the PCAOB's members were removable at will by the SEC, the Court deemed them adequately supervised to satisfy the *Edmond* subordination standard. Since the Court's decision in *Free Enterprise Fund*, the circuit courts have severed removal restrictions from other statutes to accomplish the same result.[22]

In *United States v. Arthrex, Inc.*,[23] the Supreme Court considered the constitutionality of the Patent Trial and Appeals Board (PTAB), an adjudicatory body within the Patent and Trademark Office (PTO) that uses panels of Administrative Patent Judges (APJs) to conduct *inter partes* review of claims that existing patents do not satisfy patentability standards. The Court applied the *Edmond* subordination standard and concluded that, because PTAB APJs make final decisions that no one else in the executive branch (including the PTO's director) can review and overturn, they have too much power for PTAB's structure to be constitutional. The most obvious conclusion from the Court's analysis would be that APJs are principal officers who must be appointed by the president with the advice and consent of the Senate. But the Court expressly declined to reach that conclusion. Instead, the Court claimed that such a decision was unnecessary because it was enough to say that "[o]nly an officer properly appointed to a principal office may issue a final decision binding the executive branch in the proceeding before us." To achieve that outcome, the Court severed language in the statute preventing the PTO's director from reviewing and overturning PTAB decisions. Because the PTO director is appointed by the president with the advice and consent of the Senate, the severing of that provision meant that a principal officer now possessed sufficient supervisory authority over PTAB APJs to satisfy constitutional requirements.

21. 561 U.S. 477 (2010).

22. *See, e.g., Intercollegiate Broadcasting System v. Copyright Royalty Board*, 684 F.3d 1332 (D.C. Cir. 2012); *PHH Corp. v. Consumer Financial Protection Bureau*, 83 F.3d 1 (D.C. Cir. 2016), *rev'd on other grounds*, 881 F.3d 75 (D.C. Cir. 2018) (en banc).

23. 141 S. Ct. 1970 (2021).

[3] Courts of Law and Heads of Departments

When thinking about who can appoint inferior officers, some possibilities are obvious. Courts of law obviously include Article III courts; heads of departments obviously include cabinet-level secretaries like the Secretary of the Treasury or the Secretary of Health and Human Services. Particularly given the evolution and expansion of the executive branch and independent agencies, however, who else might be eligible to appoint inferior officers is far from clear.

The United States Tax Court (Tax Court) has been the subject of some of the more interesting jurisprudence on this topic. Congress created the Board of Tax Appeals as an independent agency within the executive branch in 1924. Congress changed its name to the "Tax Court of the United States" in 1942 but retained the body's status as an independent agency in the executive branch. In 1961, Congress designated the Tax Court as an "Article I Court" but did not materially change its composition or function.[24]

The Tax Court is a trial court that performs the single function of adjudicating disputes concerning federal tax liabilities. Its judges are appointed to 15-year terms by the president with the advice and consent of the Senate and are removable only for cause. The Tax Court also employs a number of "special trial judges," who are appointed by the Chief Judge of the Tax Court and are removable at will. The special trial judges handle a more limited set of duties, including resolving small cases, but also a variety of trial matters much like magistrate judges in the Article III trial system do.

In *Freytag v. Commissioner of Internal Revenue*,[25] the Supreme Court held unanimously that Tax Court special trial judges are inferior officers who can be appointed by the Chief Judge of the Tax Court. The justices divided sharply, however, as to why. The five justices in the majority concluded that the Tax Court is a court of law represented by its Chief Judge, not a department. They reasoned that the Tax Court could not be a department, because it is not a cabinet-level agency and its sole function is to adjudicate. Indeed, the majority suggested strongly that no agency can be a department for Appointments Clause purposes unless it is a cabinet-level agency. On the other hand, the *Freytag* majority may not have intended that suggestion to be taken quite so literally, as it expressly declined to resolve whether independent agencies like the Federal Trade Commission or the Securities Exchange Commission (SEC) might be departments for this purpose. The *Freytag* majority also contended that, although the Tax Court is in the executive branch rather than the judicial branch, and although the Tax Court's judges lack life tenure and are subject to presidential removal for cause, "[t]he Tax Court exercises judicial, rather than executive, legislative, or administrative power."[26]

The four concurring justices in *Freytag*, by contrast, argued that the Tax Court is not a court of law but is instead a department for Appointments Clause purposes. In an opinion authored by Justice Antonin Scalia, the concurring justices maintained that the Tax Court could not be a court of law, because it is not an Article III court and its judges

---

24. For discussions of some of the legal conundrums presented by the Tax Court's structure, see Stephanie R. Hoffer & Christopher J. Walker, *The Death of Tax Court Exceptionalism*, 99 Minn. L. Rev. 221 (2014); Leandra Lederman, *Restructuring the U.S. Tax Court: A Reply to Stephanie Hoffer and Christopher Walker's The Death of Tax Court Exceptionalism*, 99 Minn. L. Rev. Headnotes 1 (2014).

25. 501 U.S. 868 (1991).

26. *Id.* at 890-91.

lack the constitutional safeguards that apply to Article III judges. "Such tribunals, like any other administrative board, exercise the executive power, not the judicial power of the United States."[27] Instead, they maintained that the Tax Court is a department because it is an agency "immediately below the President in the organizational structure of the Executive Branch."[28]

Many years after the *Freytag* decision, the Supreme Court settled the question they declined to resolve in that case regarding whether independent agencies could be departments for Appointments Clause purposes. In *Free Enterprise Fund v. Public Company Accounting Oversight Board*, the Court held that the SEC is a department eligible to appoint members of the PCAOB as inferior officers because the SEC "is a freestanding component of the Executive Branch, not subordinate to or contained within any other such component."[29] The five members of the SEC, acting collectively, are the "head" of that department because the SEC's powers are vested in the members jointly rather than any one of them alone.

[4] Appointment of Independent Agency Officials

The president's appointment of persons to lead the multi-member independent agencies is often more complicated than the appointment of other executive branch officials. For example, the Federal Trade Commission Act provides that the Federal Trade Commission (FTC) is to be headed by a five-person commission appointed by the president for seven-year terms with the advice and consent of the Senate.[30] No more than three of the five commissioners may be members of the same political party. To ensure that all the commissioners do not come up for reappointment at the same time, the terms are staggered. To preserve staggered terms, the president may appoint a person to an unexpired term only for the duration of that term.[31] The commissioners, rather than the president, choose their own chair.

Notwithstanding congressional efforts to preserve a strong degree of independence for some agencies, the influence of the presidential appointment power is considerable, even when dealing with an independent agency like the FTC. The length of an FTC commissioner's term stretches nearly across two presidential terms, but it provides independence only so long as the commissioner wishes to keep the seat. It is not unusual for commissioners to leave office before their terms are up, so staggered terms often are less of an inhibition on the president's influence than they might seem. The limitation on the number of commissioners from the same political party sounds like a check on the president's power, but, in reality, a president can find members of either party who are fully sympathetic with the current administration's positions.

---

27. *Id.* at 909 (Scalia, J., concurring).
28. *Id.* at 918.
29. 561 U.S. 477, 511 (2010).
30. 15 U.S.C. §§ 41, 42.
31. When an agency initially is formed, the enabling act typically provides for one term of three years, one of four years, one of five years and so on, to ensure that the commissioners sit in staggered terms from the outset. Staggering has two effects, one practical and one political: it enhances continuity at the highest agency levels over one or more presidential terms, and it prevents the president from appointing a completely new commission in a single term (unless, of course, individual commissioners resign before the expiration of their terms).

[5] Recess Appointments and Vacancies Act

The requirement of Senate approval has occasionally stymied presidents. Many nominees obtain Senate approval with few dissenting votes, but disputes between the president and the Senate over nominees have become more common over the last several presidencies. Although few presidential nominees have been rejected outright by a vote of the Senate, many more have seen their nominations withdrawn due to Senate opposition. For many years, presidents in turn utilized *recess appointments* to appoint nominees at least temporarily in the face of Senate recalcitrance.

Article II, § 2, Clause 3 of the U.S. Constitution gives presidents the authority "to fill up all Vacancies that may happen during the Recess of the Senate, by granting Commissions which shall expire at the End of their next Session." Particularly in times when travel was difficult and the Senate might be adjourned for months, the Recess Appointments Clause served as a pragmatic exception from the Senate consent requirement of the Appointments Clause. President George Washington utilized the Recess Appointments Clause numerous times, as did most if not all of his successors. Historically, much of the controversy surrounding the Recess Appointments Clause related to recess appointments of federal judges; from 1789 through 1960, presidents made more than 300 judicial recess appointments, including several Supreme Court justices. Judicial recess appointments declined substantially, however, after 1960.[32] By comparison, modern presidents from Ronald Reagan through Barack Obama frequently utilized their recess appointment authority to fill executive branch positions, particularly when members of the Senate blocked their nominees.[33]

The circumstances surrounding various recess appointments raised a number of questions regarding the proper interpretation of the Recess Appointments Clause. In *National Labor Relations Board v. Noel Canning*,[34] the Supreme Court addressed a number of those questions. For one, the Court concluded that a vacancy need not arise during a recess of the Senate to support a recess appointment. It is enough that the vacancy happens to exist.

Also in *Noel Canning*, the Court addressed at great length the timing and duration of what constitutes a recess. The Court said that the president may make recess appointments not only during the annual sine die adjournment—*i.e.*, the period between the end of one legislative session and the beginning of the next—but also during intrasession breaks of sufficient duration. Intrasession recesses of three days or fewer cannot support a recess appointment; intrasession recesses of four to nine days are "presumptively too short" but might be sufficient in "some very usual circumstance" such as "a national catastrophe... that renders the Senate unavailable but calls for an urgent

32. *See* Henry B. Hogue, Congressional Research Service, Recess Appointments: Frequently Asked Questions, CRS Report RS21308 (Mar. 11, 2015); Patrick Hein, *In Defense of Broad Recess Appointment Power: The Effectiveness of Political Counterweights*, 96 Cal. L. Rev. 235 (2008).

33. Until November 2013, a longstanding Senate rule required 60 senators to agree to end debate, known as cloture, before the Senate could hold a confirmation vote. The cloture rule thus allowed a minority of senators to block the presidential nominations they found objectionable. On November 21, 2013, a majority of senators voted to change the cloture rule to allow a simple majority vote to end debate with respect to most judicial and all executive branch nominations. Only Supreme Court nominations were excluded from that rule change, and a subsequent vote of the Senate in April 2017 ended that exclusion.

34. 573 U.S. 513 (2014).

response"; and intrasession recesses of ten days or more are adequate to support a recess appointment.[35]

Finally in *Noel Canning*, the Court considered the circumstances in which the Senate might be deemed to be in recess. In the circumstances of the case, the Senate by unanimous consent had adopted a resolution in which it declared that it would take a series of brief recesses and conduct *pro forma* sessions every few days between December 17, 2011, and January 23, 2012. The Senate did not actually conduct business at these pro forma sessions; it merely formally convened and then adjourned. President Barack Obama had made three recess appointments to the NLRB during the three-day period between two of these *pro forma* sessions. He argued before the Court that the pro forma sessions were not actual sessions of the Senate at all, but rather that the Senate was functionally in recess during the entire period from December 17 to January 23. The Court disagreed, holding that "the Senate is in session when it says it is, provided that, under its own rules, it retains the capacity to transact Senate business" and that the Senate met that standard in this case.[36]

In summary, on the one hand, the Court's decision in *Noel Canning* construed the text of the Recess Appointments Clause quite broadly, defining both "the recess" and "happen" to allow the president greater latitude to make recess appointments. However, by respecting the Senate's own rules and use of pro forma sessions, the Court's decision simultaneously gave the Senate the power to curtail substantially the president's ability to make recess appointments as the Senate so chooses. As a consequence, since the Court decided *Noel Canning*, there have been no recess appointments.

The practical curtailment of the president's recess appointment authority has done nothing to solve the ongoing problem of executive branch vacancies and delays by the Senate in confirming presidential nominees. Instead, Presidents Barack Obama, Donald Trump, and Joe Biden have relied on mechanisms outlined in the Federal Vacancies Reform Act of 1998 (Vacancies Act)[37] to fill vacant executive branch positions. The Vacancies Act provides for three classes of people who may serve as acting officials, designating the first assistant to the vacant office as the default alternative but allowing the president to choose instead either a person serving in another Senate-confirmed position or another senior officer or employee of the same agency. And, because presidents are relying more heavily on the Vacancies Act to fill vacant executive branch positions, courts have been called upon to resolve various issues regarding the Vacancies Act's meaning and application.[38] Justice Clarence Thomas has questioned whether the Vacancies Act is constitutional, suggesting that it violates the Appointments Clause by allowing the president to direct persons to serve as officers of the United States without the advice and consent of the Senate.[39]

---

35. *Id.* at 537–38.

36. *Id.* at 550.

37. 5 U.S.C. §§ 3345–49d.

38. *See, e.g., National Labor Relations Board v. SW General, Inc.*, 137 S. Ct. 929 (2017); *Hooks v. Kitsap Tenant Support Services, Inc.*, 816 F.3d 550 (9th Cir. 2016); *Guedes v. Bureau of Alcohol, Tobacco, Firearms & Explosives*, 920 F.3d 1 (D.C. Cir. 2019).

39. *SW General*, 137 S. Ct. at 945 (Thomas, J., concurring).

[B] Removal of Officers

The president's removal powers often are conditional as well. Cabinet secretaries serve at the pleasure of the president, as do most executive branch political appointees (*i.e.*, those persons who are not given civil service protection). No one should be fooled by the protocol of presidential appointments or removals and believe that, simply because a president announces in the public press that he has "asked for" the resignation of a certain person, that somehow, he could not fire that person forthwith. He can and occasionally does. The president's ability to remove other government officials is more complicated.

[1] Statutory Limitations on Removal of Most Federal Employees

For the first 100 years or so of our constitutional history, the presidential power to terminate executive branch employees was rarely at issue. In *Shurtleff v. United States*,[40] the Supreme Court broadly confirmed the president's general authority to remove executive branch personnel unless the statute creating the position provides otherwise.

In the late nineteenth century, Congress became concerned that a new president's power to summarily remove large numbers of low-ranking government employees on political grounds was interfering with the effective running of the government. The spoils system was wreaking havoc with the continuity of government operations, and the lack of personnel standards had a detrimental effect on the quality of government services. Congress reacted by passing the Civil Service Act of 1883 (often referred to as the Pendleton Act),[41] which created the Civil Service Commission to develop a professional corps of government employees who could not be removed for purely political reasons. Persons with civil service protection may be fired only for cause.[42] At the present time, approximately 80 percent of all federal employees are insulated from summary removal due to the considerable number of statutory limitations on the president's removal power and the protections afforded them under the Pendleton Act. The Office of Personnel Management now supervises most federal employees. Virtually all the state governments have similar systems.

In reaction to what many presidents and quite a few members of Congress perceived as too much insulation and too little accountability on the part of high-level civil servants, Congress enacted the Civil Service Reform Act of 1978 (CSRA),[43] which established the Senior Executive Service (SES). The SES was established to create a group of highly-qualified top managers with strong incentives and opportunities to improve the federal government.[44] These senior-level federal officers serve without the civil service job protections of other federal employees, but they are entitled to higher salaries and performance bonuses that are unavailable to other civil servants.[45] As of 2016, there

40. 189 U.S. 311 (1903). *Shurtleff* held that a customs official who did not serve a specific term by statute was removable at the discretion of the president. Among other things, the Court feared that any other result might guarantee persons like Shurtleff lifetime employment in the government.

41. 5 U.S.C. §§1101–05.

42. *See, e.g.*, David H. Rosenbloom, Federal Service and the Constitution (1971).

43. Pub. L. No. 95-454, 92 Stat. 1111 (codified at 5 U.S.C. §§101–05).

44. House Rep. No. 95-1403, 95th Cong., 2d Sess. at 101 (July 31, 1978).

45. Career and political SES appointees also have different job protections. Career SES appointees can only be removed under specific circumstances enumerated by statute and can appeal

were 9,936 SES positions.[46] A majority of these positions are held by career appointees, and the CSRA places limits on the total number of political appointees to SES positions as well as the number of political appointees in SES positions within a given agency.[47] While most federal agencies have SES positions, there are several notable exceptions, including the Federal Bureau of Investigations, the Drug Enforcement Agency, and some intelligence and financial regulatory agencies.[48]

The Civil Service Reform Act of 1978 also contained provisions establishing special protection for federal employees who face adverse action for reporting agency misconduct, known as *whistleblowers*. Congress on several occasions since then has amended and expanded the scope of whistleblower protections, including to cover federal contractors as well as private-sector employees.[49]

[2] Limitations on Removal of Officers

The parallel question of whether the Constitution also allows Congress to limit the president's power of removal has been tested in several cases, including two very different cases from the early twentieth century: *Myers v. United States*,[50] decided in 1926, and *Humphrey's Executor v. United States*,[51] decided in 1935. *Myers* involved a postmaster appointed by President Woodrow Wilson with Senate consent. Under the terms of the postal service statutes, a first-class postmaster like Frank Myers served a four-year term and could be removed during that term only with the consent of the Senate. President Wilson fired Myers without seeking Senate approval. Myers retaliated by bringing a lawsuit in the Court of Claims seeking the salary that would have been paid him had he not been removed. Chief Justice William Howard Taft (who had served as president himself) wrote the opinion for the Supreme Court and held that the statutory provision requiring Senate approval before the president could remove this kind of executive branch official was unconstitutional.

The basis for the Court's decision in *Myers* was straightforward. The Court cited the provisions of Article II that vest the executive power in the president, give the president the authority to appoint federal officers, and admonish the president to "take Care" that the laws are properly executed. The Court also surveyed at great length historical practice regarding presidential removal authority, including but not limited to its decision in the *Shurtleff* case discussed above. The Court then concluded that the president's removal

adverse decisions to the Merit Systems Protection Board; political appointees can be removed at any time and have no opportunity to appeal their termination. *See* Jacob A. Stein & Glenn A. Mitchell, 1 Administrative Law §5.07(4)(f) (2020).

46. Senate Committee on Homeland Security and Government Affairs, 114th Cong., United States Government Policy and Supporting Positions (Plum Book) 217 (Comm. Print 2016).

47. *Id.*

48. *Id.* For more information about the Senior Executive Service, see https://www.opm.gov/policy-data-oversight/senior-executive-service/.

49. *See, e.g.*, Whistleblower Protection Act of 1989, Pub. L. No. 101-12, 103 Stat. 16 (codified as amended in scattered sections of 5 U.S.C.); Whistleblower Protection Enhancement Act of 2012, Pub. L. No. 112-199, § 110, 126 Stat. 1465, 1471-72 (codified at 5 U.S.C. § 2302(b)(8)); Pilot Program for Enhancement of Contractor Protection from Reprisal for Disclosure of Certain Information, Pub. L. No. 112-239, § 828, 126 Stat. 1632, 1837 (codified at 41 U.S.C. § 4712) (2013). For a comprehensive review of the state of federal whistleblower protections, see David D. Schein, *Whistleblower Protection for Federal Contract Employees*, 29 U. Fla. J.L. & Pub. Pol'y 73 (2018).

50. 272 U.S. 52 (1926).

51. 295 U.S. 602 (1935).

power is virtually unfettered under the Constitution. Justices Brandeis, Holmes, and McReynolds dissented in *Myers*, contending that the Court's interpretation of Article II gave the president too much power over federal officers and, thus, tilted the balance of power as between the president and Congress too much in the president's favor.

Much of the Supreme Court's language in *Myers* proved to be too broad for a subsequent Court. In 1935, the same Court that rejected the centerpiece of President Franklin Delano Roosevelt's economic recovery program in the *Panama Refining* and *Schechter Poultry* cases[52] also denied his authority to ignore a statutory limitation on his power to remove a member of an independent agency. William Humphrey had been appointed to a second seven-year term on the FTC by President Herbert Hoover in 1931. Humphrey clearly disagreed with Roosevelt's ideas for the FTC, and he refused to resign at Roosevelt's request, so Roosevelt fired him on October 7, 1933. Like Myers, Humphrey sued in the Court of Claims for his salary, insisting that his "removal" by Roosevelt was invalid. Humphrey passed away before his suit reached the Supreme Court, but his estate continued to pursue the case (hence the use of the word *Executor* in the caption of the Supreme Court's opinion).[53]

Like *Myers*, *Humphrey's Executor* has both a statutory and a constitutional dimension. The Federal Trade Commission Act provides that commissioners of the FTC are to be appointed by the president with the advice and consent of the Senate, that they shall serve for staggered seven-year terms, and that they shall be removed from office by the president only for "inefficiency, neglect of duty or malfeasance in office."[54] President Roosevelt did not invoke any of these grounds in firing Humphrey. Writing for the Supreme Court, Justice George Sutherland maintained that Congress wanted to make removing an FTC commissioner difficult for a president because the FTC was to function as a neutral body of experts acting in the public interest, free from presidential interference, in certain matters of commerce and trade.

According to Sutherland, Congress's intent was easily discerned. The harder question was the statute's constitutionality. The *Shurtleff* and *Myers* opinions contained some exceptionally broad language describing the president's removal powers, and the Court apparently was not inclined to overrule those cases. Sutherland avoided the difficulty by going back to the Federal Trade Commission Act and determining that the FTC was to carry out its duties to police unfair methods of competition by exercising "quasi-legislative" and "quasi-judicial" powers. According to Sutherland, when the FTC exercises quasi-legislative powers, it functions as an "aid to" (or agent of) Congress, and when it exercises quasi-judicial powers, it functions as an aid to the courts.[55] In creating such an agency, Congress had the power to limit the president's authority to remove its leaders; the Constitution did not give the president "illimitable power of removal" over such officers. Allowing the president unfettered removal authority over officers exercising such quasi-legislative and quasi-judicial powers would violate separation of powers principles by permitting him to interfere with agents of the other two branches of government. And in this way, Humphrey was distinguishable particularly from Myers,

---

52. *See* Chapter 2, § 2.02.

53. The amount in controversy was approximately $60,000 (almost $1.3 million in modern dollars)—a healthy sum in the Great Depression. Humphrey had served about two years of a seven-year term. His yearly salary was $10,000. No wonder the executor of Humphrey's estate fought so fiercely on behalf of Humphrey's family.

54. 15 U.S.C. § 41.

55. *Humphrey's Executor*, 295 U.S. at 628–29.

whose functions as a first-class postmaster were said to be "purely executive."[56] To the extent that Chief Justice Taft's extensive analysis for the Court in *Myers* was more sweeping, Sutherland dismissed it as mere "dicta."

At first glance, this reasoning strikes many people as somewhat contrived and convoluted. Undoubtedly, the politics of the time influenced the Court.[57] It is probably not mere coincidence that *Humphrey's Executor* was handed down the same day as *Schechter Poultry.* Also, while Congress wanted some independence from the president for the FTC, it is unlikely that Congress really viewed the FTC as either its own agent or an agent of the courts. There is virtually nothing in the legislative history of the Federal Trade Commission Act supporting that characterization, although having participated in Congress's debates over the legislation as a senator, Justice Sutherland may have some special insight on this issue.

In rationalizing the decision, Justice Sutherland did a terrible disservice to agencies themselves and to generations of lawyers and law students by labeling agency powers as merely "quasi." Particularly if one thinks that the word *quasi* conveys connotations of *artificial* or *weak*, most of the remainder of this book demonstrates that there is nothing *quasi* about an agency's powers.[58] Anyone within an agency's jurisdiction violates agency requirements at their peril, as an agency's exercise of its powers can be a harrowing experience for a regulated party. Moreover, the *Humphrey's Executor* decision might be blamed for adding an unfortunate label to the lexicon of administrative law. Since the decision in *Humphrey's Executor*, many people have taken to calling independent agencies like the FTC the "headless fourth branch" of government.

Although the Court has not overruled *Humphrey's Executor* outright, the Court's reasoning in that case has not been so enduring. In one case, *Weiner v. United States*,[59] Justice Felix Frankfurter (who, as one of Roosevelt's principal New Deal advisers, presumably would have agreed with the attempted removal of Humphrey) held the removal of a member of the War Claims Commission invalid on the ground that the agency functioned essentially as a court. Since the *Weiner* decision, however, the Court's removal power jurisprudence has moved substantially away from such reasoning and relied on different theoretical justifications. Subsequently, however, the Court's removal power jurisprudence has almost entirely discarded the reasoning of *Humphrey's Executor.*

56. *Id.* at 627–28.

57. Both sides in the case held strong political feelings. Further, Justice Sutherland had participated as a senator in the debates on the Federal Trade Commission Act, the FTC's enabling legislation. Louis L. Jaffe & Nathaniel L. Nathanson, Administrative Law Cases & Materials 157–59 (4th ed. 1976). Commenting on Roosevelt's attempt to pack the Supreme Court after the *Panama Refining, Schechter Poultry*, and *Humphrey's Executor* decisions, Justice Robert Jackson (then Roosevelt's Attorney General) commented, "I really think the decision that made Roosevelt madder at the Court than any other decision was that damn little case of *Humphrey's Executor.* The President thought they went out of their way to spite him personally and they were giving him a different kind of deal than they were giving Taft." Eugene C. Gerhart, America's Advocate: Robert H. Jackson 99 (1958). For additional comments on *Humphrey's Executor*, see David M. Driesen, *Toward a Duty-Based Theory of Executive Power*, 78 Fordham L. Rev. 71 (2009).

58. Justice Jackson, dissenting in *Federal Trade Comm'n v. Ruberoid Co.*, 343 U.S. 470 (1952), noted that: "The mere retreat to the qualifying 'quasi' is implicit with confession that all recognized classifications have broken down and 'quasi' is a smooth cover which we draw over our confusion as we might use a counterpane to conceal a disordered bed." *Id.* at 487–88.

59. 357 U.S. 349 (1958).

After *Weiner*, the next major case in which the Supreme Court addressed the president's removal power was *Morrison v. Olson*,[60] discussed above. In addition to concluding that independent counsels were inferior rather than principal officers, the Court held that Congress could limit the president's removal authority by providing that only the Attorney General of the United States could remove independent counsels appointed pursuant to the Ethics in Government Act, and then only for good cause, notwithstanding that the functions of investigation and prosecution assigned to independent counsels were inherently executive. The majority held that limiting the president's ability to control the exercise of those functions in the context of the investigation and prosecution of alleged wrongdoing by an executive branch official did not "sufficiently deprive the President of control over the independent counsel to interfere impermissibly with his constitutional obligation to ensure the faithful execution of the laws." The Court distinguished its opinions in prior cases on the basis that "this case does not involve any attempt by Congress to increase its own power at the expense of the Executive Branch." The Court did not, however, articulate a standard for distinguishing purely executive officials who must be subject to presidential removal "at will" from those whom Congress may protect with a "for cause" removal limitation. Justice Antonin Scalia's passionate dissent in *Morrison* expressed concern that, without some judicially-enforced constraint on Congress's ability to limit the president's removal power, Congress would emasculate the presidency.

Another significant shift in the Supreme Court's removal power jurisprudence came in *Free Enterprise Fund v. Public Company Accounting Oversight Board*.[61] In that case, the Court considered whether a "dual for cause" restriction on the president's authority to (1) remove members of the Securities and Exchange Commission (SEC), combined with (2) the SEC's authority to remove members of the Public Company Accounting Oversight Board (PCAOB), violated the Constitution's separation of powers principles. The Court insisted that it was not rejecting its past removal power decisions, including *Humphrey's Executor* and *Morrison v. Olson*. But the Court also reasoned that, as compared with a single for cause removal restriction, a dual for cause limitation interfered even more, and too greatly, with the president's ability to take care that the laws be faithfully executed. "[I]f allowed to stand, this dispersion of responsibility could be multiplied" by adding more and more layers of insulation between the president and his subordinates. Accordingly, the Court found dual for cause restrictions unconstitutional.

Justice Breyer wrote a dissenting opinion in *Free Enterprise Fund* on behalf of himself and three of his colleagues. He disagreed that adding a second layer of insulation from potential removal would interfere with the president's ability to execute the laws. Rather, he defended that extra degree of removal protection as justified both by the need to ensure both that PCAOB adjudications are undertaken free of political influence and that the PCAOB will make decisions based on its expertise rather than for political considerations. Justice Breyer also devoted a large part of his dissent and lengthy appendices to documenting several dozen agencies and hundreds of agency officials across the federal government with similar dual for cause removal arrangements. As Justice Breyer observed, the Court's *Free Enterprise Fund* decision raised significant questions regarding the constitutionality of the actions of all of those agencies and officials.

60. 487 U.S. 654 (1988).
61. 561 U.S. 477 (2010).

In *Seila Law LLC v. Consumer Financial Protection Bureau*,[62] the Supreme Court again claimed to retain its decisions in cases like *Humphrey's Executor* and *Morrison v. Olson*, while simultaneously moving away from their reasoning and curtailing their reach. The *Seila Law* case concerned the constitutionality of the Consumer Financial Protection Bureau (CFPB), an independent agency headed by a single director who could only be removed from office for cause. The Court concluded that the CFPB's organizational structure violated separation of powers. The Court reasoned that, because Article II executive power "belongs to the President alone," lesser officers who assist the president in his duties must be accountable to him, and the ability to remove those lesser officers is necessary to ensure accountability. In considering its past removal power precedents, the Court focused upon *Myers* as providing the general rule of a broad removal power, and cast *Humphrey's Executor* and *Morrison v. Olson* as establishing mere "exceptions to the President's unrestricted removal power." One exception is for "multimember expert agencies that do not wield substantial executive power," although the Court also emphasized the FTC's partisan balance and the staggered terms of its members. The second exception is for "inferior officers with limited duties and no policymaking or administrative authority." Together, the Court said these exceptions "represent what up to now have been the outermost constitutional limits of permissible congressional restrictions on the President's removal power." In a footnote, however, the Court noted that its conclusion in 1935 "that the FTC did not exercise executive power has not withstood the test of time," which raises the question whether an agency that the Court has not already deemed to be non-executive could be found to satisfy the first exception today.

Regardless, applying these two exceptions to the CFPB, the Court said that the agency's single director could not be described as a nonpartisan body of experts with staggered terms and that the director clearly exercised policymaking authority and "core executive power" by adopting binding rules, issuing final decisions in administrative adjudications, and seeking monetary penalties against private parties in federal court. The Court also said that the CFPB's director "is not an inferior officer, and her duties are far from limited." Regarding other agencies with similar structures—*i.e.*, the Comptroller of the Currency, the Office of Special Counsel, the Social Security Administration, and the Federal Housing Finance Agency—the Court described those agencies as "isolated examples [that] are modern and contested [and] do not involve regulatory or enforcement authority remotely comparable to that exercised by the CFPB." Also, in addition to the statutory restriction on the president's removal power, the Court pointed to the CFPB director's fixed five-year term and funding outside the appropriations process as "unique" and, when combined, "even more problematic." To resolve the constitutional difficulty, the Court severed the removal restriction from the agency's enabling act and made the CFPB's director accountable to the president directly.

Subsequently, in *Collins v. Yellen*,[63] the Supreme Court relied on its decision in *Seila Law* regarding a second independent agency headed by a single director, the Federal Housing Finance Agency (FHFA), to hold that "the Constitution prohibits even 'modest restrictions' on the President's power to remove the head of an agency with a single top officer." Although the Court acknowledged that the CFPB and the FHFA were different from one another in several ways, the Court said none of those distinctions justified "a different result."

62. 140 S. Ct. 2183 (2020).
63. 141 S. Ct. 1761 (2021).

Although Congress in some instances may be able to limit the president's authority to remove high-level government officials, that power does not extend to Congress reserving a role in the removal process for itself. The Court held as much in the *Myers* case, but had another opportunity to consider the issue in *Bowsher v. Synar*.[64] In that case, the Supreme Court conducted a thorough analysis of the status of the comptroller general as the head of the General Accounting Office (now the Government Accountability Office) and concluded that there was no doubt that the comptroller general was an agent of Congress and had been such since the creation of the office in 1921. Having affirmed that finding, the Court then reviewed virtually all of the case law discussed above and concluded that "Congress cannot reserve for itself the power of removal of an officer charged with the execution of the laws except by impeachment." Coupling the holding in *Bowsher* with its earlier decision invalidating the legislative veto, *Immigration & Naturalization Service v. Chadha* (discussed in Chapter 2), the Court went on to state in the most unambiguous terms:

> To permit an officer controlled by Congress to execute the laws would be, in essence, to permit a congressional veto. Congress could simply remove, or threaten to remove, an officer for executing the laws in any fashion found unsatisfactory to Congress. This kind of congressional control over the execution of the laws ... is constitutionally impermissible.[65]

Controversies over the status of the president's removal power and separation of powers more broadly are far from over. The cases discussed in this chapter, and the additional cases discussed in Chapter 2, suggest that the Supreme Court debates over these principles will continue.

§ 3.04 Other Presidential Powers and Tools

[A] Presidential Powers Generally

In the early 1950s, during the Korean War, President Truman seized the nation's steel mills in order to avert a strike that in his opinion would have endangered the national security. Prior to the seizure, Truman had asked Congress for seizure authority and had been refused. Truman took over the mills anyway and ran them with military personnel. Most students of constitutional law know that the Supreme Court, in *Youngstown Sheet & Tube Co. v. Sawyer*,[66] held the seizure unconstitutional because Truman exceeded his presidential powers. More instructive for administrative law is the perceptive concurrence by Justice Jackson that outlined three categories of presidential power for further analysis:

> 1. When the President acts under an express or implied authorization of Congress, his authority is at its maximum, for it includes all that he possesses in his own right plus all that Congress can delegate.... If his act is held unconstitutional under these circumstances, it usually means that the Federal Government as an undivided whole lacks power....

64. 478 U.S. 714 (1986).
65. *Id.* at 726–27.
66. 343 U.S. 579 (1952).

> 2. When the President acts in absence of either a congressional grant or denial of authority, he can only rely upon his own independent powers, but there is a zone of twilight in which he and Congress may have concurrent authority, or in which its distribution is uncertain. Therefore, congressional inertia, indifference or quiescence may sometimes, at least as a practical matter, enable, if not invite, measures on independent presidential responsibility. In this area, any actual test of power is likely to depend on the imperatives of events and contemporary imponderables rather than on abstract theories of law.
>
> 3. When the President takes measures incompatible with the expressed or implied will of Congress, his power is at its lowest ebb, for then he can rely only upon his own constitutional powers minus any constitutional powers of Congress over the matter. Courts can sustain exclusive Presidential control in such a case only by disabling the Congress from acting upon the subject. Presidential claim to a power at once so conclusive and preclusive must be scrutinized with caution, for what is at stake is the equilibrium established by our constitutional system.[67]

The "zone of twilight" described by Justice Jackson is often fertile ground for enforceable executive orders and proclamations. For example, the president's power to establish certain labor management rules for federal employees has been upheld, as has an executive order prohibiting the award of government contracts to certain firms that violate what the president labeled "voluntary" wage and price controls.[68] Over time, there has been a trend to increased presidential participation in administrative process.[69]

Another power that President Bill Clinton attempted to exercise was the authority given to him by a recent Congressional statute to veto individual provisions or "line items" in congressional legislation. President Clinton, exercising this power, vetoed (or, in the parlance of the statute, "cancelled") two items in a 700-page Omnibus Budget Reconciliation Act. His action was quickly challenged in court and, on review by the Supreme Court, the Court held the line-item veto power to be unconstitutional. Although the opinion was lengthy, the ultimate conclusion was simply stated:

> [O]ur decision rests on the narrow ground that the procedures authorized by the Line Item Veto Act are not authorized by the Constitution.... If there is to be a new procedure in which the President will play a different role in determining the final text of what may "become a law," such change must come not by legislation but through the amendment procedures ... of the Constitution.[70]

[B] Unitary Executive Theory

Over the past few decades, and stretching over a number of presidential administrations, a theory of presidential power called the unitary executive has been propounded[71]

---

67. *Id.* at 635–38.

68. *See, e.g.*, *Old Dominion Branch No. 496 v. Austin*, 418 U.S. 264 (1974); *AFL-CIO v. Kahn*, 618 F.2d 784 (D.C. Cir.), *cert. denied*, 443 U.S. 915 (1979).

69. *See, e.g.*, Elena Kagan, *Presidential Administration*, 114 Harv. L. Rev. 2245 (2001); John O. McGinnis, *Presidential Review as Constitutional Restoration*, 51 Duke L.J. 901 (2001); Steven Croley, *White House Review of Agency Rulemaking: An Empirical Investigation*, 70 U. Chi. L. Rev. 821 (2003).

70. *Clinton v. City of New York*, 524 U.S. 417 (1998).

71. *See, e.g.*, Stephen G. Calabresi & Christopher S. Yoo, The Unitary Executive: Presidential Power from Washington to Bush (2008); Steven G. Calabresi & Saikrishna B. Prakash,

by some and rejected[72] by others. The theory focuses on presidential power and contends particularly that the president possesses the constitutional authority to pursue three particular actions: (1) the power to remove lower-ranking executive branch officials; (2) the power to dictate to subordinates the making of executive branch policy; and (3) the power to veto, or nullify exercises of discretion by lower-ranking persons within the executive branch.[73] The theory has historical antecedents. Prior to the drafting and ratification of the current United States Constitution, the Articles of Confederation established a weak national executive that has been characterized as "executive by committee." There is some evidence stemming from the constitutional debates and other sources that the founders wished to vest all the powers of the executive branch in a single person—the president of the United States.

The theory derives principally from the language in Article II, § 1 of the United States Constitution: "The executive Power shall be vested in the President of the United States of America." There is no question that the Framers adopted this language instead of counter proposals that would have created some kind of executive council. Article II, § 2 gives the president the authority to "require the Opinion, in writing, of the principal Officer in each of the executive Departments, upon any Subject relating to the Duties of their respective Offices." And Article II, § 3 requires that the *president* "shall take Care that the Laws be faithfully executed." Some have read the sum of these provisions as giving the president virtually unfettered authority within the executive branch. In his dissenting opinion in *Morrison v. Olson*,[74] the decision upholding the independent counsel statute discussed above in this chapter, Justice Scalia cited the Vesting Clause of Article II and noted that "this does not mean *some* of the executive power but *all* of the executive power.... The President's constitutionally assigned duties include *complete* control over the investigation and prosecution of violations of the law."[75]

Unitary executive theory has clearly influenced the Supreme Court's decisionmaking in several decisions over the past decade concerning separation of powers principles, including the *Free Enterprise Fund*, *Seila Law*, and *Arthrex* cases discussed above in this chapter. For the purposes of this book, however, perhaps the most difficult of the questions posed is whether the president has the power to dictate policy decisions made by lower-ranking officials in the executive branch even when he clearly has the power to appoint and to fire such persons. Unitary executive theory suggests the answer to this question is *yes*.[76] At least one commentator contends to the contrary that "the president may advise agency heads concerning his views on particular rules but the president has no authority to dictate regulatory decisions entrusted to them [the lower-ranking officers] by law."[77] The Court is unlikely ever to be in a position to resolve this question.

The President's Power to Execute the Laws, 104 YALE L.J. 541 (1994).

72. *See, e.g.*, Mark Tushnet, *A Political Perspective on the Theory of the Unitary Executive*, 12 U. PA. J. CONST. L. 313 (2010); Robert V. Percival, *Presidential Management of the Administrative State: The Not-So-Unitary Executive*, 51 DUKE L.J. 963 (2001).

73. *See, e.g.*, Saikrishna Prakash, *Fragmented Features of the Constitution's Unitary Executive*, 45 WILLAMETTE L. REV. 701 (2009); Christopher S. Yoo, Steven G. Calabresi & Anthony J. Colangelo, *The Unitary Executive in the Modern Era, 1945-2004*, 90 IOWA L. REV. 601 (2005).

74. 487 U.S. 654 (1988).

75. *Id.* at 705 & 711 (emphasis in the original).

76. Although she does not endorse unitary executive theory as such, Justice Elena Kagan has defended presidential authority to direct the executive branch on other grounds. *See* Elena Kagan, *Presidential Administration*, 114 HARV. L. REV. 2245 (2001).

77. Robert V. Percival, *Presidential Management of the Administrative State: The Not-So-Unitary Executive*, 51 DUKE L.J. 963 (2001); *see also* Peter L. Strauss, *Overseer, or "The Decider"? The*

[C] The Role of the Executive Order

Presidents have other mechanisms available for guiding and controlling executive action. One such device is the executive order, by which a president communicates directives to cabinet-level agencies. Presidents have claimed legal authority to issue executive orders based on Article II of the U.S. Constitution, particularly Article II, § 1, which vests "the executive Power" in the president, and Article II, § 3, which requires the president to "take Care that the Laws be faithfully executed." In defending presidential authority to issue executive orders, the Department of Justice has quoted from the *Myers* case to the effect that the president has an obligation to "supervise and guide Executive officers in their construction of the statutes under which they act in order to secure that unitary and uniform execution of the laws which Article II of the Constitution evidently contemplated in vesting general executive powers in the President alone."[78] Sometimes, legislation expressly authorizes the president to act by executive order. In other instances, Congress has ratified an executive order after the president issued it.

Although it is not entirely clear whether executive orders carry the force of law, executive orders are compelling documents that agencies ignore at their peril. For example, during the early 1970s, President Richard Nixon established a "voluntary" wage and price control program by executive order. In that order, President Nixon required that agencies deny government contracts to any firm that did not comply with the wage and price controls. In *AFL-CIO v. Kahn*,[79] the D.C. Circuit upheld the executive order's validity even though it was neither expressly authorized nor compelled by statute. The court reasoned that the federal procurement acts gave the president broad authority to manage government contracts through the device of the executive order.

The more difficult issue is whether an executive order may govern the activities of independent agencies. In its analysis of President Ronald Reagan's Executive Order 12,291, establishing cost-benefit analysis requirements for executive agencies, the Department of Justice concluded that an executive order could control the actions of independent agencies, but that "an attempt to exercise supervision of these agencies [through an executive order] would be lawful only if the Supreme Court is prepared to repudiate certain expansive dicta [in *Humphrey's Executor*] and [would trigger] a confrontation with Congress, which has historically been jealous of its prerogatives with regard to [the independent agencies]."[80] Most presidents have respected this arm's-length distance between the chief executive and the independent agencies.

[D] Office of Information and Regulatory Affairs and EO 12866

The Office of Management and Budget and its subsidiary, the Office of Information and Regulatory Affairs (OIRA), are entities within the Executive Office of the President that exercise a great deal of control over executive branch rulemaking through a series

President in Administrative Law, 75 Geo. Wash. L. Rev. 696 (2007).

78. *Myers v. U.S.*, 272 U.S. 52, 135 (1926); *see also* § 3.03[B][2].

79. 618 F.2d 784 (D.C. Cir. 1979).

80. Memorandum of the Office of Legal Counsel, Department of Justice on Implementation of Executive Order 12,291 (1981).

of executive orders, the most prominent of which is EO 12866. These executive orders have required, among other things, that agencies prepare, publish, and regularly update their regulatory agendas and that agencies submit to OIRA each "major rule," including a "regulatory impact analysis" describing the rule's anticipated costs and benefits. The OIRA review process and regulatory impact analysis are discussed at greater length in §§ 7.06 and 7.07.

[E] Presidential Signing Statements

When signing legislation, presidents have issued signing statements as a means of communicating to Congress, the courts, and federal agencies their contemporaneous views regarding legislative meaning. Although the first presidential signing statement dates back to President James Monroe, their use became substantially more common only in the twentieth century.[81] Unlike executive orders, presidential signing statements clearly lack the force and effect of law.

Some presidential signing statements merely celebrate the legislation to which they correspond, recognize persons instrumental in the legislation's enactment, or express disappointment that the legislation did not contain additional provisions that the president wanted. Other presidential signing statements represent presidential efforts to influence or guide the behavior of other governmental actors, like agency officials or judges.

One common use of presidential signing statements is as a mechanism for expressing the president's view that parts of the legislation are unconstitutional. For example, when Congress enacted some amendments to a Department of Defense appropriations act prohibiting the federal government from engaging in torture of detained persons (including those detained as enemy combatants at Guantanamo Bay, Cuba), President George W. Bush objected because, in his view, this language interfered with his prerogatives as Commander-in-Chief. Presidents have been criticized for using signing statements in this way, with critics arguing that a president should not sign a bill that he believes is unconstitutional. Defenders of this practice observe that presidential signing statements are not legally binding and that the concerns about constitutionality typically relate to potential applications of the provisions in question. At worst, they suggest that such presidential signing statements represent a determination not to enforce a statute that may or may not actually lead to nonenforcement.

Other presidential signing statements articulate the president's interpretation of statutory text, undoubtedly in an effort to influence and guide both federal agency officials and courts.[82] Former Attorney General Edwin Meese has been credited with persuading

---

81. For just a few examples of the many academic articles documenting and analyzing presidential use of signing statements across history, see Daniel B. Rodriguez, Edward H. Stiglitz & Barry R Weingast, *Executive Opportunism, Presidential Signing Statements, and the Separation of Powers*, 8 J. Legal Analysis 95, 100 (2016); Curtis A. Bradley & Eric A. Posner, *Presidential Signing Statements and Executive Power*, 23 Const. Comment. 307 (2006); Christopher N. May, *Presidential Defiance of "Unconstitutional" Laws: Reviving the Royal Prerogative*, 21 Hastings Const. L.Q. 865 (1994); Marc N. Garber & Kurt A. Wimmer, *Presidential Signing Statements as Interpretations of Legislative Intent: An Executive Aggrandizement of Power*, 24 Harv. J. on Legis. 363 (1987).

82. *See, e.g.*, John M. de Figueiredo & Edward H. Stiglitz, *Signing Statements and Presidentializing Legislative History*, 69 Admin. L. Rev. 841 (2017); Kristy L. Carroll, *Whose Statute is it Anyway? Why and How Courts Should Use Presidential Signing Statements When Interpreting Federal Statutes*, 46 Cath. U. L. Rev. 475 (1997).

the publisher of the U.S. Code Congressional and Administrative News (U.S.C.C.A.N.) to include presidential signing statements in its volumes, arguing that the president's role in the enactment process made signing statements at least as reliable an indicator of statutory meaning as other forms of legislative history.[83] However, one recent study of judicial citations to presidential signing statements found that very few judicial opinions actually cite signing statements and that, when they do, the signing statements are relied upon merely to buttress the judges' own interpretations of statutes. One exception seems to be in traditional areas of executive prerogative, such as foreign policy and national security.[84] Perhaps the paucity of judicial citations to presidential signing statements explains why the Supreme Court has not addressed the constitutional validity of presidential signing statements or the extent to which courts ought to defer to them.[85]

[F] The Special Role of the Department of Justice

The Department of Justice, under the leadership of the attorney general of the United States (AG), plays a more substantial role in the administration of executive branch agencies than any other department.[86] The Department of Justice functions as the law firm for executive branch agencies in court. The Department also functions as the principal law enforcement agency for the federal government. As the chief executive officer in the Department of Justice, the AG was one of the original members of the president's cabinet, in an office established by the 1789 Judiciary Act, although the Department of Justice itself was not established until 1870, over 100 years later.[87] The Attorney General must be someone

> learned in the law... whose duty it shall be to prosecute and conduct all suits in the Supreme Court in which the United States shall be concerned, and *to give his advice and opinion upon questions of law* when required by the President of the United States, or when requested by the heads of any departments, touching any matters that may concern their departments....[88]

It is this advice giving prerogative—the power to issue opinions—that gives the AG substantial influence over the remainder of the executive branch. In earlier times, these opinions took the form of Attorney General Opinions. In contemporary times, that function has been delegated to the Office of Legal Counsel (OLC). Regardless, the issuance of

83. *See, e.g.*, Rodriguez, Stiglitz & Weingast, *supra* note 80, at 100.

84. *See* Figueiredo & Stiglitz, *supra* note 81, at 852–65.

85. *See, e.g.*, Ronald A. Cass & Peter L. Strauss, *The Presidential Signing Statements Controversy*, 16 Wm. & Mary Bill Rts. J. 11 (2007) (discussing these issues).

86. One of the best studies of the Office of Attorney General is Daniel J. Meador, The President, the Attorney General, and the Department of Justice (1980); a fascinating shorter article on the origins of the Department of Justice is Susan L. Bloch, *The Early Role of the Attorney General in Our Constitutional Scheme*, 1989 Duke L.J. 561 (1989).

87. Bloch *supra* note 85, at 566 & 619. While this is not the place to get into the intricacies of the U.S. law enforcement organizational structure, some detail is necessary to appreciate the full scope of the Department's authority. To a certain extent, the Office of United States Attorney in each federal judicial district functions as a kind of field office for the Department of Justice in both civil and criminal matters. However, each United States Attorney is separately appointed by the president and confirmed by the Senate and consequently enjoys a fair amount of independence from the Department of Justice itself. *See, e.g.*, Peter L. Strauss, An Introduction to Administrative Justice in the United States 101 n.151 (1989).

88. Judiciary Act of 1789, ch. 20, 1 Stat. 73, 92–93.

such opinions is frequently used to settle interagency disputes or to resolve broad administrative questions that cover a number of agencies. As Professor Peter Strauss suggested at one time, "[o]nce the agencies have received advice from the Attorney General, they may lack the means to generate valid litigation that would test its correctness; but if the issue later arises in a proper dispute, say between a citizen and an agency, the Attorney General's prior expression of view would have only persuasive authority for a court."[89] While the issue is not conclusively resolved, many agencies regard these opinions to be binding on them until rescinded or removed by judicial action.[90]

§ 3.05 Ethics in Government Service

[A] Ethical Issues Arising Facing Administrative Lawyers

Ethical questions arise frequently in administrative practice both on the part of government attorneys and on the part of private practitioners. Lawyers have too often been insensitive to these concerns, probably resulting in the generally low opinion many members of the public have for lawyers in general and certain agency practitioners in particular. There may be serious limits to what statutes and rules can accomplish in this area, but there is no excuse for personal callousness on the part of individual lawyers.

There is probably no better place in this book to discuss some of the concerns that Congress, the executive branch, and the general public have expressed regarding the conduct of federal employees, and more importantly, the conduct of lawyers who work for the Federal Government. To begin with, there are numerous controls on lawyers' conduct, such as the Code of Professional Responsibility or the newer Model Rules of Professional Conduct, that apply irrespective of whether a lawyer is a government employee. Thus, no lawyer, whether in the government or in the private sector, may commit fraud or engage in illegal conduct or violate any of the other canons or rules of professional ethics. In addition, there are statutory provisions and agency rules that prohibit federal employees dealing with matters in which the employee has a financial interest. An executive order forbids employee conduct that might impair the integrity of the government.[91] The Civil Service Reform Act of 1978 provides special protections for whistleblowers.[92]

[B] The Ethics in Government Act

One of the most important problems in present-day administrative practice is the so-called revolving door phenomenon. This is the practice by which agency personnel leave government for high positions in the industries their agencies regulate, and industry

89. Strauss, *supra* note 86, at 101 n.152.

90. *See* Douglas Kmiec, *OLC's Opinion Writing Function*, 15 Cardozo L. Rev. 337 (1993).

91. Exec. Order 11,222 (codified at 3 C.F.R. § 306).

92. 5 U.S.C. § 1101. A good illustration of how some of the statutory whistleblower provisions work in practice is the discussion by Judge Patricia Wald in *Borrell v. United States International Communications Agency*, 682 F.2d 981 (D.C. Cir. 1982). *See also* § 3.03[B][1].

executives move into those same agencies for a few years as political appointees. This movement creates a number of difficulties for the agency. For example, if the revolving door is completely uncontrolled and too cozy, it can result in a "captive" agency that reflects more the interests of the businesses being regulated than the concerns of the general public. By contrast, an agency cannot function capably if its personnel are so insulated that they are totally ignorant of the regulated industry.

The revolving door phenomenon places ethical pressures on the officials exiting the government. In an attempt to curb the worst revolving door abuses, Congress in 1978 enacted the Ethics in Government Act,[93] a statute that bears close study by anyone contemplating entering or leaving government service. First, the Act requires current high-level government employees (generally those who are political appointees or serving in grades of GS-15 or higher) to file financial disclosure forms for both themselves and their close family members. Second, any employee who was personally and substantially involved in a particular matter is barred permanently from appearing in any representative capacity on that matter for any party. (Rulemaking, however, is not regarded as a particular "matter" within the scope of the act.) There are also prohibitions against a former government employee representing persons on *any* matter before his or her agency for two years after leaving the government.[94]

The Ethics in Government Act has not been uniformly praised. In fact, the statute may have the effect of reducing the number of persons interested in government service. It is not entirely clear whether the Act, even after forty years of operation, is truly effective or properly administered. Nonetheless, it is, at the very least, a statement by Congress that these matters are important.

93. Pub. L. No. 95-521, 92 Stat. 1824 as amended (codified in scattered portions of U.S.C.). Useful articles discussing government ethics in general and the Ethics in Government Act specifically include the following: Kathleen Clark, *Do We Have Enough Ethics in Government Yet? An Answer from Fiduciary Theory*, 1996 U. Ill. L. Rev. 57; ABA Committee on Government Standards, *Keeping Faith: Government Ethics & Government Ethics Regulation*, 45 Admin. L. Rev. 287 (1993); James M. Lager, *Overcoming Cultures of Compliance to Reduce Corruption and Achieve Ethics in Government*, 41 McGeorge L. Rev. 63 (2009); Alice Bartek-Santiago, *Humanizing Federal Ethics: Motivating and Mobilizing Compliance Through Creative Outreach*, 51 Creighton L. Rev. 713 (2018).

94. The Supreme Court held that the subsection of Ethics in Government Act prohibiting receipt of honoraria by government employees was unconstitutional. *See United States v. National Treasury Employees Union*, 513 U.S. 454 (1995).

Chapter 4

The Exercise of Agency Power

§ 4.01 Introduction

The topics discussed in Chapters 2 and 3 involve the legitimacy and fundamental nature of administrative agencies. But questions of delegation and executive control mostly are issues that have long been settled in existing administrative agencies. Most of the real controversies in administrative law involve the agency in action. This chapter begins an analysis of agency action by examining certain limits on agency power, including issues that are often not clearly addressed in many administrative law casebooks but that are vital to a full understanding of individual agencies and of the administrative process as a whole.

Two basic concepts should be kept in mind as you work through this chapter and the remainder of the book. First, feel free to presume for the sake of argument and understanding that your agency has no problems with the nondelegation issue—*i.e.*, that its enabling act contains a valid standard and that the powers delegated are delegated only to eligible government officials, not to ineligible delegees like private parties. Challenges to an agency's basic functions are usually resolved early in its existence. Subsequent controversies regarding such things as delegation usually arise only when the legislature gives the agency brand new authority or jurisdiction.

Second, this chapter is not an exclusive nor exhaustive statement of the limitations on agency powers but merely a review of some of those limitations that do not fit easily into later chapters. Many limitations on agency functions are explored in the chapters on decisionmaking and judicial review and are not discussed here.

Administrative agencies engage in a number of different actions. Some of those actions look a lot like the drafting and enactment of statutes. Others involve the resolution of individual claims and grievances brought by or against private parties. In *Humphrey's Executor v. United States*,[1] the Supreme Court labeled these actions respectively as "quasi-legislative" and "quasi-judicial" in character. Referring to agency actions in these terms is not meant to suggest that a pronouncement from an agency should be taken more casually than one from a legislature or a court. Nothing could be further from the truth. To the extent that an agency is functioning under a proper delegation and within the jurisdiction established by its enabling act, its pronouncements should not be regarded lightly.

1. 295 U.S. 602 (1935). *Humphrey's Executor* is discussed fully in Chapter 3, § 3.03.

§ 4.02 Agency Jurisdiction— The *Ultra Vires* Doctrine

The federal Administrative Procedure Act expressly permits a court to determine whether an agency is functioning within its jurisdiction. Sections 706(2)(A) and (C) authorize courts to set aside agency action found to be "contrary to law" or "in excess of statutory jurisdiction, authority, or limitations, or short of statutory right."[2] The authority of courts to review jurisdictional questions of this kind was established by the Supreme Court in *Crowell v. Benson*,[3] a case which is now disdained by most administrative law scholars for other reasons. If an agency is acting outside its jurisdictional limits, it is said to be functioning in an *ultra vires* manner.

The term *ultra vires* is borrowed from corporate law and must be sharply distinguished from the nondelegation doctrine.[4] A delegation analysis looks at the face of the enabling act and asks whether the statute *itself* contains a proper standard curbing unfettered agency discretion.[5] By contrast, the issue of whether an agency is acting *ultra vires* assumes that there is a proper delegation in the statute and then analyzes specific action taken by the agency to see whether that action is within the limits set by the enabling act. Courts often overturn agency action because the action is outside the agency's boundaries.

But how does one know whether an agency is functioning within its jurisdiction? Generally, this is a statutory question, based on the agency's enabling act. To the extent that the Shipping Act expressly gives the Federal Maritime Commission the authority to regulate ocean shipping but not airlines, that agency will be limited to regulating ocean shippers. Most of the time, the enabling acts are clear enough as to the substantive boundaries of an agency's jurisdiction. For example, in one of its most important *ultra vires* decisions, *Board of Governors, Federal Reserve System v. Dimension Financial Corp.*,[6] the Supreme Court determined that the Federal Reserve Board's authority to regulate "banks," as that term was defined in the underlying statute, did not give the Board the authority to regulate certain savings and loan institutions. As the Court put it: "If the statute is clear and unambiguous [with regard to an agency's authority] that is the end of the matter...." The D.C. Circuit reached a similar conclusion when it decided that the Gramm-Leach-Bliley Financial Modernization Act clearly did not give the

2. The standards of APA § 706(2) are cumulative rather than exclusive of one another. *See, e.g., Ass'n of Data Processing Service Organizations v. Board of Governors of the Federal Reserve System*, 745 F.2d 677, 683 (D.C. Cir. 1984).

3. 285 U.S. 22 (1932). This case should be approached with extreme care. It does establish the authority of courts to review an agency's jurisdiction, but much of the language in the case dealing with the concept of "constitutional" or "jurisdictional" fact (suggesting that a court can review these matters *de novo, i.e.*, with no deference whatsoever to what the agency said) is probably not acceptable today.

4. For a more complete and thought-provoking analysis comparing *ultra vires* doctrine in the contexts of corporate charters and administrative agency enabling acts, see Lars Noah, *Interpreting Agency Enabling Acts: Misplaced Metaphors in Administrative Law*, 41 WM & MARY L. REV. 1463 (2000).

5. *See* Chapter 2, § 2.02 (discussing delegation analysis and the nondelegation doctrine at length).

6. 474 U.S. 361 (1986).

Federal Trade Commission the authority to regulate law firms engaged in the practice of law as "financial institutions."[7]

But sometimes the issue is not so clear cut. The old Federal Power Commission (FPC) (now the Federal Energy Regulatory Commission) was given statutory authority to regulate rates for the interstate shipment of natural gas in 1938. For a number of reasons, the FPC believed that its authority permitted it to regulate only interstate natural gas pipelines and firmly insisted that this jurisdiction did not extend to the regulation of prices charged by natural gas *wells* whose production was sold in interstate commerce. It took a Supreme Court decision in 1954, *Phillips Petroleum Co. v. Wisconsin*,[8] to prompt the FPC to exercise its wellhead jurisdiction. The Communications Act of 1934, as amended by the Telecommunications Act of 1996, gives the Federal Communications Commission (FCC) the authority to regulate "telecommunications services" but not "information services." In the age of cable and the Internet, numerous cases have arisen over whether particular service providers fall within the FCC's regulatory jurisdiction,[9] partly because the FCC itself keeps changing its mind.[10]

Occasionally, an agency will aggressively test the limits of its jurisdiction. Examples abound. The Consumer Product Safety Commission decided that it had jurisdiction to regulate the use of aluminum electric wiring in new home construction as a safety hazard, asserting that aluminum wiring was a consumer product within the definition of the Consumer Product Safety Act. The aluminum manufacturers and the construction industry strongly objected, but eventually, a federal court of appeals determined that aluminum wiring did fit within the statutory definition of consumer product.[11] In another instance, however, the federal Food and Drug Administration (FDA) was slapped down by the Supreme Court for going beyond its jurisdictional boundaries. In *Food & Drug Administration v. Brown & Williamson Tobacco Corp.*,[12] the FDA attempted to regulate tobacco products as within the FDA's statutory power to regulate "drugs" and certain "drug delivery devices," despite decades of denying such jurisdiction. Relying largely on a history of failed congressional legislation attempting to give FDA such authority, the Court determined that Congress had effectively prohibited any FDA regulation of tobacco products, and any FDA ban on such products "would therefore plainly contradict congressional policy."[13]

Ultra vires issues mainly involve statutory interpretation and require a close look at the express language of the statute, particularly those provisions that tell the agency

---

7. *American Bar Ass'n v. Federal Trade Comm'n*, 430 F.3d 457 (D.C. Cir. 2005).

8. *Phillips Petroleum Co. v. Wisconsin*, 347 U.S. 672 (1954). In this case, the FPC declined to investigate and review the rates of a particular industry participant on the ground that the company's activities fell outside its jurisdiction. Upon appeal of that decision, the Court disagreed with the FPC's interpretation of its jurisdiction and affirmed a lower court's instruction to the FPC to review and fix the company's rates.

9. *National Cable & Telecommunications Ass'n v. Brand X Internet Services*, 545 U.S. 967 (2005); *U.S. Telecom Ass'n v. Federal Communication Comm'n*, 825 F.3d 674 (D.C. Cir. 2016); *Mozilla Corp. v. Federal Communication Comm'n*, 940 F.3d 1 (D.C. Cir. 2019).

10. *Mozilla Corp.*, 940 F.3d at 17–18 (documenting FCC vacillation over whether broadband cable and Internet services are telecommunications services or information services).

11. *Kaiser Aluminum & Chemical Corp. v. Consumer Product Safety Comm'n*, 574 F.2d 178 (3d Cir.).

12. 529 U.S. 120 (2000).

13. *Id.* at 132. Congress subsequently adopted the Family Smoking Prevention and Tobacco Control Act, Pub. L. No. 111-31, 123 Stat. 1776 (2009), granting the FDA the authority to regulate tobacco products.

what it may regulate. Statutory interpretation, in turn, often requires an examination of the enabling act's legislative history. Moreover, courts often will defer to an agency's assessment of its own jurisdiction.[14] In *City of Arlington v. Federal Communications Commission*, the Supreme Court made clear that the highly deferential *Chevron* standard of judicial review applies to a properly-adopted agency determination of the agency's own jurisdiction.[15]

Ultra vires issues arise infrequently in day-to-day agency practice. The jurisdiction of older administrative agencies is normally well established, and new jurisdictional issues usually arise only when the agency's enabling act is amended or the agency decides to test the outer limits of their jurisdiction. The more conservative agencies are careful not to push their boundaries, although this reluctance also may be because they have more than enough to do in addressing matters squarely within their purview.

§ 4.03 Agency Authority to Adopt Rules and Regulations

As part of the executive branch, any agency has the inherent power to express its views regarding the proper interpretation of a statute that the agency administers. Agencies can create a legally binding, substantive rule or regulation, however, only by issuing a *legislative rule*. An agency has the power to adopt legislative rules only if and to the extent that Congress has granted it the authority to do so.[16]

Most statutes are clear and explicit in granting, or in failing to grant, the power to issue legislative rules, but some statutes are ambiguous in this regard. The Federal Trade Commission Act, as it stood in 1973, was a good example. In the early 1960s, after nearly fifty years of making agency policy by bringing individual adjudications asserting unfair or deceptive trade practices or unfair methods of competition against individual companies, the Federal Trade Commission (FTC) decided that it would make policy by announcing broad, generally applicable rules relating to unfair and deceptive trade practices (to be known as *trade regulation rules*) rather than relying exclusively on case-by-case policy development. The only language arguably giving the FTC rulemaking power was section 6(g) of the Federal Trade Commission Act, which provided that the Commission may "[f]rom time to time ... classify corporations and ... make rules and regulations for the purpose of carrying out the provisions of ... this title."[17]

The language of section 6 created a number of interpretative difficulties. This section was placed in the Federal Trade Commission Act at a time when the two major independent agencies (the Interstate Commerce Commission and the FTC) did virtually nothing but adjudicate. For fifty years, the FTC itself had interpreted this portion of the

14. *See Chevron U.S.A. Inc. v. Natural Resources Defense Council, Inc.*, 467 U.S. 837 (1984) (holding that an agency's reasonable interpretations of ambiguity in a statute that it administers are entitled to judicial deference).

15. 569 U.S. 290 (2013). The *Chevron* standard of judicial review is discussed at length in Chapter 13, § 13.04.

16. *United States v. Storer Broadcasting Co.*, 351 U.S. 192 (1956); *National Broadcasting Co. v. United States*, 319 U.S. 190 (1943).

17. FTC Act § 6(g), codified at 15 U.S.C. § 46(g).

statute as merely giving it power to promulgate rules governing agency procedures or housekeeping matters. Thus, the agency's own longstanding interpretation and practice arguably created an inference that legislative rules were not authorized by section 6.

Nonetheless, in 1962, the FTC began issuing trade regulations separately from its conventional adjudications. In 1971, after some less-than-complimentary reports on its activities and after significant changes in FTC personnel, the FTC really began to flex its rulemaking muscles. One of its most controversial actions was a trade regulation that, in effect, ordered gasoline service stations to post octane ratings on gasoline pumps.[18] The new regulation deemed a service station's failure to post octane ratings to be an unfair or deceptive trade practice that could lead to civil penalties.[19]

When the controversy reached the federal courts in *National Petroleum Refiners Ass'n v. Federal Trade Commission*,[20] the district court reviewed the section 6 language, its legislative history, and previous FTC interpretations of the section and concluded that the FTC had rulemaking power only for "housekeeping chores and investigative responsibilities." But on appeal, the D.C. Circuit looked at these same materials (noting, for example, that nothing in the enabling act's history said the FTC could *not* make trade regulation rules) and waxed eloquent on the benefits of an agency's issuing regulations rather than doing all its policymaking by adjudication. Accordingly, the D.C. Circuit upheld the FTC's authority to promulgate legislative rules, even under the minimal language of section 6.[21]

Since *National Petroleum Refiners*, the issue is hardly worth questioning: an agency with a conventionally-worded enabling act authorizing the agency to adopt rules and regulations may exercise rulemaking powers. On the other hand, such grants are not limitless, and courts at times have been quite stingy in interpreting agency rulemaking power. For example, in *Chamber of Commerce v. National Labor Relations Board*, the Fourth Circuit concluded that the NLRB's statutory authority to address charges of unfair labor practices and to conduct representation elections did not empower the NLRB to adopt rules requiring employers to post notices informing employees of their labor rights.[22]

Congress sometimes enacts statutes that confer rulemaking power jointly on two or more agencies. Statutes of that type can be difficult to implement due to the required effort to coordinate efforts of agencies with different missions and bureaucratic cultures.

---

18. There was a rational basis for this rule. The FTC's investigation showed that consumers were purchasing inappropriate grades of gasoline because they had no idea of the gasoline's octane rating. Some were buying more expensive premium gasoline when they really didn't need it, and others were buying low octane gasoline for high performance engines and thereby doing serious damage to their cars.

19. Note that the FTC would still have to pursue an offending service station operator in an individual enforcement action to collect penalties for the violation. But if the FTC's rule were held valid, then few if any service station operators would disregard it, and the FTC's burden of establishing that the statute had been violated would be substantially reduced.

20. 482 F.2d 672 (D.C. Cir. 1973).

21. *See* Thomas W. Merrill & Kathryn Tongue Watts, *Agency Rules with the Force of Law: The Original Convention*, 116 HARV. L. REV. 467, 549–57 (2002) (documenting this history).

22. 721 F.3d 152 (4th Cir. 2013).

§ 4.04 Agency Exercise of Ajudication Power

[A] The Basic Power to Adjudicate

Federal agencies conduct millions of adjudications each year. The Social Security Administration alone adjudicates well over a million disability disputes per year. When state and local agency adjudications are included, the total number of agency adjudications in the United States probably numbers in the scores of millions. Agencies dwarf courts in terms of the number of adjudications resolved. Agencies adjudicate with respect to government personnel matters, immigration, welfare, school discipline, taxes, occupational licenses, land use, environmental permits, sanctions for violations of statutes and regulations, regulation of private labor relations, and in hundreds of other, widely-varied contexts.[23]

For several decades, virtually all that the major regulatory agencies accomplished was done through adjudication. The proliferation of agency rules and regulations (measurable by comparing the length of the *Federal Register* between, say, 1960 and 2020) began much later. The basic power of agencies to decide individual cases was rarely questioned, because virtually all enabling acts make specific reference to the agency's adjudication authority. The Federal Trade Commission Act, for example, provides that the Federal Trade Commission may police unfair or deceptive trade practices by drafting a complaint, holding a hearing, making findings of fact and issuing a cease-and-desist order.[24] Other agencies function under similar statutory language.

The Administrative Procedure Act expressly contemplates that federal administrative agencies will engage in the adjudication of various matters. Nevertheless, the Vesting Clause of Article III, § 1 vests "the judicial power" in the federal judiciary, not administrative agencies. Yet, although the Constitution thus seems to assign responsibility for the adjudicative functions of government to the courts, reading this assignment literally is impractical if not impossible. As Professor Paul Bator observed, "[e] very time an official of the executive branch, in determining how faithfully to execute the laws, goes through the process of finding facts and determining the meaning and application of the relevant law, he is doing something which functionally is akin to the exercise of judicial power."[25] Professor Gary Lawson similarly has noted that "[m] uch adjudicative activity by executive officials—such as granting or denying benefits under entitlement statutes—is execution of the laws by any rational standard, though

23. An extensive academic literature exists discussing different dimensions of agency authority to adjudicate disputes. For just a few examples, see William D. Araiza, *Agency Adjudication, The Importance of Facts, and The Limitations of Labels*, 57 Wash. & Lee L. Rev. 351 (2000); Caleb Nelson, *Adjudication in the Political Branches*, 107 Colum. L. Rev. 559 (2007); Thomas W. Merrill, *Article III, Agency Adjudication, and the Origins of the Appellate Review Model of Administrative Law*, 111 Colum. L. Rev. 939 (2011); Christopher J. Walker & Melissa F. Wasserman, *The New World of Agency Adjudication*, 107 Calif. L. Rev. 141 (2019). Additionally, for a fantastic report surveying contemporary agency adjudication practices prepared for the Administrative Conference of the United States, see Michael Asimow, *Adjudication Outside the Administrative Procedure Act*, Admin. Conf. U.S. (Sept. 16, 2016), https://www.acus.gov/sites/default/files/documents/adjudication-outside-the-administrative-procedure-act-updated-draft-report.pdf.

24. 15 U.S.C. § 45(b).

25. Paul M. Bator, *The Constitution as Architecture: Legislative and Administrative Courts Under Article III*, 65 Ind. L.J. 233 (1990).

it also fits comfortably within the concept of the judicial power if conducted by judicial officers."[26] The Seventh Amendment, which guarantees the jury trial right, is also a concern.[27]

As a consequence of the relative murkiness of the Constitution's text with respect to agency adjudicatory power, the scope of Congress's constitutional authority to allow federal government agencies to adjudicate cases and resolve disputes has been the subject of numerous Supreme Court decisions that are often difficult to reconcile with one another. Several key cases concern bankruptcy courts, which reside within the judicial branch even though they are not Article III courts, rather than administrative agencies in the executive branch. Nevertheless, the Court commonly considers precedents cases concerning the former in resolving adjudicatory power issues associated with the latter.

In *Crowell v. Benson*,[28] the Supreme Court upheld the decision of Congress in the Longshoremen's and Harbor Workers Act to replace court-adjudicated tort law with agency-adjudicated workers' compensation law. The Court reasoned that judicial review of the agency's findings provided judicial involvement in the adjudicatory system that was sufficient to safeguard the Article III and due process values implicated by the assignment of adjudicatory responsibility to an agency. The continuing validity of the holding in *Crowell* is in some doubt as a result of other changes in administrative law. At the time the Court decided *Crowell*, courts engaged in de novo review of many agency decisions. Over time, judicial review of agency adjudicatory decisions has become far more deferential, thereby undermining to some extent the reasoning in *Crowell*.

For some years, the Supreme Court determined which cases could be addressed through agency adjudication by distinguishing between public rights and private rights. In *Northern Pipeline Construction Co. v. Marathon Pipe Line Co.*,[29] the Court considered the constitutional validity of a new bankruptcy statute in which Congress modified the substantive law of contracts when a bankrupt entity is one of the contracting parties. The new statute created specialized, non-Article III bankruptcy courts, and assigned to the new bankruptcy judges the responsibility for both interpreting contracts under state law and modifying the rights of the contracting parties to reflect statutory preferences. The Court held the bankruptcy statute as written unconstitutional because it empowered non-Article III judges to resolve contract disputes. According to Justice Brennan, writing for a four-justice plurality of the Court, (1) only Article III tribunals could exercise judicial power; (2) while non-Article III tribunals, including agencies, could adjudicate *public* rights, *private* rights disputes were said to be "inherently... judicial"; and (3) all contract disputes involve private rights because contract rights have an independent antecedent source in the common law. Two justices concurred in the judgment but expressed reservations about the breadth of Justice Brennan's reasoning. Three justices dissented, arguing that plurality's reasoning did "violence" to the many prior decisions in which the Court had upheld congressional grants of power to adjudicate disputes between individuals to non-Article III tribunals.

One potential difficulty with the public/private rights distinction advanced by Justice Brennan in *Northern Pipeline* was that his definition of private rights as rights with an

26. Gary Lawson, *The Rise and Rise of the Administrative State*, 107 Harv. L. Rev. 1231 (1994).
27. *See, e.g.*, *Granfinanciera v. Nordberg*, 492 U.S. 33 (1989); *Atlas Roofing Co. v. Occupational Safety & Health Review Comm'n*, 430 U.S. 442 (1977); *see also* Ellen E. Sward, *Legislative Courts, Article III, and the Seventh Amendment*, 77 N.C. L. Rev. 1037 (1999).
28. 285 U.S. 22 (1932).
29. 458 U.S. 50 (1982).

antecedent in the common law was broad enough to encompass a high proportion of the disputes resolved by agencies. A few years later, in *Thomas v. Union Carbide Agricultural Products Co.*,[30] the Court backed away from the arguable breadth of the reasoning of the *Northern Pipeline* plurality. The *Union Carbide* case concerned a challenge to the constitutionality of an administrative program under the Federal Pesticide Act. That statute required companies to submit certain proprietary information on pesticides to the Environmental Protection Agency (EPA). The statute further provided that the EPA had to pay compensation to those companies when it used that proprietary data. The statute called for disputes over the amount of compensation to be resolved through binding arbitration conducted by private sector arbitrators. Challenging the arbitration process, the companies argued that they should be permitted to litigate their claims in an Article III court, rather than be required to submit to binding arbitration.

Making some slightly shaky distinctions relating to the earlier cases, the Court in *Union Carbide* concluded that Congress's use of binding arbitration was constitutionally permissible, although the justices disagreed as to why. Writing on behalf of a majority of the Court, Justice O'Connor observed that the distinction between public and private rights announced in the plurality opinion in *Northern Pipeline* "did not command a majority of the Court." She also noted several examples of the grave difficulties that the Court would encounter if it attempted to apply that distinction to the myriad disputes now resolved by agencies. According to Justice O'Connor, the binding arbitration in this case affected a private right, but that private right was expressly created by Congress in enacting the Federal Pesticide Act. As such, disputes concerning that private right did not require adjudication in an Article III court and could be handled properly and constitutionally through arbitration.[31] In Justice O'Connor's words, "Congress, acting for a valid legislative purpose pursuant to its constitutional powers under Article I, may create a seemingly private right that is so closely integrated into a public regulatory scheme as to be a matter appropriate for agency resolution with limited involvement by the Article III judiciary." Three other justices, in an opinion concurring in the judgment authored by Justice Brennan, argued instead that the statutory compensation scheme at issue in *Union Carbide* "should be viewed as involving a matter of public rights" rather than private ones, and distinguished *Northern Pipeline* on that basis.[32]

Not long at all after the Court's *Union Carbide* decision, in *Commodity Futures Trading Commission v. Schor* in 1986,[33] Justice O'Connor seemed to repudiate outright much of the reasoning of *Northern Pipeline*. The *Schor* case concerned the constitutional validity of a Commodity Futures Trading Commission (CFTC) regulation that empowered the agency to adjudicate common law counterclaims when a party files an action before the agency claiming that a commodity broker has violated CFTC rules and seeking reparations for the violation. If the Court had applied the *Northern Pipeline* test, it undoubtedly would have held the CFTC's regulation unconstitutional, since the counterclaims the CFTC sought to adjudicate arose as a result of antecedent state common law rights long recognized and enforced by courts. Indeed, two justices reached that very conclusion in *Schor*, in a dissenting opinion by Justice Brennan (the author of the *Northern*

30. 473 U.S. 568 (1985).

31. The Court's decision in *Union Carbide* provided additional impetus to Congress' enactment of the Administrative Dispute Resolution Act in 1990, discussed in Chapter 8.

32. Justice Stevens concurred separately to argue that the companies lacked standing to challenge the statute, as they did not claim that the EPA had used any of its data without first obtaining consent. Standing doctrine is discussed in Chapter 12.

33. 478 U.S. 833 (1986).

Pipeline plurality opinion). By contrast, Justice O'Connor, again writing for the Court's majority, distinguished *Northern Pipeline* by concluding that the CFTC deals only with a "particularized area of law," whereas bankruptcy judges may face a much broader array of state law claims. Justice O'Connor was relatively casual about the public/private right distinction in her opinion, suggesting that "the public rights doctrine reflects simply a pragmatic understanding that when Congress selects a quasi-judicial method of resolving matters that could be conclusively determined by the Executive and Legislative Branches, the danger of encroaching on the judicial powers is less than when private rights, which are normally within the purview of the judiciary, are relegated as an initial matter to administrative adjudication." She then went on to uphold the constitutionality of the CFTC's adjudication of common law counterclaims on two grounds: first, that the CFTC's exercise of jurisdiction did not threaten the role of the independent judiciary within the constitutional scheme; and second, that Schor implicitly consented to the CFTC's exercise of jurisdiction over the common law counterclaim in his case by filing his action for reparations arising out of the same set of transactions.

In *Stern v. Marshall*,[34] the justices again debated at length the extent to which Congress can assign adjudication of a class of disputes to a governmental body other than an Article III court. The case concerned whether Congress could authorize Article I bankruptcy courts, in the context of bankruptcy proceedings, to adjudicate counterclaims in the form of common law tort actions that ordinarily would be adjudicated in state courts. The Court held that Congress could not reallocate adjudication of private right disputes like common law tort actions in this way. However, the majority in *Stern* included language suggesting that it is more willing to acquiesce in congressional decisions to allow the adjudication of some common law claims by expert agencies. Specifically, the majority referred to cases like *Union Carbide* and *Schor* as illustrations of an exception to the prohibition on reallocation of adjudication of private rights to non-Article III tribunals. The majority said the exception was limited "to cases in which the claim at issue derives from a federal regulatory scheme, or in which resolution of the claim by an expert government agency is deemed essential to a limited regulatory objective within the agency's authority." With those and other words, the Court suggested strongly that it would be likely to uphold the vast majority of congressional assignments of adjudicatory responsibilities to administrative agencies.

By comparison, the dissenting justices in *Stern* advocated a multi-factor "practical effect" standard to decide whether Congress had good reasons to assign a class of disputes to a non-Article III tribunal. In every case in which the Court has used this type of functional reasoning, it has upheld the congressional assignment of adjudicative functions to bodies other than Article III courts. Consequently, the Court's reasoning in *Stern* does not appear to be a major obstacle to agency adjudicatory power. Many observers interpreted *Stern* as indicating that at least a majority of the justices, and perhaps even all of them, were willing to continue to acquiesce in congressional decisions to reallocate adjudication of private rights issues to agencies when the class of disputes is limited to those that relate so closely to a regulatory regime that it makes sense to reallocate their adjudication to the agency that holds the responsibility to implement and administer that regime.

Notwithstanding *Stern*'s seeming consensus among the justices regarding agency adjudicatory power, the various opinions in *Oil States Energy Services, LLC v. Green's*

34. 564 U.S. 462 (2011).

Energy Group, LLC[35] suggest that the justices continue to be divided with respect to the circumstances in which Congress may shift adjudicative power from Article III courts to agencies. *Oil States* raised the question whether Congress could assign decision-making responsibility regarding the validity of patents from courts to a newly-created agency, the Patent and Trademark Appeals Board (PTAB), that is part of the Patent and Trademark Office (PTO). Since the PTO implements a complicated regulatory regime by, among other things, making initial decisions to grant patents, the case seemed to be a good example of one in which the Court would uphold the reallocation based on its conclusion that adjudication of disputes with respect to the validity of patents was closely related to the regulatory regime implemented by the PTO.

In fact, the *Oil States* Court did uphold the reallocation of adjudicatory authority at issue, seven justices to two. But the different opinions authored in the case suggested greater disagreement among the justices. The Court upheld the adjudicatory authority of the PTAB based on a conclusion that disputes regarding patent validity were public rights disputes. The opinion for the majority suggested, however, that at least some of the participating justices might not have upheld the statute if they had concluded that disputes over patent validity concerned private rather than public rights. Three of the justices who joined the majority opinion also concurred separately to argue that the PTAB's adjudicatory powers would have been constitutional even if disagreements over the validity of patents were characterized as private right disputes—thus suggesting that the remaining four justices in the majority felt otherwise. Two justices dissented, arguing that Congress cannot reallocate authority to adjudicate public rights disputes from Article III courts to agencies in circumstances in which there is reason to believe that agencies lack sufficient independence to be confident that they will adjudicate the disputes in an unbiased way. In summary, the opinions in *Oil States* suggest that the justices are divided three ways with respect to the power of Congress to reallocate the authority to adjudicate disputes from Article III courts to agencies.

Harmonizing these cases or even relying on them to predict how the Court might resolve the next case in this area of the law is difficult. We surely have not seen the last debate over or application of the public/private rights distinction.

[B] Penalty Assessments and Other Remedial Powers of Agencies

As agencies adjudicate various controversies within their jurisdiction, what power do they have to grant remedies or to penalize wrongdoers? Early case law suggested that administrative agencies had no right to assess civil penalties, because giving agencies that power would confer excessive discretion upon them. For example, the Federal Trade Commission Act, which was adopted in 1914 to create the Federal Trade Commission (FTC) and entrust it with the responsibility for investigating and adjudicating violations of that statute's prohibition against unfair or deceptive trade practices, requires the FTC to go to court to seek penalties for noncompliance. More contemporary organic statutes often give administering agencies the power to assess financial penalties. For example, the Occupational Safety and Health Act authorizes the Administrator of the Occupational Safety and Health Administration to "assess and recover a civil penalty

35. 138 S. Ct. 1365 (2017).

of not more than $25,000 per day for each violation" under specified circumstances.[36] In *National Independent Coal Operators' Ass'n v. Kleppe*,[37] the Supreme Court approved the assessment of flexible monetary civil penalties under the Federal Coal Mine Safety and Health Act,[38] a statute much like the Occupational Safety and Health Act.

However, the penalties should be proportionate to the actual violation. The Supreme Court made the proposition somewhat clear in *United States v. Bajakajian*.[39] In *Bajakajian*, an international traveler attempted to board a flight carrying more than $350,000. He was detained and cited for failure to report to Customs officials that he was carrying more than $10,000 in currency. The traveler pleaded guilty to this offense. However, as an additional citation, the government attempted to declare the entire amount of $357,144 forfeited because the traveler willfully violated the statute and the funds were directly "involved in" the offense. On review, the Court concluded that the forfeiture constituted punishment and as such it fell within the Excessive Fines Clause of the Eighth Amendment to the U.S. Constitution. Because the amount of the forfeiture was deemed to be excessive, it was overturned by the Court. *Bajakajian* is something of an outlier in this context,[40] but nevertheless demonstrates an outer boundary to financial punishment in the agency context.

An agency's organic statute may authorize other remedies. The FTC, for example, has the power to issue *cease and desist* orders to persons found to have committed unfair or deceptive trade practices. These orders are similar to injunctions and have been uniformly upheld by the courts. Many agencies find the device of the consent order (by which a party refuses to admit liability but agrees to discontinue the practice) helpful. Some agencies that engage in economic regulation of a particular industry may order restitution of overcharges. Still other agencies may suspend or revoke permits or licenses, or bar parties from doing business with the agency for some period of time. There is little doubt that an agency may do any of these things so long as Congress approves.

The more difficult question is not whether an agency may assess penalties, issue cease and desist orders, or otherwise punish offenders, but rather whether a party is subject to instant discipline if she refuses to pay the penalty, defies an order, or otherwise declines to comply. In other words, do agencies have the inherent authority to *enforce* their sanctions? In some cases, as for example, when a party is requesting permission from the agency to do something, such as asking the Federal Communications Commission for a broadcast license, the agency may sanction the party by merely denying the license. But in many instances, the agency may not enforce civil sanctions without seeking judicial assistance. If compliance by the private party is not voluntary, agencies generally must ask an appropriate court to enforce the penalty or sanction against the party. In other words, a separate court proceeding is required, even if that proceeding is short and sweet. Judges are rarely happy with people who defy the legitimate commands of administrative agencies.

---

36. 42 U.S.C. § 7413(b).

37. 423 U.S. 388 (1976).

38. 30 U.S.C. § 813(a).

39. 524 U.S. 321 (1998).

40. For that matter, Congress effectively overturned *Bajakajian* when it enacted the USA PATRIOT Act, designating the smuggling of large amounts of cash as a crime in and of itself. *See, e.g.*, *United States v. Del Toro-Barboza*, 673 F.3d 1136 (9th Cir. 2012); *United States v. Jose*, 499 F.3d 105 (1st Cir. 2007).

Unusual among agencies, the Internal Revenue Service has the power to assess and collect many financial penalties in the same manner that it does taxes, including through the levy and seizure of property. Also, officials from federal, state, and local agencies in various contexts are authorized to seize property through a controversial practice known as civil asset forfeiture.

[C] Agencies and Criminal Sanctions

May an agency put someone in jail? The short answer is no; no agency has *independent* authority to impose criminal penalties of any sort. However, this blurs an issue that many lawyers and law students never quite grasp. Even if the agency itself may not put your client in jail, your client still may go to jail for willfully violating an agency's rules and regulations if the agency's organic statute expressly provides for criminal penalties and if a court determines that the violation was intentional.[41] Forgetting this basic proposition can have drastic consequences for lawyer and client alike.

The criminal violation process works as follows. Consider that a typical agency enabling act permits an agency to develop a regulatory program through its rulemaking authority. For example, the Environmental Protection Agency (EPA) is permitted under the Clean Air Act[42] to develop rules restricting the amount of sulfur oxide emissions from coal-burning power plants. The Clean Air Act permits the assessment of civil monetary penalties and authorizes both criminal fines and jail sentences for violators who intentionally violate the statute (or, by derivation, the agency's rules implementing the statute). Assume that the EPA writes a rule setting the maximum discharge of sulfur oxide at 1 part per cubic foot of total air emissions from a particular type of power plant. Assume further that XYZ, Inc., a corporation subject to the Clean Air Act and to this rule, knows about the rule and intentionally permits emissions from its plant totaling 126 parts per cubic foot.

The EPA may do one of two things: it may use its own enforcement authority to assess civil penalties against XYZ, or it may refer the case to the Department of Justice for criminal prosecution. To the extent that the agency has already compiled data on XYZ's pollution control practices, that information will probably be introduced at trial. Granting that XYZ has all the procedural rights given to criminal defendants (such as right to counsel, proof beyond a reasonable doubt, etc.), it must still defend against the EPA's charges. If the government can prove both the violation itself and the requisite state of mind for criminal conviction (intentional violation), XYZ and its officers potentially face jail sentences as well as fines.

This scenario was not always so. Before the turn of the twentieth century, in *Interstate Commerce Commission v. Brimson*,[43] the Supreme Court stated in dicta that an agency "could not, under our system of government, and consistently with due process of law, be invested with authority to compel obedience to its orders by a judgment of

---

41. Some people have become concerned that agencies are imposing punishments traditionally reserved for the criminal justice system. *See* Jason M. Day, *The Intertwining of Administrative Actions and the Criminal Justice System*, 4 Tex. Tech. J. Tex. Admin. L. 99 (Spring, 2003). Not every regulatory statute with the potential for criminal punishment requires a finding of willfulness. *See, e.g., United States v. Thompson/Center Arms Co.*, 504 U.S. 505 (1992).

42. 42 U.S.C. §§ 7401–26.

43. 154 U.S. 447 (1894).

fine or imprisonment." Some early readers of *Brimson* took this comment to mean that no criminal sanctions whatsoever could flow from a violation of an agency requirement even if the criminal action was brought in a proper court.

Not quite fifteen years after *Brimson*, however, the Court decided *United States v. Grimaud*,[44] mainly to remove this uncertainty. Mr. Grimaud had intentionally violated a Department of Agriculture order forbidding grazing of cattle on national forest land without a permit. Charged with a criminal violation in federal court, he argued that the Department did not have the constitutional power to define the terms of any crime—*i.e.*, that an agency rule could not be used as the substantive basis for a criminal conviction. The Court disagreed and upheld the conviction based upon very simple reasoning: It is Congress that authorizes the criminal penalty by making any violation of a proper agency rule unlawful. Thus, the authority for the criminal sanction springs from the legislature and not from the agency itself even if the agency writes the rule upon which the conviction is based.

An administrative action and a criminal proceeding may go forward at the same time in most instances, and the government agency involved and the prosecutor of the criminal action may share information on the same case as the two go forward. The courts have made quite clear that there has always been significant overlap between the regulatory and criminal laws of the United States. While a court may have discretion to stay a parallel civil or administrative proceeding pending the outcome of a criminal case, it generally is not required to do so.[45]

[D] Agency Regulation of Attorney Conduct

Regardless of specialty, the behavior of all U.S. lawyers, including administrative law practitioners, is governed by ethics rules. The American Bar Association (ABA) first adopted "Canons of Professional Ethics" setting forth general principles of ethical conduct for attorneys in 1908. Subsequently, in 1969, the ABA created a Model Code of Professional Responsibility that substantively was similar to the Canons. Many states adopted variations of the Model Code. In the 1970s, motivated in part by the Watergate scandal, the ABA spent a great deal of time and effort attempting to develop a new set of ethical constraints better attuned to the practice of law in the United States in the latter half of the twentieth century. Those efforts led to the 1983 adoption of the Model Rules of Professional Conduct. The ABA has continued periodically to review and amend the Model Rules. Variations of the Model Rules have been adopted by all fifty states and the District of Columbia. A few federal administrative agencies have incorporated aspects of the Model Rules into their own rules of practice and procedure. Nevertheless, because lawyers who practice before agencies must be admitted in at least one state, the Model Rules have a significant effect on their behavior as lawyers.

At least one jurisdiction, the District of Columbia, has modified the Model Rules of Professional Conduct for members of the D.C. Bar. Although based on the Model Rules, the D.C. rules include special provisions directed specifically toward lawyers whose practices involve government service or who take and then leave government service (the so-called "revolving door"). Because so many lawyers in D.C. have administrative

44. 220 U.S. 506 (1911).

45. *See, e.g.*, *United States v. Kordel*, 397 U.S. 1 (1970); *United States v. Stringer*, 535 F.3d 929 (9th Cir. 2008); *Securities & Exchange Comm'n v. Dresser Industries, Inc.*, 628 F.2d 1368 (D.C. Cir. 1980).

agency practices, the D.C. rules may provide a model for regulating the conduct of lawyers in other states with a heavy administrative practice.

Additional formal constraints on lawyer behavior in the context of administrative practice may exist, depending on the agency.[46] Most agencies have the power to regulate the conduct of attorneys who appear before the agency. Congress made this clear a number of years ago when it enacted a portion of Title 5 of the *United States Code* that is rarely reproduced in administrative law casebooks. Title 5 U.S.C. § 500(d)(2) provides that the APA "does not authorize or limit the discipline, including disbarment, of individuals who appear in a representative capacity before an agency."[47]

Some agencies have used this provision and other portions of their own organic statutes to promulgate ethical rules for attorneys, strictly for their respective agencies. The Securities and Exchange Commission, for example, has adopted regulations providing standards of professional conduct for lawyers who practice before that agency.[48] Similarly, the Internal Revenue Service's "Circular 230" regulations impose ethical standards of professional behavior for tax attorneys.[49] The now-defunct Interstate Commerce Commission had a code of professional behavior that had been used on occasion as the basis for agency-imposed discipline. In one instance, the ICC ordered a six-month suspension for a lawyer who represented two clients with conflicting interests before the Commission without the permission or knowledge of those clients. The lawyer challenged the authority of the ICC to administer any discipline whatsoever and pursued that challenge into the D.C. Circuit. In a decision dripping with incredulity and sarcasm, the court very nearly held his appeal frivolous, noting that the existence of 5 U.S.C. § 500 makes it abundantly clear that an agency may discipline attorneys who appear before it and who engage in improper conduct.[50]

In short, agencies have tremendous authority to regulate the behavior of lawyers who practice before them. New agency lawyers should take special care to determine whether any agency before which they will be practicing has a special code of ethics and to ascertain the terms of that code prior to engaging in practice before the agency. Even if no special code exists, lawyers should never forget the applicability of the applicable state Rules of Professional Conduct to administrative practice.

---

46. For general scholarly discussion of ethical conduct in the administrative context over time, see, *e.g.*, Arthur Best, *Shortcomings of Administrative Agency Lawyer Discipline*, 31 EMORY L.J. 535 (1982); Harold Levinson, *Professional Responsibility Issues in Administrative Adjudication*, 2 BYU J. PUB. L. 219 (1988); Lars Noah, *Sham Petitioning as a Threat to the Integrity of the Regulatory Process*, 74 N.C. L. REV. 1 (1995); Keith R. Fisher, *The Higher Calling: Regulation of Lawyers Post-Enron*, 37 U. MICH. J.L. REFORM 1017 (2004); Eli Wald, *Federalizing Legal Ethics, Nationalizing Law Practice, and the Future of the American Legal Profession in a Global Age*, 48 SAN DIEGO L. REV. 489 (2011).

47. Another part of that same provision, 5 U.S.C. § 500(b), precludes agencies from requiring more than mere admission to a state bar as a qualification for practicing before the agency.

48. *See* Securities and Exchange Commission, Final Rule: Implementation of Standards of Professional Conduct for Attorneys, 68 Fed. Reg. 6296-01 (2003); *see also* Thomas Lee Hazen, *Administrative Law Controls on Attorney Practice—A Look at the Securities and Exchange Commission's Lawyer Conduct Rules*, 55 ADMIN. L. REV. 323 (2003). For some general discussion of many of these issues, see Harold Levinson, *Professional Responsibility Issues in Administrative Adjudication*, 2 BYU J. PUB. L. 219 (1988).

49. 31 C.F.R. §§ 10.0-10.93; *see also* JONATHAN G. BLATTMACHR, MITCHELL M. GANS & DAMIEN RIOS, THE CIRCULAR 230 DESKBOOK: RELATED PENALTIES, REPORTABLE TRANSACTIONS, WORKING FORMS (Practicing Law Inst. 2021).

50. *Polydoroff v. Interstate Commerce Comm'n*, 773 F.2d 372 (D.C. Cir. 1985).

§ 4.05 Agency Acquisition of Information—An Overview

[A] Congress' and the Courts' Recognition of Agency Need for Information

One of the ways an agency first begins to exercise its powers is by demanding information from persons within its jurisdiction. This desire for information is not surprising, because it is axiomatic that agencies cannot function without information. But it is equally axiomatic that many persons regulated by administrative agencies dislike providing information, particularly information that touches on sensitive personal or business matters. Congress and the courts have acknowledged these tensions, but have generally resolved the issues in favor of the agencies—in clear recognition that agencies simply cannot perform their missions without a great deal of information.

There are basically four devices available to most agencies for obtaining information as discussed below.

[B] Recordkeeping Requirements

Agencies often adopt rules that require people to maintain and preserve certain records. Perhaps the best-known example of a recordkeeping requirement is the multitude of records that must be kept by persons who seek to deduct business, investment, or personal expenses on their tax returns. Note that these requirements merely oblige a person to document their deductions and maintain those records, but not necessarily to turn them over to the government. Records such as these get into the hands of the government under normal circumstances only when a dispute arises between the private party and the agency.

[C] Reporting Requirements

Many statutes and agency regulations require persons to file periodic reports with the agency. One of the best-known examples of a reporting requirement is the annual income tax return, by which taxpayers inform the IRS of their yearly income, expenditures, and associated tax liabilities. Another example pertains to persons holding federal licenses—*e.g.*, television broadcast licenses or hydroelectric power licenses—who must file periodic reports on their activities. These reports are typically much more detailed even than the information requested by the IRS to determine one's tax liabilities. The failure to file the required reports commonly results in penalties that may be imposed separately from any other penalty.

[D] Subpoenas

Most administrative agencies have the power to issue their own subpoenas through language in their organic statutes and through § 555(d) of the Administrative Procedure Act. Many state agencies have parallel subpoena power. A subpoena may simply require the presence of an individual before some kind of agency hearing to give testimony (the classic subpoena *ad testificandum*) or may be issued in the form of a subpoena *duces tecum*, which requires that individual to appear as well as to present to the agency certain specified records. When an agency is engaged in a formal adjudication, it frequently invokes its own discovery rules to take depositions or to submit interrogatories as a device for acquiring information.

[E] Physical Inspections

Many agencies can do their job only if they can actually view the operations of a business. For example, the government decided long ago that many aspects of coal mine health and safety could be policed only by on-premises inspections of operating coal mines. In some instances, the Environmental Protection Agency can determine whether certain industries are releasing impermissible amounts of air or water pollution only by looking at the factory. For these reasons, many agencies conduct periodic, and usually unannounced, inspections of persons and businesses within their jurisdiction.

[F] Other Forms of Information Gathering

There are many other ways that an agency acquires information. Often, when an agency conducts a major rulemaking, it is given reams of data by interested persons who submit comments on the proposed rules. Frequently, that information is useful for other agency purposes as well, and not just for the rule under consideration. When agencies open participation in adjudications to persons other than the original parties, they may acquire considerable material in the nature of *amicus curiae* (friend of the court) briefs. Moreover, agency personnel closely follow the activities of regulated industries through congressional hearings and investigations, adding to the agency's store of knowledge. In reality, an agency's problem is frequently too much information and too little analysis, rather than the other way around.

In 1978, Congress enacted the Inspector General Act and created a wholly new entity within most major federal agencies, the Inspector General (IG).[51] Under the IG Act, each major federal agency now contains an IG appointed by the president with the advice and consent of the Senate. Among other things, the IG is empowered to conduct audits within the agency, investigate instances of fraud and abuse in the agency's programs and to report on and make various recommendations relating to those audits or investigations to the agency head. Agency inspectors general are also required to report periodically to Congress.

Since the inception of the Offices of Inspector General, IGs have become a power to be reckoned with in many major agencies. Subsequent amendments to the Inspector

51. Pub. L. No. 95-452, 92 Stat. 1101 (1978). The IG Act is set out at 5 U.S.C. Appendix. For more information on the work of and issues related to inspectors general, see Paul C. Light, Monitoring Government: Inspectors General and the Search for Accountability (1993); William S. Fields & Thomas E. Robinson, *Legal and Functional Influences on the Objectivity of the Inspector General Audit Process*, 2 Geo. Mason Ind. L. Rev. 97 (1993); Michael R. Bromwich, *Running Special Investigations: The Inspector General Model*, 86 Geo. L.J. 2027 (1998); Shirin Sinnar, *Protecting Rights from Within? Inspectors General and National Security Oversight*, 65 Stan. L. Rev. 1027 (2013); Andrew McCanse Wright, *Executive Privilege and Inspectors General*, 97 Tex. L. Rev. 1295 (2019).

General Act in 1988 and 2008 have only strengthened the powers of IGs. The investigating powers of IGs have created a whole new structure of information gathering and employee discipline within agencies. While, in theory, an IG is an officer who deals with the internal governance of each agency, because so many IG reports eventually become public knowledge, the activities of the IGs have also become an important source of information about the agency for both Congress and the general public. Many state and municipal governments have established their own IGs.[52]

§ 4.06 Recordkeeping and Reporting Requirements

[A] Information Requests Generally

The primary source of recordkeeping and reporting requirements is the rules and regulations of the agency in question. Congress occasionally writes such requirements into an agency's enabling act. Even when it does so, however, it typically sets out the requirements in fairly sketchy terms. The particulars of any information gathering requirement generally are respected by persons regulated by the agency. One of the reasons these requirements are not often questioned is that, as will be seen, there are not many plausible grounds on which a person can resist keeping records or making reports if the agency requires her to do so.

Around the beginning of the twentieth century, the Supreme Court wrote a number of opinions, often under the pen of Justice Oliver Wendell Holmes, containing language that raised doubts about the scope of an agency's power to compel private parties to provide information. In *Harriman v. Interstate Commerce Commission*,[53] after the Interstate Commerce Commission sought information for the purpose of recommending legislation, Justice Holmes suggested that an agency could compel the production of information only when the agency is able to allege a "specific breach of the law." Specific legislation giving the Interstate Commerce Commission broader investigatory powers later eroded the *Harriman* holding.[54]

Agency information-gathering continued to trouble Justice Holmes as late as the 1920s when he wrote what has become one of the classic (but little followed) decisions in this area, *Federal Trade Commission v. American Tobacco Co.*[55] In *American Tobacco*, the FTC asked for "all" letters and telegrams received by a company from its jobbers over a one-year period. The request stemmed from an FTC investigation into the company's business practices, although there was no ongoing enforcement action. The case is famous mainly for Justice Holmes's comment that an agency's general power to investigate and to request documents does not permit "fishing expeditions into private papers on the possibility that [the papers] may disclose evidence of crime."[56] Justices

52. *See, e.g.*, Patricia Salkin & Zachary Kansler, *Ensuring Public Trust at the Municipal Level: Inspectors General Enter the Mix*, 75 ALB. L. REV. 95 (2012).

53. 211 U.S. 407 (1908).

54. *Smith v. Interstate Commerce Comm'n*, 245 U.S. 33 (1917).

55. 264 U.S. 298 (1924).

56. *Id.* at 306.

Holmes's fishing expedition dicta seems to be invoked whenever private persons seek to resist agency requests for information. Such efforts generally are unsuccessful, however.

Since the 1940s, the Supreme Court has been much more accepting of agencies' efforts to obtain information from parties within their jurisdiction. In *Endicott Johnson Corp. v. Perkins*,[57] the Supreme Court considered a subpoena from the Secretary of Labor seeking records relating to payrolls in certain plants under a company to determine whether they violated federal minimum wage requirements, but only for the purpose of ascertaining whether the company was eligible to be awarded a government contract, and not due to any actual allegations of impropriety. The company declined to comply with the subpoena, contending that the payroll records were not relevant to any particular matter pending before the agency. The Court held that that, since "[t]he evidence sought by the subpoena was not plainly incompetent or irrelevant to any lawful purpose of the Secretary in the discharge of her duties," the Secretary's need for the payroll records was for the agency rather than the courts to decide.[58] The courts' job was to enforce the agency's subpoena. The Supreme Court extended the same principle to other agencies in subsequent cases.[59]

The basic legal framework applicable to judicial enforcement of agency subpoenas has not changed appreciably in several decades. That framework makes it difficult for any private party to win a subpoena enforcement dispute with a federal agency. The agency must have statutory authority to issue the subpoena, but courts tend to interpret statutory grants of subpoena power broadly.[60] The materials sought must be relevant to a lawful purpose within the agency's jurisdiction, but that requirement is also interpreted permissively. The agency needs to show only the "possible relevance" of the materials to some plausible agency investigation.[61] A party who wants to resist enforcement of an agency subpoena has a realistic prospect of success only when it can raise a statutory or constitutional objection that is unique to the statute at issue or the nature of the materials requested.[62] Parties sometimes succeed in persuading a court that a subpoena imposes an unreasonable burden, but the remedy is limited to a judicial requirement that the agency narrow the scope of the subpoena or identify the materials sought with greater specificity.[63]

In 2017, in *McLane Co., Inc. v. Equal Employment Opportunity Commission*,[64] the Supreme Court held that district court decisions to grant or deny subpoenas requested by an agency are subject to review through application of the abuse of discretion standard. The Court also used the case as an opportunity to review and to restate the criteria a district court should use to decide whether to grant such a subpoena.

A district court is not to use an enforcement proceeding as an opportunity to test the strength of the underlying complaint. Rather, a district court should satisfy itself that

57. 317 U.S. 501 (1943).

58. *Id.* at 509.

59. *See, e.g., United States v. Morton Salt Co.*, 338 U.S. 632 (1950); *Oklahoma Press Publishing Co. v. Walling*, 327 U.S. 186 (1946).

60. *See, e.g., United States v. Exxon Corp.*, 628 F.2d 70 (D.C. Cir. 1980).

61. *Federal Trade Comm'n v. Texaco, Inc.*, 555 F.2d 862 (D.C. Cir. 1977).

62. *See, e.g., Equal Employment Opportunity Comm'n v. Lutheran Social Services*, 186 F.3d 959 (D.C. Cir. 1999); *In re Sealed Case*, 121 F.3d 729 (D.C. Cir. 1997).

63. *See, e.g., United States v. Theodore*, 479 F.2d 749 (4th Cir. 1973).

64. 137 S. Ct. 1159 (2017).

the charge is valid and that the material requested is "relevant" to the charge. It should do so cognizant of the "generous[s]" construction that courts have given the term "relevant." If the charge is proper and the material requested is relevant, the district court should enforce the subpoena unless the employer establishes that the subpoena is "too indefinite," has been issued for an "illegitimate purpose," or is unduly burdensome.[65]

[B] Limitations Imposed by the Paperwork Reduction Act

Congress has become much more sensitive to the burdens of government reporting and recordkeeping requirements in recent years. In 1980, Congress passed the Paperwork Reduction Act (PRA)[66] in an attempt to limit the proliferation of agency requests for information or agency demands that records be kept. Briefly stated, the PRA forbids an agency from conducting or sponsoring the collection of information from private persons without first obtaining clearance for that request from the Office of Information and Regulatory Affairs (OIRA)—a subsidiary agency within the Office of Management and Budget (OMB) created by the PRA for the purpose of overseeing its requirements. OIRA may not approve any *information collection request* for more than three years at a time, and no person may be sanctioned or penalized in any way for refusing to comply with an information request that has not been approved by OIRA.[67] OIRA also reviews and has the authority to disapprove of *collection of information requirements* contained in new agency regulations as they go through the notice-and-comment rulemaking process. OIRA supervises other federal agencies in the dissemination, including electronic dissemination, of information to the general public. And OIRA oversees the compilation and publication of statistics, supervises agency archives and agencies' protection of private and confidential information.

The theory behind the PRA is that OIRA will closely scrutinize all agency information gathering and will approve agency requests sparingly. There is a serious question whether the PRA has accomplished that purpose. When the Act initially took effect, OIRA essentially grandfathered all existing government forms and recordkeeping requirements. There has been very little empirical study of the Act's effectiveness since its enactment. Although the 1995 amendments may be viewed as a congressional vote of confidence in the concept of paperwork reduction, the PRA is far broader than a mere paperwork approval process. Many people continue to be somewhat cynical as to the Act's true value.[68]

---

65. *Id.* at 1165 (internal citations and quotation marks omitted).

66. 44 U.S.C. §§ 3501–20.

67. For a good discussion of the Act, see William Funk, *The Paperwork Reduction Act: Paperwork Reduction Meets Administrative Law*, 24 Harv. J. on Legis. 1 (1987).

68. *See, e.g.*, Andrew L. Levy, Note: *The Paperwork Reduction Act of 1980: Unnecessary Burdens and Unrealized Efficiency*, 14 J.L. & Com. 99 (1994).

§ 4.07 Agency Subpoenas

[A] Some General Considerations

Subpoenas are authorized in an agency's enabling act and through § 555(d) of the Administrative Procedure Act (APA) which provides:

Agency subpoenas *authorized by law* shall be issued to a *party* on request and, when required by rules of procedure, on a statement or showing of *general relevance and reasonable scope* of the evidence sought. On contest, the court shall sustain the subpoena or similar process or demand to the extent that it is found to be in accordance with law. In a proceeding for enforcement, the court shall issue an order requiring the appearance of the witness or the production of the evidence or data within a reasonable time under penalty of punishment for *contempt* in case of contumacious failure to comply.

This language, read carefully, tells us a great deal about agency subpoena practice. Working through the following questions is a good way to solve any subpoena problem:

1. Does an agency have subpoena power?
2. Who may invoke the agency's subpoena power?
3. What showing is necessary to obtain a subpoena?
4. To whom may a subpoena be addressed?
5. What may a subpoena compel?
6. Are there any ways to defend against a subpoena, and most importantly, what is the price paid for resisting a subpoena without a proper basis?

The APA as well as various agency organic statutes, relevant case law, and common sense answer these questions.

[B] Who May Issue Subpoenas?

An agency has the authority to issue subpoenas only if its organic statute or some other statutory provision outside the APA gives it the power to do so. Note the statutory language of APA § 555(d), that agency subpoenas must be "authorized by law." Congress has given virtually all major federal regulatory agencies subpoena power. By comparison, many state and local government agencies, particularly the lower-echelon agencies, lack subpoena power. An agency's organic statute and other relevant statutes must be closely examined before reaching a conclusion that the agency has subpoena authority.

[C] Who May Utilize an Agency's Subpoena Power and What Showing Is Necessary to Obtain a Subpoena?

Under the APA, either the agency itself or a "party" (as defined in § 551 of the APA)[69] may utilize the agency's subpoena power. The showing necessary to obtain a subpoena

69. Section 551(3) defines party as "a person or agency named or admitted as a party, or properly seeking and entitled as of right to be admitted as a party, in an agency proceeding, and a person admitted by an agency as a party for limited purposes."

is normally presumed if the requester is a party to an action. There are times, however, when grounds for issuing a subpoena are questioned. Possible grounds for resistance are detailed in subsection [E] below. Most agencies use similar forms for their subpoenas. The illustration below is a subpoena form to appear and testify at a hearing used by the Department of Labor.

(06/2015) Administrative Subpoena to Appear and Testify at a Hearing Page 1 of 3

United States Department of Labor
OFFICE OF ADMINISTRATIVE LAW JUDGES

In Re:

(Plaintiff/Complainant/Claimant)

v.

OALJ Case No:

(Defendant/Respondent/Employer/Carrier)

SUBPOENA TO APPEAR AND TESTIFY AT A HEARING

To:
Address
City State Zip Code

YOU ARE COMMANDED to appear at the time, date, and place set forth below to testify at a formal hearing in the above captioned proceeding. When you arrive, you must remain at the location of the proceeding until the judge or a court officer allows you to leave. If you are an organization that is not a party in this case, you must designate one or more officers, directors, or managing agents, or designate other persons who consent to testify on your behalf about the following matters, or those set forth in an attachment:

Place of Testimony: Date:

Time:

YOU MUST ALSO BRING WITH YOU the following documents, electronically stored information, or objects (blank if not applicable):

The provisions of Code of Federal Regulations (CFR) 29 C.F.R. §§18.56(c) and 18.52(a), relating to your protection as a person subject to a subpoena, and 29 CFR §§18.56(d) and 18.56(e), relating to your duty to respond to this subpoena and the potential consequences of not doing so, are attached.

This subpoena is issued upon the application of (indicate attorney/representative for named party):

(Person requesting subpoena) (Address and Telephone Number)

Firm Name
Name Address
Bar Number City
Phone Number State Zip Code

If this subpoena commands the production of documents, electronically stored information, or tangible things, a copy of this subpoena must be served on each party before it is served on the person to whom it is directed. 29 C.F.R. §18.56(b)

IN WITNESS WHEREOF the undersigned United States Administrative Law Judge has hereunto set his/her hand and caused the seal of the United States Department of Labor to be affixed.

Signature of U.S. Administrative Law Judge Date To be valid, a raised USDOL Seal must appear here

(06/2015) Administrative Subpoena to Appear and Testify at a Hearing — Page 2 of 3

NOTICE: This subpoena is only valid in proceedings before the Office of Administrative Law Judges or Office of Workers' Compensation Programs. To be valid, this subpoena must bear a raised United States Department of Labor (USDOL) seal, and the signature of a Department of Labor (DOL) administrative law judge.

Rules of Practice and Procedure for Administrative Hearings Before the Office of Administrative Law Judges
[Code of Federal Regulations, Title 29, Part 18]

29 C.F.R. §18.56 Subpoenas
(c)(3) *Motion to quash or modify subpoena*. Provides that the person against whom the subpoena is directed may file a motion to quash or modify the subpoena, setting forth why the subpoena should be withdrawn or why it should be limited in scope. Pursuant to 29 CFR §18.33(d), the Party that requested the subpoena must file a response within 14 days after such motion is served.

(e) *Failure to comply*. Provides that if the person fails to comply with a subpoena, the party adversely affected by the failure may, when authorized by statute or law, apply to the appropriate district court to enforce the subpoena.

29 C.F.R. §18.22 Representation
(b) *Categories of representation*. Provides that any person compelled to testify in a proceeding in response to a subpoena may be accompanied, represented, and advised by a qualified representative.

29 C.F.R. §18.52 Protective orders
(a) *In general*. Upon motion by a party or person from whom discovery is sought, and for good cause shown, the administrative law judge may make an order to protect a party or person from annoyance, embarrassment, oppression, or undue burden or expense, including one or more of the following:
(1) Forbidding the disclosure or discovery;
(2) Specifying terms, including time and place, for the disclosure or discovery;
(3) Prescribing the discovery method of discovery other than the one selected by the party seeking discovery;
(4) Forbidding inquiry into certain matters, or limiting the scope of disclosure or discovery to certain matters;
(5) Designating the persons who may be present while discovery is conducted;
(6) Requiring that the deposition be sealed and opened only on the judge's order;
(7) Requiring a trade secret or other confidential research, development or commercial information not be revealed or be revealed only in a specified way; and,
(8) Requiring the parties simultaneously file specified documents or information in sealed envelopes, to be opened as the judge directs.

18 U.S.C. §1505 Obstruction of proceedings
Whoever acts with an improper purpose, including making a false or misleading statement or by withholding, concealing, altering or destroying a document or other information, or by threats or force influences, obstructs or impedes the due an proper administration of law under which any pending proceeding before an agency of the United States, shall be fined and imprisoned not more than 5 years.

HIPAA NOTICE: In regard to the Privacy of Individually Identifiable Health Information under the Health Insurance Portability and Accountability Act of 1996, if this subpoena does not bear a raised USDOL seal and the signature of a DOL administrative law judge, it is not valid under 45 C.F.R. §§164.512(e), 164.512(f) or 164.512(l).

Federal Rules of Civil Procedure [Applied by 29 C.F.R. §18.10(a)]
Rule 45 Subpoena
(c) Protecting a Person Subject to a Subpoena.

(c)(1) Provides that the party or attorney responsible for issuing and serving a subpoena must take reasonable steps to avoid imposing undue burden or expense on a person subject to the subpoena and the issuing court must enforce this duty and impose an appropriate sanction on a party or attorney who fails to comply.
(c)(2) Provides that, unless ordered to appear for a deposition or hearing, a person ordered to produce documents, electronically stored information, or tangible things, or to permit inspection of premises, need be present at the place of production or inspection. The person subject to the subpoena may also object to producing the documents, electronically stored information, or tangible things, or to permit inspection of premises, by giving written notice to the party or attorney responsible for issuing and serving the subpoena. The written objection must be made before the date of requested performance or 14 days from receiving the subpoena, whichever is earlier.
(c)(3) Provides that the person subject to the subpoena may file a motion to quash (stop) or limit the scope of a subpoena because there is not enough time to comply with the subpoena, the person would incur substantial expense requiring travel more than 100 miles to comply, privileged or protected matter would be disclosed, or other undue burden would result.

(d) Duties in Responding to a Subpoena.
(d)(1) Requires that the person responding to the subpoena produce documents as they are kept in the ordinary course of business or must organize and label them to correspond to the categories in the subpoena. If the subpoena does not specify a form for producing electronically stored information, the person responding must produce it in the form in which it is usually maintained or in another reasonably usable form.
(d)(2) Require that a person withholding subpoenaed information because it is privileged information or subject to protection as trial-preparation material must expressly make such claim and describe the nature of the withheld documents, communications, or tangible things in a manner that, without revealing the privileged or protected information, will enable the parties to assess the claim of privilege or protection.

(e) Contempt. Provided that a U.S. District Court may hold a person in contempt if the person fails to obey the subpoena without adequate excuse, such as those reasons in Rule 45(c)(3).

Because an agency subpoena is so easy to obtain and often looks deceptively simple, it is sometimes taken casually. Treating an agency subpoena casually is one of the most dangerous things a lawyer can do. Always remember: *in most circumstances, an agency subpoena has just as much power and authority as a subpoena issued by a court.*

(06/2015) Administrative Subpoena to Appear and Testify at a Hearing Page 3 of 3

PROOF OF SERVICE

On ______ I received this subpoena and served it pursuant to 29 CFR §18.56(b) as follows:

Person served (print name) ______ Date of Service ______

Place of Service ______ Manner of Service ______

☐ I have also tendered to the witness fees for one day's attendance and the mileage allowed by law, in the amount of $ ______

☐ I have not tendered witness fees for one day's attendance and for the mileage allowed by law.

DECLARATION OF SERVER

I declare under penalty of perjury under the laws of the United States of America that the foregoing information contained in the Proof of Service is true and correct.

Address:

Signature of Server ______ Date ______

Name of Server (Print Name) ______ City: ______ State: ______ ZIP: ______

[D] What May a Subpoena Compel and to Whom May It Be Addressed?

As noted, a subpoena may be used to compel the attendance of a particular person at a hearing (sometimes referred to by its classic Latin name, *subpoena ad testificandum*). Alternatively, a subpoena may be issued in the form of a *subpoena duces tecum*, requiring that person to appear at the hearing and to produce certain specified records. Most of the questions concerning a subpoena's scope and direction have been addressed by the Supreme Court and answered broadly.

Two cases decided by the Supreme Court during World War Two make this abundantly clear. In *Endicott Johnson Corp. v. Perkins*,[70] decided in 1943, the Court dealt with a subpoena issued by the Department of Labor under the authority conferred on the Department by the Walsh-Healey Act.[71] The Walsh-Healey Act gives the Department of Labor the authority to police minimum wage and labor standards among private companies that obtain government contracts. The company resisted the subpoena by invoking Justice Holmes's "fishing expedition" language from *Federal Trade Commission v. American Tobacco Co.*,[72] the Fifth Amendment and, most importantly, by claiming that the agency had no jurisdiction over the company. Nonetheless, the Court permitted the subpoena to be enforced and summarily rejected the fishing expedition and Fifth Amendment claims. The Court spent most of its time on the narrower question

70. 317 U.S. 501 (1943).
71. 41 U.S.C. §§ 35–45.
72. 264 U.S. 298 (1924). This case is discussed at greater length in § 4.06[A].

of whether the agency exceeded its jurisdiction in issuing the subpoena. Jurisdictional arguments, the Court held, simply did not apply to subpoena enforcement cases. The time to argue about jurisdiction is when and if the agency decides to bring an enforcement action, not when it is merely requesting information.

The leading decision on the subject of administrative subpoenas, *Oklahoma Press Publishing Co. v. Walling,*[73] was decided three years later, and said almost exactly the same thing. In *Oklahoma Press*, the newspaper argued that, as a newspaper, it was not subject to the Fair Labor Standards Act and, more importantly, the subpoena had been issued before the Department of Labor had any grounds for believing the newspaper had violated the statute. The Supreme Court paid no attention to either argument, pointing out that the jurisdictional argument had been addressed in *Endicott Johnson* and that an agency subpoena does not have to be supported by the kind of probable cause necessary to obtain a search warrant. Subpoenas may be used to develop facts, even when the agency is not yet certain it has a case.

These two decisions were enough to give the agencies the broadest possible powers of inquiry. But possibly to reemphasize that point, the Court, in 1957, granted certiorari in *Civil Aeronautics Board v. Hermann,*[74] reversing the Ninth Circuit's quashing of an agency subpoena on the grounds that less drastic information gathering techniques should be used before an agency resorts to a subpoena. The Supreme Court, *per curiam*, thought differently. The subpoenas had been reviewed by the hearing examiner, the CAB itself, and a federal district judge. Each of these entities had determined that (1) the subpoenas described the documents requested, (2) with sufficient particularity, (3) were reasonable in scope, and (4) were not found to be oppressive (*i.e.*, overly burdensome). As a consequence, the Court ordered the subpoenas enforced.

Part of what happened in *Hermann* springs from comments in dicta by Justice Holmes in the *American Tobacco* case to the effect that a subpoena cannot be so broad and oppressive that it disrupts a company's ability to carry on its business. Obviously, a company could not long survive if an agency is able to seize all of its original and current accounts receivable records. There is additional language in *American Tobacco* and other cases, stating that a subpoena must be particularized and cannot simply request "all" of a company's records.

Modern technology has reduced the burden of providing records in response to a subpoena, at least as compared to the days of *American Tobacco*. The "burden" of scanning or making photocopies of documents has not persuaded many courts to find compliance with a large record request to be oppressive. A subpoena's request for documents still must be particularized. But an examination of the actual subpoena in the *Hermann* case suggests that the sum total of the requests came very close to a request for all of the company's records.[75] The *Hermann* decision has led many observers of the agency subpoena process to conclude that all of a company's records can be requested if one simply creates an itemized list of records—even if that list eventually totals 100 percent of the contents of a company's files.

---

73. 327 U.S. 186 (1946).

74. 353 U.S. 322 (1957) (*per curiam*).

75. The text of the subpoena can be found in the circuit decision, *Hermann v. Civil Aeronautics Board*, 237 F.2d 359 (9th Cir. 1956), *rev'd*, 353 U.S. 322 (1957), and included, among many other things: all general ledgers, all audit reports, all bank statements and canceled checks, all correspondence between Hermann and a long list of other companies, all individual personnel and payroll records, etc.

[E] May a Subpoena Be Resisted?

A private party resists an agency subpoena at his or her peril. The mechanics of the enforcement process, at least on the federal level, are relatively simple. Once an agency determines that voluntary compliance with the subpoena is not forthcoming, it refers the matter to the Justice Department. Justice lawyers file a *show cause* action in an appropriate federal district court against the person subject to the subpoena. A private party who cannot show proper cause for noncompliance with the subpoena and who continues to resist is likely to be hit with a contempt of court citation. Lawyers who participate in frivolous resistance may face sanctions, including the payment of the government's attorney's fees and bar discipline.

Smart lawyers think through the subpoena process as a component of overall case strategy. Give some thought to whether you want to break your sword on a generally futile resistance action when you could be marshaling a more plausible attack against the agency on other grounds, such as whether the violation actually occurred. Remember that no matter what the case law says, negotiation is always possible. Don't forget the penalties, both monetary and professional, for bringing frivolous actions.

§ 4.08 Physical Inspections

Agencies, particularly agencies concerned with public health and safety, must, as a matter of course, conduct hundreds of thousands of inspections of premises. There are certain aspects of health and safety compliance that can be enforced only by taking a close look at a factory or a private residence. Most of these inspections do not result in controversy.

The Supreme Court generally recognizes that the Fourth Amendment, prohibiting unreasonable searches and seizures, applies to the inspection of premises. Yet, the Court also has concluded that inspections by regulatory agencies are at least a little bit different from searches conducted by the police. Recall that the Fourth Amendment provides:

> The right of the people to be secure in their persons, houses, papers, and effects, against [i] *unreasonable* searches and seizures, shall not be violated, and no [ii] *Warrants shall issue*, but [iii] upon *probable cause*, [iv] supported by *Oath or Affirmation* and [v] *particularly describing* the place to be searched, and the persons or things to be seized.[76]

The italicized portions of the quoted language identify the crucial elements of the Fourth Amendment and provide a good issue-spotting outline for resolving an administrative search question. First, is the inspection an "unreasonable" search? If the answer is "no," the inquiry is at an end. If the answer is "yes," a person who is about to be searched has the right to refuse the search. If the search is refused, you must analyze the amendment's warrant requirements: first, a warrant must be obtained (generally, from a federal magistrate-judge for federal agency inspections); second, the warrant must be supported by a sworn affidavit from someone in the agency (typically, the person who

76. Emphasis and bracketed materials added.

wishes to conduct the inspection); and third, that affidavit must explain with some precision the necessity for the search.

A series of cases from the late 1960s and the 1970s generally governs this area of administrative practice. Before 1967, no administrative lawyer had to worry about these issues because the Supreme Court had consistently held administrative inspections per se reasonable and therefore not subject to the warrant requirements of the Fourth Amendment.[77] In 1967, however, the Court changed its mind and decided, in two companion cases, *Camara v. Municipal Court of the City and County of San Francisco*[78] and *See v. City of Seattle*,[79] that administrative inspections were searches within the meaning of the Fourth Amendment, that they were not always reasonable, and that in certain circumstances, a warrant would be required.

The *Camara* case concerned the inspection of a private residence for housing code violations. The occupant of an apartment refused to allow a warrantless search, refused two days later, and refused a third time sixteen days later. The purpose of the inspection was to enforce a restriction against use of the ground floor for residential purposes. Rather than merely addressing the circumstances before it, however, the Court described the case broadly as requiring it to reexamine "whether administrative inspection programs, as presently authorized and conducted, violate Fourth Amendment rights." The Court articulated as its starting point the premises that the Fourth Amendment is not limited to circumstances in which criminal behavior is suspected and that, "except in certain carefully defined classes of cases, a search of private property without proper consent is 'unreasonable' unless it has been authorized by a valid search warrant." Based on these premises, the Court concluded that "the warrant procedure" is needed in the context of housing inspections. On the other hand, the Court expressly disagreed with the argument "that warrants should issue only when the inspector possesses probable cause to believe that a particular dwelling contains violations of the code being enforced." Instead, the Court acknowledged the need for "routine periodic inspections" in certain administrative contexts and held that "area inspections"—in the context of the case, presumably inspections pursuant to a warrant authorizing inspection of all structures in an area—are reasonable. "'[P]robable cause' to issue a warrant to inspect must exist if reasonable legislative or administrative standards for conducting an area inspection are satisfied with respect to a particular dwelling. Such standards ... will not necessarily depend upon specific knowledge of the condition of the particular dwelling."

The *See* case was different from *Camara* in two important respects: first, that it involved a warehouse rather than a personal residence; and second, that the ordinance authorizing the inspection was much narrower. The ordinance in *Camara* authorized "employees of the City departments or City agencies ... to enter, at reasonable times, any building ... to perform any duty imposed upon them." The ordinance in *See* authorized the Fire Chief to "enter all buildings and premises, except the interior of dwellings, as often as may be necessary for the purpose of ascertaining and causing to be corrected any conditions liable to cause fire." The Court framed the *See* case as concerning "whether *Camara* applies to similar inspections of commercial structures that are not used as private residence." As in *Camara*, the Court in *See* held that a warrant was required before the Fire Chief could enter a locked warehouse. Again, however, the Court denied that

77. The prototype case is *Frank v. Maryland*, 359 U.S. 360 (1959). It was *Frank* that was expressly overruled by the subsequent *See* and *Camara* decisions discussed in this chapter.

78. 387 U.S. 523 (1967).

79. 387 U.S. 541 (1967).

obtaining a warrant required a demonstration of probable cause to believe that the law was being violated. The Court added further, "We do not in any way imply that business premises may not reasonably be inspected in many more situations than private homes, nor do we question such accepted regulatory techniques as licensing programs which require inspections prior to operating a business or marketing a product."

Two decisions after *Camara* and *See* demonstrated the Court's willingness to make exceptions from the principles adopted in those cases given the right circumstances. In *Colonnade Catering Corp. v. United States*,[80] the Supreme Court unanimously held that "the long history of the regulation of the liquor industry during pre-Fourth Amendment days, first in England and later in the American Colonies," made the holding in *See* inapplicable to searches to determine whether liquor bottles had been refilled or altered. "Congress has broad power to design such powers of inspection under the liquor laws as it deems necessary to meet the evils at hand." Not long after, the Court applied *Colonnade Catering* to a firearms dealer in *United States v. Biswell*.[81] Although the Court recognized that "[f]ederal regulation of the interstate traffic in firearms is not as deeply rooted in history as is governmental control of the liquor industry," the Court said that "close scrutiny of this traffic is undeniably of central importance to federal efforts to prevent violent crime and to assist the States in regulating the firearms traffic within their borders.... Large interests are at stake, and inspection is a crucial part of the regulatory scheme." The *Biswell* Court particularly distinguished the regulatory circumstances of *See*. It observed that, in *See*, warrants could give privacy a measure of protection with little if any threat to the effectiveness of the inspection system. In *Biswell*, by contrast, "if inspection is to be effective and serve as a credible deterrent, unannounced, even frequent, inspections are essential. In this context, the prerequisite of a warrant could easily frustrate inspection." Further, the Court in *Biswell* observed in the firearms context that, "[w]hen a dealer chooses to engage in this pervasively regulated business and to accept a federal license, he does so with the knowledge that his business records, firearms, and ammunition will be subject to effective inspection." According to the Court, the "urgent federal interest[s]" furthered by regulatory inspections of firearms dealers meant that the comparative "possibilities of abuse and the threat to privacy are not of impressive dimensions." For these reasons, and under these circumstances, the Court said that no warrant was required.

Given the pervasiveness of federal government regulation in a variety of business and industrial settings, the *Biswell* Court's theory of implied consent could have become the rule rather than the exception. For example, many if not most businesses that hire employees do so with the knowledge that Occupational Safety and Health Administration inspectors may check up on their health and safety arrangements. In *Marshall v. Barlow's, Inc.*, however, the Court declined to expand the exception it created in *Colonnade Catering* and *Biswell* to a more mundane regulatory setting. The *Barlow's* case concerned the permissibility of unannounced workplace inspections without a warrant under the Occupational Safety and Health Act. To the extent that statute authorized warrantless inspections, the Court declared it to be unconstitutional. Nevertheless, the Court emphasized that "[p]robable cause in the criminal law sense is not required" in order to obtain a warrant. Instead, quoting *Camara*, the Court said that "probable cause justifying the issuance of a warrant may be based not only on specific evidence of an existing violation but also on a showing that 'reasonable legislative or administrative

80. 397 U.S. 72 (1970).

81. 406 U.S. 311 (1972).

standards for conducting an inspection are satisfied with respect to a particular [establishment].'" According to the Court in *Barlow's*, a warrant would be appropriate so long as the agency could demonstrate that "a specific business has been chosen for a... search on the basis of a general administrative plan for the enforcement of the Act derived from neutral sources."

Cases after these generally fall into two categories: those in which the Court concludes that a warrant is required because an agency has broad regulatory powers,[82] and those in which the Court permits warrantless inspections because the agency has narrow regulatory power with respect to an industry historically subject to pervasive regulation.[83] Unless the businesses to be inspected are "closely regulated," if an administrative agency—whether federal, state, or local—wishes to conduct a physical inspection of private premises, the agency must obtain a warrant unless the agency may avail itself of some other recognized exception to the warrant requirement.

As ominous as cases like *Camara* and *See* might seem from the perspective of agency enforcement personnel, those decisions have not impeded most subsequent agency inspection efforts. The vast majority of agency inspections do not raise objections. In other words, when the agency inspector presents herself at someone's door, she generally receives entry. Remember that anyone may voluntarily give up a constitutional right, and if that consent/waiver is knowing and intelligent, that's the end of the matter.

Of course, there are gradations of awareness of Fourth Amendment rights in terms of agency inspections. By now, presumably, most businesspeople are aware of *Camara*, *See*, and other cases discussed above. They may occasionally refuse to admit an inspector on constitutional grounds. Most non-businesspeople are unaware of their right to refuse admittance, and the Court has never contemplated a requirement that agency inspectors inform private parties of their constitutional rights under the Fourth Amendment.[84]

A good lawyer should think of the advantages and disadvantages of counseling his or her clients to refuse entry to an agency inspector. A refusal may simply mean that the inspector makes a quick stop in a magistrate judge's office and returns with a warrant. The extra effort may make that inspector a little more grouchy when she does gain admittance, although agencies generally will deny any retaliatory intent. Regardless, many inspectors are voluntarily admitted by people who understand their rights fully.

§ 4.09 An Agency's Use of Information as a Sanction

If we accept the idea that agencies are to look out for the public interest, it makes sense that an agency occasionally will have to warn the general public when dangerous conditions exist, no matter what impact that warning may have on a particular company or industry. Capsules that look like normal painkillers but contain cyanide have to

---

82. *See, e.g., City of Los Angeles v. Patel*, 135 S. Ct. 2443 (2015); *G.M. Leasing Corp. v. United States*, 429 U.S. 338 (1977).

83. *See, e.g., New York v. Burger*, 482 U.S. 691 (1987); *Donovan v. Dewey*, 452 U.S. 594 (1981).

84. *See, e.g., United States v. Thriftimart, Inc.*, 429 F.2d 1006 (9th Cir. 1970) (indicating no need for agency inspectors to inform a company official of his right to refuse entry).

be taken off the market instantly, and purchasers must be warned immediately. There is no time for elaborate investigations and extensive fact-finding proceedings prior to the announcement.

Occasionally, agencies release information to the press as a kind of sanction against a particular business or industry. The Consumer Product Safety Commission, not too many years ago, made a number of public comments on the safety of skateboards long before they had completed an investigation of their safety. In other circumstances, an agency's announcement may have nothing to do with health or safety. It could concern business practices that the agency does not approve of and would like to see halted. Some business enterprises are so delicate that a simple announcement that the company is under agency investigation for, say, unfair trade practices or impermissible securities transactions can harm a company.

Agency press releases are a double-edged sword. If there is a true danger, virtually no one would question the agency's right to tell the public. But what if the agency is wrong? Adverse publicity can kill a business without any opportunity for that business to contradict the release. Is it possible for a company to go into court to enjoin an adverse press release? The general rule is no. Most courts reason that an agency has a duty to warn the public in many instances, even when it does not yet have all the facts necessary to pursue a conventional enforcement action.[85]

In a few cases, courts have permitted injunctions when the company can prove that it has been improperly singled out, or when the agency is conducting some kind of vendetta against it or when the agency has deliberately misrepresented the facts.[86] These cases, however, are vanishingly rare, and their reasoning has never been reviewed by the Supreme Court.[87] This is one instance when court-ordered relief is not likely to be forthcoming. Is there anything else that can be done? One possibility, if an attorney has advance warning of the adverse press release, is to try to negotiate a number of things with the agency such as:

1. a delay of the release until corrective action can be taken; or
2. cancellation of the release if corrective action can immediately take care of the problem; or
3. an agreement to have the agency release accompanied by some kind of response on the company's part.

On occasion, the agency itself may be helpful. A few agencies have recognized the truly awesome power of their press releases and have voluntarily limited their own actions by rule. The Consumer Product Safety Commission, for example, typically gives an affected company notice and an opportunity to comment prior to issuing a press release except when an emergency exists.[88] Most agencies are not so kind. This is one area in which private clients are simply at the mercy of the agency.

---

85. *See, e.g., Ajay Nutrition Foods, Inc. v. Food and Drug Admin.*, 378 F. Supp. 210 (D.N.J. 1974), *aff'd*, 513 F.2d 625 (3d Cir. 1975).

86. *See, e.g., Silver King Mines, Inc. v. Cohen*, 261 F. Supp. 666 (D. Utah 1966); *B.C. Morton International Corp. v. Federal Deposit Insurance Corp.*, 305 F.2d 692 (1st Cir. 1962).

87. One administrative law scholar who has touched on these issues is Lars Noah, *Administrative Arm-Twisting in the Shadow of Congressional Delegations of Authority*, 1997 Wis. L. Rev. 873.

88. 16 C.F.R. § 115.15(c).

Chapter 5

Constitutional Due Process and Agency Decisionmaking

§ 5.01 An Introduction to Constitutional Due Process

[A] Issues Pertaining to Due Process

The typical course in administrative law concentrates on agency procedure. For this and other less frequently articulated reasons, many administrative law professors spend some amount of time on issues of constitutional due process. However much these issues interest the academics, it is entirely possible for an administrative law *practitioner* to spend thirty or forty years in practice without ever encountering a constitutional due process issue. Keep in mind that the Constitution sets procedural *minimums* for administrative agencies at every level of government. By contrast, the procedural rules governing day-to-day administrative practice grow out of the applicable administrative procedure act and additional procedures implemented by the individual agencies. Most of the time, the combination of a jurisdiction's administrative procedure act requirements and an agency's internal procedures far exceed the constitutional threshold. For this reason, constitutional due process claims in practice are relatively rare.

Nonetheless, notions and understandings associated with, if not required by, constitutional due process animate many administrative law practices and conversations. Any student of administrative law thus is well served by having a basic understanding of the basic structure of and issues associated with constitutional due process. A close look at some of the cases and concepts will pay dividends in many areas far removed from day-to-day agency practice. One benefit is the insights into the Supreme Court's decisional process provided by the procedural due process cases. Another benefit is the exposure these cases bring to the fascinating historical evolution of deliberately ambiguous constitutional language. Due process at the beginning of the twenty-first century is a very different concept from due process in the late 1800s.

Before getting into specific cases and issues, it is a good idea to think through some fundamentals of constitutional law. First, when the Supreme Court declares a matter to be of constitutional dimension, that pronouncement may not be altered except by constitutional amendment or by the Supreme Court's overruling of the earlier decision. Second, when the Court speaks on a matter of constitutional dimension, that pronouncement applies to all levels of government throughout the United States. These are the messages of *Marbury v. Madison*[1] and other early Supreme Court decisions. It

1. 5 U.S. (1 Cranch) 137 (1803).

is always surprising how many law students and lawyers forget these basic propositions when working through more sophisticated administrative law problems.

Another fundamental often disregarded is the language of the Constitution. When working with a procedural due process problem on the federal or state level, you apply the Due Process Clause of either the Fifth Amendment (federal level) or the Fourteenth Amendment (state level). Those clauses state:

> *Fifth Amendment*: "No person... [shall] be deprived of life, liberty, or property, without due process of law...."
>
> *Fourteenth Amendment*: "[N]or shall any State deprive any person of life, liberty, or property, without due process of law...."

Because the language of these provisions is virtually identical, courts typically apply cases interpreting them interchangeably.

How do you spot due process issues? There are a number of ways to work through a problem, but it may be helpful to think through the issues with the following progression of questions:

1. *Whether* due process, of any kind, is required?
2. *When* is the process due?
3. *How much* process is due?

While a bit simplistic, these questions reflect the foundational issues of due process analysis, and thus form the basis for virtually every due process issue that is likely to arise, either in an administrative law course or out in practice. Like most simple concepts, they warrant further explanation.

[B] *Whether*

This is the threshold analysis. It must be answered in the affirmative before moving on to the other two questions. It relates directly to the language of the Fifth and Fourteenth Amendment Due Process Clauses as recited above. If the question is whether some amount of process is due, then the answer to that question will only be "yes" if an agency is seeking to deprive someone of a *life, liberty*, or *property interest*.

In practical terms, administrative due process questions involve either *liberty* or *property* as separate and distinct categories of protected interests. Notwithstanding the text of the Fifth and Fourteenth Amendments, *life* is generally restricted to the matter of capital punishment and is mostly just ignored as a third, distinct category of protected interests in the administrative due process context.[2] On some occasions, courts and scholars have spoken of "life, liberty, or property" as a holistic representation of interests deemed important enough to be protected, rather than as individual categories of protected interests. Regardless, to be eligible for procedural protections of constitutional due process, you must be able to identify a protected due process interest. Identifying a protected due process interest—whether liberty or property—is not necessarily easy.

---

2. One intriguing case, however, involved certain plaintiffs arguing that certain custodial practices followed by a nursing home deprived the nursing home patients of "life." *Town Court Nursing Center v. Beal*, 586 F.2d 280 (3d Cir. 1978), *rev'd*, 447 U.S. 773 (1980).

Because due process is triggered by either a liberty interest or a property interest, it is tempting to try to draw distinct, categorical lines between the two. This is rarely a productive exercise in the abstract. Many of the cases in this area speak in terms of one or the other. Being able to identify precedent that categorizes the interest one is seeking to defend as either a liberty interest or a property interest may be helpful. Nevertheless, the truly important distinction is between something that *is* a protected due process interest and something which *is not* a protected due process interest.

Also, do not forget that the deprivation of a protected due process interest must be at the hands of the government, not at the hands of private persons. This is the requirement of *state action*.[3] In most administrative law problems, state action is a given, because the action under review is normally that of a government agency.

[C] *When*

This is a question of *timing—i.e.*, at what point in the agency's decisionmaking process must the required process be provided. There are certain instances when the Supreme Court has directed that due process requires certain procedures to be provided before a person may be initially deprived of a protected due process interest, and other instances when the Court has permitted some or all of the procedures required by due process to be given after that initial deprivation. This *when* question is to be analyzed simultaneously with the next question, concerning *how much* process is due.

[D] *How Much*

The *how much* process question gets into the specific elements of an agency's procedures. For example, an agency may choose merely to give persons notice of some proposed agency action and an opportunity to submit responsive arguments or evidence in writing. Another agency dealing with a different matter may permit an oral hearing, but without the right to examine directly or cross-examine witnesses. In at least one case, the Supreme Court has determined that the Due Process Clause requires the opportunity to examine directly and cross-examine witnesses.

Supreme Court case law, discussed below, suggests that the minimum due process required (if any process whatsoever is due) is at least notice *plus* some opportunity to respond either in writing or orally. As a result, notice and opportunity to respond is a starting point for analysis of the *how much* question.

Recall again that you do not move into questions regarding when or how much process will be due until you first determine that a protected due process interest is at stake. That threshold analysis requires an understanding of some of the more prominent Supreme Court decisions.

3. Anyone who is unclear as to this factor should review the discussion of the state action requirement in, *e.g.*, *Jackson v. Metropolitan Edison Co.*, 419 U.S. 345 (1974) (actions in terminating utility services by a private utility that was merely licensed to do business by a state agency was not state action under the Fourteenth Amendment).

§ 5.02 The *Londoner* and *Bi-Metallic* Decisions

Before moving on to some of the more sophisticated due process problems, most administrative law courses begin with an analysis of two Supreme Court opinions written in the early part of the twentieth century. Although these cases are principally of historical interest, they are sufficiently foundational that the distinction they establish—between agency adjudication that may give rise to procedural due process concerns and agency rulemaking that virtually never will—continues to come up in contemporary cases, though mostly in connection with state and local actions rather than federal ones.[4]

In *Londoner v. City of Denver*,[5] the Court confronted state agency action in the context of local government assessments for making street improvements. A municipal agency, the Board of Public Works in Denver, Colorado, was permitted to order street paving when a majority of the abutting landowners requested that a particular street be paved. The paving was paid for by special property tax assessments based on the proportionate benefit enjoyed by the individual landowners after paving—*i.e.*, each individual assessment reflected the length of the particular landowner's frontage on the newly-paved street as compared with the other landowners. Also, the special assessments were made against all landowners whose property abutted the newly-paved street, not just those who requested the paving. All the landowners were given notice of the specific dollar amounts of their individual assessments, but they were permitted to object to these assessments only in writing. There was no provision whatsoever for an oral proceeding.

The aggrieved landowners who objected to the special assessments took the dispute to court, arguing that the Fourteenth Amendment's Due Process Clause gave them the right to an oral hearing. The Supreme Court agreed. The Court acknowledged the notice and opportunity to present objections and complaints in writing, but declared (without much analysis) that, in these circumstances, something more was required for the aggrieved landowners. The additional procedure involved at least "the right to support his allegations by [oral] argument, however brief; and, if need be, by proof, however informal."[6]

In terms of the three-step due process analysis described above, *Londoner* is not a *whether* case. Rather, it is a *how much* case, because neither the Court nor the City of Denver disputed that the landowners were entitled to—and, in fact, had already been given—some kind of hearing. The question addressed by the Court was whether the procedures already afforded were sufficient, and its conclusion was that they were not. The *Londoner* Court determined that some degree of what we now refer to as "orality" must be provided and some mechanism allowing the landowners to put evidence into the record must be furnished. The Court did not, however, prescribe in any detail the procedural mechanisms necessary to satisfy these two requirements, nor did the Court

4. *See, e.g., Onyx Properties, LLC v. Board of County Commissioners*, 838 F.3d 1039 (10th Cir. 2016); *Grand River Enterprises Six Nations v. Pryor*, 425 F.3d 158 (2d Cir. 2005); *75 Acres, LLC v. Miami-Dade County*, 338 F.3d 1288 (11th Cir. 2003).

5. 210 U.S. 373 (1908).

6. *Id.* at 386.

demand elaborate procedures. Rather, the Court demanded only a little more process "however brief and however informal."

The *Londoner* case is not the end of the story, however. Seven years later, *Londoner* was followed by a striking decision written by Oliver Wendell Holmes, *Bi-Metallic Investment Co. v. State Board of Equalization.*[7] Like *Londoner*, the case began in Denver, Colorado. This time it involved a generic or across-the-board increase of approximately 40% in the valuation of all taxable real estate in the city of Denver.[8] In other words, no determinations were made regarding individual property values, and particularized facts and circumstances were irrelevant in this instance. The government simply increased the valuation of *all* taxable property by 40%. The decision was made by a Denver Board of Equalization that did not hear from individual landowners prior to making its decision. One of the landowners, invoking the *Londoner* decision, argued that he had a due process right to be heard orally, in some fashion, before the decision was made.[9]

The Court held that no process was due the taxpayers in *Bi-Metallic*. Justice Holmes acknowledged the existence of the *Londoner* decision, but distinguished that case based on (1) the huge numbers of people to which the Board would have had to give individualized hearings, (2) the fact that the landowners were also voters in Denver and could vote to remove their elected representatives if they did not like the Board's actions, and (3) the generic, across-the-board nature of the Board's decision, with no individualized determinations of the specific valuation of particular plots of land whatsoever.

Unlike *Londoner*, *Bi-Metallic* is a true *whether* case, and a case that answered the *whether* question in the negative: no process was due. Recall that, in an analysis of constitutional due process, if the answer is that no process is due, any further inquiry into the timing of the agency decision or the elements of due process is superfluous.

But *Bi-Metallic* is different from most *whether* cases in that it does not ask whether a protected due process liberty or property interest is at stake. Rather, the *Bi-Metallic* opinion typically is cited for the proposition that when an agency functions in a *legislative* capacity—that is, when it makes a generic, across-the-board rule—the Due Process Clause does not attach, and the agency is not required to provide individualized procedures.

The distinction between rulemaking and adjudication drawn by *Londoner* and *Bi-Metallic* can be explained in three ways. First, it can be explained on the purely pragmatic basis that the kind of procedural safeguards due process requires for individualized government determinations would be prohibitively expensive and time-consuming if

7. 239 U.S. 441 (1915).

8. One of the reasons many students have difficulty understanding *Bi-Metallic* is that they do not understand the basic mechanism of state property taxation. Described briefly, the process works like this. First, taxable property is identified and given a valuation—*e.g.*, the house and lot at 123 Cedar Street shall be valued at $15,000. Valuation traditionally was and is something considerably less than fair market value, although most governments have moved to something closer to a fair market value level of valuation. Second, having valued each unit of taxable property, the government decides how much tax to assess against each dollar of valuation. For instance, the government might assess 2 cents per dollar of valuation, which in this hypothetical would yield a tax liability of $15,000 × $.02, or $300. Finally, the landowner is sent a bill for that amount of tax—$300. Taxes can be raised either by increasing the rate of taxation (*e.g.*, from 2 cents to 3 cents per dollar of valuation) or by increasing the valuation of property (which is what occurred in *Bi-Metallic*). The taxpayer is allowed to contest that final tax bill mainly with arguments, such as "my house is not worth that much" or "your arithmetic is wrong."

9. 239 U.S. at 445.

they were required when a large number of people will be affected by agency action. This concern was mentioned specifically in *Bi-Metallic* itself and fits well with the Supreme Court's frequent emphasis on pragmatic considerations in the due process context.

Second, the *Londoner/Bi-Metallic* distinction can be explained based on the nature of the disputed facts on which a government action is based. All government actions necessarily are based on a large number of findings or assumptions concerning many facts. The factual underpinnings of government actions frequently are disputed. As Prof. Kenneth Culp Davis famously observed, however, the nature of the disputed facts varies widely depending upon whether the government action in question is legislative or adjudicative in nature.[10] Agency adjudicative decisions typically concern questions of unique and individualized historical facts regarding who did what to whom, where, how, why, and with what motive or intent—*i.e.*, adjudicative facts. By contrast, legislation (and rulemaking like it) typically is based on factual determinations that are not unique to particular individuals or their past conduct, but instead are more generalized across a larger group.

Third, the *Londoner/Bi-Metallic* distinction can be explained based on the theory of government that underlies the U.S. Constitution. Prof. John Hart Ely argued that the Constitution is principally concerned with providing process of two types: procedural fairness in the resolution of individual disputes, and ensuring broad participation in the larger processes and distributions of government.[11] The political process can be trusted to protect large classes of people from agency actions adverse to their interests, subject only to the crucial caveats that the judiciary must ensure that the political process can work effectively by enforcing such political rights as freedom of speech and the process of representation. The judiciary must protect insular minorities from the potential for systematic discrimination by the majority, for example by enforcing the Equal Protection Clause. When government singles out individuals for adverse action, the political process provides little protection. Those individuals so singled out can be protected only by forcing the government to use a decisionmaking process that ensures fairness to the individual. That is the purpose of the Due Process Clause.

§ 5.03 The Impact of *Goldberg v. Kelly*

For much of the nation's history, the kinds of interests protected from arbitrary government deprivation by the Due Process Clause were relatively narrow. The Supreme Court relied primarily on a traditional common law definition of property. If an individual owned some object of value like a house or a car, she had a property interest protected from arbitrary government deprivation by the Due Process Clause. The more abstract liberty included not only freedom from incarceration but also other traditional freedoms, such as the opportunity to choose one's occupation ("with proper regard for all reasonable regulations")[12] or the choice of parents to send their children to private rather than public schools.[13] Yet, when Dorothy Bailey sought a hearing before losing

10. Kenneth Culp Davis, *An Approach to Problems of Evidence in the Administrative Process*, 55 Harv. L. Rev. 364, 402-10 (1942).

11. John Hart Ely, Democracy and Distrust: A Theory of Judicial Review (1980).

12. *New State Ice Co. v. Liebmann*, 285 U.S. 262, 280 (1932).

13. *Pierce v. Society of Sisters*, 268 U.S. 510, 535 (1925).

her civil service job with the federal government for her alleged association with the Communist Party, the reviewing court rejected her due process claim with the following brief analysis: "It has been held repeatedly and consistently that Government employ is not 'property' and that in this particular it is not a contract. We are unable to perceive how it could be held to be 'liberty.' Certainly it is not 'life.'"[14]

Courts in those days declined to explore the precise contours of property or liberty as separate rights and instead emphasized a distinction between *rights* and *privileges*. By this analysis, while common law rights warranted due process protection, other interests created by statute and drawing from government resources were mere privileges falling outside the range of the Due Process Clause. Hence, for example, when the Mayor of New Bedford, MA, fired a policeman for disagreeing with him publicly on a matter of public importance, Justice Oliver Wendell Holmes, Jr., then serving on the Massachusetts Supreme Judicial Court, dismissed the policeman's due process claim with the observation that he "may have a constitutional right to talk politics, but he has no constitutional right to be a policeman."[15]

While the Supreme Court occasionally tinkered with agency due process in the decades after the *Londoner* and *Bi-Metallic* decisions, what is sometimes referred to as the "due process explosion" did not begin until the Court's 1970 decision in *Goldberg v. Kelly*.[16] *Goldberg* remains one of the fundamental cases in this area and warrants close scrutiny by anyone seeking to understand procedural due process. It also represents something of a high-water mark in the Court's procedural due process jurisprudence, so lawyers and students should be careful about over-applying its pronouncements.

The facts of *Goldberg* were complicated initially and became even more convoluted as the case worked its way through the lower federal courts, because the agency being sued by the welfare recipients changed its mind as to how termination proceedings should be conducted as the case was being litigated. Although the agency initially argued that no process was due, midway through the litigation, the agency overhauled its own procedures and, in doing so, identified additional procedures that it would be willing to provide the recipients.

The dispute arose out of certain state-based welfare programs and out of the program known as Aid to Families with Dependent Children (AFDC), a program established by federal statute but largely administered through state welfare agencies and subsequently replaced during the Clinton administration by the more limited Temporary Assistance for Needy Families program. In its simplest terms, AFDC provided money for families with children when the family's income fell below a certain level. People received AFDC money by qualifying under certain statutory criteria, including level of income, number of dependent children, and the absence of an able-bodied supporting parent. Once a person could show that he or she qualified, the agency was required to provide monetary support, assuming funds were available. The agency normally had no discretion to deny the benefits if a person was qualified under the statutory criteria. In 1996, Congress abolished the AFDC program and replaced it with the Temporary Assistance for Needy Families (TANF) program. States are now given block grants and permitted to create and administer welfare programs of their own choosing that do not necessarily have to be consistent with the former AFDC program. However, because *Goldberg*

14. *Bailey v. Richardson*, 182 F.2d 46, 57 (D.C. Cir. 1950), *aff'd per curiam*, 341 U.S. 918 (1951).
15. *McAuliffe v. City of New Bedford*, 29 N.E. 517, 517 (1892).
16. 397 U.S. 254 (1970).

is a constitutional decision, it follows that any state welfare program that is modeled after AFDC would have to abide by the principles articulated by the Supreme Court in *Goldberg*.

Grounds for termination of AFDC benefits also varied. In most cases, recipients were terminated because they no longer met the statutory criteria. Occasionally, welfare agencies terminated benefits for other reasons, such as improper use of the funds. For example, one of the plaintiffs in *Goldberg* was threatened with termination because she refused to sue her absent spouse for child and spousal support. Another *Goldberg* plaintiff was terminated because he refused to participate in a drug counseling and rehabilitation program.

A number of recipients who were either terminated or threatened with termination filed suit against the State of New York (the administering agency) in federal district court in New York, arguing, among other things, that termination without a pre-termination hearing was unconstitutional. Before the *Goldberg* lawsuit was filed, New York provided no process whatsoever. The agency had simply issued notices of termination. After the *Goldberg* lawsuit was filed, the state adopted new rules that gave recipients (1) notice of termination, (2) reasons for the termination, and (3) if requested by the recipient, either a review of the case by an office supervisor or an opportunity for the terminated recipient to comment on the termination in writing. In some cases, the recipient would be able to have the case reviewed and to respond. After termination, the state promised recipients a fairly elaborate oral hearing with direct examination and cross-examination of witnesses, among other procedures.

In *Goldberg v. Kelly*, the Supreme Court held both sets of procedures unconstitutional. The Court, in a majority opinion authored by Justice Brennan, required elaborate pre-termination hearing procedures as a matter of constitutional law. *Goldberg* is simultaneously a *whether*, *when*, and *how much* case. Although *Goldberg* is not favored by the current Supreme Court, it remains highly important because it sets the outer limits for constitutional due process. The Court's reasoning warrants close examination.

First, the Court determined that AFDC benefits are a statutory "entitlement" constituting a protected interest under the Fifth and Fourteenth Amendments. The Court reached this conclusion by noting that AFDC benefits, in the modern American economic system, are far more than mere gratuities or *privileges*, which the state can provide or terminate solely in its discretion. Indeed, the Court hinted in a footnote that these statutory entitlements comprise a new form of property that deserve just as much constitutional protection as the more traditional forms of property ownership—*e.g.*, a car or a piece of real estate.[17]

The Court's rhetoric arguably swept much more broadly in defining protected due process interests than merely categorizing AFDC benefits as property.

---

17. This proposition originated from two law review articles written just a few years before *Goldberg* was decided: Charles A. Reich, *Individual Rights and Social Welfare: The Emerging Legal Issues*, 74 Yale L.J. 1245 (1965), and Charles A. Reich, *The New Property*, 73 Yale L.J. 733 (1964). In his majority opinion, Justice Brennan was also careful to move away from an outmoded distinction, discussed below, that things that a court can label a "privilege" are not protected by the Constitution, while something that a court is willing to label a "right" is deserving of a great deal of protection. Expunge those terms from your administrative law vocabulary. In 1988, Justice Brennan wrote a law review article that articulated some of his thinking in constructing the *Goldberg* opinion. William J. Brennan, Jr., *Reason, Passion, and "The Progress of the Law,"* 10 Cardozo L. Rev. 3 (1988).

> Relevant constitutional restraints apply as much to the withdrawal of public assistance benefits as to disqualification for unemployment compensation, or to denial of a tax exemption, or to discharge from public employment. The extent to which procedural due process must be afforded the recipient is influenced by the extent to which he may be "*condemned to suffer grievous loss*," and depends upon whether the recipient's interest in avoiding that loss outweighs the governmental interest in summary adjudication.[18]

In a footnote, the Court suggested a laundry list of other possible protected due process interests including farm subsidies, airline routes, defense contracts, and social security pensions. While the Court did not address the interests inherent in applying for AFDC benefits in the first instance, it held squarely that *termination* of these benefits was a protected constitutional interest. Thus, the Court's answer to the *whether* question was a most emphatic "yes," and then some.

The Court could have stopped there if it wished, simply by holding that a total absence of process or even the procedures offered to recipients by the State of New York after the *Goldberg* lawsuit was filed were not enough. This would have permitted the state officials to experiment with new procedures and possibly to return to the Court in subsequent litigation if the recipients were not satisfied with the new procedures. Such a disposition would have been entirely consistent with the way the Court generally handles cases.

The Court, however, did not stop with a simple declaration of unconstitutionality. It addressed and resolved both of the other questions. On the question of timing (*when*), the Court determined that the due process must be afforded *prior* to termination, reasoning that AFDC benefits were so important as to mean the difference between survival and starvation—between life and death—for the recipients. In the Court's parlance, AFDC benefits satisfied a "brutal need,"[19] and without those benefits, recipients would suffer a "grievous loss" and might even die. Some welfare experts believe that such is not really the case, and that a number of welfare programs exist to provide basic subsistence, even if a person has lost his or her AFDC benefits.

The Court went on to hold that, because the need for AFDC benefits is so important and the risks involved in the government's making a wrong decision are so dire, due process must be provided not only before benefits are terminated, but that process must also be extraordinarily detailed (the *how much* issue). As a matter of constitutional law, Justice Brennan required that the pre-termination hearing contain the following elements:

- Notice;
- An oral hearing, including the opportunity to present evidence and to confront and cross-examine adverse witnesses;
- The right to retained counsel (although not appointed counsel);
- Compilation of a record;
- The use of that record as the exclusive basis for a decision;
- An impartial decisionmaker; and

18. *Goldberg*, 397 U.S. at 262-63 (emphasis added) (quoting *Joint Anti-Fascist Refugee League Committee v. McGrath*, 341 U.S. 123, 168 (1951)).

19. The Court's references to "grievous loss" and "brutal need" in *Goldberg* are now regarded as bits of Brennan-esque hyperbole that were not really necessary to the decision. The Supreme Court has never again held that a government benefit rose to the level of satisfying a "brutal need" such that its deprivation would represent a "grievous loss."

- A decision accompanied by a statement of reasons and evidence relied upon by the decisionmaker (although not necessarily the sort of formal findings and conclusions that a trial judge must make).

Most students who read *Goldberg* today do not fully appreciate the nature of the case as a landmark. No case before or since *Goldberg* has required more procedures as a matter of constitutional due process law. This type of Supreme Court decision often has the effect of carving its requirements in granite, either until the Constitution is amended or until the Court overrules the decision. In the case of *Goldberg*, neither has occurred. Thus, the Court's reasoning deserves even more explication.

Undoubtedly, the Court regarded notice and some kind of hearing as fundamental. New York had not offered such procedures at the outset but did so in the revised hearing procedures that it drafted and proposed after the *Goldberg* litigation began. Justice Brennan was clear that he wanted an oral hearing mainly because he did not believe that the typical AFDC recipient was likely to be able to handle a purely written proceeding. For an oral hearing to be meaningful, confrontation and cross-examination of witnesses would seem important. Allowing an agency to base its final decision on external materials and information, rather than solely on the record produced by the hearing, would likewise undercut the entire hearing process. Some degree of neutrality in the hearing officer also seems desirable, although the Court did not require complete independence. The hearing officer could be an agency employee so long as she was not involved in the case initially. Reasons for the decision must be given, especially if a decision is to be taken to a higher authority for review, and also to ensure that the decision was based on the record rather than external materials and information. A lawyer, trained in the adversary process, would be useful and at least must be permitted to represent the claimant at the hearing, even if the Court perceived a constitutional right to appointed counsel to be a step too far.

At first glance, this sounds great; but there are some flaws in the Court's reasoning. As Justice Hugo Black observed in dissent, such extensive hearings are expensive and time-consuming. Providing them may detract severely from the agency's primary mission of delivering AFDC benefits to qualified recipients in need. As Black saw it, in a society of finite resources, every dollar spent on elaborate, trial-type hearings was a dollar less that could be given to qualified AFDC beneficiaries.

Second, think about the dispute resolution aspects of this case. The Court in *Goldberg* mandated essentially an adversarial, trial-type proceeding (notwithstanding the fact that Justice Brennan kept referring to a *Goldberg*-type hearing as an "informal" process) without requiring a lawyer.[20] But how can lay people—particularly lay

20. This is another point with which some students have difficulty. Remember that this is a due process case interpreting the Fifth and Fourteenth Amendments. It is the Sixth Amendment that guarantees counsel in a criminal trial. In *Gagnon v. Scarpelli*, 411 U.S. 778 (1973), a decision that imposed virtually the same due process elements on probation revocation proceedings that had been mandated for parole revocation in *Morrissey v. Brewer*, 408 U.S. 471 (1972), the Court addressed the issue of counsel: "presumptively, it may be said that counsel should be provided in cases where, after being informed of his right to counsel, the probationer or parolee makes such a request." By contrast, in *Walters v. National Ass'n of Radiation Survivors*, 473 U.S. 305 (1985), the Court upheld a Civil War vintage statute prohibiting attorneys from recovering fees in excess of $10 per case for representing veterans before the Veterans Administration. In *Walters*, the Court relied heavily on statistics that suggested that cases handled by lawyers do not show a greater degree of success than cases handled by nonlawyers or by the claimant veterans themselves. The Court structured its discussion in terms of the "risk of erroneous deprivation" factor set out in *Mathews*

people who, in the Court's own judgment, were ill equipped to deal adequately with a purely paper proceeding—be expected to effectively and efficiently build a record, cross-examine adverse witnesses, persuade a neutral hearing officer, or read a final decision with enough sophistication to decide whether to pursue an appeal? Without the participation of dispute resolution professionals, such as lawyers, does the complicated hearing process envisioned by the Court in *Goldberg* become nearly meaningless? Most of these questions have no immediate answer. It is unlikely that the Supreme Court had any real interest in seeking the answers. Nonetheless, these questions were readily apparent to many after *Goldberg* was decided and should be pondered as we examine the next landmark procedural due process case, *Mathews v. Eldridge*, explored in § 5.05, below.

Perhaps because of questions such as these, and the resulting criticism of *Goldberg*, the Supreme Court quickly lost whatever affection it may have had for that decision. Yet the Court has never garnered the votes to overrule the decision outright. Consequently, the Court instead has found ways to work around it by carefully distinguishing the facts and circumstances of subsequent cases, and thus substantially constraining *Goldberg's* reach.[21]

§ 5.04 Interests Protected by Due Process

For at least a brief period of time, *Goldberg* represented what administrative law scholars sometimes have referred to as the *due process revolution*.[22] Perhaps unsurprisingly given its sweeping rhetoric, in the several years immediately following *Goldberg*, the Court decided a surprisingly large number of cases involving a wide range of government decisionmaking in which it determined that at least some process was due, including:

- driver license revocation (*Bell v. Burson*);[23]
- parole revocation (*Morrissey v. Brewer*);[24]
- termination of a state university teacher's contract in a *de facto* tenure setting (*Perry v. Sindermann*);[25]
- certain prisoner's rights (*Wolff v. McDonnell*);[26]

---

v. Eldridge (discussed *below*) and concluded that the statistics show that a lawyer's presence or absence in a claim for veterans benefits did not significantly affect the risk of error.

21. *See, e.g.*, Richard J. Pierce, Jr., *The Due Process Counterrevolution of the 1990's?*, 96 Colum. L. Rev. 1973 (1996).

22. The phrase was coined by a distinguished and not-unsympathetic appeals court judge, Henry Friendly (of the Second Circuit), in one of the classic articles on administrative due process. Henry J. Friendly, *Some Kind of Hearing*, 123 U. Pa. L. Rev. 1267 (1973). As Judge Friendly put it, after *Goldberg*, the tendency was to ask: "If there, why not here?" On the other hand, Judge Friendly was also critical of *Goldberg*, observing that hearings can take many forms and that the goal should be to devise procedures that are fair, feasible, and appropriate to the task at hand, rather than to constitutionalize a one-size-fits-all approach to agency adjudication.

23. 402 U.S. 535 (1971).

24. 408 U.S. 471 (1972).

25. 408 U.S. 593 (1972).

26. 418 U.S. 539 (1974).

- misconduct suspension of a public school student for ten days or less (*Goss v. Lopez*).[27]

This is an illustrative list, rather than exhaustive one. Simultaneously, the lower federal courts, following the lead of the Supreme Court, rapidly expanded the number of private interests accorded due process protection.[28]

By 1976, the membership of the Supreme Court had changed significantly. President Nixon, who ran on a platform of express distaste for the Warren Court, had the opportunity to appoint three new members of the Court, including the Chief Justice, Warren Burger. Some remaining justices, of course, had never been happy with *Goldberg*. The Court began searching for some way to stop the flood of due process cases before the "explosion" got completely out of hand.

Importantly, the Court has not overturned the early post-*Goldberg* decisions that expanded the range of protected interests beyond those recognized historically.[29] Nevertheless, the Court has so often distinguished and contextualized those cases that lawyers should take care not to read them too expansively. For example, although *Goldberg* spoke sweepingly of grievous losses and brutal needs in defining protected interests, the Court quickly returned to a more categorical approach of identifying protected interests in terms of either liberty interests or property interests (although those categories were defined more broadly than before).

[A] Property Interests and Entitlement Theory

Two companion cases decided on the same day in 1972, *Board of Regents of State Colleges v. Roth*[30] and *Perry v. Sindermann*,[31] illustrate the contemporary understanding of property interests. Both Roth and Sindermann were professors at state colleges, and neither had tenure. Roth was hired for a fixed term of one year and was not rehired for the following year. He expected to be rehired, but the college never gave him any assurance that he would be retained beyond the one year. Sindermann similarly had been employed for four years under a series of one-year contracts and likewise expected to be rehired. In his case, however, the college had published an official faculty guide stating

---

27. 419 U.S. 565 (1975).

28. *Caulder v. Durham Housing Authority*, 433 F.2d 998 (4th Cir. 1970) (concerning eviction from public housing).

29. Although the Court has never overruled *Goldberg*, Congress enacted a statute in 1996 that seems to have that effect. *See* Personal Responsibility and Work Opportunity Reconciliation Act, Pub. L. No. 104-193, 110 Stat. 2105 (1996) (codified in scattered sections of 42 U.S.C.). That statute abolished the AFDC program, which gave an individual an entitlement to benefits if she met specified eligibility criteria, and created instead a system of block grants to states for "temporary assistance for needy families." The statute also declared unequivocally that it "[should] not be interpreted to entitle any individual ... to assistance under any state program funded under this part." By eliminating the statutory entitlement to subsistence benefits that was the predicate for the Court's holding in *Goldberg*, Congress arguably removed federal welfare programs from the scope of due process protection. *See, e.g.*, Christine N. Cimini, *Welfare Entitlements in the Era of Devolution*, 9 Geo. J. on Poverty L. & Pol'y 89 (2002). *But see Cleveland Board of Education v. Loudermill*, 470 U.S. 532 (1985) (rejecting state legislature's efforts to limit due process protections as a condition of entitlement, contending that "[t]he right to due process 'is conferred, not by legislative grace, but by constitutional guarantee'").

30. 408 U.S. 564 (1972).

31. 408 U.S. 593 (1972).

that, although the college had no tenure system, it wanted each faculty member "to feel that he has permanent tenure as long as his teaching services are satisfactory and as long as he displays a cooperative attitude toward his co-workers and his superiors, and as long as he is happy in his work." Neither Roth nor Sindermann were given a hearing or even a statement of reasons for why they were not rehired. Both sued their respective colleges claiming their due process rights had been violated and seeking a hearing.

The Court held that Sindermann's continued employment was a property interest protected from arbitrary government deprivation by due process, but Roth's was not. In *Roth*, the Court explained its holding by contending that property interests stem from "legitimate claim[s] of entitlement" that "are created and… defined by existing rules or understandings that stem from an independent source such as state law—rules or understandings that secure certain benefits and that support claims of entitlement to those benefits." Roth could point to no such independent source, so lacked a protected property interest in his continued employment.[32] By contrast, notwithstanding his lack of formal tenure status, Sindermann could point to the faculty guide, and thus could claim "legitimate reliance upon guidelines promulgated by" his government employer as the basis for his entitlement to continued employment at the college.

The definition of property interests as entitlements rooted in "existing rules or understandings that stem from an independent source" is not limited to state law entitlements. The AFDC benefits at issue in *Goldberg* were interests created by federal statute. Other post-*Goldberg* due process cases involve similar property interests in the form of statutory entitlements established by Congress as well.[33]

In *Brock v. Roadway Express, Inc.*,[34] the Court applied the reasoning of *Roth* and *Sindermann* as the basis for holding that an employment contract between two private parties can give the employer a property interest that is protected by due process. The case involved an attempt by the Department of Labor (DOL) to apply the "whistleblower" protection provision of the Surface Transportation Assistance Act of 1982. That provision authorized the DOL to order a trucking company to reinstate a previously fired employee if the agency determined that the employee was fired because he reported a safety violation to the Department of Transportation. In this instance, Roadway had fired a driver, putatively for inadequate performance of his responsibilities. The DOL ordered Roadway to reinstate the employee based on the DOL's determination that Roadway actually had fired the employee for reporting safety violations to the Department of Transportation, contrary to the statute. The justices disagreed sharply on how much procedure the DOL was required to use before it could order the employee's reinstatement, but the Court was unanimous in holding that the employer had a property interest protected by the Due Process Clause. A collective bargaining agreement between the employer and the employee's union, which gave the employer the right to fire any employee for cause, created the property interest that the DOL could not take away without providing due process. The Court reached a similar conclusion with little discussion in *Federal Deposit Insurance Corp. v. Mallen*,[35] which concerned an FDIC order suspending the employment of the president of a federally insured bank who was indicted.

32. *See also Bishop v. Wood*, 426 U.S. 341 (1976) (holding that "mere" employment by a government body is not a protected interest.)

33. *See, e.g., Mathews v. Eldridge*, 424 U.S. 319 (1976) (concerning social security disability benefits). This case is discussed at great length in § 5.05 below.

34. 481 U.S. 252 (1987).

35. 486 U.S. 230 (1988).

In 2005, the Court revisited the issue of property interests in the context of enforcement of domestic violence restraining orders. In *Town of Castle Rock v. Gonzales*,[36] the petitioner, a woman estranged from her husband, obtained a restraining order from a state court ordering the husband, among other things, to stay at least 100 yards from the family home. The husband disobeyed the order, kidnapped the couple's three children, and ultimately murdered the children. The wife sued the town of Castle Rock, asserting that the town's police department customarily disregarded such orders and often failed to enforce them, thereby depriving her of due process.[37] In an opinion authored by Justice Scalia, the Court determined that the wife did not have a protected property interest in the enforcement of the protective order. Justice Scalia reviewed earlier case law including *Roth* to note that a property interest is an entitlement, not an abstract need or desire, and such entitlements are "defined by existing rules or understandings that stem from an independent source such as state law."[38] The benefit here was not a protected interest because "a benefit is not a protected entitlement if government officials may grant or deny it in their discretion."[39] Looking closely at the Colorado statutes and applicable case law, and refusing to defer to the Tenth Circuit's view of these issues,[40] the Court determined that nothing in the Colorado law made enforcement of protective orders *mandatory*. Accordingly, as a matter of state government discretion, there was no protected interest at stake.

[B] Liberty Interests: Prisoners' Rights and Stigma Plus

Because liberty obviously implicates freedom from incarceration, one area in which the Supreme Court has repeatedly considered the implications of due process is the rights of prisoners, and particularly prisoners' conditions of confinement. Jurisprudence on this issue is complex, and detailed treatment of the many complicated cases involving the due process rights of prisoners is more appropriate for a book on criminal law or prisoners' rights than for a book on administrative law.

In *Wolff v. McDonnell*,[41] the Supreme Court rejected the argument that prisoners lacked a protected liberty interest in prison disciplinary procedures. The case concerned the validity of procedures for depriving prisoners of "good-time credits." Echoing its rhetoric regarding entitlements and property rights, the Court held,

---

36. 545 U.S. 748 (2005).

37. The wife asked for money damages under 42 U.S.C. § 1983 (the federal statute that permits a monetary recovery against state officers who violate constitutional rights under color of law).

38. *Town of Castle Rock*, 545 U.S. at 756.

39. *Id.*

40. While not terribly relevant to administrative law, this concept of deference to a federal circuit court's construction of state law grows out of an important civil procedure concept first articulated in *Erie Railroad v. Tompkins*, 304 U.S. 64 (1938) (application of state substantive law to federal court cases arising in diversity). Following the *Erie Railroad* decision, the Supreme Court decided to let the federal circuit courts make the final determination of what state law said. Here, however, Justice Scalia determined that this was not a case requiring deference to state law but rather a matter of federal constitutional law (*i.e.*, what constituted a protected interest under the United States Constitution).

41. 418 U.S. 539 (1974).

> It is true that the Constitution itself does not guarantee good-time credit for satisfactory behavior while in prison.... *But the State having created the right to good time and itself recognizing that its deprivation is a sanction authorized for major misconduct*, the prisoner's interest has real substance and is sufficiently embraced within Fourteenth Amendment "liberty" to entitle him to those minimum procedures appropriate under the circumstances and required by the Due Process Clause to insure [sic] that the state-created right is not arbitrarily abrogated.[42]

In *Sandin v. Conner*,[43] the Court arguably shifted direction and curtailed prisoners' due process rights when it held that a prisoner who was serving an indeterminate sentence of 30 years to life did not have a constitutionally protected liberty interest in his challenge to a prison decision to place him in segregated confinement. According to the Court in *Sandin*, prison conditions give rise to a protected liberty interest only when they impose an "atypical and significant hardship on the inmate in relation to the ordinary incidents of prison life." In *Wilkinson v. Austin*,[44] the Court held unanimously that placing a prisoner in a Supermax prison deprives the prisoner of a liberty interest. The *Wilkinson* Court noted in passing, however, that the claim of a liberty interest in that case was somewhat weak given that the prisoner was already confined and thus had suffered a loss of liberty from the initial incarceration.

The federal circuit courts' varying efforts to apply *Sandin*'s guidance illustrate the complexity of ascertaining liberty interests in the context of prisoners' rights. In *Aref v. Lynch*,[45] the D.C. Circuit observed that the Supreme Court has not established a baseline for evaluating exactly when segregated confinement imposes an atypical and significant hardship, and that the circuit courts have adopted different approaches to filling that void:

- the Third, Sixth, and Tenth Circuits consider administrative confinement as the baseline;
- the Fourth Circuit considers the general prison population as a baseline;
- the Seventh Circuit looks to conditions "at the harshest facility in the state's most restrictive prison";
- the Second Circuit has found that special confinement of even a relatively short period (*e.g.*, 180 days or 305 days) gives rise to a protected liberty interest;
- the Fifth Circuit has held that segregation "can never implicate a liberty interest unless it 'inevitably' lengthens a prisoner's sentence"; and
- the D.C. Circuit employs "a multi-factor approach" to determining the baseline that takes into account confinement conditions relative to administrative segregation as well as the duration of the segregation generally and as compared to similarly-situated prisoners, but also recognizes that less severe conditions can give rise to liberty interests if they are prolonged or indefinite.

The Supreme Court has always recognized, however, that liberty interests protected by due process are far more extensive than arbitrary incarceration. In *Wisconsin v.*

42. *Id.* at 557 (emphasis added).
43. 515 U.S. 472 (1995).
44. 545 U.S. 209 (2005).
45. 833 F.3d 242 (D.C. Cir. 2016).

Constantineau,[46] the Court held a Wisconsin statute unconstitutional as violating due process because it authorized a police chief to post a notification in all liquor stores declaring an individual to be a habitual drunkard without providing that individual an opportunity to challenge that official characterization. The Court described posting such a notification as "such a stigma or badge of disgrace that procedural due process requires notice and an opportunity to be heard."

Similarly, in *Goss v. Lopez*,[47] the Court held that public school students were deprived of a liberty interest when they were suspended from school for alleged misconduct without being provided an opportunity to challenge the charges against them. As in *Constantineau*, the liberty interest was reputational. The *Goss* Court recognized that charges of misconduct "could seriously damage the students' standing with their fellow pupils and their teachers as well as interfere with later opportunities for higher education and employment."

The Court subsequently retreated somewhat from its construction of liberty for due process purposes. In *Paul v. Davis*,[48] the Court considered a due process challenge against a police chief's widespread distribution of flyers identifying certain people by name and mug shot as active shoplifters. Davis's name and photograph were included because he had been arrested for shoplifting, although his guilt or innocence remained undetermined, and he was not provided an opportunity to challenge his inclusion on the flyers. The Court rejected Davis's due process claim, saying that "reputation alone, apart from some more tangible interests such as employment" was insufficient to establish a protected liberty interest. The Court suggested that state tort law provided adequate protection for reputational interests.

Courts since have derived from the *Paul* case a *stigma plus* standard for identifying liberty interests protected by the Due Process Clause. Stigmatizing an individual alone does not constitute deprivation of a liberty interest. Rather, the stigma plus standard requires the government to simultaneously label someone in a stigmatizing way and deprive the individual of something tangible. Thus, in *Siegert v. Gilley*,[49] the Supreme Court rejected a claim by a clinical psychologist that his former federal employer harmed his reputation and violated his due process rights by providing a negative review of his work performance to a prospective employer. The Court held that the psychologist lacked a protected due process liberty interest. The alleged reputational injury alone was inadequate, and the potential impairment of future employment opportunities was insufficiently tangible to satisfy the stigma plus test.

46. 400 U.S. 433 (1971).
47. 419 U.S. 565 (1975).
48. 424 U.S. 693 (1976).
49. 500 U.S. 226 (1991).

§ 5.05 How Much Process— *Mathews v. Eldridge*

No one doing any work in the area of administrative due process can afford to disregard *Mathews v. Eldridge.*[50] The setting of the case was not very different from that of *Goldberg.* The Social Security Administration (at one time a component of the Department of Health and Human Services, but now an independent agency) is charged with the administration of the social security system, including a program that pays social security disability insurance (SSDI) benefits to persons who qualify and who are no longer able to work. Persons employed in the United States pay into the social security system through payroll deductions (called "FICA"). Persons who have paid into the system for the requisite number of calendar quarters (forty quarters at the time the *Mathews* case arose) are eligible to claim disability benefits if, during their working careers, they become disabled to the point where they are not capable of gainful employment. This is not a workers' compensation system; the injury or illness does not have to be suffered on the job to trigger social security disability benefits. Rather, it is a form of salary insurance that an eligible person receives in monthly payments from the social security system until she again becomes capable of gainful employment.

In *Mathews*, SSDI benefits were terminated after notice and the opportunity to respond in writing. After termination, the recipient was given a trial-type hearing. If the claimant prevailed, retroactive benefits would be paid. The claimant argued that this form of process was constitutionally insufficient. The Supreme Court disagreed.

The bottom line of *Mathews* is straightforward enough. The Court held that, while an SSDI termination proceeding does trigger some kind of due process (or, more accurately, the government in *Mathews* did not dispute the *whether* aspects of the case), Mr. Eldridge was not entitled to any more due process than he had already received. The Court reached this conclusion mainly by distinguishing *Goldberg* and *Mathews.*

Some commentators find it difficult to accept a number of the distinctions. The Court was unwilling to equate the brutal need for AFDC benefits and SSDI benefits. As the Court reiterated in *Mathews*, AFDC recipients are "on the very margin of subsistence." The Court maintained such is not the case for persons who have their SSDI benefits terminated. Also, in the Court's view, an AFDC proceeding was more likely to turn on specific factual disputes where an oral hearing might be beneficial, while SSDI benefits were more a matter of evaluating medical evidence that had already been committed to paper. According to the Court, oral hearings generally are less necessary when the resolution of the dispute depends primarily on a paper record.

The *Mathews* Court's comments on evidence are the one part of the decision that puzzles many people who deal regularly with SSDI termination proceedings. In practice, SSDI assessments generate a lot of documentation, and many decisions turn on that documentation. But many cases involve medical evidence and expert witnesses presented by each side. Frequently, the issue becomes one of which expert to believe,

---

50. 424 U.S. 319 (1976). The reader should also consider all of the more recent cases cited and discussed in Richard J. Pierce, Jr., *The Due Process Counterrevolution of the 1990s?*, 96 Colum. L. Rev. 1973 (1996).

which is a question that is particularly suitable for a face-to-face oral confrontation and often difficult to resolve solely on the basis of documentary evidence. Moreover, there appears to be nothing in the *Mathews* record that supports the Court's conclusion that a paper hearing process was sufficient as an across-the-board proposition. The Court apparently reached this conclusion without much factual or statistical support. On the other hand, reaching this conclusion allowed the Court to decide *Mathews* the way it wanted without having to overrule *Goldberg*.

Regardless, the most significant part of *Mathews* is not the ultimate disposition of the case itself. Differences do exist between SSDI and AFDC eligibility determinations, and a great deal of due process already was afforded in the challenged procedures. Moreover, having conceded the *whether* question, the Court did have a certain amount of leeway in addressing the *when* and *how much* issues. What is important, and what everyone reading *Mathews* and dealing with a procedural due process question in the future must address, is the three-part test first articulated in *Mathews* by which all federal courts now evaluate challenges to agency procedures. Since the *Mathews* decision, due process questions have been weighed in terms of three factors:

1. the private interest affected by agency action;
2. the risk of error inherent in the agency's existing procedures; and
3. the government's interest in maintaining the existing procedures weighed in terms of both fiscal and administrative burdens that might be encountered if new procedures were mandated.

Remember: this test is a Supreme Court pronouncement and must be addressed any time you deal with an administrative due process question. For example, if you are writing a brief in federal court on an administrative due process issue, it is likely that you will organize the brief on the basis of these three factors. *Mathews* is now almost 50 years old, and the Court has not altered its basic formula or suggested a desire to replace its approach.

Factor one has three components. First, *identify* the "thing" (*i.e.*, the interest) with which the government is tampering. Is it AFDC benefits, a job, a driver's license, a person's reputation, or something else? Second, *discuss* whether this thing is either a protected property or a liberty interest. A discussion of approaches for making this determination follows below. Third, if the thing in question is a protected property or liberty interest, then *consider* how important the thing is to a person's well being or survival.

Factor two requires an evaluation of the agency's procedures to determine whether those procedures lead to accurate results.[51] The touchstone for this assessment, however, is not total accuracy. Instead, this inquiry really blends an analysis of (1) the protected interest involved and its importance to the private person, and (2) whether the procedures already offered assure to some reasonable degree that the government's decision is correct. Additionally, in considering the latter of these two elements, it is important to specify the additional procedures sought, and how they would improve decisional

51. A classic law review article takes up administrative procedures along the same lines as *Mathews*, but uses a slightly different vocabulary: "accuracy," "efficiency," and "acceptability." Roger C. Cramton, *A Comment on Trial-Type Hearings in Nuclear Plant Siting*, 58 VA. L. REV. 585 (1972).

accuracy. Again, keep in mind the Court's language. The articulated test is "the risk of erroneous deprivation."

Factor three requires an analysis of what the Court refers to alternatively as the *public* interest or the *government* interest. The Court seems to view the two terms as being synonymous, although one can disagree with the Court on this point. A government agency may worry only about its budget and not give a hoot for establishing a fair procedure for those whose lives the agency affects. By contrast, the public may have just as strong an interest in ensuring that agencies implement a fair and accurate decisional process as it does in guarding against unreasonable expenditures of government money. On the other hand, procedure is not free, and funds expended to provide additional procedures must come from somewhere. In factor three, the Court usually (although not always) describes the public interest in terms of an interest in the public fisc and the cost of additional procedures.

What the justices were really getting at in factor three was not clearly articulated in the *Mathews* opinion itself. Recall Justice Black's point in *Goldberg*: How much do we want to burden the agency, both financially and administratively, simply to insure an additional increment of fairness or accuracy? The Court was quick to point out in *Mathews* that "[f]inancial cost alone is not a controlling weight in determining whether due process requires a particular procedural safeguard .... But the Government's interest, and hence that of the public in conserving scarce fiscal and administrative resources is a factor that must be weighed."

Mathews was a watershed case. Since then, the Court has not overturned any of the due process protections decided during the explosion years, but it has sent repeated, clear signals in *Mathews* and in subsequent cases that it does not intend to go too much further. For example, there is no case that extends beyond the protections provided by *Goldberg*. The case that is probably closest to *Goldberg* in terms of mandating strict procedure is *Morrissey v. Brewer* (parole revocation).[52] When someone loses a parole hearing, he or she goes back to jail.

Also since *Goldberg*, the Court has taken a number of cases in which it finessed the *whether* question (*i.e.*, refused to deem the interest either a property or liberty interest) by examining how much process the recipient was given and deeming that sufficient. For example, in *Board of Curators of the University of Missouri v. Horowitz*,[53] the Court reviewed the expulsion from a state medical school of a fourth-year medical student. Throughout the *Horowitz* opinion, the Court seemed to view the failure of Ms. Horowitz to satisfy academic criteria as the reason for the expulsion. It was obvious that the Court felt totally uncomfortable second-guessing the academic determinations of a medical faculty and simply affirmed Ms. Horowitz' expulsion. In reaching this result, the Court refused to reach the question of whether attendance at a state-supported medical school was a property or liberty interest and held instead that the procedures afforded Ms. Horowitz were more than adequate, even if she had a property or liberty interest in medical school attendance.

Observing that the Court was able to avoid resolving the *whether* question in *Horowitz* by finding the amount of process provided to be adequate is not the same as suggesting that the Court reached the wrong decision in that case. Ms. Horowitz's clinical

52. The procedures required for parole revocation in *Morrissey v. Brewer*, 408 U.S. 471 (1972), are virtually identical to the *Goldberg* procedures, but the Court has never gone beyond *Goldberg*.

53. 435 U.S. 78 (1978).

performance was reviewed at various times by: (1) the medical school faculty, (2) a Council of Evaluation (three times), (3) an appeals board consisting of seven practicing physicians, (4) a faculty coordinating committee, (5) the medical school's Dean, and (6) the University Provost. By any standard, Ms. Horowitz received considerable process from the University. If one views due process, in part, as the making of a *careful* decision, it is difficult to find fault with the University of Missouri's procedures.

For a time after *Mathews v. Eldredge*, the justices flirted with another approach to the *how much* process question in the context of statutory entitlements known as the "bitter with the sweet" model. When Justice (later Chief Justice) William Rehnquist joined the Supreme Court in 1972, he was unhappy with decisions like *Goldberg v. Kelly* in which the Court had expanded both the definition of protected property interests to include statutory entitlements and the procedural protections an agency would have to provide before depriving a person of such entitlements. Justice Rehnquist understood, however, that the Court's commitment to stare decisis principles made overruling *Goldberg* unlikely. Instead, he suggested the following: if a person relies on a statute as the basis for a right that is protected by due process, then that person must accept the procedural contours of the right (*i.e.*, the bitter) along with the substantive contours of that right (*i.e.*, the sweet) as prescribed by the legislature.

In *Arnett v. Kennedy*,[54] the Supreme Court considered the due process claim of a non-probationary federal civil service employee who was fired for falsely and publicly accusing his boss of attempted bribery. The employee received only a post-termination opportunity for an evidentiary, trial-type hearing, as provided by statute. Justice Rehnquist wrote the opinion of the Court representing a three-justice plurality, holding that the employee's property interest in his government employment was limited to the procedural protections granted by Congress when it strengthened statutory job protections for civil service workers. As explained by the plurality opinion, "where the grant of a substantive right is inextricably intertwined with the limitations on the procedures which are to be employed in determining that right, a litigant ... must take the bitter with the sweet." Although two other justices agreed with the judgment against the employee on the ground that the procedures offered by the relevant statute satisfied due process, they sided with the four dissenting justices in rejecting Justice Rehnquist's bitter with the sweet model.

Subsequently, however, in *Bishop v. Wood*,[55] the Court evaluated the due process claim of a permanent-status policeman fired for cause, and this time, a five-justice majority seemed to embrace the bitter with the sweet approach to procedural due process. Although the opinion of the Court written by Justice John Paul Stevens was not a model of clarity, it arguably rejected the policeman's due process claim because, although the relevant state and local statutes articulated the circumstances justifying termination, they did not grant him a right to a hearing and instead left evaluation of the grounds for discharge to a city manager. At least, that is how the dissenting justices in *Bishop* characterized the majority's opinion.

The Court clearly and unequivocally rejected the bitter with the sweet approach in *Cleveland Board of Education v. Loudermill*.[56] The case concerned the claim of a state civil servant that he was fired in violation of his right to procedural due process. In

54. 416 U.S. 134 (1974).
55. 426 U.S. 341 (1976).
56. 470 U.S. 532 (1985).

this case, an eight-justice majority of the Court determined that Mr. Loudermill had a protected property interest in his employment and required that he be given at least a minimal pre-termination due process opportunity to explain his position. He had been given none by the state. According to the Court, "[w]hile the legislature may elect not to confer a property interest in [public] employment, it may not constitutionally authorize the deprivation of such an interest, once conferred, without appropriate safeguards." As if that were not clear enough, the Court also offered the following reasoning:

> [T]he "bitter with the sweet" approach misconceives the constitutional guarantee.... The point is straightforward: the Due Process Clause provides that certain substantive rights—life, liberty, and property—cannot be deprived except pursuant to constitutionally adequate procedures.... Were the rule otherwise, the Clauses would be reduced to a mere tautology. "Property" cannot be defined by the procedures provided for its deprivation any more than can life or liberty. The right to due process "is conferred, not by legislative grace, but by constitutional guarantee."[57]

Justice Rehnquist dissented from the Court's decision in *Loudermill*, defending the bitter with the sweet model and arguing that a majority of the justices had adopted it in *Arnett v. Kennedy.*

The war on terrorism and national security concerns have sparked a number of important judicial decisions regarding the *how much* process question. The Supreme Court's decision in *Hamdi v. Rumsfeld*,[58] is illustrative. Mr. Hamdi was born in the United States and eventually arrested by U.S. authorities in Afghanistan where, according to the government, he took up arms on behalf of the Taliban. In a lengthy opinion, the Court first determined that the United States government does have the power to detain enemy combatants under congressional authority enacted in 2002 which permitted the president to use "all necessary and appropriate force" against persons who were associated with the September 11, 2001 terrorist attacks.

Regardless, Mr. Hamdi asserted that he had a right under the Due Process Clause to challenge his enemy combatant status. The Court performed a standard *Mathews* three-part analysis to conclude that Hamdi did have a right to bring such a challenge. With regard to the threshold issue (private interest affected), the Court concluded that the case implicated one of the "most elemental of liberty interests—the interest in being free from physical detention by one's own government." Not even war, the government interest asserted, trumped this particular private interest.

With regard to the risk of an erroneous determination (the second of the three factors in the *Mathews* standard), the Court reviewed the procedures suggested by the government and determined that they did not satisfy due process requirements. The Court ultimately required that a person in Hamdi's position, at the very least, be given "notice of the factual basis for his classification, and a fair opportunity to rebut the government's factual assertions before a neutral decisionmaker." However, the Court was willing to accept certain constraints on the hearing process. For example, it conceded that the admission of hearsay evidence might be necessary. It was willing to permit some kind of presumption in favor of the government's assertions. Nonetheless, it went on to reiterate its fundamental holding: even terrorism does not warrant deprivation of

57. *Id.* at 541.

58. 542 U.S. 507 (2004).

at least the requirements of notice, some kind of hearing, and an independent decision maker.[59]

Justice Scalia authored a dissenting opinion in *Hamdi*, joined by Justice Stevens, in which he questioned the applicability of the *Mathews* standard in cases involving national security and freedom from incarceration. He focused his analysis instead on the Constitution's Suspension Clause, Art. I, § 9, cl. 2, and seemed genuinely baffled that the Court would rely instead on the "sort of 'judicious balancing'" outlined in *Mathews*, "a case involving... *the withdrawal of disability benefits!*" (emphasis in original).

In another case concerning the intersection of the Due Process Clause and national security, along with immigration, *Kerry v. Din*,[60] the Court considered the procedural obligations of the State Department when it denied a visa application from the spouse of a U.S. citizen. The applicant received only a brief statement indicating that the denial was required by a provision of the Immigration and Nationality Act that referred to several potential bases for denying a visa. The apparent reason for the denial was the applicant's prior position as a civil servant in the government of Afghanistan at the time it was controlled by the Taliban, although the State Department did not specify that this was the reason for the denial. With Justice Scalia writing for the Court, a three-Justice plurality held that the State Department did not violate Din's due process rights.

Justice Scalia spoke sweepingly about the scope of the Due Process Clause in his opinion for the Court in *Kerry v. Din*. He referred to the narrow scope of due process and of the procedures required by due process described by Coke in 1797 and by Blackstone in 1769 as if those descriptions were determinative in the present day. Coke and Blackstone were referring to the Magna Carta, but Justice Scalia expressed the view that their descriptions also applied to the Due Process Clause because Coke and Blackstone were widely accepted as the leading authorities on due process at the time of the founding. According to Justice Scalia, Coke and Blackstone described the scope of due process as applying only to traditional forms of property and to liberty defined only to include the literal loss of physical freedom. Justice Scalia also suggested that the Court's decisions in cases like *Goldberg* and *Loudermill*, expanding the scope of protected due process interests and authorizing courts to require the government to provide procedures beyond those prescribed by statute, were illegitimate. In short, Justice Scalia's opinion suggested that at least some justices might be inclined to overrule many of the Court's contemporary due process decisions.

Justices Anthony Kennedy and Samuel Alito, writing in concurrence in *Kerry v. Din*, used different reasoning to support a judgment in favor of the government. They found it unnecessary to address the broad constitutional issues discussed by the plurality. Assuming without deciding that Din had an interest protected by due process, the concurring justices concluded that the State Department's reference to a specific statutory provision as the basis for its decision was adequate to satisfy due process in the circumstances of the case. Unlike the plurality, the concurring justices referred repeatedly to national security to support their unwillingness to confer on the applicant greater procedural rights than the extremely limited procedures provided by the relevant statute.

---

59. As might be expected, *Hamdi* generated an enormous amount of commentary. *See, e.g.*, Cass R. Sunstein, *Administrative Law Goes to War*, 118 Harv. L. Rev. 2663 (2005); Erwin Chermerinsky, *Enemy Combatants and Separation of Powers*, 1 J. Nat'l Security L. & Pol'y 73 (2005). Hamdi was eventually released under an agreement that he relinquish his U.S. citizenship.

60. 576 U.S. 86 (2015).

The four dissenting justices in *Kerry v. Din*, with Justice Breyer writing the opinion, expressed the view that the spouse of the applicant had a liberty interest protected by the Due Process Clause under the broad headings of the "fundamental right" to marry and the "fundamental right" of a U.S. citizen to live in the United States. The dissenting justices contended that the State Department had deprived the spouse of the applicant of those protected interests without due process by failing to provide adequate notice of the grounds for denial and an explanation of its decision to deny the visa application. The dissenting justices also suggested that the State Department was required to provide the applicant with some kind of hearing at which the applicant could contest the stated basis for the decision, or at least an explanation of its decision not to provide such a hearing.

These cases are hardly the last word from the Court regarding *how much* process must be provided to satisfy the Due Process Clause. The Court decides new procedural due process cases frequently. For lawyers, the important challenge often is how to relate new fact patterns to the existing case law.

§ 5.06 Resolving Administrative Due Process Issues

[A] Approaches

The *whether*, *when*, and *how much* questions help with spotting due process issues but do not really help resolve them.[61] There are a number of ways to work through due process issues. The following discussion contains some suggestions for doing so. One thing that is certain is that it is hard to talk about these concepts in the abstract.

You may find the following discussion almost impenetrable if you have not read the previous sections, because it refers to the important due process cases by name. This section is not the place to begin. Anyone who arrives at this point without understanding the analysis of the landmark cases discussed in the preceding sections should go back to the beginning of the chapter. Application of the *whether*, *when*, and *how much* questions will help you understand the fundamentals and identify some of the basic issues, but you need to take your analysis several steps further to complete a full-blown resolution of any new due process question.

[B] Resolving a *Whether* Issue

Recall that the place to begin is with the language of the Fifth and Fourteenth Amendments and that the term *life* almost never figures into an administrative due process question because it is generally reserved for capital punishment cases. Thus, the

61. This is an elementary point that is too often lost on law students. Issue spotting is the process of identifying and categorizing legal questions by area of the law. Issue resolution, by contrast, is the analysis of a particular body of law to attempt to reach conclusions as to the validity of an agency's action. In other words, issue resolution is a matter of predicting how a court faced with this issue might decide it.

question becomes: Does your client have a property or liberty interest protected by the Constitution?

As the discussion earlier in this chapter demonstrates, the Supreme Court's robust procedural due process jurisprudence has produced a few broadly-applicable principles for identified protected property and liberty interests. Property interests include entitlements created by statutes, regulations, or other independent sources. Liberty interests extend to a person's reputation, although only if the stigma imposed by government action is accompanied by the deprivation of something more tangible as well. Because the Court often speaks of property or liberty as though they are distinct categories, students often strive mightily to distinguish between the two. In the context of administrative due process, that's rarely a productive inquiry. The Supreme Court never has made up its mind on the distinction. Instead, the goal ought to be simply whether the interest in question is protected.

A case-by-case analysis of the procedural due process cases illustrates the difficulty of drawing hard and fast lines in defining what is a protected interest. Given the sheer number of cases in this area, the best way to resolve the *whether* question often is simply to search the cases for those most analogous to the facts and circumstances at hand. Consider the following lists:

	Due Process Required	No Due Process Required
1.	termination of non-probationary government employment[62]	termination of government employee's security clearance[63]
2.	termination of a state university professor in a system with actual or de facto tenure[64]	termination of a state university professor on a one year contract[65]
3.	automatic revocation of a driver's license because driver has no insurance[66]	automatic revocation of a driver's license after 3 suspensions in 10 years[67]

62. *Cleveland Board of Education v. Loudermill*, 470 U.S. 532 (1985); *Stone v. Federal Deposit Insurance Corp.*, 179 F.3d 1368 (Fed. Cir. 1999).

63. *Department of the Navy v. Egan*, 484 U.S. 518 (1988); *Cafeteria Workers v. McElroy*, 367 U.S. 886 (1961); *Gargiulo v. Department of Homeland Security*, 727 F.3d 1181 (Fed. Cir. 2013); *Kercade-Melendez v. Aponte-Roque*, 829 F.2d 255 (1st Cir. 1977).

64. *Perry v. Sindermann*, 408 U.S. 593 (1972); *Collins v. Marina-Martinez*, 894 F.2d 474 (1st Cir. 1990).

65. *Board of Regents of State Colleges v. Roth*, 408 U.S. 564 (1972); *Omosegbon v. Wells*, 335 F.3d 668 (7th Cir. 2003); *Batra v. Board of Regents of University of Nebraska*, 79 F.3d 717 (8th Cir. 1996).

66. *Bell v. Burson*, 402 U.S. 535 (1971). *But see Fowler v. Benson*, 924 F.3d 247 (6th Cir. 2019) (holding that indigent individuals do not have a protected due process interest in maintaining their driver's licenses when state law requires the licenses to be suspended due to unpaid court debt).

67. *Dixon v. Love*, 431 U.S. 105 (1977). *But see Scott v. Williams*, 924 F.2d 56 (4th Cir. 1991) (finding a protected due process interest against an automatic suspension of a driver's license upon release from a rehabilitation facility for drug addiction).

4. individualized tax assessment[68]	tax liability due to across-the-board increase in assessed property values[69]
5. posting of a drunkard list[70]	posting of a shoplifters list[71]

This is an incredible jumble; it is extremely difficult to make heads or tails out of these cases without subjecting each to close scrutiny, because the distinctions between the cases on either side of the list often seem minute.

Another way to evaluate the *whether* question is to recognize that the Court has recognized certain generic exceptions to any expectation that the Due Process Clause applies. For example:

a. *Waiver.* Anyone can voluntarily relinquish or waive a right to administrative procedures.[72] Attending a hearing only to object to the procedure provided may not constitute a waiver,[73] but otherwise failing or refusing to participate in administrative procedures may prevent a litigant from bringing a procedural due process claim challenging those procedures.[74]

b. *Emergency.* Whether emergencies serve as a justification for dispensing with due process is a more difficult question. Many due process cases addressing emergencies exist, including cases involving adulterated food,[75] jockeys suspected of drug use,[76] and unsafe coal mines.[77] However, a close analysis of each of the emergency cases suggests that what the Court is addressing in these cases is the *when* question—deciding that post-decisional due process alone is adequate—rather than carving out an exception to the *whether* question. In each instance, the private party got at least some due process after the government action.

---

68. *Londoner v. City of Denver*, 210 U.S. 373 (1908).

69. *Bi-Metallic Investment Co. v. State Board of Equalization*, 239 U.S. 441 (1915).

70. *Wisconsin v. Constantineau*, 400 U.S. 433 (1971). *But see Collins v. Hall*, 991 F.Supp. 1065 (N.D. Ind. 1997) (distinguishing and declining to apply *Constantineau* where a drunkard list was withdrawn with only damage to reputation and without other tangible consequences).

71. *Paul v. Davis*, 424 U.S. 693 (1976).

72. *See, e.g., National Independent Coal Operators' Ass'n v. Kleppe*, 423 U.S. 388 (1976). This case concerned the waiver of a statutory right to a formal hearing if a mine operator failed to request a hearing. An organization representing mine operators had argued that the Mine Safety and Health Review Administration was required to provide a hearing even in the absence of a request. The Supreme Court acknowledged that the statute gave the mine operators the right to a hearing, but only if they requested one. Although *Kleppe* is a statutory case rather than a constitutional one, the Court's assessment of the waiver concept could extend to constitutional procedural due process rights. *See also Reno v. Flores*, 507 U.S. 292 (1993) (concluding procedural due process satisfied in allowing detained undocumented juveniles to waive a hearing before an immigration judge).

73. *See, e.g., Baird v. Board of Education for Warren Community Unit School District No. 205*, 389 F.3d 685 (7th Cir. 2004); *Riggins v. Board of Regents of University of Nebraska*, 790 F.2d 707 (8th Cir. 1986).

74. *See, e.g., Krentz v. Robertson*, 228 F.3d 897 (8th Cir. 2000); *Fern v. Thorp Public School*, 532 F.2d 1120 (7th Cir. 1976).

75. A classic example is *North American Cold Storage Co. v. Chicago*, 211 U.S. 306 (1908), involving contaminated chickens. The Court said simply that the company's right to due process could not stand in the way of an emergency confiscation of the chickens to protect the public health.

76. *Barry v. Barchi*, 443 U.S. 55 (1979).

77. *Hodel v. Virgina Surface Mining Ass'n*, 452 U.S. 264 (1981).

Moreover, contrary cases abound. For example, in *Johnson v. City of Saginaw*,[78] the Sixth Circuit considered the case of a restaurant owner whose water service was cut off without a hearing as part of a police effort to prevent violence after a shooting outside her premises, allegedly as a result of a confrontation between attendees at a party hosted at the restaurant. Although the City defended its action as based on a need for "quick action" and provided post-deprivation procedures that resulted in water service being reestablished, the court found that "there was nothing preventing the City from exercising other lawful options to address the emergency" and concluded that circumstances did not excuse the lack of pre-deprivation due process.

In short, approach this potential exception from due process requirements cautiously.

c. *Legislative-type actions.* The Supreme Court has never overruled its decision in *Bi-Metallic*, so we must cope with Justice Holmes' notion that when an agency is exercising its legislative powers, the Due Process Clause does not apply.[79] Some states have taken *Bi-Metallic* to mean that there are virtually no procedural restrictions on agency rulemaking, including such things as notice and publication requirements. The federal government provides at least notice and opportunity to comment in writing for agency rulemaking under the Administrative Procedure Act, and many states do as well.

In *Atkins v. Parker*,[80] food stamp recipients objected to certain notice that they had received from a food stamp agency after Congress changed the percentage of a household's income that would be disregarded in computing food stamp eligibility from 20 to 18 percent. The recipients argued that they should have had advanced notice of the legislative change and precise notice of the change in the dollar amount of their individual benefits. The Supreme Court disagreed, commenting that "[t]he procedural component of the due process clause does not impose a constitutional limitation on the power of Congress to make substantive changes in the law of entitlement to public benefits." Courts have applied this principle to uphold federal and state legislation adjusting or eliminating a variety of government benefits, including state Medicaid benefits,[81] state employment benefits for veterans,[82] and federal welfare benefits.[83]

It is equally clear that agencies may simplify adjudicatory proceedings by dealing generically with certain issues or aspects of the proceeding through rulemaking. For example, in *United States v. Storer Broadcasting Co.*,[84] the Federal Communications Commission, by rule, limited the number of television stations any one person could own. Storer argued that such a generic limitation deprived it of its right to due process in an individual licensing proceeding. The Supreme Court disagreed, holding the FCC had power to deal with many issues by rulemaking and did not have to grant a hearing when an otherwise valid rule completely forecloses the application.

Similarly, in *Heckler v. Campbell*,[85] the agency had promulgated general medical-vocational guidelines to be used in social security disability hearings, rather than

78. 980 F.3d 497 (6th Cir. 2020).

79. *See, e.g.*, *Onyx Properties, LLC v. Board of County Commissioners*, 838 F.3d 1039 (10th Cir. 2016); *Grand River Enterprises Six Nations, Ltd. v. Pryor*, 425 F.3d 158 (2d Cir. 2005); *Hotel & Motel Ass'n of Oakland v. City of Oakland*, 344 F.3d 959 (9th Cir. 2003).

80. 472 U.S. 115 (1985).

81. *See, e.g.*, *Pashby v. Delia*, 709 F.3d 307 (4th Cir. 2013).

82. *See, e.g.*, *Hoffman v. City of Warwick*, 909 F.2d 608 (1st Cir. 1990).

83. *See, e.g.*, *Oliver v. Ledbetter*, 821 F.2d 1507 (11th Cir. 1987).

84. 351 U.S. 192 (1956).

85. 461 U.S. 458 (1983).

relying on the testimony of vocational experts case by case. The Supreme Court upheld the guidelines, even though they foreclosed a particular applicant from introducing certain evidence at a hearing. In *Heckler*, the Court stated: "It is true that the statutory scheme contemplates that disability hearings will be individualized determinations based on evidence adduced at a hearing. But this does not bar the Secretary from relying on rulemaking to resolve certain classes of issues."

Also, in *Lopez v. Davis*,[86] the Bureau of Prisons had adopted regulations implementing an early release program for prisoners who successfully completed a substance abuse program and, as part of those regulations, categorically excluded from eligibility prisoners convicted of felony firearms offenses. Although the challengers claimed that the agency should be allowed to rely only on case-by-case assessments of eligibility for early release, the Court disagreed and said that "[t]he Bureau is not required continually to revisit 'issues that may be established fairly and efficiently in a single rulemaking proceeding.'"

d. *No adjudicatory facts to be found.* The Supreme Court never has required an agency to engage in totally superfluous action. When a hearing would be meaningless, the Due Process Clauses do not require one. This is the message of *Dixon v. Love* and a few other cases.[87] The late Professor Kenneth Culp Davis liked to distinguish between what he calls *legislative facts* (concerning generic historical conditions, market conditions, the overall state of an industry, etc.) and *adjudicative facts* (illustrating the who, what, where, why, and when facts applicable to a particular individual). In doing so, he suggested that, when an agency is dealing with legislative facts, no individualized due process is required.[88]

e. *When a "privilege" is at stake.* Although distinguishing between rights and privileges has proven enormously challenging,[89] some people still like to argue that rights trigger due process while privileges are matters of grace for which the government need provide nothing. The Supreme Court has made abundantly clear that the right/privilege doctrine is no longer a useful concept in its deliberations. *Goldberg* signaled the Court's distaste for this distinction. *Board of Regents of State Colleges v. Roth* and subsequent cases have referred to it as a useless, "wooden" doctrine.[90] Some state courts may continue to consider mere privileges as an exception from due process requirements.

f. *Private action.* Recall that the Due Process Clause is not triggered unless the action in question is taken by the government. The Supreme Court has reiterated this point on several occasions. For example, the Court has held that termination of utility services by a private utility company carries no obligation to provide the customer with due process, even though termination of services by a municipally-owned utility requires

86. 531 U.S. 230 (2001).

87. *See supra* note 67; *see also, e.g., Weinberger v. Hynson, Westcott & Dunning, Inc.*, 412 U.S. 609 (1973).

88. *See, e.g.*, Kenneth Culp Davis, *The Requirement of Opportunity to Be Heard in the Administrative Process*, 51 YALE L.J. 1093 (1942); Kenneth Culp Davis, *Judicial Notice*, 55 COLUM. L. REV. 945 (1955); Kenneth Culp Davis, *The Requirement of a Trial-Type Hearing*, 70 HARV. L. REV. 193 (1956); Kenneth Culp Davis, *Facts in Lawmaking*, 80 COLUM. L. REV. 931 (1980).

89. For example, consider the discussion of the distinction between rights and privileges in the context of agency adjudicatory powers more generally in § 5.03.

90. *But see Kerry v. Din*, 576 U.S. 86 (2015) (Breyer, J., dissenting) (accusing Justice Scalia's opinion for the Court of attempting to resurrect the distinction between rights and privileges in the context of procedural due process).

some pre-termination due process.[91] Similarly, the Court declined to recognize a due process obligation on the part of private insurers who withheld payments for disputed medical treatment pending an independent review to evaluate whether the treatment in question was reasonable or necessary.[92] Although insurance companies are heavily regulated, so their procedures had at least the tacit approval of state officials, the Court found "mere approval or acquiescence of the State" insufficient to impose a due process obligation on private insurers.

These different approaches may all be useful in answering the primary question of whether a private person is due any process. But this is only the first question. Recall that once you resolve the *whether* question in the affirmative, you must deal with the questions of *when* and *how much.*

[C] Resolving a *When* Issue

Unlike the question of *whether* a private person has a protected liberty or property interest at stake, the *when* and *how much* issues are usually discussed simultaneously. They tend to blend with each other, and no one should expect to find a bright line between the two concepts. Nonetheless, they are separate inquiries, and both must be analyzed to complete the due process inquiry.

As noted earlier in this chapter, the Supreme Court on some occasions has held that

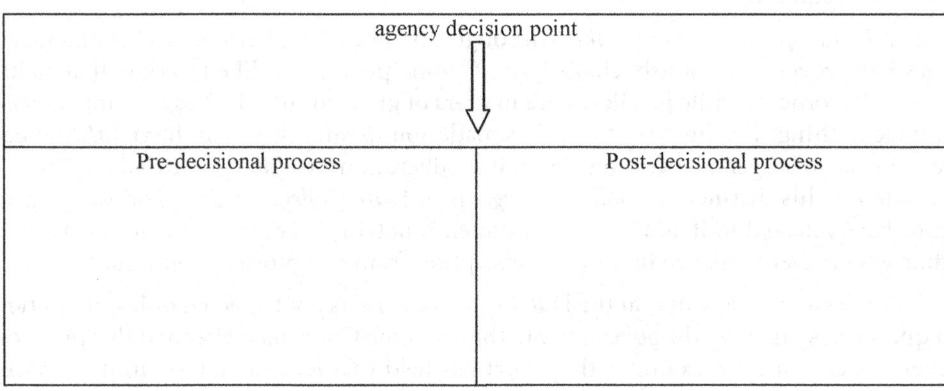

due process requires certain procedures to be provided *pre-deprivation* (*i.e.*, before a person may be initially deprived of a protected due process interest). In other cases, the Court has permitted some or all of the procedures required by due process to be given

91. *Compare Jackson v. Metropolitan Edison Co.*, 419 U.S. 345 (1974) (private utility—no due process), *with Memphis Light, Gas & Water Division v. Craft*, 436 U.S. 1 (1978) (public utility—due process required). A federal circuit court recently determined that the American Bar Association's law school accreditation function triggered a "common law" obligation to employ fair procedures in making accreditation decisions. In this instance, the ABA was given accreditation powers by the United States Department of Education. *Thomas M. Cooley Law School v. American Bar Ass'n*, 459 F.3d 705 (6th Cir. 2006).

92. *See American Manufacturers Mutual Insurance Co. v. Sullivan*, 526 U.S. 40 (1999).

post-deprivation (*i.e.*, after that initial deprivation). The timing of due process can best be visualized by keeping in mind the following chart:

Any fact pattern can be evaluated by placing procedures afforded by the agency before it acted on the left side of the chart and procedures afforded by the agency after it acted on the right side of the chart. Doing this facilitates a comparison of the facts at hand with the case law that analyzes when the process is due.

Pursuing this exercise does not completely resolve the issue. The Court has never been completely clear on the timing question. Nevertheless, again, a case-by-case analysis can go a long way toward solving a new problem. Courts tend to be skeptical of a total lack of due process prior to the agency decision. Note that the few cases in which the Court has permitted all of the procedures to be delayed until after the decision tend to involve emergencies or similar circumstances where requiring more procedure prior to the deprivation would interfere with the need to protect the physical wellbeing of someone or something, like *North American Cold Storage* (involving contaminated chickens) and *Barry v. Barchi* (concerning a racehorse trainer drugging a horse).

A common thread in these cases is an assessment of the impact of termination on the individual. For example, recall that in *Goldberg v. Kelly*, the Court emphasized that AFDC recipients relied on those benefits for basic subsistence and might starve while waiting for their benefits to be restored. (The Court used terms like "grievous loss" and "brutal need.") By contrast, in *Mathews v. Eldridge*, the Court concluded that the recipient of Social Security Disability Insurance benefits had other resources available to ensure that his basic needs were met. Consequently, a temporary deprivation pending a post-decisional hearing was of less concern. In *Wisconsin v. Constantineau*,[93] including a person's name on a list of drunkards would damage the person's reputation immediately once the list was posted. In *Morrissey v. Brewer*,[94] a post-deprivation evaluation of a decision to revoke parole would have to be conducted from a jail cell. No amount of post-deprivation procedure can cure some injuries.

If the harm of a temporary deprivation can be remedied effectively by a post-decisional hearing, however, the Court seems not to worry too much about what precedes the agency's action. Even in these cases, the Court will probably not tolerate a *total* absence of due process.

Another question should be addressed at this point in the timing analysis. Occasionally, two individuals seek a government license that, for technical reasons, is mutually exclusive, such as television broadcast licenses or hydroelectric projects. If an agency hears initially from only one claimant and decides in that person's favor, the second claimant is effectively excluded from the process. The Supreme Court addressed this issue in *Ashbacker Radio Corp. v. Federal Communications Commission*,[95] a case in which the FCC heard from one applicant, granted the license to that applicant and then granted a hearing to the second applicant only to tell the second applicant that he could not have the license because it had already been awarded. The Court determined that an agency must hear from both applicants simultaneously in any situation involving a "mutually exclusive" license in order to give both applicants a "meaningful hearing." A significant number of cases consider the circumstances in which the

93. 400 U.S. 433 (1971).

94. 408 U.S. 471 (1972).

95. 326 U.S. 327 (1945).

Ashbacker doctrine requiring consolidated consideration of mutually exclusive applications applies.[96] *Ashbacker* is not a constitutional decision. It was based on the Court's construction of the language of the Communications Act. Although the courts have considered and sometimes applied the doctrine in other contexts with similar statutes,[97] it is not at all clear that the present Supreme Court would have any interest in converting the *Ashbacker* doctrine into a constitutional requirement under the Due Process Clause. Nevertheless, evaluating *Ashbacker* doctrine considerations in conjunction with the when question may be worthwhile depending upon the subject matter of the matter at hand. Most agencies deal with the problem of multiple applications for an exclusive license by announcing that they will receive applications and by establishing a cut-off date for those applications. Applicants who file after the cut-off date will not be heard, but timely applications will be heard simultaneously and will be disposed of on a comparative merit basis.

[D] Resolving a *How Much* Issue

Whenever the *whether* question is resolved in the affirmative, some amount of procedure must be provided. Determining *how much* procedure or what kind of hearing must be given to an individual requires an analysis of all three *Mathews* factors. To begin this inquiry, you should establish some generic boundaries and then proceed to a case-by-case analysis.

Judge Henry Friendly suggested that the rock-bottom minimum due process would be notice plus some opportunity to comment.[98] For example, in *Goss v. Lopez*,[99] the Supreme Court merely required notice plus an opportunity for the student to comment orally prior to suspension. The Court mentioned several times that this procedure was intended to provide at least some due process for the student while minimally interfering with the work of the school administrators. *Goss* comprises one of the shortest lists of procedures ever mandated by the Court.

The most extensive collection of procedures ever required by the Court as a matter of constitutional due process is in *Goldberg v. Kelly*. These procedures are set out in § 5.03, *above*, and include among other things, a neutral decision-maker, the opportunity to present evidence orally and to confront adverse witnesses, an exclusive record, and a decision in writing. Generic terms for such procedures are *trial-type* or *evidentiary* hearing. The longstanding trend among due process cases suggests, however, that the Court has no interest in ever going beyond *Goldberg*. Indeed, the Court appears now mainly to be concerned with cutting back on *Goldberg* without actually overruling the case. The trend of the Court is away from elaborate, constitutionally-mandated procedures. Fewer, rather than more, procedures seem to be the preference.

Once the boundaries of due process have been established, problem solving is simply a matter of fitting the new fact pattern in between *Goldberg* and *Goss*, with the

96. *See, e.g., Bachow Communications, Inc. v. Federal Communications Comm'n*, 237 F.3d 683 (D.C. Cir. 2001); *Western Radio Service Co., Inc. v. Glickman*, 123 F.3d 1189 (9th Cir. 1997); *Rainbow Broadcasting Co. v. Federal Communications Comm'n*, 949 F.2d 405 (D.C. Cir. 1991).

97. *See, e.g., ANR Pipeline Co. v. Federal Energy Regulatory Comm'n*, 205 F.3d 403 (D.C. Cir. 2000); *Altamont Gas Transmission Co. v. Federal Energy Regulatory Comm'n*, 965 F.2d 1098 (D.C. Cir. 1992); *Central Freight Lines, Inc. v. United States*, 669 F.2d 1063 (5th Cir. 1982).

98. *See, e.g.*, Henry J. Friendly, *Some Kind of Hearing*, 123 U. Pa. L. Rev. 1267 (1973).

99. 419 U.S. 565 (1975).

understanding that, for most agency actions, the Court will likely not go as far as *Goldberg* in writing new procedures but probably will require something more than the minimal procedures of *Goss*. Moreover, the *when* question blends into this inquiry. One of the reasons the Court tolerated the more limited pre-deprivation procedures in *Mathews* was because a more extensive, trial-type hearing was granted after the deprivation in a setting where the benefits that had been denied could be restored retroactively.

Most of the preceding discussion has focused on the minimum due process procedures required by the Constitution. A legislature may grant far more procedures than the Court has ever required. For example, the trial-type, formal adjudication procedures written into the federal Administrative Procedure Act[100] include several more elements—for example, testimony under oath and verbatim transcript of oral testimony—than the Court required in *Goldberg*.[101] Even in the absence of a statute, an agency, as a matter of its own discretion, can give persons more procedural protections than the Constitution requires. Many federal agencies do so.

§ 5.07 Substantive Due Process in Administrative Law

Constitutional law courses teach us that government action must be not only procedurally correct, but also must satisfy certain notions of intrinsic fairness. We usually refer to this concept of intrinsic fairness as *substantive due process*. Traditionally, substantive due process has not had much of an impact on administrative law, mainly because there are other, subconstitutional doctrines available for the Supreme Court to use in resolving cases without turning every administrative law question into a constitutional concern. For example, the Administrative Procedure Act requires an agency to stay within the boundaries of its organic statute and to give reasons for its actions. An agency's interpretations of the statutes governing its actions and the reasons an agency offers in support of those actions, to a certain extent, are subject to examination by reviewing courts. This book describes those and many other principles that constrain substantive agency action.

While court-developed concepts such as stare decisis, res judicata, and estoppel have comparatively little utility in day-to-day agency practice, agencies are held to some degree of consistency in their policymaking, whether the policy is made by rule or through successive adjudications. Agencies are allowed to change their minds, and thus their policies, but not without justification or explanation. For example, in *Encino Motorcars, LLC v. Navarro*,[102] in considering a Department of Labor regulation that changed the agency's longtime policy of treating car dealership service advisors as "salesmen" exempt from the Fair Labor Standards Act's minimum wage and maximum hour requirements, the Court summarized the law as follows:

---

100. It should be noted that the full requirements of formal adjudication in §§ 554, 556, and 557 of the federal Administrative Procedure Act are applied in relatively few actual agency adjudications when compared to informal agency adjudications discussed in Chapter 9.

101. For example, compare the procedures required in *Goldberg* with those outlined in §§ 556–557 of the APA.

102. 579 U.S. 211 (2016).

> Agencies are free to change their existing policies as long as they provide a reasoned explanation for the change. When an agency changes its existing position, it need not always provide a more detailed justification than what would suffice for a new policy created on a blank slate. But the agency must at least display awareness that it is changing position and show that there are good reasons for the new policy. In explaining its changed position, an agency must also be cognizant that longstanding policies may have engendered serious reliance interests that must be taken into account. In such cases it is not that further justification is demanded by the mere fact of policy change; but that reasoned explanation is needed for disregarding facts and circumstances that underlay or were engendered by the prior policy. It follows that an unexplained inconsistency in agency policy is a reason for holding an interpretation to be an arbitrary and capricious change from agency practice. An arbitrary and capricious regulation of this sort is itself unlawful....[103]

This reasoning is based on statutory standards of review set out in the APA, however, rather than constitutional requirements. Even so, the consistency demanded of agencies by statute has its roots in the concept of fundamental fairness, which is a central ingredient of due process.

Laws that are unduly vague have sometimes been declared to violate due process and, thus, are void as a consequence of that vagueness. Courts generally have recognized that *void for vagueness* doctrine may apply to agency rulemaking.[104] In other words, an agency's regulations may be constitutionally defective if they are not written with sufficient precision and accuracy. Nevertheless, most agency regulations do not involve contexts where courts are particularly concerned about vagueness.[105] In *Village of Hoffman Estates v. Flipside, Hoffman Estates, Inc.*,[106] the Supreme Court cautioned against applying void for vagueness doctrine in pre-enforcement facial challenges to agency rules, observing particularly that "the regulated enterprise may have the ability to clarify the meaning of the regulation by its own inquiry, or by resort to an administrative process." Void for vagueness doctrine also is less strict in the contexts of economic regulation and rules leading to civil rather than criminal penalties,[107] although the Court has also held "that the most exacting vagueness standard should apply" in cases concerning the deportation of immigrants.[108] In short, practitioners should not rely heavily on void for vagueness doctrine as a basis for challenging agency regulations. They are better off mastering the principles and doctrines of agency rulemaking discussed in the next chapter so that they may be able to participate effectively in the rulemaking process.

---

103. *Id.* at 2125–26 (internal quotation marks, citations, and brackets omitted).

104. *See, e.g., Federal Communications Comm'n v. Fox Television Stations, Inc.*, 567 U.S. 239 (2012) (evaluating a void for vagueness challenge to an agency regulation); *Sweet Home Chapter of Communities for a Great Oregon v. Babbitt*, 1 F.3d 1 (D.C. Cir. 1993) (acknowledging that an agency regulation can in theory be void for vagueness).

105. *See, e.g., American Iron & Steel Institute v. Occupational Safety & Health Admin.*, 182 F.3d 1261 (11th Cir. 1999) (observing that void for vagueness doctrine is applied "outside of the First Amendment context only rarely").

106. 455 U.S. 489 (1982).

107. *See id.* at 498–99; *see also Kolender v. Lawson*, 461 U.S. 352 (1983).

108. *See, e.g., Sessions v. Dimaya*, 138 S. Ct. 1204 (2018); *Jordan v. DeGeorge*, 341 U.S. 223 (1951).

Chapter 6

Agency Decisionmaking: Choosing Between Rulemaking and Adjudication

§ 6.01 Introduction

This chapter begins an analysis of material that is central to most law school courses in administrative law and crucial to an administrative law practitioner. Agencies conduct their business by making decisions. Lawyers need to know a great deal about how agencies make those decisions. Sometimes the decisions have broad policy implications for all persons who are regulated by the agency. Sometimes the decisions affect only a single individual.

On the federal level, most agencies have a national jurisdiction and, by definition, have large numbers of persons and companies under their control. Consider, for example, the millions of people affected by the Social Security Administration and the Internal Revenue Service, or the thousands of firms regulated by the Securities and Exchange Commission. Because agencies are generally required to treat similarly situated persons in a consistent manner, even agency pronouncements that seem to affect only one person may in reality reflect broader agency policy. As a consequence, most lawyers who practice before any of the federal agencies pay close attention to virtually anything the agency says, irrespective of either the label that the pronouncement carries or the person to whom that pronouncement is addressed. In other words, in practice, you typically heed every nuance and pay attention to every raised eyebrow on the part of the agency. Even decisions nominally limited to a single fact pattern and a single individual may be very helpful in predicting future agency behavior. An appreciation of the subtleties of an agency's behavior is what separates the skilled agency practitioner from the merely mediocre.

This same principle—that you do not disregard anything an agency says—holds true for state administrative agencies, although one of the primary difficulties in some state administrative practices is obtaining information from the agency. Some states, for example, have no general requirement that agency rules or decisions be published. By contrast, federal agencies generate so much material that the information is nearly impossible to collate and index, much less to master in its entirety.

Most federal and state agencies use two procedural vehicles for announcing agency policy: rulemaking and adjudication. This chapter begins our general policymaking analysis by examining the limitations on an agency's decision whether to choose rulemaking or adjudication to announce major policy decisions. These days, most agencies use an amalgam of rules and adjudication for policymaking. In *Securities & Exchange*

Commission v. Chenery Corp.,[1] the Supreme Court made clear that, when Congress gives an agency both rulemaking and adjudication powers, the choice between those procedural vehicles belongs to the agency. The case law in this area is not terribly complicated, but it is sometimes difficult to understand without grasping some of the elementary distinctions between rulemaking and adjudication.

§ 6.02 Some Basic Distinctions Between Rulemaking and Adjudication

On the federal level, *rulemaking* and *adjudication* are defined by the Administrative Procedure Act (APA). Under § 551(5), rulemaking is the "agency process for formulating, amending, or repealing a rule"; § 551(4) in turn defines a rule as "the whole or part of an agency statement of general or particular applicability and future effect designed to implement, interpret, or prescribe law or policy or describing the organization, procedure, or practice requirements of an agency," followed by a list of specific types of agency actions, like ratemaking, that are included. This chapter will concentrate on the use of rulemaking or adjudication to make law or policy, rather than the use of these devices to prescribe agency procedures.

Two aspects of this definition are particularly notable. The first is its emphasis on rules and rulemaking under the APA being of either *general or particular applicability*. Supreme Court precedents under the Due Process Clause had previously distinguished rulemaking and adjudication by reference to whether the pronouncement in question affected a small or large number of people.[2] That distinction can be a challenging one to apply, however, as illustrated by the example of ratemaking that the APA expressly classifies as rulemaking: ratemaking focuses on the rates charged by a single service provider to its entire customer base. Accordingly, the APA definition instead emphasizes the *future effect* of rules and rulemaking, as contrasted with the orientation toward past actions or events inherent in adjudication.[3]

Basic rulemaking procedure on the federal level involves a process of public notice and opportunity for comment called, unsurprisingly, *notice-and-comment rulemaking*. An agency announces a proposed rule, receives and considers comments from interested persons on that rule, and promulgates a final rule, normally effective no sooner than thirty days after the final rule is announced.[4] While this process has been criticized for being insufficiently accessible to the general public, it has the advantage of permitting any interested person (virtually anyone who cares to write into the agency) to comment on a proposed rule, and requires the agency at least to consider the comments it receives. Also, the final rule, in most instances, must be published in the *Federal Register*, so everyone in the United States, at least in theory, receives notice of the rule at the time of its publication. A person regulated by an agency has at least thirty days to clean

1. 332 U.S. 194 (1947).
2. *Compare Londoner v. Denver*, 210 U.S. 373 (1908), *with Bi-Metallic Investment Co. v. State Board of Equalization*, 239 U.S. 441 (1915).
3. *See Bowen v. Georgetown University Hospital*, 488 U.S. 204, 216 (1988) (Scalia, J., concurring) (drawing attention to this aspect of the APA's definition of rule).
4. 5 U.S.C. § 553. For more on rulemaking procedure, see Chapter 7, § 7.02, *below*.

up his act before finding himself in violation of some new agency policy if that policy is announced in a rulemaking.

Under APA § 551(7), adjudication is the "agency process for the formulation of an order." For this purpose, APA § 551(6) defines an order residually, as: "the whole or part of a final disposition, whether affirmative, negative, injunctive, or declaratory in form, of an agency in a matter *other than* rulemaking but including licensing" (emphasis added). Given such a broad definition, it is difficult to itemize all of the possible routes for obtaining an agency order.

In the context of these definitions, it would seem that any agency action labeled an order would be the product of adjudication, and that a rule could only be the product of rulemaking. Neither assumption is quite accurate, however. Some agencies, such as the Federal Communications Commission, attach the "order" label to rulemaking actions. Lawyers must take care, therefore, not to put too much credence in the agency's label. Moreover, much like courts in a common law system, agencies adopt legal "rules"—as in policies intended to guide private behavior—through case-by-case adjudication.

Procedurally, adjudication can be either a *trial-type proceeding*, with oral evidentiary hearings (and thus, sometimes referred to alternatively as simply an evidentiary hearing),[5] or what many law professors choose to call *informal adjudication*.[6] As a policymaking tool, the Achilles' heel of adjudication is twofold: first, it frequently involves only a small number of participants; and second, orders are not normally required to be published in the *Federal Register* in the same fashion as proposed rules. Although many agencies regularly announce their orders, and although many proprietary information services publish almost everything an agency issues, agency adjudicative orders carry few formal publication requirements. Because agency orders arising from adjudication are typically written in the same form as judicial opinions, spotting a new agency policy when the announcement of that new policy is buried in an adjudicative order forces a lawyer to resort to common law techniques for analyzing cases. You have to worry about which language is *holding*, which is *dicta*, whether new adjudication *X* overrules old adjudication *Y* and the like. Worst of all, the grain of the new policy can get drowned in the chaff of a factual recitation. Highly experienced agency lawyers will spot these changes easily. Neophyte lawyers have a much harder time identifying new policy in the context of adjudication. Lay persons are almost never aware of the impact of an agency order unless it happens to affect them personally.

---

5. Discussed extensively in Chapter 8.

6. Informal adjudication is discussed in Chapter 9. It is not a term of art in administrative practice. Think of informal adjudication as an agency decision that results from a process that is *neither* a rulemaking nor a trial-type proceeding. For a discussion on how an emergence of informal, nonadversarial procedures in adjudications as well as the rise of rulemaking have contributed to the growth of administrative state, see Richard E. Levy & Sidney A. Shapiro, *Special Issue on the History of the Trial: Administrative Procedure and the Decline of the Trial*, 51 KAN. L. REV. 473 (2003).

§ 6.03 The Many Advantages of Rules and Rulemaking

Comparing rulemaking and adjudication, it is not difficult to understand why rulemaking is usually viewed as a superior device for announcing agency policy preferences. The legislative history of the federal Administrative Procedure Act (APA) demonstrates that the entire statute was molded around the distinctions between rulemaking and adjudication. The drafters of the APA expected that rulemaking would be the vehicle "primarily concerned with policy considerations."[7] An APA adjudication, by contrast, was viewed primarily as a device for applying agency policy preferences to individual cases. For many decades, legal scholars and judges have extolled the virtues of the rulemaking over adjudication for agency policymaking.[8] Commentators have identified several different advantages of rulemaking over adjudication as a source of generally applicable rules governing primary behavior.[9]

Rulemaking produces *higher quality rules* than adjudication. When an agency acts through adjudication, it has before it only the parties to the particular dispute and the evidence those parties submit. Traditionally, that evidence focuses primarily or exclusively on the specific, historical facts related to those parties and their disagreement. The fact pattern on which the agency bases its pronouncement may be widely generalizable, but it also may be entirely idiosyncratic. The agency has no way of knowing whether the fact pattern before it is applies broadly to many parties or only superficially to a few. Other common fact patterns may suggest that entirely different policy choices would be better.

The process of adopting a general rule of conduct should not be based primarily on resolution of a particularized set of historical facts. The primary purposes of legal rules are to guide future conduct and to provide reasonable clarity and objective criteria for application in adjudicatory proceedings. The process of adopting a general rule of

---

7. Attorney General's Manual on the Administrative Procedure Act 9 (1947). This distinction, of course, is not the only basis for drafting an administrative procedure act. The Florida APA chooses to base most of its central distinctions on whether an agency action substantially affects individuals irrespective of the label that is placed on the procedure at issue. If the action has a substantial effect on private persons, the agency may be forced to conduct more formal proceedings to reach its decision. Fla. Stat. § 120.54. *See also* William F. Fox, Jr. & Leonard Carlson, A *Comparison of the Federal and Florida Systems of Administrative Procedure*, 1980 Fla. B.J. 699. Although a new Model State Administrative Procedure Act (MSAPA) was adopted in 2010, the 1981 version of the MSAPA recommended that an agency "as soon as feasible and to the extent practicable, adopt rules to supersede principles of law or policy lawfully declared by the agency as the basis for its decisions in particular cases." The commentary in the 1981 version of the MSAPA was much more forceful than anything seen in the decisions of the United States Supreme Court: "Only by the enactment of a statutory provision [such as] recommended here, therefore, can agencies be forced to codify in rules principles of law or policy they may lawfully declare in decisions in particular cases.... Without such a provision they will be free, in many situations, to make their most controversial policies on a case-by-case basis in adjudications, and thereby avoid on a permanent basis rulemaking procedures and legislative and gubernatorial review." Commissioners' Comment to the MSAPA.

8. *See, e.g., National Petroleum Refiners Ass'n v. Federal Trade Comm'n*, 482 F.2d 672 (D.C. Cir. 1974); David L. Shapiro, *The Choice of Rulemaking and Adjudication in the Development of Administrative Policy*, 78 Harv. L. Rev. 921 (1965).

9. Kristin E. Hickman & Richard J. Pierce, Administrative Law Treatise § 4.08 (6th ed. 2018) (detailing nine advantages of rulemaking over adjudication).

conduct should be oriented toward considering evidence relevant to those goals, not based primarily on the resolution of a particularized set of historical facts, as in adjudication. An agency contemplating the announcement of a general rule of conduct should ask itself, "How can we direct the future conduct of regulated parties or beneficiaries in ways that will further our statutory mission?" An adjudication rarely yields meaningful, high-quality evidence relevant to such a question.

Rulemaking also enhances the *political accountability* of agency policymaking. Before an agency can make a binding policy decision through the rulemaking process, it must notify the public of its proposed rule and solicit comments from interested parties. This process of public notice and comment also enables interested parties who oppose or support the proposal to alert the president and members of Congress to the proposal's existence and to express their views of the agency's proposal to those politically-accountable officials. This, in turn, allows the president and Congress to communicate their own views concerning the proposed policy decision to the agency and, through the process of presidential and congressional oversight, to influence agency resolutions of policy disputes.[10] By contrast, when an agency announces a policy decision in the context of resolving a particular adjudicatory dispute, the public typically has no prior notice or opportunity to comment, and neither do the president and Congress, so those politically accountable officials have much less ability to influence the agency's policy decision.

Rulemaking often is more *efficient* than adjudication. Rulemaking eliminates the need to engage in expensive and time-consuming adjudicatory hearings to relitigate recurring issues. For example, imagine that an agency believes a particular practice that is widespread among industry participants violates statutory requirements. If the agency tries to prohibit the practice through adjudication, it must begin by bringing an enforcement action against a single party: engaging in discovery, marshalling evidence, subpoenaing witnesses, cross-examining adverse witnesses, and so on, all of which are time consuming and expensive. Even if the agency is pleased with the outcome of a particular adjudication, the policy that the agency announces in the course of resolving the adjudication (*i.e.*, that the particular practice in question violates statutory requirements) binds only the single party in question. Maybe other, similarly-situated industry participants will choose to comply rather than risk being pursued by the agency themselves. But those other parties may choose instead not to comply and to force the agency to go through the same process all over again. They may hope that the agency will change its mind regarding the policy in question with the passage of time, or maybe they think that they will be able to distinguish their circumstances adequately from the prior decision. When adjudications turn on facts that are generalizable across all industry participants, the adjudication process can be unnecessarily duplicative and extremely wasteful of resources.

If an agency proceeds instead with a rulemaking, it begins by issuing a notice of proposed rulemaking in which the agency describes its proposal and the reasons for it. The agency makes available to the public the studies and other evidence regarding the widespread industry practice on which its proposal is based. Interested members of the public have the opportunity to submit comments on the agency's proposal. The most valuable comments will go far beyond lawyers' arguments to include studies and other

10. *See* Matthew D. McCubbins, et al., *Administrative Procedures as Instruments of Political Control*, 3 J.L. ECON. & ORG. 243 (1987).

evidence both supporting and contradicting the agency's views, bolstering and criticizing the agency's studies, and proposing more effective or less intrusive alternatives to the agency's proposal. After satisfying the APA's procedural requirements, the agency will produce a rule that binds and likely will alter the behavior of all industry participants without further delay or consumption of agency resources. In theory, a particular industry participant may choose not to comply, and the agency will be forced to pursue enforcement of its rule through adjudication of that individual case. But that adjudication will be simplified substantially by the existence of the rule.

Other advantages of rulemaking over adjudication fall under the general heading of *fairness*. Rulemaking often is perceived simply as fairer than adjudication. Rulemaking gives parties affected by the rules adopted thereby with clearer advanced notice of which conduct the agency considers to be permissible or impermissible. Rulemaking reduces the incidence and magnitude of the sorts of inconsistencies that are often common among adjudications presided over by different agency adjudicators. And rulemaking allows all potentially-affected members of the public an opportunity to participate in the process of developing the policies that affect them.

Private parties should be able to discern what conduct is permitted or prohibited by an agency rule. Yet, as all lawyers discover early in law school, stating the legal "rule" announced in an adjudicatory opinion is often difficult, whether that opinion comes from an Article III court or an administrative agency. Even if an agency emphasizes the broad basis for a new policy in an adjudicatory opinion, the agency also must discuss the specific facts and arguments presented in the case. The reader can never be certain that the policy in question applies to every industry participant or instead is tied to one or more of the facts unique to the particular case. Even if the opinion is unusually clear in that respect, industry participants may have a hard time determining the precise conduct that satisfies the agency's new policy. Rulemaking can provide clearer answers to questions of this type, which enhances the fairness of the administrative process.

Rulemaking also enhances fairness by giving all potentially affected members of the public an opportunity to participate in the process of formulating the rules that affect them and with which they must comply. By contrast, when an agency announces a generally applicable rule in the process of adjudicating a particular dispute, only the parties to the dispute have a role in shaping the resulting legal "rule," even if that rule ultimately affects thousands of regulated parties or beneficiaries who had no opportunity to participate in the process of that rule's formulation. Even if the agency invites other interested parties to participate through the submission of amicus briefs, such opportunities for participation are likely to be narrower in scope than is common in rulemaking.

§ 6.04 The Supreme Court's View: The *Chenery* Saga

Despite the acknowledged superiority of rulemaking as a vehicle for agency policymaking, many agencies persist in preferring to make policy through adjudication. Both before and after the enactment of the Administrative Procedure Act (APA), the National

Labor Relations Board and the Federal Trade Commission, among others, assiduously avoided rulemaking and continued to announce their policy choices in adjudications.[11]

The Supreme Court has criticized agencies that persist in engaging in policymaking and announcing legal "rules" through adjudication rather than through rulemaking.[12] Nevertheless, in the landmark *Securities & Exchange Commission v. Chenery Corp.*,[13] the Supreme Court made clear that, when Congress gives an agency both rulemaking and adjudication powers, the choice between those procedural vehicles belongs to the agency. This holding remains a core principle of administrative law doctrine.

The *Chenery* case grew out of an exercise by the Securities and Exchange Commission (SEC) of its authority under an obscure New Deal statute, the Public Utility Holding Company Act of 1935 (PUHCA).[14] That statute gave the SEC the power to police mergers and acquisitions among large holding companies that had acquired many of the nation's private utilities after the First World War.

There are many ways to read the *Chenery* saga. For one thing, it is a good example of the lengths to which people will go to pursue an argument when there is a great deal of money at stake. It tells us a lot about protracted administrative litigation and those things that can happen to a case when the case itself outlives agency commissioners and Supreme Court justices. The full *Chenery* road map through the federal courts looks like this:

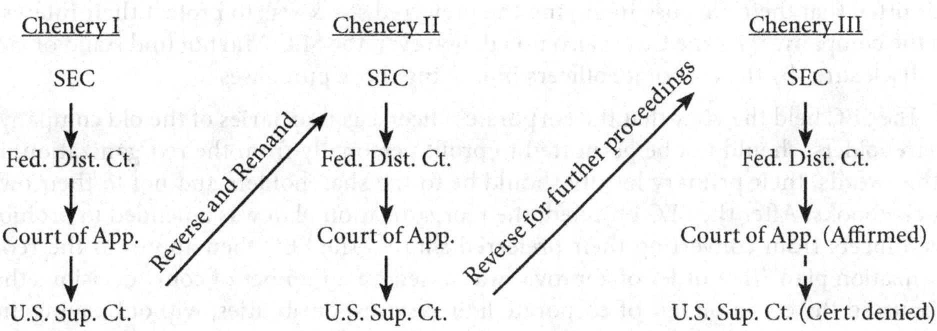

11. Two classic articles on this topic are Colin S. Diver, *Policymaking Paradigms in Administrative Law*, 95 Harv. L. Rev. 393 (1981), and David Shapiro, *The Choice of Rulemaking or Adjudication in the Development of Administrative Policy*, 78 Harv. L. Rev. 921 (1965). For a more recent discussion of some of the concerns related to agency choice in policymaking form, as well as potential means for addressing these concerns, see M. Elizabeth Magill, *Agency Choice of Policymaking Form*, 71 U. Chi. L. Rev. 1383, 1442–47 (2004).

12. *See, e.g., Allentown Mack Sales & Service, Inc. v. National Labor Relations Board*, 522 U.S. 359 (1998); *cf. Mohawk Industries, Inc. v. Carpenter*, 558 U.S. 100 (2009) (acknowledging the values of the rulemaking process over case-by-case adjudication in the context of expanding the collateral order doctrine).

13. *Securities & Exchange Comm'n v. Chenery Corp.*, 332 U.S. 194 (1947). This case is *Chenery II.* The case known as *Chenery I*, discussed below, is also a landmark and can be found at 318 U.S. 80 (1943). The third *Chenery* is not so well known but ended with a denial of certiorari by the Supreme Court at 340 U.S. 831 (1950).

14. Pub. L. No. 74-333, 49 Stat. 803 (1935), *repealed by* Public Utility Holding Company Act of 2005, Pub. L. No. 109-58, 119 Stat. 972 (2005).

This chapter deals mainly with what the Supreme Court had to say about rulemaking versus adjudication in *Chenery II*, but an analysis of that decision requires a quick explanation of *Chenery I*.

In *Chenery I*, an existing utility holding company, called the Federal Water Service Corporation, sought to comply with PUHCA by reorganizing into the Federal Water and Gas Corporation. The officers of the existing company filed an elaborate reorganization plan with the SEC, which PUHCA tasked with reviewing such transactions. After a lengthy analysis of the proposed reorganization plan, the SEC objected to a portion of the plan by which the officers of the original corporation, who had bought preferred stock of the original corporation (Federal Water Service) on the market, would see their preferred shares (along with the preferred shares of other shareholders) converted into the common stock of the reorganized holding company (Federal Water & Gas).

Many first-time readers of *Chenery I* become intimidated at this point because they are unfamiliar with corporate transactions. They are not alone, as many experienced lawyers are just as unfamiliar with the finer points of corporate transactions. Stated a little more colloquially, the corporate officers thought that the company was a good investment. Their plan would allow them to retain control over the company and its activities, and they expected to make a lot of money as a result of the reorganization. Obviously, a great deal of money was at stake here; the road map alone is evidence of that.[15] The Supreme Court acknowledged in *Chenery I* that the corporate officers were able to buy the shares in question on the market for a bargain price, and they "frankly admitted that their purpose in buying the preferred stock was to protect their interests in the company."[16] As the Court also noted, however, the SEC "did not find fraud or lack of disclosure" by the corporate officers in making those purchases.

The SEC held the view that the corporate officers, as fiduciaries of the old company's shareholders, should not be permitted to profit personally from the reorganization. In other words, their primary loyalty should be to the shareholders and not to their own pocketbooks. After the SEC objected, the reorganization plan was amended to prohibit the officers from converting their preferred shares. The SEC then approved the reorganization plan. That order of approval was based on a number of court decisions that discussed the common law of corporate fiduciary responsibilities, without paying any attention to the statute (PUHCA) or legislative history underlying the SEC's authority to review the transaction in the first instance. The disgruntled corporate officers then took the SEC to court.

In *Chenery I*, the Supreme Court held that the SEC's reliance on court decisions as the basis for its order was wrong because, in the Court's opinion, the SEC had misinterpreted the thrust of those decisions. The cases relied on by the SEC forbade officers to trade in stock of their own company only in instances in which there was fraud or mismanagement on the part of the officers; again, the SEC found no such fraud or mismanagement in this case. Before the Court, the SEC claimed that the terms of PUHCA

---

15. It is always helpful to try to look behind the printed appellate opinions in any casebook to try to determine exactly why people were in a dispute and why they were pursuing matters so strenuously before the agency and later in court. This behind-the-scenes analysis is really the only way anyone can understand how the lawyers in the case began thinking through the dispute. Litigation is incredibly costly these days and was similarly expensive in the 1940s. The *Chenery* cases were not *pro bono* or *in forma pauperis*, so it is clear that large amounts of money were involved. Knowing this may help explain a great deal about this case that is not found in any of the *Chenery* opinions.

16. *Chenery I*, 318 U.S. at 84–85.

itself supported its decision. But the Court held that "an administrative order cannot be upheld unless the grounds upon which the agency acted in exercising its powers were those upon which its action can be sustained." And, because the court decisions on which the SEC relied were inapposite, the Court invalidated the SEC's decision and remanded the case to the SEC for further proceedings. As something of an aside, the Court in its opinion noted that the SEC had never issued any *rules or regulations* under the statute that would forbid the corporate officers' purchase of the preferred shares.

On remand, the SEC arrived at the same conclusion as it had the first time. It disapproved the reorganization so long as the corporate officers were permitted to convert their preferred shares to common stock in the new company. But this time, the SEC did not rely on common law fiduciary principles to justify its decision. Instead, as the Court put it in *Chenery II*, the SEC "recast" its decision in terms of PUHCA's language, purpose and legislative history. The corporate officers attacked this new determination as well, arguing that Supreme Court's decision in *Chenery I* gave the SEC only two choices on remand:

1. The Commission could engage in rulemaking and issue a rule forbidding stock purchase by corporate officers in the midst of a reorganization. The rule would, of course, be purely prospective and thereby could not govern the reorganization of Federal Water Service; or
2. The SEC could simply accept the Supreme Court's reversal and approve the reorganization as proposed.

In *Chenery II*, the Supreme Court upheld the SEC's rejection of the corporate officers' reorganization plan. The Court disagreed with the corporate officers' argument that its decision in *Chenery I* mandated a rulemaking. Instead, the Court concluded that an agency "in its informed discretion" could choose either rulemaking or adjudication as the vehicle for announcing new policy. The Court concluded that the new, statutory rationale provided by the SEC was a valid basis for its adjudicative decision.

In other words, the SEC did not have to engage in rulemaking and adopt a rule on corporate officer stock purchases before it could enforce its new policy in an adjudication, *i.e.*, the *Chenery* case. The Court in *Chenery II* recognized that there might be times when the agency would have to confront problems that it simply had not foreseen and, thus, had not addressed through rulemaking. Alternatively, sometimes the problems an agency is called upon to address are too specialized to permit the drafting of good rules of general applicability. As the Court noted, "In those situations, the agency must retain power to deal with the problem on a case-to-case basis if the administrative process is to be effective." The Court also acknowledged that, given the nature of adjudication, "such action might have a retroactive effect," but observed that "[e]very case of first impression has a retroactive effect, whether the new principle is announced by a court or by an administrative agency" and that "such retroactivity must be balanced against the mischief of producing a result which is contrary to a statutory design or to legal or equitable principles."[17]

Justice Robert Jackson wrote a scathing dissent in *Chenery II* in which he accused the Court of reducing judicial review of administrative orders "to a mere feint" and putting "most administrative orders over and above the law."[18] He expressed particular concern

---

17. *Chenery II*, 332 U.S. at 203.
18. *Id.* at 210 (Jackson, J. dissenting).

that the stock purchases of the Chenery corporate officers were legal when they were made, and that the SEC had required them to forfeit their property without warning, without compensation, and without a clear basis in the law other than as an exercise of executive discretion. Quoting Justice Benjamin Cardozo, Jackson said that "Law as a guide to conduct is reduced to mere futility if it is unknown and unknowable."[19] Concluding, Jackson maintained that the Court's *Chenery II* decision was "an ominous one to those who believe that men should be governed by laws that they may ascertain and abide by, and which will guide the action of those in authority as well as those who are subject to authority."[20] He maintained further that the only way to explain the difference in result between *Chenery I* and *Chenery II* was "a fundamental change in prevailing philosophy," presumably alluding to the intervening change in Supreme Court personnel.[21]

Jackson's concerns are understandable when one considers his background. He was known, among other things, for his staunch defense of procedural due process as a check against government overreach. In the midst of the *Chenery* saga, Jackson helped draft the charter that formed the legal basis for the Nuremberg Trials and served as the United States Chief Prosecutor in prosecuting Nazi war criminals.[22] Those experiences undoubtedly heightened his sensibilities regarding the importance of the rule of law and the dangerous potential of arbitrary exercises of governmental power—both themes that his dissent touched upon.

At the same time, legitimate explanations exist for the actions of both the SEC and the Supreme Court in the *Chenery II* decision. The Supreme Court was not that many years removed from the threat of President Franklin Delano Roosevelt's plan to pack the Court in his favor by adding several new justices. The SEC was one of the principal New Deal agencies, and PUHCA (the statute governing the *Chenery* dispute) was viewed at the time as an important tool for breaking up some unusually large and very powerful energy conglomerates, over which the states were exercising no meaningful control. Remember that the *Chenery* controversy started in the early 1940s when the power of the SEC was just being established, even though the case took well over ten years to resolve completely. As an agency, the SEC was finding its own footing, and may not yet have had a good enough sense of how best to effectuate its policy preferences.

Finally, the APA itself was new. It did not exist at the time the SEC acted, it went into effect only one year prior to the *Chenery II* decision, and it had not yet been fully explicated by the courts. Older agencies, such as the Federal Trade Commission, had rarely promulgated rules and still functioned effectively. While the *legislative history* of the APA strongly suggests using rulemaking to make policy, the statute itself provides procedures for both rulemaking and adjudication, and clearly contemplates that agencies might use either or both without articulating a preference between them in the language of the statute itself.

---

19. *Id.* at 217.
20. *Id.*
21. Three *Chenery I* justices, namely Justices Harlan Stone, Owen Roberts, and James Byrnes, had departed and were replaced by Justices Fred Vinson, Harold Burton, and Wiley Rutledge.
22. For an interesting perspective on Justice Jackson's Nuremberg experience, see NOAH FELDMAN, SCORPIONS: THE BATTLES AND TRIUMPHS OF FDR'S GREAT JUSTICES (2010).

§ 6.05 *Chenery II* and Retroactivity

Although controversial for reasons explained in Justice Jackson's dissent, the principle announced in the Supreme Court's *Chenery II* decision—that agencies given the power to act through both rulemaking and adjudication are allowed to choose for themselves between those procedures without interference by the courts—has proven quite durable and remains black letter administrative law today. The SEC has grown to embrace rulemaking, although it also sometimes acts and makes policy through adjudication as well. Most agencies follow the same pattern. A few notable holdouts exist, however, and they continue to raise questions regarding the fairness of adjudicative policymaking.

The National Labor Relations Board (NLRB), even to this day, prefers to make policy through adjudication rather than through rulemaking. On occasion, the NLRB has twisted itself into a pretzel with its steadfast refusal to engage in rulemaking. Its practices, however, have offered the Supreme Court the opportunity to further explore the implications of *Chenery II* for the choice between rulemaking and adjudication as competing mechanisms for agency policymaking. An old but often cited case, *NLRB v. Wyman-Gordon Co.*,[23] remains illustrative.

The difficulty presented by the *Wyman-Gordon* controversy become apparent when one considers some basic concepts of judicial decision making. Recall that when a *court* decides a case, it may frame its disposition of the case in three ways:

1. Make the decision fully retroactive;
2. Make the decision applicable to the parties to the case and to future persons similarly situated through the doctrine of stare decisis; or
3. Make the decision prospective only (*i.e.*, applicable to persons in the future, but not applicable to the parties who brought the lawsuit).

The first alternative really is not an option for an agency. Even when *courts* render decisions, they rarely make their decisions fully retroactive. The Supreme Court occasionally makes a decision fully retroactive based upon the notion that the Court does not "make" constitutional rights but merely "discovers" rights in the Constitution itself. For example, the Court made its classic right to counsel case, *Gideon v. Wainwright*,[24] retroactive. But *Gideon* was unusual in this regard. Fully retroactive *agency* action is even more rare, if it exists at all. In *Bowen v. Georgetown University Hospital*,[25] the Court explicitly rejected outright retroactivity for agency rulemaking, absent express authorization from Congress.

The second of the above alternatives is classic common law judicial method. But some people are troubled by this method when a court decides to change one of its decisional principles. If a *court* uses the common law method for announcing the new principle and reversing the old one, one of the parties before the court will be penalized by her good faith reliance on the old principle. In all likelihood, the loser in the case will have had no advance warning that the reviewing court was going to change its mind. The legal instability and inequity of such outcomes are why the courts follow a doctrine

23. 394 U.S. 759 (1969).
24. 372 U.S. 335 (1963).
25. 488 U.S. 204 (1988) (discussed at greater length in Chapter 7, § 7.09). *Bowen* contained a strong general pronouncement: "Retroactivity is not favored in the law." *Id.* at 208.

of stare decisis in the first instance. The Supreme Court in *Chenery II* was not overly troubled by such an outcome in the *agency* context, but such a result may not seem entirely fair to onlookers.[26]

Which leads us to the third alternative: announcing the new principle as purely prospective—*i.e.*, not governing the parties before it, but controlling on all cases in the future. At one time, the Supreme Court followed this approach on occasion respecting its own decisions, but cases in the 1990s effectively ended that practice.[27] The NLRB continues to follow this approach, however, with the Supreme Court's approval.

Such was the choice confronting the NLRB in *Excelsior Underwear, Inc.*,[28] and leading in turn to the *Wyman-Gordon* case. In *Excelsior*, the NLRB decided that it would be a good idea for employers to provide to union organizers a list of the names and addresses of employees who are eligible to vote in what is frequently referred to as a unit election. These elections, with votes cast by eligible employees, determine whether the employees want a union and which union they prefer to represent them. Because the NLRB at that time did not make substantive rules, it announced a brand new principle in the *Excelsior* adjudication: in the future, a failure to furnish a list of employees would be deemed an unfair labor practice leading to sanctions against the employer. However, because the NLRB sympathized with the Excelsior Company, which obviously had relied on the absence of any such principle when it engaged in the collective bargaining at issue, the NLRB made the disclosure of the list of employees mandatory only for *future* bargaining unit elections and not to the party to the adjudication before it. Even though the employee-disclosure requirement has become known to labor lawyers as the *Excelsior* list, the new requirement was never imposed on the Excelsior Company itself.

When the Wyman-Gordon Corporation became involved in a union election, the company refused to give over the list. Brought before the NLRB in an enforcement action and charged with an unfair labor practice, the company argued that the *Excelsior* list requirement was not enforceable as agency policy. The requirement could not be binding on it as an adjudicative order because it had not been made applicable to the Excelsior Company in the *Excelsior* adjudication, and thus had no stare decisis effect. As an agency rule with future effect, however, the requirement of an employee list had not been properly promulgated because the NLRB had not utilized the proper rulemaking procedures in adopting it. A fractured Supreme Court upheld the NLRB's action, but with a majority of the justices disapproving of how the NLRB had accomplished its ends. Justices Douglas

26. One author argues that the fairness concern is the only one justifying a judicial review of the agency's rulemaking/adjudication. *See* William D. Araiza, *Agency Adjudication, the Importance of Facts, and the Limitations of Labels*, 57 WASH. & LEE L. REV. 351 (2000); *see also* Jason Nichols, *"Sorry! What the Regulation Really Means Is . . .": Administrative Agencies' Ability to Alter an Existing Regulatory Landscape Through Reinterpretation of Rules*, 8 TEX. L. REV. 951 (2002). Another author offers several potential approaches for addressing concerns related to *Chenery II*, which may prove especially relevant given the Supreme Court's recent decision in *Kisor v. Wilkie*, 139 S. Ct. 2400 (2019). *See* Aaron L. Nielson, *Beyond Seminole Rock*, 105 GEO. L.J. 943 (2017). For additional, extensive commentary on *Chenery II*, see Russell L. Weaver & Linda D. Jellum, *Chenery II and the Development of Federal Administrative Law*, 58 ADMIN. L. REV. 815 (2006). For discussion of the potential upsides of retroactive decisions in the larger context of ex post lawmaking, see Donald T. Hornstein, *Resiliency, Adaptation, and the Upsides of Ex Post Lawmaking*, 89 N.C. L. REV. 1549 (2011).

27. *See, e.g., Reynoldsville Casket Co. v. Hyde*, 514 U.S. 749 (1995); *Harper v. Virginia Department of Taxation*, 509 U.S. 86 (1993). Arguably, however, the courts have adopted other mechanisms for mitigating the negative effects of adjudicative retroactivity. *See* Elizabeth Earle Beske, *Backdoor Balancing and the Consequences of Legal Change*, 94 WASH. L. REV. 645 (2019).

28. 156 N.L.R.B. 1236 (1966).

and Harlan simply dissented, contending that the NLRB—and the Court's support for the Board's position—had "trivialized" the presumption in the APA favoring rules as the appropriate vehicle for announcing policy shifts. The plurality opinion, representing four justices, concluded that the NLRB had not abused its broad *Chenery* discretion, but was also exceptionally critical of what the NLRB had done. Justice Fortas, who announced the Court's decision, wrote with unusual force: "The rule-making provisions of [the APA] which the Board would avoid were designed to assure fairness and mature consideration of rules of general application. There is no warrant in law for the Board to replace the statutory scheme with a rulemaking procedure of its own invention." Clearly, these four justices, too, would have overturned the NLRB's action but for the fact that, in this particular instance, the NLRB had issued a specific order to Wyman-Gordon to furnish the list of employees. That order had to be obeyed by the company, even if the policy announced in the *Excelsior* case had no effect. The remaining three justices concurred in the result of the decision but declined Fortas's harsh criticism of the NLRB.

Wyman-Gordan might have been perceived as a nudge by the Supreme Court toward requiring agencies to utilize rulemaking and denying them a choice of procedures in some instances. Moreover, a few years later, in *Morton v. Ruiz*,[29] the Supreme Court again was sharply critical of an agency's use of adjudication. In that case, the Court rejected a Bureau of Indian Affairs (BIA) adjudicative order adopting a new policy regarding the eligibility of Native Americans for general assistance benefits. Documenting numerous examples of inconsistencies in the BIA's explanation and application of its policy, the Court strongly suggested that the BIA utilize rulemaking to adopt clearer eligibility requirements, further calling into question the ongoing vitality of *Chenery II*'s holding in favor of agency procedural choice.

Suggestions that the Court might be whittling away at *Chenery II* ended quickly thereafter with the Supreme Court's decision in *NLRB v. Bell Aerospace Co.*[30] Here again, as in *Wyman-Gordon*, the NLRB utilized an adjudicatory hearing to announce a broader rule of general applicability, this time concluding that even workers properly classified as "managerial employees" are nevertheless covered by the National Labor Relations Act. Relying particularly on the plurality and dissenting opinions in *Wyman-Gordon*, the court of appeals had held that, although the NLRB possessed the authority to interpret the statute to include managerial employees, the agency could only adopt such a rule through rulemaking, not through adjudication. The Supreme Court unanimously rejected that conclusion. Although the Court acknowledged that rulemaking might yield a better result, it insisted that "[t]he views expressed in *Chenery II* and *Wyman-Gordon* make plain that the Board is not precluded from announcing new principles in an adjudicative proceeding and that the choice between rulemaking and adjudication lies in the first instance within the Board's discretion."[31]

Notwithstanding *Chenery II*, an agency's ability to act retroactively through adjudication is not unlimited. The Supreme Court in *Chenery II* indicated that retroactive application of rules adopted through adjudication might be impermissible if "the ill effect of the retroactive application of a new standard" outweighed statutory interests. In *Retail, Wholesale & Department Store Union v. NLRB*,[32] the D.C. Circuit attempted to clarify *Chenery II* and articulate some parameters limiting an agency's discretion to

29. 415 U.S. 199 (1974).
30. 416 U.S. 267 (1974).
31. *Id.* at 294–95.
32. 466 F.2d 380 (D.C. Cir. 1972).

impose rules retroactively through adjudication. In particular, the D.C. Circuit identified several factors that courts should consider in balancing the inequities of retroactive application against the statutory interests advanced thereby:

1. whether the particular case is one of first impression,
2. whether the new rule represents an abrupt departure from well established practice or merely attempts to fill a void in an unsettled area of law,
3. the extent to which the party against whom the rule is applied relied on the former rule,
4. the degree of the burden which a retroactive order imposes on a party, and
5. the statutory interest in applying a new rule despite the reliance of a party on the old standard.[33]

Where these factors weigh against retroactivity, the alternative is that of the NLRB in *Wyman-Gordon* and *Bell Aerospace*: make the decision prospective only, *i.e.*, applicable to persons in the future but not applicable to the parties who brought the lawsuit. Some other circuits have adopted the *Retail, Wholesale* factors,[34] while others have pursued alternative standards for evaluating when agency policymaking through adjudication should be applied prospectively only.[35] Most recently, these factors have played a prominent role in judicial evaluation of adjudicatory decisions by the Board of Immigration Appeals.[36]

§ 6.06 Solving a Rulemaking Versus Adjudication Problem

Rulemaking versus adjudication problems come up more on law school and bar examinations than in practice. Most major federal agencies make their most consequential policy choices through rulemaking rather than adjudication. Practicing lawyers know that the National Labor Relations Board (NLRB) is going to continue to make the vast bulk of its policy by adjudication unless Congress changes the agency's mind.

Thus, looking at the issue from the perspective of the agency lawyer is a good place to start. Assume that you are a Federal Trade Commission (FTC) lawyer who is charged with developing some consumer protection principles for American supermarkets. We know that the FTC has the authority both to adjudicate and to make substantive rules. Thus, the agency may clearly proceed by rule or by order.

The FTC has the power to sanction supermarkets for engaging in what the enabling act calls unfair or deceptive trade practices. If the Commission chooses adjudication, it will bring an agency enforcement proceeding against a supermarket by charging that store with an unfair trade practice (*i.e.*, engaging in the retail practices that the FTC wants to stop). If the enforcement staff prevails at the agency level and in court, it will

33. *Id.* at 390.

34. *See, e.g., Montgomery Ward & Co., Inc. v. Federal Trade Comm'n*, 691 F.2d 1322 (9th Cir. 1982); *Laborers' International Union of North America, AFL-CIO v. Foster Wheeler Corp.*, 26 F.3d 375 (1982); *National Labor Relations Board v. Wayne Transportation*, 776 F.2d 745 (7th Cir. 1985).

35. *See, e.g., Microcomputer Technology Institute v. Riley*, 139 F.3d 1044 (5th Cir. 1998).

36. *See, e.g., Garfias-Rodriguez v. Holder*, 702 F.3d 504 (9th Cir. 2012); *Velasquez-Garcia v. Holder*, 760 F.3d 571 (7th Cir. 2014).

walk away with one reported judicial-style decision, presumably containing a description of what the store did that the FTC doesn't like. In the context of this action, it might be possible to persuade the FTC and the courts to penalize the store in some fashion during the adjudication as having engaged in an unfair/deceptive trade practice.

After a few such cases, there will be a body of FTC case law in place that makes the FTC's point very clearly. Because American businesses pay close attention to regulatory agencies, you can be assured that by the time the third or fourth enforcement action is completed, virtually all supermarkets in the United States will have gotten the message. People in business become very quickly aware of agency sanctions against other companies.

Notice, however, that the agency's actions have essentially trapped a few companies who were doing things that they did not realize were unfair trade practices until the FTC and the courts spoke. By contrast, trying to be gentle with the few stores who get caught in the agency's net can put the agency in the same dilemma as that in which the NLRB found itself in the *Excelsior* case discussed above in this chapter. If they forgive the targeted stores, they might have difficulty enforcing the new policy against other stores. At a minimum, penalizing some stores and not others for the same practices may strike many observers as unfair.

Would it make sense to try to write a rule? The bottom line on this issue is clearly established: Whether an agency adjudicates or engages in rulemaking, its choice of procedure is almost certain to be upheld by the courts in light of *Chenery II*.

Accordingly, the answer comes down to the practicalities of the situation. Are supermarkets throughout the United States too different from each other for an agency to write a meaningful rule? Obviously, it depends on what sort of practice the agency is trying to stop; but everyone who has shopped for groceries will acknowledge that supermarkets across the country are more alike than they are different. Supermarkets all have common traffic patterns, use shopping carts, have checkout stands and the like. A general rule might be an effective way to control the abusive practice.

Second, what will happen to the offending supermarkets? If the agency intends to declare the offending marketing practices unfair or deceptive trade practices and to seek fines or other sanctions for their violation, a rulemaking will be perceived as fairer, if for no other reason than that it gives supermarkets at least thirty days to mend their ways before they are placed in jeopardy of a penalty.

In the long run, the agency's choice may not matter, because it can take a great deal of comfort from the fact that no matter what choice is made, it is unlikely to be turned around on judicial review. Still, agency lawyers should recall the admonition of the Supreme Court in *NLRB v. Wyman-Gordon*, also discussed above in this chapter: APA rulemaking is designed to assure fairness and mature consideration of rules of general application. To the extent that the agency accepts this admonition, it really ought to consider proceeding by rule as part of its obligation to the public. Although the context may be somewhat different, future agency lawyers should remember the suggestion to prosecutors in the old Model Code of Professional Responsibility: "The responsibility of a public prosecutor differs from that of the usual advocate; his duty is *to seek justice*, not merely to convict."[37]

---

37. Model Code of Prof'l Responsibility EC 7-13 (1980). The current Model Rules of Professional Conduct state it a little differently but make much the same point: "A prosecutor has the responsibility of a minister of justice and not simply that of an advocate." Model Rules of Prof'l Conduct R. 3.8 cmt. (2021).

Chapter 7

Rulemaking

§ 7.01 Introduction

The preeminent administrative law scholar of the twentieth century, Kenneth Culp Davis, called agency rulemaking "one of the greatest inventions of modern government."[1] Not everyone feels that way. Justice Antonin Scalia, also a well-known professor of administrative law before joining the judiciary, took a less enthusiastic view, suggesting in 1981 that "the bloom [was] off the rulemaking rose."[2] Many private citizens and most practicing lawyers view agency rulemaking more in terms of whose ox is being gored by the agency. Environmental groups gloat when the EPA tightens air pollution control standards; the regulated industries cringe. Domestic oil producers are happy when the executive branch places import restrictions on foreign petroleum; motorists who may be faced with higher gasoline prices are far less enthusiastic.

Few people get terribly excited about the rulemaking procedure. But as we will see, it is difficult to challenge the substance of an agency rule successfully in court because the Supreme Court has admonished federal courts to defer to an agency's policymaking judgments. Lawyers know that there are many bases for challenging an agency rule. You can argue that the rule's substantive provisions are contrary to the meaning of the statute. You can also claim that the reasons the agency offers for its discretionary choices show a lack of reasoned decisionmaking.[3] Or you can argue that the agency failed to follow the required rulemaking procedures properly. Nevertheless, remember one of the cardinal rules of agency practice: if you don't like what an agency is proposing to do, the place to win your fight is at the agency. You are much less likely to get any great satisfaction out of a reviewing court.

1. Kenneth Culp Davis, Cases, Text and Problems on Administrative Law 241 (6th ed. 1977). A good survey of rulemaking scholarship over the past several decades includes the following: Wendy Wagner, William West, Thomas McGarity & Lisa Peters, *Dynamic Rulemaking*, 92 N.Y.U. L. Rev. 183 (2017); Aaron Nielson, *In Defense of Formal Rulemaking*, 75 Ohio St. L.J. 237 (2014); Cary Coglianese, Heather Kilmartin & Evan Mendelson, *Transparency and Public Participation in the Federal Rulemaking Process: Recommendations for the New Administration*, 77 Geo. Wash. L. Rev. 924 (2009); Richard J. Pierce, Jr., *Rulemaking and the Administrative Procedure Act*, 32 Tulsa L.J. 185 (1996); Cornelius M. Kerwin, Rulemaking (1994); E. Donald Elliott, *Re-inventing Rulemaking*, 41 Duke L.J. 1490 (1992); Colin S. Diver, *Policymaking Paradigms in Administrative Law*, 95 Harv. L. Rev. 393 (1981); James V. DeLong, *Informal Rulemaking and the Integration of Law and Policy*, 65 Va. L. Rev. 257 (1979); William F. Pedersen, *Formal Records and Informal Rulemaking*, 85 Yale L.J. 38 (1975).

2. Antonin Scalia, *Making Law Without Making Rules*, Reg. Mag. 25 (July/Aug. 1981).

3. Occasionally, an agency regulation deemed by a court to be lacking in its demonstration of reasoned decisionmaking will be remanded to the agency for further explanation without being vacated. For just one perspective on this remedy, see Daniel B. Rodriguez, *Of Gift Horses and Great Expectations: Remand Without Vacatur in Administrative Law*, 36 Ariz. St. L.J. 599 (2004).

This chapter examines the procedures for making agency rules and the legal developments that brought us to that status quo. It also describes other developments that affect agency rulemaking. The chapter concludes with a few basic techniques for writing agency rules. Because any statement of agency rulemaking is not complete without some discussion of how the courts react to rules, statements on judicial review of agency rulemaking are interspersed throughout the chapter. Readers seeking a thorough understanding of judicial review of agency action should also read Chapters 10 through 13.

§ 7.02 The Impact of *Florida East Coast Railway* and *Vermont Yankee* on Rulemaking Procedure

[A] Sources of Rulemaking Procedure

Three sources of authority prescribe the procedures for agency rulemaking: Congress, typically through the Administrative Procedure Act (APA), but occasionally through an agency's organic statute; the agency itself, through its discretion to establish its own internal procedural requirements, although those requirements must comply with the governing statute; and the courts, through cases interpreting statutory requirements. Congress's power is virtually unfettered in this regard. Remember the cardinal rule of administrative law that agencies are creatures of Congress and may function only insofar as Congress gives them authority to do so. Once established, however, agencies typically enjoy a great deal of discretion, particularly in establishing the details of their decisionmaking procedures. Agencies frequently give affected persons more process than either the APA or their organic statutes require.

A trickier question is the extent to which courts may impose additional rulemaking procedures on the agency apart from whatever is required by the APA, the relevant organic statute, and the agency's own rules. Make no mistake about this point: the general rule is that courts cannot require agencies to follow rulemaking procedures beyond those imposed by statute. On the other hand, courts play a substantial role in interpreting the statutes that govern agency rulemaking procedures—especially when, like the APA, those statutes are written in such a way as to leave them open to interpretation.

[B] *Florida East Coast Railway* and the Demise of Formal Rulemaking

Most contemporary rulemaking follows the procedures imposed by § 553 of the APA. These are not the only rulemaking procedures prescribed in the APA, however. At the end of § 553(c), the APA provides that "[w]hen rules are required by statute to be made on the record after opportunity for an agency hearing, sections 556 and 557 of this title apply instead of this subsection." APA §§ 556 and 557, in turn, provide a set of procedures that an agency must use in what is commonly known as *formal rulemaking*. These procedures are similar to those of § 553 in many ways, but they include one very significant difference: an agency engaged in formal rulemaking must conduct an oral evidentiary hearing, including the taking of testimony under oath and the cross-examination of witnesses—procedures closely analogous to a judicial trial (or perhaps a congressional committee hearing). In fact, APA §§ 556 and 557 also provide the procedures governing formal adjudication by agencies, discussed in Chapter 8.

When Congress initially adopted the APA, adjudication rather than rulemaking was the norm for agency policymaking. Beginning in the 1960s, however, facing rising caseloads and pressure to develop more definite standards to guide regulated party behavior, federal agencies began to embrace rulemaking, first gradually and then with enthusiasm. Also in the 1960s and 1970s, Congress adopted legislation creating new agencies, like the Environmental Protection Agency and the National Highway Traffic Safety Administration, and expanding the powers of others, like the Food and Drug Administration. In many instances, Congress required these agencies to utilize rulemaking. Most agencies believed they were required to use formal rulemaking, yet the hearing procedures for formal rulemaking contained in APA §§ 556 and 557 were notoriously time consuming and expensive. In one famous example, the Food and Drug Administration spent twelve years in an unsuccessful attempt to use formal rulemaking to adopt a rule to determine whether peanut butter must contain 87.5% or 90% peanut content.

The Supreme Court dramatically altered that procedural landscape in *United States v. Florida East Coast Railway.*[4] The case concerned the now-abolished Interstate Commerce Commission (ICC) and its attempt to deal with a chronic, nationwide shortage of railroad freight cars that was hurting the national economy. A preliminary investigation by the ICC revealed that one of the reasons for the shortage was that many railroads were hoarding freight cars, in part because it was simply cheaper to pay rent on the borrowed cars than to either buy new cars or risk not having cars available when needed. To make a very long story short, the ICC promulgated rules requiring railroads that kept freight cars belonging to other companies to pay an incentive charge for the use of the cars. The ICC believed that this incentive charge would persuade railroads to return freight cars not in use to their proper owners as quickly as possible and also to purchase new cars. The affected companies challenged the rules in court on both substantive and procedural grounds, but the Supreme Court took up only the procedural issue.

The relevant portion of the Interstate Commerce Act stated that the ICC could promulgate rules "after hearing."[5] A number of railroads, including Florida East Coast, argued that this statutory language required the ICC to adopt rules only after a full-blown trial-type proceeding conducted under the terms of §§ 556 and 557 of the APA, a procedure often referred to as *formal rulemaking.* And, in fact, the ICC interpreted the statute that way at first, conducting two formal, oral evidentiary hearings before issuing a third notice of proposed rulemaking and declining to hold a third hearing.[6] Before the Court, however, the government argued that it was not required to follow the procedures of APA §§ 556 and 557.

4. 410 U.S. 224 (1973).

5. Interstate Commerce Act § 1(14)(a), 24 Stat. 379 (1887). This provision was codified originally at 49 U.S.C. § 1(14)(a), later recodified at 49 U.S.C. § 10101(14)(a), and finally repealed in 1995.

6. Although the Court resolved the case on different grounds, the ICC justified its failure to conduct a third oral evidentiary hearing on the basis that APA § 556(d) authorizes agencies to forego such hearings if parties affected by the rule would not be prejudiced. Since the ICC had already held two such hearings in the rulemaking and allowed parties to submit written comments and evidence in response to the third notice of proposed rulemaking, the ICC maintained that no one was prejudiced by the lack of yet another hearing.

The Supreme Court resolved the procedural issue in the ICC's favor, holding that the ICC was not required to conduct oral evidentiary hearings under APA §§ 556 and 557 at all before promulgating the rule. According to the Court, § 553(c) of the APA requires an oral evidentiary hearing as outlined in APA §§ 556 and 557 only when the agency's enabling act or other statute specifically requires the agency's rules to be made "on the record after opportunity for an agency hearing." If lower courts or litigants thought that the mere use of the word *hearing* in the Interstate Commerce Act triggered the formal hearing requirements of the APA, they were wrong, because the Interstate Commerce Act did not contain the additional language, "on the record after opportunity for agency hearing."

The problem, to the extent one sees it as such, with the Supreme Court's decision in *Florida East Coast Railway* is that few if any statutes actually include the magic words "on the record after opportunity for agency hearing" in commanding agencies to engage in rulemaking. Many of those statutes predate the *Florida East Coast Railway* decision, and agencies implementing those statutes clearly understood them as requiring formal rulemaking procedures under APA §§ 556 and 557 prior to the Court's decision in this case. Nevertheless, after the Court's decision, those same agencies were and are no longer obligated to use formal rulemaking procedures in adopting rules under those statutes.

Congress rarely (if ever) requires formal rulemaking. The Copyright Royalty Board seemingly uses formal rulemaking procedures in making its determinations regarding the terms and rates of royalty payments for copyrighted works, although its decisionmakers are called judges.[7] There is no problem with hybrid or even formal rulemaking when it springs from legislative action or is a choice made by an agency. Except in those rare instances in which Congress has mandated formal rulemaking, today, virtually no agency conducts formal, oral evidentiary hearings under APA §§ 556 and 557 when engaging in rulemaking.

[C] "Hybrid" Rulemaking and *Vermont Yankee*

Florida East Coast Railway dealt with the two polar positions in agency rulemaking under the APA—informal rulemaking procedures under APA § 553 and formal rulemaking procedures under APA §§ 556 and 557. Is there anything in between? Of course there is.

Many agencies use procedures sometimes referred to as *hybrid rulemaking*. Hybrid rulemaking is not a statutory term of art; it is not mentioned in the APA and cannot be associated with a precise set of rulemaking procedures. Rather, the term is used to describe some combination of rulemaking procedures that is neither limited to those of APA § 553 nor as elaborate and time-consuming as APA §§ 556 and 557. Legislatures, including but not limited to Congress, at times have required hybrid rulemaking by statute by particular agencies or in certain contexts. Additionally, because the APA provides a floor rather than a ceiling of agency procedural requirements, agencies can and often do provide procedures beyond those required by statute when they believe the additional procedures serve a useful purpose.

---

7. *See* Andrew D. Stephenson, Note, Webcaster II: *A Case Study of Business to Business Rate Setting by Formal Rulemaking*, 7 Hastings Bus. L.J. 393, 405 (2011) (characterizing the procedures utilized by the Copyright Royalty Board as formal rulemaking under the APA). For another perspective on formal rulemaking, see Aaron Nielson, *In Defense of Formal Rulemaking*, 75 Ohio St. L.J. 237 (2014).

The more difficult question in the aftermath of *Florida East Coast Railway* was whether a reviewing court could order an agency to adopt hybrid rulemaking procedures when the agency chose not to do so and when Congress did not include such a requirement in the agency's organic statute. In 1978, the Supreme Court decided *Vermont Yankee Nuclear Power Corp. v. Natural Resources Defense Council, Inc.*,[8] a case that holds very plainly and simply that courts may not impose rulemaking procedures on agencies beyond those set out in APA § 553 or another statute.

> Absent constitutional constraints or extremely compelling circumstances, the administrative agencies should be free to fashion their own rules of procedure and to pursue methods of inquiry capable of permitting them to discharge their multitudinous duties.[9]

In other words, the rulemaking procedures set out in APA § 553 are the only ones that a court may require an agency to follow, unless Congress by statute demands that the agency do more or unless the agency itself chooses, in its discretion, to provide more.

But this is working through *Vermont Yankee* backward. The initial dispute in the case stemmed from actions taken by the Nuclear Regulatory Commission (NRC) in issuing a construction permit to Vermont Yankee Nuclear Power Corporation to begin building a nuclear power plant.[10] During the elaborate evidentiary proceedings that led to the issuance of the construction permit, a number of issues arose involving the disposal of the power plant's high-level radioactive waste and various other environmental concerns.

Recall that an agency has discretion to make new policy in either a rulemaking or an adjudication, so the NRC could have disposed of some of these issues in Vermont Yankee's license adjudication. It chose, however, to initiate a rulemaking for some of the environmental problems, and it is this rulemaking that led to the dispute finally resolved by the Supreme Court.

The NRC proposed to deal with certain power plant environmental effects through promulgation of what has since become known as the S-3 Table (a set of engineering and operating standards by which, in the Commission's judgment, the negative environmental consequences of nuclear waste disposal would be held to acceptable minimums). The NRC promulgated the S-3 Table after the following proceedings:

1. A notice of proposed rulemaking;
2. An oral hearing permitting interested persons to present their views to the NRC (including some questioning from the NRC's members, but not including all of the formal rulemaking procedures required by APA §§ 556 and 557);

---

8. 435 U.S. 519 (1978).

9. *Id.* at 543 (internal quotation marks and citations omitted).

10. *Vermont Yankee* is easier to follow if you understand the NRC licensing process that was in effect when *Vermont Yankee* was decided. Constructing nuclear power plants is expensive and controversial. Banks and other lending institutions are reluctant to lend money to a project without an assurance that the plant will be completed and the loans paid off through sales of electricity. To help applicants obtain funding—and to provide close monitoring of projects from start to finish—the NRC divided its licensing process into two parts. First, an applicant applied for permission to construct the plant by filing an elaborate set of documents, including an environmental impact statement, blueprints, engineering specifications, and many other things. After lengthy review, the NRC could grant permission (the construction permit) to start construction. Second, the plant could not begin operations until it completed yet another process with the NRC and obtained an operating license.

3. An opportunity afforded the participants to review not only all documents but also the written transcript from the oral hearing; and
4. An opportunity to file supplemental written comments thirty days after the written transcript from the oral hearing was made available to the public.

Some of the parties—including the Natural Resources Defense Council, an environmental organization—decided that these procedures were inadequate and asked the NRC to provide an opportunity for discovery and cross-examination before making the final rule. Because the NRC steadfastly refused to agree to any additional process, the D.C. Circuit vacated the S-3 table for procedural deficiencies and remanded the matter back to the NRC for further proceedings. The Supreme Court granted certiorari and proceeded, unanimously, to write one of the strongest opinions of the past several decades, reversing the circuit court and holding squarely that APA § 553 procedures are, under normal circumstances, all that an agency need follow.

Vermont Yankee can be understood on a number of different grounds. First, it may be seen as simply a reiteration of the doctrine stated in *Florida East Coast Railway*, that it is up to Congress and the agencies themselves, rather than the courts, to decide what rulemaking procedures are necessary or appropriate. Second, it is up to the agency's discretion, rather than that of the courts, to decide to extend more process than Congress requires. But readers should be aware of third potential dimension. After many years, the Supreme Court may have become impatient with what it perceived as excessively free-wheeling decisionmaking on the part of the D.C. Circuit that intruded too extensively into agency policy prerogatives. To a certain extent, *Vermont Yankee* was a message to the D.C. Circuit to back off.[11]

Is there any daylight in *Vermont Yankee* that might permit a reviewing court to require an agency to use procedures beyond those required by APA § 553? In a manner of speaking, the answer is "no." To this day, the Supreme Court continues to adhere to the holding of *Vermont Yankee*, that courts may not impose rulemaking procedures on agencies that Congress has not required by statute.[12] On the other hand, since the Court's decisions first in *Florida East Coast Railway* and then in *Vermont Yankee*, the federal circuit courts have interpreted the text of APA §§ 553 and 706(2)(A) more expansively to require agencies to shoulder a greater procedural burden than the APA's drafters likely anticipated in connection with those provisions (although, arguably, the APA's drafters also anticipated that agencies would be using the formal rulemaking procedures of APA §§ 556 and 557). As discussed below, the key difference is that contemporary procedural requirements are at least loosely linked to the APA's text.

---

11. One year later, the D.C. Circuit took up the same issue, the validity of the S-3 Table. This time, the only possible argument was on substantive grounds, whether the NRC rule was arbitrary and capricious under APA § 706(2)(A). The circuit court held the table invalid as arbitrary agency action. The Supreme Court again reversed in an opinion filled with language that could have left no possible doubt that the Court wanted the D.C. Circuit to stop micromanaging the NRC. *See Baltimore Gas & Electric Co. v. Natural Resources Defense Council, Inc.*, 462 U.S. 87 (1983).

12. *See, e.g., Little Sisters of the Poor Saints Peter & Paul Home v. Pennsylvania*, 140 S. Ct. 2367 (2020); *Perez v. Mortgage Bankers Ass'n*, 575 U.S. 92 (2015).

§ 7.03 Basic Rulemaking Procedure Under the APA

[A] Triggering of Rulemaking Process

How does an agency begin a rulemaking? The rulemaking process can be triggered in many ways.[13] The agency may be commanded by its organic statute to adopt rules to resolve a particular issue or address a certain topic. Much of the legislation passed by Congress expressly calls for agencies to promulgate rules and regulations, although the agency often has a great deal of discretion in determining what the final rules look like. On occasion, when it thinks rules need to be adopted especially quickly for some reason, Congress may provide in a statute for an agency to adopt interim-final rules that will remain in place until the agency gets around to promulgating its own regulatory program.[14] Quite often, an agency will determine that rules are needed when its own investigative processes show the need for additional regulatory activity in some area. Occasionally, requests by private citizens will prompt an agency to pursue a rulemaking. Section 553(e) of the Administrative Procedure Act (APA) gives any "interested person the right to petition for the issuance, amendment, or repeal of a rule."

The definition of a rule in the federal APA is broad. The APA defines a rule, in part, as "the whole or a part of an agency statement of general or particular applicability and future effect designed to implement, interpret, or prescribe law or policy or describing the organization, procedure, or practice requirements of an agency...."[15]

By contemporary practices, the APA's normal rulemaking procedures are found in § 553.[16] Many people refer to these procedures as *notice-and-comment rulemaking.* Technically, from the perspective of the APA as written, these procedures also represent

---

13. One issue not discussed in this chapter is the refusal of an agency to make a rule and whether that refusal is reviewable in court. In *Heckler v. Chaney*, 470 U.S. 821 (1985), the Supreme Court held that an agency's refusal to launch an enforcement action was not reviewable, because such decisions are committed to agency discretion. *See* discussion of *Heckler* in Chapter 10, § 10.05[D]. While *Heckler* did not involve a refusal to make a rule, many commentators have acknowledged its impact on the rulemaking process. *See* Ronald M. Levin, *Understanding Unreviewability in Administrative Law,* 74 MINN. L. REV. 689, 762–73 (1990). Shortly thereafter, however, the D.C. Circuit held that such a refusal can be reviewed in some circumstances. *See American Horse Protection Ass'n v. Lyng*, 812 F.2d 1 (D.C. Cir. 1987). The Supreme Court subsequently implicitly endorsed the D.C. Circuit's holding in *Massachusetts v. Environmental Protection Agency*, 549 U.S. 497 (2007).

14. For example, Congress did this with in Health Care Portability and Accountability Act of 1996 with respect to group health insurance plan requirements, see 26 U.S.C. § 9833, and in the Healthy Forests Restoration Act of 2003 concerning efforts to reduce the threat of destructive wildfires by streamlining the permitting process for harvesting timber in national forests. *See* 16 U.S.C. § 6515.

15. APA § 551(4). *See* JEFFREY S. LUBBERS, A GUIDE TO FEDERAL AGENCY RULEMAKING (American Bar Ass'n 4th ed. 2006). *See also* C.M. KERWIN, RULEMAKING: HOW GOVERNMENT AGENCIES WRITE LAW AND MAKE POLICY (2d ed. 1999). Another factor in agency rulemaking that must not be discounted is the role that agency lawyers play. It is a highly important topic, if somewhat understudied by legal scholars. For a pair of excellent studies, see Christopher J. Walker, *Inside Agency Statutory Interpretation*, 67 STAN. L. REV. 999 (2015), and Thomas O. McGarity, *Government Lawyering: The Role of Government Attorneys in Regulatory Agency Rulemaking*, 61 LAW & CONTEMP. PROBS. 19 (1998).

16. For an interesting perspective on the climate of contemporary federal agency rulemaking, see Lisa Schultz Bressman, *Procedures as Politics in Administrative Law*, 107 COLUM. L. REV. 1749 (2007).

informal rulemaking, as compared to the more formal rulemaking procedures of APA §§ 556 and 557. Because the APA's formal rulemaking procedures now are rarely used, and the informal rulemaking procedures of APA § 553 have become more demanding in their requirements, many lawyers will describe notice-and-comment rulemaking colloquially as formal or formalized rulemaking. To understand this crucially important vehicle for agency decisionmaking, it is important to begin with a quick walk-through of § 553's important provisions.

[B] The Scope of § 553

The APA imposes certain preliminary limitations on the scope of the procedural requirements of § 553. First, note a key limitation on the applicability of the APA itself, set out in the definition of *agency* provided by § 551(1). If the entity that is acting is not an agency as defined by that provision, then § 553 cannot impose a procedural burden on that entity. Not every governmental body is an agency under the APA, and a substantial jurisprudence exists exploring the boundaries of that definition.[17] For the purposes of this Chapter, we assume that we are dealing with a governmental body that fits within the definition of agency.

A second set of preliminary exemptions from § 553 procedures is set out in § 553(a). Agencies with activities having to do with military or foreign affairs, or instances in which an agency deals with management or personnel or public property, loans, grants, benefits or contracts are exempt from § 553 procedures. A quick reading of § 553(a) could give the impression that these exemptions are themselves completely free of all controls. Such is not the case. For example, a substantial body of statutes, case law, and regulations exists that pertains to government contracts and grants. In many instances, those matters are subject to even tighter procedures than the APA might impose. The exemptions in § 553(a) simply mean that the APA's rulemaking provisions do not apply to those activities.[18]

Moreover, no one should lose sight of what the agencies themselves may choose to do, irrespective of the commands of the APA. For example, the Department of Defense may choose to use notice-and-comment rulemaking procedures when it engages in rulemaking, even if the APA does not demand that it do so. Also, an exemption from the rulemaking procedures of § 553 does not necessarily exempt an agency from other portions of the APA. For example, an agency may still have to publish its rules in the *Federal*

---

17. The Supreme Court has held, for example, that the president is not an agency, absent clear congressional intent to make him so. *See Franklin v. Massachusetts*, 505 U.S. 788 (1992). The Library of Congress and the Government Publishing Office (formerly the Government Printing Office) are not agencies because they fall within the legislative branch. *See, e.g., Ethnic Employees of the Library of Congress v. Boorstin*, 751 F.2d 1405 (D.C. Cir. 1985); *Mayo v. U.S. Government Printing Office*, 9 F.3d 1450 (9th Cir. 1993). The U.S. Sentencing Commission is not an agency because it falls within the judicial branch, although the Sentencing Commission's organic statute expressly requires it to follow the procedures of APA § 553. *See, e.g., United States v. Lopez*, 938 F.2d 1293 (D.C. Cir. 1991); *see also* Kristin E. Hickman & Richard J. Pierce, Jr., Administrative Law Treatise § 1.2 (6th ed. 2018) (describing case law regarding the definition of agency in much greater depth).

18. For academic perspectives of § 553(a) over time, see, *e.g.*, Arthur E. Bonfield, *Public Participation in Federal Rulemaking Relating to Public Property, Loans, Grants, Benefits, or Contracts*, 118 U. Pa. L. Rev. 540 (1970); Arthur E. Bonfield, *Military and Foreign Affairs Function Rulemaking Under the APA*, 71 Mich. L. Rev. 221 (1972); Kathryn E. Kovacs, *A History of the Military Authority Exception in the Administrative Procedure Act*, 62 Admin. L. Rev. 673 (2010).

Register or demonstrate that its rules are the product of reasoned decisionmaking, even if those regulations do not have to be promulgated under the § 553 procedures.[19]

[C] The Notice Requirement

The first procedural requirement of APA § 553 is that the agency must give notice to affected persons of its intent to adopt a rule. Under normal circumstances this notice is placed in the *Federal Register.* This notice is referred to, both statutorily and in practice, as a *notice of proposed rulemaking.* In theory, if an agency can give personal notice to all affected people (*e.g.*, in a situation where only ten companies are affected by a rule), individual notice is sufficient. But identifying with certainty all of the people who would be affected by an agency rule is likely to be difficult, which leaves publication in the *Federal Register* as the only practical alternative.

The notice of proposed rulemaking has a number of mandatory ingredients:

1. A statement of the time, place, and nature of any public rulemaking proceedings;
2. A reference to the legal authority under which the agency proposes the rule; and
3. Either the terms or substance of the proposed rule or a description of the topics and issues involved in the proposal.[20]

In satisfaction of these requirements, a notice of proposed rulemaking typically will include an invitation to submit written comments on the rule, along with a cutoff date for submitting comments. It will also tend to specify the statutory provisions that the proposed rule is intended to implement and from which the agency derives its authority to act. Beyond the deadline for submitting comments, however, the crucial parts of the notice for persons affected by the rule are the specific language of the proposed rule and the introductory description that precedes it. In fact, although the statutory requirements for a notice of proposed rulemaking may seem sparse, contemporary notices are often quite lengthy in the content they include. At least in part, lengthy notices of proposed rulemaking are a product of judicial interpretation of APA §§ 553 and 706(2)(A) after the Supreme Court's *Florida East Coast Railway* did away with most formal rulemaking.

For example, one line of federal circuit court cases requires final regulations to be a *logical outgrowth* of the notice of proposed rulemaking—or, to phrase it slightly differently, requires a notice of proposed rulemaking to sufficiently foreshadow the final regulations to come. On its face, APA § 553 requires only a "description of the subjects and issues involved" in the rulemaking. That phrase says nothing about how detailed that description must be or how much final rules must resemble the original proposal. The circuit courts have held repeatedly, however, that the opportunity for public participation in the rulemaking process required by § 553(c) is only meaningful if the notice of proposed rulemaking adequately informs interested parties of the eventual content

19. This is as good a place as any to confront a habit of terminology that sometimes confuses people new to administrative law concepts. The APA uses and defines only the term *rule.* That definition is set out in § 551(4) and is discussed in Chapter 6, § 6.2. Most practitioners and agency personnel use the term *regulation* interchangeably with *rule*, particularly after agency rules have been promulgated. The Government Publishing Office, charged with the publication of the *Federal Register* and the *Code of Federal Regulations*, normally uses the term *regulation* only for those agency statements that are codified in the C.F.R. Generally, the term *rule* encompasses many more agency pronouncements than the term *regulation*, but there are no formal limitations on the scope of the latter term.

20. 5 U.S.C. § 553(b)(1)–(3).

of the final regulations. If an agency changes course or otherwise deviates too far from its original proposal in response to comments it receives, a court may deem its notice of proposed rulemaking to be inadequate. To avoid this result, the agency must issue a second notice of proposed rulemaking and allow interested parties another opportunity to comment on the new proposal.[21]

Another notice requirement imposed by courts interpreting APA § 553 holds that an agency make available to the public any studies or data relied upon by the agency in developing the rule. "An agency commits serious procedural error when it fails to reveal portions of the technical basis for a proposed rule in time to allow for meaningful commentary."[22] The D.C. Circuit's decision in *Portland Cement Ass'n v. Ruckelshaus*[23] illustrates the concern. In that case, the D.C. Circuit considered a challenge to an Environmental Protection Agency (EPA) rule governing cement plants. In its notice of proposed rulemaking, the EPA stated only that its proposal was based on testing conducted by the EPA or its contractors. The EPA did not reveal the details of the tests or the testing methodology employed until after the time for submitting comments on the proposal had passed, and the proposed standard was adopted by the agency over the objections of industry participants. When industry members finally obtained the testing methodology details, they raised concerns about serious deficiencies in the agency's sampling techniques. But because the EPA had already finalized the rule, those concerns were submitted to the reviewing court rather than to the agency. The D.C. Circuit rejected the EPA's rule, holding that "[i]t is not consonant with the purpose of a rulemaking proceeding to promulgate rules on the basis of inadequate data, or on data that, [to a] critical degree, is known only to the agency."[24] Again, this requirement derives from the belief that such information is necessary if the opportunity for public participation mandated by APA § 553(c) is to be meaningful. Courts applying *Portland Cement* have limited its scope, however, for example, by requiring parties challenging the rule to demonstrate that they were prejudiced by any nondisclosure.[25]

---

21. *See, e.g., Empire Health Foundation for Valley Hospital Medical Center v. Azar*, 958 F.3d 873 (9th Cir. 2020); *Mid Continent Nail Corp. v. United States*, 846 F.3d 1364 (Fed. Cir. 2017); *Council Tree Communications, Inc. v. Federal Communications Comm'n*, 619 F.3d 235 (3d Cir. 2010); *Shell Oil Co. v. Environmental Protection Agency*, 950 F.2d 741 (D.C. Cir. 1991); *Chocolate Manufacturers Ass'n of U.S. v. Block*, 755 F.2d 1098 (4th Cir. 1985).

22. *Connecticut Light & Power Co. v. Nuclear Regulatory Comm'n*, 673 F.2d 525 (D.C. Cir. 1982) (holding, however, that the lack of references to available studies in that case was not fatal to the rule because the technical background had been the subject of extensive adversarial dialogue for several years).

23. 486 F.2d 375 (D.C. Cir. 1973).

24. In *American Radio Relay League v. Federal Communications Comm'n*, 524 F.3d 227 (D.C. Cir. 2008), now-Justice Brett Kavanaugh authored a dissenting opinion in which he expressed the view that *Portland Cement* violates *Vermont Yankee*. For a debate over that issue, compare Jack M. Beermann & Gary Lawson, *Reprocessing Vermont Yankee*, 75 Geo. Wash. L. Rev. 856 (2007), with Richard J. Pierce, Jr., *Waiting for Vermont Yankee III, IV, and V? A Response to Beermann and Lawson*, 75 Geo. Wash. L. Rev. 902 (2007).

25. *See, e.g., Personal Watercraft Industry Ass'n v. Department of Commerce*, 48 F.3d 540 (D.C. Cir. 1995) (declining to invalidate a rule for the agency's failure to publish a study on which it relied where the petitioner did not question the study's methodology or findings or identify comments that it would have submitted regarding the study had it been given the opportunity to do so); *Community Nutrition Instititute v. Block*, 749 F.2d 50 (D.C. Cir. 1984) (refusing to find prejudice where new studies merely expanded on, confirmed, and corrected a methodological flaw in information that the agency had included in the notice of proposed rulemaking, and where the challenging party did not suggest that the new data was in any way defective).

It is rare for an agency to describe only the subject matter of a proposed rule. Normally, the agency includes the text of the rule that it proposes to issue. This permits far more pointed and specific comments to be submitted by interested persons. When an agency realizes that a problem exists within its jurisdiction, but does not yet have sufficient information to write a full-blown proposed rule, it generally refrains from publishing a proposed rule and instead publishes either (1) a Notice of Inquiry, which includes a broad description of the area and issues for which it may write some kind of rule, or (2) an Advanced Notice of Proposed Rulemaking. While neither of these two terms are specifically addressed by the APA, they have evolved from agency custom and practice over the last several decades. Examples of each appear frequently in the *Federal Register.*

The following illustration is an extract from an agency notice of proposed rulemaking, which was published in the *Federal Register.*

Federal Register / Vol. 84, No. 16 / Thursday, January 24, 2019 / Proposed Rules **321**

(b) * * *

(1)The QHP issuer must comply with applicable requirements in § 155.221 of this subchapter.

* * * * *

Dated: December 14, 2018.

Seema Verma,

Administrator, Centers for Medicare & Medicaid Services.

Dated: December 18, 2018.

Alex M. Azar II,

Secretary, Department of Health and Human Services.

[FR Doc. 2019–00077 Filed 1–17–19; 4:15 pm]

BILLING CODE 4120–01–P

DEPARTMENT OF COMMERCE

National Oceanic and Atmospheric Administration

50 CFR Part 217

RIN 0648–BI44

Taking and Importing Marine Mammals; Taking Marine Mammals Incidental to U.S. Air Force Launches and Operations at Vandenberg Air Force Base, California

AGENCY: National Marine Fisheries Service (NMFS), National Oceanic and Atmospheric Administration (NOAA), Commerce.

ACTION: Proposed rule; request for comments.

SUMMARY: NMFS has received a request from the U.S. Air Force (USAF) for authorization to take marine mammals incidental to launching space launch vehicles, intercontinental ballistic and small missiles, and aircraft and helicopter operations at Vandenberg Air Force Base (VAFB) from March 2019 to March 2024. As required by the Marine Mammal Protection Act (MMPA), NMFS is proposing regulations to govern that take, and requests comments on the proposed regulations. NMFS will consider public comments prior to making any final decision on the issuance of the requested incidental take regulations and agency responses will be summarized in the final notice of our decision.

DATES: Comments and information must be received no later than February 22, 2019.

ADDRESSES: You may submit comments, identified by NOAA–NMFS–2018–0047, by any of the following methods:

- *Electronic submissions:* submit all electronic public comments via the Federal eRulemaking Portal, Go to *www.regulations.gov/#!docketDetail;D=NOAA-NMFS-2018-0047*, click the "Comment Now!" icon, complete the required fields, and enter or attach your comments. Alternately, electronic comments may be emailed to *ITP.laws@noaa.gov*.
- *Mail:* Submit comments to Jolie Harrison, Chief, Permits and Conservation Division, Office of Protected Resources, National Marine Fisheries Service, 1315 East-West Highway, Silver Spring, MD 20910–3225.

Instructions: Comments sent by any other method, to any other address or individual, or received after the end of the comment period, may not be considered by NMFS. All comments received are a part of the public record and will generally be posted for public viewing on *www.regulations.gov* without change. All personal identifying information (*e.g.*, name, address, etc.), confidential business information, or otherwise sensitive information submitted voluntarily by the sender may be publicly accessible. Do not submit Confidential Business Information or otherwise sensitive or protected information. NMFS will accept anonymous comments (enter "N/A" in the required fields if you wish to remain anonymous). Attachments to electronic comments will be accepted in Microsoft Word, Excel, or Adobe PDF file formats only.

FOR FURTHER INFORMATION CONTACT: Jordan Carduner, Office of Protected Resources, NMFS; phone: (301) 427–8401.

SUPPLEMENTARY INFORMATION:

Availability

A copy of the USAF's application and any supporting documents, as well as a list of the references cited in this document, may be obtained online at: *www.fisheries.noaa.gov/permit/incidental-take-authorizations-under-marine-mammal-protection-act*. In case of problems accessing these documents, please call the contact listed above (see **FOR FURTHER INFORMATION CONTACT**).

Purpose and Need for Regulatory Action

This proposed rule would establish a framework under the authority of the MMPA (16 U.S.C. 1361 *et seq.*) to allow for the authorization of take of marine mammals incidental to launching space launch vehicles, intercontinental ballistic and small missiles, and aircraft and helicopter operations at VAFB.

We received an application from the USAF requesting the five-year regulations and authorization to take marine mammals. Take would occur by Level B harassment incidental to launch noise and sonic booms. Please see "Background" below for definitions of harassment.

Legal Authority for the Proposed Action

Section 101(a)(5)(A) of the MMPA (16 U.S.C. 1371(a)(5)(A)) directs the Secretary of Commerce to allow, upon request, the incidental, but not intentional taking of small numbers of marine mammals by U.S. citizens who engage in a specified activity (other than commercial fishing) within a specified geographical region for up to five years if, after notice and public comment, the agency makes certain findings and issues regulations that set forth permissible methods of taking pursuant to that activity and other means of effecting the "least practicable adverse impact" on the affected species or stocks and their habitat (see the discussion below in the "Proposed Mitigation" section), as well as monitoring and reporting requirements. Section 101(a)(5)(A) of the MMPA and the implementing regulations at 50 CFR part 216, subpart I, provide the legal basis for issuing this proposed rule containing five-year regulations, and for any subsequent LOAs. As directed by this legal authority, this proposed rule contains mitigation, monitoring, and reporting requirements.

Summary of Major Provisions Within the Proposed Rule

Following is a summary of the major provisions of this proposed rule regarding space launch activities. These measures include:

- Required acoustic monitoring to measure the sound levels associated with the proposed activities.
- Required biological monitoring to record the presence of marine mammals during the proposed activities and to document responses to the proposed activities.
- Mitigation measures to minimize harassment of the most sensitive marine mammal species.

Background

Sections 101(a)(5)(A) and (D) of the MMPA (16 U.S.C. 1361 *et seq.*) direct the Secretary of Commerce to allow, upon request, the incidental, but not intentional, taking of small numbers of marine mammals by U.S. citizens who engage in a specified activity (other than commercial fishing) within a specified geographical region if certain findings are made and either regulations are issued or, if the taking is limited to harassment, a notice of a proposed authorization is provided to the public for review.

A close reading of § 553(b) indicates that there are some exceptions to the notice requirement, paraphrased as

(A) when the agency is promulgating *interpretative rules, general statements of policy*, or *rules of agency organization, procedure, or practice*; and

(B) when the agency asserts what is known as the *good cause exception*, finding (and incorporating that finding and a brief statement of reasons for it in the rules issued) that notice is *impracticable, unnecessary*, or *contrary to the public interest*.

These exceptions are discussed below and in Chapter 9.

[D] Consideration of Comments

One of the hallmarks of rulemaking under the APA is solicitation of comments from all interested persons. This means very simply that an agency must accept comments from anyone who makes the effort to write a letter or submit a comment online at regulations.gov. Most agency comments are submitted in writing, although certain agencies, either because of a statutory requirement in their organic statute or through their own discretion, will conduct oral hearings to permit the submission of comments.

The more difficult question is what the agency must do with these comments. Section 553(c) of the APA requires agencies to *consider* the comments they receive, but it does not define the term. This is not a totally hollow requirement. Courts have interpreted APA § 553 as requiring agencies to respond to all significant comments they receive in the statement of basis and purpose that accompanies a final rule. In *United States v. Nova Scotia Food Products Corp.*,[26] for example, the Second Circuit invalidated a Food and Drug Administration regulation imposing time, temperature, and salinity requirements for the processing of hot-processed smoked fish on the ground that the agency had neglected to respond to comments it received objecting to the regulations. Of particular concern for the court was the agency's failure even to acknowledge a comment that the regulation's requirements, if applied to whitefish, were not only unnecessary to ensure product safety but also would destroy the commercial feasibility of the product. Said the court, "It is not in keeping with the rational process to leave vital questions, raised by comments which are of cogent materiality, completely unanswered. The agencies certainly have a good deal of discretion in expressing the basis of a rule, but the agencies do not have the prerogative of obscurantism reserved to legislatures." Courts recognize that comments are written with a particular point of view and, more often than not, are pieces of advocacy rather than models of objectivity. One court has stated bluntly that neither agencies nor courts "need ... accept at face value the self-serving comments of interested members of the [affected] industry."[27] Notably, however, that court also required the agency in question to respond to the comments in question with more than "unsupported and unconvincing assertions."[28]

Cynics who represent clients before federal agencies would probably say that consideration of comments for many agencies merely means logging the comments as they come in and tossing them into an appropriate filing cabinet; others are less cynical.[29] It is abundantly clear that an agency is not bound absolutely by the comments, nor is an agency totally restricted to the comments in formulating a final rule. It can

26. 568 F.2d 240 (2d Cir. 1977).

27. *National Tire Dealers & Retreaders Ass'n v. Brinegar*, 491 F.2d 31, 39–40 (D.C. Cir. 1974).

28. *Id.* at 40.

29. For insights into public participation, see Mariano-Florentino Cuéllar, *Rethinking Regulatory Democracy*, 57 ADMIN. L. REV. 411 (2005); Cary Coglianese, *Citizen Participation in Rulemaking: Past, Present, and Future*, 55 DUKE L.J. 943 (2006).

invoke its own expertise in writing a rule, even if the comments all suggest a contrary result. However, if an agency takes this approach, it must explain its reasoning clearly. A reviewing court will be exceptionally suspicious of an agency rule that disregards all the comments it receives.

[E] Promulgating a Final Rule

This step completes the basic rulemaking process. The step contains two important components—the first regarding content, and the second concerning publication of the rule.

First, after considering the comments and other matter in the rulemaking record, the agency must prepare "a concise general statement of [the] basis and purpose" of the final rule.[30] The statement of basis and purpose, often referred to as the *preamble*, is published along with the final rule in the *Federal Register.* But even though it is published only as a preamble, the basis and purpose statement is a crucial part of the rulemaking process, both for its capacity to explain the agency's thinking to affected parties and also in the event the rule is challenged in court by those parties.

The drafters of the APA saw the basis and purpose statement as an important part of the final rule, but they did not specify what it should contain. The legislative history of APA § 553(c) suggests that Congress intended to require agencies to go beyond merely a formal explanation for a rule. Committee reports describe the scope of the required undertaking in language that suggests some duty to discuss the factual basis for a rule and the reasoning process that links those factual predicates to a set of expected effects consistent with one or more statutory goals. "The agency must analyze and consider all relevant matter presented. The required statement of the basis and purposes of rules issued should not only relate to the data so presented but with reasonable fullness explain the actual basis and objectives of the rule."[31]

Courts have taken this requirement seriously, because the preamble is sometimes one of the few pieces of information by which a court can evaluate a rule if the validity of the rule is challenged before the agency has the opportunity to enforce it. For example, in *Automotive Parts & Accessories Ass'n v. Boyd,*[32] the District of Columbia Circuit looked at the words *concise* and *general* in the rule's statement of basis and purpose and concluded,

> These adjectives must be accommodated to the realities of judicial scrutiny, which do not contemplate that the court itself will, by a laborious examination of the record, formulate in the first instance the significant issues faced by the agency and articulate the rationale of their resolution. We do not expect the agency to discuss every item of fact or opinion included in the submissions made to it in informal rule making. We do expect that, if the judicial review which Congress has thought it important to provide is to be meaningful, the "concise general statement of ... basis and purpose" mandated by [the APA]

30. 5 U.S.C. § 553(c).

31. S. Doc. No. 79-248, at 259 (1946). The Attorney General's Manual on the APA notes that the statement is not to be in the nature of formal findings and conclusions (such as a federal district judge prepares in issuing a decision in a civil bench trial) but is mainly intended to "advise the public" of the basis and purpose of the rule. Department of Justice, Attorney General's Manual on the Administrative Procedure Act 32 (1947).

32. 407 F.2d 330 (D.C. Cir. 1968).

> will enable us to see what major issues of policy were ventilated by the informal proceedings and why the agency reacted to them as it did.[33]

In short, although the court promised not to be too demanding about it, the court also refused to do the agency's job for it, just to preserve a rule. The court was also careful to note that the reason for the basis and purpose statement is simple: it is to demonstrate to the public and, more importantly, to reviewing courts that the agency has done its job "in a manner calculated to negate the dangers of arbitrariness and irrationality in the formulation of rules for general application in the future."[34]

No court today would uphold a major agency rule that includes only a brief preamble. To have any reasonable prospect of obtaining judicial affirmance of a major rule, an agency must set forth the basis and purpose of the rule in a detailed statement in which the agency refers to the evidentiary basis for all factual predicates, explains its method of reasoning from factual predicates to the expected effects of the rule, relates the factual predicates and expected effects of the rule to each of the statutory goals or purposes the agency is required to further or to consider, responds to all major criticisms contained in the comments on its proposed rule, and explains why it has rejected at least some of the most plausible alternatives to the rule it has adopted. This demanding judicial definition of the statement of basis and purpose required by APA § 553(c) can be understood as the product of decades of judicial attempts to give content to several related APA provision, including most particularly APA § 706(2)(A), which compels a court to "hold unlawful and set aside agency action" that is "arbitrary" or "capricious."[35] Failure to satisfy this understanding of APA §§ 553(c) and 706(2)(A) has become a frequent basis for judicial reversal of agency rules.[36]

Second, under normal circumstances, the rule must be published at least thirty days before it goes into effect.[37] Recall that this was one of the reasons why the Supreme Court has so strongly favored rulemaking for the announcement of new agency policy.[38] It gives someone subject to the new rule at least a month to get things in order before being in violation of the rule.

Congress realized, however, that on occasion, an agency will need to move faster than that. Note carefully the exceptions in APA § 553(d) to the thirty-day publication requirement:

1. A substantive (as opposed to procedural) rule that *grants or recognizes an exemption* or *relieves a restriction*. These are instances in which the agency is easing up on a regulated party rather than imposing some new regulatory burden. Obviously, parties will welcome implementation as quickly as possible.
2. Interpretative rules and statements of policy.

---

33. *Id.* at 338 (ellipses in original).

34. In *Independent U.S. Tanker Owners Committee v. Dole*, 809 F.2d 847 (D.C. Cir. 1987), the D.C. Circuit reversed an agency for an inadequate statement of reasons for the rule, but did not depart in any substantial way from the Circuit's earlier language in *Boyd*.

35. 5 U.S.C. § 706(2)(A); *see also Motor Vehicle Manufacturers Ass'n of the United States, Inc. v. State Farm Mutual Automobile Insurance Co.*, 463 U.S. 29 (1983). The arbitrary and capricious standard and the *State Farm* decision are discussed in Chapter 13.

36. *See, e.g., Prometheus Radio Project v. Federal Communications Comm'n*, 373 F.3d 372 (3d Cir. 2004); *American Gas Ass'n v. Federal Energy Regulatory Comm'n*, 888 F.2d 136 (D.C. Cir. 1989); *cf. Gatewood v. Outlaw*, 560 F.3d 843 (8th Cir. 2009) (upholding the agency rule but describing at length the requirements for doing so).

37. 5 U.S.C. § 553(d).

38. *See* cases discussed in Chapter 6.

3. Upon a *finding of good cause* included in the publication of the final rule.

The following illustration is a portion of a final rule announced in the *Federal Register.*

380 Federal Register / Vol. 84, No. 17 / Friday, January 25, 2019 / Rules and Regulations

DEPARTMENT OF LABOR

Occupational Safety and Health Administration

29 CFR Part 1904

[Docket No. OSHA–2013–0023]

RIN 1218–AD17

Tracking of Workplace Injuries and Illnesses

AGENCY: Occupational Safety and Health Administration (OSHA), Labor.

ACTION: Final rule.

SUMMARY: To protect worker privacy, the Occupational Safety and Health Administration (OSHA) is amending the recordkeeping regulation by rescinding the requirement for establishments with 250 or more employees to electronically submit information from OSHA Forms 300 and 301. These establishments will continue to be required to maintain those records on-site, and OSHA will continue to obtain them as needed through inspections and enforcement actions. In addition to reporting required after severe injuries, establishments will continue to submit information from their Form 300A. Such submissions provide OSHA with ample data that it will continue seeking to fully utilize. In addition, OSHA is amending the recordkeeping regulation to require covered employers to submit their Employer Identification Number (EIN) electronically along with their injury and illness data submission, which will facilitate use of the data and may help reduce duplicative employer reporting. Nothing in the final rule revokes an employer's duty to maintain OSHA Forms 300 and 301 for OSHA inspection. These actions together will allow OSHA to improve enforcement targeting and compliance assistance, decrease burden on employers, and protect worker privacy and safety.

DATES: This final rule becomes effective on February 25, 2019.

Collections of information: There are collections of information contained in this final rule. (*See* Section XI, Paperwork Reduction Act). Notwithstanding the general date of applicability that applies to all other requirements contained in the final rule, affected parties do not have to comply with the collections of information until the Department of Labor publishes a separate document in the **Federal Register** announcing that the Office of Management and Budget has approved them under the Paperwork Reduction Act.

ADDRESSES: In accordance with 28 U.S.C. 2112(a)(2), OSHA designates Edmund Baird, Acting Associate Solicitor of Labor for Occupational Safety and Health, Office of the Solicitor, Room S–4004, U.S. Department of Labor, 200 Constitution Avenue NW, Washington, DC 20210, to receive petitions for review of the final rule.

FOR FURTHER INFORMATION CONTACT:

For press inquiries: Frank Meilinger, OSHA Office of Communications, telephone: (202) 693–1999; email: *meilinger.francis2@dol.gov.*

For general and technical information: Amanda Edens, Director, Directorate of Technical Support and Emergency Management, telephone: (202) 693–2300; email: *edens.mandy@dol.gov.*

SUPPLEMENTARY INFORMATION:

Table of Contents

Citation Method

In the docket for this rulemaking found at *http://www.regulations.gov,* every submission was assigned a document identification (ID) number that consists of the docket number (OSHA–2013–0023) followed by an additional four-digit number. For example, the document ID number for the proposed rule is OSHA–2013–0023–1922. Some document ID numbers include one or more attachments, such as one of the submissions by the National Institute for Occupational Safety and Health (NIOSH). (*See* Document ID OSHA–2013–0023–2003).

When citing exhibits in the docket in this preamble, OSHA includes the term "Document ID" followed by the last four digits of the document number; the attachment number or other attachment identifier, if applicable (designated as "A," followed by the number of the attachment); page numbers, if applicable; and, in a limited number of cases, a footnote number (designated as "Fn"). In a citation that contains two or more document ID numbers, the document ID numbers are separated by semi-colons. For example, a citation referring to an attachment to the National Association of Home Builders' comments and the second attachment to the United Steelworkers' comments would be indicated as follows: (Document ID 2044–A1, pp. X–X; 2086–A2, p. X).

The exhibits in the docket, including public comments, supporting materials, meeting transcripts, and other documents, are listed on *http://www.regulations.gov.* All exhibits are listed in the docket index on *http://www.regulations.gov,* but some exhibits (*e.g.,* copyrighted material) are not available to read or download from that website. All materials in the docket are available for inspection at the OSHA Docket Office, Room N–3508, U.S. Department of Labor, 200 Constitution Avenue NW, Washington, DC 20210; telephone (202) 693–2350.

I. Background

A. Introduction

OSHA's regulation at 29 CFR part 1904 requires employers with more than 10 employees in most industries to keep records of occupational injuries and illnesses at their establishments. Employers covered by these rules must record each recordable employee injury and illness on an OSHA Form 300, which is the "Log of Work-Related Injuries and Illnesses," or equivalent. Employers must also prepare a supplementary OSHA Form 301 "Injury and Illness Incident Report" or equivalent that provides additional details about each case recorded on the OSHA Form 300. At the end of each year, employers are required to prepare a summary report of all injuries and illnesses on the OSHA Form 300A, which is the "Summary of Work-Related Injuries and Illnesses," and post the form in a visible location in the workplace.

The recordkeeping regulation also requires establishments with 250 or more employees that are currently

§ 7.04 The Good Cause Exception and Interim-Final Rulemaking

[A] The Good Cause Exception

Section 553(b)(B) of the Administrative Procedure Act (APA) exempts rules from notice-and-comment rulemaking procedures "when the agency finds (and incorporates the finding and a brief statement of reasons therefor in the rule issued) that notice and public procedure thereon are impracticable, unnecessary, or contrary to the public interest." Agencies that successfully invoke this good cause exception are able to adopt rules that are legally binding yet lack the procedures described above. The language raises both a procedural question and a substantive one, neither of which the courts have answered consistently.

Procedurally, the text of APA § 553(b)(B) on its face requires the agency to assert and justify its claim of good cause both explicitly and contemporaneously when it publishes the associated rule. Yet, the courts have not always enforced this requirement. For example, in *Bohner v. Daniels*,[39] the Bureau of Prisons claimed that its statement that it was publishing a regulatory change with only post-promulgation notice and comment "in order to solicit public comment while continuing to provide consideration for early release to qualified inmates" constituted a good cause claim. The court found the language insufficient to invoke the exception. By contrast, other courts have deemed similarly inexplicit language adequate as an assertion of good cause.[40]

Even if a court finds a short and inexplicit statement to be a valid declaration of good cause, however, the court may not think that the statement provides adequate explanation to satisfy the APA.[41] In other words, it may not be enough for an agency merely to claim good cause. Rather, courts typically require an agency to justify its finding of good cause with both specificity and particularity.[42] Courts often consider brief and generic declarations of the need for immediate agency action or guidance as inadequate to sustain a finding of good cause.[43] Although the length of an agency's explanation in support of its good cause finding is not necessarily determinative, the likelihood of an agency's success in claiming the good cause exception is often directly related to the amount of detail the agency offers.

Substantively, APA § 553(b)(B) allows a claim of good cause where an agency finds notice-and-comment rulemaking procedures to be "impracticable, unnecessary, or contrary to the public interest." Because this language uses the disjunctive "or," the contemporaneously-written Attorney General's Manual on the APA and a number of judicial opinions assume that an agency must establish good cause within the parameters of three separate and distinct categories of justifications. The Attorney General's Manual defines notice and comment as impracticable when "due and timely execution of [an agency's] functions would be impeded by" those procedures. Notice and comment are

39. 243 F. Supp. 2d 1171 (D. Or. 2003).

40. *See, e.g., National Customs Brokers & Forwarders Ass'n of America v. United States*, 59 F.3d 1219 (Fed. Cir. 1995).

41. *See, e.g., Utility Solid Waste Activities Group v. Environmental Protection Agency*, 236 F.3d 749 (D.C. Cir. 2001).

42. *See, e.g., Natural Resources Defense Council, Inc. v. Evans*, 316 F.3d 904 (9th Cir. 2003).

43. *See, e.g., Zhang v. Slattery*, 55 F.3d 732 (2d Cir. 1995).

unnecessary if the rule is "a minor rule or amendment in which the public is not particularly interested." Notice and comment are contrary to the public interest if "the interest of the public would be defeated by any requirement of advance notice."[44]

In sum, the good cause exception exists primarily to give agencies flexibility to deal with emergencies, to fix typographical errors, and to impose rules in advance of public notice on those rare occasions in which advance notice would undermine the rule itself. Courts thus sometimes uphold agency invocations of the good cause exception and sustain legally-binding agency rules in emergency situations or when a statutory deadline makes it impossible or inadvisable for the agency to pursue the notice-and-comment rulemaking process before issuing the rule. For example, the D.C. Circuit sustained an agency assertion of good cause for revised airline pilot certification regulations in the months after terrorists hijacked several commercial airlines and used them to attack the World Trade Center and the Pentagon in 2001.[45] Similarly, the Ninth Circuit upheld an agency's good cause claim for air safety regulations in response to a wave of fatal air tour accidents.[46]

On other occasions, however, courts are stingy and demanding in their interpretation of what the good cause exception requires. For example, in *Mack Trucks, Inc. v. Environmental Protection Agency*,[47] the D.C. Circuit rejected the EPA's argument that it had good cause to postpone notice and comment to permit manufacturers of heavy-duty diesel engines to sell engines that did not comply with previously-issued emissions limits by paying a nonconformance fee. The sole purpose and effect of the rule would have been to allow a particular manufacturer that had attempted unsuccessfully to comply with the emissions limits to continue to sell engines while continuing to work toward compliance through technological innovation. The court began by referring to its many opinions in which it had held that the good cause exception was to be narrowly construed. It then rejected the agency's suggestion that the public would not be harmed by allowing the manufacturer to continue to sell its engines while working toward compliance, saying the agency's argument "misstate[d] the statutory criterion. The question is not whether *dispensing* with notice and comment would be contrary to the public interest, but whether *providing* notice and comment would be contrary to the public interest" (emphasis in original).

Although the courts routinely claim their intent to construe the good cause exception narrowly, agencies regularly claim good cause to issue rules without notice and comment. According to a 2012 report issued by the Government Accountability Office, 35 percent of 568 major rules and 44 percent of the roughly 30,000 nonmajor rules adopted between 2003 and 2010 lacked notice and comment. Agencies asserted the good cause exception for 77 percent of major rules and 61 percent of nonmajor rules published without those procedures.[48]

---

44. Department of Justice, Attorney General's Manual on the Administrative Procedure Act 30–31 (1947).

45. *Jifry v. Federal Aviation Admin.*, 370 F.3d 1174 (D.C. Cir. 2004).

46. *Hawaii Helicopter Operators Ass'n v. Federal Aviation Admin.*, 51 F.3d 212 (9th Cir. 1995).

47. 682 F.3d 87 (D.C. Cir. 2012).

48. United States Government Accountability Office, Report to Congressional Requesters, Federal Rulemaking: Agencies Could Take Additional Steps to Respond to Public Comments, GAO-13-21 (Dec. 2012).

[B] Interim-Final Rulemaking

Agencies that issue rules without prior notice and comment under the good cause exception often label those rules as *interim-final rules*. Agencies couple their issuance of immediately-effective interim-final rules with a request for comments on whether to reissue the interim-final as a permanent, final rule with or without changes. When agencies have stated plausible grounds for issuing legally-binding rules that are effective immediately without notice and comment, the sequence of interim-final rule followed by a permanent, final rule that has been shaped by post-promulgation notice and comment represents a practical compromise between the need for temporal urgency and the desirability of public participation in the rulemaking process. Courts have struggled, however, in their efforts to find an appropriate remedy when they find an agency's reliance on the good cause exception to be misplaced, but the agency has used notice and comment procedures in the meantime to finalize the interim-final rule in question.[49]

In some instances in which an agency has issued an interim-final rule, then invited and considered comments in finalizing the rule, and a court subsequently has concluded that the agency lacked good cause, courts have found the agency's procedural error harmless based on a perception that the agency acted with an "open mind" in considering the comments received.[50] In other cases, courts have held that the procedural invalidity of an interim-final rule likewise rendered the succeeding final regulation invalid, theorizing that allowing an agency to cure the inadequacy of a good cause claim through post-promulgation notice and comment threatens to eviscerate the APA rulemaking procedures.[51]

In *Little Sisters of the Poor Saints Peter and Paul Home v. Pennsylvania*,[52] the Supreme Court rejected the open mind standard. The case concerned an interim-final rule exempting certain religious and conscientious objectors from a regulatory requirement under the Affordable Care Act that employers provide contraceptive coverage to their employees through their group health plans. In issuing the interim-final rule, the promulgating agencies had requested comments. After considering the comments received, the agencies issued a final rule that left the terms of the interim-final rule largely unchanged, but the agencies responded to the comments received in the preamble to the final rule. After finding that the government lacked good cause, the Third Circuit rejected the final rule as procedurally inadequate on the ground that the lack of changes in the rule demonstrated that the agencies did not review the comments with an open mind. Citing its *Vermont Yankee* decision, discussed above in this chapter, the Supreme Court rejected the open mind standard on the ground that the APA's text does not require open-mindedness.

Other language in the Court's opinion suggested it did not much care whether the agency sought comments before or after it issued legally-binding regulations, with or

49. For a more thorough analysis of this issue, see Kristin E. Hickman & Mark Thomson, *Open Minds and Harmless Errors: Judicial Review of Postpromulgation Notice and Comment*, 101 Cornell L. Rev. 261 (2014).

50. *See, e.g., United States v. Reynolds*, 710 F.3d 498 (3d Cir. 2013); *Mortgage Investors Corp. of Ohio v. Gober*, 220 F.3d 1375 (Fed. Cir. 2000); *Advocates for Highway & Auto Safety v. Federal Highway Admin.*, 28 F.3d 1288 (D.C. Cir. 1994).

51. *See, e.g., Air Transportation Ass'n of America v. Department of Transportation*, 900 F.2d 369 (D.C. Cir. 1990); *Natural Resources Defense Council, Inc. v. Environmental Protection Agency*, 683 F.2d 752 (3d Cir. 1982).

52. 140 S. Ct. 2367 (2020).

without a good cause claim. Yet, the Court's reasoning in this regard was brief, and the particular circumstances of the case—a politically charged substantive question, debated at length by the agencies and the public over a decade—suggest that a broad reading of this part of the Court's decision is probably inadvisable. The open mind standard is no longer available for interim-final rulemaking coupled with invalid good cause claims. Nevertheless, in more run-of-the-mill circumstances, it seems likely that courts will continue to struggle, rather than allowing agencies to reorder at will the procedural steps for notice-and-comment rulemaking laid out in APA § 553.

§ 7.05 Negotiated Rulemaking

Not all agencies have had a happy experience with notice-and-comment rulemaking. The submission of comments in written form sometimes makes it difficult to develop a dialogue on all the relevant issues. The invitation to all *interested persons* sounds nice in theory, but in reality, most rulemakings usually only receive a small number of comments from parties with the sophistication and resources to engage with the process—at the federal level, often trade associations, industry organizations, or other special interest groups that have a true stake in the outcome of the rule.[53] More importantly, the comments tend to come in only after the agency has expended considerable effort in writing a proposed rule and tend to focus on the defects and deficiencies in the proposed rule—to poke holes in the rule by way of destructive, rather than constructive criticism. Finally, any well-financed group that feels abused by the final rule will, in all likelihood, try to tie up implementation of the rule in court.

Some agencies have experimented with the agency rulemaking process to make it work better for their needs. One such effort is referred to as *negotiated rulemaking* or *regulatory negotiation* (or, more colloquially, as "reg neg"). Developed in the 1980s, this approach attempted to satisfy more of the groups directly affected by the rules and to stave off some of the instant litigation that is triggered by disgruntled parties as soon as the rules are issued in final form.[54] One of the pioneers of this technique was the Environmental Protection Agency, though it is by no means the only agency to use it. The idea was to bring those parties and groups particularly interested in the rulemaking around a table to discuss and negotiate a possible rule, even in advance of the agency's publishing a notice of proposed rulemaking. The Administrative Conference of the United States (ACUS) endorsed and recommended procedures for negotiated rulemaking in 1982, and later commissioned empirical and theoretical studies of the process.[55]

---

53. The ability to submit comments online through the eRulemaking Program, located at regulations.gov, has helped to make the comment process a little more accessible and democratic, but not all agencies participate in that program.

54. *See, e.g.*, Philip J. Harter, *Negotiating Regulations: A Cure for Malaise*, 71 Geo. L.J. 1 (1982); Daniel J. Fiorino & Chris Kirtz, *Breaking Down Walls: Negotiated Rulemaking at EPA*, 4 Temp. Envt. L. & Tech. J. 29 (1985).

55. *See, e.g.*, Recommendations of the Administrative Conference, 47 Fed. Reg. 30,701, 30,708-10 (July 15, 1982) (publishing ACUS Recommendation No. 82-4, Procedures for Negotiating Proposed Regulations). One of the primary sources of background material on negotiated rulemaking is a thick volume compiled by ACUS. *See* ACUS, Negotiated Rulemaking Sourcebook (2d ed. 1995).

As one might expect, the process was not without its impediments. In particular, statutes such as the Government in the Sunshine Act[56] and the Federal Advisory Committee Act[57] contain language that seemed to get in the way of negotiating rules. While none of these impediments halted a bona fide negotiated rulemaking in those agencies that were committed to the process, it made a number of other agencies a little hesitant about trying out this new concept. As a result, in late 1990, Congress decided that the entire matter needed legislative clarification and, for the first time in years, wrote extensive amendments to the APA that are known as the Negotiated Rulemaking Act of 1990.[58]

The Negotiated Rulemaking Act, reauthorized by Congress in 1996 and now a fully legitimate component of the APA, is not particularly complicated and may be best understood as an adjunct to normal notice-and-comment rulemaking for those instances in which an agency determines that negotiated rulemaking would be a good thing. No agency is required to utilize negotiated rulemaking. No agency is required to publish either a proposed or a final rule merely because it is the product of negotiated rulemaking. And an agency's decision either to use or to forego negotiated rulemaking is exempt from judicial review as being totally within the agency's discretion.[59]

Negotiated rulemaking is commenced with the agency making an initial determination that a particular rulemaking setting is a good prospect for the procedure. The Negotiated Rulemaking Act suggests that the agency consider, among other things, whether (1) a rule is needed; (2) a limited number of identifiable interests will be significantly affected by the rule; (3) the agency will be able to convene a balanced and representative committee of persons who will negotiate in good faith; and (4) the negotiating process will not delay promulgation or implementation of a final rule.[60]

Note that these criteria hint at some of the advantages and disadvantages of negotiated rulemaking. A rulemaking that will affect vast numbers of diversely situated persons is probably not a good prospect for negotiated rulemaking. A negotiated rulemaking will not proceed smoothly if it has too many participants. One successful project at the Department of Transportation involved the Federal Aviation Administration (FAA) making a rule involving maximum hours of flying time for pilots and other flight

56. 5 U.S.C. § 552b. *See* the discussion of the Sunshine Act *infra*, Chapter 14, § 14.05.

57. 5 U.S.C. App. The Federal Advisory Committee Act requires an agency to establish and publicize the appointment of a federal advisory committee if it intends to meet with more than one private sector individual on more than a single occasion to discuss agency policy making and to receive advice and recommendations on that policy from the private sector. The statute's purposes are to give notice to all interested persons that the agency is consulting with private sector persons, and to avoid the appearance of secret meetings with favored groups. For two excellent articles about the Federal Advisory Committee Act that grew out of projects commissioned by ACUS, see Steven P. Croley & William F. Funk, *The Federal Advisory Committee Act and Good Government*, 14 Yale J. on Reg. 451 (1997); Steven P. Croley, *Practical Guidance on the Applicability of the Federal Advisory Committee Act*, 10 Admin. L.J. Am. U. 111 (1996). For a more recent perspective on the Federal Advisory Committee Act in action, see Gregory Morrison, *Science in the Modern Administrative State: Examining Peer Review Panels and the Federal Advisory Committee Act*, 82 Geo. Wash. L. Rev. 1654 (2014).

58. Pub. L. No. 101-648, 104 Stat. 4969, amended by the Administrative Dispute Resolution Act of 1996, Pub. L. No. 104-320, now codified at 5 U.S.C. §§ 56–70.

59. 5 U.S.C. § 570. This section states: "Any agency action relating to establishing, assisting, or terminating a negotiated rulemaking committee under this subchapter shall not be subject to judicial review."

60. 5 U.S.C. § 563(a).

crew. A rule was necessary; a small number of parties or groups were actually affected by the proposals, all of whom were strongly and capably represented by trade associations; and, in the judgment of the FAA, a negotiation would likely speed up implementation, rather than delay it.[61] The Negotiated Rulemaking Act permits the agency to obtain the services of a *convener* to assist in making these threshold determinations.[62]

Once a decision is made to proceed with negotiated rulemaking, the agency must publish a notice in the *Federal Register* announcing the project, describing the subject of the negotiated rulemaking, setting out a list of the persons that it believes are proper participants and inviting other persons to apply for seats around the negotiating table.[63] To a certain extent, this may be one of the Achilles' heels of the negotiated rulemaking process. To be effective, the negotiation must involve a relatively small and relatively manageable group of participants. But few federal agency rulemakings affect only a small number of people. Obviously, not everyone who might be affected can participate. One device for dealing with the problem of too many people is to look to trade associations and special interest groups as representatives of the individuals actually affected by the rulemaking. There is no reason to have all licensed airline pilots around the table if they can be adequately represented by the Airline Pilots Association. The Negotiated Rulemaking Act limits membership on the committee to twenty-five members unless the agency determines that a larger group must be formed to represent adequately all significant interests. At least one member must be a representative of the agency.[64]

After publication of the notice and a final agency decision to commence the negotiated rulemaking process, the committee is formed and begins to deliberate under the guidance of what the Negotiated Rulemaking Act calls a *facilitator*.[65] The facilitator may be a private sector person or a government employee, but whoever is nominated must be approved by the committee. The facilitator chairs the negotiating sessions and keeps the records of the proceeding. If the committee reaches a consensus on the text of a rule, it transmits this consensus to the agency in the form of a proposed rule. The text of the proposed rule may then be handled through the conventional notice-and-comment rulemaking process, but with the *Federal Register* notice including information on the preceding negotiation. If the negotiation fails, as many of them do, the agency is at least armed with guidance from the committee on future pitfalls in its rulemaking.[66]

After several decades of negotiated rulemaking, the procedure remains somewhat obscure and less utilized than its proponents would like. Relying in part on empirical data, scholars have debated whether negotiated rulemaking actually achieves its purported benefits.[67] As Prof. Jeff Lubbers has documented, agency use of negotiated

---

61. This is one of the projects described in Neil Eisner, *Regulatory Negotiation: A Real World Experience*, 31 FED. B. NEWS & J. 371 (1984).

62. 5 U.S.C. § 563(b). According to the statute, a convener is "a person who impartially assists an agency in determining whether establishment of a negotiated rulemaking committee is feasible and appropriate in a particular rulemaking." 5 U.S.C. § 562(3).

63. 5 U.S.C. § 564.

64. 5 U.S.C. § 565.

65. 5 U.S.C. § 566(c) & (d).

66. One of the real contributions of the *ACUS Sourcebook* is a number of communications from facilitators reporting on both successful and unsuccessful negotiations.

67. *See, e.g.*, William Funk, *Bargaining Toward the New Millennium: Regulatory Negotiation and the Subversion of the Public Interest*, 46 DUKE L.J. 1351 (1997); Cary Coglianese, *Assessing Consensus: The Promise and Performance of Negotiated Rulemaking*, 46 DUKE L.J. 1255 (1997); Philip J. Harter, *Assessing the Assessors: The Actual Performance of Negotiated Rulemaking*, 9 N.Y.U. ENVTL. L.J. 32 (2000); Laura L. Langbein & Cornelius M. Kerwin, *Regulatory Negotiation Versus*

rulemaking, which was never exactly robust, has declined.[68] At the same time, the 1996 permanent reauthorization of the Negotiated Rulemaking Act at least signals congressional approval of the process. Even if only a few agencies use it successfully, it remains available as an alternative to the traditional notice-and-comment process.

§ 7.06 Other Statutory Controls on Agency Rulemaking

Congress has imposed many restrictions on agency rulemaking outside of the APA. We discuss some of these at greater length in Chapter 14. In certain circumstances, the Government in the Sunshine Act[69] may require some of the agency's deliberations to be conducted in open meetings. If the agency's action is a major federal action significantly affecting the quality of the environment, the agency may have to complete an environmental impact statement under the National Environmental Policy Act.[70] If the new rule imposes additional record keeping or reporting requirements on affected persons, the agency may have to comply with the clearance procedures for new federal forms imposed by the Paperwork Reduction Act.[71] In 1995, Congress enacted amendments to the Paperwork Reduction Act that some commentators believed substantially strengthened the role of the Office of Information and Regulatory Affairs (the supervising entity for that statute). Those amendments also deal more effectively with electronic forms and electronic information.[72]

Even if none of the above apply, agencies are required to comply with the Regulatory Flexibility Act,[73] as amended by the Small Business Regulatory Enforcement Fairness Act of 1996.[74] With the 1996 amendments, the Regulatory Flexibility Act has become one of the most important general requirements imposed on agency rulemaking apart from the APA itself. *RegFlex*, as regulatory lawyers often call the Regulatory Flexibility Act, was enacted to force agencies to make periodic comprehensive reviews of their regulatory activities by publishing a semi-annual agenda of proposed and continuing rulemaking. These agendas, published in the *Federal Register*, are a good source of information on many different agency proceedings and generally include a brief

---

Conventional Rule Making: Claims, Counterclaims, and Empirical Evidence, 10 J. Pub. Admin. Research & Theory 599 (2000); Cary Coglianese, *Assessing the Advocacy of Negotiated Rulemaking: A Response to Philip Harter*, 9 N.Y.U. Envtl. L.J. 386 (2001); Andrew P. Morriss, et al., *Choosing How to Regulate*, 29 Harv. Envtl. L. Rev. 179 (2005).

68. Jeffrey S. Lubbers, *Achieving Policymaking Consensus: The (Unfortunate) Waning of Negotiated Rulemaking*, 49 S. Tex. L. Rev. 987 (2008).

69. 15 U.S.C. § 552b (described in detail in Chapter 14).

70. 42 U.S.C. §§ 4321–47.

71. 44 U.S.C. §§ 3501–20.

72. Paperwork Reduction Act of 1995, Pub. L. No. 104-13, 109 Stat. 163 (codified at 44 U.S.C. §§ 3501–20). A good commentary on the 1995 changes is Jeffrey S. Lubbers, *Paperwork Redux: The (Stronger) Paperwork Reduction Act of 1995*, 49 Admin. L. Rev. 111 (1997).

73. 5 U.S.C. §§ 601–12.

74. Pub. L. No. 104-121, §§ 201–53, 110 Stat. 847, 857 (Mar. 29, 1996) (codified in scattered sections of 5 U.S.C., 15 U.S.C., and 28 U.S.C.). An excellent commentary on the 1996 Act is Thomas O. Sargentich, *Recent Developments: Regulatory Reform and the 104th Congress: The Small Business Regulatory Enforcement Fairness Act*, 49 Admin. L. Rev. 123 (1997).

statement of what the rule encompasses, a chronology of rulemaking activities and proposed rulemaking completion dates. For anyone with clients who are anticipating rules to be issued, it can be a helpful publication. Agencies always have trouble setting these agendas.[75]

In addition, RegFlex requires agencies to consider the impact their rules have on small businesses and to discuss that impact in the preamble to the rules prior to promulgation. While this requirement apparently is not an independent ground on which to attack the validity of a rule, it does give certain agency rulemaking a new dimension.[76]

In 1996, Congress enacted the Small Business Regulatory Enforcement Fairness Act arguably to give additional teeth to the RegFlex concept. Briefly stated, the SBREFA provides the following:

- Judicial review for: (a) the contents of the agency's RegFlex analysis; (b) the agency's certification that the rule does not have an impact on small entities; (c) any agency delay in completing its RegFlex analysis; and (d) the agency's periodical review of its regulations. The statute permits judicial review of these issues to be sought by aggrieved parties up to a year *after* the final agency action.[77]
- New requirements for the drafting of rules including so-called plain English language and the preparation of handbooks to guide compliance on the part of small businesses.
- The establishment in the Small Business Administration of a "Small Business and Agriculture Regulatory Enforcement Ombudsman." This office is supposed to work with every other federal agency to see that each agency is properly attentive to the concerns of small business.
- Amendment of the Equal Access to Justice Act to permit small entities to recover attorneys' fees against an agency when agency action is attributable to excessive and unreasonable demands in the agency's performance of its enforcement obligations.

Not all commentators were sanguine about the SBREFA. Professor Thomas Sargentich, for example, contended that the Act merely imposed an array of new procedural and analytical burdens and legal constraints on agencies "already struggling mightily to meet minimal performance standards."[78] Others viewed the Act more favorably. For lawyers representing small entities before federal agencies, it expanded their leverage.

Also in 1996, Congress adopted the Congressional Review Act (CRA).[79] Under the CRA, no "major" rule can take effect until sixty legislative days after the promulgating

---

75. For a discussion of agendas and many other issues, see Sidney A. Shapiro, *Agency Priority Setting and the Review of Existing Agency Rules*, 48 ADMIN. L. REV. 370 (1996).

76. *Compare Small Refiner Lead Phase-Down Task Force v. Environmental Protection Agency*, 705 F.2d 506 (D.C. Cir. 1983) (rule might be struck down if there is a defect in Regflex analysis), *with Thompson v. Clark*, 741 F.2d 401 (D.C. Cir. 1984) (a failure in the Regflex analysis may not be an independent ground for declaring a rule invalid but may help support an argument that a rule is otherwise arbitrary and capricious).

77. 5 U.S.C. § 611.

78. Sargentich, *supra* note 74, at 137. For a lengthy article arguing against the policy wisdom of treating small business differently, see Richard J. Pierce, Jr., *Small Is Not Beautiful: The Case Against Special Regulatory Treatment of Small Firms*, 50 ADMIN. L. REV. 537 (1998).

79. 110 Stat. 868 (1996) (codified at 5 U.S.C. §§ 801–808). For a thorough description of the statute's history, purpose, and terms, see Paul J. Larkin, Jr., *Reawakening the Congressional Review Act*, 41 HARV. J.L. & PUB. POL'Y 187 (2018).

agency submits to Congress and the Comptroller General a copy of the rule, a concise general statement relating to the rule, and other information, including any cost-benefit analysis relating to the rule. During that sixty-day period, Congress can veto the rule by enacting a joint resolution of disapproval subject to presentment to and potential veto by the president. The CRA establishes a special expedited procedure for enacting a joint resolution of disapproval. That expedited procedure eliminates the potential for opponents of the resolution to use tactics like a filibuster or introduction of amendments to try to forestall the resolution's enactment. The critical term "major rule" is defined broadly to include rules that would cause "a major increase in cost or prices" and rules that would have "significant adverse effects on competition, employment, investment productivity, innovation," or global competitiveness. If Congress disapproves an agency rule by passing a joint resolution under the CRA, the issuing agency is prohibited by statute from adopting future rules that are "substantially the same" as the disapproved rule. The CRA also includes a provision limiting the availability of judicial review for failure to comply with statutory requirements.[80]

The CRA initially had limited effects on agency rulemaking. Between 1996 and 2017, Congress vetoed only one rule. Issued by the Occupational Safety and Health Administration in the last days of the Clinton Administration, the rule in question imposed extensive new obligations on employers to prevent and compensate employees for workplace ergonomic injuries. The ergonomics rule was potentially quite costly and highly controversial, and Congress rejected it by joint resolution under the CRA in the early days of the George W. Bush Administration. Otherwise, throughout that twenty-year period, members of Congress would occasionally introduce resolutions seeking to reject various agency rules, but none of those efforts were successful.

In 2017, in the early days for the Trump Administration, Congress used the CRA's joint resolution mechanism to veto several rules issued in the last weeks of the Obama Administration, bringing new attention to the CRA as a statutory tool for congressional oversight and influence over agency rulemaking. Congress subsequently rejected Consumer Finance Protection Bureau regulations regarding arbitration agreements in 2017 and indirect auto lending in 2018. In 2021, Congress employed the CRA to disapprove of regulations adopted by the Equal Employment Opportunity Commission, the Environmental Protection Agency, and the Comptroller of the Currency in the closing months of the Trump Administration.

80. Legal scholars have debated how to interpret the CRA's judicial review provision. *See, e.g.*, Michael J. Cole, *Interpreting the Congressional Review Act: Why the Courts Should Assert Judicial Review, Narrowly Construe "Substantially the Same," and Decline to Defer to Agencies Under* Chevron, 70 ADMIN. L. REV. 53 (2018); Paul J. Larkin, Jr., *The Congressional Review Act and Judicial Review*, 39 YALE L. & POL'Y REV. INTER ALIA 1 (2021).

§ 7.07 Supervision of Executive Branch Rulemaking by the Office of Management and Budget and Office of Information and Regulatory Affairs

The Office of Management and Budget (OMB) evolved from the Bureau of the Budget, established within the Treasury Department by Congress in 1921 "to assemble, correlate, revise, reduce, or increase" the budget of and monitor expenditures by the executive branch. With this power, the Bureau of the Budget quickly became instrumental as a sort of informational clearinghouse, helping presidents discern what various government agencies were doing and influence their actions. Under President Franklin D. Roosevelt, the Bureau of the Budget moved from the Treasury Department to the Executive Office of the President. Richard Nixon transformed the Bureau of the Budget into OMB and gave it certain nonbudgetary powers over federal government agencies as part of a larger executive reorganization plan. President Gerald Ford expanded OMB review of agency actions for their inflationary impact (a big concern in the 1970s). President Jimmy Carter issued Executive Order (E.O.) 12044, which replaced the Nixon and Ford agency oversight programs with a requirement that agencies first analyze and consider the costs of proposed rules as well as possible alternatives and then select from the "least burdensome of the acceptable alternatives."

The Office of Information and Regulatory Affairs (OIRA) is a subsidiary agency within OMB. Congress established OIRA in the Paperwork Reduction Act of 1980.[81] Under that statute, OIRA is responsible for monitoring and reducing the burden of paperwork across the federal government and also with respect to private entities. Over time, OIRA has acquired additional administrative responsibility over various statutes that govern agency behavior, including but by no means limited to the Information Quality Act. OIRA has also assumed responsibility for the OMB's duties under various E.O.s issued from the Reagan Administration onward.[82]

OMB is led by a Director, and OIRA is led by an Administrator, both of whom are appointed by the president with the advice and consent of the Senate. OMB and OIRA continue to be designated on government organizational charts as a part of the Executive Office of the President. Over time, OMB and OIRA have become central institutions in the executive branch, with power and influence ranging far beyond their original, more limited functions. Following on the actions of his predecessors, President Reagan took the single most important step toward systematic presidential control of administrative agencies in 1981 when he issued E.O. 12291,[83] superseding President Carter's E.O. 12044 and providing for the OMB and OIRA to play an expanded supervisory role in directing agency rulemaking efforts. Among other provisions, E.O. 12291 required agencies to prepare and submit to OMB each *major rule*, including a *regulatory impact analysis*

81. Pub. L. No. 96-511, 94 Stat. 2812 (1980) (codified at 44 U.S.C. § 3501 *et seq.*).

82. For an article documenting OIRA's history much more thoroughly, authored by a key government official involved in its establishment as part of a special issue of the Administrative Law Review celebrating OIRA's thirtieth anniversary, see Jim Tozzi, *OIRA's Formative Years: The Historical Record of Centralized Regulatory Review Preceding OIRA's Founding*, 63 Admin. L. Rev. 37 (2011).

83. 46 Fed. Reg. 13,193 (Feb. 19, 1981).

describing the rule's anticipated costs and benefits. E.O. 12291 also articulated criteria for agencies to apply as part of their regulatory decisionmaking, including limiting their regulatory actions to those for which "the potential benefits to society for the regulation outweigh the potential costs to society." Finally, E.O. 12291 required agencies to publish twice each year a *regulatory agenda*, providing certain basic information about proposed regulations they intended to issue. Four years after he issued E.O. 12291, President Reagan issued E.O. 12498, expanding significantly the regulatory agenda requirements.

In 1993, President Clinton replaced both E.O. 12291 and E.O. 12498 with E.O. 12866,[84] which continues to provide the framework for the current system of OMB and OIRA review of executive branch rulemaking. E.O. 12866 borrows heavily from its Reagan-era predecessors. E.O. 12866 requires agencies to submit all *significant regulatory actions* to OIRA for review and clearance, with significance defined by reference to $100 million of economic impact, inconsistency with other regulatory actions, and "novel legal or policy issues." E.O. 12866 fine-tuned the regulatory planning mechanisms of its predecessor E.O.s, requiring agencies, under OIRA's supervision, to develop a *unified regulatory agenda* and a *regulatory plan* communicating numerous details regarding their regulatory intentions, goals, and priorities. Finally, E.O. 12866 directed each agency to appoint a *regulatory policy officer* to work on regulations within the agency and serve as the liaison with OIRA.

Additionally, E.O. 12866 articulates a philosophy and principles of regulation that requires agencies to do the following:

- Issue "only such regulations as are required by law, are necessary to interpret the law, or are made necessary by compelling public need, such as material failures of private markets to protect or improve the health and safety of the public, the environment, or the well-being of the American people";
- Adopt regulations only after a thorough assessment of the costs and benefits—quantitatively to the extent feasible and qualitatively where quantifying is difficult—for both the agency's proposal as well as available regulatory alternatives, "including the alternative of not regulating";
- Select the regulatory alternatives that "maximize net benefits (including potential economic, environmental, public health and safety, and other advantages; distributive impacts; and equity), unless a statute requires another regulatory approach";
- Identify clearly the problem that regulations are intended to address, the significance of that problem, and "whether existing regulations ... have created, or contributed to, the problem that a new regulation is intended to correct" and, if so, whether the existing regulations should be modified;
- Base regulations on the best available "scientific, technical, economic and other information concerning the need for, and consequences of, the intended regulation";
- Consider the impact of proposed regulations on State, local, and tribal governments, seek the views of those governments' officials, and harmonize Federal regulatory efforts with those governments' regulatory and other functions; and
- Draft regulations "to be simple and easy to understand, with the goal of minimizing the potential for uncertainty and litigation arising from such uncertainty."

84. 58 Fed. Reg. 51,735 (Sept. 30, 1993). For a concise review of requirements that an agency must consider when adopting a rule, see Mark Seidenfeld, *A Table of Requirements for Federal Administrative Rulemaking*, 27 FLA. ST. U. L. REV. 533 (2000).

The Bush, Obama, Trump, and Biden administrations have all issued supplementary Executive Orders with additional requirements, some of which have since been retracted. But E.O. 12866 continues to govern OMB and OIRA oversight of executive branch regulatory efforts. Note that the requirements of E.O. 12866 generally are not statutory, nor are many of them expressly set out in agency organic statutes. Nonetheless, because it is an executive order, the executive branch agencies are governed by its terms.[85]

E.O. 12866, its predecessors, and other associated executive orders have had a major impact on federal rulemaking, including but not limited to the rigors of regulatory impact analysis and greater political coordination of executive branch rulemaking efforts. Critics of E.O. 12866 suggest that OIRA has accumulated so much power through the regulatory review and clearance process that it has become in essence a "super agency" with powers clearly not contemplated by Congress when it first established OIRA.[86] Proponents tout the benefits of OIRA's interagency coordination function,[87] as well as the merits of regulatory impact analysis and of presidential oversight over the executive branch.[88] Whatever your personal evaluation, keep in mind that OIRA is now a strong voice in rulemaking and will likely continue as such for the foreseeable future.

§ 7.08 Ex Parte Contacts and Bias in Agency Rulemaking

[A] Ex Parte Contacts

By now, it should be apparent that federal agencies promulgate a multitude of rules that affect a substantial number of people. A difference of only a few words or a slightly altered technical standard or computational formula can mean millions of dollars in costs or savings for American industry or assistance to the beneficiaries of social welfare programs. There is intense lobbying on agency rules both inside and outside the administrative agencies. This lobbying takes place on different levels and in different settings. A great deal of the lobbying effort in Congress is directed toward amending or repealing agency organic statutes. At the agency level, hundreds of informal contacts occur on a day-to-day basis because of the close relationship between many agencies and representatives of industry or other special interests. The so-called revolving door by which high-level private sector officials take government positions and government

85. Regulations adopted by independent agencies historically have been exempted from OIRA review by the terms of E.O. 12866 itself, although some of the E.O.'s regulatory planning provisions apply to independent agencies.

86. *See, e.g.*, Daniel A. Farber & Anne Joseph O'Connell, *The Lost World of Administrative Law*, 92 Tex. L. Rev. 1137 (2014); *see also* Lisa Heinzerling, *Inside EPA: A Former Insider's Reflections on the Relationship Between the Obama EPA and the Obama White House*, 31 Pace Envtl. L. Rev. 337 (2014) (describing and criticizing OIRA's role in the regulatory process).

87. *See* Cass R. Sunstein, *The Office of Information and Regulatory Affairs: Myths and Realities*, 126 Harv. L. Rev. 1838 (2013).

88. *See, e.g.*, Christopher C. DeMuth & Douglas H. Ginsburg, *White House Review of Agency Rulemaking*, 99 Harv. L. Rev. 1075 (1986); John D. Graham, *Saving Lives through Administrative Law and Economics*, 157 U. Pa. L. Rev. 395 (2008).

administrators move out into the private sector is another mechanism of communication (and possible conflicts of interest).

Long before agencies promulgate rules, they typically send signals to affected persons before making any kind of formal announcement in the *Federal Register.* Agency officials invite contact by making speeches before trade associations and other private sector groups. Trade publications with inside-the-agency sources often publish agency plans long before an agency might wish to have the activity made public. To a certain extent, these activities are healthy, necessary, and inevitable. But on the other hand, they can be harmful to the public interest if an agency listens only to one pressure group or accedes to the interests of only a segment of the industry it regulates.

When an agency acts as an adjudicatory body, the APA rules on unilateral or ex parte contacts with agency decision-makers are rather clear. Ex parte contacts in an adjudication are generally forbidden.[89] By contrast, one of the major goals in agency rulemaking is to encourage the agency to seek and listen to as wide a spectrum of opinion and expertise as possible when it is contemplating a rule. The main drawback with ex parte contacts is that they can go unrebutted and thus may carry more weight than they really should. Worst of all, they are often made in secret, thus, contributing to the sleaze element in administrative practice.

When important issues representing millions of dollars are at stake, ex parte contacts in agency rulemaking can become not only ugly, but also downright unfair if not properly handled. The Administrative Procedure Act is silent on this type of ex parte contact, but the federal courts, and particularly the D.C. Circuit, have occasionally taken up these issues and written a few opinions from which we can glean the dimensions of the problem, even if we cannot articulate many hard, fast rules on ex parte contacts in agency rulemaking.

In the mid-1970s, the Federal Communications Commission (FCC) began paying more attention to cable television and subscription television activities. After a long investigation, the Commission decided to promulgate some rules setting out certain programming limitations for these broadcasters. The new rules, as almost always happens, were immediately challenged in court.[90] The FCC went through the conventional rulemaking process and compiled a massive record. Comments and other information put into that record are always accessible to the public, and it is on the basis of that record that the Commission fashions the final rule.

However, in the case of the cable programming rules, a number of persons, mainly representatives of different segments of the industry, talked to individual commissioners and various FCC staff members in secret one-on-one sessions where they made additional comments on the rules. When the FCC finally promulgated the rules, it justified the rules only on the basis of the public record. The Commission neglected to mention even that the ex parte contacts had taken place. It said absolutely nothing about the substance of those contacts.

In *Home Box Office, Inc. v. Federal Communications Commission,*[91] the D.C. Circuit found these secret, off-the-record activities intolerable, vacated the rules and remanded the rulemaking proceeding to the Commission because it found the rules themselves fatally tainted by the ex parte contacts. As Judge Skelly Wright, speaking for the court, put it,

---

89. *See infra* Chapter 8, §8.05, for a discussion of ex parte contacts in agency adjudications.

90. Challenges to FCC rulemaking are taken directly and exclusively to the United States Court of Appeals for the District of Columbia Circuit.

91. 567 F.2d 9 (D.C. Cir.), *cert. denied*, 434 U.S. 829 (1977).

> [W]here, as here, an agency justifies its actions by reference only to information in the public file while failing to disclose the substance of other relevant information that has been represented to it, [the court] must treat the agency's justifications as a fictional account of the actual decision making process and must perforce find its actions arbitrary.[92]

Think carefully about what the court was saying in *Home Box Office*. Is the factor of secrecy the important thing? In other words, would it have sufficed for the FCC to disclose these contacts, and perhaps, even to disclose the substance of the conversations? According to the *Home Box Office* court, the answer is "no." It is very important, in the court's view, that statements and representations be weighed in the give-and-take of an open rulemaking proceeding, a proceeding in which all interested persons may participate. Merely docketing the contacts would probably not be enough.

Home Box Office caused a stir in all agencies, not just the FCC, because the general understanding among agency personnel prior to that decision was that ex parte contacts in rulemaking proceedings were generally permitted. Worse, some of the court's comments in the case seemed almost to force an agency into *formal* rulemaking procedures just to avoid any hassle with off-the-record comments.

Just three months later, however, another panel on the D.C. Circuit tried to put a few things right. In *Action for Children's Television v. FCC* (*ACT*), a three-judge panel that included Judge George MacKinnon, the dissenter in *Home Box Office*, struck a more moderate tone.[93] *ACT* involved FCC rules for television programs directed mainly toward children. In this instance, the Commission refused to promulgate a rule because it was convinced that voluntary standards and compliance efforts worked out by the networks would suffice. These voluntary efforts were proposed by network representatives in undisclosed meetings with individual commissioners. The general public had no knowledge of the meetings or of the substance of the proposals, and it had no opportunity to comment on the networks' proposals prior to the FCC's cancellation of the rulemaking.

The cancellation of the rulemaking was taken to court, where *Home Box Office* was cited as a basis for vacating the Commission's actions. It is apparent from some of the dicta in the *ACT* opinion that this D.C. Circuit panel was not happy with some of the broader comments in *Home Box Office*. The *ACT* panel refused to find the ex parte contacts impermissible and knocked down a few straw men on the way to its decision.

> If we go as far as *Home Box Office*... why not go further to require the decision maker to summarize and make available for public comment every status inquiry from a Congressman or any germane material—say a newspaper editorial—that he or she reads on their evening-hour ruminations? In the end, why not administer a lie-detector test to ascertain whether the required summary is an accurate and complete one?[94]

The *ACT* decision appears to be based on practicality: How can these things be policed meaningfully by a reviewing court? The decision seems also to be based on the idea that no individual profited from the ex parte contacts. In other words, this was an instance in which the agency decided to do nothing, rather than a case of someone having secret conversations that enabled him to get a positive agency benefit like a broadcast license.

92. *Id.* at 55–6.
93. 64 F.2d 458 (D.C. Cir. 1977).
94. *Id.* at 477.

The most important opinion on ex parte communications to address informal, notice-and-comment rulemakings is *Sierra Club v. Costle.*[95] The case concerned a new Environmental Protection Agency (EPA) rule governing sulfur dioxide emissions from electric generating plants, and the participation of EPA decisionmaking personnel in extensive meetings with members of the House and Senate and government officials from the White House, the Department of Energy, and several offices within the Executive Office of the President, as well as industry representatives. Several environmental groups argued that the EPA's final rule was illegally tainted by these ex parte communications, labeling the meetings as nothing more than "political arm-twisting." The D.C. Circuit disagreed.

The D.C. Circuit held in *Sierra Club* that the EPA had complied with its only duty with respect to the meetings, that of placing in the public record those communications "of central relevance to the rulemaking." The court recognized that the APA prohibits ex parte communications only in formal rulemakings and formal adjudications. It acknowledged the Supreme Court's holding in *Vermont Yankee* that courts cannot compel agencies to adopt procedures beyond those required by statute or by the Constitution. The court noted that the prohibition on ex parte communications derived from the Due Process Clause applies only to adjudications of individual rights and not to the kinds of broad policy disputes at issue in rulemakings. Indeed, the court concluded that not only was it not wrong for agency officials to participate in meetings like the ones at issue but, to the contrary, such meetings are highly desirable, and maybe even constitutionally protected. "Our form of government simply could not function effectively or rationally if key executive policy makers were isolated from each other and from the Chief Executive."[96] While there was a strong suggestion from the court, based on the statutory language controlling EPA rulemaking, that all such meetings and contacts be docketed in the rulemaking record, the contacts themselves were not seen by the court as a proper basis on which to overturn the agency action.

Courts continue to apply the principles announced in *Sierra Club* in evaluating ex parte communications today. In *State of New Mexico v. Environmental Protection Agency*,[97] for example, the D.C. Circuit reaffirmed its holding from *Sierra Club*, concluding that agency discussions with the Office of Management and Budget are permissible even if they induce changes in an agency rule, so long as the agency can justify its rule "entirely by reference to the record before it." Courts in other cases have concluded that congressional pressure to adopt a rule does not impermissibly taint the rule.[98]

Ex parte contacts often cause problems for young lawyers. On the one hand, you have an ethical obligation to represent your client zealously within the bounds of the law. On the other hand, you do not dare poison a client's case by engaging in impermissible ex parte contacts. There is no easy answer to these questions. You might begin with two separate presumptions: in adjudications and formal rulemaking, you should presume that unilateral contacts are always forbidden; in informal rulemaking, absent special constraints in the agency rules, the statute, or relevant case law, you may presume that there is no absolute barrier to ex parte contacts, although you always want to be as sensitive as possible to negative fall-out. Be aware, however, that agency organic statutes or

95. 657 F.2d 298 (D.C. Cir. 1981).

96. *Id.* at 406.

97. 114 F.3d 290 (D.C. Cir. 1997).

98. *See, e.g., Radio Ass'n on Defending Airwave Rights, Inc. v. U.S. Department of Transportation, Federal Highway Admin.*, 47 F.3d 794 (6th Cir. 1995); *Strickland v. Commissioner, Maine Department of Human Services*, 48 F.3d 12 (1st Cir. 1995).

agency regulations may contain special requirements regarding ex parte contacts, and you should take care to determine whether such is the case on any matter that would involve your engaging with agency personnel in this regard. One rule of thumb followed by most of the careful lawyers in the District of Columbia is that you should not do anything that would embarrass you or your client if your actions became a front-page story in the *Washington Post* the next day.

[B] Agency Bias

One of the concerns of agency decisionmaking is that the decisionmakers be fair to all parties concerned. Does that mean that a decider must be completely neutral or totally free from preconceived notions about the controversy? In one case, a member of the Federal Trade Commission (FTC), Michael Pertschuk, made speeches condemning network advertising practices in children's programs prior to his appointment to an FTC rulemaking involving children's advertising. The D.C. Circuit, in *Ass'n of National Advertisers v. Federal Trade Commission*,[99] held that statements such as these were not sufficient to disqualify an agency decision maker, even though a different standard might apply to, for instance, a federal judge.

The court's reasoning was straightforward. First, there is a long-standing presumption of administrative regularity. It takes a great deal to prove actual bias on the part of an administrator. Second, "[t]he legitimate functions of a policymaker, unlike an adjudicator, demand interchange and discussion about important issues.... The mere discussion of policy or advocacy on a legal question, however, is not sufficient to disqualify an administrator." In other words, it is in the nature of persons charged with making policy to have ideas and value judgments and to want to advocate those conclusions. Thus, there is to be no disqualification of an administrator without "the most compelling proof that he is unable to carry out his duties in a constitutionally permissible manner."

Given this language, it is difficult to say that *National Advertisers* establishes a test for disqualification. At present, the standard may differ, depending on the nature of the rulemaking procedures used. In informal rulemaking, it appears to be virtually impossible to disqualify a decisionmaker for bias. When an agency either employs more extensive, hybrid procedures or uses formal rulemaking procedures, more neutrality may be required.[100]

99. 627 F.2d 1151 (D.C. Cir. 1979).

100. *See, e.g.*, Peter L. Strauss, *Disqualification of Decisional Officials in Rulemaking*, 80 Colum. L. Rev. 990 (1980).

§7.09 Retroactivity and Agency Rules

Congress can enact retroactive statutes as long as it makes its intent to do so clear and has a rational purpose for the retroactivity.[101] State legislatures likewise can enact retroactive statutes.[102] Such authority is not limitless; for example, the constitutional prohibition of ex post facto law applies to limit retroactive legislation in the criminal law context.[103]

Courts also routinely engage in retroactive lawmaking. Retroactive lawmaking by judges occurs whenever a court announces and applies a new common law rule in the process of deciding a case. The Supreme Court long ago recognized as fictional the traditional claim that judges merely "find" rather than make law.[104] Of course, it follows that agencies with the power to adjudicate cases can engage in retroactive lawmaking by replicating the practice of the courts. An agency can announce a new legal "rule" in an opinion resolving an adjudicatory dispute and apply that same "rule" retroactively to the parties before it. The Court has upheld this practice,[105] although most lower courts apply a multi-factor balancing test to determine whether applying a new legal rule adopted through agency adjudication would be inequitable such that the rule should be applied prospectively only.[106]

Until 1988, the law concerning the power of agencies to adopt legal rules with retroactive effect was the same whether an agency announced the rule in the process of adjudicating a case or through the rulemaking process. An agency could give its rules retroactive effect unless a court concluded that retroactivity served no legitimate purpose and was unfair, and courts evaluated the arguments regarding the inequity of retroactive application similarly.[107] The Court's decision in *Bowen v. Georgetown University Hospital*[108] changed that approach.

In *Georgetown University Hospital*, the Department of Health and Human Services (HHS) promulgated rules that set limits on the reimbursable costs under the Medicaid program. While the details of the rules are too complex to be set out here, it is enough to understand that HHS had promulgated a cost schedule in 1981, excluding wages paid by government hospitals. In 1983, this rule was successfully challenged in court on the ground that HHS had not followed proper notice-and-comment rulemaking procedures in promulgating the 1981 cost schedule. In 1984, HHS promulgated a final rule that essentially reinstated the 1981 schedule and attempted to recoup payments made between 1983 and 1984. In the Court's own words: "In effect, [HHS] had promulgated a

101. *See, e.g., United States v. Carlton*, 512 U.S. 26 (1994); *Pension Benefit Guarantee Corp. v. R.A. Gray & Co.*, 467 U.S. 717 (1984); *Welch v. Henry*, 305 U.S. 134 (1938); *see also* Charles B. Hochman, *The Supreme Court and the Constitutionality of Retroactive Legislation*, 73 Harv. L. Rev. 692 (1960).

102. *See, e.g., General Motors Corp. v. Romein*, 503 U.S. 181 (1992).

103. *See, e.g., Satterlee v. Matthewson*, 27 U.S. 380 (1829); *Calder v. Bull*, 3 U.S. 386 (1798). Additionally, the Supreme Court has prohibited Congress from skirting the prohibition by enacting civil penalties that are essentially criminal sanctions. *See Burgess v. Salmon*, 97 U.S. 381 (1878).

104. *See, e.g., Linkletter v. Walker*, 381 U.S. 618 (1965).

105. *See, e.g., Securities & Exchange Comm'n v. Chenery Corp.*, 332 U.S. 194 (1947). This case is discussed at length in Chapter 6, §6.04.

106. *See, e.g., Retail, Wholesale & Dep't Store Union, AFL-CIO v. National Labor Relations Board*, 466 F.2d 380 (D.C. Cir. 1972); *E.L. Wiegand Div. v. National Labor Relations Board*, 650 F.2d 463 (3d Cir. 1981); *Velasquez-Garcia v. Holder*, 760 F.3d 571 (7th Cir. 2014).

107. *See, e.g., Citizens to Save Spencer County v. U.S. Environmental Protection Agency*, 600 F.2d 844 (D.C. Cir. 1979).

108. 488 U.S. 204 (1988).

rule retroactively, and the net result was as if the original rule had never been set aside." Georgetown University Hospital challenged the retroactive application of the rule.

Although HHS attempted a number of justifications for this retroactivity, the department ran into a totally unsympathetic Supreme Court. The Court took a journeyman approach to this issue. It began by stating the unexceptional proposition that agencies have power to issue legislative rules only if and to the extent Congress has conferred that power. From that proposition, the Court reasoned, "A statutory grant of legislative rulemaking power will not, as a general matter, be understood to encompass the power to promulgate retroactive rules unless that power is conveyed by Congress in express terms." The Court then looked at the applicable organic statute and could find nothing in either the express language of the statute or its legislative history giving HHS permission to write retroactive rules. Thus, the Court held squarely, "Our interpretation of the Medicare Act compels the conclusion that [HHS] has no authority to promulgate retroactive cost-limit rules."

Justice Antonin Scalia wrote a strong concurrence in *Georgetown University Hospital* that has had enduring significance.[109] Justice Scalia believed that the Administrative Procedure Act (APA) provided independent confirmation of the majority's holding in *Georgetown University Hospital.* Recall that APA § 551 defines a rule as a statement of general or particular applicability "and future effect."[110] Taking a commonsense approach to the problem, Justice Scalia noted that the concept of future effect generally precludes engaging in retroactive rulemaking. Nevertheless, Justice Scalia observed that retroactivity can take different forms. He interpreted the Court's opinion in *Georgetown University Hospital* as prohibiting only regulations that alter "the *past* legal consequences of past actions" without authorization. By comparison, the "secondary retroactivity" or regulations that alter only the *future* legal consequences of past actions are both common and entirely permissible unless that secondary retroactivity is deemed arbitrary and capricious under APA § 706(2)(A). Justice Scalia also went on to emphasize that the concept of no retroactivity applies only to rulemaking—that an agency may, in proper circumstances, create a retroactive effect through adjudication. Beyond that, however, any agency that believes it absolutely must have retroactive rulemaking authority may simply apply to Congress for the requisite authority.

Permissible versus impermissible degrees of retroactivity are not always easy to discern. In *Landgraf v. USI Film Products,*[111] the Supreme Court tussled with the difficult task of determining just when a statute or rule is being applied retroactively. As Justice Stevens, writing for the Court, noted:

> A statute does not operate "retrospectively" merely because it is applied in a case arising from conduct antedating the statute's enactment or upsets expectations based in prior law. Rather, the court must ask whether the new provision attaches new legal consequences to events completed before its enactment. The conclusion that a particular rule operates "retroactively" comes at the end of a process of judgment concerning the nature and extent of the change in the law and the degree of connection between the operation of the new rule and a relevant past event. Any test of retroactivity will leave room for disagreement

109. *See id.* at 216–25 (Scalia, J., concurring).

110. 5 U.S.C. § 551(4).

111. 511 U.S. 244 (1994).

in hard cases, and is unlikely to classify the enormous variety of legal changes with perfect philosophical clarity.[112]

Justice Stevens went on, however, to recognize the Court's decision in *Georgetown University Hospital* and note the now-usual assumption that agency rules have only prospective effect and may not be applied retroactively unless Congress permits such retroactivity in the underlying statute.

§ 7.10 Estoppel Against the Government

[A] WARNING!

Probably no other area of administrative law traps young lawyers more quickly than estoppel—*i.e.*, the legal principle that when a private person makes a decision or takes a position, he or she may be prevented from a change of mind at some later point in time. It is a topic that may not come up in an administrative law course but may become vitally important to a neophyte practitioner who is counseling clients in agency matters.

To make sure no one misunderstands the fundamental rule: absent extraordinary circumstances, the government may not be estopped. Rely on advice given by agency personnel at your own peril.

[B] The Estoppel Case Law

The Supreme Court has not vacillated in this area. An important early case in this area is *Federal Crop Insurance Corp. v. Merrill.*[113] Merrill was a wheat farmer in Idaho who applied for crop insurance under the Federal Crop Insurance Act. The Act was administered by a government corporation, the Federal Crop Insurance Corp. (FCIC), that used local agents to carry out most of the program's terms. In this case, Merrill and other farmers worked through the Bonneville County Agricultural Conservation Committee, the local agent for the FCIC.

The FCIC had on its books certain rules that prohibited the insuring of any reseeded crops. The FCIC, however, accepted Merrill's application for insurance, leading Merrill to believe that his reseeded crops were fully insured. The FCIC said nothing to Merrill about the exception for reseeded crops, although the exception was plainly stated in the *Federal Register* announcement of the FCIC's rules. Merrill's crops were destroyed by drought, and the Corporation refused to pay, citing the exception in its regulations. Merrill did not go quietly. He brought a lawsuit against the FCIC on the theory that a private insurance company, having accepted the application, would be estopped from denying coverage for something not personally disclosed to the insured party.

The Supreme Court disagreed. Although a private party likely would be estopped in circumstances like these, the Court refused to invoke the doctrine of estoppel against a government agency on the ground that public policy requires that a different principle be applied to the government. First, the Court reasoned, whether Merrill had actual

112. *Id.* at 270 (internal citations omitted).
113. 332 U.S. 380 (1947).

knowledge or not, he was on notice along with everyone else in the country as to the terms of the FCIC's rules when those rules were published in the *Federal Register.* As the Court put it, publication of rules in the *Federal Register* constitutes notice to all persons wherever situated as of the time of publication.

Second, said the Court, permitting estoppel to be used against the federal government could prove to be a very serious impediment to efficient government operations. The government is such a vast operation and has so many employees (roughly three million civilian employees in the last decade of the twentieth century) that it cannot possibly know of all the representations made in its name. The only legitimate source of information for agency rules is the text of the rules themselves. Good faith reliance on either erroneous advice or a misreading of the rules (what some students like to call an "honest mistake") is simply irrelevant.

The *Merrill* principle remains good law. Occasionally, language contrary to the no estoppel rule creeps into the Supreme Court's language. For example, in *Heckler v. Community Health Services,*[114] the Court declined to adopt what it termed "a flat rule that estoppel may not in any circumstances run against the government." Justice O'Connor quoted this language a year later in a separate concurrence in *United States v. Locke,*[115] a mineral leasing case where long-term leaseholders relied on the representations of a Department of Interior employee; the Court, however, disposed of the case on other grounds. In *Locke,* Justice O'Connor seemed to be willing to entertain an estoppel argument (unfortunately it had not been raised below, but might, according to O'Connor, be brought up on remand) involving what she described as the extinguishing of "a vested property interest that has been legally held and actively maintained for more than twenty years."

Probably to put an end to any speculation that might have been prompted by these two pronouncements, the Court in 1990 wrote yet another estoppel opinion that essentially confirmed everything that had been said in *Merrill* and reemphasized the proposition that there is to be no estoppel against the government. In *Office of Personnel Management v. Richmond,*[116] the Court reviewed a case in which a retired civilian employee of the Department of the Navy had qualified for disability payments from the government. Congress had passed a statute in 1982 that provided expressly for termination of disability payments to any retired person who earns in another job pay equivalent to at least 80 percent of his government salary before retirement. The law before 1982 was more complicated. It provided that the disability pay cutoff was not triggered unless the retired person met the 80 percent test in two consecutive years.

In 1986, four years after the statutory change, Mr. Richmond wanted to work overtime at his current job. He inquired at the agency. An agency employee gave him an erroneous opinion based on the law prior to 1982. Richmond worked the overtime, had his disability benefits cut off, and took his benefits claim to federal court. In a strong opinion by Justice Kennedy, the Supreme Court once again affirmed the *Merrill* principle. This time the Court went further by speculating on the possible impact of a legal principle that permitted the government to be estopped.

---

114. 467 U.S. 51 (1984).
115. 471 U.S. 84 (1985).
116. 496 U.S. 414 (1990).

> To open the door to estoppel claims would only invite endless litigation over both real and imagined claims of misinformation by disgruntled citizens .... [Moreover,] [a] rule of estoppel might create not more reliable advice, but less advice. The natural consequence of a rule that made the Government liable for the statements of its agents would be a decision to cut back and impose strict controls upon Government provision of information in order to limit liability. Not only would valuable information programs be lost to the public, but the greatest impact of this loss would fall on those of limited means, who can least afford the alternative of private advice.[117]

The Supreme Court has offered no hint that it might become more amenable to estoppel against the government any time soon.

[C] Dealing with Estoppel as a Practitioner

The *Merrill* and *Richmond* holdings must give civil servants a great deal of comfort. Most civil servants are conscientious and reliable, but they are human, and they do not always receive the best guidance from their leadership. Nonetheless, dealing with the Court's estoppel doctrine is a challenge for private sector practitioners.

To begin with, consider the other side of the coin. Most agency practitioners have a problem just the opposite of *Merrill* and *Richmond.* Most of the time, it is difficult, if not impossible, to get the agency to say anything to you. Agency personnel may not return telephone calls. They may fail to answer emails or letters, or take months to respond. When you do receive a response, it may be incomplete and unhelpful. Even when an agency has some procedure for issuing guidance, such as rulings or interpretations, the delay in obtaining one of these may be so long that your client cannot afford to wait.

How do you deal with agency silence regarding the issue that confronts you and your client? More often than not, you simply have to make do with whatever is at hand. You try to find as much published agency guidance and data as possible. You make a stab at interpreting the relevant statutory and regulatory text as well as any case law on point. You evaluate the political and philosophical climate that exists in the agency. You can, occasionally, find former agency employees who are willing to hazard a guess on your problem. Eventually, you cover yourself with an opinion letter to the client that has a sufficient number of disclaimers in it to absolve yourself of most malpractice consequences. It may seem uncertain and unsatisfying, but in the end, lawyers are paid for their judgment and expertise in the face of legal uncertainty.

What happens if your client insists on obtaining something from the agency? The first thing you should try to do is to reduce the matter on which you seek agency advice to the narrowest possible legal question. In other words, if your problem involves topics A, B, C & D, try to use publicly available and undisputed information such as statutory language, legislative history, existing agency regulations, and other published agency guidance to answer your questions regarding, say, topics A, C, & D. If there is still an informational gap with regard to topic B, you then have fewer questions to ask when you contact the agency to see what agency personnel have to say.

Using as much publicly available material as you can find should give you a very good idea of the parameters of the problem and should leave only a small portion of

117. *Id.* at 433–34.

your problem to ad hoc agency advice. Once you have done the maximum possible narrowing of the issues on your own and have decided to seek agency advice, the best way to deal with that advice is to think through a spectrum of possibilities, keeping the Court's estoppel doctrine firmly in mind. For example:

1. Oral advice from an agency employee may tell you what agency personnel think but should not be relied upon, especially if that oral advice appears to cut against your own interpretation of agency rules. Oral advice that confirms what you have previously worked out may be a little comfort, but remember that if you are later proven wrong, you cannot use the advice as an excuse.

2. Written advice in the form of a letter or email may be better but will usually be more difficult to obtain. Think through this issue from the standpoint of the agency. The agency has the discretion *not* to use the *Merrill* defense. There are some situations in which an agency may choose to honor a written pronouncement as a matter of fairness to the private party, even if the pronouncement is inconsistent with agency policy. Obviously, the higher the rank of the writer, the greater the potential reliability. But continue to keep in mind the Court's estoppel doctrine. There is virtually no distinction in the estoppel case law between oral and written advice or the rank of the officer giving the bad advice.

3. Many agencies have established procedures by which they will give advice that the agency agrees in advance to honor. For example, the Internal Revenue Service will issue letter rulings to persons on request. The Service considers itself bound by the terms of the letter ruling only for the person making the request. Nonetheless, a smart administrative lawyer knows that agencies tend not to indulge in abrupt shifts in position and that they try to treat similarly situated persons in a similar fashion. If your client has a tax situation precisely the same as the recipient of a letter ruling, you might decide to place at least some reliance on the ruling, absent any other signals that the agency is in the process of changing its position. Again, however, you will not be able to rely on such agency representations in court.

The difficulty with personalized decisions such as letter rulings is that they are incredibly time-consuming. Your application for a ruling may take a long time to prepare, and it may take an enormously long time for an agency to respond. Many problems in agency practice cannot wait the typical six months to a year for the agency to take action on an individual petition for clarification.

4. An agency declaratory order is another possibility. Under § 554(e) of the APA, an agency has the discretion to issue a declaratory order to terminate a controversy or remove uncertainty in cases that would otherwise be subject to a trial-type hearing. A declaratory order under the APA is the functional equivalent of the declaratory judgment in federal court civil practice. The declaratory order device is not always available, however. Agencies have to promulgate a rule establishing the procedure, and the proceedings can be as expensive, time-consuming and adversarial as any other evidentiary hearing. Nonetheless, when issued, a declaratory order binds the agency just as much as any other order it issues.[118]

---

118. For a good general article on agency declaratory orders, see Emily S. Bremer, *The Agency Declaratory Judgment*, 78 Ohio St. L.J. 1169 (2017).

§ 7.11 Rulemaking in the States

No one should leave a course in administrative law thinking that the federal Administrative Procedure Act (APA) is the only way an administrative system can be structured. The 1946 federal APA was a great improvement in its time, but it has rarely been amended by Congress, in part because it works relatively well and in part because Congress has been far too busy with other more pressing matters. When Congress wants to deviate from the APA's procedures, it normally writes the different procedures in an individual agency's organic statute. Although many of the modern state systems of administrative law were inspired by the federal APA, a great deal of innovation in administrative law has taken place at the state level.

Consequently, state rulemaking practices and procedures are quite diverse. Some states have relatively primitive administrative procedure acts; others have statutes that are more sophisticated and well-considered. One likely reason for the diversity is the Supreme Court's decision in *Bi-Metallic Investment Co. v. State Board of Equalization*,[119] which held that the Constitution's Due Process Clause did not apply to agency rulemaking and suggested that a citizen's remedy for bad rulemaking is to replace the decision-makers in the next election. *Bi-Metallic*'s holding gives states tremendous latitude in designing their rulemaking procedures. Some states still do not publish agency rules in a generally available publication, thus requiring regulated parties to contact the agency to obtain the text of the rules. Some states do not require notice and comment for agency rules on the assumption that disgruntled individuals can always have the rules reviewed in a specific agency enforcement proceeding or in a court action.

In an effort to achieve some degree of uniformity at the state level, the National Conference of Commissioners on Uniform Laws promulgated a model state APA that provides for notice-and-comment rulemaking similar to the federal approach.[120] Notice of the proposed rule must be published at least thirty days before the rule's adoption, the agency must specify a public comment period of at least 30 days as well, and the agency must consider and incorporate into the record any information received in response. Also, prior to adoption of a rule, an agency must perform a regulatory analysis of the rule. On final promulgation, the agency must issue an explanatory statement along with the rule itself, including the agency's reasons for not accepting arguments made by the comments.

The only proper way to deal with state administrative rulemaking is to check the provisions of the state's APA. Most state administrative procedure acts are at least similar to the federal APA and interpretations thereof, however, so most things discussed in this Chapter will have relevance to both state and federal administrative practice.

---

119. 239 U.S. 441 (1915). *Bi-Metallic* is extensively discussed in Chapter 5, § 5.02. For a comprehensive discussion of state rulemaking, see ARTHUR BONFIELD, STATE ADMINISTRATIVE RULEMAKING (1986).

120. *See* Article 3, §§ 301–18 of the Model Act in Appendix B.

§ 7.12 Drafting Agency Rules

Most administrative law casebooks spend a great deal of time on the "law" of the administrative process without devoting much time to some of the things that lawyers work with every day. One such gap is the lack of attention paid to the techniques of drafting agency rules.

There are a number of reasons for this lapse. It is very difficult to communicate information on drafting techniques apart from actually drafting a rule. It is difficult to talk about drafting without having a specific drafting assignment to focus on. It is difficult to draft a rule without knowing a great deal about the administrative agency that is going to promulgate that rule. For all of these reasons, drafting is one of those things that most people learn by doing.

Nonetheless, regulatory drafting instruction could be improved. Before he left office, President Jimmy Carter became very concerned that agency regulations were so poorly written that they could not be understood by those people who were subject to their commands, or even by reviewing courts. Saddest of all, they often could not be fully grasped even by the agencies who wrote them. To cope with these problems, President Carter issued an executive order directing executive branch agencies to write their regulations in plain English. This Executive Order was rescinded by President Ronald Reagan, although most agencies continue to try to write regulations that can be understood.

On the federal level, regulatory drafting has achieved some uniformity simply from the way the *Federal Register* is organized. For example, publication of agency rules begins with the part of the *Code of Federal Regulations* affected, followed by a title for the rule (*e.g.*, "resales of restricted and other securities"), the name of the agency (Securities and Exchange Commission) and the type of action taken ("final rule"). This introductory information is then followed by a summary of the action, names and telephone numbers of persons within the agency to contact for further information and the preamble to the rule.

The preamble, frequently used as the statement of basis and purpose in a final substantive rule, is often filled with information on the background of the rule, the agency's reasons for promulgating the rule and an explanation of comments received both in favor and opposed to the rule. The preamble is followed by the text of the rules themselves, followed by the name of the agency officer in charge of the promulgation and the date of promulgation.

But that's just the format. How about drafting the text of the rules themselves? The Plain Writing Act of 2010[121] and Executive Order 13,563[122] both require regulation drafters to use plain language, defined by statute as "writing that is clear, concise, well-organized, and follows other best practices appropriate to the subject or field and intended audience."[123] An informal group of federal employees known as the Plain Language Action and Information Network has developed and published the *Federal Plain Language Guidelines* and maintains a website at www.plainlanguage.gov to facilitate

121. Pub. L. No. 111-274, 124 Stat. 2861 (2010) (codified at 5 U.S.C. § 301 note).
122. 76 Fed. Reg. 3821 (Jan. 18, 2011).
123. 5 U.S.C. § 301 note sec. 3(3).

compliance with the Plain Writing Act.[124] In 2017, the Administrative Conference of the United States adopted recommendations on plain language in regulatory drafting that included following those guidelines.[125]

Also, the Government Printing Office, publisher of the *Federal Register*, has published a guide called the *GPO Style Manual*[126] that is some help when faced with a regulatory drafting project. As its title suggests, the *GPO Style Manual* offers principally information about the style and formatting preferences of the GPO, rather than concrete advice about how to draft regulatory preambles and regulations substantively. Nevertheless, it is a useful tool to have in your drafting arsenal.

Many fledgling writers do not understand the proper use of ambiguity in regulation drafting. Ambiguity is a defect when you mean thirty days and write "month" because some months are longer or shorter than thirty days. By contrast, ambiguity may be required when a drafter cannot foresee completely the application of the regulation and intends to adopt a more open-ended standard rather than a bright-line rule. When the *Uniform Commercial Code* uses the term "good faith," when Congress establishes a standard of "public convenience and necessity" in an organic statute, or when a court talks about a duty of "reasonable" care, each of these entities is using *purposeful* or *deliberate* ambiguity.[127]

Agency rules are, by definition, supposed to be more detailed and more specific than statutes. The purpose of agency rules is to clarify and resolve statutory ambiguity, not create more ambiguity. Nevertheless, deliberate ambiguity is not necessarily problematic in regulatory drafting. You may intentionally incorporate an ambiguous phrase or open-ended standard such as *good faith* in a rule. But you should have a very good reason for being deliberately ambiguous. Without a reason behind it, regulatory ambiguity does a great disservice to those regulated parties who are trying to modify their conduct to comply with the rule. If you do not intend deliberate ambiguity, then choose your words carefully to avoid inadvertent ambiguity.

The purpose of this book is not to offer a primer on regulation drafting. Just remember that writing agency rules requires as much or perhaps even more care and thought as judges put into judicial opinions or as the legislatures put into drafting their statutes. State and federal agency regulations affect hundreds of thousands of people. The vast bulk of these regulations are never construed by courts or reviewed by legislatures. The only thing that makes them work is careful drafting.

§ 7.13 Solving Rulemaking Problems

As everyone should recognize by now, agencies have vast discretion in formulating policy. More often than not, in "real life," an agency rule is going to stand as written. In law school courses and on bar examinations, agency rules are sometimes a little more

124. *See* Federal Plain Language Guidelines (Mar. 2011), *available at* https://plainlanguage.gov/media/ FederalPLGuidelines.pdf.

125. Admin. Conf. of the U.S., Recommendation 2017-3, *Plain Language in Regulatory Drafting*, 82 Fed. Reg. 61,728 (Dec. 29, 2017).

126. GPO, Legal Drafting Style Manual (undated).

127. *See, e.g.*, F. Reed Dickerson, Legal Drafting (1981).

difficult to predict. The following are just a few hints in the nature of a checklist for working through rulemaking problems.

(A) *Identify the format* that the agency is using for announcing its policy. Recall a theme discussed in Chapter 6: an agency may announce new policy either by rule or by adjudication, and its choice is not likely to be disturbed by a reviewing court. If the device being used is rulemaking, consider the following:

(B) *Separate* the issues into (1) the *procedure* for promulgating the rule; (2) the contents of the rule—*i.e.*, its *substance*; and (3) the *explanation* offered by the agency in support of the rule—*i.e.*, evidence that the rule was the product of reasoned decisionmaking.

(1) *Procedural Issues:*

(a) Determine the procedures that the agency has used or is using. Assuming that the requirements of APA § 553 apply, make sure that all the elements of § 553 are present. Skipping § 553 procedures may mean that the rule is procedurally defective and, thus, that a court might be persuaded to vacate it. Remember, however, the message of *Vermont Yankee*: unless Congress (through the phrase "on the record" in the organic statute) or the agency (through its own discretion) sets up special rulemaking procedures, the notice-and-comment rulemaking procedures set out in APA § 553 are the *maximum* procedures to be followed, absent due process concerns or "extremely compelling circumstances."[128] For all practical purposes, you will not encounter problems that meet those exceptional conditions. When all a statute mentions is a "hearing" or otherwise merely authorizes an agency to adopt rules and regulations, an agency need only abide by § 553 procedures.

(b) Consider whether the one of the *exemptions* from notice-and-comment rulemaking procedures applies to the rule at issue. If the agency has relied on the good cause exception, that reliance should be explicit. But remember also to distinguish between *legislative rules* and those that are exempt from notice-and-comment rulemaking procedures—especially interpretative rules and policy statements, but also procedural rules—both for purposes of evaluating the agency's compliance with the procedural requirements of APA § 553 but also for later when you evaluate the substance of and explanation supporting the agency's rule. The APA and the courts impose very few procedural demands on interpretative rules, policy statements, and procedural rules. But recall that distinguishing between legislative rules that must be adopted using notice-and-comment rulemaking procedures and exempt interpretative rules, policy statements, and procedural rules can be difficult. Occasionally, an agency will use notice-and-comment procedures even where the rule arguably is exempt, whether from an abundance of caution if the agency is unclear regarding the proper characterization of the rule or because the agency feels that public comment would be useful even if it is not required.

---

128. *Vermont Yankee Nuclear Power Corp. v. Natural Resources Defense Council, Inc.*, 435 U.S. 519 (1978).

(c) Read the *organic statute*. Some organic statutes impose additional procedures on agency rulemaking, whereas other organic statutes authorize fewer or alternative procedures. If Congress commands an agency to promulgate rules following specific procedures set out in its organic statute, the agency must follow those instructions. Relatedly, if an agency has adopted regulations providing for specific rulemaking procedures beyond those required by APA § 553 and fails to follow those regulations in adopting a rule, the agency will be deemed to have violated its own internal procedural requirements, and a court may be receptive to invalidating the rule.

(2) *Substance Issues:*

Compare what the rule says with the agency's authority under the organic statute. Agencies may only adopt legislative rules when Congress gives them the authority to do so. If the language of the rule exceeds the limits of the organic statute, an agency is acting in excess of statutory authority. The Securities and Exchange Commission lacks the authority to adopt rules governing pharmaceutical manufacturing, and the Food and Drug Administration likewise lacks the power to write rules governing the marketing and sale of securities to investors. Agency rules that exceed statutory authority are invalid, and a court will set such rules aside.

(3) *Reasoned Decisionmaking:*

Review the agency's statement of basis and purpose, also known as the regulatory preamble. The preamble is a crucial part of any rulemaking. If the agency has not provided a reasoned and rational explanation either for making a rule or for rescinding an existing rule, a court will overturn the agency's action as arbitrary and capricious. Recall that courts take a "hard look" at the rulemaking record.[129]

In the final analysis, although agency rulemaking may seem procedurally simple, it can be fraught with difficulties for lawyers, whether they are inside or outside the agency. You can cope more effectively with the issues you will encounter as a law student and as a practitioner if you first explore some of the rudiments of agency rulemaking discussed in this chapter and if you organize your issue resolution along the lines suggested by the preceding outline. One thing you can count on as a matter of certainty, whether it be as a lawyer or as a citizen of the United States in the twenty-first century, you will encounter—and be forced to consider—large numbers of agency rules for the rest of your life.

---

129. *See Motor Vehicle Manufacturer Ass'n of the United States, Inc. v. State Farm Automobile Insurance Co.*, 463 U.S. 29 (1983).

Chapter 8

APA Formal Adjudication Proceedings

§ 8.01 Introduction

Some lawyers make fundamental mistakes in agency lawyering by assuming that agency adjudications track the civil trial process. There are many similarities, but there are also a number of crucial differences. That is not to say that good trial skills are of no use in agency hearings. They are of tremendous importance. Even so, a lawyer who does not fully grasp the differences between a trial and an agency hearing may compromise a client's case.

This chapter covers a number of matters relevant to *formal* adjudications under the Administrative Procedure Act (APA) in federal agencies. It is important to recognize that not all, or even most, agency adjudications are formal in the manner described in this chapter. As discussed in Chapter 9, most agency adjudications are *informal*, but that label covers a wide range of hearing procedures, some of which are even more extensive than those provided in the context of APA formal adjudication.[1] Still, understanding the procedures outlined for formal adjudication under the APA is useful for appreciating the procedures used in different types of hearings. Also, state evidentiary hearings often resemble their federal counterparts, although there appears to be a greater degree of informality in many state procedural systems.[2]

Accordingly, this chapter walks you through the important statutory provisions in the federal Administrative Procedure Act (APA). It then takes an administrative hearing apart piece by piece to make sure that you have a good understanding of the nuances of agency proceedings. Finally, it examines—again piece by piece—the process of making a decision based on an evidentiary hearing and provides some insights into how to draft an initial decision. Some of this material is standard fare for administrative law courses; other parts, especially the material on strategy and tactics and the suggestions on drafting an initial opinion, are new. All of it, however, is essential for a successful agency practice.

1. For consideration of formal adjudication procedures in contexts falling outside of the APA, see, *e.g.*, Christopher J. Walker & Melissa F. Wasserman, *The New World of Agency Adjudication*, 107 Cal. L. Rev. 141 (2019); Michael Asimow, *Adjudication Outside the Administrative Procedure Act*, Admin. Conf. U.S. (Sept. 16, 2016).

2. The provisions for evidentiary hearings in the *Model State Administrative Procedure Act* are set out in Article 4 thereof. *See* Appendix B. For those of you contemplating practice in a specific state, make absolutely sure you check your own state administrative procedure act. Not all states have adopted the Model Act. Keep in mind the admonitions in the text about looking closely at enabling acts and agency rules.

§ 8.02 An APA Roadmap

[A] Trial-Type Procedures

A judicial trial in a civil proceeding traditionally includes a long list of procedural safeguards:

- Timely and adequate notice of issues and contentions;
- An effective opportunity to confront adverse witnesses;
- Oral presentation of arguments;
- Oral presentation of evidence;
- Cross-examination of adverse witnesses;
- Disclosure of opposing evidence;
- The right to retain an attorney;
- A decision based solely on the evidence adduced at the trial;
- A determination based on findings of fact and conclusions of law; and
- A decision by an impartial decisionmaker.[3]

The Administrative Procedure Act (APA) describes a process of formal adjudication that includes and adapts these elements to the agency context:

- Notice of legal authority and matters of fact and law asserted, *see* § 554(b);
- An oral evidentiary hearing presided over by the agency, one of the members of the body that comprises the agency, or an Administrative Law Judge, each of whom must be impartial and can be disqualified for bias, *see* § 556(b);
- Limitations on the adjudicator's ex parte communications with the parties and with persons inside or outside the agency, *see* §§ 554(d) & 557(d)(1);
- A right to representation by an attorney or other authorized representative, *see* § 555(b);
- The proponent of an order has the burden of proof, *see* § 556(d);
- A party is entitled to present oral or documentary evidence, *see* § 556(d);
- A party is entitled "to conduct such cross-examination as may be required for a full and true disclosure of the facts," *see* § 556(d);
- An order can be issued only on the basis of the record adduced at the hearing, *see* § 556(d);
- A party is entitled to a transcript of evidence that shall be the exclusive record for decision, *see* § 556(e); and
- The decision must include "findings and conclusions, and the reasons or basis therefor, on all the material issues of fact, law, or discretion presented on the record." *See* 557(c)(3)(A).

This is tedious stuff, but it's vitally important. Understanding the sections that follow requires appreciating precisely what the APA permits and forbids. In reading through

---

3. *See, e.g., Goldberg v. Kelly*, 397 U.S. 254 (1970).

this material, keep in mind that agency organic statutes and agency regulations have an important impact on agency adjudications. For example, to the extent that an agency provides formal rules of evidence or specific discovery tools, it will do so by rule. The APA has little to say about these two things except to mention that neither rules of evidence nor elaborate discovery is mandatory under the APA.

Agency organic statutes sometimes add to the provisions of the APA, particularly in the area of intra-agency review of initial decisions. Formal adjudications before agencies are often, although not always, adversarial, and tend to be similar to, but not identical with, civil bench trials in federal court. Be alert for both the similarities and the differences. One thing you will not have to spend much time with in this area is constitutional due process. You will find, as you work through the APA provisions in greater detail, that Congress has provided far more due process by statute than the Supreme Court has ever required as a matter of constitutional law.[4]

[B] The Scope of APA Formal Adjudication

Begin the analysis by refreshing your recollection of the definition of *agency* in § 551(1) and *order* in § 551(6).[5] Next read thoroughly §§ 554, 555, 556, 557 and 558. These portions of the APA are the provisions that govern trial-type, usually oral, evidentiary proceedings. The place to begin is § 554 (adjudications). With certain exceptions, agencies subject to the APA are to conduct adjudications when the agency's decisionmaking proceedings are "required by statute to be determined on the record after opportunity for an agency hearing," with certain exceptions.

Not all components of the federal government are covered by the APA. There is no easy way to get a sense of which agency proceedings are covered other than to read the organic statutes and procedural regulations of individual agencies. As a general matter, evidentiary hearings are often granted for major federal licenses and for agency actions that terminate important federal benefits, such as civil service employment or social security disability payments.

The Supreme Court has not been of very much help in making this threshold determination. *Wong Yang Sung v. McGrath*,[6] an immigration case decided shortly after enactment of the APA, is a good statement of the trials and tribulations of getting a uniform agency procedure act through Congress. The Court seemed to suggest that §§ 556–57 hearings, including the requirement that the prosecutorial function be separated from the judicial function, are to be the rule rather than the exception in any instance in which individual rights (such as exclusion and deportation) are affected. But

---

4. Many law professors ask students to compare the procedures mandated for certain welfare benefit terminations set out in *Goldberg v. Kelly*, 397 U.S. 254 (1970), with the procedures set out in APA §§ 556–57. The APA list is longer, including such things as testimony under oath, a much more independent decider (an administrative law judge) and a verbatim transcript. For the *Goldberg* list, see *supra* Chapter 5, § 5.03.

5. *Order* is a kind of catch-all category that includes virtually any kind of agency decision that is not rulemaking, and expressly including licensing decisions. To this extent, the concept of order is a residual definition. If an agency makes a decision, and if that decision does not result in a rule, the agency has made an order.

6. 339 U.S. 33, *modified in*, 339 U.S. 908 (1950).

Congress overruled *Wong Yang Sung* legislatively just a few months after the decision by amending the statute to restrict the right to a hearing in certain immigration matters.[7]

Subsequently, in *United States v. Florida East Coast Railway*,[8] the Court interpreted § 553(c) of the APA to hold that the mere use of the word "hearing" in an organic statute was not enough to trigger formal rulemaking. Because APA § 554(a) uses virtually identical language as § 553(c) in describing when APA §§ 554, 556, and 557 apply to agency adjudications, the lower courts have struggled to determine whether the holding of *Florida East Coast Railway* should carry over to the adjudication context.

In 1978, the United States Court of Appeals for the First Circuit decided *Seacoast Anti-Pollution League v. Costle*,[9] a case involving the Clean Water Act's requirement that nuclear power plants obtain water pollution discharge permits.[10] That statute is administered by the Environmental Protection Agency (EPA), but the statute is unclear on its face regarding whether the EPA must use formal adjudication procedures in deciding whether to issue discharge permits. The statute requires "an opportunity for public hearing," which is meaningfully different from the phrase "on the record after opportunity for an agency hearing" that was so important to the Supreme Court in *Florida East Coast Railway*. In *Seacoast*, the First Circuit adopted a presumption in favor of formal adjudication under APA §§ 556–57 unless the organic statute says something expressly to the contrary and, on that basis, decided that the Clean Water Act required those procedures in connection with discharge permit determinations.[11]

Other federal circuit courts reached different conclusions, however, regarding APA formal adjudication procedures. The D.C. Circuit, in *United States Lines v. Federal Maritime Commission*,[12] took the opposite tack from the First Circuit in *Seacoast*. There, the controversy was over the Federal Maritime Commission's (FMC) approval of an anti-competitive agreement. The statute requiring FMC approval did not expressly use the language "on the record after opportunity for hearing," so the court decided that formal adjudication was not required. In *City of West Chicago v. U.S. Nuclear Regulatory Commission*,[13] the Seventh Circuit concluded that the Atomic Energy Act's failure to include the words "on the record after opportunity for an agency hearing" or provide some other clear indication of congressional intent to require formal adjudication under APA §§ 556–57 meant that the agency was not required to use those procedures. In an earlier case, the Seventh Circuit court had previously reached the same conclusion as the First Circuit in *Seacoast* regarding the language of the Clean Water Act.[14] In *City of West Chicago*, however, the Seventh Circuit expressly rejected its prior decision in favor of a presumption against requiring formal adjudication unless the governing statute uses the "magic words"—on the record—or Congress otherwise "clearly indicate[s] its intent to trigger the formal,

---

7. For some recent commentary suggesting that *Wong Yang Sung* should be revived, see William Funk, *The Rise and Purported Demise of Wong Yang Sung*, 58 ADMIN. L. REV. 881 (2006).

8. 410 U.S. 224 (1973). *Florida East Coast* is discussed extensively in Chapter 7, § 7.02.

9. 572 F.2d 872 (1st Cir. 1978).

10. 33 U.S.C. §§ 1251 *et seq.*

11. The First Circuit was not a voice in the wilderness on this point. At least one other circuit, considering the same statute at issue in *Seacoast*, came to essentially the same conclusion. *Marathon Oil Co. v. Environmental Protection Agency*, 564 F.2d 1253 (9th Cir. 1977).

12. 584 F.2d 519 (D.C. Cir. 1978).

13. 701 F.2d 632 (7th Cir. 1983).

14. *U.S. Steel Corp. v. Train*, 556 F.2d 822 (7th Cir. 1977). The Seventh Circuit in *U.S. Steel* relied principally on APA § 558 to hold that licensing applications should be evaluated "in accordance with sections 556 and 557" irrespective of APA § 554. The courts have moved away from that reading of § 558 as well.

on-the-record hearing provisions of the APA." The Fifth Circuit likewise interpreted the hearing requirement of the Clean Water Act as requiring only a written exchange of views and data rather than the oral evidentiary hearing anticipated by APA §§ 556 and 557.[15]

The D.C. Circuit took a completely different approach to the problem in *Chemical Waste Management, Inc. v. Environmental Protection Agency.*[16] The case concerned a challenge to the validity of a procedural rule in which the EPA specifically declined to provide an opportunity for oral presentation of evidence and cross-examination of witnesses in adjudications to require "corrective action" based on an agency determination that a waste disposal permit holder has released hazardous waste into the environment. The relevant statute, the Solid Waste Disposal Act, required the EPA to conduct a "public hearing" before issuing a corrective action order. In upholding the EPA's rule, the D.C. Circuit invoked the Supreme Court's deferential two-step approach for evaluating agency interpretations of statutes articulated in *Chevron U.S.A. Inc. v. Natural Resources Defense Council, Inc.*[17] Applying the *Chevron* standard, the D.C. Circuit concluded that the term "public hearing" was insufficient to demonstrate that Congress had clearly indicated an intention that the EPA use APA formal adjudication procedures and that the EPA's procedural rule interpreting that language was reasonable, and thus worthy of judicial deference.

The clear judicial trend is against requiring formal adjudication procedures under APA §§ 556 and 557. No case exemplifies this shift more than the First Circuit's 2003 decision in *Dominion Energy Brayton Point, LLC v. Johnson,*[18] in which the court overruled its earlier *Seacoast* decision. The case required the court to look at the same Clean Water Act language ("an opportunity for public hearing") as it had in *Seacoast.* This time, however, the First Circuit followed the D.C. Circuit's lead from *Chemical Waste Management* and concluded that the Supreme Court's *Chevron* doctrine, requiring judicial deference to an agency's construction of ambiguity in a statute the agency administers, trumped the First Circuit's prior presumption in favor of formal adjudication. Much like the D.C. Circuit's decision in *Chemical Waste Management* before it, the *Dominion Energy* opinion is a straightforward application of *Chevron*'s two-step analytical approach. First, the court determined that the statutory reference to a "public hearing" was ambiguous. Then the court decided that the EPA's alternative procedures represented a reasonable interpretation of the public hearing requirement.[19]

Notwithstanding the trend in the courts, many agencies continue to use formal adjudication procedures under APA §§ 556 and 557, or something quite similar, whether because they always have or because their organic statute more expressly requires them to do so. Moreover, the above line of cases is not where the analysis of the scope of APA § 554 ends. Section 554 also provides exceptions for certain proceedings, including for military and foreign affairs,[20] for certain federal personnel matters, and for certification of worker representatives.[21] The provision also includes two exceptions involving

---

15. *Taylor v. District Engineer, U.S. Army Corps of Engineers,* 567 F.2d 1332 (5th Cir. 1978).
16. 878 F.2d 1477 (D.C. Cir. 1989).
17. 467 U.S. 837 (1984). The *Chevron* standard for evaluating agency statutory interpretations is discussed at length in Chapter 13.
18. 443 F.3d 12 (1st Cir. 2006).
19. The EPA did its own, parallel *Chevron* analysis when it issued the final rule that dispensed with formal adjudication for discharge permits.
20. Section 553 rulemaking also contains a military and foreign affairs exception.
21. Don't be misled by this exception. The federal labor statutes contain elaborate due process requirements. One successful labor lawyer of the author's acquaintance, with considerable work

courts (where a person gets a trial *de novo* in court or where the administrative agency is functioning only as an agent for the court), and one, slightly strange exception for proceedings in which the agency decision is based on inspections, tests or elections.[22] The exceptions are construed narrowly, so the requirement that an agency proceed in a dispute by adjudication will normally apply to many, if not most, of the individual disputes processed by the various agencies.

[C] The Hearing

In anticipation of the hearing, APA § 554(b) requires that affected persons be given specific notice of the hearing, including time, place, nature of the hearing, legal authority for convening the hearing, and in most circumstances, particularized information on the issues presented. The section also promotes settlement by requiring an agency to receive pre-hearing submissions, which may lead to a disposition of the controversy by consent.

Section 556 of the APA sets out the requirements for a hearing. Although that statute allows for the hearing to be presided over by the agency or one or more of its members, typically, an administrative law judge presides over an oral evidentiary hearing under § 556. The presiding officer admits documentary evidence and testimony under oath, permits direct and cross-examination of witnesses, rules on evidentiary objections, and so forth. Although it need not be adversarial, it is this part of the hearing process that most closely resembles a civil bench trial in federal court. Section 556(d) imposes the burden of proof on "the proponent of a rule or order." The hearing record is to be the sole basis for the ultimate decision.

The overwhelming number of formal adjudications conducted by federal agencies have a substantial oral component. But not all hearings need necessarily be oral, even if they fit within the other strictures of APA §§ 556–557. In initial licensing proceedings, which are subject to §§ 556–557 procedures because of specific language to that effect in § 558, APA § 556(d) provides expressly that "an agency may, when a party will not be prejudiced thereby, adopt procedures for the submission of all or part of the evidence in written form."[23] When including this provision, the drafters of the APA had in mind procedures used by the Interstate Commerce Commission and the Department of Agriculture prior to the enactment of the APA, sometimes referred to as *shortened procedure* or *modified procedure*.

---

before the National Labor Relations Board, has practiced for many years in a heavily proceduralized agency setting without ever referring to or even having read the APA itself.

22. The *Attorney General's Manual* provides a number of obscure examples, such as locomotive inspections and the grading of grain by the Department of Agriculture. The sense of this provision is that the inspection or test is everything. The idea of this exception is that while it's not impossible to summon the inspector or tester into a hearing and require that person to swear under oath that she graded the grain in such a fashion or inspected the locomotive on such and such a date, the hearing wouldn't really provide anything meaningful that was not already provided in the report itself. As the *Manual* puts it: "The surest way to ascertain what is the grade of grain is for a skilled inspector to test it...." Department of Justice, Attorney General's Manual on the Administrative Procedure Act 45 (1947). Reasonable people might differ over this conclusion, however. Even experts occasionally make mistakes. There seems to be little reason to exclude these matters from the hearing process when other administrative hearings involve frequent clashes between experts as to the accuracy of a test or evaluation.

23. APA § 556(d).

Even if the entire case cannot be reduced to paper submissions, many issues can be disposed of without an oral hearing in the same way that courts dispose of a great many pretrial issues through the devices of stipulation and summary judgment. A number of agencies incorporate summary judgment rules in their procedural systems, although it is difficult to tell whether these devices are used as frequently as they are in civil trials.[24]

Section 554(d) provides for strict separation of functions. This is one of the more important aspects of this portion of the APA. Agency employees who may be involved in gathering information and serving as the agency equivalent of prosecutor or investigator must be separate and distinct from agency employees designated to preside over hearings. When an administrative law judge serves as the presiding officer, he or she must be guaranteed even more separation and decisional independence than that required by § 554. To enhance this separation, § 554 prohibits ex parte contacts between the parties and the presiding officer. Additional provisions governing ex parte contact are contained in § 557(d)(1). These issues are discussed in greater depth later in this chapter.

[D] The Agency Decision

The outcome of an agency adjudication is referred to as an *order*. The process by which a hearing record is converted into an order is set out in § 557. Under normal circumstances, the Administrative Law Judge (ALJ) writes an initial decision that is reviewed by higher-ups in the agency if parties object to the initial decision. The agency decision is accompanied by formal findings of fact and conclusions of law (normally prepared by the ALJ but occasionally subject to modification within the agency) and is subject to judicial review.

The APA provides expressly that an initial decision must reveal the ALJ's ultimate decision on the issues, show the ALJ's rulings on objections and exceptions and be accompanied by "findings and conclusions, and the reasons or basis therefore, on all the material issues of fact, law, or discretion presented on the record."[25] This is a point at which many students with little or no trial experience become confused. What are findings and conclusions? How does an ALJ structure this part of the decision?

Findings are generally findings of fact: the who, what, where and when aspects of a case. Because the initial decision must be based on the entire record, an ALJ likely will not feel free simply to disregard any piece of evidence contained in the record without explaining the reasons for doing so. *Conclusions* are conclusions of law—*i.e.*, those parts of a decision in which the ALJ either applies fact to law or decide questions of pure law (*e.g.*, whether the agency's interpretation of the governing statute comport with the statute's terms).

There is no specific format for a decision. Some judges utilize two outline headings, *Findings of Fact*, and *Conclusions of Law* and write individually numbered paragraphs

24. *See* Ernest Gellhorn & Glen Robinson, *Summary Judgment in Administrative Adjudication*, 84 Harv. L. Rev. 612 (1971). This report was used as the basis for an Administrative Conference recommendation that all agencies that conduct evidentiary hearings adopt a summary judgment rule. For a contrary perspective, see Alexander I. Platt, *Is Administrative Summary Judgment Unlawful?*, 44 Harv. J.L. & Pub. Pol'y 239 (2021); Alexander I. Platt, *Unstacking the Deck: Administrative Summary Judgment and Political Control*, 34 Yale J. on Reg. 439 (2017).

25. APA § 557(c).

within these headings. Other judges write what looks very much like an appellate opinion, which they label *findings and conclusions.* The actual structure or appearance of the decision is not nearly as important as understanding the judge's reasoning.

Section 556(e) of the APA makes clear that a decision in a §§ 556–557 formal adjudication is to be based exclusively on the record of the hearing. The record consists of the "transcript of testimony and exhibits, together with all papers and requests filed in the proceeding." The Supreme Court made the exclusivity requirement a matter of constitutional due process for AFDC termination hearings in *Goldberg v. Kelly.*[26]

The reasons for this requirement are obvious. Trial-type, oral evidentiary hearings are important to the participants. All the participants should know before the initial decision is prepared exactly what the presiding officer is going to rely upon for the decision.

Moreover, it is a recognition that agency adjudication is an adversarial process before a neutral decisionmaker. The parties create the record, so an agency record is just as bad or good as the hearing participants (and their lawyers) make it. An ALJ cannot add to the record after it is formally closed. Lawyers should take comfort from this requirement. They have a great deal to do with the record's composition and thereby with the ultimate decision.

Good lawyers, however, also recognize that the exclusivity requirement contains pitfalls. Once the record closes, that's it. The record is reopened only on petition to the ALJ. These requests are often denied. You must get all of your material into the record before it closes, or risk a decision based upon less material than you think necessary. Don't let the ALJ close the record if you believe important things are still missing. Even if you don't get everything in at the hearing, documents and other material may still be submitted in writing with the judge's permission and with copies to opposing counsel.

[E] Right to Counsel

The APA leaves no doubt on the right of participants to have counsel. Section 555(b) indicates, "A person compelled to appear ... is entitled to be accompanied, represented and advised by counsel, or, if permitted by the agency, by other qualified representative. A party is entitled to appear in person or by or with counsel or other qualified representative in an agency proceeding." Note, however, that this means only that a person may retain counsel, not that counsel will be provided. The Supreme Court has never required appointed counsel in administrative adjudications because they are regarded as civil proceedings.[27] In some instances, attorneys' fees may be recovered from the agency.

Congress on some occasions has imposed statutory limitations on the fees that attorneys can charge in representing claimants to certain government benefits. The Supreme Court generally has upheld such limitations against legal challenges. In a 1985 opinion, *Walters v. National Ass'n of Radiation Survivors,*[28] the Court reviewed a case in which veterans challenged a statutory limitation of $10 for attorneys' fees that could be paid for representing veterans before the Veterans Administration, now the Department of

26. 397 U.S. 254 (1970).

27. The constitutional requirements associated with agency adjudications are discussed in Chapter 5.

28. 473 U.S. 305 (1985).

Veterans Affairs (VA). This limitation had been inserted after the Civil War to prevent unscrupulous lawyers from gouging helpless veterans as they pursued their veterans' benefits. The dollar amount had never been changed by Congress. Veterans who had been exposed to nuclear bomb explosions in the 1950s challenged the $10 limit on fees on the basis of the Fifth Amendment's Due Process Clause and the First Amendment, claiming that it deprived them of their constitutional right to retain counsel of their choice in VA matters. Writing for the Court, Justice William Rehnquist held that the $10 limit did not infringe the Constitution. In this instance, the Court simply applied the three-part standard from *Mathews v. Eldridge*.[29] Under that standard, the Court concluded that the government had an interest in maintaining a certain procedural informality and ensuring that any benefits awarded would be paid to veterans rather than to attorneys, and that interest was entitled to "great weight." The Court also said that the veterans failed to show that retained counsel would significantly improve the likelihood of receiving benefits in VA proceedings.

Subsequently, in *U.S. Department of Labor v. Triplett*,[30] the Supreme Court upheld agency regulations prohibiting lawyers from receiving any fees for helping claimants obtain benefits under the Black Lung Benefits Act. The Court in *Triplett* observed that, when it decided *Walters*, it "assumed that the fee limitation would make attorneys unavailable to claimants, but nevertheless upheld the statute because attorneys were not essential to vindicate the claims." In this instance, the Court turned that observation into a requirement, that the Court would only consider overturning the fee limitation if it could be shown "(1) that claimants could not obtain representation, and (2) that this unavailability of attorneys was attributable to the Government's fee regime." More than anecdotal evidence was required, and again the litigants in this case simply failed to satisfy the burden imposed upon them by the Court.

In addition, recall that, in *Wolff v. McDonnell*,[31] the Court recognized that some agency proceedings may be so delicate (in that instance, hearings involving internal prison discipline) that the agency may justify even the *exclusion* of lawyers. Attorneys in a garden-variety federal agency practice are unlikely to experience such settings. The vast number of agency proceedings are attended by lawyers.

The Agency Practice Act[32] forbids agencies to set any requirements for admission to practice for attorneys other than admission to the bar of at least one state. A few agencies permit nonlawyer representatives to practice before them, such as certified public accountants or enrolled agents who become qualified to practice before the Internal Revenue Service.[33] Although there are no uniform professional conduct rules for federal agency practitioners, many agencies have their own standards of ethics for practitioners.[34]

29. 424 U.S. 319 (1976). The *Mathews* standard is discussed in Chapter 5.

30. 494 U.S. 715 (1990).

31. 418 U.S. 539 (1974). The *Wolff* case is discussed in Chapter 5.

32. 5 U.S.C. § 500 (1999). For more information, ACUS maintains a continuously-updated, electronic sourcebook on Federal Administrative Procedure that includes a discussion of the Agency Practices Act. *See* https://https://sourcebook.acus.gov/wiki/Agency_Practice_Act/view.

33. The Internal Revenue Service rules are codified at 31 C.F.R. pt. 10.

34. For academic discussion of the legal and ethical obligations of lawyers in agency practice, see, *e.g.*, George M. Cohen, *The Laws of Agency Lawyering*, 84 Fordham L. Rev. 1963 (2016); Lawrence G. Baxter, *Reforming Legal Ethics in a Regulated Environment: An Introductory Overview*, 8 Geo. J. Legal Ethics 181 (1995); Michael P. Cox, *Regulation of Attorneys Practicing Before Federal Agencies*, 34 Case W. Res. L. Rev. 173 (1984).

§ 8.03 Evidence

[A] Formal Rules of Evidence

The Administrative Procedure Act (APA) was never intended, on its own, to incorporate the court-based Federal Rules of Evidence. These complicated evidence rules were designed to govern decisionmaking by juries. They are premised on the belief that lay jurors are likely to misuse certain types of potentially-relevant evidence if they become aware of that evidence. Irrespective of whether the Federal Rules of Evidence serve that purpose well, they are less appropriate for application to agency adjudications.

Other than a specific provision on official notice discussed in the next subsection, the APA speaks only in § 556(d) of "the exclusion of irrelevant, immaterial, or unduly repetitious evidence" and a decision supported by "reliable, probative, and substantial evidence."[35] The APA's legislative history makes clear that the use of terms like *relevant* and *material* in § 556(d) was meant to invoke notions of efficiency and common sense, rather than providing a basis for imposing technical rules of evidence. The House Report points out that "[t]hese are ... principles usually applied tacitly and resting mainly upon common sense which people engaged in the conduct of responsible affairs instinctively understand."[36] At bottom, Congress seemed to view formal rules of evidence as applicable mainly to civil jury trials, not agency adjudications before presumably expert ALJs. This conclusion was echoed by Judge Richard Posner, writing for the Seventh Circuit, in *Peabody Coal Co. v. Director, Office of Workers' Compensation Programs.*[37]

> The rules of evidence are primarily designed to protect jurors, viewed as naive or inexperienced factfinders, from being muddled or inflamed by misleading, prejudicial, unreliable, confusing, or repetitious evidence. The reason these rules are not applicable to agencies is that being staffed by specialists the agencies are assumed to be less in need of evidentiary blinders than lay jurors or even professional, though usually unspecialized judges. Evidence that might merely confuse a lay fact-finder may be essential to the exercise of expert judgment by a specialized professional adjudicator.[38]

Even so, some agencies, such as the Federal Trade Commission and the National Labor Relations Board—agencies that regularly engage in large numbers of evidentiary hearings—have decided to use formal rules of evidence when practicable. Many agencies that have adopted evidence rules have referenced aspects of the Federal Rules of Evidence in doing so.[39] Regardless, neither the APA, nor the Supreme Court, requires an agency to adopt formal rules of evidence. Indeed, in one of the principal Supreme Court decisions on point, the Court took the opposite view.

Richardson v. Perales[40] involved a claim for social security disability benefits filed by Pedro Perales. The statute requires that a claimant demonstrate that he is disabled

---

35. 5 U.S.C. § 556(d).

36. H.R. Rep. No. 1980, 79th Cong., 2d Sess., at 270 (1946).

37. 165 F.3d 1126 (7th Cir. 1999).

38. *Id.* at 1128–29.

39. *See, e.g.*, Richard J. Pierce, *Use of the Federal Rules of Evidence in Federal Agency Adjudications*, 39 Admin. L. Rev. 1 (1987); William H. Kuehnle, *Standards of Evidence in Administrative Proceedings*, 49 N.Y.L. Sch. L. Rev. 829 (2004).

40. 402 U.S. 389 (1971).

and unable to engage in gainful employment. Mr. Perales asserted that he had suffered a back injury on the job that prevented him from working. He filed a claim after seeing his own physician. The agency processed the claim and eventually denied it, triggering an evidentiary hearing request by Mr. Perales. Prior to the hearing, the following information came to the agency:

1. The report of an initial examination by Dr. Lampert, a consulting neurologist, who could find no objective evidence of a medical injury.
2. An examination by Dr. Morales, Perales' personal physician, whose report diagnosed Perales' injury as "back sprain-lumbro sacral spine, moderately severe, ruptured disk not ruled out."
3. An examination, commissioned by the agency, by Dr. Langston, who reported that Perales was not really injured.
4. An examination, again commissioned by the agency, by Dr. Bailey, a psychiatrist with a sub-specialty in neurology, who concluded that Mr. Perales had a "paranoid personality, manifested by hostility ...."
5. A second report based on electromyography studies by Dr. Langston and by a Dr. Mattson, both of whom concluded that Perales' problem was not job related or disabling.

After the agency denied the claim several times, Mr. Perales asked for, and received, an oral evidentiary hearing. The agency introduced various hospital records and the written reports filed by Drs. Langston, Bailey, Mattson and Lampert. The only one of these physicians to appear at the hearing and give oral testimony, however, was Mr. Perales's own doctor, Dr. Morales. Instead, the agency gave all of the written reports to yet another physician, a Dr. Leavitt, who reviewed all the records and testified orally as what the agency termed a medical adviser. Dr. Leavitt examined all the evidence and then offered an expert opinion on Mr. Perales' medical condition. Dr. Leavitt testified that in his opinion, Mr. Perales was suffering a "mild low-back syndrome of musculo-ligamentous origin." In other words, in Dr. Leavitt's opinion, Mr. Perales was not hurt badly enough to receive social security disability benefits. But because Dr. Leavitt himself had not examined Mr. Perales, but merely reviewed the statements of the other physicians, his testimony was also hearsay testimony. Following presentations by counsel, the social security hearing examiner (ALJ) agreed with Dr. Leavitt's conclusion and denied the Mr. Perales's benefits claim. To fully understand *Perales*, it helps to know that the federal courts are authorized to review only whether the agency decision is supported by *substantial evidence*.[41] The substantial evidence standard is fairly deferential. The reviewing court examines the entire record of the proceeding and determines if "more than a mere scintilla" of evidence supports the agency's decision.[42] If so, the court must uphold the agency's action.

In *Perales*, the Supreme Court looked first at the Social Security Act, a statute that provides expressly for the receipt by an ALJ of evidence that might be "inadmissible under rules of evidence applicable to court procedure." This statutory provision deals only with the introduction of evidence, however, and not with the use to which evidence is put in reaching a final agency decision. According to the Court, the decision against Mr. Perales rested solely on uncorroborated hearsay—something that the Court

41. The substantial evidence standard is discussed in depth in Chapter 13.
42. *Universal Camera Corp. v. National Labor Relations Board*, 340 U.S. 474 (1951).

in an earlier decision, *Consolidated Edison Co. v. National Labor Relations Board*,[43] had suggested would not be sufficient, by itself, to support an agency decision. The Court refused to apply this aspect of *Consolidated Edison* to the *Perales* case, although it did not expressly overrule the earlier case. Instead, the Court walked through the various reports described above, alluded to the fact that each of the reporting physicians did examine Mr. Perales (even if they were not available for cross-examination at the hearing), cited the figures on the enormous workload of the Social Security Administration, and refused to condemn the ALJ's reliance on Dr. Leavitt as a "medical adviser." At several points, the Court mentioned the reliability and probative worth of written medical reports and noted that Mr. Perales's lawyer could have subpoenaed the examining physicians and did not do so. The Court did not completely dispose of the case. Instead, it remanded the case to the district court for a determination of whether, given the Court's opinion in *Perales*, the agency decision was supported by substantial evidence. Nevertheless, the Court left little doubt as to its own sentiments on the issue.

The key lesson to take from *Perales* is that, irrespective of what the Federal Rules of Evidence might have to say about it, hearsay can come into agency hearings. Indeed, hearsay may be a substantial part of the proof. Most courts will not reject agency decisions merely because information that could be excluded in court comes onto a hearing record. You must be able to deal with this as an administrative lawyer without being devastated by the absence of formal rules of evidence.

[B] Official Notice

One other type of evidence specifically mentioned in the APA is *official notice*, also sometimes labeled *administrative notice*. APA § 556(e) provides, "When an agency decision rests on official notice of a material fact not appearing in the evidence in the record, a party is entitled, on timely request, to an opportunity to show the contrary." Although § 556(e) applies only to formal proceedings under the APA, the general principles that it expresses apply to all types of agency proceedings, including informal rulemaking as well as informal adjudication. This is because no administrator can possibly evaluate a question of fact, law, or policy without drawing upon her previous experiences and thinking of her general knowledge outside of any formal administrative record. Established facts merge with existing understandings and basic reasoning. Official notice should not be viewed lightly. When it is taken, however, it becomes just as much a basis for the final decision as anything else in the record.

The statutory authorization for official notice gives rise to two additional, related questions: (1) what sorts of things may be subject to official notice, and (2) how does official notice relate to and compare with judicial notice? The 1947 Attorney General's Manual on the APA discusses official notice as a concept that is designed to circumvent the time-consuming efforts involved in proving "what is obvious and notorious."[44] It is equally clear from the Manual and the other legislative history of the APA that official notice is intended to be broader than the related concept of judicial notice. Consequently, at a minimum, anything that is a proper subject of judicial notice may also be officially noticed in agency proceedings.

43. 305 U.S. 197 (1938).

44. Department of Justice, Attorney General's Manual on the Administrative Procedure Act 79 (1947).

Explicating judicial notice, and thus official notice, requires some understanding of the distinction between *legislative facts* and *adjudicative facts* developed by Professor Kenneth Culp Davis.[45] Generally speaking, adjudicative facts usually answer the questions of who did what, where, when, how, why, or with what motive or intent. In other words, adjudicative facts are the kinds of facts that typically would be given to the jury in a jury trial. By comparison, legislative facts do not usually concern the immediate parties but are the general facts, broadly applicable, that help a decisionmaker decide questions of law, policy, and discretion. To offer an example in the context of a common adjudicatory hearing—that of a social security disability proceeding—adjudicative facts might include the claimant's age, the number of years the claimant has paid into the social security system, or the nature of the claimant's specific injury, whereas legislative facts might include the knowledge that a majority of employed persons in the United States contribute to the social security system.

Perhaps unsurprisingly, it is much easier to take both judicial notice and official notice of legislative facts than adjudicative facts. Rule 201, Federal Rules of Evidence, limits the taking of judicial notice to a fact that is "not subject to reasonable dispute because it (1) is generally known within the trial court's territorial jurisdiction; or (2) can be accurately and readily determined from sources whose accuracy cannot reasonably be questioned." The same Rule 201 provides specifically that it governs judicial notice of adjudicative facts only, not legislative facts, so judicial notice of legislative facts is not limited to the above two categories. Also, courts typically evaluate legislative factfinding de novo but adjudicative factfinding under the clearly erroneous standard.[46] Thus, although "the precise demarcation ... is not always easily identified,"[47] federal courts often have recognized and applied the distinction between legislative facts and adjudicative facts in conjunction with Rule 201.[48]

Again, agencies generally are not bound to follow the Federal Rules of Evidence, so understanding Rule 201 only represents a conceptual starting point for thinking about official notice in agency hearings. One very important difference between courts and agencies is the latter's policymaking role. Recall that agencies have a choice between rulemaking and adjudication as the format for making policy choices.[49] The availability of that choice blurs even further the dividing line between legislative and adjudicative factfinding. Remember also that agencies are supposed to be experts in what they do. They accumulate a vast store of information in files, libraries, and other reservoirs of information. An administrative law judge (ALJ) hearing a matter involving medical evidence might like to know the statistics on congestive heart failure among white males between the ages of 40 and 55 that the ALJ knows is available in agency records. Why force the parties to submit evidence of such statistics when opening an agency file drawer may provide the information? Correspondingly, agency officials make predictions and exercise judgment based at least partly on the expertise and judgment derived

45. Kenneth Culp Davis, *An Approach to Problems of Evidence in the Administrative Process*, 55 Harv. L. Rev. 364 (1942); *see also* Kristin E. Hickman & Richard J. Pierce, Jr., Administrative Law Treatise §§ 9.5 & 9.6 (6th ed. 2018).

46. *See, e.g., United States v. Miller*, 982 F.3d 412 (6th Cir. 2020); *West Alabama Women's Center v. Williamson*, 900 F.3d 1310 (11th Cir. 2018).

47. *United States v. Gould*, 536 F.2d 216 (8th Cir. 1976).

48. *See, e.g., Robinson v. Liberty Mutual Insurance Co.*, 958 F.3d 1137 (11th Cir. 2020); *United States v. Lopez*, 880 F.3d 974 (8th Cir. 2018); *Oriental Financial Group, Inc. v. Cooperativa de Ahorro y Crédito Oriental*, 832 F.3d 15 (1st Cir. 2016).

49. This choice is discussed at length in Chapter 6.

from their own experiences. What would be the point in requiring them to set aside and ignore that expertise when deciding matters before the agency?

The requirement of APA § 556(e), that parties be given an opportunity to respond, mitigates the potential for agency overuse of official notice. Section 556(e) does not describe the nature of that opportunity, however. Agencies may introduce the facts that they consider in connection with a particular matter through any of (1) evidence at the hearing, (2) a statement for the first time in an ALJ's report, or (3) a statement for the first time in the agency's final report. Parties can exercise the right to respond conferred by § 556(e) at any of these times as well, whether as an opportunity to submit contrary evidence or in the form of argument in a brief or in an application for rehearing. Each of these approaches may be appropriate depending upon the circumstances. Critical variables in evaluating whether parties have been given adequate opportunity to respond are the degree to which the facts in question are adjudicative or legislative, the degree of doubt or certainty regarding the facts in question, and the degree of effect on the decision that those facts have. More procedural protections are necessary for adjudicative facts than for legislative ones, more for disputed or debatable facts than for those that seem indisputable, and more for facts that importantly affect the decision than for peripheral or background facts. When the facts in question are adjudicative, disputed, and critical, the opportunity to present evidence at a hearing typically is required. By contrast, the opportunity to respond to legislative facts that seem indisputable or are peripheral to the decision of the ALJ or the agency typically can come later in the administrative process.[50]

The Supreme Court has only occasionally addressed issues of official notice in the administrative process, with variable results, some of which may be attributable to changed attitudes over time. In 1937, in *Ohio Bell Telephone Co. v. Public Utilities Commission of Ohio*,[51] the Court refused to accept the taking of official notice involving land values and price trends by the Ohio Public Utilities Commission in a telephone rate case, because, in the words of Justice Cardozo, the agency decision was based on "facts not spread upon the record." Part of the Court's concern in that case may have been attributable to the Commission's refusal to reveal the sources of its information rather than that the Commission proposed to officially notice facts.

Regardless, eight years later, in *Market Street Railway v. Railroad Commission*,[52] the Court approved an agency's taking of official notice involving the potential effects on traffic of a rate reduction in street car and bus fares. In *Market Street*, Justice Jackson appears to have been persuaded by the expertise of the agency. "We cannot say that it is a denial of due process for a commission so experienced ... to draw inferences as to the probable effect on traffic of a given rate decrease on such a record as we have here."

In *Federal Power Commission v. Transcontinental Gas Pipe Line Corp.*,[53] the Supreme Court declined to allow the transportation and direct sale of natural gas from Texas to a New York utility company based at least partly on concerns about the implications

---

50. In the context of formal rulemaking, the Supreme Court has held that oral presentation of evidence and opportunity to cross-examine the sources of that evidence are not required when the contested issues of fact are general rather than specific to a particular party. *See United States v. Florida East Coast Railway Co.*, 410 U.S. 224 (1973); *United States v. Allegheny Ludlum Steel Corp.*, 406 U.S. 742 (1972).

51. 301 U.S. 292 (1937).

52. 324 U.S. 548 (1945).

53. 365 U.S. 1 (1961).

for future natural gas pricing. The Court rejected an argument that the agency "should have adduced testimonial and documentary evidence to the effect that [its] forecast would come true." Instead, the Court declared firmly that "we think that a forecast of the direction in which future public interest lies necessarily involves deductions based on the expert knowledge of the agency."

In *Federal Communications Commission v. National Citizens Committee for Broadcasting*,[54] the Court spoke in terms of "judgmental or predictive" facts rather than legislative facts or adjudicative facts in upholding regulations limiting common ownership of radio and television broadcasting stations and newspapers. In adopting the regulations, the agency exempted most of the existing instances of common ownership. A lower court had set aside the regulations for insufficient factual evidence supporting them, but the Court disagreed. The Court acknowledged that certain factual determinations were involved in the agency's decision—"e.g., whether a divestiture requirement would result in trading of stations with out-of-town owners; whether new owners would perform well as existing cross-owners, either in the short run or in the long run; whether losses to existing owners would result from forced sales; whether such losses would discourage future investment in quality programming; and whether new owners would have sufficient working capital to finance local programming." The Court held, however, that "[i]n such circumstances complete factual support in the record for the [agency's] judgment or prediction is not possible or required; 'a forecast of the direction in which future public interest lies necessarily involves deductions based on the expert knowledge of the agency.'"

The message of these cases seems clear. Official notice is permitted on many things that might not necessarily be proper topics of judicial notice. A careful ALJ will be cautious about moving too far beyond the judicial limits for official notice of facts. The more compelling matter from the standpoint of fairness is the opportunity to respond. For the party who is adversely affected by the taking of some official notice, all that may be necessary is to give that person the opportunity to respond. Presumably, the party could mount a two-pronged attack: first, that official notice of this particular fact is impermissible; and second, that the fact itself is not accurate. Most ALJs are careful with such matters.

[C] Burden of Proof

The APA addresses burden of proof in the first sentence of § 556(d): "Except as otherwise provided by statute, the proponent of a rule or order has the burden of proof."[55] The House Report on the APA equates the term *proponent* with the entity initiating the hearing.[56] In other words, an agency commencing an enforcement proceeding has the burden of proof, but a person seeking a federal license has the burden of showing her suitability for the license.

The APA does not expressly distinguish between *burden of going forward* and *burden of persuasion*, even though this distinction is an important one.[57] On this topic, the APA's legislative history is not much help. The Senate Report on the APA makes clear

54. 436 U.S. 775 (1978).
55. 5 U.S.C. § 556(d).
56. 1 H.R. Rep. No. 79-1980, at 270 (1946).
57. *See, e.g.*, Kenneth S. Braun, et al., McCormick on Evidence, §§ 336–44 (8th ed. 2020).

that drafters of the APA recognized the matter of allocation of proof by pointing out that while the proponent has both the burden of coming forward and the burden of persuasion on the basic point of the hearing, other parties may bear the burden on other matters sought to be proved.[58]

Until 1994, courts and commentators were unanimous in concluding that the APA imposed the burden of production, but not the burden of persuasion, on the proponent of a rule or order. In *Director, Office of Workers' Compensation Programs v. Greenwich Collieries*,[59] the Court held that the APA imposes both burdens on the proponent. The Court said that the term "burden of proof" had been ambiguous throughout much of the nation's history, but that by 1946, when Congress adopted the APA, the term clearly included both the burden of production and the burden of persuasion. Accordingly, the Court attributed to Congress that understanding of the burden of proof.[60]

[D] Standard of Proof

As thorough as the APA is on certain aspects of agency practice, it says absolutely nothing about the standard of proof applicable in trial-type proceedings. In the context of jury trials, there are three standards of proof: (1) *beyond a reasonable doubt*, used almost exclusively in a criminal setting and with litigation; (2) *clear and convincing*; and (3) *preponderance of the evidence*. Although the precise meaning of these terms is elusive, definitions can be found in model jury instructions and in the various treatises on evidence. These standards have had little practical impact on administrative proceedings.

In *Steadman v. Securities & Exchange Commission*,[61] the Supreme Court considered the implications of the standards of proof for jury trials in the context of administrative proceedings. The case involved a registered broker who was sanctioned by the SEC for violating various provisions of the securities laws. One of the sanctions imposed on the broker included a permanent prohibition on affiliating with registered investment advisers or investment companies and a one-year prohibition on affiliating with any securities broker or dealer. The broker challenged the sanctions in part because the SEC had applied the preponderance of the evidence standard to his disciplinary proceeding. He argued that when an agency takes action affecting the professional status of a person functioning in a setting regulated by the agency, the agency should be held to the higher standard of proof, specifically the clear and convincing evidence standard.

The Supreme Court rejected this proposition. The Court noted that the APA does not include a standard of proof requirement. The Court also observed that the APA's language on burden of proof and evidence tends to lean toward the minimum amount of evidence necessary to show to a reviewing body that the agency decision is supported by substantial evidence (which is a standard of judicial review with respect to administrative action, not a standard of proof for an agency hearing). *Steadman* is not a difficult

---

58. S. Rep. No. 79-752, at 207–09 (1945).

59. 512 U.S. 267 (1994).

60. Leading evidence scholars would find this conclusion surprising. A leading evidence treatise has described the modern understanding of the burden of proof as "encompass[ing] two separate burdens of proof. One burden is that of producing evidence [and] [t]he second is the burden of persuading the trier of fact that the alleged fact is true." Braun, et al., *supra* note 57, at § 336.

61. 450 U.S. 91 (1981).

decision to understand. The Court was straightforward in its holding. Absent a statutory requirement, or perhaps an agency rule of practice,[62] the only standard of proof to be applied in agency proceedings is the preponderance of the evidence standard.

§ 8.04 Administrative Law Judges and Decisional Independence

[A] Appointing and Protecting ALJs

According to Administrative Procedure Act (APA) § 556(b), evidentiary hearings may be presided over by "(1) the agency; (2) one or more members of the body which comprises the agency; or (3) one or more *administrative law judges* appointed under section 3105 of [Title 5]" (emphasis added). Prior to the enactment of the APA in 1946, evidentiary hearings were conducted by presiding officers called *hearing examiners*. The people serving this function had few job protections. They tended to be subject to pressures and disciplinary actions within their agencies that influenced how they decided cases. On many occasions, the person who served as the hearing examiner might be the same person who had conducted the initial investigation and written the initial complaint. As a result, many hearing examiners found themselves functioning in both a judicial and a prosecutorial capacity in the same case. Viewed from a contemporary perspective, this approach sounds terribly biased, insensitive, and perhaps even callous on the part of the agencies. Yet it was only after agencies began to proliferate and to conduct more and more evidentiary hearings that issues questioning the duties and independence of the hearing examiners officers arose.

The APA clarified many of these points by insisting on a strict separation of functions, segregating enforcement personnel from those who conduct hearings, and establishing heavy restrictions on ex parte contacts between the presiding officer, the rest of the agency, and the parties to the adjudication. APA § 554(d) provides expressly that agency personnel with investigative or prosecutorial responsibilities "may not, in that or a factually related case, participate or advise in the decision ... except as witnesses or counsel in public proceedings." That same provision also prohibits agency investigators or prosecutors from supervising those who preside over hearings.

To shore up this emphasis on the decisional independence of those who oversee evidentiary hearings, control over many of the personnel matters relating to presiding officers was taken out of the hands of the individual agencies and transferred to the Civil Service Commission, now the Office of Personnel Management. In 1972, the title of those officials who preside over formal agency hearings was changed as well. The Civil Service Commission, by rule, changed the term from hearing examiner to *administrative law judge*, a change that was codified in APA § 556(b) and elsewhere in Title 5 of the United States Code in 1978.[63] Also, while the ALJs remain assigned to specific

62. One basis for the Court's decision in *Steadman* was the fact that the SEC had always used the preponderance standard in disciplinary proceedings.

63. 5 U.S.C. § 3105. For a discussion of the separation of functions doctrine, see Benjamin W. Mintz, *Administrative Separation of Functions: OSHA and the NLRB*, 47 CATH. U. L. REV. 877 (1998).

agencies, negative personnel actions against ALJs are now handled by the Merit Systems Protection Board.[64] The rules of the Office of Personnel Management and the Merit Systems Protection Board make removing or disciplining ALJs difficult. To that extent, ALJs are fairly well insulated from specific agency pressures, although ALJs assigned to the Social Security Administration (the largest single group of ALJs in the federal government) have frequently complained about undue agency pressure to dispose of cases quickly and without thorough consideration.[65]

Assignment of ALJs to specific agencies is something that has been debated at length on the federal level.[66] To a certain extent, an agency assignment still leaves the ALJs at the mercy of the agencies for things such as office assignments and staff support. By contrast, removing ALJs from individual agencies and assigning them to a central board which would then farm out individual judges to agencies on a case-by-case basis would diminish their expertise in specific areas of regulation. This issue continues to be debated at the federal level, but every attempt so far to create an independent corps of ALJs for federal agencies has failed to get out of Congress.

Although evidentiary hearings under APA §§556 and 557 formal adjudication procedures are conducted by ALJs, many relatively formal hearings that fall outside of the APA are overseen by "mere" administrative judges, or AJs.[67] Many lawyers do not appreciate the distinction between the two categories of agency adjudicators. Although AJs perform many of the same function as ALJs, they are hired directly by the agencies that employ them rather than the Office of Personnel Management, and they lack the formal legal protections given to ALJs. Moreover, unlike ALJs, AJs are not prohibited by statute from engaging in ex parte communications with agency officials, discussed below.

Many states maintain a central pool of administrative law judges available for assignment to any agency that requires an adjudication. Florida is one example.[68] Minnesota[69]

---

64. 5 U.S.C. §7521.

65. For a specific case on point, see *Ass'n of Admin. Law Judges v. Heckler*, 594 F. Supp. 1132 (D.D.C. 1984). For more extensive narrative commentary, see, *e.g.*, Jerry L. Mashaw & Richard Merrill, The American Public Law System 239–50 (2d ed. 1985). Professor Mashaw has done extensive research and writing in the work of the social security system. *See, e.g.*, Jerry L. Mashaw, Social Security Hearings and Appeals (1978) (with others). For additional insight into the ALJs and their problems, see Daniel J. Gifford, *Federal Administrative Law Judges: The Relevance of Past Choices to Future Directions*, 49 Admin. L. Rev. 1 (1997). The system found in many state processes of assigning ALJs from a central pool of judges is extensively analyzed in Allen C. Hoberg, *Administrative Hearings: State Central Panels in the 1990s*, 46 Admin. L. Rev. 75 (1994).

66. *See, e.g.*, Richard E. Levy & Robert L. Glicksman, *Restoring ALJ Independence*, 105 Minn. L. Rev. 39 (2020); Malcolm C. Rich & Alison C. Goldstein, *The Need for a Central Panel Approach to Administrative Adjudication: Pros, Cons, and Selected Practices*, 39 J. Nat'l Ass'n Admin. L. Judiciary 1 (2019); Charles H. Koch, Jr., *Policymaking by the Administrative Judiciary*, 56 Ala. L. Rev. 693 (2005); Paul R. Verkuil, et al., *Report for Recommendation 92-7, The Federal Administrative Judiciary*, *in* 2 Administrative Conference of the United States, Recommendations and Reports 779 (1992).

67. For excellent discussions of the issues associated with AJs, see Christopher J. Walker & Melissa F. Wasserman, *The New World of Agency Adjudication*, 107 Cal. L. Rev. 141 (2019); Kent Barnett, *Against Administrative Judges*, 49 U.C. Davis L. Rev. 1643 (2016).

68. *See* Fla. Stat. §120.75. Florida calls its central pool of ALJs the Division of Administrative Hearings. *See also* https://doah.state.fl.us/ALJ/.

69. *See* Minn. Stat. §14.48. Minnesota calls its central pool of ALJs the Office of Administrative Hearings. *See also* https://mn.gov/oah/.

and New Jersey[70] are others. These systems seem to work well, although the opponents of a similar change on the federal level suggest that the typical state adjudication is far less complicated than one at the federal level. Agency-specific expertise has its advantages. A central assignment facility has different advantages.[71]

[B] Separation of Functions

Although the APA provides for a separation of functions, and thus decisional independence for ALJs, it seems clear that the Supreme Court does not consider the separation of functions to be especially important for decisional legitimacy if a legislature fails to provide for it. At one time, the Court seemed as though it might take the separation of functions seriously. Shortly after Congress enacted the APA, in *Wong Yang Sung v. McGrath*,[72] the Court considered a challenge to the procedures used to adjudicate disputes over the potential deportation of noncitizens. Congress had not explicitly required the Commissioner of Immigration or the Board of Immigration Appeals to use the APA's formal adjudication procedures in deportation proceedings. The Court concluded that the deportation procedures afforded by the agency in that case were flawed for the inadequacy of a separation of functions, as the agency officials responsible for adjudicating deportation disputes reported to officials who had enforcement responsibilities.

The Court suggested in *Wong Yang Sung* that it might require APA formal adjudication procedures as the constitutional floor for adjudicating important matters like deportation cases. Nevertheless, Congress subsequently adopted amendments to the Immigration and Nationality Act overruling *Wong Yang Sung* by establishing procedures specific to the immigration context that again had agency officials with responsibility for adjudicating deportation disputes report to officials with enforcement responsibilities. In *Marcello v. Bonds*,[73] the Court upheld those amendments as constitutional against a due process challenge, backing away from its dicta in *Wong Yang Sung*, and emphasizing "the longstanding practice in deportation proceedings" as well as "the specific considerations applicable to deportation which the Congress may take into account in exercising its particularly broad discretion in immigration matters."

In other contexts, the Court has upheld instances of combined functions as well. The Court's most comprehensive treatment of the subject was its decision in *Withrow v. Larkin*.[74] In that case, a physician licensed to practice medicine in Wisconsin was subject to a disciplinary hearing because he allegedly performed abortions in violation of state law. The hearing took place before the state's Medical Examining Board, an entity that had first investigated the doctor's conduct and then presided over the administrative hearing regarding the allegations. The Court decided that this combination of functions in a single entity was constitutional, mainly because the doctor could not specify any

70. *See* N.J.S.A. § 52:14F-1 & -4. New Jersey calls its central pool of ALJs the Office of Administrative Law. *See also* https://www.nj.gov/oal/.

71. *See* James F. Flanagan, *Redefining the Role of the State Administrative Law Judge: Central Panels and Their Impact on State ALJ Authority and Standards of Agency Review*, 54 ADMIN. L. REV. 1355 (2002).

72. 339 U.S. 33 (1950).

73. *See Marcello v. Bonds*, 349 U.S. 302 (1955) (upholding the amendments to the Immigration and Naturalization Act's procedures as constitutional).

74. 421 U.S. 35 (1975).

actual bias on the part of the Board. The Justices presumed regularity and integrity on the part of the Board, absent some showing to the contrary. The Court acknowledged that "a 'fair trial in a fair tribunal is a basic requirement of due process,'" whether the tribunal is a court or an agency. But the Court said that demonstrating an unconstitutional risk of bias purely based on a combination of functions,

> must overcome a presumption of honesty and integrity in those serving as adjudicators; and it must convince that under a realistic appraisal of psychological tendencies and human weakness, conferring investigative and adjudicative powers on the same individuals poses such a risk of actual bias or prejudgment that the practice must be forbidden if the guarantee of due process is to be adequately implemented.[75]

Much more recently, if somewhat more tangentially, in 2018, in *Lucia v. Securities & Exchange Commission*,[76] the Court held that SEC ALJs are inferior officers whose appointments must be made consistently with the Appointments Clause, rather than mere employees of the SEC. In 2021, in *United States v. Arthrex, Inc.*,[77] the Court held that the structure of the Patent Trial and Appeal Board was unconstitutional for relying on Administrative Patent Judges to issue final decisions without giving the Director of the Patent and Trademark Office review authority over those decisions. The consequences of these decisions for ALJ decisional independence and the formal separation of functions at administrative agencies are worth watching.

The Court's disinterest in the separation of functions does not mean that the Court is completely callous about these issues. When actual bias has been shown in an individual case, the Court has not hesitated to strike down agency action.[78]

§ 8.05 Bias and Ex Parte Contacts in Agency Proceedings

[A] Bias and Disqualification

[1] Need for Impartiality

Due process requires a neutral, or unbiased, adjudicatory decisionmaker. No one wants important disputes to be decided by people who cannot approach the issues with an open mind. One of the reasons for the separation of functions discussed in § 8.04, *above*, is to avoid the appearance of bias in favor of the agency that might occur if someone performed several different functions that crossed the line between enforcement and adjudication.

Even beyond the separation of functions, the Administrative Procedure Act (APA) itself recognizes the importance of avoiding the appearance of bias by permitting parties to sidestep agency adjudicators who may not be impartial. According to APA § 556(b), "On the filing in good faith of a timely and sufficient affidavit of personal bias or other

75. *Id.* at 47.
76. 138 S. Ct. 2044 (2018). *See* Chapter 3, § 3.03.
77. 141 S. Ct. 1970 (2021).
78. *See Gibson v. Berryhill*, 411 U.S. 564 (1973).

disqualification of a presiding or participating employee, the agency shall determine the matter as a part of the record and decision in the case."[79] In other words, the agency will evaluate and dispose of a motion to disqualify an agency decisionmaker for bias and will do so on the same record as the rest of the case. Under normal circumstances, an issue of bias does not give rise to a wholly separate proceeding, but proceeds to judicial review along with the remainder of the dispute.

Analyzing any question of bias is easier if you recognize and carefully distinguish between the different types of bias that may affect an agency hearing. Some kinds of bias are simply permissible, even if private parties whose cases are being adjudicated find them troubling. For example, most bias that agency practitioners encounter is ideological—*e.g.*, a prejudgment or point of view about a question of law or policy or about legislative facts that help answer a question of law or policy.[80] This sort of bias is rarely, if ever, disqualifying.

Three forms of bias are particularly impermissible in the adjudicatory context: *personal interest bias*, *prejudgment* regarding adjudicative facts, and *personal bias or prejudice*. Before examining the nuances of these issues, however, be aware of the bottom line: for anyone seeking to overturn an agency action because of bias of any kind, this is one of the most difficult fights in the book. It is rare that a court will find either prejudgment or personal bias or prejudice to a sufficient degree to disqualify a particular decisionmaker from overseeing an agency adjudication. Recall the adage: "He who shoots at the king should aim carefully." Charging a judge or other agency adjudicator with bias and not winning a disqualification on that point will guarantee you a very uncomfortable hearing. Understand also that, even if you do show bias, you will not automatically win your case. Successfully arguing that a particular adjudicator is biased merely disqualifies that person from hearing your case. The case itself will then simply be reassigned and proceed before another, unbiased adjudicator.

[2] Personal Interest Bias

Bias based on a decisionmaker's personal interest is easy to understand. A person who stands to gain or lose personally and somewhat directly from the outcome of an agency adjudication is disqualified from participating in the decisionmaking process by reason of that personal interest. The Supreme Court has addressed this concern on several occasions.

For example, in *Gibson v. Berryhill*,[81] the Court considered the makeup of a state board charged with licensing optometrists, which board was staffed entirely by already-licensed optometrists. A federal district court held that admitting new optometrists could dilute the earnings of the existing optometrists in the state, thereby giving the members of the board a personal financial stake in the issue of new licenses. The Supreme Court affirmed that decision, holding that a personal financial interest in the outcome of an adjudicatory decision does not even have to be a direct interest if that interest is sufficient to suggest possible bias.

---

79. 5 U.S.C. § 556(b).

80. The distinction between legislative facts and adjudicative facts is discussed in § 8.03[B], above.

81. 411 U.S. 564 (1973).

The Court reached a similar conclusion in *North Carolina State Board of Dental Examiners v. Federal Trade Commission*,[82] when the Court held that a state agency controlled by dentists could not prohibit non-dentists from providing teeth whitening services. In that case, the Court repeatedly emphasized the risk that an agency controlled by active market participants with conflicts of interest might engage in "private self-dealing" instead of acting to further the public good unless the agency was actively supervised by state officials who were not active market participants.

Nevertheless, the Court's concern about the appearance of personal interest bias does not necessarily preclude the government from privatizing certain adjudications. In *Schweiker v. McClure*,[83] the Court considered a government delegation of certain Medicare benefit determinations to hearing officers employed by insurance companies. A lower court found an "intolerable risk" that the hearing officers would be biased against the persons claiming benefits and in favor of their insurance company employers. The Supreme Court disagreed and upheld the scheme because both the Medicare benefits and the hearing officers' salaries were paid from government funds. The Court said there was no evidence that either the insurance companies or the hearing officers were impermissibly biased against claimants to benefits.

[3] Prejudgment Bias

Agency adjudicators can be disqualified for prejudging disputed issues of adjudicative fact, which again typically concern who did what to whom, where, when, how, why, and with what motive or intent. Advance knowledge of adjudicative facts that are at issue in a particular adjudication alone is not enough to disqualify someone from making those findings of fact. Disqualification comes from a precommitment to particular factual findings.

Issues of prejudgment bias usually involve people at the top of the agency. These are the employees who make public statements on behalf of the agency, including their own views as to what the agency should be doing. Cabinet secretaries, the commissioners or other heads of independent agencies, and general counsels often are asked to and do speak in public as agency representatives. At least some of those people are final decisionmakers, for example in reviewing initial decisions on behalf of an agency. Many or even most of the cases of bias in this category involve agency officials who publicly express particular points of view before sitting on actual cases.

A classic case in this area is *Cinderella Career & Finishing Schools, Inc. v. Federal Trade Commission*.[84] Federal Trade Commissioner Paul Rand Dixon joined the Federal Trade Commission (FTC) in acting on a cease-and-desist proceeding against a for-profit school that stood accused of misrepresentations and false advertising for not living up to its promises to its students. After sixteen days of hearings, a hearing examiner recommended dismissal of the charges. The FTC, with Dixon participating, instead issued a cease-and-desist order on six of thirteen charges. Dixon's participation in the proceedings came after he had made a speech to the National Newspaper Association criticizing newspapers for carrying advertisements "that offer college educations in five weeks, fortunes by raising mushrooms in the basement, getting rid of pimples

82. 135 S. Ct. 1101 (2015).
83. 456 U.S. 188 (1982).
84. 425 F.2d 583 (D.C. Cir. 1970).

with a magic lotion, or becoming an airline's hostess by attending a charm school.... Granted that newspapers are not in the advertising policing business, their advertising managers are savvy enough to smell deception when the odor is strong enough." The D.C. Circuit Court of Appeals concluded that Dixon had to be disqualified. According to the court, "[Dixon] was sensitive to theory but insensitive to reality" when he later declined to recuse himself from the school's case by suggesting that disqualification was not required "for trifling causes" but rather was left to "the discretion and sound judgment of the administrator himself." Worse, the court said, his actions indicated that he was "indifferent" to the court's pronouncements on bias. The court determined that it had to speak in these terms because "of Mr. Dixon's flagrant disregard of prior [court] decisions."

Do not conclude that it is easy to disqualify agency personnel. By comparison, consider the Tenth Circuit's more recent decision in *Zen Magnets, LLC v. Consumer Product Safety Commission*.[85] The Tenth Circuit rejected allegations that Consumer Product Safety Commission (CPSC) members either prejudged or showed personal interest bias in adjudicating whether a product sold by a manufacturer, Zen, posed a "substantial product hazard" as defined in the Consumer Product Safety Act. Zen sold small rare-earth magnets, which reportedly have caused serious injuries and death when swallowed by children. After first issuing a notice of proposed rulemaking to adopt a safety standard requiring manufacturers to make small rare-earth magnets larger or their magnetic strength weaker, the CPSC brought a complaint against Zen. The CPSC decided that the magnets sold by Zen posed a substantial product hazard irrespective of any warnings or age recommendations. Prior to that decision, at a hearing on the rulemaking, three members of the CPSC made various public statements about safety issues associated with small rare-earth magnets. Two of those members specifically distinguished the rulemaking from the adjudication, maintaining that the two types of proceedings involved "different factual elements and different standards of proof." A third CPSC member delivered "an impassioned statement" at the rulemaking hearing that addressed the dangers of small rare-earth magnets, his love of and fears for his own children, and the loss suffered by the family of a child injured by small rare-earth magnets. A few years earlier, after a federal district court enjoined Zen from selling magnets it had acquired from another company, that same third member had applauded the injunction as "put[ting] the rule of law and the safety of children above the profits sought by Zen."

Before the Tenth Circuit, Zen argued that the three CPSC members demonstrated prejudgment by their public statements, and thus violated Zen's due process rights. The court concluded, however, that the "context and content" of the CPSC members' statements did not show prejudgment. The court carefully traced their statements to the rulemaking, rather than the adjudication, and noted other statements distinguishing the rulemaking from the adjudication. Regarding the third CPSC member who spoke of his own children, the court said that "simply expressing sympathy for the family of a child who had died swallowing the magnets ... did not reflect prejudgment of the issues" in the adjudication. The statement regarding the prior litigation was unrelated to the adjudication and likewise did not show prejudgment.

85. 968 F.3d 1156 (10th Cir. 2020).

[4] Personal Bias or Prejudice

Personal bias or prejudice easily supports disqualification of an adjudicatory decisionmaker. People tend to think of personal bias or prejudice in terms of hostility toward the party in question, whether arising from a prior bad relationship or from the party's personal characteristics (*e.g.*, race, gender, religion, or ethnic origin). But personal bias can include favoritism toward a party, perhaps due to a close friendship or other affectionate relationship.

When assessing claims of personal bias or prejudice, a key difficulty lies in determining the degree or the source of the alleged bias based on ambiguous evidence. Many cases have required courts to evaluate bias claims based on things that decisionmakers have said in the course of adjudicating the matters before them, and to distinguish statements that are merely ill-advised or unprofessional from those that exhibit true bias or prejudice. Consider, for example, *Bieber v. Department of the Army*.[86] In this case, an administrative judge for the Merit Systems Protection Board heard an appeal from an employee's removal from government service for insubordination, disrupting the workplace, and making a false statement concerning his supervisor. The employee's actions stemmed from (1) his objections to casual clothing worn by his co-workers that the employee found inappropriate, and (2) his complaints that his supervisors failed to provide adequate guidance regarding the appropriateness of the clothing in question. During the hearing, the administrative judge made comments like "I really think what people wear to work is no concern of their fellow employees" and "why didn't [the employee] just shut up?," and also said repeatedly that he could not understand why the employee "continued to be obsessed with [the dress code issue]." In considering whether those claims demonstrated bias, the Federal Circuit Court of Appeals held that the administrative judge's remarks, "while in some instances inappropriate," did not demonstrate the sort of "deep-seated ... antagonism that would make fair judgment impossible."

As already noted, however, having a strong attitude favoring a particular policy position or interpretation of the law—sometimes referred to as *viewpoint bias*—typically is not disqualifying. A key case in this regard is *National Labor Relations Board v. Pittsburgh Steamship Co.*[87] In that case, a hearing examiner for the NLRB had found witnesses for the employer to be uniformly untrustworthy and witnesses for the complaining union to be uniformly reliable. The NLRB adopted the hearing examiner's findings. A lower court had held that "the unvarying repudiation of every witness for [the employer] because of falsity, evasion, or faint recollection, along with consistent exaltation of every union witness as truthful, forthright, and accurate" reflected undue bias and "destroy[ed] completely any confidence that might otherwise be placed in" the agency's decision. The Supreme Court disagreed, finding that the adjudication's transcript showed "thoughtful and discriminating evaluation of the facts" and holding that "total rejection of an opposed view cannot of itself impugn the integrity or competence of a trier of fact."

86. 287 F.3d 1358 (Fed. Cir. 2002).
87. 337 U.S. 656 (1949).

[B] Ex Parte Contacts in Adjudicatory Hearings

The APA contains a number of express provisions on ex parte contacts. APA § 551(14) defines ex parte communication as "an oral or written communication not on the public record with respect to which reasonable prior notice is not given, but it shall not include requests for status reports on any matter or proceeding covered by this chapter."[88] The APA then proceeds to prohibit ex parte communications to or from any agency decisionmaker concerning the merits of any formal adjudication (or formal rulemaking). Specifically, APA § 554(d) provides that agency employees who preside over formal adjudicatory hearings, including ALJs, may not consult "a person or party on a fact in issue, unless on notice and opportunity for all parties to participate."[89] At first glance, the language looks a little cumbersome, but it's really fairly easy to outline.

1. Remember that ex parte contacts go both ways; parties are prohibited from contacting the agency deciders, and the agency deciders are prohibited from contacting the parties.

2. Understand that this does not prohibit you from saying "good morning" to an ALJ. Ex parte contacts are those contacts that relate "to the merits of the proceeding." Requests for status reports are expressly permitted. Private communications concerning procedure or timing also do not violate the statutory prohibition on ex parte contacts. At the same time, it makes no difference whether contacts relating to the merits are made orally or in written form. Either type of contact regarding the merits is forbidden.

3. Agency employees have an express obligation to docket and explain all ex parte contacts or attempts at ex parte contacts in the hearing record.

Courts do not like ex parte contacts and may deal quite harshly with abuses of these rules. In one instance, the D.C. Circuit vacated an agency action because the agency heard from an interested company in secret, after the record was ostensibly closed and other companies had concluded their participation.[90] In another particularly bad case of ex parte communications, one of two competing applicants for a television broadcasting license sent each of the commissioners of the Federal Communications Commission (FCC) private written submissions purporting to prove contested material facts, bought them meals, and gave them Christmas turkeys. The reviewing court vacated the license the FCC had awarded to the participant in question on the ground that the licensing proceeding "involved ... resolution of conflicting private claims to a valuable privilege, and that basic fairness requires such a proceeding to be carried on in the open."[91]

Even among agency personnel, ex parte communications may threaten the validity of an agency action. The FCC, for example, draws some tight distinctions between decisional and nondecisional staff and prohibits contacts between the two categories of employees on matters subject to formal hearing requirements.[92] In *Seacoast Anti-Pollution League v. Costle*,[93] an Environmental Protection Agency (EPA) presiding officer listened to some EPA scientists off the record. The agency action was vacated because of these contacts.

---

88. 5 U.S.C. § 551(14).
89. 5 U.S.C. § 554(d).
90. *United States Lines, Inc. v. Federal Maritime Comm'n*, 584 F.2d 519 (D.C. Cir. 1978).
91. *Sangamon Valley Television Corp. v. United States*, 269 F.2d 221 (D.C. Cir. 1959).
92. 47 C.F.R. §§ 1.1200–1.1216.
93. 572 F.2d 872 (1st Cir. 1978).

On the other hand, ex parte contacts will not automatically destroy every case. APA § 706 instructs reviewing courts to take "due account ... of the rule of prejudicial error"—*i.e.*, to recognize that some errors are harmless and do not require the court to invalidate agency action. In some instances, courts have held ex parte communications harmless. For example, in *Ludwig v. Astrue*,[94] the Ninth Circuit reached such a conclusion notwithstanding having labeled the ex parte communication in question "egregious." In this case, after an ALJ completed a hearing in a Social Security disability case, an agent from the Federal Bureau of Investigation (FBI) told the ALJ that the applicant was faking his disability. The ALJ notified the applicant's attorney but refused to give the attorney an opportunity to cross-examine the FBI agent or to assure the attorney that the ALJ would not give the FBI agent's statement any weight. The ALJ concluded that the applicant was not disabled. In his opinion, the ALJ said that he had not given the FBI agent's statement "significant weight." The court expressed concern about the statement because it went to the heart of the case and because the FBI agent was considered more credible than the applicant himself. The court also said that the ALJ committed error both by listening to the FBI agent's statement and by not giving the applicant's counsel an opportunity to cross-examine the FBI agent. Nevertheless, the court held that the ALJ's error was harmless because the record contained ample evidence to support finding that the applicant had lied in his testimony.

Regardless, when it comes to ex parte contacts, be cautious. You have an ethical obligation to represent your clients zealously, but failing to follow the rules can backfire on both your client and you—with your client potentially losing its case, and you finding yourself possibly the subject of bar disciplinary action. Remember that the ethical command tells you to represent your clients zealously *within* the bounds of the law.

§ 8.06 Review of an Initial Decision Within the Agency

Virtually all federal agencies provide for review of an initial adjudicative decision within the agency. Administrative Procedure Act (APA) § 557(b) acknowledges this by providing that, "[o]n appeal from or review of the initial decision, the agency has all the powers which it would have in making the initial decision except as it may limit the issues on notice or by rule."[95] The *Attorney General's Manual on the Administrative Procedure Act* makes clear that this language was intended to communicate the agency's almost unfettered authority to do anything it wishes in reviewing an initial decision. The agency may review only those things objected to by the parties, or it may set aside the entire decision and make its own findings with or without the taking of additional evidence.[96]

In practice, however, matters typically are more closely confined on intra-agency review. Most agencies pay close attention to the initial decision for at least two reasons.

---

94. 681 F.3d 1047 (9th Cir. 2012).

95. 5 U.S.C. § 557(b).

96. Department of Justice, Attorney General's Manual on the Administrative Procedure Act 84–85 (1947). For additional discussion on the issues involved with what is called intra-agency review, see Russell L. Weaver, *Appellate Review in Executive Departments and Agencies*, 48 Admin. L. Rev. 251 (1996).

First, as a practical matter, agencies do not have the time or the resources to completely reconsider every case that is appealed by the losing party. Second, the Supreme Court requires the agency to give consideration particularly to the findings of fact of the administrative law judge (ALJ), and thus places some constraints on what the agency can do with the case after the ALJ has conducted the initial hearing.

The Supreme Court has paid considerable attention to the weight to be given the ALJ's decision in the agency decisional process. In its landmark decision in *Universal Camera Corp. v. National Labor Relations Board*,[97] the Supreme Court reviewed a case in which a worker alleged that he had been unlawfully discharged by his employer because he filed a grievance against the company. The discharged worker invoked several of the federal labor statutes as protection against this kind of retaliatory termination. The employer said the worker was fired because he had a fist fight with the company's personnel manager. The ALJ believed the company's witnesses; the NLRB reversed and upheld the employee's side of the story.

The question that reached the Supreme Court was how much weight an ALJ's findings must be given on intra-agency review. In this case, the reviewing body was the Board itself, consisting of the NLRB's five members. In an opinion authored by Justice Frankfurter, the Court conceded that the Board did not need to treat the ALJ's decision in the same way that an Article III court might treat the findings of a special master. As Justice Frankfurter stated, an ALJ's findings are "not as unassailable as a master's." Nor did the Board have to approach the ALJ's findings as an appellate court would deal with the findings of a trial court—*i.e.*, reversing the ALJ's findings only if the Board determined that the ALJ's findings were *clearly erroneous*.

At the same time, the Board could not just disregard the ALJ's findings. Surely, the findings of someone who presided over the evidentiary hearing, heard the witnesses, and presumably reviewed the entire record was deserving of some weight. The Court noted especially that the Board should pay at least some attention to "the [ALJ's] opportunity to observe the witnesses he hears and sees... [that] the Board does not."

Justice Frankfurter's opinion in *Universal Camera* was not precise in describing how much weight the Board should give the ALJ's findings. Rather, Justice Frankfurter was describing the substantial evidence standard that the NLRB had to satisfy in reaching a decision regarding the employee's claim. To satisfy the substantial evidence standard, he said that the NLRB could not merely rely upon some of the evidence presented and instead had to consider the whole record, including the ALJ's decision and other contrary evidence. Regardless, the unspoken message of this aspect of the Supreme Court's decision in *Universal Camera* seems to be that agency officials engaged in intra-party review of an initial decision should be careful when reversing an ALJ who has heard the witnesses, when the ALJ's findings turn heavily on the credibility of the witnesses and when credibility is a significant factor in the case.

97. 340 U.S. 474 (1951).

§ 8.07 Alternative Dispute Resolution in Federal Agencies

In late 1990, Congress enacted some important amendments to Title 5 of the United States Code that greatly broaden the procedural options for federal agency disputes. The statute is cited as the Administrative Dispute Resolution Act (ADR Act).[98] It made virtually all of the procedural vehicles available in private sector dispute resolution also available to agencies. The ADR Act survived some tangential attacks and was permanently reauthorized in 1996. In essence, Congress merely codified what had become a growing number of agency experiments in ADR over the preceding years.[99] In 1998, a presidential memorandum signed by President Clinton established the Interagency ADR Working Group to assist federal agencies in developing and implementing alternative dispute resolution programs.[100]

To a certain extent, the ADR Act was a strange development because administrative agencies themselves were supposed to be alternative dispute resolution entities. Federal and state agencies were given adjudication responsibilities because the courts were not up to dealing expeditiously with the many adjudications arising from administrative governance in a large and complex society.

The ADR Act confirmed that the APA's formal adjudication process itself is cumbersome and time-consuming. Congress determined that many disputes could be resolved by some mechanism other than the elaborate evidentiary hearing process described in detail in this chapter. Under the ADR Act, agencies are permitted—in appropriate circumstances—to employ ADR devices to resolve disputes.

Nothing about the ADR Act is compulsory. Agencies use these alternative mechanisms at their election and only after careful consideration.[101] Moreover, the parties to the dispute must agree to their use. The ADR Act's general authority states that "an agency may use a dispute resolution proceeding for the resolution of an issue in controversy that relates to an administrative program, if the parties agree to such proceeding."[102] This voluntary component was a major concession to the possibility that

---

98. Pub. L. No. 101-552, 104 Stat. 2736, codified at 5 U.S.C. §§ 581 *et seq.*

99. For a discussion of these experiments, see Philip J. Harter, *Dispute Resolution and Administrative Law: The History, Needs, and Future of a Complex Relationship*, 29 Vill. L. Rev. 1393 (1983). The ADR Act reflects a strong recommendation from the Administrative Conference of the United States (ACUS) that agencies adopt ADR techniques. *See* Recommendations of the Administrative Conference Regarding Administrative Practice and Procedure, 51 Fed. Reg. 25,641 (1986) (documenting adoption of ACUS Recommendation 86-3, Agencies' Use of Alternative Means of Dispute Resolution). ACUS produced a good—and lengthy—compendium of ADR materials in ACUS, Sourcebook: Federal Agency Use of Alternative Means of Dispute Resolution (1990), and maintains a continuously-updated, electronic sourcebook on Federal Administrative Procedure that includes extensive discussion of alternative dispute resolution under the ADR Act. *See* https://sourcebook.acus.gov/wiki/Administrative_Dispute_Resolution_ Act/view; *see also* Robin J. Evans, Note, *The Administrative Dispute Resolution Act of 1996: Improving Federal Agency Use of Alternative Dispute Resolution Processes*, 50 Admin. L. Rev. 217 (1998).

100. More information about the Interagency ADR Working Group is available at adr.gov.

101. *See* 5 U.S.C. § 572(b) (listing factors for agencies to consider in deciding whether to use alternative dispute resolution methods).

102. Legal scholars have suggested that courts may have the power to compel participation in nonbinding alternative dispute resolution processes where states have, by local rule or statute, given them that power, notwithstanding the terms of the ADR Act. Amy M. Pugh & Richard A. Bales,

some alternative dispute resolution techniques, specifically arbitration, could run afoul of the nondelegation doctrine's prohibition on the use of private persons to make government decisions.

In at least two separate instances, the Supreme Court has approved the use of alternatives that employ private sector persons. In *Schweiker v. McClure*,[103] the Court approved the use of hearing examiners employed by private insurance carriers to dispose of claims filed under the Social Security Administration's Medicare program. The use of these private adjudicators was attacked on due process rather than delegation grounds, and the Court upheld their use without addressing the potential nondelegation issue. In *Thomas v. Union Carbide Agricultural Products Co.*,[104] the Court approved the use of binding, private sector arbitration in disputes arising out of the payment of compensation for the use of company data in the registration of pesticides by the Environmental Protection Agency. In this instance, the Court held that not all disputes involving a government agency had to be tried in an Article III court.

The ADR Act permits agencies to employ "conciliation, facilitation, mediation, fact-finding, minitrials, arbitration, the use of ombuds, or any combination thereof" in resolving disputes.[105] Most of these proceedings will be presided over by what the Act calls a *neutral*. Neutrals may be either agency employees or private persons who are acceptable to the parties as unbiased and who are bound by certain statutory requirements of confidentiality with regard to the proceeding.[106]

It is obvious that Congress did not want many lawsuits arising out of the mere decision to use ADR, so an agency's decision to use ADR is committed to its discretion. Of course, the final agency action may be reviewable, but the decision to use ADR techniques is generally exempt from judicial review. Arbitral awards will be reviewed by a court under the terms of the Federal Arbitration Act, rather than under the APA.[107]

The ADR Act is not a perfect statute. There is no perfect form of dispute resolution, whether it be ADR, formal adjudication under APA §§556 and 557, or agency adjudication outside the APA. Probably the ADR Act's biggest contribution is that it gives federal agencies all the dispute resolution techniques that have been available in the private sector for years.

The Inherent Power of the Federal Courts to Compel Participation in Nonbinding Forms of Alternative Dispute Resolution, 42 Duq. L. Rev. 1 (2003) (arguing that courts have the power to compel participation in nonbinding alternative dispute resolution processes where states have, by local rule or statute, given them that power, notwithstanding the terms of the ADR Act). Subsequent case law interpreting the Appointments Clause may call these suggestions into question. *See* C. Scott Maravilla, *Private Judges, Public Law: The Unconstitutionality of Binding Arbitration Under the Alternative Dispute Resolution Act After* Lucia v. SEC, 35 Ohio St. J. on Disp. Resol. 63 (2019).

103. 456 U.S. 188 (1982).

104. 473 U.S. 568 (1985). This case is discussed at greater length in Chapter 4.

105. 5 U.S.C. §§571(3) & (6), 572(a).

106. 5 U.S.C. §583.

107. 5 U.S.C. §581. The Federal Arbitration Act, 9 U.S.C. §§10 *et seq.*, has been amended appropriately.

Chapter 9

Informal Agency Action

§ 9.01 Introduction

It may come as a surprise to some readers to find one of the shortest chapters in this book devoted to agency activities that comprise the vast majority of all administrative action.[1] The problem is that it is very difficult to generalize about these agency actions, other than to call attention to supportive provisions in the Administrative Procedure Act (APA) and to survey court decisions affecting informal agency action.

There is not even a great deal of agreement on the labels to be applied to informal agency action. Technically, notice-and-comment rulemaking is informal relative to the formal procedures of APA §§ 556 and 557, and any agency adjudication that is not governed by those same procedures might be labeled informal as well. Yet the procedures for notice-and-comment rulemaking that have evolved over the past fifty years are substantial, as are the procedures for many supposedly informal agency adjudications—to the point that even experienced practitioners will describe those agency actions as formal simply to distinguish them from the bulk of agency actions that are even more informal.

§ 9.02 Guidance: Interpretative Rules and Policy Statements

Chapter 7 of this book discussed agency rulemaking at great length, explaining the shift from formal rulemaking under §§ 556 and 557 of the Administrative Procedure Act (APA) to contemporary notice-and-comment rulemaking under APA § 553, and the various procedural burdens that the courts have interpreted the APA as imposing upon that technically "informal" rulemaking process. *Legislative rules* adopted according to this process are generally described as carrying *the force of law*, meaning that they are binding upon all who fall within their scope and must be followed in order to avoid the imposition of penalties or other legal consequences.

Agencies commonly put forth other types of less formal pronouncements that do not purport to carry the same legal force and that nevertheless can be extremely valuable to

1. Although the term "informal" has not always held constant meaning in the administrative law context, at the time the Administrative Procedure Act was adopted, it was said that as much as 90 percent of administrative action was informal. *Hearings Before the Subcomm. of Comm. on the Judiciary on S.674, S.675, & S.918*, 77th Cong., 1st Sess. 804 (1941) (testimony of Dean Acheson). The same assumption holds true today as well. *See, e.g.*, Todd D. Rakoff, *The Choice Between Formal and Informal Modes of Administrative Regulation*, 52 Admin. L. Rev. 159 (2000).

private parties seeking to understand what an agency thinks about the laws it administers and how an agency intends to proceed in implementing and administering statutes under its authority. In practical terms, these less formal pronouncements carry a host of different labels that often vary from agency to agency—*e.g.*, opinion letters, enforcement or guidance manuals, staff advice, frequently asked questions (FAQs), just to name a few. Lawyers who practice regularly before administrative agencies sometimes will refer to these different pronouncements collectively as *nonlegislative rules* or, even more commonly, *guidance*. Section 553 of the APA, in exempting these pronouncements from notice-and-comment rulemaking procedures, refers to them as *interpretative rules* and *policy statements*.

Unfortunately, distinguishing between legislative rules (those that carry the force of law and must follow notice-and-comment rulemaking procedures) and interpretative rules or policy statements (that do not) is one of the most difficult issues in administrative law. For example, APA § 551 merely defines rule without drawing any distinctions between types of rules. The *Attorney General's Manual on the APA* makes some distinctions, but mainly by way of illustration. The Manual defines a substantive rule (*i.e.*, a legislative rule) as

> rules, other than organizational or procedural rules ... issued by an agency pursuant to statutory authority and which implement the statute, as, for example, the proxy rules issued by the [SEC] pursuant to § 14 of the Securities Exchange Act of 1934. Such rules have the force and effect of law.

The *Manual* then defines interpretative rules as "rules or statements ... to advise the public of the agency's construction of the statutes and rules which it administers." Policy statements are defined as "statements ... to advise the public prospectively of the manner in which the agency proposes to exercise a discretionary power."[2]

For most issues encountered by a practitioner in the administrative law space, the major task is to distinguish substantive or legislative rules from other pronouncements, because that is the distinction that matters for APA purposes. Trying to distinguish interpretative rules from policy statements is a waste of time, as both types of nonlegislative rules are exempt from APA procedural requirements.

In drawing the distinction between legislative and nonlegislative rules, the Supreme Court has offered only minimal assistance in the way of a final, categorical pronouncement. In *Chrysler Corp. v. Brown*,[3] a case better known for its relevance to the Freedom of Information Act,[4] the Court noted that most distinctions drawn by reviewing courts have been by negative inference rather than by positive definition—*e.g.*, a rule is legislative if it is not an interpretative rule or a policy statement. Otherwise, the Court made only relatively abstract pronouncements about legislative rules carrying the force of law, affecting "individual rights and obligations,"[5] and having to comply with APA procedural requirements.

Chrysler Corp. contained some hints that the way an agency labels a rule may have some influence on a reviewing court because courts are often fairly deferential to agency pronouncements. Hence, early on, courts simply looked to whether a rule, by its own

2. Department of Justice, Attorney General's Manual on the Administrative Procedure Act 30 n.3 (1947).
3. 441 U.S. 281 (1979).
4. The Freedom of Information Act is discussed in Chapter 14, § 14.02.
5. *See also Morton v. Ruiz*, 415 U.S. 199 (1974) (using similar language).

terms, was "an authoritative implementation" under the relevant statute, such that "in an enforcement action an agency need prove only that the defendant's conduct was contrary to the rule."[6] In other words, if the rule on its face purported to carry such a legal effect, then it was a legislative rule. Courts and others realized, however, that agencies have an incentive to avoid APA procedural requirements and yet substantially influence the actions of regulated parties by labeling rules as nonlegislative while treating those rules in practice as conclusive. Accordingly, courts have declined repeatedly to accept agency characterizations at face value, and instead conduct their own inquiries into whether rules are legislative or nonlegislative.[7]

Affecting individual rights and obligations sounds like a potentially useful formulation at first blush. But anyone involved in agency practice quickly realizes that virtually all agency pronouncements affect individual rights and obligations as a practical matter, if not overtly in a legal sense. Consider, for example, letter rulings issued by the Internal Revenue Service. These letter rulings have never been considered to have the force and effect of law, although they affect at least the individual party who requests the ruling. Moreover, because of the Freedom of Information Act, they are released publicly in redacted form, and similarly situated taxpayers will frequently (and wisely) take them into consideration in evaluating their own obligations under the tax laws.

Statutory language can be difficult to interpret and susceptible of more than one possible meaning. Statutes rarely, if ever, expressly address every possible application or resolve the full range of circumstances within their scope. Congress frequently fails to define statutory terms or adopts open-ended standards rather than bright-line rules. On some level, agency pronouncements that define the undefined or designate the applicability of open-ended standards to particular facts and circumstances merely interpret statutory language, clarify existing law, or describe how the agency proposes to enforce a statute. Prudent regulated parties scour even the most casual agency pronouncements for clues and hints as to the agency's interpretations, policy preferences, and goals, and adjust their behavior accordingly. Yet courts are rightly wary of characterizing every agency action that might influence the behavior of private parties as a legislative rule subject to the requirements of notice-and-comment rulemaking for fear of discouraging agencies from issuing informal guidance. As D.C. Circuit Judge Stephen Williams noted in *American Mining Congress v. Mine Safety & Health Administration*,[8]

> The protection that Congress sought to secure by requiring notice and comment for legislative rules is not advanced by reading the exemption for "interpretive rule" so narrowly as to drive agencies into pure ad hocery—an ad hocery, moreover, that affords less notice, or less convenient notice, to affected parties.

In the absence of anything definitive from the Supreme Court, the lower courts have settled on standards that attempt to identify pronouncements that agencies do not freely admit possess legal effect but that carry sufficient weight that notice and comment should be required. For identifying interpretative rules, the Fifth Circuit relies on a standard that borrows from *Chrysler Corp.* by asking whether the guidance at issue imposes rights and obligations on regulated parties and also whether the rule leaves

6. William T. Mayton, *A Concept of a Rule and the "Substantial Impact" Test in Rulemaking*, 33 Emory L.J. 889 (1984).

7. *See, e.g.*, *Hemp Industry Ass'n v. Drug Enforcement Agency*, 333 F.3d 1082, 1087 (9th Cir. 2003); *Zhang v. Slattery*, 55 F.3d 732, 746 (2d Cir. 1995).

8. 995 F.3d 1106 (D.C. Cir. 1993).

the agency and its decisionmakers free to exercise discretion or, conversely, binds the agency as well as regulated parties.[9] Most circuits, however, use a test that derives from the D.C. Circuit's opinion in *American Mining Congress* that asks "if Congress has delegated legislative power to the agency and if the agency intended to exercise that power in promulgating the rule," and relies on several elements to identify the agency's intent to act legislatively:[10]

- Whether the rule is necessary to provide legislative basis for an enforcement action or conferral of benefits;
- Whether the rule revokes or alters an existing legislative rule;
- Whether the agency has explicitly invoked its legislative authority; or
- Whether the rule in question seeks to interpret a legislative rule that itself is too vague or open-ended to provide independent support for the alleged interpretative rule.[11]

For policy statements, the courts typically rely upon a "binding norm" standard that, in its analysis if not its label, strongly resembles the Fifth Circuit's standard for evaluating interpretative rules. In *Pacific Gas & Electric Co. v. Federal Power Commission*,[12] the D.C. Circuit stated that, unlike legislative rules, a general statement of policy "does not establish a 'binding norm.' It is not finally determinative of the issues or rights to which it is addressed." In subsequent cases,[13] the D.C. Circuit elaborated and expanded the binding norm standard by articulating two criteria for identifying a policy statement: first, that the purported policy statement "not impose any rights and obligations on" regulated parties and, second, that it "leave[] the agency and its decisionmakers free to exercise discretion." Courts applying the binding norm standard sometimes also consider whether agency guidance alleged to be policy statements operate only prospectively.[14]

None of these standards is a model of clarity or offers a bright line for distinguishing legislative rules from informal guidance. Nevertheless, they at least provide a common phraseology for comparing and contrasting agency pronouncements and framing arguments for and against characterizing guidance as a legislative rule, and thus subject to notice-and-comment rulemaking procedures, or as a nonlegislative interpretative rule or policy statement, and thus exempt from those requirements. The practical reality of day-to-day administrative practice requires being aware of even informal and

---

9. *Texas Savings & Community Bankers Ass'n v. Federal Housing Finance Board*, 201 F.3d 551 (5th Cir. 2000); *Professionals & Patients for Customized Care v. Shalala*, 56 F.3d 592 (5th Cir. 1995).

10. *American Mining Congress*, 955 F.2d at 1109. 1112.

11. This last element was not articulated in the *American Mining Congress* decision, but rather evolved later. *See, e.g.*, *Catholic Health Initiatives v. Sebelius*, 617 F.3d 490 (D.C. Cir. 2010); *Hoctor v. U.S. Department of Agriculture*, 82 F.3d 165 (7th Cir. 1996). Meanwhile, the D.C. Circuit in *American Mining Congress* also suggested that publication in the Code of Federal Regulations would make a rule legislative, but later backed away from that element to suggest it is only a potential indicator and is insufficient on its own to be determinative, because agencies are encouraged under certain circumstances to publish even nonlegislative rules in the Code of Federal Regulations. *See, e.g.*, *Hemp Industry Ass'n*, 333 F.3d at 1087 n.5.

12. 506 F.2d 33 (D.C. Cir. 1974).

13. *Community Nutrition Institute v. Young*, 818 F.2d 943 (D.C. Cir. 1987); *American Bus Ass'n v. United States*, 627 F.2d 525 (D.C. Cir. 1980).

14. *See, e.g.*, *Chamber of Commerce of United States v. U.S. Department of Labor*, 174 F.3d 206 (D.C. Cir. 1999); *Mada-Luna v. Fitzpatrick*, 813 F.2d 1006 (9th Cir. 1987).

nonbinding agency pronouncements and fashioning one's behavior and expectations in the face of such guidance.

§ 9.03 Informal Adjudication

One problem with the term *adjudication* is that it frequently suggests—to persons unfamiliar with the terminology of the Administrative Procedure Act (APA)—some type of elaborate, time-consuming, trial-type adversarial proceeding. In reality, the bulk of informal agency adjudications are relatively quick decisions. More importantly, the term does not really convey the wide spectrum of procedures used in informal action, which can run the gamut from almost no procedures whatsoever to a process that is nearly as elaborate as hearings under APA §§ 556 and 557.

Two examples provide a good illustration of the significant differences in informal agency procedures. Most actions taken by the Social Security Administration involve accepting, reviewing and processing various benefits applications. Occasionally, some of these actions result in an applicant's sitting down with an agency employee for a face-to-face conversation, but others are handled solely on the basis of a few pieces of paper. These applications result in some kind of decision, and the agency normally gives reasons for its decision. This action fits within the definition of *order* in the APA, and yet, the procedures afforded the applicants are skeletal at best. The applicant may, at a later point in time, get a trial-type proceeding, but the initial determination for benefits is informal.

Similarly, the Board of Veterans' Appeals (BVA), which is part of the Department of Veterans Affairs, decides thousands of disability cases each year. A full, formal evidentiary hearing under APA §§ 556–557 is not required by statute. Nonetheless, the procedures the BVA uses include most of the elements of trial-type formal adjudication. One of the distinctions between BVA procedures and formal adjudication is the absence of an administrative law judge. Most of the other BVA procedures are nearly the same as those required under §§ 556 and 557.[15]

In a 2016 report to the Administrative Conference of the United States, Professor Michael Asimow recognized the fallacy of attempting to divide agency adjudications into strictly formal and informal categories. Instead, he described three categories of agency adjudications—Types A, B, and C—two of which would be regarded as informal from the perspective of the APA.

> "Type A adjudication" refers to adjudicatory systems governed by the adjudication sections of the [APA]. With a few exceptions, Type A hearings are presided over by administrative law judges (ALJs). The term "Type B adjudication" refers to adjudication by federal administrative agencies through evidentiary hearings required by statute, regulation, or other source of law, that are not governed by the adjudication provisions of the APA. The hearings in Type B adjudication are presided over by administrative judges (AJs), although these officials are known by many other titles (or by the agency heads without the assistance of AJs).... The term "Type C adjudication" means adjudication by

15. *See, e.g.*, William F. Fox, The United States Board of Veterans' Appeals: The Unfinished Struggle to Reconcile Speed and Justice During Intra-Agency Review (2004).

> federal administrative agencies that does not occur through legally required evidentiary hearings.[16]

Asimow observed further that the borders between each of these adjudication types are blurry in practice. He contended that labeling particularly Type B adjudication as informal, while perhaps technically correct as a matter of APA interpretation, "creates a false picture of Type B adjudication." According to Asimow, "in some cases, Type B adjudication is even *more* formal than the familiar, trial-type adjudication procedure prescribed by the APA. In contrast, some Type A adjudication ... is *less* formal than many Type B schemes."[17]

[A] Statutory Provisions Affecting Informal Adjudication

Chapter 8 discussed briefly the potential for a paper hearing process even under the constraints of APA §§ 556 and 557. Recall that, under § 556(d), an agency is permitted to adopt procedures for the submission of all evidence in written form when it is determining claims for money or benefits or passing on applications for initial licenses. This is not, strictly speaking, informal agency action, but rather an exception within the formal adjudication process. Nonetheless, it does permit an agency that otherwise must follow APA §§ 556 and 557 to establish something other than a full-blown trial-type process for certain specified agency actions.

Separately, APA § 555(e) provides,

> [P]rompt notice shall be given of the denial in whole or in part of a written application, petition, or other request of an interested person made in connection with any agency proceeding. Except in affirming a prior denial or when the denial is self-explanatory, the notice shall be accompanied by a brief statement of the grounds for denial.

The *Attorney General's Manual on the Administrative Procedure Act* states that § 555(e) "has no application to matters which do not relate to rulemaking, adjudication or licensing. Generally, it is not applicable to the mass of administrative routine unrelated to those proceedings."[18] On its face, however, this provision would seem to impose at least some minimal burden of explanation on informal agency adjudications. In the few cases when courts have reviewed agency action under § 555(e), however, they have not found the burden of explanation imposed by that provision to be very great. An agency need only "explain why it chose to do what it did" and "evince reasoned decisionmaking."[19]

---

16. Michael Asimow, *Adjudication Outside the Administrative Procedure Act* (Sept. 16, 2016), available at https://www.acus.gov/sites/default/files/documents/adjudication-outside-the-administrative-procedure-act-updated-draft-report.pdf.

17. *Id.* at 2–3. For additional discussion and analysis of contemporary "informal" agency adjudications, see Michael Sant'Ambrogio, *Private Enforcement in Administrative Courts*, 72 Vand. L. Rev. 425 (2019); Emily Bremer, *The Exceptionalism Norm in Administrative Adjudication*, 2019 Wis. L. Rev. 1351.

18. Attorney General's Manual on the Administrative Procedure Act 70 (1947).

19. *Ark Initiative v. Tidwell*, 749 F.3d 1071, 1076 (D.C. Cir. 2014); *see also City of Colorado Springs v. Solis*, 589 F.3d 1121, 1134 (10th Cir. 2009) (finding an "admittedly ... terse" explanation to be "sufficient" for APA purposes). *But see Gillette v. Federal Energy Regulatory Comm'n*, 737 F.2d 883 (10th

Beyond § 555(e), there is virtually nothing else in the APA governing informal agency adjudication. Individual agency enabling acts may impose other statutory requirements or constraints, but those provisions are thus limited to the agencies to which they apply and have no bearing on federal administrative procedure generally. Agencies are not totally insensitive to issues of fair dealing. Many agencies have adopted internal agency rules and regulations that provide more procedures than may be mandated by either the APA or the agency's enabling act. It is simply impossible to generalize about these matters. Such matters can be properly understood only in a specific agency context.

The *Model State Administrative Procedure Act* takes a slightly different approach to informal agency adjudication.[20] The *Model Act* first requires an agency to conduct an adjudicative proceeding as its process for issuing an order.[21] However, the *Model Act* then establishes a number of choices depending on the matter in controversy. An agency proceeds by what the *Model Act* calls a formal adjudicative hearing unless a separate statute or agency rule permits an alternative proceeding.[22] The alternative proceedings recognized by the *Model Act* include a conference hearing, which may be utilized in situations in which there is no disputed issue of material fact.[23] Another alternative is what the *Model Act* calls an emergency adjudicative proceeding. In circumstances that pose an immediate danger to the public health, safety, or welfare, an agency may issue an emergency order with virtually no due process afforded prior to the order.[24]

The attempt of the *Model Act* to deal with informal agency action by express statutory provisions stands in dramatic contrast to the deliberate refusal of the federal APA to address informal adjudication directly (apart, of course, from the minimalist provisions in § 555).[25]

[B] Judicial Control of the Substance of Informal Adjudication

Reviewing courts ordinarily are deferential to the substance of even informal agency adjudication. Among many other decisions, the Supreme Court's opinions in *Vermont Yankee Nuclear Power Corp. v. Natural Resources Defense Council, Inc.*[26] and *Motor Vehicle Manufacturers Ass'n of the United States, Inc. v. State Farm Mutual Automobile Insurance Co.*[27] admonished the federal judiciary that reviewing courts should avoid

---

Cir. 1984) (holding that a person who requests a commission waiver is entitled to a statement sufficiently detailed to permit a court to review the agency action).

20. The Model State Administrative Procedure Act is set out in full text in Appendix B.

21. Model State Admin. P. Act § 102 (2010).

22. *Id.* § 401.

23. *Id.* § 102.

24. *Id.* § 407.

25. Dean Acheson, a well-known Washington lawyer (and later Secretary of State in the Truman Administration), chaired the 1941 Attorney General's Committee on Administrative Procedure (whose report ultimately led to the enactment of the Federal APA). Mr. Acheson commented that the Committee had deliberately avoided codifying informal procedures to avoid overly formalizing that process: "It was perfectly clear to us that that was not the thing to do; that that would not be of service to the citizen; that it would not be of service to the Government and it was an entirely futile thing to do so...." *Hearings Before Subcomm. of Comm. on the Judiciary on S.674, S.675 and S.918*, 77th Cong., 1st Sess. 804 (1941).

26. 435 U.S. 519 (1978).

27. 463 U.S. 29 (1983).

substituting their judgment for the scientific and technical determinations and discretionary choices of administrative agencies.[28] But such pronouncements do not mean that an agency's actions are unreviewable. At bottom, the APA imposes a duty on a court to set aside any agency action that it finds arbitrary and capricious, even if the court cannot substitute its judgment on certain matters for that of the agency.

The Supreme Court addressed judicial review of informal agency adjudication in *Citizens to Preserve Overton Park, Inc. v. Volpe,*[29] a case in which the Secretary of Transportation decided to release federal funds to construct a highway through a municipal park in Memphis, Tennessee. *Overton Park* is a landmark Supreme Court administrative law opinion that carries significance for many of the chapters in this book. For the purposes of this chapter, however, it suffices to know that a statute required the Secretary, before releasing funds for road construction, to consider alternatives to the routing of the highway through the park and to ensure that steps were taken to minimize environmental damage. In particular, the statute prohibited the Secretary from approving any road project that would use public parkland unless "no feasible and prudent alternative to the use of such land" existed and plans had been made "to minimize harm" to the park.[30] The challenging parties in this case complained that the Secretary had made no record demonstrating the basis for such determinations, or even if he had made them at all in authorizing the release of funds.

After establishing its own jurisdiction to review the Secretary's actions under the arbitrary and capricious standard of APA §706(2)(A), the Supreme Court concluded that the administrative record submitted by Department of Transportation (DOT) for judicial review was not sufficient for the Court to reach any conclusions as to the validity of the Secretary's actions. Stated another way, the Court decided that the DOT had provided insufficient explanation in support of its informal adjudication of the application for highway funds.

Because of deficiencies in the record, the Supreme Court remanded the case for further explanation of the Secretary's actions. The Court noted that a decision stemming from informal agency action need not be accompanied by formal findings and conclusions (as would be required in formal adjudication). Nevertheless, the Court held that the agency was required to provide the court with the *reasons* for its action. At the same time, the Court realized that the remand gave the DOT a perfect opportunity simply to concoct plausible explanations for its actions long after the decision was made, so the Court took the additional step of cautioning the agency that any new explanation proffered on remand would be reviewed suspiciously as merely a "post hoc" rationalization. In the event a lower court found the agency's demonstration of its reasons to be inadequate, the Supreme Court further authorized that court to require agency officials to submit themselves to discovery, including testimony and cross-examination under oath. The desire of agency officials to avoid the discovery process is a powerful incentive to produce an administrative record sufficient to support judicial review.

---

28. Actually, the second Supreme Court decision in the *Vermont Yankee* dispute made this even clearer. *See Baltimore Gas & Electric Co. v. Natural Resources Defense Council, Inc.*, 462 U.S. 87, 103 (1983) ("[A] reviewing court must remember that the [Nuclear Regulatory Commission] is making predictions, within its area of special expertise, at the frontiers of science. When examining this kind of scientific determination, as opposed to simple findings of fact, a reviewing court must generally be at its most deferential.").

29. 401 U.S. 402 (1971).

30. 23 U.S.C. §138(a).

Overton Park made other contributions to review of informal action. The decision in essence requires that a court reviewing agency action take what courts and scholars since have termed a *hard look* at the agency record to determine whether the agency has complied with relevant statutes and whether proper procedures have been followed. If this hard look shows that the agency has explained itself properly and has not abused its discretion or violated any mandatory procedures, the reviewing court's work is finished.[31]

Some years after the Supreme Court's decision in *Overton Park*, and after the Court declared in *Vermont Yankee* that courts could not impose procedural burdens on agencies beyond those contained in congressionally-enacted statutes, some commentators suggested that *Overton Park*'s requirement that agencies provide reviewing courts with an administrative record sufficient to support judicial review was inconstant with *Vermont Yankee*. The Court dismissed this concern in *Pension Benefit Guaranty Corp. v. LTV Corp.*[32]

The Pension Benefit Guaranty Corporation (PBGC) is a government corporation that becomes responsible for the payment of certain corporate pension benefits when the private businesses are not able to pay them. In this case, the PBGC determined that certain pension plans initially in existence between LTV and some of its labor force were to be restored, even though LTV had been reorganized in bankruptcy. The court of appeals had invalidated the PBGC's restoration orders in part because the PBGC's procedures did not afford LTV an adequate opportunity to participate in the PBGC's decisionmaking process by failing to apprise LTV of either the PBGC's reasoning in support of its orders or the material on which the PBGC based its decision.

In reversing the court of appeals and upholding the PBGC's orders, the Supreme Court maintained that, contrary to LTV's assertions, very little tension existed between the Court's *Overton Park* and *Vermont Yankee* opinions. *Vermont Yankee* continues to stand for the proposition that courts may not impose specific procedural requirements on agencies beyond those required by statute. *Overton Park* simply requires an agency to provide a reviewing court with a record adequate for judicial review, not necessarily a record compiled through the use of specific procedures.

Some informal agency adjudications are totally subject to agency discretion and will never (or almost never) be reviewed by courts. Some examples are an agency's decision to terminate an investigation and an agency's decision not to proceed with an enforcement matter. Chapter 10, § 10.05 discusses this kind of nonreviewability. Although there are some minor exceptions not applicable here, nonreviewability, by definition, means that a party cannot seek recourse from the courts for an adverse agency decision.

Agency action that is categorically non-reviewable must be dealt with *inside* the agency or in the legislative branch, rather than through the courts. One way to approach actions that are not reviewable is to accept that agencies are composed of human beings, most of whom try to perform their duties in good faith and who are subject to the limitations placed on them by Congress and by the courts. Considerable tension between

---

31. A number of administrative law scholars believe that the principles of *Overton Park* and like cases place a number of curbs on totally unfettered agency discretion. *See, e.g.*, Mariano-Florentino Cuellar, *Auditing Executive Discretion*, 82 Notre Dame L. Rev. 227 (2006); Barry Friedman, *The Politics of Judicial Review*, 84 Tex. L. Rev. 257 (2005). Others disagree. *See, e.g.*, Jacob Gersen & Adrian Vermeule, *Thin Rationality Review*, 114 Mich. L. Rev. 1355 (2016).

32. 496 U.S. 633 (1990).

the regulators and the regulated often exists, but few instances exist of downright ugly, malicious, or truly irrational behavior on the part of government officials that cannot be challenged in some fashion or that will not be corrected at some other level within the agency.

Agency supervisors often reverse improper decisions by low-echelon agency employees. Agency inspectors general are authorized by statute to investigate allegations of unacceptable agency behavior.[33] On the federal level, Congress has authorized the Government Accountability Office (GAO) to investigate agency actions upon the request of individual members of Congress. Some state legislatures have offices, much like the GAO, that perform similar duties on the state level. So, even if you cannot challenge the substance of an agency decision in court, you are not completely powerless.

[C] Judicial Control of Informal Adjudication Procedure

There are three grounds on which a court may review the procedural aspects of informal action: (1) whether the procedure is compatible with constitutional due process; (2) whether the action complies with procedures set out in the agency's organic statute or in the APA; and (3) whether the procedure complies with existing agency procedural regulations. The only way to examine the second and third of these grounds is to look closely at the applicable statutes and rules of individual agencies. Obviously, a violation of either the statutes or the rules governing agency action may invalidate the action itself.

The issue of whether an agency's informal action procedures satisfy constitutional due process requires a brief reminder of the cases and materials analyzed in Chapter 5. There is no need to repeat that material here, except to point out that the procedural requirements of the Due Process Clause do not apply to most informal agency adjudications, because those actions do not implicate the life, liberty, or property interests that constitutional due process protects. For those informal agency adjudications that concern protected interests, after 1976 and the Court's decision in *Mathews v. Eldridge*,[34] a court will review agency procedures by balancing the following three elements:

1. the private interest affected;
2. the risk of error inherent in the existing procedures; and
3. the interest of the government.

But this, of course, analyzes only the constitutional minimums placed upon informal agency adjudication. Neither agencies nor legislatures need confine themselves to minimum procedures if they believe that more process is necessary to insure fair and accurate decisions. Many years ago, Professor Kenneth Culp Davis identified what he considered to be four necessary ingredients for an acceptable system of informal agency adjudication procedures: (1) parties should be apprised of and have an opportunity to comment on evidence against them; (2) agencies should be as open as possible in reaching their decisions; (3) any action should be accompanied by a basic statement of findings and reasons; and (4) agencies should try, insofar as possible, to remain consistent

---

33. *See* the Inspector General Act, 5 U.S.C. App. §§1–12 (2000).
34. 424 U.S. 319 (1976).

through the application of precedent to their decisions. Professor Davis believed that agency ombuds and advisory opinions would also contribute to fairness in the adjudicative decisionmaking process.[35]

Each of these elements is addressed elsewhere in this book, and each is generally considered to be a central facet of fair administrative procedure. Notice is probably the first among equals and is required by the APA when an agency commences a formal adjudication regarding a specific individual as well as when an agency initiates a rulemaking.[36] Virtually all agencies provide reasons for their decisions, and courts normally require consistency in agency action.[37] On occasion, however, lawyers will encounter agency process that lacks one or more of these elements. If a court challenge is impossible, you can still try to deal with agency personnel on an individual basis; you may be able to invoke internal corrective devices such as an intra-agency appeal or a plea to the agency's inspector general or other ombuds; or you can try to take your problem to the legislature for correction. These are not perfect solutions for agency abuses, but they at least provide some minimal leverage for persons aggrieved by informal agency action.

---

35. Kenneth Culp Davis, Cases, Text & Problems on Administrative Law 514 (6th ed. 1977).

36. *See* Chapter 7 for a discussion of rulemaking procedures and Chapter 8 for a discussion of agency adjudication procedures.

37. *See* Chapter 13 for a discussion of consistency and reasoned decisionmaking. For a slightly different perspective, see Thomas O. Sargentich, *Informal Agency Decision Making: Problems of Delay and Public Information*, 3 Admin. L.J. 223 (1989). For yet another look at informal adjudication, see Ronald J. Krotoszynski, Jr., *Taming the Tail that Wags the Dog: Ex Post and Ex Ante Constraints on Informal Adjudication*, 56 Admin. L. Rev. 1057 (2004).

Chapter 10

Judicial Review of Agency Action: Reviewability

§ 10.01 An Analytical Framework for Judicial Review Issues

The Constitution, statutes, case law, and in some instances even agency regulations impose a variety of limitations on whether and under what circumstances judicial review of agency action is available. New attorneys often get themselves into trouble by approaching an agency case with the assumption that courts review and set aside vast numbers of agency decisions. This is simply not the case.

Readers of this book should understand one very important message: courts review a relatively small percentage of agency decisions and set aside an even smaller subset of the agency decisions they review. The permissible grounds for overturning agency action are narrow, giving courts very little room to maneuver in most cases. The place to win your case is at the agency. Do not expect a court to reward sloppy or casual lawyering at the agency level.

On the other hand, judicial review can have a disproportionate impact on agency action, because a court's holding in one case will often affect large numbers of individual agency actions. An adverse court decision may undo years of agency time, effort, and resources. The mere possibility of judicial review often prompts agencies to adjust their practices to avoid a negative outcome. Thus, courts remain an important component of federal agency practice.

Before a reviewing court can even consider the merits of a legal claim against an agency action, challenging parties and their lawyers must first overcome a number of obstacles sometimes referred to collectively as *justiciability limitations*. These limitations can be summarized as concerning a series of simple questions:

1. *Whether* the case may be taken to court.
2. *When* is judicial review appropriate (discussed in Chapter 11)?
3. *Who* can take the case to court (discussed in Chapter 12)?
4. *What kind* of review will the court perform on the merits (discussed in Chapter 13)?

This chapter is concerned with the *whether* issues. The components of the *whether* inquiry are (1) jurisdiction, (2) form of action, (3) sovereign immunity, and (4) preclusion. Each of these components will be discussed in order.

§ 10.02 Jurisdiction

[A] Generally

On the federal level, any problem involving judicial review of agency action must begin with this inquiry. Recall some fundamental propositions of our system of government and, particularly, what you learned about federal courts in other law school courses. First, federal courts are courts of limited jurisdiction. Second, the limits on that jurisdiction are imposed by Article III of the Constitution as well as 28 U.S.C. § 1331, which, among other things, limit the federal courts to a consideration of cases or controversies arising under the laws, treaties or Constitution of the United States. Congress has also enacted certain jurisdictional limitations on the federal courts apart from this basic command, including, for example, the amount in controversy requirement for diversity of citizenship actions. By contrast, state courts are usually courts of general jurisdiction, so the highly technical questions involved in establishing federal jurisdiction may not be necessary in state court.[1]

For judicial review of agency action, these principles mean that no one may enter federal court unless Congress has enacted a statutory permission to use the federal courts.[2] Administrative law scholars have developed a term, *nonstatutory review*, that suggests that there may be instances in which a person injured by agency action can enter federal court without an underlying jurisdictional statute. When law professors use the term *nonstatutory review*, they are usually talking about federal court jurisdiction that is found outside the agency's organic statute.[3]

Do not be confused by this terminology. Stick with the fundamental requirements for getting into federal court. Every case filed in a federal court requires a jurisdictional statute. That statement of jurisdiction must appear on the face of your complaint. You find those statutes in different places in the *United States Code*. Another approach is to think through a jurisdictional problem along the following lines. If you want to get into federal court, there are essentially two places to look for jurisdictional authority: (1) the organic statute and (2) the general jurisdictional statutes set out in Title 28 of the U.S.C., such as 28 U.S.C. § 1331 (basic federal question jurisdiction) or 28 U.S.C. § 1337 (jurisdiction arising out of any act of Congress regulating commerce).

---

1. It may be theoretically possible to enter federal court to challenge the action of a federal agency in the context of a lawsuit based on diversity of citizenship. However, this almost never happens, because the *arising under* language in 28 U.S.C. § 1331 normally includes the actions of all federal agencies. By contrast, diversity jurisdiction has been used frequently as a basis for testing the validity of state administrative action in federal court. *See, e.g., Burford v. Sun Oil Co.*, 319 U.S. 315 (1943).

2. It is conceivable that no statute is necessary to trigger the original jurisdiction of the Supreme Court because that jurisdiction is set out expressly in Article III and does not require congressional action. There are, however, very few instances in which federal agency action fits within that jurisdictional category.

3. For a discussion of the history of *nonstatutory review*, see Kathryn E. Kovacs, *Revealing Redundancy: The Tension Between Federal Sovereign Immunity and Nonstatutory Review*, 54 Drake L. Rev. 77 (2005); *see also* Adrian Vermeule, *Our Schmittian Administrative Law*, 122 Harv. L. Rev. 1095 (2009) (discussing the doctrine in a broader context).

[B] Organic Statutes and Jurisdiction

Most federal organic statutes of any vintage, and virtually all modern organic statutes, contain language providing for judicial review. Under most circumstances, these are the provisions to be invoked in challenging agency action. That is, look first at the organic statute for a grant of subject matter jurisdiction and go to the general jurisdictional statutes in Title 28 only if the organic statute is silent.

Be aware, of course, that few practitioners take any chances here; defects in subject matter jurisdiction are fatal and may be brought up at any stage of the litigation by either party or by the court itself. Most lawyers challenging agency action write an allegation of jurisdiction that invokes as many jurisdictional statutes as may plausibly relate to the case.

There is no particular rhyme or reason for Congress' selection of various routes for judicial review. The selection of a judicial review scheme depends very heavily upon the views of judicial review held by the members of Congress who draft that particular enabling act. Consider the following examples: (1) disputes out of the Securities and Exchange Commission generally go into federal district court; (2) most disputes coming out of the Federal Energy Regulatory Commission go into an appropriate federal court of appeals (the circuits), depending on the geographical location of the original dispute; (3) most disputes involving the Federal Communications Commission may be taken only into the United States Court of Appeals for the District of Columbia Circuit. These agencies are all major federal regulatory agencies that perform similar regulatory tasks for different industries within the United States. They are all independent agencies and were created around the same time. The headquarters of each agency is in Washington, D.C., although some of the agencies have regional offices that transact a certain amount of agency business. The businesses that each agency regulates are scattered throughout the United States. There is no discernible reason, other than the whim of the legislators, that explains the vastly different routes of judicial review established for each agency.

Congress can make things even more complicated. Consider, for example, the jurisdictional provisions governing challenges to the actions of the Environmental Protection Agency (EPA) under the Clean Air Act:[4]

1. Pre-enforcement challenges to EPA rulemaking may be taken to an appropriate circuit;
2. Challenges to certain specific EPA actions, such as the promulgation of national emission standards, may be taken only to the D.C. Circuit;
3. EPA subpoena enforcement actions are docketed in a federal district court in which the subpoenaed person resides; and
4. Certain EPA orders prohibiting retaliatory actions against employees may be enforced in appropriate federal district courts.

The message of this recitation is plain. Even within a single organic statute, such as the Clean Air Act, Congress may include a multiplicity of jurisdictional provisions. Moreover, Congress may, in some instances, make a certain jurisdictional provision mandatory—*i.e.*, may forbid persons from using other statutory routes for judicial review. Lawyers who invoke an impermissible jurisdictional statute will find their case

4. 42 U.S.C. §7607(b).

dismissed for lack of jurisdiction. That kind of dismissal may not hurt if the case can be refiled in the proper court before the statute of limitations runs out, but the lawyer who filed the case will look very silly in any event. Pay close attention to the jurisdictional provisions in agency organic statutes.

[C] Review Under General Jurisdictional Statutes

The most frequently invoked general jurisdictional statute providing for review of agency action is 28 U.S.C. § 1331, which now provides, "The district courts shall have original jurisdiction of all civil actions arising under the Constitution, laws, or treaties of the United States."[5] Prior to October 1976, § 1331 was not as useful as it is today because it limited district court jurisdiction to cases in which the amount in controversy was in excess of $10,000. Accordingly, it was possible to have federal agency action that arguably did not fit within any jurisdictional statute because the amount in controversy was not large enough.

Because of this pre-1976 loophole, a claimant—attempting to have the Social Security Administration re-open a previously denied claim for benefits—invoked the Administrative Procedure Act (APA) itself as an alternative jurisdictional basis for challenging the agency's action.[6] APA § 702 provides, in part, "A person suffering legal wrong because of agency action... is entitled to seek judicial review thereof." Because the APA is a congressional enactment and because that portion of § 702 sounds very much like a guarantee of judicial review, it was at least arguable that Congress was writing, for federal agency action, a grant of jurisdiction for cases involving the APA. Yet, by not explicitly conferring jurisdiction on the federal courts (or even using the word jurisdiction), this language from APA § 702 does not resemble that of conventional jurisdictional statutes like 28 U.S.C. § 1331. Most organic statute jurisdictional provisions contain the same sort of language as 28 U.S.C. § 1331.

The Supreme Court took up this question in *Califano v. Sanders*.[7] The question could have been a tricky one for the Court, which often has been reluctant to cut off judicial review of agency action. In October 1976, however—just before *Sanders* was decided—Congress repealed the $10,000 amount in controversy jurisdictional limitation in 28 U.S.C. § 1331. The elimination of that limitation made § 1331 essentially a catch-all or residual jurisdictional statute. In other words, to the extent that someone has a claim arising out of the laws, treaties, or Constitution of the United States (and virtually any challenge to federal agency action fits this language), a federal district court may hear the claim without worrying about the dollar amount of the claim. Arguably liberated by the amendment to 28 U.S.C. § 1331, the Court was then free to hold squarely in *Sanders* that "the APA does not afford an implied grant of subject-matter jurisdiction permitting federal judicial review of agency action."

In summary, between 28 U.S.C. § 1331 and organic statute jurisdictional provisions, the jurisdictional component of *whether* agency action may be challenged in court usually is not a problem for someone seeking to pursue such a case.

---

5. If an organic statute rests on the Commerce Clause, it is also possible to invoke 28 U.S.C. § 1337. Civil rights claims may come in under 28 U.S.C. § 1343.

6. The Social Security Act contains its own jurisdictional provision for cases of denied benefits. The claimant here had not challenged the original denial, so he could not use that provision.

7. 430 U.S. 99 (1977).

§ 10.03 Venue, Service of Process, and Limitations Periods

It is not enough to identify a proper federal jurisdictional statute. A litigator who wishes to challenge agency action must resolve the issues of *venue* and *service of process*, and additionally must invoke some type of remedial mechanism that the court can use to grant the relief sought. Venue and service of process are seldom major points of dispute when suing federal agencies. An organic statute may contain specific venue provisions, such as in the Clean Air Act, discussed above. In instances where the organic statute is silent on venue, 28 U.S.C. § 1391(e) provides that venue is proper in any federal judicial district where (1) the defendant resides, (2) a substantial part of the events or omissions giving rise to the claim occurred, or a substantial part of property that is the subject of the action is situated, or (3) the plaintiff resides, if no real property is involved. This is one of the broadest venue provisions on the books and makes it possible in many cases to do a little forum shopping.

Service of process is equally uncomplicated, although you must work carefully through Rule 4 of the Federal Rules of Civil Procedure to make sure all persons are properly served. For most actions involving a federal agency, Rule 4 provides for service on the United States attorney in the district in which the action is brought and service by certified or registered mail on the Attorney General in Washington. If the case involves a lawsuit against an agency or officer of the United States, the plaintiff must serve the U.S. Attorney, the Attorney General and the agency itself. If the case involves an attack on an agency order when the agency is not named as a party to the lawsuit, the agency must also be notified by registered or certified mail.[8]

When the relief sought is simply an injunction asking the court to halt the challenged agency practice or a request that the court make a declaration as to the validity of the agency action, there is normally no problem. Section 703 of the Administrative Procedure Act (APA) now expressly permits a court to utilize "any applicable form of legal action including actions for declaratory judgments or writs of prohibitory or mandatory injunction or habeas corpus...." In addition, the agency's action can normally be challenged in the context of a defense to an agency's civil or criminal enforcement action.

This last proposition, while generally true, is not unlimited in its scope, however. For example, many organic statutes contain provisions limiting judicial review of agency rules to a brief period, like 30 or 60 days. Additionally, 28 U.S.C. § 2401(a) provides that "every civil action commenced against the United States shall be barred unless the complaint is filed within six years after the right of action first accrues." Courts have interpreted these limitations provisions as cutting off judicial review of certain challenges against agency regulations brought outside the applicable limitations period even in the context of a defense to an agency's civil enforcement action.[9]

On the other hand, when the scope and effect of an explicit statutory limit on judicial review is unclear and the courts perceive a significant risk of unfairness if the statutory limit is given broad effect, the courts will sometimes strain to interpret the limitations provision narrowly. Such was the case in *Adamo Wrecking Co. v. United States*.[10]

---

8. Fed. R. Civ. P. 4(i)(2)(a).
9. *See, e.g.*, *Herr v. U.S. Forest Service*, 803 F.3d 809 (6th Cir. 2015).
10. 434 U.S. 275 (1978).

That case concerned the government's criminal prosecution of a company, Adamo Wrecking, for violating an emission standard issued by the Environmental Protection Agency (EPA) under the Clean Air Act. The statute explicitly limited the right to judicial review of any emission standard to the 30-day period following the standard's issuance. Although that 30-day period had long since elapsed, as part of its defense, Adamo Wrecking claimed that the emission standard itself was invalid (rather than merely arguing that it had not committed the offense in question). The EPA invoked an earlier Supreme Court decision, *Yakus v. United States*,[11] for the proposition that once the time has passed for challenging the agency's rulemaking, a reviewing court should not consider attacks on the validity of the rule in a subsequent enforcement action. In other words, according to the EPA, the only thing Adamo Wrecking should have been able to argue was whether it committed the act in question, not whether the EPA's emission standard was validly promulgated.

The Supreme Court held in favor of Adamo Wrecking, but only on narrow grounds. The Court held that the statute of limitations precluded a court from considering any of the "familiar inquiries which arise in the course of an administrative review proceeding," such as whether the regulation satisfied statutory procedural requirements or was arbitrary and capricious under APA §706(2)(A) for lack of reasoned decisionmaking, except in response to a petition for review filed within the statutory limitations period.[12] "Not only is the [EPA] Administrator's promulgation of the [emission] standard not subject to judicial review in the criminal proceeding, but no prior notice of violation from the Administrator is required as a condition for criminal liability." The Court nevertheless noted that Congress had neither prescribed criminal sanctions for all violations of the Clean Air Act nor limited judicial review of the applicability of emission standards. Thus, the Court allowed Adamo Wrecking's challenge to go forward on the narrow basis that what the EPA in this case had labeled an emission standard was, in fact, not an emission standard at all as that term was used in the 30-day limitations provision. Consequently, the 30-day limitations period for challenging emission standards did not apply to the regulation challenged by Adamo Wrecking. The Court then went on to reach the merits, determined that the EPA's rule was invalid, and ordered the district court to dismiss the indictment.

Although essentially treating the issue before it as a question of statutory interpretation, the *Adamo Wrecking* decision placed great emphasis on the fact that the proceedings concerned criminal rather than civil liability. The Court also seemed to disfavor the Clean Air Act's extremely short, 30-day time limit for challenging an emission standard. Justice Lewis Powell, writing in concurrence, thought that the 30-day limitations period might be *unconstitutional* because many parties affected by an emission standard would be unlikely to become aware of its existence in time to seek judicial review. The majority did not adopt this reasoning, but the Court's narrow interpretation of the statutory limit in this case was undoubtedly influenced by the same fairness concerns that led Powell to question the provision's constitutionality.

Regardless of whether or not the reasoning of the Court's decision in *Adamo Wrecking* might be limited to criminal cases or extremely short time limits, one thing is clear: lawyers who represent clients with regular business before particular agencies should

11. 321 U.S. 414 (1944).
12. These types of challenges are discussed in Chapters 7 and 13, respectively.

challenge rules within the time frame established by Congress. Waiting until the agency attempts to enforce the rule may choke off some of the client's available arguments.

Federal courts no longer place a great deal of stock in the now-obsolete concept of *form of action*, and § 703 makes clear that *form of action* is not to be an insuperable barrier to mounting a challenge to agency action. A party challenging agency action may invoke any remedy within the court's power to grant. Labels, such as *mandamus*, *injunction*, *declaratory judgment* and the like, are less important than the ground on which the action is challenged. Of course, you should also consider the matter of sovereign immunity, particularly if the remedy your client seeks is monetary relief.

§ 10.04 Sovereign Immunity

In years past, administrative law courses spent significant time on sovereign immunity, because the Supreme Court on numerous occasions blocked challenges to agency action on the ground that the government was sovereign and had not consented to being sued. Many times, challenging parties had to invoke various legal fictions such as, for example, in *Ex parte Young*,[13] that an agency officer who is acting in excess of statutory authority (*ultra vires*) loses the cloak of immunity given to government officers. Another case on this point, *Larson v. Domestic & Foreign Commerce Corp.*,[14] resulted in a Supreme Court opinion permitting a lawsuit against an agency official in his personal capacity based on "unconstitutional administration."

In 1976, Congress amended § 702 of the Administrative Procedure Act to eliminate the defense of sovereign immunity in cases in which the plaintiffs are seeking relief "other than money damages." So, those actions that seek only injunctive or declaratory relief no longer have to face a sovereign immunity defense.

But what if the client wants money damages? If you are suing for some kind of constitutional violation and if you seek a judgment against a federal officer or employee personally—*i.e.*, out of his or her personal pocketbook—you may be able to invoke the *Bivens* remedy.[15] However, a *Bivens*-type recovery is only against the employees and may not be satisfied out of the federal treasury. Most government employees are effectively judgment proof because their only income is their salary. Moreover, as the Supreme Court acknowledged in *Ashcroft v. Iqbal*, it "has been reluctant to extend *Bivens* liability 'to any new context or new category of defendants.'"[16]

Those clients who seek to recover money damages satisfied out of the federal treasury must proceed under one of the statutes—such as the Federal Tort Claims Act or the

---

13. 209 U.S. 123 (1908).

14. 337 U.S. 682 (1949).

15. *Bivens v. Six Unknown Named Agents of Federal Bureau of Narcotics*, 403 U.S. 388 (1971) (when federal agents violate a citizen's constitutional rights and the citizen seeks money damages against the individual agents, a court may fashion a common-law remedy, even if Congress has not enacted a statute permitting such relief).

16. 556 U.S. 662, 675 (2009) (quoting *Correctional Services Corp. v. Malesko*, 534 U.S. 61, 68 (2001)).

Tucker Act—by which Congress has relaxed the doctrine of sovereign immunity. These statutes are tricky and have a number of exceptions that must be confronted.[17]

§ 10.05 Preclusion

[A] Section 701 of the APA

Even when you find a proper jurisdictional statute and resolve all the issues previously discussed in this chapter, the action still may not be reviewable according to § 701 of the Administrative Procedure Act (APA). Section 701(a) distinguishes between two types of preclusion: (1) matters that are precluded *by statute*, and (2) matters that are precluded because they are *committed to agency discretion*. Further, as a matter of doctrine, preclusion by statute can be *express* or *implied*.

Preclusion deals with the subject matter of a dispute, rather than the parties to the action. In a setting involving preclusion, it often makes no difference who brings the case to court; if the issue is precluded from review, a court may not act. Of course, exceptions exist where preclusion is specific to particular groups of litigants. Regardless, preclusion is a door-closing proposition. Courts are powerless to act on a matter that is properly precluded.

Nevertheless, take some comfort from the fact that the vast bulk of agency actions are reviewable in some fashion. Since *Abbott Laboratories v. Gardner*,[18] decided in 1967, the Supreme Court has interpreted the APA as embodying a presumption in favor of judicial review. Thus, the cases that are precluded under § 701 are, by definition, the exceptions. Also, be aware that courts do not take kindly to being told that they cannot examine action taken by the executive branch. Remember the message of *Marbury v. Madison*[19] and the exceptionally strong views of Chief Justice John Marshall that the Supreme Court plays a critical role as a component of the federal government.

[B] The Presumption in Favor of Judicial Review

Abbott Labs was a case involving a challenge by various drug companies to certain labeling requirements imposed on them by the Food and Drug Administration. The Court, at the urging of the government, looked closely at whether there was any statute or part of a statute that might be interpreted as somehow precluding the Court from reviewing the companies' claims at that point in time. The Court, finding no such pronouncement, held that there was no statute expressly prohibiting judicial review and that there was most certainly no "showing of clear and convincing evidence" of any intent on the part of Congress to restrict review.

---

17. There are instances in which the doctrine of sovereign immunity will prohibit lawsuits against state administrative agencies in federal court. Those issues are beyond the scope of this chapter and this book. Some excellent discussion of these matters may be found in Roger C. Hartley, *Enforcing Federal Civil Rights Against Public Entities After* Garrett, 28 J.C. & U.L. 41 (2001); Roger C. Hartley, Alden *Trilogy: Praise and Protest*, 23 HARV. J.L. & PUB. POL'Y 323 (2000).

18. 387 U.S. 136 (1967).

19. 5 U.S. (1 Cranch) 137 (1803).

Even as it nodded toward various justiciability limitations imposed by the APA's judicial review provisions, the Court in *Abbott Labs* recognized the background presumption of reviewability that provides the foundation for much of administrative law:

> Early cases in which this type of judicial review was entertained have been reinforced by the enactment of the Administrative Procedure Act, which embodies the basic presumption of judicial review to one suffering legal wrong because of agency action or adversely affected or aggrieved by agency action within the meaning of a relevant statute, 5 U.S.C. § 702, so long as no statute precludes such relief or the action is not one committed by law to agency discretion, 5 U.S.C. § 701(a).... The legislative material elucidating that seminal act manifests a congressional intention that it cover a broad spectrum of administrative actions, and this Court has echoed that theme by noting that the Administrative Procedure Act's generous review provisions must be given a hospitable interpretation.... [O]nly upon a showing of clear and convincing evidence of a contrary legislative intent should the courts restrict access to judicial review.[20]

The Court has reiterated this presumption on numerous occasions since 1967. Four years after the Court's decision in *Abbott Labs*, in *Citizens to Preserve Overton Park, Inc. v. Volpe*,[21] in responding to a claim that the decision of the Secretary of Transportation to permit the use of federal funds to construct a highway through a municipal park was precluded from judicial review, the Court invoked the presumption in favor of review as well as the principle that this presumption can be overcome only by clear and convincing evidence to the contrary.

In *Dunlop v. Bachowski*, the Court considered whether the language of the Labor-Management Reporting and Disclosure Act precluded judicial review of a Labor Department investigation and decision not to bring a civil action to set aside a questionable union election. Rejecting such an interpretation, the Court described the agency's "heavy burden of overcoming the strong presumption that Congress did not mean to prohibit all judicial review of his decision," and the "clear and convincing evidence" of legislative intent necessary to satisfy that burden.[22]

In *Bowen v. Michigan Academy of Family Physicians*, in allowing a challenge by physicians to Medicare regulations governing health care reimbursements, the Court observed that, "from the beginning our cases have established that judicial review of a final agency action by an aggrieved person will not be cut off unless there is persuasive reason to believe that such was the purpose of Congress."[23] The Court in that case refused to infer such congressional intent from statutory silence regarding judicial review.

In *Sackett v. Environmental Protection Agency*, in responding to the government's argument that judicial review of an EPA compliance order would make enforcement of the Clean Water Act less efficient, the Court observed, "The APA's presumption of judicial review is a repudiation of the principle that efficiency of regulation conquers all."[24] In *U.S. Army Corps of Engineers v. Hawkes Co., Inc.*, having found agency jurisdictional determinations under the Clean Water Act to be final agency action, the Court again

20. *Abbott Labs*, 387 U.S. at 140 (internal citations and quotation marks omitted).
21. 401 U.S. 402 (1971).
22. 421 U.S. 560 (1975).
23. 476 U.S. 667 (1986) (internal quotation marks and brackets omitted).
24. 566 U.S. 120, 130 (2012).

declined to infer from statutory silence congressional intent to preclude judicial review "given 'the APA's presumption of reviewability for all final agency action.'"[25]

Lawyers should take care not to overread these bold statements in favor of judicial review of agency action. Many of the doctrines discussed in this book reflect the Supreme Court's reluctance to intrude too deeply into the sphere of agency discretion. These bold statements in favor of judicial review stand alongside many others of a Supreme Court that has an aversion to intruding too deeply into agency prerogatives. Nevertheless, they do make plain that the Court is equally reluctant to accept an argument that federal courts cannot review a dispute over agency action at all.

[C] Statutory Preclusion

Notwithstanding the Supreme Court's presumption in favor of reviewability, the Court occasionally has concluded that Congress has precluded judicial review by statute. The application of APA § 701(a)(1) statutory preclusion analysis normally requires identification of a statute outside the APA that expressly prohibits a court from reviewing an agency decision, although on occasion, the preclusion of judicial review may be implied.

Most statutory preclusion provisions are obvious from the face of the statute. There are a number of these statutes in the *United States Code.* Consider, for example, a provision pertaining to judicial review of payments to farmers under the Agricultural Adjustment Act of 1938, as amended:

> The facts constituting the basis for... any payment under the wheat, feed grain, upland cotton, extra long staple cotton, and rice programs authorized by [the Act],... when officially determined in conformity with the applicable regulations prescribed by the Secretary [of Agriculture] or by the Commodity Credit Corporation, shall be final and conclusive and shall not be reviewable by any other office or agency of the Government.[26]

Another example comes from the Internal Revenue Code known as the Anti-Injunction Act, which provides in pertinent part:

> Except as provided in [other specified sections of the statute], no suit for the purpose of restraining the assessment or collection of any tax shall be maintained in any court by any person, whether or not such person is the person against whom such tax was assessed.[27]

Even when the Supreme Court encounters such statutes, it often is reluctant to accept the preclusion as a total barrier to judicial review. Consider, for example, language considered by the Court in *Johnson v. Robison*,[28] a seemingly-sweeping statutory provision that, until 1988, precluded judicial review of Veterans Administration (VA) decisions regarding veterans benefits. That provision provided in relevant part:

---

25. 136 S. Ct. 1807, 1816 (2016) (quoting *Sackett*, 566 U.S. at 129).

26. 7 U.S.C. § 1385; *see also Olenhouse v. Commodity Credit Corp.*, 42 F.3d 1560 (10th Cir. 1994) (discussing the preclusive effect of this provision).

27. 26 U.S.C. § 7421(a); *see also, e.g., CIC Services, LLC v. Internal Revenue Service*, 141 S. Ct. 1582 (2021) (concerning the scope of this limitation on judicial review).

28. 415 U.S. 361 (1974).

> [T]he decisions of the [VA] on any question of law or fact… providing benefits for veterans… shall be final and conclusive and no other official or any court of the United States shall have power or jurisdiction to review any such decision by an action in the nature of mandamus or otherwise.[29]

The case concerned a plaintiff who had done alternative service in lieu of serving in the military. He argued that the VA's refusal to give persons who performed alternative service the same benefits as were given to persons who served in the military was a violation of his constitutional rights under the First and Fifth Amendments. The Court looked closely at the statutory language and determined that the preclusion limited judicial review only of day-to-day benefits determinations, and not to constitutional challenges against the validity of the organic statute on its face.

Given the Supreme Court's frequent reluctance to read express statutory language as precluding judicial review, one would think that it would never find statutory preclusion when a statute is silent regarding reviewability. Such thinking would be mistaken. On occasion, the Supreme Court has seen fit to infer from a statute's structure or legislative history the requisite evidence of congressional intent to preclude judicial review. *Block v. Community Nutrition Institute*,[30] is particularly illustrative of the Court's occasional willingness to infer preclusive intent without express statutory language. *Block* concerned a challenge brought by consumers against milk market orders issued by the Secretary of Agriculture. Milk market orders set minimum prices for milk as part of the federal government's price support program for the dairy industry. The statute expressly provided for judicial review of challenges to milk market orders by milk producers and milk "handlers" (*i.e.*, middlemen between producers and consumers), but was silent regarding suits brought by consumers. Notwithstanding that statutory silence, the Court read the statute as precluding consumers from challenging milk marketing orders, emphasizing that "[w]hether and to what extent a particular statute precludes judicial review is determined not only from its express language, but also from the structure of the statutory scheme, its objectives, its legislative history, and the nature of the administrative action involved."[31] Although it recognized the presumption in favor of reviewability of agency action adopted in *Abbott Labs v. Gardner*, the Court said "[t]hat presumption does not control in cases such as this one, however, since the congressional intent to preclude judicial review is 'fairly discernible' in the detail of the legislative scheme." Irrespective of the validity of the consumers' challenge to the milk market orders, the Court said that "Congress simply did not intend for consumers to be relied upon to challenge agency disregard of the law."

The Court's willingness to infer preclusive intent from a statute's structure, objective, and history has on other occasions been overshadowed by its concerns about fairness. *Bowen v. Michigan Academy of Family Physicians*[32] offers an instructive example. The Department of Health and Human Services issued a rule implementing the Medicare program by providing for different levels of payment for similar physicians' services. A group of physicians challenged the rule as inconsistent with statutory requirements. The Medicare statute included language that provided for judicial review of some types of claims and denied reviewability for other types of claims under the statute, but the

---

29. *Id.* at 365, n.5. This provision was repealed by the Veterans Benefits and Program Improvement Act of 1988, Pub. L. No. 100-689, 120 Stat. 1461.
30. 467 U.S. 340 (1984).
31. *Id.* at 345.
32. 476 U.S. 667 (1986).

relevant provision was silent regarding the reviewability of the physicians' particular claim. Given the Supreme Court's willingness to infer nonreviewability from statutory silence in the *Block* case only two years prior, one might have expected the same outcome in *Bowen*. Instead, the Court turned back to the "strong presumption that Congress intends judicial review of administrative action." Although it recognized the presumption could be overcome by "a specific congressional intent to preclude judicial review that is 'fairly discernible in the detail of the legislative scheme,'" quoting *Block*, the Court said "[t]he mere fact that some acts are made reviewable should not suffice to support an implication of exclusion as to others. The right to review is too important to be excluded on such slender and indeterminate evidence of legislative intent." The Court seemed particularly intent on the fact that, unless challenges like that brought by the physicians were allowed, the substantive and procedural validity of substantial and broadly-applicable new regulations in effect would be unreviewable by a court of law. Calling the government's position to the contrary "extreme," the Court found it improper "to think [Congress] intended that there be no forum to adjudicate statutory and constitutional challenges to regulations promulgated by the Secretary."

In short, questions regarding statutory preclusion in general, and implied preclusion of the sort discussed in the *Block* and *Bowen* cases, are highly case-specific. Although the Court consistently recognizes both the presumption in favor of judicial review of agency action and the rebuttability of that presumption, these cases depend heavily on careful consideration of the particular statute and agency action in question.

[D] Action Committed to Agency Discretion

Section 701(a)(2) of the APA recognizes that judicial review of certain agency actions is precluded because those actions have been *committed to agency discretion by law*. As difficult as it may be to discern whether or under precisely which circumstances statutory language precludes judicial review under APA § 701(a)(1), the committed to agency discretion language of APA § 701(a)(2) is positively cryptic. Much of the APA is oriented toward the understanding that agencies routinely exercise discretion, and the APA clearly contemplates judicial review as a check against agency arbitrariness in the exercise of that discretion, yet APA § 706(2)(A) simultaneously suggests that some such discretionary exercises are unreviewable simply by virtue of being discretionary. Prof. Ronald Levin suggests that those involved in drafting the APA must have known that the committed to agency discretion language was ambiguous. Levin documents that, rather than pursue clearer statutory language in the APA, different parties in the APA's enactment process loaded the APA's legislative history with statements supporting their competing views of the provision's meaning.[33]

It is perhaps unsurprising, therefore, that the Supreme Court has struggled to settle on a single standard for what it means to commit agency action to agency discretion by law, despite several opportunities to do so. One such case was *Citizens to Preserve Overton Park v. Volpe*,[34] involving a challenge to a decision by the Secretary of Trans-

---

33. Ronald M. Levin, *Understanding Unreviewability in Administrative Law*, 74 Minn. L. Rev. 690, 695–99 (1990).

34. 401 U.S. 402 (1971). For a particularly rich description and analysis of this case, see Peter Strauss, *Revisiting* Overton Park: *Political and Judicial Controls Over Administrative Actions Affecting the Community*, 39 UCLA L. Rev. 1251 (1992).

portation to extend federal funding in support of a new highway to be built through a public park. The Federal Aid to Highway Act required a determination by the Secretary that no "feasible and prudent" alternative route existed other than the planned route through the park. Despite extensive engagement among federal, state, and local officials and numerous public hearings concerning the new highway's route, opponents of the plan challenged the Secretary's decision to support the plan with federal funding as violating the APA.

The government raised several arguments in its defense in *Overton Park*, including that the decision to authorize funding for the highway was not reviewable because it was committed to agency discretion by law as described in APA § 701(a)(2). The government noted that the statute did not provide expressly for judicial review. The statute also did not require the Secretary to provide reasons, utilize particular procedures, or even create an administrative record. Hence, argued the government, the Secretary's decision was entirely discretionary.

The Supreme Court disagreed. Acknowledging the APA's presumption in favor of reviewability of final agency action, recognized just a few years earlier in *Abbott Labs*, the Court turned to the legislative history of the APA to gain some understanding of the committed to agency discretion exception. Quoting from that legislative history, the Court said that the APA's presumption of reviewability applies "except in those rare instances where 'statutes are drawn in such broad terms that in a given case there is *no law to apply*.'"[35] And the Court concluded that, by referring to the avoidance of highways through public parks when a "feasible and prudent" alternative exists, the statute provided sufficient law for a court to apply on judicial review. "Plainly, there is 'law to apply' and thus the exemption for action 'committed to agency discretion' is inapplicable."[36] The Court went on to require the agency either to provide an administrative record sufficient to facilitate judicial review or, alternatively, to allow the district court on remand to give the challenging parties the opportunity to examine the decisionmaker to determine his reasons for authorizing funding of the highway.[37]

The "no law to apply" formulation of the APA's committed to agency discretion exception from judicial review is at least as difficult to understand as the exception itself. Recall that, in Chapter 2, we considered the Supreme Court's repeated assertions under the nondelegation doctrine that congressional delegations of discretionary authority to agencies are only constitutional if they establish intelligible principles that limit agency discretion and guide agency behavior. Of course, the Supreme Court has rarely found that a statute's delegation does not set forth intelligible principles. Nevertheless, if a statute provides such intelligible principles, then how can it be said that the statute commits an issue to agency discretion by offering no law to apply?

The Court had an opportunity to provide some clarity regarding what it meant to have no law to apply several years later in *Heckler v. Chaney*,[38] but really just sowed more confusion. The case concerned a decision by the Food and Drug Administration (FDA) not to investigate states' use of prescription drugs for a purpose for which they were not intended, to administer the death penalty by lethal injection. The FDA is

35. *Overton Park*, 401 U.S. at 410 (emphasis added) (quoting S. REP. 752, 79TH CONG., 1ST SESS. 26 (1945)).

36. For one reaction to this formulation of the committed to agency discretion exception, see Kenneth Culp Davis, "*No Law to Apply*," 25 SAN DIEGO L. REV. 1 (1988).

37. This aspect of the *Overton Park* decision is discussed at greater length in Chapter 9, § 9.03[B].

38. 470 U.S. 821 (1985).

required by statute to ensure that all "new drugs" are "safe and effective" for use under the conditions prescribed or suggested in the drugs' official labeling. The FDA generally does not prohibit unapproved uses of approved drugs. Chaney had filed a petition with the FDA alleging that the drugs that the states were using were not safe and effective for lethal injection use because they caused extreme pain prior to death and demanding that the FDA investigate and pursue enforcement actions to eliminate this unapproved use of the drugs. The FDA declined to take the requested actions for a few years. First, the FDA was reluctant to interfere with state uses of drugs for state purposes explicitly authorized by state statutes. Second, the FDA questioned whether it possessed the authority to prohibit unapproved uses of otherwise approved drugs. Finally, as a matter of policy, the FDA preferred to focus its enforcement resources on circumstances that posed a serious danger to the public health or demonstrated a blatant scheme to defraud.

The Court upheld the FDA's decision not to pursue the requested investigation and enforcement actions. The *Chaney* case is known principally for announcing an analytical framework for evaluating judicial review of agency inaction, as discussed in the next section of this chapter. Nevertheless, the decision is also notable for its discussion of the committed to agency discretion limitation of APA § 701(a)(2). The Court reiterated its statement from *Overton Park* that an action is committed to agency discretion only in the "rare case" where "there is no law to apply." The Court then paraphrased that statement as referring to a situation in which there is "no meaningful standard against which to judge the agency's exercise of discretion." This alternative formulation of "no law to apply" as "no judicially manageable standard" prompted some observers to suggest that the Court had actually changed its interpretation of APA § 701(a)(2) from a narrow and formalistic focus on judicial review with little real world heft to a more pragmatic and functional approach.[39]

Regardless, just a few years later, in *Webster v. Doe*,[40] the Court again took up the question of whether a statute limited judicial review by committing a particular act to agency discretion. In this case, the Court considered a decision by the Central Intelligence Agency (CIA) to fire a security officer with that agency solely on the basis of his sexual orientation. The terminated employee argued that his dismissal exceeded the CIA's statutory authority and was arbitrary and capricious under the APA. He also raised a number of constitutional due process issues. In addressing the issue at hand, the Court cited both the *Overton Park* "no law to apply" and the *Chaney* "no meaningful standard" formulations for APA § 701(a)(2). In this instance, however, the Court then focused its attention on the organic statute's very loose language regarding the CIA Director's discretion to terminate any employee "whenever he shall deem such termination necessary or advisable in the interest of the United States." This language, in the Court's view, "fairly exudes deference to the Director, and appears to us to foreclose the application of any meaningful judicial standard of review," thus barring judicial review of the employee's statutory claims. At the same time, however, the Court held the employee's constitutional claims to be reviewable because there was no clear congressional intent to block review of constitutional issues.

Justice Antonin Scalia wrote an interesting dissenting opinion in *Webster* that has come to influence how the Court evaluates the committed to agency discretion question.

39. *See, e.g.*, Ronald M. Levin, *Understanding Unreviewability in Administrative Law*, 74 MINN. L. REV. 689 (1990).

40. 86 U.S. 592 (1988).

He was quite critical of the Court's careful parsing of the statute's text as a means of evaluating whether there was no law to apply or no meaningful standard by which to review the agency's action. According to Justice Scalia, that sort of statutory analysis is more the province of APA § 701(a)(1), which asks whether "*statutes* preclude judicial review."[41] Treating the committed to agency discretion limitation of § 701(a)(2) as a statutory inquiry as well would be redundant. Consequently, Justice Scalia maintained that the phrase "committed to agency discretion *by law*" in § 701(a)(2) "was intended to refer to 'the common law of judicial review of agency action'—a body of jurisprudence that had marked out, with more or less precision, certain issues and certain areas that were beyond the range of judicial review." He offered as examples "principles ranging from the 'political question' doctrine, to sovereign immunity..., to official immunity, to prudential limitations upon the courts' equitable powers, to what can be described no more precisely than a traditional respect for the functions of the other branches." This sort of emphasis on whether the agency action at hand was "of the sort that is traditionally unreviewable" would "operate[] to keep certain categories of agency action out of the courts." Justice Scalia went on to explain why he would find both the statutory and the constitutional challenges in this case unreviewable.

Although Justice Scalia's opinion in *Webster* was merely a dissent joined by none of his colleagues, the Court later adopted his notion of interpreting committed to agency discretion by reference to areas of traditional unreviewability in *Lincoln v. Vigil*.[42] This case concerned a decision by the Indian Health Service to discontinue a regional program serving disabled Native American children and reallocate its funding to a broader national effort to help the same population. The relevant statute allocated an annual lump-sum appropriation to the Indian Health Service and gave it broad discretion to use the appropriated funds to improve Native American health. The beneficiaries of the regional program challenged the decision to discontinue it on both APA and constitutional grounds. The Court held that the APA claims were unreviewable under APA § 701(a)(2). Although quoting the "no meaningful standard against which to judge" language from its earlier decisions, the reason offered for the Court's holding echoed Justice Scalia's explanation in *Webster*: "The allocation of funds from a lump-sum appropriation is another administrative decision traditionally regarded as committed to agency discretion." Having decided that the challengers' statutory claims were unreviewable, the Court nevertheless remanded the case for consideration of the constitutional arguments raised because the lower courts had not addressed them, so the record was inadequate for "mature consideration of [those] issues."

So where does the Supreme Court's meandering over the committed to agency discretion leave us? The Court has never repudiated and continues to recite the "no law to apply" and "no meaningful standard by which to judge" formulations of the committed to agency discretion inquiry, but also has embraced Justice Scalia's notion that some agency actions simply are "of the sort that is traditionally unreviewable." Consequently, lower courts continue to evaluate agency claims that particular actions are unreviewable as having been committed to agency discretion by reference to all of the above—parsing statutory language for evidence of the extent to which particular decisions have been left to agency discretion, but also contemplating whether the action in question involves an area of traditional unreviewability. Accordingly, litigants and their

41. Statutory preclusion under APA § 701(a)(1) is discussed in the immediately preceding subsection of this chapter.

42. 508 U.S. 182 (1993).

attorneys are well advised to approach these questions from all directions as well, pending further clarification by the Court, if it ever comes.

[E] Discretion Not to Act

With the exception of *Heckler v. Chaney*, all of the cases described above regarding the preclusion and committed to agency discretion limitations on judicial review imposed by APA § 701(a) have involved agency decisions to take particular actions. Agency decisions not to pursue certain actions represent a challenging subset of cases under § 701(a). Accordingly, they have developed their own unique jurisprudence among the cases exploring the scope of § 701(a), with different results for enforcement decisions as opposed to decisions not to pursue a rulemaking.

[1] Discretion Not to Pursue Enforcement

In 1975, the Supreme Court decided *Dunlop v. Bachowski*,[43] a case in which a participant in a union election had complained to the Department of Labor about potential violations of the Labor-Management Reporting and Disclosure Act of 1959. Upon the receipt of such a complaint, the statute provided, in pertinent part, that "[t]he Secretary shall investigate such complaint and, if he finds probable cause to believe that a violation... has occurred and has not been remedied, he shall, within sixty days after the filing of such complaint, bring a civil action against the labor organization as an entity." After investigation, the Labor Department sent the complainant a letter declining to pursue an enforcement action. The complainant challenged the agency's nonenforcement decision, asking that the court order the agency to file suit to set aside the union election in question. The Department defended its refusal on the ground that "the structure of the statutory scheme, its objectives, its legislative history, the nature of the administrative action involved, and the conditions spelled out with respect thereto, combine to evince a congressional meaning to prohibit judicial review of his decision" and also that his decision was "an unreviewable exercise of prosecutorial discretion." The Court disagreed and held that the agency's refusal to act was reviewable. The Court found that the statute limited the scope of judicial review but did not prohibit it outright. The Court acknowledged that Congress intended to rely on the agency's "special knowledge and discretion" in deciding when to pursue actions challenging the validity of a union election. Accordingly, the Court was emphatic that "the reviewing court is not authorized to substitute its judgment for the decision of the [agency] to bring suit." Yet, given the lack of an outright prohibition against judicial review in the statute, the Court also required the agency to "provide the court and the complaining witness with copies of a statement of reasons supporting [its] determination."

Many federal circuit courts interpreted the *Bachowski* decision broadly and, in its wake, ordered agencies to take actions they did not want to take, much to the delight of many public interest groups. The situation changed dramatically in 1985 when the Court decided *Heckler v. Chaney*.[44] Recall that the case concerned the FDA's refusal to investigate and pursue enforcement against states' off-label use of prescription drugs to administer the death penalty by lethal injection. The FDA justified its decision both because of

43. 421 U.S. 560 (1975).
44. 470 U.S. 821 (1985).

doubts regarding its authority to prohibit unapproved uses of otherwise approved drugs and because it preferred to focus its enforcement efforts on circumstances that posed a serious danger to the public health or demonstrated a blatant scheme to defraud.

Notwithstanding its decision in *Bachowski*, the Court in *Chaney* recognized a presumption of unreviewability of agency inaction in the enforcement context. The Court offered three reasons for this presumption. First, the Court acknowledged that agencies cannot realistically be expected to pursue every violation of statutes within their jurisdiction. Agency decisions whether to initiate enforcement actions are usually based on a complicated balancing of several factors, such as the efficient allocation of limited agency resources, the likelihood of success, and the relationship of a particular action to the agency's overall enforcement strategy. Second, the Court saw less need for judicial review in the context of enforcement inaction because, unlike when agencies act, inaction does not involve agencies exercising coercive power over individual rights. Third, the Court took notice of a close analogy between agency decisions not to act and exercises of prosecutorial discretion that courts have traditionally declined to review.

The presumption of unreviewability adopted by the Court in *Chaney* is a rebuttable one. In footnotes, the Court described three circumstances that might be sufficient to rebut the presumption. First, if an agency declines to act based "solely" on its belief that it lacks jurisdiction, the Court suggested that judicial review could be pursued regarding the agency's jurisdictional determination. Second, if an agency "consciously and expressly" adopts a policy that is so extreme as to represent an abdication of its statutory responsibilities, the Court suggested that judicial review might be available to consider whether the agency's position was not committed to agency discretion. Third, the Court expressly noted that its opinion did not address agency decisions not to engage in rulemaking. Distinguishing the circumstances before it from those of *Bachowski*, the Court also referred to situations in which a statute couples the language of command—*e.g.*, "the agency shall"—with a justiciable standard. The statute at issue in *Chaney* used more permissive language, and the Court's comparison of the two statutes had the effect of limiting *Bachowski*'s scope significantly.

Remember that *Chaney* goes only to the initial decision whether to take action. A refusal to commence an enforcement action is not normally reviewable under *Chaney*. If, however, an agency proceeds with enforcement, the enforcement action itself will normally be subject to judicial review under the traditional standards discussed in this chapter and in Chapters 12 and 13.

[2] Discretion Not to Make a Rule

Recall that the Supreme Court's decision in *Heckler v. Chaney* expressly did not apply to agency decisions not to pursue rulemaking. Agencies sometimes refuse to promulgate rules even after they have been asked to do so by various private groups. Is such a refusal reviewable or is it committed to agency discretion under § 701(a)(2)?

Shortly after the Supreme Court's decision in *Heckler v. Chaney*, the United States Court of Appeals for the District of Columbia Circuit addressed this question in *American Horse Protection Ass'n v. Lyng*.[45] The Department of Agriculture adopted regulations under the Horse Protection Act to prohibit certain devices and methods associated with a practice known as "soring"—which trained horses to adopt a high-stepping gait, but

45. 812 F.2d 1 (D.C. Cir. 1987).

at the risk of great pain and potential injury. Concerns were raised that the regulations were inadequate, and the Association met with agency officials and suggested a rulemaking. The agency declined, however, to pursue a new rulemaking pending further studies. When the agency's inaction was challenged, the D.C. Circuit decided that judicial review was not precluded.

In reaching its conclusion regarding reviewability, the D.C. Circuit turned directly to *Chaney* and the three reasons offered by the Supreme Court for its presumption in favor of unreviewability of nonenforcement decisions. Two of those reasons applied in the rulemaking context as well: the "expertise and coordination" in allocating agency resources and the comparative lack of coercive power over individual rights inherent in declining to act. But the third reason for the *Chaney* presumption—the analogy of agency nonenforcement decisions to traditionally unreviewable prosecutorial discretion—did not apply in the rulemaking context. Whereas exercises of enforcement discretion occur often and in large numbers, and tend to be based on considerations of fact, "[r]efusals to institute rulemakings... are likely to be relatively infrequent and more likely to turn upon issues of law." Moreover, unlike for nonenforcement decisions, APA §§ 553(e) and 555(e), respectively, require agencies to accept petitions for rulemaking from interested persons and provide "a brief statement of the grounds for denial" of the same. According to the D.C. Circuit, those provisions "provide a focus for judicial review" and "suggest that Congress expected that agencies denying rulemaking petitions must explain their actions." For these reasons, the court concluded that decisions not to pursue rulemaking were reviewable under the arbitrary and capricious standard of APA § 706(2)(A).[46] The court went on to hold that the agency "ha[d] not presented a reasonable explanation" for its decision not to act on the petition for more extensive soring regulations. The court did not, however, order the agency to institute rulemaking proceedings, and instead merely remanded for the agency to either explain itself better or initiate a rulemaking.

Since the D.C. Circuit's decision in the *American Horse Protection* case, other federal circuit courts have adopted the same approach of reviewing agency decisions not to pursue rulemakings using the APA § 706(2)(A) arbitrary and capricious standard.[47] Additionally, the Supreme Court in *Massachusetts v. Environmental Protection Agency*[48] adopted the holding and reasoning of the D.C. Circuit with respect to the Environmental Protection Agency's failure to promulgate rules regulating greenhouse gas emissions from new motor vehicles under the Clean Air Act. According to the Court in that case, "EPA has offered no reasoned explanation for its refusal to decide whether greenhouse gases cause or contribute to climate change.... We hold that EPA must ground its reasons for action or inaction in the statute."[49] The explanatory bar in this context is not very high. Nevertheless, some explanation is required, and courts will review those explanations for reasoned decisionmaking.

---

46. The APA § 706(2)(A) arbitrary and capricious standard is discussed at length in Chapter 13.

47. *See, e.g., International Union v. Chao*, 361 F.3d 240 (3d Cir. 2004); *Maier v. U.S. Environmental Protection Agency*, 114 F.3d 1032 (10th Cir. 1997); *O'Keeffe's, Inc. v. U.S. Consumer Product Safety Comm'n*, 92 F.3d 940 (9th Cir. 1996).

48. 549 U.S. 497 (2007).

49. *Id.* at 534–35.

Chapter 11

Judicial Review: Timing Doctrines

§ 11.01 Introduction

This chapter covers questions of *when* judicial review can be had. These issues are often referred to as the *timing* issues because their resolution does not prohibit judicial review but simply establishes the point in time when a court can get its hands on the matter. Nevertheless, these questions must be resolved before a court gets to the merits of a controversy. The four timing issues discussed in this Chapter have universally-accepted labels: primary jurisdiction, finality, and ripeness and exhaustion.

Briefly stated, *primary jurisdiction* doctrine concerns whether a court can be the first avenue of resolution of a dispute, or whether the dispute must be given to an agency first and taken into court only when the agency has concluded its action. The boundaries between judicial responsibilities and agency responsibilities are not always clear and often depend upon expert analysis of fact patterns. Consequently, courts sometimes use primary jurisdiction doctrine to give an agency the initial responsibility of deciding whether an overlap that is likely to lead to conflicts actually exists. Stated a bit simplistically, primary jurisdiction is like a fork in the road. Principles of primary jurisdiction determine which fork a particular dispute must follow. As explained below, primary jurisdiction is less of a barrier to judicial review than it once was.

The doctrines of *finality*, *ripeness*, and *exhaustion* also involve issues of the timing of judicial review. Their analysis often overlaps, but they are analytically distinct from one another and rely on separate standards. *Finality* focuses on whether agency action is complete in the sense that it carries legal consequences. *Ripeness* asks whether the issues in dispute are sufficiently matured to permit a court to review the case—*i.e.*, whether there is a properly-framed *legal* issue in the case that the court may review. *Exhaustion* asks whether a person currently before the agency must stay within the agency until all possible agency procedures or levels of decision making are completed—*i.e.*, exhausted.

These three doctrines interact with one another in various ways. Many disputes at the agency level have not exhausted agency level procedures, are not final, and are not ripe, so all three doctrines apply to limit the availability of judicial review. Conversely, a case that has exhausted all procedures at the agency level typically will be final and ripe for judicial review as well. Yet, an issue may be ripe for judicial review and may even satisfy finality requirements, even though additional procedures are available at the agency. The availability of those additional procedures raises a possible exhaustion problem and may impede reviewability. In other cases that have not exhausted agency level procedures, courts may review the merits anyway because exhaustion sometimes is merely a matter of judicial policy that leaves judges with a fair amount of discretion. Meanwhile, on some occasions, cases that satisfy both finality and exhaustion requirements may not be ripe for judicial review and must await further agency action before courts can consider them.

A great illustration of the significant overlap among the doctrines of finality, ripeness, and exhaustion is the decision of the D.C. Circuit Court of Appeals in *Ticor Title Insurance Co. v. Federal Trade Commission*.[1] The court dismissed the petition for review as premature, and the three members of the panel all agreed with the court's disposition of the case. Yet, the judges disagreed completely regarding the basis for that disposition. One judge concluded that the agency action was final and ripe but that review was premature because the petitioner had not yet exhausted administrative remedies. One judge concluded that the action was final and that the petitioner had exhausted administrative remedies but that review was premature because the action was not yet ripe. The third judge concluded that the action was ripe for judicial review and the petitioner had exhausted administrative remedies but that review was premature because the action was not yet final.

The main thing to remember is that finality, ripeness, and exhaustion all can be used to postpone (or, perhaps more accurately, to block outright) judicial review. All three doctrines must be analyzed as you consider *when* a court may pass judgment on the matter.

§ 11.02 Primary Jurisdiction

[A] Analysis of the Fundamentals

Primary jurisdiction is a somewhat obscure and difficult concept of administrative law that is often confused and misapplied by both courts and practitioners.[2] Hence, it frequently confuses law students as well. Most of the confusion can be dispelled, however, by focusing on the fundamentals.

Primary jurisdiction issues arise as the disputing parties try to decide who should resolve their dispute—an agency or a court. If the party seeking formal dispute resolution goes first to the agency, primary jurisdiction typically will not be an issue. All subsequent questions regarding the timing of judicial review will turn on application of the doctrines of finality, ripeness, and exhaustion, not on primary jurisdiction principles. Sometimes, however, a party with a grievance will try to go to court first, completely avoiding the agency. When that happens, the issue of primary jurisdiction must be considered.

Stated concisely, the doctrine of primary jurisdiction requires that a dispute that falls within the jurisdiction of a government agency should be taken first to that agency, even if the case or certain issues within the case might in theory be taken into court initially. At one time, invoking primary jurisdiction doctrine was the near exclusive means by

1. 814 F.2d 731 (D.C. Cir. 1987).

2. For more recent academic analysis of primary jurisdiction doctrine, see, *e.g.*, Diana R.H. Winters, *Restoring the Primary Jurisdiction Doctrine*, 78 Ohio St. L.J. 541 (2017); Richard J. Pierce, Jr., *Primary Jurisdiction: Another Victim of Reality*, 69 Admin. L. Rev. 431 (2017). For historical perspective on this topic, see, *e.g.*, Louis L. Jaffe, *Primary Jurisdiction*, 77 Harv. L. Rev. 1037 (1964); Israel Gonvisser, *Primary Jurisdiction: The Rule and Its Rationalizations*, 65 Yale L.J. 315 (1956).

which a court could seek and obtain the views of an agency regarding issues within the agency's expertise and responsibility when the court wanted that perspective in trying to resolve a dispute before it.

Occasionally, Congress specifically requires courts to apply the primary jurisdiction doctrine to a class of disputes. One example is Title VII of the Civil Rights act of 1964, which provides for Equal Employment Opportunity Commission resolution of unlawful employment practice claims and requires persons aggrieved by unlawful employment practices to obtain permission from that agency before filing a civil action against an employer in federal court.[3]

In most cases, however, the doctrine of primary jurisdiction is judge-made. Although courts considering primary jurisdiction issues will carefully consider the applicable organic statute and how it interacts with the Administrative Procedure Act, at least at the federal level, no general primary jurisdiction statute as such exists. Consequently, attorneys considering primary jurisdiction questions should be sensitive to the underlying goals and tensions inherent in the doctrine. Congress established administrative agencies to deal with certain types of problems because courts were not always up to the task at hand. Unlike courts, agencies are expected to be experts in the scientific or other technical matters within their jurisdiction. Frequently, the resolution of a case can be enhanced by a proper understanding of the dispute's scientific or technical aspects. This is something at which an agency is usually more skilled than is a court.

On the other hand, Congress also expressly confers upon the courts the jurisdiction to resolve issues concerning a wide variety of different subject matters. For example, a statute gives federal district courts the authority to resolve disputes between parties who are citizens of different states when the amount in controversy exceeds the sum of $75,000 (*i.e.*, diversity jurisdiction).[4] Another statute permits federal district courts to decide cases that arise under a statute, a treaty, or the U.S. Constitution (*i.e.*, federal question jurisdiction).[5] Yet another statute allows federal district courts to hear cases involving interstate commerce or the federal antitrust statutes.[6] Thus, many disputes may go straight to court under one or another of these jurisdictional statutes, rather than to an arguably appropriate agency. In each of the primary jurisdiction cases discussed in this chapter, the party seeking judicial review without first going to an agency invoked an appropriate jurisdictional statute, so the party at least theoretically was entitled to be in court in the first instance. In most of these cases, however, the Supreme Court instead required the party to go to the agency for initial resolution of the dispute.

[B] The *Abilene Cotton* and *Western Pacific* Cases

The Supreme Court's first significant pronouncement regarding primary jurisdiction came in 1907 in *Texas & Pacific Railway v. Abilene Cotton Oil Co.*[7] The Court's opinion in *Abilene Cotton* is long and written in an older judicial style that can be hard to read. In substance, however, the case is not so complicated. A shipper of goods and a railroad contracted to carry those goods disagreed about whether the railroad was

3. 42 U.S.C. § 2000e-5.
4. 28 U.S.C. § 1332.
5. 28 U.S.C. § 1331.
6. 28 U.S.C. § 1337.
7. 204 U.S. 426 (1907).

charging reasonable rates (*i.e.*, prices) to haul the shipper's freight. Armed with this grievance, the shipper chose to go directly into a federal district court to challenge the reasonableness of the rates, even though Congress in the Interstate Commerce Act had given the Interstate Commerce Commission (ICC) statutory authority to determine the reasonableness of interstate freight rates.

Before Congress established the ICC, a federal district court was the only place where a shipper could challenge a railroad's rates. In going to court, the shipper invoked the statute generally giving the federal district courts original jurisdiction over matters concerning interstate commerce, 28 U.S.C. §1337. Additionally, the Interstate Commerce Act expressly stated Congress's intent not to "in any way abridge or alter the remedies existing at common law or by statute" and authorized persons suffering injury at the hands of a railroad regulated by the ICC to bring suit against the railroad in federal district court. In its *Abilene Cotton* decision, the Supreme Court conceded that the shipper had the theoretical right to be in district court in the first instance.

Notwithstanding that statutory and common law backdrop, a fundamental purpose of the Interstate Commerce Act was to produce a certain national uniformity in the rates that railroads charged their customers for hauling freight. The Court in *Abilene Cotton* concluded that the ICC had been set up expressly to handle rate disputes and had special expertise on matters such as rail transportation and freight rates. Just as importantly, the Court reasoned that the ICC was a federal agency with national jurisdiction over the nation's transportation industry whose decisions and policies would have nationwide scope and effect. Allowing a single federal district court take the first look at this kind of dispute could lead to literally hundreds and possibly thousands of conflicting and inconsistent court decisions on what constituted a reasonable rate. By contrast, ICC decisionmaking could ensure a uniform approach throughout the country. For these reasons, the Court in *Abilene Cotton* invoked the doctrine of primary jurisdiction and ordered the district court to dismiss the case with an invitation to the parties to take their grievance to the ICC for resolution. If one or another of the parties disliked what the ICC did, they could always return to the courts for judicial review of the agency's action.

Abilene Cotton was a relatively unusual, and comparatively straightforward, case because the parties only raised one issue and the Court held that the agency had primary jurisdiction over that issue. The agency's resolution of the issue would be subject to judicial review. In disposing of the case in this way, the Court surrendered all power over the dispute, at least until the agency resolved the matter and one or both parties sought judicial review.

More frequently, primary jurisdiction is held to apply only to one or more of several issues that must be resolved in the process of adjudicating a dispute. In such cases, the court retains jurisdiction to adjudicate the dispute, including initial resolution of all issues not referred to the agency, but the court defers its decisionmaking process until the agency resolves the referred issues.[8]

8. In *Reiter v. Cooper*, 507 U.S. 258 (1993), the Supreme Court reaffirmed the principle that a court retains the power to resolve a dispute even when it refers an issue to an agency for its initial resolution. Whether to retain jurisdiction or dismiss the case without prejudice is left to the court's discretion.

This more typical effect of primary jurisdiction is illustrated by another significant early case regarding the doctrine, *United States v. Western Pacific Railroad Co.*[9] The essence of the *Western Pacific* case was quite similar to that of *Abilene Cotton*: a shipper (in this instance, the federal government) wanted to ship goods via railroad, and the shipper and the railroad disagreed over the reasonableness of the railroad's rates for hauling the freight. The details, however, demonstrate the greater complexity of the dispute and the Supreme Court's handling of it.

Under the Interstate Commerce Act, railroads set their prices by filing tariffs (schedules of prices) with the ICC. There are two basic components to these prices, *i.e.*, the nature of the commodity to be shipped, and the distance traveled. Applying the first component requires a railroad to determine into which commodity classification the goods are to be placed. The classifications depend on such factors as density, perishability and dangerousness. In other words, a good that is highly perishable or extremely dangerous to transport will cost more to ship than a good that does not have those characteristics. Once the good is placed into an appropriate classification, the railroad then determines the number of miles the good is to be shipped and arrives at the final price to be charged for the shipment.

In the *Western Pacific* case, the goods that the federal government wanted to ship were napalm bombs, and the government and the railroad disagreed over the proper classification of those goods. The railroad insisted that the napalm should be classified as "incendiary bombs," which was a classification that triggered a higher price than the classification sought by the government, "gasoline in drums." In other words, the railroad would make more money for shipping the napalm bombs if they were classified as incendiary bombs instead of gasoline in drums. Meanwhile, the government would pay less if the napalm bombs were classified as gasoline in drums. Given that the government shipped a significant amount of napalm, the amount of money in controversy was considerable.

The government insisted on paying the lower price for the shipments, so the railroad filed suit against the government in the Court of Claims (now the United States Court of Federal Claims), seeking reimbursement for the higher price. The railroad's lawsuit bypassed the ICC entirely. On review, the Supreme Court determined that the doctrine of primary jurisdiction applied such that the ICC held primary jurisdiction to interpret the tariff and determine which rate applied to the napalm balms. The Court of Claims retained the ultimate power to resolve the overall dispute between the government and the railroad, but that court was required to suspend its decisionmaking process and refer to the ICC the question of which tariff provision applied to the shipment in question. According to the Supreme Court in *Western Pacific*,

> "Primary jurisdiction" ... applies where a claim is originally cognizable in the courts, and comes into play whenever enforcement of the claim requires the resolution of issues which, under a regulatory scheme, have been placed within the special competence of an administrative body; in such a case the judicial process is suspended pending referral of such issues to the administrative body for its views.[10]

As in *Abilene Cotton*, the Supreme Court based its holding in *Western Pacific* primarily on the ICC's greater expertise in interpreting freight tariffs. Although tariff

9. 352 U.S. 59 (1956).
10. *Id.* at 63–64.

interpretation is an issue solely of law, and thus falls within traditional understandings regarding judicial competence, the ICC had been the body that originally determined the appropriateness of the tariff classifications and corresponding rates based on its detailed evaluation of the costs of shipping different categories of freight. The ICC possessed specialized knowledge of the factors that had prompted it in the first place to draw the distinctions reflected in the tariff. That same knowledge would be useful in deciding which rate in the tariff applied to a particular type of goods.

On the other hand, the Court in *Western Pacific* stopped short of holding that all issues of tariff interpretation were within the ICC's primary jurisdiction, and instead distinguished between different types of tariff interpretation questions. The Court also declined to draw bright lines in defining when primary jurisdiction applied to require a reviewing court to refer particular issues to the relevant agency. According to the Court in *Western Pacific*,

> No fixed formula exists for applying the doctrine of primary jurisdiction. In every case the question is whether the reasons for existence of the doctrine are present and whether the purposes it serves will be aided by its application in the particular litigation.[11]

Because the Court has not articulated a clear standard for evaluating primary jurisdiction issues, case law applying the doctrine can be confusing and difficult to reconcile.

[C] Avoiding Delays Associated with Primary Jurisdiction

One significant disadvantage to referring issues to agencies through the application of the primary jurisdiction doctrine is the significant delays the practice imposes on judicial resolution of the underlying disputes. Agencies can respond to such referrals by initiating a rulemaking or an adjudication to resolve an issue referred by a court. Those agency-level proceedings can take months or even years to complete.[12] Perhaps unsurprisingly, courts and litigants have found various ways of avoiding such delays.

In contemporary case law, courts often extend substantial deference to agency interpretations of law. The cases and doctrines counseling judicial deference to agency interpretations of law—*Chevron*, *Skidmore*, *Mead*, and *Auer*, to name the most well-known—are discussed in Chapter 13. In particular, the *Chevron* doctrine considers ambiguities in statutory meaning to represent delegations of policymaking discretion to agencies and requires courts to defer to reasonable agency interpretations of statutes resolving such ambiguities.[13] At least in theory, one of the many effects of the *Chevron* doctrine of judicial deference to agency interpretations of statutory meaning should be to increase the number of cases in which courts send questions to agencies under the primary jurisdiction doctrine. In other words, given the intersection of *Chevron* deference and primary jurisdiction doctrine, courts should ask agencies to resolve questions of statutory meaning when (1) the statutory language supports more than one reasonable interpretation, (2) the outcome of the case before the court turns on the choice between or among the competing alternative interpretations, and (3) the agency has not

11. *Id.* at 64.
12. For extended discussions of rulemaking and adjudication procedures, see Chapters 7 and 8.
13. *Chevron U.S.A. Inc. v. Natural Resources Defense Council, Inc.*, 467 U.S. 837 (1984).

previously expressed an interpretation of the statutory language at stake.[14] Often, however, this is not what happens. Reviewing courts instead will adopt their own interpretations of ambiguous, agency-administered statutes, but with the understanding that agencies remain free thereafter to adopt a different interpretation as long as the agency's interpretation is reasonable.[15]

Correspondingly, the Supreme Court has relied on *Chevron* deference in declining to refer an issue to an agency. In *Reiter v. Cooper*,[16] the Court considered the applicability of the primary jurisdiction doctrine in connection with a disagreement between a motor carrier and a shipper in connection with a contract to ship goods. The litigation featured an array of claims and counterclaims. The motor carrier argued that the primary jurisdiction doctrine required certain of the shipper's claims to go first to the ICC rather than a court. The Supreme Court disagreed. The Court observed that the ICC had previously concluded that it lacked jurisdiction over the same issue. On that basis, the Court found the ICC's prior interpretation of the relevant statutory provision to be "reasonable" and thus "binding" on the Court under *Chevron*.

One way that courts have avoided the delays associated with primary jurisdiction has been to ask agencies instead to address issues of interpretation in amicus briefs, which then may be eligible for deferential review by the courts. An agency can file an amicus brief with a court taking a position on an issue without having to follow the time-consuming procedures that often burden agency rulemakings or adjudications. Thus, by requesting an amicus brief, a court can obtain the agency's views regarding an issue in a timely manner. The Supreme Court has consistently approved of, and has itself even relied on, this practice.[17]

In most circumstances, the parties to a dispute can waive primary jurisdiction simply by not raising the issue in a timely manner. In *Northwest Airlines, Inc. v. County of Kent*,[18] the Supreme Court evaluated a dispute over airport user fees between commercial airlines and the local authorities of the county that owned the airport. In its opinion, the Court noted that the lower courts could have referred the reasonableness of the fees to the Department of Transportation. Since none of the parties had briefed the question, however, the Court declined to invoke primary jurisdiction and refer the case to the agency. Several federal circuit courts have held expressly that primary jurisdiction, its label notwithstanding, is not jurisdictional and is waivable.[19]

---

14. *See* Kristin E. Hickman & Richard J. Pierce, Jr., Administrative Law Treatise §16.4 (6th ed. 2018).

15. *See, e.g., National Cable & Telecommunications Ass'n v. Brand X Internet Services*, 545 U.S. 967 (2005). This and other cases concerning judicial deference to agency legal interpretations are discussed in Chapter 13.

16. 507 U.S. 258 (1993).

17. *See, e.g., Kasten v. Saint-Gobain Performance Plastics Corp.*, 568 U.S. 1, 14–15 (2011); *Chase Bank v. McCoy*, 562 U.S. 195, 214 (2011); *Long Island Care at Home, Ltd. v. Coke*, 551 U.S. 158, 161 (2007); *Auer v. Robbins*, 519 U.S. 452, 461–62 (1997); *see also* Richard J. Pierce, Jr., *Primary Jurisdiction: Another Victim of Reality*, 69 Admin. L. Rev. 431 (2017) (highlighting the practice).

18. 510 U.S. 355 (1994).

19. *See, e.g., CSX Transporation Co. v. Novolog Bucks County*, 502 F.3d 247 (3d Cir. 2007); *U.S. v. Henri*, 828 F.2d 526 (9th Cir. 1987); *Gross Common Carrier, Inc. v. Baxter Healthcare Corp.*, 51 F.3d 703 (7th Cir. 1995). *But see MCI Telecommunications Corp. v. Teleconcepts, Inc.*, 71 F.3d 1086 (3d Cir. 1995) (invoking primary jurisdiction doctrine where a state legislature expressly by statute gave a state administrative agency exclusive authority to resolve the issue, even though the parties did not raise the primary jurisdiction question).

§ 11.03 Finality

[A] Statutory Foundation

Finality doctrine derives principally from § 704 of the federal Administrative Procedure Act, which provides as follows:

> Agency action made reviewable by statute and final agency action for which there is no other adequate remedy in a court are subject to judicial review.

This language is relatively clear on its face but still leads to problems when it becomes necessary to determine when *final agency action* has occurred.

Sometimes statutes dictate when agency action is reviewable. For example, the Federal Trade Commission Act expressly authorizes judicial review of Federal Trade Commission cease and desist orders when a challenge is filed within sixty days after service of the order.[20] The Freedom of Information Act allows judicial review when an agency fails to comply with certain statutory deadlines.[21] A number of agencies have provisions in their regulations stating that particular actions by particular agency components constitute final agency action for the purposes of judicial review. When a case falls under one of those provisions, there is usually no question that the agency action in question is final. Both agencies and courts tend to accept these pronouncements at face value.

Problems can arise when neither a statute nor an agency rule makes a definitive pronouncement about when judicial review of a particular agency action should occur. In such cases, what does it mean for agency action to be final? Of course, even if a particular agency action satisfies the finality requirement, ripeness and exhaustion may still apply to postpone judicial review. Remember that all of these doctrines are premised on the idea that a court generally should not interfere with ongoing agency operations. It is one thing for a court to review a case after the agency is finished with it. It is much more intrusive for a court to take a case out of the agency before agency action is completed.

[B] The *Bennett v. Spear* Two-Part Test

Prior to 1997, the Supreme Court evaluated the finality of agency action by considering various nonexclusive factors. Among the considerations were whether the agency action in question represented the agency's "definitive" position; the extent to which its effects were "direct and immediate," for example, on the challenging party's day-to-day operations; and the legal force of the agency action, including whether it carried an expectation of immediate compliance.[22]

In 1997, in *Bennett v. Spear*,[23] the Court synthesized and reduced its prior finality analysis to a two-part inquiry. The Court did not acknowledge the shift or repudiate its previous jurisprudence. Nevertheless, the two-part test articulated by the Court in *Bennett v. Spear* drives contemporary finality analysis. According to the Court,

---

20. 15 U.S.C. § 45(c).

21. 5 U.S.C. § 552(a)(6)(C). *See infra* Chapter 14, § 14.02.

22. *E.g., Federal Trade Comm'n v. Standard Oil Co. of Calif.*, 449 U.S. 232 (1980); *Abbott Labs v. Gardner*, 387 U.S. 136 (1967); *Frozen Food Express v. United States*, 351 U.S. 40 (1956).

23. 520 U.S. 154 (1997).

> As a general matter, two conditions must be satisfied for agency action to be "final." First, the action must mark the consummation of the agency's decision-making process—it must not be of a merely tentative or interlocutory nature. And second, the action must be one by which rights or obligations have been determined, or from which legal consequences will flow.[24]

The case itself concerned the finality of a *biological opinion* issued by the Fish and Wildlife Service (FWS) under the Endangered Species Act. Specifically, that statute requires that, when any federal agency action might adversely affect a threatened or endangered species, the agency seeking to pursue that action must formally consult with FWS. In such cases, FWS must provide the requesting agency with a written biological opinion explaining how the proposed action will affect the species or its habitat. If FWS finds that the agency action in question will jeopardize or adversely modify the habitat of a threatened or endangered species, the biological opinion must set out "reasonable and prudent alternatives" that FWS believes will avoid that consequence. Also, if FWS concludes that no jeopardy or adverse habitat modification will result from the agency action in question, or if the biological opinion offers reasonable and prudent alternatives, FWS must issue a separate *incidental take statement* that specifies the terms and conditions under which the requesting agency may "take" (*i.e.*, harm) the species.

The biological opinion in *Bennett v. Spear* concluded that an irrigation project operated by the Bureau of Reclamation in northern California and southern Oregon threatened two species of endangered fish, the Lost River Sucker and the Shortnose Sucker, and required as reasonable and prudent alternatives the maintenance of higher minimum water levels on reservoirs in the area of the irrigation project. The Bureau of Reclamation promised to follow the biological opinion. Irrigation districts and ranchers who relied on the reservoirs for their own water needs challenged the reasoning and conclusions of the biological opinion. The government asserted that the case was unreviewable because the biological opinion was not final agency action. The Supreme Court disagreed.

Applying the two-part test described above, the Supreme Court had little difficulty concluding that the FWS biological opinion at issue in *Bennett v. Spear* was final agency action. The government conceded that the biological opinion represented the consummation of FWS's decisionmaking, thus satisfying the first prong of the two-part test. Regarding the second prong, the government maintained that the biological opinion was merely advisory, but the Court rejected that argument. According to the Court, the biological opinion "alter[ed] the legal regime" to which the agency requesting the biological opinion was subject, because that agency could pursue its intended course of action "if (but only if) it complie[d] with the prescribed conditions." The government acknowledged that agencies rarely failed to follow the conclusions and recommendations of FWS biological opinions. If the recipient agency were to decide not to comply with the terms of a biological opinion, the agency employees who pursued such contrary acts would be vulnerable to civil and criminal penalties. Accordingly, the biological opinion had "direct and appreciable legal consequences."

Although the Supreme Court's earlier finality pronouncements clearly emphasized the pragmatic, day-to-day impacts of agency actions as well as their legal consequences, the two-part *Bennett v. Spear* test arguably narrowed the scope of finality doctrine in a more legalistic direction. Some federal circuit courts of appeals have applied it that

24. *Id.* at 177–78.

way, for example, suggesting that agency action lacks legal consequences for purposes of the second prong of the *Bennett v. Spear* test unless it carries the force and effect of law in a manner that would render the agency's action eligible for *Chevron* deference.[25] The Court's more recent finality decisions instead have emphasized the more pragmatic approach of the earlier cases, even under the banner of *Bennett v. Spear*.

The first of those two decisions came in *Sackett v. Environmental Protection Agency*,[26] in which the Supreme Court considered the finality of an *administrative compliance order* (Order) issued by the Environmental Protection Agency (EPA). The Sacketts were owners of residential property in Idaho that was located near a lake but separated from the water by several other lots with permanent buildings on them. In preparing to build a house, the Sacketts filled in part of their land with dirt and rock. The EPA sent the Sacketts an Order declaring their property to be wetlands subject to EPA jurisdiction under the Clean Water Act. The Order required the Sacketts to restore the site in compliance with an EPA-approved restoration work plan and under the EPA's supervision. Failing to comply with the Order would have exposed the Sacketts to potential financial penalties in future enforcement proceedings for violating the Clean Water Act and, additionally, for violating the Order itself. The EPA refused the Sacketts' request for an administrative hearing to contest the Order. Yet, the EPA also maintained that the Order was not final agency action because it invited the Sacketts to "engage in informal discussion" of the Order's terms and requirements and to let the agency know if they thought any of the allegations contained in the Order were inaccurate.

Applying the two-part test from *Bennett v. Spear*, the Supreme Court concluded the Order in *Sackett* was final agency action for which judicial review was available without further delay. The Court concluded that the first prong—consummation of the agency's decisionmaking process—was satisfied because, among other things, parties subject to EPA administrative compliance orders have no right to a formal administrative hearing to address the factual findings or determinations upon which such orders are based. The informal engagement regarding terms and requirements or errors in the allegations that the EPA offered the Sacketts was irrelevant because it did not entitle the Sacketts to further agency-level review of the Order's validity. Turning to the second prong of the two-part test—legal consequences and determination of rights or obligations—the Court observed that the Order required the Sacketts to restore their property in accordance with an agency-approved plan or face penalties for noncompliance. The Court also noted that, under a related provision of the Clean Water Act, the issuance of the Order made obtaining important permits from the United States Army Corps of Engineers considerably more difficult. The Court rejected the EPA's argument that deferring judicial review of the Order until after the EPA brought an enforcement action against the Sacketts would enhance regulatory efficiency.

Just a few years later, in *U.S. Army Corps of Engineers v. Hawkes Co., Inc.*,[27] the Supreme Court used similar reasoning regarding another agency determination that

---

25. *See, e.g.*, *Air Brake Systems, Inc. v. Mineta*, 357 F.3d 632 (6th Cir. 2004). The Sixth Circuit in *Air Brake Systems* stopped just short of this conclusion, carefully describing eligibility for *Chevron* deference as a "*sufficient* legal consequence," rather than a *necessary* one for establishing finality. On the other hand, the *Air Brake Systems* court went on to say that the Supreme Court's post-*Bennett v. Spear* curtailment of *Chevron*'s scope in *United States v. Mead Corp.*, 533 U.S. 218 (2001), meant that "less agency action ... may qualify for federal-court review" under the two-part finality test. For discussion of *Chevron* deference and the Court's *Mead* decision, see Chapter 13.

26. 566 U.S. 120 (2012).

27. 578 U.S. 590 (2016).

property fell within the scope of the Clean Water Act. In this instance, the Army Corps issued a document known as an *approved jurisdictional determination* expressing its conclusion that the plaintiffs' property was subject to Clean Water Act permitting requirements. After the challengers filed suit, the agency claimed that its action was not final. Again, the Supreme Court disagreed unanimously.

According to the Supreme Court, the approved jurisdictional determination in *Hawkes* represented the consummation of agency decisionmaking because the Army Corps issued the determination only "after extensive factfinding ... regarding the physical and hydrological characteristics of the property," the determination typically would "not [be] revisited if the permitting process move[d] forward," and the determination would "remain valid for a period of five years" according to the Army Corps. By comparison, judicial determinations designated as *preliminary*, rather than approved, were described by the Army Corps as "advisory in nature" and simply indicative that "there may be waters of the United States on a parcel of property." The possibility that the Army Corps might revise an approved judicial determination within the specified five-year period based on new information did not alter the finality of the determination.

Turning to the second prong of the *Bennett v. Spear* two-part test, the Court in *Hawkes* identified several "direct and appreciable consequences" of approved jurisdictional determinations. A negative determination provided a five-year safe harbor from any enforcement action, while a positive determination deprived the land owner of the benefits of the safe harbor. Positive determinations also included warnings that, if land owners discharged pollutants onto their property without first obtaining a permit from the Army Corps, they risked substantial civil and criminal penalties. The Court rejected the alternative of violating the Clean Water Act and defending the violation by arguing that the land did not fall within the scope of the Act because pursuing that path risked large penalties. The Court also dismissed as an alternative applying to the Army Corps for a permit to do something with the land that was otherwise prohibited, observing that the permitting process was "arduous, expensive, and long."

In short, notwithstanding the comparatively narrow framing of the two-part test of *Bennett v. Spear* relative to the open-ended, nonexclusive list of factors that the Supreme Court had previously employed, more recent unanimous applications by the Court of that two-part test have allowed parties who disagree with the government to have access to judicial review at a relatively early stage in an agency's decisionmaking process. The decisions are consistent with the Court's pragmatic insistence that parties be able to obtain judicial review of agency actions without first having to risk suffering a penalty or a collateral cost of a government decision or to endure the cost and delay of an expensive and lengthy administrative decisionmaking process. Lower courts have cited *Sackett* and *Hawkes* in holding in favor of the immediate reviewability of issues that they might previously have found to be not final based on a more legalistic approach to the two-part test of *Bennett v. Spear*.[28]

28. *See, e.g., Rhea Lana v. Department of Labor*, 824 F.3d 1023 (D.C. Cir. 2016); *Texas v. Equal Employment Opportunity Comm'n*, 827 F.3d 372 (5th Cir. 2016).

§ 11.04 Ripeness

[A] Implications of Comparative Expertise

Any inquiry into ripeness asks whether the issue that is presented to the court is sufficiently mature and crystallized to be appropriate for judicial consideration and disposition. In other words, ripeness analysis looks at the characteristics of the issue to be presented to the court.

In contemplating ripeness doctrine, it may help to remember that judges are not pharmacologists or safety engineers or experts in television broadcasting. Agencies do possess that expertise, so they are the ones Congress has tasked with resolving scientific and technical questions like whether a particular pollutant is truly harmful to human health, whether a mine roofing bolt is strong enough, or whether one radio station's broadcast signal will interfere with that of another station. Courts generally lack the expertise to resolve complex scientific and technical questions.

By and large, the best courts can do is assess whether an agency's determinations on such questions were authorized by statute, whether the agency's determinations were made in compliance with required procedures, whether the agency has explained its determinations sufficiently, and whether the agency's determinations appear to be reasonable in light of the administrative record. The courts' approach to the ripeness question arguably speaks to these limitations.

[B] The Two-Part *Abbott Labs* Test

Virtually every case involving ripeness begins with a reference to the landmark case in this area, *Abbott Laboratories v. Gardner*.[29] In this case, the Supreme Court articulated the two-part test that the courts have applied ever since for evaluating whether challenges to agency actions are ripe for judicial review.

In *Abbott Labs*, the Supreme Court considered a pre-enforcement challenge to regulations promulgated by the Food and Drug Administration (FDA) to implement amendments to the Federal Food, Drug, and Cosmetic Act. In the late 1950s and early 1960s, Congress conducted an extensive investigation of the pharmaceutical industry, resulting in several significant amendments to that statute. Among the amendments, Congress sought to alter the practice followed by virtually all pharmaceutical manufacturers of discouraging the sale of generic drugs.

Generic drugs are produced and marketed in bulk to retail stores to be sold under the retail store's name. Because they are sold in bulk and because the manufacturer does not incur any advertising and promotion costs, generic drugs tend to sell for far less per pill than the pharmaceuticals sold under the manufacturer's brand name. For many years, pharmaceutical companies tried to encourage the sale of brand name drugs by promoting those brand names among doctors and other health care professionals. These promotional activities were accompanied by large-scale advertising programs designed to enhance the name-recognition of their branded products to the detriment of the generic products. At the same time, because pharmaceutical manufacturing is

29. 387 U.S. 136 (1967).

heavily regulated by the FDA, the safety, effectiveness or chemical composition of the generic drugs was virtually identical to that of the brand name drugs.[30]

In its investigation of the pharmaceutical industry, Congress determined that one reason that doctors did not prescribe generic drugs more often was that doctors simply did not know the generic name for many drugs. By comparison, those heavy advertising campaigns led to instant recognition and recall of the brand names. Consequently, doctors just wrote prescriptions for the brand name drugs rather than the generic ones. Congress concluded that it could encourage the sale of generic drugs by educating physicians about the generic names. To accomplish this goal, Congress amended the Federal Food, Drug, and Cosmetic Act to require drug companies to include a drug's generic name in parentheses alongside the brand name used by that particular manufacturer in all the literature and advertising for that particular product. The statute was somewhat unclear, however, regarding how often the generic name had to be inserted. When the FDA promulgated regulations under the amendments, it decided to require the use of the generic name *every time* the drug's name was used. The drug companies objected to this every-time rule on the grounds that nothing in the statute's amendments required an every-time format. In other words, in the view of the companies, the FDA was acting *ultra vires—i.e.*, in excess of statutory authority.

Recall that *Abbott Labs* concerned a *pre-enforcement* challenge to agency regulations. The every-time rule at issue was so new that the FDA had not yet brought individual enforcement actions against individual companies. When the pharmaceutical companies challenged the every-time rule in court, the government argued that the dispute was not ripe for judicial review because the agency had not yet charged even a single company with violating the every-time rule. The pharmaceutical companies countered with the argument that they would prefer not to be charged with violating FDA regulations, that they felt obliged to comply with the every-time rule even if the rule were later to be deemed invalid, and that changing all of their containers and labels to comply with the every-time rule would be very expensive.

In this posture, *Abbott Labs* came before the Supreme Court. The Court decided that the case was ripe for review and, in doing so, formulated the two-part test that continues to drive ripeness analysis today:

1. Whether the issue presented to the court is *fit* for review;

   and

2. Whether withholding review would impose a substantial *hardship* on the party seeking review.

The two factors are not difficult to parse. In evaluating fitness, a reviewing court looks at the issue presented and determines whether it is the sort of legal issue that courts are particularly equipped to resolve. In *Abbott Labs*, the challenge to the every-time rule was of the sort that courts address every day, whether the agency's action was *ultra vires*, or outside the boundaries of statutory authority. In analyzing this sort of question, a court will look to the statute's terms, its legislative history, the agency's explanation for the rule, the language of the rule itself, and similar elements. Using this

30. This part of the *Abbott Labs* fact pattern can seem almost unintelligible to lay people. Think of it this way: One way to identify a drug is simply by reference to the chemical formula for that particular substance, in the manner you may have learned in high school chemistry—*e.g.*, aspirin is $C_9H_8O_4$. Another way to identify the product is by its generic name—*e.g.*, aspirin is *acetylsalicylic acid*. A third way to identify a drug is by a major manufacturer's brand name—*e.g.*, Bayer® Aspirin.

approach in *Abbott Labs*, the Supreme Court decided that whether the FDA had the statutory authority to adopt the every-time rule was a fit question for judicial review. The Court additionally emphasized that the every-time rule was "final agency action" as that term is used in § 704 of the Administrative Procedure Act, further supporting the conclusion that the case was fit for judicial review.[31]

The hardship factor addresses the specific impact on the party challenging the rule. In particular, the Court in *Abbott Labs* recognized that requiring regulated parties to either (1) comply with a rule that they believe is invalid, or (2) risk an enforcement action and the associated penalties for failure to comply is antithetical to the rule of law. The Court determined that the drug companies' printing expenses incurred in complying with the rule and the monetary penalties they would face if they refused to comply were a sufficient hardship.

The Supreme Court's decision in *Abbott Labs* was accompanied by its decisions in two companion cases, decided on the same day, in which ripeness was also an issue. Both concerned the FDA's interpretation of statutory provisions governing the use of color additives in food, drugs and cosmetics.

In *Gardner v. Toilet Goods Ass'n*,[32] the Court considered a challenge to regulations providing that diluents were color additives, meaning that they fell within a statutory requirement of FDA clearance for their use in food, drugs, and cosmetics. As in *Abbott Labs*, manufacturers sought declaratory and injunctive relief against the regulations before they could be enforced. Applying the two-part test from and similar reasoning to *Abbott Labs*, the Court held that the diluent regulations were ripe for judicial review. The Court observed that the regulations were "self-executing" and had "an immediate and substantive impact." The Court specifically found that trying to contest the validity of the regulations through noncompliance and enforcement would pose a "substantial" burden upon the manufacturers, and it upheld the lower court's finding that the manufacturers would suffer an irreparable injury if enforcement of the regulations was not enjoined. Dissenting justices argued that issues before the Court "should not be adjudicated in the abstract," but the Court responded that the facts and circumstances of a specific FDA enforcement action in this instance would not necessarily facilitate its consideration of the legal question at bar.

By contrast, in *Toilet Goods Ass'n v. Gardner*,[33] the Court reached the opposite conclusion with respect to ripeness. The statute prohibited the use of color additives altogether without FDA certification. The challenged regulation provided that the FDA Commissioner "may immediately suspend certification service" to any person who refused to allow free access to manufacturing facilities, processes, and formulae to FDA inspectors. Although the regulation was final, and the parties framed the issue before the Court as "a purely legal question"—whether the FDA had the statutory authority to adopt the regulation—the Court concluded that assessing the regulation's validity was "not appropriate for judicial resolution" in a pre-enforcement suit for declaratory and injunctive relief.

---

31. As discussed in § 11.03 above, finality analysis has changed substantially since the time of the *Abbott Labs* decision. Finality is not essential for an agency action to be considered ripe for judicial review. Nevertheless, when assessing finality as part of the fitness prong of the ripeness inquiry, courts follow the approach described in § 11.03.

32. 387 U.S. 167 (1967).

33. 387 U.S. 158 (1967).

Regarding the fitness prong of the *Abbott Labs* two-part test, the Court in *Toilet Goods* noted that the regulation at issue was permissive rather than mandatory. The regulation did not compel the FDA Commissioner to suspend a manufacturer's certification; it merely authorized him to do so. The legal issue of the regulation's substantive validity could arise conceivably in a wide variety of circumstances, depending upon how and under what conditions the Commissioner chose to exercise the discretionary power granted by the regulation. The Court expressed that its ability to address the legal issue raised in the case would be enhanced greatly by the factual context of a specific attempt to enforce the regulation. The Court would then be able to consider such contextual facts as the reason for the inspection and the manufacturer's justification for limiting an inspector's access to its facilities, processes, or formulae. Given the generality of the regulation and the array of potential circumstances in which the agency might attempt to apply and enforce it, the Court was of the view that it would need to elaborate extensively on the permissible scope of agency inspections under the statute and the Fourth Amendment.

Turning to the hardship prong of the two-part ripeness test, the Court found that the hardship imposed on additive manufacturers by a decision not to proceed with pre-enforcement judicial review would be less severe than the hardship to the drug manufacturers subject to the regulation at stake in *Abbott Labs*. If a manufacturer refused access to an FDA inspector, and if the FDA Commissioner then chose to exercise the discretionary authority provided by the regulation, then the sanction would consist "only" of a suspension of the manufacturer's certification, which then would be subject to judicial review. In other words, according to the Court, unlike in *Abbott Labs*, neither the regulation nor the decision not to proceed with judicial review would alter a manufacturer's day-to-day conduct of its business.

[C] Ripeness and Government Benefits

The *Abbott Labs* test continues to govern judicial assessments of ripeness and to allow pre-enforcement judicial review of many agency actions. Somewhat more recently, however, the Court seems to have restricted the availability of pre-enforcement judicial review for rules and regulations that determine the eligibility for government benefits rather than impose regulatory burdens.

In *Reno v. Catholic Social Services, Inc.*,[34] a five-justice majority of the Supreme Court reduced, and maybe even eliminated, the availability of pre-enforcement judicial review of agency rules and regulations concerning eligibility for government benefits. In the Immigration Reform and Control Act of 1986,[35] Congress established an administrative process through which certain immigrants illegally present in the United States could obtain legal residency by filing an application within a statutory 12-month period. The statutory criteria for eligibility included "continuous physical presence" and "continuous unlawful presence" in the United States, "except for brief, casual, and innocent absences." The Immigration and Naturalization Service (INS)[36] issued two regulations

34. 509 U.S. 43 (1993).

35. Pub. L. No. 99-603, 100 Stat. 3359 (1986).

36. The INS ceased to exist in 2003 when Congress transferred most of its functions to three new agencies within the Department of Homeland Security: U.S. Citizenship and Immigration Services, U.S. Immigration and Customs Enforcement, and U.S. Customs and Border Protection.

defining these terms in ways that excluded from the program many immigrants who otherwise seemed eligible. One of the regulations defined "brief, casual, and innocent absences" to include only absences from the United States that the INS formally authorized. In other words, under that regulation, crossing the border for a few hours one time to visit family would make an undocumented immigrant ineligible to participate in the program. The other regulation excluded from consideration for legal residency any undocumented immigrant who left the United States for any period of time if the immigrant reentered using facially-valid documentation. Two separate lawsuits challenged the validity of these regulations before the Supreme Court.

The Court started its analysis of the ripeness issue in Catholic Social Services by quoting extensively from the *Abbott Labs* and *Toilet Goods* cases. Yet, the Court did not mention the two-part fitness and hardship test from *Abbott Labs* or analyze the ripeness issue in the same way. The Court only briefly questioned the hardship imposed on undocumented immigrants by the INS's rules. Rather, the Court seemed categorically to distinguish regulations that specify criteria for benefit eligibility from regulations that impose regulatory burdens on private parties. According to the Court, the immigration regulations at issue in Catholic Social Services "impose[d] no penalties for violating any newly-imposed restriction, but limit[ed] access to a benefit created by the Reform Act but not automatically bestowed on eligible aliens." The Court then concluded that regulations governing benefit eligibility are not ripe for judicial review until a prospective applicant takes "the affirmative steps that he could take before the [agency] blocked his path by applying the regulation to him." Ordinarily, that condition would be satisfied when the agency formally denied the application on the ground that the regulation rendered him ineligible. In this case, however, the Court said that an agency action short of formally denying the application could be sufficient to establish ripeness. The parties in the case had alleged that the INS had engaged in a practice called "front desking" in which legal assistants were instructed to summarily reject applications that seemed to them to be ineligible. An application that was front desked would never be formally submitted, so could never be formally denied. The Court held that a challenge brought by an immigrant whose application was rejected through front desking would be ripe for judicial review. Nevertheless, because the record before the Court lacked evidence that particular challengers had been front desked, the Court remanded the case. "Because only those class members (if any) who were front-desked have ripe claims ... we ... remand ... for proceedings to determine which class members were front-desked."

Justice O'Connor wrote an opinion in *Catholic Social Services* in which she concurred with the Court's judgment for reasons unrelated to ripeness but disagreed with the Court's ripeness analysis. She maintained that the dispute over the regulations' validity became ripe once the application period had expired and an individual who otherwise claimed to be eligible had sought an extension of time to apply on grounds that the INS's eligibility regulations were invalid. According to Justice O'Connor, the denial of the opportunity to apply for the benefit in question was sufficient to establish ripeness.

Dissenting justices in *Catholic Social Services* castigated the majority for disregarding the Abbott Labs two-part test emphasizing fitness and hardship. The dissenters argued that the challenge to the INS's regulations was ripe as soon as the INS issued them. The mere existence of the regulations injured prospective applicants by deterring them from filing timely applications to alter their immigration status, undermining congressional intent. Individual immigrants who otherwise would have been eligible for a change in their residency status were afraid of being deported or suffering other consequences if they applied and were found ineligible due to the allegedly invalid regulations.

The *Catholic Social Services* decision shows that the Supreme Court regards ripeness doctrine as a meaningful limitation on the availability of judicial review. The Court in *Catholic Social Services* arguably created a ripeness test for persons who are seeking agency benefits that is different and more restrictive than the ripeness test applied to the *Abbott* plaintiffs who were asking, in essence, not to be regulated. Yet, nothing in *Abbott Labs* suggested that rules that confer benefits could never be attacked until the challenging party first applied for those benefits. The majority opinion in *Catholic Social Services* both quoted *Abbott Labs* extensively and said nothing outright to support the conclusion that it was creating a new ripeness test deliberately. Instead, the majority went out of its way to suggest congruence between *Abbott Labs* and its conclusion in *Catholic Social Services.*

§ 11.05 Exhaustion

[A] An Analytical Framework for Exhaustion Issues

The basic premise of exhaustion doctrine is that parties aggrieved by the actions of agency officials should pursue available administrative procedures before asking the courts to intervene. Much like finality and ripeness, the purpose of the exhaustion requirement is to prevent premature judicial review, both to conserve judicial resources and to permit agency officials to resolve cases in their own time and under their own procedures without unwarranted interference from the courts.

In some instances, exhaustion issues are resolved either by the agency's organic statute or, alternatively, by procedural regulations that the agency has adopted in implementing that statute. A statute or regulation may state expressly that a certain matter constitutes final agency action once it has been addressed by a particular body or official within the agency. Some statutes and regulations specify outright the timing for when parties subject to a particular agency action may seek judicial review. In the absence of a statutory provision or regulation directly on point, courts may require the exhaustion of administrative procedures as a matter of judicial policy and common law.

In contemplating whether an exhaustion issue exists, it often helps to look at the agency's organizational chart. You will likely find something such as the following diagram:

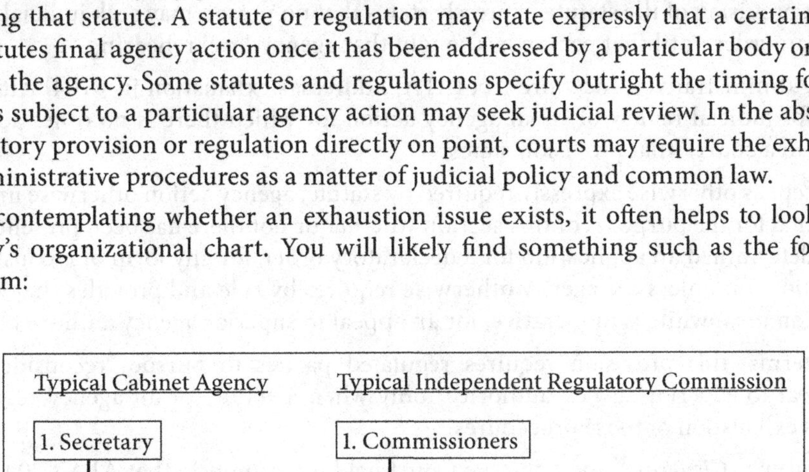

Although not every agency has this precise organization, the diagram reflects a common agency structure. As a general rule, if your case is anywhere below the first level, you may have to cope with an exhaustion argument because agency officials at higher echelons of authority have not yet acted upon your case. Presumably, those officials have the authority to review the matter and, if necessary, to reverse a decision made by someone at a lower level within the agency. If your case is at the fourth or fifth levels, in all likelihood, you will have to continue to pursue your remedies within the agency.

If you cannot find a provision governing the timing of judicial review in the agency's organic statute or procedural regulations, examining the agency's organizational chart and identifying the component of the agency that is currently handling your case may help you evaluate the likelihood of exhaustion doctrine limiting the availability of judicial review.

[B] Statutory Exhaustion

For many years, the duty to exhaust administrative procedures existed only as a judge-made doctrine that was subject to judge-made exceptions. More recently, the Supreme Court has recognized that statutes can impose and define the scope of the exhaustion requirement. Although common law exhaustion doctrine continues to apply and have powerful effects where it has not been modified by statute, that doctrine now is subject to statutory exceptions that take precedence in the circumstances in which such statutes apply. In other words, a statute can either exempt a class of actions from the exhaustion requirement or can impose a stronger version of the exhaustion requirement.

For example, the Natural Gas Policy Act of 1978[37] says that if the Federal Energy Regulatory Commission issues an order under that statute, a person aggrieved by the order has thirty days to apply to the Commissioner of that agency for rehearing. The relevant provision of the statute expressly states that no person may seek judicial review of such an order until that person has sought that agency-level rehearing.

The Administrative Procedure Act (APA) addresses exhaustion in §704. After providing for judicial review of "final agency action for which there is no other adequate remedy in a court," that provision states,

> Except as otherwise expressly required by statute, agency action otherwise final is final for the purposes of this section whether or not there has been presented or determined an application for a declaratory order, for any form of reconsideration, or, unless the agency otherwise requires by rule and provides that the action meanwhile is inoperative, for an appeal to superior agency authority.[38]

By its terms, this provision requires regulated parties to pursue "reconsideration" or "appeal to superior agency authority" only when a statute or an agency regulation requires exhaustion of those procedures.

In *Darby v. Cisneros*,[39] the Supreme Court held unanimously that APA §704 means what it says. Department of Housing and Urban Development (HUD) regulations provided that a hearing officer's decision became final in 30 days. The regulations authorized parties subject to decisions by hearing officers to request review by the HUD Secretary.

---

37. 15 U.S.C. §3416(a).
38. 5 U.S.C. §704.
39. 509 U.S. 137 (1993).

The regulations also gave the Secretary discretion over whether to review hearing officer decisions. In this instance, a hearing officer found that Darby had engaged in "sham" transactions that improperly circumvented HUD regulations and debarred Darby from participating in HUD programs for 18 months. Darby did not petition the HUD Secretary to review the hearing officer's decision, and the HUD Secretary did not exercise his discretion to review that decision on his own motion. Instead, after 30 days had passed and the hearing officer's decision became final, Darby sought judicial review. HUD argued that Darby's petition should be dismissed because he had failed to pursue the administrative remedy of petitioning the HUD Secretary for review of the hearing officer's decision. The Supreme Court concluded that the plain language of APA § 704 allowed Darby's case to proceed.

According to the Court in *Darby*, under APA § 704, courts can only require parties to seek further review within the agency before proceeding to court in only two situations: (1) when further intra-agency review is required by statute, or (2) when agency rules require further intra-agency review and the agency's action is effectively stayed pending that intra-agency review. Otherwise, once an agency takes an action that is final for APA purposes, a court cannot require a party aggrieved by that action to exhaust optional administrative appeals. APA § 704 thus authorizes a court to require exhaustion of an available administrative appeal only if that remedy is required by statute or by agency rule as a prerequisite to the availability of judicial review.

The Court's decision in *Darby* has the salutary effect of forcing federal agencies to describe the nature and effect of available intra-agency appeals clearly and explicitly in their rules. Most agencies have the discretion to make available a wide variety of procedures for intra-agency review of actions that are, or become, final in the absence of such review. Those procedures can be either optional or mandatory. Before *Darby*, some agencies attempted to have it both ways—*i.e.*, to describe an intra-agency review procedure as optional but then to seek dismissal of a petition for judicial review of an agency action if a party declined to avail itself of the putatively optional administrative appeal. After *Darby*, that option was not available to an agency in a proceeding governed by the APA. Agencies can make an intra-agency review procedure a mandatory prerequisite to the availability of judicial review only by describing it as such in agency rules and by providing that the action that is subject to the intra-agency review procedure "meanwhile is inoperative." If the agency simply makes such a procedure available, a party can obtain judicial review of an otherwise final action without first pursuing the available intra-agency review procedure, except in the relatively unusual case in which a statute makes exhaustion of the intra-agency review procedure a prerequisite to the availability of judicial review. In the post-*Darby* world, a party to an agency proceeding should be able to distinguish between optional and mandatory intra-agency review procedures simply by reading the applicable provisions of statutes and agency rules.

[C] Common Law Exhaustion

In the absence of a specific statutory provision or agency regulation on point, courts generally follow a basic presumption that matters should remain within an agency until *all* levels of agency decisionmaking have been pursued. If, however, a litigant wishes to move into court without first exhausting agency remedies, a court will analyze the propriety of judicial review in light of various factors gleaned from the case law.

In *McCarthy v. Madigan*,[40] the Supreme Court discussed its approach to exhaustion doctrine at great length, including its reasons for embracing a robust presumption in favor administrative exhaustion as well as its recognition that some exceptions from the doctrine are appropriate. First, the Court acknowledged that Congress can decide for itself by statute when judicial review of a particular agency action should be available. "Where Congress specifically mandates, exhaustion is required." Even where Congress does not so provide, and "sound judicial discretion governs," the Court said that "appropriate deference to Congress' power to prescribe the basic procedural scheme under which a claim may be heard in a federal court requires fashioning of exhaustion principles in a manner consistent with congressional intent and any applicable statutory scheme."

The Court proceeded in *McCarthy* to offer two principal justifications for requiring the exhaustion of administrative procedures before pursuing judicial review of agency action as a matter of judicial common law. The first was rooted in the Court's perceptions of congressional preference and comparative agency expertise in the administration of government programs. When Congress tasks an agency with implementing a particular statutory scheme, the courts should presume that Congress wants that agency to have "primary responsibility" over the administration of the government program in question. Agencies have their own specialized expertise, which is what prompts Congress to give them authority over government programs in the first instance. Exhaustion doctrine respects the role that agencies play and the expertise they bring to bear by giving agencies the opportunity to handle matters within their sphere and to fix their own mistakes. Judicial intrusion at too early a stage in the administrative process undermines agency authority and weakens agency effectiveness.

The second justification offered by the Court in support of a general policy of requiring administrative exhaustion was grounded in concerns about judicial efficiency. Giving agencies the chance to fix their own errors results in fewer cases that must be heard by the courts. When challenges to agency action come to the courts, the exhaustion requirement allows agencies to develop more complete administrative records that facilitate the judicial review process.

On the other hand, the *McCarthy* Court pragmatically recognized that, in some instances, requiring administrative exhaustion is unwarranted. "[F]ederal courts must balance the interest of the individual in retaining prompt access to a federal judicial forum against countervailing institutional interests favoring exhaustion." To that end, the Court identified "at least" three potential exceptions from common law exhaustion requirements: (1) where "requiring resort to the administrative remedy [would] occasion undue prejudice to subsequent assertion of a court action"; (2) where there exists "some doubt as to whether the agency was empowered to grant effective relief"; and (3) "where the administrative body is shown to be biased or has otherwise predetermined the issue before it."

The *McCarthy* case itself concerned a claim by a federal prisoner that his constitutional rights had been violated when prison authorities neglected to provide him with adequate medical care for needs resulting from a back operation and a history of psychiatric problems. The Court held that the prisoner was not required to exhaust

40. 503 U.S. 140 (1992). *McCarthy* is not the only case in which the Court has outlined the policies behind and exceptions from common law exhaustion requirements. *See also*, e.g., *McKart v. United States*, 395 U.S. 185 (1969).

the administrative remedies made available by the Bureau of Prisons as a prerequisite to filing suit for damages. In reaching that conclusion, based on the understanding of exhaustion doctrine described above, a six-justice majority of the Court noted (1) the importance of allowing petitioners access to the courts to redress violations of their constitutional rights, (2) the high risk that the petitioner in this case would lose access to the courts by missing one of the many short filing deadlines in the Bureau's procedural rules, (3) the unavailability of money damages as a result of pursuing the administrative remedy, and (4) the fact that the administrative procedures would not create a record that would be of significant help to a court in evaluating the merits of the prisoner's case. Three concurring justices would have resolved the case based solely on the fact that the administrative procedure could not produce the only remedy the petitioner sought—money damages.

In identifying "at least" three potential exceptions from common law exhaustion requirements, the Supreme Court in *McCarthy* did not foreclose the possibility that other circumstances might similarly excuse a failure to exhaust administrative remedies. For example, the Court recognized in *McCarthy* that agencies often lack and even disclaim outright the authority to examine constitutional issues, leaving judicial review as the only avenue of relief for litigants seeking to raise constitutional challenges to agency action. In some cases, courts have declined to require exhaustion of administrative remedies in cases raising legitimate constitutional challenges to an agency's actions or procedures.[41] In other cases raising such claims, however, courts have declined to waive common law exhaustion requirements so that agencies have the opportunity to address the concerns of regulated parties as best they can within their jurisdiction and pursue other remedies at their disposal, and otherwise to allow fuller development of the case record consistent with agency procedural requirements.[42]

The Court in *McCarthy* offered an exception from common law exhaustion requirements for circumstances in which agency bias or predetermination of the outcome would render pursuit of administrative remedies "inadequate." The courts have long expressed a willingness to excuse a litigant's failure to exhaust administrative remedies if pursuing them would be an exercise in futility.[43] The courts have often, however, limited the futility exception to those circumstances in which an adverse decision is certain. In *Greene v. Meese*, for example, the Seventh Circuit opined,

> Lightning may strike; and even if it doesn't, in denying relief the [agency] may give a statement of its reasons that is helpful to the district court in considering the merits of the claim.[44]

41. *See, e.g., Bangura v. Hansen*, 434 F.3d 487 (6th Cir. 2006); *Wilkins v. United States*, 279 F.3d 782 (9th Cir. 2002).

42. *See, e.g., Bonhometre v. Gonzales*, 414 F.3d 442 (3d Cir. 2005).

43. *See, e.g., Weinberger v. Salfi*, 422 U.S. 749 (1975); *Brown v. Secretary of Health & Human Services*, 46 F.3d 102 (1st Cir. 1995).

44. 875 F.2d 639, 641 (7th Cir. 1989).

Chapter 12

Judicial Review of Agency Action: Standing

§ 12.01 Basic Concepts

Standing is the most prominent among the potential barriers to getting your case into court. Standing doctrine responds to a single, arguably straight-forward question: *who* can obtain judicial review of an otherwise reviewable agency action. At its most basic, when the Court takes up a standing issue, it examines whether the persons bringing the lawsuit have what the Court in *Baker v. Carr*[1] described as "such a personal stake in the outcome of the controversy as to assure that concrete adverseness which sharpens the presentation of the issues upon which the court so largely depends for illumination of difficult constitutional questions."

Of course, the standing inquiry is more complicated than that. The Supreme Court alone has decided hundreds of standing disputes, and the justices have often disagreed in those cases. Identifying when the requisite circumstances exist to confer standing has produced a body of law that suffers from inconsistency, unreliability, and inordinate complexity. Courts have blended constitutional reasoning, statutory reasoning, and prudential reasoning in a tangled mess with several different, if overlapping, strands. It is simply impossible to reconcile and synthesize all of the Court's many standing decisions. Often, though not always, the better strategy is to approach standing doctrine in segments, rather than collectively. Consequently, this chapter aims to provide a basic sketch of contemporary standing doctrine. You should be aware, however, that this chapter really only scratches the surface of the topic.

As you read through this Chapter, you should be aware that the question of whether a plaintiff has standing to get into federal court is a proposition far different from the question of whether that same person might be permitted to participate in federal agency action (*i.e.*, at the agency level). Also keep in mind that the case or controversy requirement of Article III is only the bare minimum required when establishing that a particular party has standing in a given case. Congress occasionally adds to constitutional limitations by writing statutory standing provisions. For example, § 702 of the Administrative Procedure Act (APA) provides that "[a] person suffering legal wrong because of agency action, or adversely affected or aggrieved by agency action within the meaning of a relevant statute, is entitled to seek judicial review thereof."[2] Congress has also included standing requirements in a number of organic statutes. For example, a common provision in a number of environmental protection statutes limits standing to bring pre-enforcement challenges to agency rules *solely* to persons who have

1. 369 U.S. 186 (1962).
2. 5 U.S.C. § 702.

participated in the *agency's rulemaking* for the rule that they are attempting to challenge in court.[3] Congress cannot grant standing where the Constitution prohibits it. But although the federal courts have never considered themselves absolutely bound by Congress's ideas of who ought to have standing, they generally tend to defer to congressional pronouncements, even when those pronouncements concern who may come into federal court.[4]

§ 12.02 The *ADAPSO* Framework

Modern standing doctrine consists of both constitutional and statutory requirements. Constitutional standing requirements derive from Article III, section 2 of the U.S. Constitution, which limits federal court jurisdiction to "cases" and "controversies." Beyond constitutional standing requirements, the courts for many years have recognized certain statutory and prudential limitations on plaintiff standing in federal court.

The starting point for modern standing doctrine comes principally from the Supreme Court's decision in *Ass'n of Data Processing Service Organizations v. Camp* (*ADAPSO*),[5] although a companion case decided on the same day in 1970, *Barlow v. Collins*,[6] also allowed the Court to elaborate *ADAPSO*'s two-pronged approach. *ADAPSO* began when companies that sold data processing services challenged regulations issued by the Comptroller of the Currency that permitted banks to begin selling these services. Concerned about the competition, the data processing companies asserted that they would lose money if banks got into the data processing business and that the Comptroller's new regulations violated the Bank Service Corporation Act of 1962.[7] The plaintiffs in *Barlow* were tenant farmers who alleged a pocketbook injury stemming from regulations of the Department of Agriculture that affected the farmers' subsidy payments. The farmers argued that the new rules exceeded the Department's jurisdiction.

Prior to 1970, the Supreme Court's standing jurisprudence suggested that, to establish standing, a potential plaintiff would need to demonstrate a *legal right*—*i.e.*, a legally-protected interest established at common law or by statute that was at stake in the litigation.[8] The Court applied the legal right test to deny standing in many cases. The Court unequivocally abandoned the legal right test in *ADAPSO* and replaced it with a two-pronged inquiry, although without expressly overruling any of its previous decisions.

3. *See, e.g.*, Clean Air Act, 42 U.S.C. § 7607 (1990).

4. *Associated Industries of New York State, Inc. v. Ickes*, 134 F.2d 694 (2d Cir.), *vacated on other grounds*, 320 U.S. 707 (1943) (consumers of coal were "persons aggrieved" as defined in the statute and had standing to challenge certain actions of the Department of the Interior relating to the coal industry).

5. 397 U.S. 150 (1970).

6. 397 U.S. 159 (1970).

7. 12 U.S.C. § 1864 (1962). The Act provides: "[n]o bank service corporation may engage in any activity other than the performance of bank services for banks."

8. *See, e.g.*, *Joint Anti-Fascist Refugee League Committee v. McGrath*, 341 U.S. 123 (1951); *Perkins v. Lukens Steel Co.*, 310 U.S. 113 (1940); *Tennessee Electric Power Co. v. Tennessee Valley Authority*, 306 U.S. 118 (1939).

The framework for standing analysis described in *ADAPSO* is relatively simple to state: in order to get into federal court to challenge federal agency action,[9] a petitioner must allege that

1. the challenged agency action has caused the petitioner "injury in fact, economic or otherwise"; *and*
2. the interest the petitioner seeks to protect is arguably within the zone of interests to be protected or regulated by the statute or constitutional provision at issue in the case.

Although both of these components must be satisfied, they also operate somewhat independently of one another.

The first component relates to the constitutional requirement that courts resolve cases or controversies. Echoing the "personal stake" requirement of past cases like *Baker v. Carr*, the Court said that "[t]he question of standing is related only to whether the dispute sought to be adjudicated will be presented in an adversary context and in a form historically viewed as capable of judicial resolution." In this regard, the Court said that not only harms to legal interests would suffice, but also harms to "aesthetic, conservational, and recreational as well as economic values."[10] The sweeping scope of this last phrase was largely dicta, as the interest at stake in *ADAPSO* was an economic one in the form of anticipated reduced profits due to increased competition.

The second component of the *ADAPSO* framework added what has become known as "zone of interests" standing to the injury in fact requirement long associated with Article III of the Constitution. In *ADAPSO*, the Court acknowledged that, particularly "[w]here statutes are concerned, the trend is toward enlargement of the class of people who may protest administrative action." The Court also said that Congress can resolve the statutory standing "question one way or another," within the boundaries of Article III. With those thoughts in mind, the Court looked at the statutory provisions that authorized to the agency action in question, not in terms of the narrow legal rights they specifically created, but in terms of the general range of interests that Congress was attempting to address and accommodate. Thus, the Court framed the statutory standing question as "whether the interest sought to be protected by the complainant is arguably within the zone of interests to be protected or regulated by the statute or constitutional guarantee in question."

Considering the zone of interests at hand, the Court considered three statutes: the Bank Service Corporation Act and the National Bank Act, under which the agency had acted, and the Administrative Procedure Act (APA), which applies to most agency actions. APA §702 grants standing to any person "adversely affected or aggrieved by the agency action within the meaning of a relevant statute." The Court interpreted this provision as requiring consideration of the interest recognized by all other statutes applicable to an agency action to determine whether a party is adversely affected or aggrieved. The Court found that both the Bank Services Act and the National Bank Act indicated some concern by Congress about the potential adverse effects of allowing banks to participate in nonbanking activities like data processing. The Court noted that neither statute was designed to protect a particular group, but it held that the "general

9. Note carefully that this is a test for challenges to federal agency action. The more elementary "personal stake in the outcome" test governs challenges to state administrative agencies brought in federal court.

10. *ADAPSO*, 397 U.S. at 154 (internal quotation marks omitted).

policy" of those statutes brought competitors to banks within the zone of interests arguably protected.

As mentioned, the Supreme Court had another occasion to apply *ADAPSO*'s two-part framework for standing analysis in the *Barlow* case decided the same day. In this case, a group of tenant farmers tried to challenge regulations adopted by the Department of Agriculture implementing the Food and Agriculture Act of 1965 that allowed landlords to require the tenant farmers to assign future proceeds from a federal agricultural assistance program as security for their lease payments. According to the challengers, the regulation gave landlords extreme leverage over tenant farmers that landlords could use to force tenant farmers to obtain all of their financing from their landlords. The tenants could not assert any legally-protected interest that the regulation affected, and the relevant statute did not specifically extend standing to tenant farmers. Nevertheless, applying its *ADAPSO* framework, the Court easily found that the farmers' financial concerns gave them "the personal stake and interest that impart[ed] concrete adverseness required by Article III" of the Constitution. The Court also concluded, based on the statute's language and history, that Congress intended to protect the interests of tenant farmers, which placed them "clearly within the zone of interests protected by the Act." Accordingly, the Court held that the tenant farmers satisfied both constitutional standing and statutory zone of interests standing requirements.

Most members of the Court agreed with the framework for standing analysis described in *ADAPSO*. Justice William Brennan, joined by Justice Byron White, wrote an opinion concurring in part and dissenting in part with respect to both *ADAPSO* and *Barlow*. They argued that grafting the zone-of-interests component onto the personal injury requirement previously recognized as imposed by Article III came too close to forcing the plaintiff to try his or her entire case on the merits in the context of a preliminary motion to dismiss for lack of standing. Regardless, the Court has refined the application of the *ADAPSO* two-part framework for the last several decades without suggesting that there is anything fundamentally wrong with it.

§ 12.03 Constitutional Standing

[A] The Three-Part Test for Constitutional Standing

The Supreme Court has interpreted the case or controversy requirement of Article III as limiting standing to raise a claim in federal court to those plaintiffs who satisfy three elements. First, as the Court indicated in *ADAPSO*, a plaintiff must establish that she has suffered an injury to a legally-protected interest. Although the *ADAPSO* decision signaled the Court's interest in broadening the types of injuries that are justiciable, the Court does not accept all injuries as sufficient to qualify as an injury in fact for standing purposes. Concrete and particularized injuries qualify, while abstract or generalized injuries do not. Second, a plaintiff must demonstrate a causal connection between her injury and the conduct that gives rise to her complaint. In other words, the plaintiff's injury must be fairly traceable to the defendant's actions. Finally, a plaintiff must show that a decision by the courts in her favor will likely redress her injury.

Although the Court has frequently reiterated these three requirements—*injury in fact, causation*, and *redressability*—the courts have struggled to apply them consistently. The following subsections considers each of the three requirements in turn.

[B] Injury in Fact

Recall that the Supreme Court in *ADAPSO* declared that justiciable injuries could be "aesthetic, conservational, and recreational as well as economic," suggesting a tremendous range of interests that the Court was willing to protect. The Court's vast standing jurisprudence has addressed injuries of various types—economic injuries,[11] injuries to taxpayers,[12] reputational injuries,[13] political injuries,[14] environmental injuries,[15] informational injuries,[16] injuries to privacy,[17] and procedural injuries,[18] to name a few.

Notwithstanding the breadth of that rhetoric, the Court recognizes only some kinds of alleged injuries as sufficient to satisfy the injury in fact element of constitutional standing. Several issues routinely arise in cases evaluating the injury in fact requirement, including whether injuries that are shared with many people qualify as injuries in fact and how certain an alleged future injury must be to count as an injury in fact for standing purposes.

One important standing case that illustrates at least some of these questions, and challenges often associated with asserting environmental injuries, is *Lujan v. Defenders of Wildlife*.[19] The case concerned the Endangered Species Act (ESA), which requires federal agencies to consult with the Department of the Interior (DOI) before pursuing actions that may jeopardize the continued existence or habitat of endangered or threatened species. After years of discussion and debate, the DOI issued a rule stating that the ESA did not apply to the funding of projects outside the United States. The ESA contains a citizen suit provision broadly authorizing "any person" to seek judicial review of agency actions in conflict with the ESA. In this instance, Defenders of Wildlife challenged the rule and claimed standing on behalf of two of its members engaged in studying particular endangered species whose habitats were threatened by dam projects in Sri

11. In addition to the *ADAPSO* case, discussed above, other cases that have concerned economic injuries and standing include *Sprint Communications Co., LP v. APCC Services, Inc.*, 554 U.S. 269 (2008); *Vermont Agency of Natural Resources v. United States ex rel. Stevens*, 529 U.S. 765 (2000); and *Clarke v. Securities Industry Ass'n*, 479 U.S. 388 (1987).

12. *See, e.g., DaimlerChrysler Corp. v. Cuno*, 547 U.S. 332 (2006); *Flast v. Cohen*, 392 U.S. 83 (1968); *Frothingham v. Mellon*, 262 U.S. 447 (1923). Taxpayer standing is discussed in §12.05[C] below.

13. *See, e.g., Meese v. Keene*, 481 U.S. 465 (1987); *Joint Anti-Fascist Refugee League Committee v. McGrath*, 341 U.S. 123 (1951).

14. *See, e.g., Gill v. Whitford*, 138 S. Ct. 1916 (2018); *Department of Commerce v. U.S. House of Representatives*, 525 U.S. 316 (1999); *United States v. Hays*, 515 U.S. 737 (1995).

15. *See, e.g., Massachusetts v. Environmental Protection Agency*, 549 U.S. 497 (2007); *Friends of the Earth, Inc. v. Laidlaw Environmental Services (TOC), Inc.*, 528 U.S. 167 (2000); *Lujan v. National Wildlife Federation*, 497 U.S. 871 (1990); *Sierra Club v. Morton*, 405 U.S. 727 (1972).

16. *See, e.g., Federal Election Comm'n v. Akins*, 524 U.S. 11 (1998); *Lewis v. Casey*, 518 U.S. 343 (1996); *United States v. Richardson*, 418 U.S. 166 (1974).

17. *See, e.g., Clapper v. Amnesty International*, 568 U.S. 398 (2013).

18. *See, e.g., Summers v. Earth Island Institute*, 555 U.S. 488 (2009).

19. 504 U.S. 555 (1992).

Lanka and Egypt funded in part, respectively, by the U.S. Bureau of Reclamation and the U.S. Agency for International Development.[20] In the litigation, the two members had submitted affidavits alleging that they each had a personal and professional interest in observing a particular endangered species (the Asian leopard and the Nile crocodile, respectively); that they each had visited the habitat of that species in the past; that they each planned to visit the habitat to further observe the species in the future; that the habitat of each species was threatened by the dam projects in question; and that the DOI rule injured the two affiants by allowing U.S. agencies to fund projects outside the United States that threatened the habitats of the endangered species the affiants wanted to observe.

Six justices agreed that Defenders of Wildlife lacked standing to seek review of the DOI's rule, but two of those justices declined to join part of the plurality opinion's discussion of standing and wrote separately in concurrence.[21] Writing for the Court, Justice Antonin Scalia offered several reasons for the Court's holding, but only two were clearly supported by all six of the justices who joined parts of his opinion. One of those reasons, and the narrowest rationale in support of the holding, was that Defenders of Wildlife failed to provide evidence sufficient to demonstrate that one of its members would suffer an imminent, judicially cognizable injury in fact. The affidavits submitted were inadequate because the mere intention to travel to observe a species of its habitat at some unspecified future date was "simply not enough" to demonstrate that the alleged injury was "actual or imminent, not conjectural or hypothetical."

Six justices also supported the conclusion that the statutory provision authorizing "any person" to challenge agency actions violating the ESA was unconstitutional as applied to *Defenders of Wildlife*. The Supreme Court rarely holds federal statutes unconstitutional. It had never before rejected as unconstitutional a statutory provision authorizing a specific class of persons to seek judicial review of agency action. On this occasion, however, the Court held that Congress cannot confer standing on someone who does not establish the elements regularly applied the Court to establish standing under Article III of the Constitution. Although the Court has held that statutes creating legal rights may provide a basis for constitutional standing when those rights are injured, the Court in *Defenders of Wildlife* declined to put the ESA's citizen suit provision into that category. Justices Anthony Kennedy and David Souter wrote a concurring opinion in which they agreed with Justice Scalia's reasoning on this point, but they also discussed Congress's power to confer standing by statute—for example, by creating "statutory rights that differ from traditional common law rights" and "by defin[ing] injuries and articulat[ing] chains of causation that will give rise to a case or controversy where none existed before."

The petitioner in *Defenders of Wildlife* had also offered three "nexus" theories in support of its standing argument. "Ecosystem nexus" holds that any person who uses any part of an integrated ecosystem would be injured by actions that impair part of that ecosystem. "Animal nexus" similarly theorizes that any person who is interested in observing an endangered species, including at a zoo, would be injured by acts that adversely

20. Although third parties generally cannot claim standing to sue based on injuries suffered by others, the Supreme Court has recognized an exception for organizations challenging agency actions on behalf of their members. Third-party standing and associational standing are discussed in §12.05[B] below.

21. Justice John Paul Stevens also concurred in the judgment on other grounds, but he thought that Defenders of Wildlife had standing to challenge the DOI's rule.

affect the species' survival. "Professional nexus" posits that any person with a professional interest in an endangered species, whether as a research biologist, as a zookeeper, or otherwise, would be injured by actions that adversely affect the species' survival. Justice Scalia rejected those theories as "beyond all reason" and merely "an ingenious academic exercise in the conceivable" as well as "pure speculation and fantasy" rather than the sort of "factual showing of perceptible harm" demanded by the Court. Nevertheless, Justice Stevens concurring in the judgment and two dissenting justices accepted these theories, and Justices Kennedy and Souter suggested they might be receptive to such arguments in other circumstances.

Although the Court's opinion in *Defenders of Wildlife* suggested that the justices were inclined to severely restrict access to judicial review for environmental petitioners, such has not always been the case. In fact, the Court embraced an arguably more expansive approach to environmental injuries and standing in *Friends of the Earth, Inc. v. Laidlaw Environmental Services (TOC), Inc.*[22] The case concerned a citizen suit by an environmental group against a company claiming that the company was violating its emissions permit and the Clean Water Act by, among other things, discharging excess amounts of mercury into the Tyger River. The environmental group submitted affidavits of members stating that they had stopped engaging in activities like fishing, swimming, boating, and hiking in or near the river because of concerns about the impact of the discharges. The company argued that the environmental group and its members lacked standing to sue, in part because there had been "no demonstrated proof of harm to the environment" from the discharges. The Court disagreed, holding that changes by plaintiffs in their recreational use of a river based on "reasonable" concerns about pollution caused by the defendant were sufficient to qualify as injury in fact, irrespective of whether the claimed violations actually degraded the quality of the river's water. The fact that the plaintiffs in question "use[d] the affected area and [were] persons 'for whom the aesthetic and recreational values of the area [were] lessened'" as a result of the defendant's actions was sufficient to demonstrate injury in fact.

The Court's decisions in a pair of cases concerning the Fair Credit Reporting Act (FCRA) offer interesting analysis of the injury in fact requirement and Congress's ability to create standing by statute. The FCRA imposes various procedural requirements on "consumer reporting agencies" that are intended to reduce the risk of inaccurate reports. The FCRA also provides that consumer reporting agencies that willfully violate statutory requirements are liable for statutory and punitive damages to the individuals about whom they report, and creates a private right of action for individuals who are the subject of inaccurate reports to seek those penalties. In the first case, *Spokeo, Inc. v. Robins*,[23] the Court considered a website, Spokeo, that performed computerized database searches to compile profiles of individuals upon request, and thus, arguably, was a consumer reporting agency as defined by the FCRA. The plaintiff in this case, Robins, claimed that Spokeo willfully failed to follow the procedures required by the FCRA in gathering information and putting together his profile. The result, according to Robins, was that the profile of him that Spokeo assembled was inaccurate, not precisely in a negative way, but nevertheless in a way that could affect his employment or romantic prospects. (The profile described Robins as married with children, in his 50s, with a job, relatively affluent, and holding a graduate degree, all of which Robins claimed were incorrect.) The Court recognized that the injury of which Robins complained was based

22. 528 U.S. 167 (2000).
23. 136 S. Ct. 1540 (2016).

in the FCRA. The Court also labeled the harm Robins suffered as "intangible." Neither of those circumstances was disqualifying per se. Nevertheless, the Court insisted that "Congress' role in identifying and elevating intangible harms does not mean that a plaintiff automatically satisfies the injury-in-fact requirement whenever a statute grants a person a statutory right and purports to authorize that person to sue to vindicate that right." The question for the Court was whether the injury to Robins was sufficiently concrete to establish standing—a question the lower court had not addressed. As the Court observed, not all inaccuracies are injurious. "An example that comes readily to mind is an incorrect zip code. It is difficult to imagine how the dissemination of an incorrect zip code, without more, could work any concrete harm." Accordingly, the Court remanded the case and instructed the lower court to evaluate whether the injury suffered by Robins was concrete enough to satisfy Article III.

Subsequently, in *TransUnion LLC v. Ramirez*,[24] a class of 8185 subjects of inaccurate credit reports filed a class action lawsuit for damages against the firm that generated the reports. The inaccurate credit reports all contained the same error, reporting that the individual subject's name and a name on the Treasury Department's terrorist watch list were "a potential match." The Court held that 1853 of the class members had standing to pursue damages against the firm because the firm had sent the inaccurate reports on those class members to third parties, thereby causing those class members "concrete" harm. The firm had not sent the inaccurate credit reports regarding the other 6332 class members to third parties, however, so the Court declared that they had not suffered the concrete harm necessary to support a claim to standing. According to the Court, it was not even clear that those class members even knew about the inaccurate reports. The Court said that the harm that might be caused by potential future dissemination of the inaccurate credit reports was too remote to support a claim for damages, although such harm might be sufficient to establish standing to seek an injunction against the firm to prevent it from creating or distributing inaccurate reports about those class members in the future.

[C] Causation

Demonstrating an injury in fact is not enough to establish standing under Article III. The plaintiff must also demonstrate that the challenged action caused the injury in question. Determining whether a particular action "caused" a particular injury can be difficult. The complicated relationships addressed by contemporary regulatory actions result in a nearly infinite cascade of consequences. Courts must limit their assessment of causation in some way for purposes of constitutional standing. Consequently, although the causal relationship need not be immediately proximate, courts generally require the causal chain to be relatively direct and the sequence of events between the act and the injury to be based on relatively logical and proximate relationships.[25] Conversely, a causal relationship is insufficient if it is insubstantial, remote, tenuous, or speculative.[26]

As with every other aspect of its standing jurisprudence, the Supreme Court's decisions regarding the causation element of the Article III standing inquiry cannot always

24. 141 S. Ct. 2190 (2021).
25. *Warth v. Seldin*, 422 U.S. 490 (1975).
26. *Allen v. Wright*, 468 U.S. 737 (1984).

be reconciled with one another. Of course, a completely predictable pattern of judicial assessments of causation is likely impossible. Some gray area regarding the causation requirement is probably inevitable. As is often the case, the Supreme Court has neither attempted to explain nor even acknowledged the inconsistencies in its evaluation of causation.

To establish causation, plaintiffs must allege facts fairly tracing their injuries to the defendants' allegedly wrongful actions.[27] For this reason, establishing causation can be challenging when the alleged injury arises from governmental regulation of another party's conduct. For example, an agency action might authorize a third party to engage in an activity that is likely to injure the petitioner. Alternatively, an agency action could change the incentives of third parties, prompting them to act in ways that are likely to injure the petitioner. Under these circumstances, evaluating causation necessarily requires an assessment of probability: how likely is it that the agency's action will result in the alleged injury?

Requiring certainty in this context would be unrealistic. No court can predict with certainty how third parties will respond to agency actions. Sometimes, the Supreme Court has assessed causation based on a realistic assessment of the likely consequences of the agency's action. For example, in a number of cases, the Court has recognized the standing of economic competitors to challenge agency decisions allowing new firms to enter an existing marketplace.[28] Such was the case in the *ADAPSO* decision discussed above.[29] Authorizing new firms to enter a marketplace does not directly injure existing market participants. The only way the latter can be harmed is if one or more new firms take advantage of the authorization to begin competing so that existing market participants must either lose customers or lower prices to avoid that eventuality. Predicting precisely which particular market incumbents will be injured in this way is often difficult. New firms are likely to enter some but not all geographic markets, and some will be better able to compete than others. On the other hand, it is highly likely that authorizing new entrants into a marketplace will injure one or more existing market participants in this way. The Court does not require existing market participants to prove with substantial certainty that they will suffer injury from competitors authorized by the agency's action. It is enough to establish causation that the agency has authorized the competition and that injury to one or more existing market participants is likely.

In other cases, the Court has evaluated causation in pragmatic, probabilistic terms. On occasion, this approach has resulted in the Court granting standing based on causal relationships that seem rather remote, tenuous, and speculative. For example, in *Bryant v. Yellen*,[30] residents of the Imperial Valley region of California challenged the manner in which the Interior Department was administering a statutory provision limiting the availability of irrigation water. The residents argued that, if properly applied, the statute would allow them to profit by acquiring land at less than its fair market value and then reselling the land at market value. In other words, their alleged injury was the loss of the expected profits from land speculation that the government arguably was required to facilitate. Yet, the probability that any particular resident would purchase any of the

27. *Warth*, 422 U.S. at 505.

28. *See, e.g., National Credit Union Admin. v. First National Bank & Trust Co.*, 522 U.S. 479 (1998); *Clarke v. Securities Industry Ass'n*, 479 U.S. 388 (1987).

29. The Court's decision in *Ass'n of Data Processing Service Organizations v. Camp (ADAPSO)*, 397 U.S. 150 (1970), is discussed particularly in § 12.02.

30. 447 U.S. 352 (1980).

land for less than its fair market value was really quite low due to many contingencies. For instance, the residents did not demonstrate that they possessed the financial wherewithal to buy the land. The current owners of the land might not want to sell at below-market prices. If they did, it is likely that many purchasers would compete to buy the land. Nevertheless, the Court concluded that they had established causation because land that *might* become available for sale at less than fair market value if the statute were administered as the petitioners wished almost certainly *would not* become available for sale at less than fair market value if the statute were not so administered.

By contrast, on other occasions, the Court has been unwilling to overlook many contingencies. Consider the Court's decision in *Simon v. Eastern Kentucky Welfare Rights Organization*.[31] In this case, the Supreme Court addressed whether an Internal Revenue Service ruling allowing hospitals to deny more than emergency services to indigent citizens and still retain tax exempt status in fact caused hospitals in the plaintiffs' area to deny the plaintiffs non-emergency care. The plaintiffs claimed that, but for the ruling, the hospitals would be more likely to provide the plaintiffs with additional services. Given all the factors that a hospital might consider in electing to pursue such a policy and evidence suggesting the variability of hospital dependence upon the special tax benefits conferred by exempt status, the Court held that the link between the IRS ruling and the hospitals' actions was too speculative to satisfy the causation element of constitutional standing.

In *Clapper v. Amnesty International USA*,[32] the Supreme Court held that no petitioner had standing to obtain judicial review of the constitutionality of a provision of the Foreign Intelligence Surveillance Act (FISA) allowing the government, with judicial authorization, to listen to the conversations of noncitizens who are outside the United States at the time of the conversation. Even though the statute requires judicial authorization before the government can listen to a conversation, the FISA court had never denied such a request. The petitioners in the case were foreign correspondents, lawyers representing noncitizens accused of terrorist acts, international human rights organization personnel, and others who believed that government had listened to their conversations. They alleged future injuries in the form of their expectation that the government would listen to some of their conversations and injuries from actions taken to make it more difficult for the government to do so. The Supreme Court held that their future injuries were too speculative, and in doing so, specified that the alleged future injuries must be "certainly impending" both to satisfy the injury in fact requirement and the causation requirement for Article III standing. The Court reasoned particularly that, even if the government was listening to the petitioners' conversations, it might be doing so under statutory authority other than FISA.

If taken literally, the "certainly impending" language from *Clapper* would make establishing causation substantially more difficult for anyone relying on either a probable injury or an expected future injury as a basis for standing. That outcome seems improbable, given the Supreme Court's past inconsistency and unpredictability regarding the causation question. It seems more likely that *Clapper* decision was a consequence of the national security implications of that case.

---

31. 426 U.S. 26 (1976).
32. 568 U.S. 398 (2013).

[D] Redressability

Often, causation and redressability are functionally indistinguishable. If the challenged action causes the challenged injury, then a court can redress the injury by invalidating the action. On occasion, however, the redressability requirement of Article III standing is harder to establish, even if it is obvious that the challenged action caused the injury.

The first case in which the Supreme Court addressed redressability independently of causation was *Lujan v. Defenders of Wildlife*,[33] also discussed above. Again, the petitioners in that case challenged the validity of a rule issued by the Department of the Interior (DOI) concluding that the Endangered Species Act did not require federal agencies to consult DOI before funding overseas projects that might harm endangered species. After concluding that the petitioners had failed to establish an injury in fact, the Court also held that the injury they had alleged—potential harm to the overseas habitats of two particular species caused by dam projects funded by federal agencies—was not redressable by judicial review of the DOI's rule. According to Justice Antonin Scalia on behalf of the four-justice plurality, the DOI was the only agency that was a party to the case, so a decision invalidating the DOI's rule would be binding only with respect to the DOI, and not the agencies actually funding the projects in question. Even if the agencies funding the dam projects withdrew that funding as a result of judicial invalidation of the DOI's rule, the U.S. government was providing only part of the funding for the projects. Another government could provide the missing funding in support of the projects, the dams would be built, and the anticipated habitat destruction would occur irrespective of the remedy requested in this case.

The two dissenting justices in *Defenders of Wildlife* objected to this reasoning. They argued that the Court should not just "assume that agencies at least will not try to follow the law." They also contended that, if the Court were to invalidate the DOI's rule, then principles of collateral estoppel would preclude the other agencies from subsequently litigating the interpretation advanced by that rule. The dissenters also argued that the U.S. government's financial contribution to the two dam projects was sufficiently large, and the availability of alternative sources of funding sufficiently limited, that withdrawal of funding from the United States government could very well make a difference.

The Court adopted a significantly more relaxed approach to redressability in *Massachusetts v. Environmental Protection Agency*.[34] In that case, the Court held that Massachusetts had standing to obtain judicial review of an EPA decision to deny a petition which, if granted, would have initiated a rulemaking to establish limits on emissions from automobiles that contribute to global warming. The Court determined that a loss of land along the Massachusetts coastline represented a justiciable injury in fact to the state, then held that the injury was caused by the agency's action. The EPA did not dispute that a causal relationship exists between automobile emissions and global warming. Instead, the EPA argued that any action it could take to curtail automobile emissions would have only a limited effect on global warming because emissions from automobiles represent only a fraction of all emissions in the United States, and increasing emissions in other countries would likely offset any potential decrease in U.S. emissions. The Court rejected the EPA's argument.

33. 504 U.S. 555 (1992).
34. 549 U.S. 497 (2007).

> [The EPA's] argument rests on the erroneous assumption that a small incremental step, because it is incremental, can never be attacked in a federal judicial forum. Yet accepting that premise would doom most challenges to regulatory action.... While it may be true that regulating motor-vehicle emissions will not by itself reverse global warming, it by no means follows that we lack jurisdiction to decide whether [the] EPA has a duty to take steps to slow or reduce it.[35]

The Court's most recent standing decision illustrates that the potential for redress need not be substantial to suffice. In *Uzuegbunam v. Preczewski*,[36] the Court considered a claim that interpretations of a state university's speech policy by university police violated the First Amendment rights of two people who endeavored to make speeches on controversial subjects at the university. The university had responded to the complaints of the prospective speakers by rescinding its speech policy, which the university argued made the case moot. In an effort to keep the case going, the plaintiffs asked for nominal damages of one dollar to redress their injury. That strategy worked. The Court held that an award of one dollar would redress the asserted injury, and thus that the petitioners satisfied both standing and mootness. Chief Justice John Roberts dissented and argued that an award of nominal damages does not provide meaningful redress. He expressed the concern that the majority's position would turn the members of the Court "advice columnists," calling to mind the Court's historic refusal to issue advisory opinions.

[E] Procedural Standing

Justice Antonin Scalia's plurality opinion for the Court in *Lujan v. Defenders of Wildlife*[37] raised an issue that had not previously received much attention: in what circumstances can a party obtain judicial review of agency action based on an injury to "procedural rights?" When parties seek judicial review of agency action on grounds that they have been denied adequate notice, an adequate hearing, or an adequate explanation of the reasons for the action in question, the implicit assumption typically is that, had the parties affected by the action been given the proper procedures, the agency might have acted differently. Because agencies often have a great deal of discretion and courts tend to review their factfinding and interpretive choices deferentially, however, that implicit assumption is quite speculative. According to at least one major study, although some judicial remands of agency actions lead to major changes, in many instances, agencies simply fix their procedural errors on the way to pursuing precisely the same course of action.[38] In theory, that uncertainty might raise doubts about a plaintiff's ability to satisfy both the injury-in-fact and redressability requirements for Article III standing.

In *Defenders of Wildlife*, Justice Scalia made a specific point of characterizing the case as not seeking to assert and enforce procedural requirements that the Department of the Interior had failed to follow. Nevertheless, in conjunction with that observation, Justice Scalia dropped a footnote in which he posited the following:

> There is this much truth to the assertion that "procedural rights" are special: The person who has been accorded a procedural right to protect his concrete

35. *Id.* at 524–25.

36. 141 S. Ct. 792 (2021).

37. 504 U.S. 555 (1992).

38. *See* Peter H. Schuck & E. Donald Elliott, *To the Chevron Station: An Empirical Study of Federal Administrative Law*, 1990 Duke L.J. 984.

> interests can assert that right without meeting all the normal standards for redressability and immediacy. Thus, under our case law, one living adjacent to the site for proposed construction of a federally licensed dam has standing to challenge the licensing agency's failure to prepare an environmental impact statement, even though he cannot establish with any certainty that the statement will cause the license to be withheld or altered, and even though the dam will not be completed for many years.[39]

On the other hand, as discussed earlier in this chapter, the Court's holding that the petitioners in *Defenders of Wildlife* lacked standing more clearly rested on other reasoning. Moreover, as Justice Scalia noted further, the procedural claim raised by the *Defenders of Wildlife* petitioners in that case lacked a connection to the concrete interests he said were essential to support to support a claim to procedural standing.

Subsequent cases discussing procedural standing have continued to emphasize the need to have concrete interests at stake in order to claim standing based on a procedural injury. For example, in *Summers v. Earth Island Institute*,[40] the Court considered a challenge by several environmental advocacy groups to U.S. Forest Service rules exempting certain small timbering projects in national forests from notice and comment procedures. The Court held that most of the groups lacked standing because no members of those groups alleged that they personally would be subject to imminent injury by any application of the rules. The government had conceded, however, that one organization originally had standing based on an affidavit in which a member claimed that he had often visited and planned to visit again soon the site of one of the timbering projects, and that he would have submitted comments regarding that project had he been given the opportunity. The government then reached a settlement with that member regarding the particular project that was the subject of his affidavit, prompting the Court to declare that the organization in question no longer had standing to challenge the Forest Service rules. The settlement with the member had removed the only concrete interest established in the case. The lack of any remaining concrete interest precluded the organization from continuing to claim procedural standing.

[F] Standing on the Part of State Governments

Do individual states have standing to sue federal administrative agencies in federal court? The Supreme Court has often denied standing to states seeking to challenge the constitutionality of federal statutes when a state attempts to assert only the interests of its citizens.[41] All of that changed in 2007 with the Supreme Court's decision in *Massachusetts v. Environmental Protection Agency*.[42]

Interested parties had filed a petition urging the Environmental Protection Agency (EPA) to begin a rulemaking to regulate emissions of greenhouse gases under the Clean Air Act. The Environmental Protection Agency (EPA) denied the petition and offered

39. *Id.* at 572 n.7; *see also Massachusetts v. Environmental Protection Agency*, 549 U.S. 497 (2007) (recognizing that litigants can claim standing to assert procedural rights "without meeting all the normal standards for redressability and immediacy" if they can demonstrate concrete interests protected by the procedural rights in question).

40. 555 U.S. 488 (2009).

41. *See, e.g., Commonwealth of Massachusetts v. Laird*, 400 U.S. 886 (1970).

42. 549 U.S. 497 (2007).

two reasons for its decision: first, that it lacked the power to regulate greenhouse gases; and second, even if it had such power, it was exercising its discretion not to take regulatory action. A consortium of states, local governments, and private groups challenged the EPA's decision, asserting that the agency had abdicated its regulatory responsibilities under the Clean Air Act. Specifically, the petitioners argued that the EPA had failed to regulate greenhouse gas emissions, including carbon dioxide emissions from automobiles. The EPA responded in part by claiming that the petitioners lacked standing.

Although petitioners in the case asserted various different types of injuries, the Supreme Court focused its analysis exclusively on the injuries claimed by Massachusetts. A five-justice majority of the Court held that Massachusetts as a sovereign state had standing to obtain judicial review of the EPA's decision. Writing for the Court, Justice John Paul Stevens observed that "states are not normal litigants for the purpose of invoking federal jurisdiction." Consequently, he said, Massachusetts "[was] entitled to special solicitude in [the Court's] standing analysis."

In considering the possibility of actual injury to Massachusetts as a state, the Court concluded that the "harms associated with climate change are serious and well recognized." Examining some of the scientific studies on climate, the Court found a strong consensus among respected scientists regarding global warming and the harms that stem from it, including a sharp rise in sea levels. Rising seas, according to the Court, "have already begun to swallow Massachusetts' coastal land." Because Massachusetts owns much of this land, it was able to demonstrate a particularized injury in fact.

Moving on to the causation element, the Court concluded that the EPA's failure to regulate automobile emissions was a substantial element in the chain of causation. Regarding an adequate remedy, the Court said that, "while it may be true that regulating motor-vehicle emissions will not by itself *reverse* global warming, it by no means follows that we lack jurisdiction to decide whether EPA has a duty to take steps to *slow* or *reduce* it." Hence, the current and potential harm to Massachusetts by way of the EPA's inaction gave the state standing to challenge the EPA's action.

Chief Justice John Roberts, joined by Justices Antonin Scalia, Clarence Thomas, and Samuel Alito, dissented, disagreeing sharply with the majority's analysis. He contended, quite correctly, that there was no basis in the Court's precedent for according special status to states as litigants. He also rejected the conclusion that Massachusetts had established a concrete injury for two reasons. First, he said that the loss of coastal land was part of the generalized harm to "humanity at large" caused by global warming, and thus was insufficiently particularized to represent injury in fact. Second, he contended that Massachusetts' alleged injury was not "actual or imminent," "real or immediate," or "certainly impending," but rather was "pure conjecture" based on flawed scientific models.

It is difficult to know just how seriously to take the Court's suggestion in *Massachusetts v. EPA* that states are unique petitioners. But for that factor, a majority of the justices might have decided that the petitioners in that case failed to establish standing. The dissenters in *Massachusetts v. EPA* argued that the majority's "special solicitude" to Massachusetts as a state reflected "an implicit concession that petitioners cannot establish standing on traditional terms." Justice Stevens's majority opinion additionally emphasized that Congress had authorized the specific type of challenge brought against the EPA and that the alleged injury was a procedural one. Whether the Court would accord states special status for standing purposes without the presence of these two additional factors is uncertain.

Regardless, the holding in *Massachusetts v. EPA* has become popular among state attorneys general. Many important administrative law cases now arise because state attorneys general of one political party challenge actions taken by a presidential administration of the other political party. Applications of *Massachusetts v. EPA* by federal circuit courts in these cases have been mixed.

For example, in *Government of Manitoba v. Bernhardt*,[43] the D.C. Circuit Court of Appeals held that Missouri lacked standing to challenge an agency action based on the agency's failure to comply with the National Environmental Policy Act. The court held that Missouri had waived its right to sue based on an injury to the state itself. The court then rejected Missouri's claim that it had standing to sue on behalf of its citizens. The court noted that the Supreme Court had long held that states cannot bring suits on behalf of their citizens against the United States. The D.C. Circuit went on to characterize the Supreme Court's opinion in *Massachusetts v. EPA* as recognizing only the right of a state to challenge federal action based on injury to the state's sovereign interests.

By comparison, in *Texas v. Equal Employment Opportunity Commission*,[44] the Fifth Circuit Court of Appeals held that Texas had standing to challenge an EEOC policy statement taking the position that states refusing to hire people with criminal records were in violation of Title VII of the Civil Rights Act. Texas claimed that the policy statement violated the Administrative Procedure Act as a legislative rule lacking notice-and-comment rulemaking procedures. Complicating the case, the EEOC does not possess statutory authority to issue legislative rules in the first instance. Instead, the EEOC refers cases to the Department of Justice when it believes Title VII has been violated, but the EEOC cannot force the Department of Justice to bring such an action. Nevertheless, Texas claimed as its injury the need to either change its laws to comply with the policy statement or risk being the subject of a lawsuit by the Department of Justice. The court agreed that Texas had established standing and went on to hold the policy statement unlawful as an invalidly-promulgated legislative rule.

Regardless, the "special solicitude" the Supreme Court extended to the states in *Massachusetts v. EPA* has resulted in state governments more often being able to establish standing to challenge federal government action. In this regard, the Court's recent decision in *California v. Texas*,[45] represents an exception to this trend. In that case, a seven-justice majority of the Supreme Court held that neither individuals nor state governments had standing to challenge the constitutionality of the Affordable Care Act (ACA). The ACA as originally enacted required individuals purchase health insurance and imposed a penalty on those who failed to do so. In an earlier case, the Supreme Court had held that Congress lacked the power under the U.S. Constitution's Commerce Clause to compel individuals to purchase health insurance, but the Court upheld a penalty imposed by the ACA for failing to purchase health insurance as an exercise of Congress's taxing power under Article I, § 8, because the penalty produced at least some revenue for the government. Congress subsequently amended the ACA and set the penalty for failing to purchase health insurance at $0. Individual plaintiffs and states then sued, claiming that the elimination of the penalty meant that the ACA was no longer an exercise of the taxing power, and thus was unconstitutional. The Supreme Court concluded that the individual plaintiffs lacked standing because the lack of an actual penalty severed any causal connection between the ACA's penalty provision and the

43. 923 F.3d 173 (D.C. Cir. 2019).
44. 933 F.3d 433 (5th Cir. 2019).
45. 141 S. Ct. 2104 (2021).

claimed economic injury from being required to purchase health insurance. If the statute imposes no penalty, then there is no means of enforcing the purchase mandate.

By comparison, the state petitioners in *California v. Texas* asserted two types of injuries: the increased costs of providing health care to some of their citizens, and the resulting increased administrative costs. Again, however, the Court rejected those arguments on grounds that neither injury was caused by the amended penalty provision. According to the Court, "the States have not demonstrated that an unenforceable mandate will cause their residents to enroll in valuable benefits programs that they would otherwise forgo. It would require far stronger evidence than the States have offered here to support their counterintuitive theory of standing, which rests on a 'highly attenuated chain of possibilities.'" The states also contended that the penalty provision was not severable from the rest of the ACA, and thus that they should be able to establish standing by demonstrating they suffered injuries as a result of other provisions of the ACA, not merely injuries associated with the amended penalty provision. The Court declined to consider that argument because the states had not raised it before the lower courts.

§ 12.04 Refinements to Zone of Interests Standing

Since establishing the *zone of interests* approach to statutory standing in the *ADAPSO* case, the Supreme Court has had several occasions to revisit and refine that doctrine. As with so much else in the standing area, the Court's analysis in these cases has sometimes seemed inconsistent. In part, this may be due to the statutory basis for the zone of interests inquiry. Although associated with Administrative Procedure Act (APA) § 702, zone of interests standing requires a reviewing court to examine particularly the organic statute that provides the basis for the agency action under challenge. Every organic statute is different, resulting in highly particularized evaluations that cannot help but be somewhat unpredictable.

In *Clarke v. Securities Industry Ass'n*,[46] the Court reviewed a case in which an association of securities dealers challenged a decision by the Comptroller of the Currency to allow banks to open discount brokerage offices outside their home states. The securities dealers contended that the Comptroller's decision violated the terms of § 36 of the McFadden Act, which itself was part of the National Bank Act. The Comptroller conceded that the securities dealers suffered injury in fact, but he argued that they nevertheless lacked standing because the interest they sought to protect—avoiding the competitive harm that would ensue if banks were allowed to open out-of-state discount brokerage offices—fell outside the zone of interests that Congress sought to protect with the McFadden Act.

Writing for the Court and a five-justice majority, Justice Byron White offered the following summary of the zone of interests standard:

> In cases where the plaintiff is not itself the subject of the contested regulatory action, the [zone of interests] test denies a right of review if the plaintiff's interests are *so marginally related to or inconsistent with* the purposes implicit in the

46. 479 U.S. 388 (1987).

statute that it cannot reasonably be assumed that Congress intended to permit the suit. The test is not meant to be especially demanding; in particular, there need be no indication of congressional purpose to benefit the would-be plaintiff.[47]

In evaluating the case at bar, the Court therefore looked not only to § 36 of the McFadden Act but rather to "the overall context of the National Bank Act" and its overall statutory purposes. The Court determined that the National Bank Act showed a concern for preventing banks "from gaining monopoly control over credit and money," and that the Comptroller's actions would put the securities dealers in competition with banks. From these two determinations, the Court inferred that "'Congress [has] arguably legislated against the competition that [the securities dealers seek] to challenge' by limiting the extent to which banks can engage in the discount brokerage business" and that Congress therefore "intended [the petitioners] to be relied upon to challenge agency disregard of the law." Chief Justice William Rehnquist and Justices Sandra Day O'Connor and John Paul Stevens concurred in the judgment but criticized the majority opinion for a "wholly unnecessary exegesis on the 'zone of interests' test," offering instead their view that a "straightforward" analysis of the text and legislative history of the McFadden Act showed that Congress intended nonbank competitors like the securities dealers to be beneficiaries of that statute.

Given the breadth of the Court's framing of the zone of interests inquiry in the *Clarke* case, its decision a few years later in *Air Courier Conference v. American Postal Workers Union*[48] was surprising. Union members challenged an action by the U.S. Postal Service that permitted private couriers to deliver letters to government postal services in other countries. The effect of this action is to take what had been a monopoly out of the hands of the postal service, which would in turn lose business, which would in turn result in layoffs of postal service employees. Once again, the Court was willing to accept that the union's members suffered injury in fact, but the Court denied standing on the basis of a zone of interest analysis.

One difference between *Clarke* and *Air Courier* lay in the Court's framing of the zone of interests question. Whereas the *Clarke* decision said that "no indication of congressional purpose to benefit the would-be plaintiff" was required, the *Air Courier* decision said that the question was whether the plaintiff's injury fell "within the 'zone of interests' *sought to be protected*" (emphasis added) by the statute in question, which is a narrower inquiry. Another critical aspect of the Court's reasoning in *Air Courier* was its definition of exactly what statute was relevant for purposes of evaluating whether the union and its members fell within the zone of interests. Whereas the Court in *Clarke* looked at the purposes of the entire National Bank Act, rather than merely the provision of the McFadden Act that gave rise to the challenge, the Court in *Air Courier* adopted a much more limited stance.

The Postal Service action under challenge in *Air Courier* was taken in interpretation of the Private Express Statute of 1792, which established the Postal Service's statutory monopoly. That statute had been reenacted as part of a more extensive Postal Reorganization Act, which additionally included several provisions addressing labor-management

47. *Id.* at 399–400 (emphasis added). Justice John Paul Steven wrote a concurring opinion, joined by two of his colleagues, agreeing that the securities dealers had standing, but on narrower grounds than the majority.

48. 498 U.S. 517 (1991).

relations, employee pay, and working conditions at the Postal Service. Just as the Court in *Clarke* considered the entire National Bank Act, the union in *Air Courier* maintained that the Court should consider the entirety of the Postal Reorganization Act in conducting its zone of interests analysis. The Court disagreed and maintained instead that the only relevant statute was that "whose violation is the gravamen of the complaint," which in this case was the Private Express Statute alone. According to the Court, the Private Express Statute was intended by Congress to protect "the Government's capital investment in the post roads, not the jobs of as-yet virtually nonexistent postal employees." Consequently, the union and its members fell outside the zone of interests.

The holding in *Air Courier* makes sense to the extent that it requires some relationship between the statute that evidences Congress's consideration of a particular group's interests and the statute that provides the basis for that same group's challenge to an agency's action on the merits. Without some such limitation, the zone of interests standard for statutory standing would be essentially meaningless. Nevertheless, the line drawn by the Court in *Air Courier* is a difficult one to draw. Determining whether two statutes are sufficiently related to allow a petitioner to obtain standing under one to make a challenge on the merits under the other often will be quite difficult. Perhaps for this reason, since its decision in *Air Courier*, the Court has backed away from this requirement and moved closer to its framing of the zone of interests inquiry in the *Clarke* case.[49]

In *Match-E-Be-Nash-She-Wish Band of Pottawatomi Indians v. Patchak*,[50] the Supreme Court unanimously described and applied a version of the zone of interests standard that is easy to satisfy but relatively limitless so long as a plaintiff is able to satisfy the requirements for constitutional standing. In this case, exercising authority conferred by the Indian Reorganization Act, the Department of the Interior gave a piece of land in trust to a Native American tribe so that the tribe could construct and operate a casino. The owner of nearby property who did not want to live near a casino challenged the agency's action. The purpose of the Indian Reorganization Act was to advance the interests of Native Americans, not to protect the property rights of their neighbors. Quoting *Clarke* for the proposition that the zone of interests requirement "is not meant to be especially demanding," Justice Elena Kagan wrote that the Court looks only to ensure that a plaintiff's interests are not "so marginally related to or inconsistent with the purposes implicit in the statute that it cannot reasonably be assumed that Congress intended to permit the suit." She then characterized the Indian Reorganization Act and the property acquisition in question as having much to do with land use and described how "the statute's implementation centrally depends upon the projected use of a given property." As a neighboring landowner, Patchak's interests in the case likewise concerned how the land would be used. Accordingly, he fell "within the zone ... protected or regulated by the statute."

---

49. *See, e.g.*, *National Credit Union Admin. v. First National Bank & Trust Co.*, 522 U.S. 479 (1998) (reiterating the rhetoric from *Clarke* that the Court "should not inquire whether there has been a congressional intent to benefit the would-be plaintiff").

50. 132 S. Ct. 2199 (2012).

§12.05 Prudential Standing

[A] Generally

Beyond the requirements of constitutional standing and statutory standing, the Supreme Court has recognized certain other limitations on who may raise a claim in federal court. As the Court summarized in *Allen v. Wright*,[51]

> Standing doctrine embraces several judicially self-imposed limits on the exercise of federal jurisdiction, such as the general prohibition on a litigant's raising another person's legal rights, the rule barring adjudication of generalized grievances more appropriately addressed in the representative branches, and the requirement that a plaintiff's complaint fall within the zone of interest protected by the law invoked.[52]

Following this rhetorical lead, courts routinely grouped all of these limitations on plaintiff standing under the label of *prudential standing*. The three most commonly recognized prudential standing categories are third-party standing, generalized grievances, and the zone of interests standing requirement discussed above.[53]

Many years later, in *Lexmark International, Inc. v. Static Control Components, Inc.*,[54] Justice Antonin Scalia observed that "prudential standing" is a bit of a misnomer. First, he noted that zone of interests standing is not a function of judicial prudence but instead is statutorily required. "Whether a plaintiff comes within the zone of interests is an issue that requires us to determine, using traditional tools of statutory interpretation, whether a legislatively conferred cause of action encompasses a particular plaintiff's claim." In this same spirit, one can easily argue that other prudential standing doctrines, like the limitation on taxpayer standing discussed below, are merely different applications of the injury-in-fact requirement for constitutional standing under Article III. Nevertheless, the courts continue to use the prudential standing label, so its permutations beyond zone of interests standing are worth exploring.

[B] Third-Party Standing

May one person assert the rights of another person in federal court? Usually, the answer is an unequivocal no. In a few limited circumstances, however, the Court has permitted—or suggested—that it might permit the assertion of one person's rights by another. For example, in *Craig v. Boren*,[55] the Court permitted a bar owner to assert the rights of young men in Oklahoma between the ages of 18 and 21 to drink beer containing 3.2% alcohol. Under an Oklahoma statute, women over 18 were permitted to buy beer; men had to be 21. Reaching the merits, the Court decided that this was an impermissible gender discrimination under the Equal Protection Clause.

In virtually all other cases in which the Court has permitted third-party standing, there has been a much closer relationship between the plaintiff and the person whose

51. 468 U.S. 737 (1984).
52. *Id.* at 751.
53. *See* §§12.02 and 12.04.
54. 572 U.S. 118 (2004).
55. 429 U.S. 190 (1976).

rights are being advanced. In *Singleton v. Wulff*,[56] a plurality of four justices thought that obstetricians should be permitted to assert the rights of their pregnant patients in attacking a federal prohibition on the use of Medicaid funds for abortions. In *Eisenstadt v. Baird*,[57] the relationship at issue was also physician-patient (prescribing contraceptives for minors). Despite these specific exceptions, the Court will usually forbid most attempts to use third-party standing.

The Court has recognized an important exception to the prudential limitation against third-party standard for certain instances in which organizations assert injuries suffered by their members or other stakeholders, also known as *associational standing*. Although at one time, the Court expressed concerns about allowing "special interest" organizations to claim standing based on the interests of their members,[58] the Court overcame those concerns in *Hunt v. Washington Apple Advertising Commission*.[59] In that case, the Court recognized the standing of a membership association to bring suit on behalf of its members if three requirements are satisfied: "(a) its members would otherwise have standing to sue in their own right; (b) the interests it seeks to protect are germane to the organization's purpose; and (c) neither the claim asserted nor the relief requested requires the participation of individual members in the lawsuit."

The three-part test described by the Court in *Hunt* is only partially prudential in nature. In *United Food & Commercial Workers Union Local 751 v. Brown Group Inc.*,[60] the Court unanimously characterized the first element of the three-part *Hunt* test as compelled by the Constitution's Article III. The Court characterized the second element of the *Hunt* test as "at the least, complementary to the first." But the Court characterized the third *Hunt* element as prudential, "best seen as focusing on these matters of administrative convenience and efficiency, not on the elements of a case or controversy within the meaning of the Constitution." As a result of this characterization, the Court in the *United Food* case held that Congress could authorize third-party unions to sue an employer for backpay on behalf of its employees.

[C] Taxpayer Standing

As previously noted in this chapter, as a general rule, the injury asserted by a plaintiff must be particularized to satisfy the requirements for constitutional standing. A corresponding principle of prudential standing holds that generalized grievances are inadequate to establish standing. A particular subset of the cases concerning generalized grievances falls under the label of taxpayer standing. Since its 1923 decision in *Frothingham v. Mellon*,[61] the Supreme Court generally has refused to recognize the standing of any person to challenge government action purely on the ground that the person is a taxpayer whose tax dollars are somehow being misspent. In *DaimlerChrysler Corp. v. Cuno*,[62] a unanimous Supreme Court extended the reasoning of *Frothingham*, holding that state taxpayers and municipal taxpayers could not rely on their status as taxpayers

56. 428 U.S. 106 (1976).
57. 405 U.S. 438 (1972).
58. *See, e.g.*, *Sierra Club v. Morton*, 405 U.S. 727 (1972).
59. 432 U.S. 333 (1977).
60. 517 U.S. 544 (1996).
61. 262 U.S. 447 (1923).
62. 547 U.S. 332 (2006).

to claim Article III standing to challenge state and local tax exemptions intended to persuade businesses to locate their facilities within a particular state.

The Supreme Court made an exception to this understanding in *Flast v. Cohen*,[63] a 1968 case involving an attack on certain Department of Health, Education and Welfare (HEW) payments to religious schools. (HEW was later split into two different cabinet level departments: the Department of Health and Human Services and the Department of Education.) The plaintiffs in *Flast* attacked the payments under the First Amendment's Establishment Clause, but the only injury they could allege involved their status as taxpayers and the expenditure of funds derived from tax revenues.

Upon consideration, the Court articulated a two-part test that opens the window of taxpayer standing only slightly. According to the Court in *Flast*, taxpayer plaintiffs must allege (1) a connection between their status as taxpayers and the legislation they are attacking (*i.e.*, the legislation must call for spending dollars raised through taxes) and (2) a connection between their status as taxpayers and the constitutional infringement alleged (*i.e.*, that an absolute prohibition on the expenditure of tax dollars, such as the Establishment Clause, is being violated). The *Flast* plaintiffs satisfied both parts of this test.

Since *Flast*, however, the Court has been scrupulously careful to restrict the test described in that decision to cases with nearly identical facts. The Court has never overturned *Flast*, but also has refused to extend its reasoning to different circumstances that might at first blush seem to satisfy *Flast*'s requirements. For example, taxpayer challenges to Vietnam War expenditures were rejected in 1974.[64]

In 2011, the Supreme Court once again addressed taxpayer standing and concluded that the taxpayers lacked standing to go forward with their federal court lawsuit. In *Arizona Christian School Tuition Organization v. Winn*,[65] a number of Arizona taxpayers objected to the state's granting of tax credits for the support of "school tuition organizations." While a somewhat complex topic, these school tuition organizations funded scholarships for Arizona students to attend private schools, including schools that were created and operated by religious organizations. The plaintiff-taxpayers objected to this action as a violation of the Establishment Clause and invoked basic standing principles and the special rule of *Flast v. Cohen* as the basis for their standing to sue.

A five-justice majority in *Winn* applied both the three-part test for constitutional standing discussed earlier in this chapter and *Flast*. Regarding constitutional standing, and illustrating the tremendous overlap between prudential standing and constitutional injury-in-fact, the Court noted that mere status as a taxpayer ordinarily is insufficient to establish standing. Moreover, the Court was unwilling to discern any palpable, specific injury to the State of Arizona due to the program. For that matter, the taxpayers failed to show that merely permitting the tax credits would result in an increase to their individual state tax liabilities. In rejecting the argument that standing was conferred under the Establishment Clause exception in *Flast*, the Court claimed a significant difference between the tax *credits* at issue in this case and the specific government *expenditures* that were at issue in *Flast*.[66] The Court commented that, "[w]hen the

63. 392 U.S. 83 (1968).

64. *United States v. Richardson*, 418 U.S. 166 (1974); *Schlesinger v. Reservists*, 418 U.S. 208 (1974).

65. 563 U.S. 125 (2011).

66. For what it is worth, any tax professor can tell you that tax credits and government expenditures are functionally equivalent from an economic perspective.

government declines to impose a tax ... there is no such connection between dissenting taxpayers and alleged [acts in violation of the Establishment Clause.]" Consequently, "any financial injury remains speculative."[67] Notably, although Justices Antonin Scalia and Clarence Thomas joined the majority opinion, they also wrote separately in favor of overruling *Flast* altogether.

67. *Id.* at 1447.

Chapter 13

Judicial Review: On the Merits

§ 13.01 Introduction

After all the requirements outlined in Chapters 10, 11, and 12 are satisfied, only then will a court to agree to review the merits of a challenge against an agency action. At this stage, several potential arguments may be raised to persuade a court to set aside an agency action as exceeding the scope of the agency's statutory authority or as otherwise invalid as a matter of law.

Inexperienced lawyers think that this is the point at which any and all defects in an agency case will be remedied. In practice, it rarely works out that way. Many agency decisions never reach review by a court of law because the losing party cannot afford judicial review or concludes that the costs of litigation outweigh the burden of living with arguably illegitimate or erroneous agency actions. Many cases that try to go to court and obtain judicial review will be waylaid by the doctrines discussed in Chapters 10, 11, and 12. Only a small number of agency cases ever reach the merits stage. Moreover, the standard remedy for some types of Administrative Procedure Act violations is for the court simply to remand the matter back to the agency for additional, corrective proceedings. It is not uncommon for courts to declare that the party challenging an agency's action is the outright winner, but very few agency actions suffer that end.

You should always keep in mind that persuading a court to overturn agency action is rarely easy. Courts tend to be fairly deferential toward agencies as finders of fact, interpreters of law, and deciders of policy. Courts review most (though not all) arguments for overturning agency actions with an attitude of deference toward agencies. If you dispute the facial constitutionality of the organic statute or agency action itself, the courts will not defer to the agency. Likewise, if you claim an agency has failed to follow procedural requirements contained in the Administrative Procedure Act (APA), the courts will examine those arguments for itself (*i.e.*, de novo). But if you challenge agency action on the basis of flawed fact finding, misinterpretation of ambiguous statutory or regulatory text, or flawed or inconsistent policy decisions, then you should expect courts to give agencies a fair amount of latitude.

In other words, any attempt to predict the outcome of judicial review on the merits should begin with an assumption that the court is more likely *not* to overturn an agency decision. After that, the analysis can proceed in any number of ways. Most lawyers try first to identify the applicable legal requirements and issues raised by the agency's action, and then to consider the standards by which courts evaluate the same. Just do not expect a lot of bright lines or clear answers. This type of analysis requires careful framing and attention to detail. This whole area, like so much of lawyering, is a matter of predictions and probabilities.

All of that said, in approaching judicial review on the merits, framing is critical. It is not enough to complain that an agency action is unreasonable. The court will simply ask, unreasonable in what way? It is the lawyer's job to identify and frame specific arguments based on constitutional or statutory requirements and judicial common law. Building from statutory text, the courts have fashioned a number of principles that in turn shape challenges to and judicial review of agency actions in many cases.

As usual, the best place to begin is with the agency's organic statute. Many organic statutes contain provisions governing judicial review. For example, many organic statutes instruct reviewing courts to ascertain whether particular agency actions are supported by *substantial evidence.* If the organic statute is silent regarding judicial review, or even if it is not, the APA provides a host of potential grounds for challenging agency actions.

Generally speaking, agency actions can be challenged on any (or all) of several grounds:

- the decision is based on a finding of fact that is not adequately supported by the available evidence;
- the agency action is inconsistent with the substantive provisions of the agency's organic statutes and regulations;
- the procedures the agency used were inadequate;
- the agency did not engage in reasoned decisionmaking—*i.e.*, it did not adequately explain why it acted as it did, or the action represents an unexplained departure from past agency precedent.

Each of these grounds is discussed at some length below.

§ 13.02 Judicial Review Under the APA

Section 706 of the Administrative Procedure Act (APA) addresses the scope and standards of judicial review of agency action. It provides as follows:

> To the extent necessary to decision and when presented, the reviewing court shall decide all relevant questions of law, interpret constitutional provisions, and determine the meaning or applicability of the terms of an agency action. The reviewing court shall—
>
> (1) compel agency action unlawfully withheld or unreasonably delayed; and
>
> (2) hold unlawful and set aside agency action, findings, and conclusions found to be—
>
> (A) arbitrary, capricious, an abuse of discretion, or otherwise not in accordance with law;
>
> (B) contrary to constitutional right, power, privilege, or immunity;
>
> (C) in excess of statutory jurisdiction, authority, or limitations, or short of statutory right;
>
> (D) without observance of procedure required by law;
>
> (E) unsupported by substantial evidence in a case subject to sections 556 and 557 of this title or otherwise reviewed on the record of an agency hearing provided by statute; or

(F) unwarranted by the facts to the extent that the facts are subject to trial de novo by the reviewing court.

In making the foregoing determinations, the court shall review the whole record or those parts of it cited by a party, and due account shall be taken of the rule of prejudicial error.[1]

Courts have recognized that the standards outlined in this provision are not mutually exclusive but rather are cumulative.[2] For example, according to the Supreme Court's decision in *Motor Vehicle Manufacturers Ass'n of the United States, Inc. v. State Farm Mutual Automobile Insurance Co.*,[3] agency exercises of policymaking discretion typically fall under the purview of the APA § 706(2)(A) arbitrary and capricious standard, which is deferential and does not allow a court to substitute its own judgment for that of the agency.[4] It is fairly obvious that agency actions that are not authorized by an agency's organic statute exceed statutory authority and, correspondingly, are not in accordance with law, and thus are arbitrary and capricious as well.[5] But agency actions that fall within statutory authority as a matter of mere interpretation still can be arbitrary and capricious under *State Farm*, and thus must be set aside as well.[6] Wherever the precise line between statutory interpretation and policymaking discretion falls, when traditional tools of statutory interpretation fail and policymaking takes over, the arbitrary and capricious standard comes into play.

Beyond setting out the basic parameters of judicial review, the APA says very little about what the different elements of § 706 mean or how they relate to one another. Terms like *substantial evidence* or *arbitrary* and *capricious* are not defined within the APA. Some of these terms were used in other statutes or at common law before the APA was adopted. Otherwise, courts have simply groped their way through the application of APA § 706 on a case-by-case, argument-by-argument basis.

---

1. 5 U.S.C. § 706.

2. *See, e.g., Ass'n of Data Processing Service Organizations v. Board of Governors of the Federal Reserve System*, 745 F.2d 677 (D.C. Cir. 1984); *Olenhouse v. Commodity Credit Corp.*, 42 F.3d 1560 (10th Cir. 1994).

3. 463 U.S. 29 (1983).

4. *See also, e.g., Department of Commerce v. New York*, 139 S. Ct. 2551 (2019).

5. *See, e.g., California Communities Against Toxics v. Environmental Protection Agency*, 928 F.3d 1041 (D.C. Cir. 2019); *Northwest Environmental Advocates v. U.S. Environmental Protection Agency*, 537 F.3d 1006 (9th Cir. 2008); *see also* Emily Hammond Meazell, *Deference and Dialogue in Administrative Law*, 111 COLUM. L. REV. 1722, 1733 (2011) ("Although these standards differ in their phrasing, each attempts to pair judicial deference with a reasoned decisionmaking requirement.").

6. *See, e.g., Peter Pan Bus Lines, Inc. v. Federal Motor Carrier Safety Admin.*, 471 F.3d 1350 (D.C. Cir. 2006) (citing cases supporting this proposition); *cf. Negusie v. Holder*, 555 U.S. 511 (2009) (concluding that the statute was ambiguous but remanding without evaluating the reasonableness of the agency's interpretation because the agency had based its action on its belief that the statute was unambiguous).

§ 13.03 Judicial Review of Agency Factual Determinations

[A] Introduction

Agencies routinely make findings of fact. In the context of adjudication, agency factfinding typically concerns the same sorts of questions about *who* did *what* to whom, *where*, *when*, and *why*. For example, the National Labor Relations Board (NLRB) might find that foreman X punched worker Y in the nose in the State Street plant on a particular day when Y was picketing the plant during a labor disruption. Factfinding also occurs in the rulemaking context, although the sorts of *legislative facts* on which agencies base their rules are a little different from *adjudicative facts*.[7] For example, the Environmental Protection Agency once determined that a level of 1 gram per gallon of lead in gasoline is the highest level that can be tolerated without endangering human health.

The standards of review listed in Administrative Procedure Act (APA) § 706 are relevant for judicial review of agency factfinding. They are the *arbitrary and capricious* standard of § 706(2)(A), the *substantial evidence* standard described in § 706(2)(E), and the de novo standard mentioned in § 706(2)(F).

Little needs to be said about de novo review of agency factfinding. In rare circumstances, agency findings of fact are made subject to de novo review expressly in an agency organic act.[8] Alternatively, in *Citizens to Preserve Overton Park, Inc. v. Volpe*,[9] the Supreme Court observed that de novo review may be appropriate where the agency's adjudicatory proceeding offered inadequate factfinding procedures, but acknowledged that such circumstances do not arise often. A reviewing court engaged in de novo review need not consider the agency's findings of fact. The case comes into the court as if there were no decision at the agency level. The court is perfectly free to substitute its judgment for any of the agency's findings and conclusions.

By comparison, an extensive jurisprudence exists discussing and applying the substantial evidence standard and the arbitrary and capricious standard. Each is discussed below in turn.

[B] Substantial Evidence Review

The substantial evidence standard has been around for a long time. It is the standard of review specified in a number of organic statutes as well as one of the standards recognized in APA § 706. Unless an agency's organic statute provides otherwise, the express language of APA § 706(2)(E) and Supreme Court precedent make clear that it applies only to formal agency action conducted under APA §§ 556 and 557.[10]

---

7. Kenneth Culp Davis, *An Approach to Problems of Evidence in the Administrative Process*, 55 Harv. L. Rev. 364 (1942).

8. *See, e.g.*, 26 U.S.C. § 6015(e)(7) (prescribing de novo review for United States Tax Court review of Internal Revenue Service determinations regarding taxpayer joint and several liability).

9. 401 U.S. 402 (1971); *see also Camp v. Pitts*, 411 U.S. 138 (1973) (acknowledging *Overton Park* and the possibility of de novo review, but declining to find such circumstances in the case at bar).

10. *See, e.g., Pitts*, 411 U.S. at 140-141 (1973); *Citizens to Preserve Overton Park*, 401 U.S. at 414.

Contemporary understandings of the substantial evidence standard begin with the Supreme Court's landmark decision in *Universal Camera Corp. v. National Labor Relations Board.*[11] The *Universal Camera* decision is renowned in part because of the eloquent rhetoric of Justice Felix Frankfurter writing for the Court. But it is influential additionally because it was written just after the APA was enacted and it determined that Congress's use of the term *substantial evidence* in the then-new APA was consistent with Congress's use of the same term in other, prior statutes. In other words, according to the Court, because substantial evidence as a statutory term predated the APA, Congress intended it to carry the same meaning in the context of both organic statutes and the APA. Prior to the Court's *Universal Camera* decision, some had speculated that Congress might have had something different in mind when it included the substantial evidence term in APA § 706. After a lengthy exposition of the APA's legislative history, the Court in *Universal Camera* concluded otherwise and interpreted substantial evidence in the APA context as synonymous with earlier usages of the term.

In describing the substantial evidence standard, Justice Felix Frankfurter in *Universal Camera* said that it,

> is more than a mere scintilla. It means such relevant evidence as a reasonable mind might accept as adequate to support a conclusion. Accordingly, it must do more than create a suspicion of the existence of the fact to be established.... [I]t must be enough to justify, if the trial were to a jury, a refusal to direct a verdict when the conclusion sought to be drawn from it is one of fact for the jury.[12]

Be careful with the statement relating to directed verdicts. Justice Felix Frankfurter obviously knew what he had in mind, but one of the more dangerous practices in working with administrative law concepts is drawing too many analogies between agency action and court litigation. The best way to think about substantial evidence when evaluating the adequacy of the evidence in an administrative case is to compare the administrative record in question with those of other cases applying the substantial evidence standard, rather than considering trials in Article III courts.

Nevertheless, the import of Justice Frankfurter's words is that Congress intended substantial evidence review to be quite deferential. The Court acknowledged that earlier attempts at substantial evidence review by the federal courts had been too casual and lacking in appropriate rigor, resulting in expressions of congressional dissatisfaction. At the same time, the Court cautioned against treating the substantial evidence standard as "a body of rigid rules assuring sameness of applications." Instead, the Court said that "Congress expressed a mood" in articulating "a standard for judgment."

Beyond this, *Universal Camera* made a major contribution to the *process* of substantial evidence review. The Court appreciated that substantial evidence review in cases like this one occurs in two stages. The first stage is the one where the facts are gathered—*i.e.*, the proceeding before the administrative law judge (ALJ), although ALJs in those days were referred to as hearing examiners. The second stage is where the agency makes its final decision. With regard to the first stage, the Court determined that, while the findings of fact submitted by an ALJ to higher-ups in an agency could be set aside in certain circumstances by reviewing personnel within the agency, the ALJ's findings are important and cannot be totally disregarded. On this point, the Court reasoned that agency action involves all the expertise within an agency, not merely that of its

11. 340 U.S. 474 (1951).
12. *Id.* at 477.

ALJs. The persons in the agency above the ALJ (*i.e.*, those who perform an agency-level reviewing function) are permitted to consider the dispute in light of their own expertise as well as being required to attend to the ALJ's pronouncements. Still, the Court cautioned agencies to be sensitive to an ALJ's findings on issues such as the credibility of witnesses, because it is the ALJ who presides over the evidentiary hearing and who hears and sees the witnesses.[13] The ALJ's findings are not beyond questioning, but the Court in *Universal Camera* required both agencies and reviewing courts to give careful consideration to the ALJ's conclusions.

Moreover, the Court in *Universal Camera* said that, in evaluating the substantiality of the evidence, it is not enough that the record contains some evidence supporting the agency's decision. Language at the end of §706 requires the reviewing courts to consider "the whole record or parts of it cited by a party."[14] Prior to *Universal Camera*, a typical reviewing court would merely review an administrative record until it identified some evidence (more than a mere scintilla, of course) that supported the agency's decision. At that point, the court could halt its review and declare the agency decision to be supported by substantial evidence. *Universal Camera* rejected this approach, holding instead that a court performing substantial evidence review must consider the administrative record as a whole, including the evidence opposing the agency's decision as well as supporting it, to determine whether the decision is supported by substantial evidence.

Notwithstanding its holding in *Universal Camera* that a reviewing court should consider the whole administrative record to determine the substantiality of the evidence supporting an agency's decision, in a companion case, *National Labor Relations Board v. Pittsburgh Steamship Co.*,[15] the Court cautioned against interpreting that mandate too literally. The lower court had rejected the agency's decision for its reliance on the conclusions of a hearing examiner who found all of the employer's witnesses untrustworthy and all of the union's witnesses reliable, suggesting bias. "Painstakingly" reviewing the administrative record for itself, the lower court had concluded that the agency's factual inferences were so outweighed by contrary evidence as to be unsupported by substantial evidence. The Supreme Court declined to conduct for itself a similarly thorough review of the administrative record, opting instead to "adhere to the usual rule of non-interference where conclusions of Circuit Courts of Appeals depend on appreciation of circumstances which admit of different interpretations."

Despite the cautionary note sounded by the Court in *Pittsburgh Steamship*, in 1998, in *Allentown Mack Sales & Service, Inc. v. National Labor Relations Board*,[16] the Supreme Court engaged in a very extensive (some might say nit-picking) review of a decision by the National Labor Relations Board to conclude that the agency's decision was not supported by substantial evidence. In an opinion for the majority written by Justice Antonin Scalia, who was a former administrative law professor undoubtedly familiar with *Universal Camera*, the Court dug into the record to discuss specific testimony by individual witnesses at the hearing before the ALJ and to compare the manner in which the ALJ and the NLRB dealt with that testimony. The Court itself weighed some of the witness testimony in terms that are more often found in decisions by ALJs themselves:

---

13. This point is also discussed in Chapter 8.
14. 5 U.S.C. §706.
15. 340 U.S. 498 (1951).
16. 522 U.S. 359 (1998).

> Allentown [the company and a party to the action] would reasonably have given great credence to Mohr's [an employee/witness] assertion of lack of union support, since he was not hostile to the union, and was in a good position to assess antiunion sentiment.... It seems to us [the Supreme Court] that Mohr's statement has undeniable and substantial probative value on the issue of "reasonable doubt."[17]

The Court went on to conclude that the legal standard established by the NLRB for evaluating an employer's actions (known as the "reasonable doubt" test) was rational and consistent with the statute. But the Court found the NLRB's decision regarding Allentown's actions to be fatally flawed as unsupported by substantial evidence on the record as a whole. Justice Stephen Breyer, himself a former professor of administrative law, wrote a dissent accusing the majority of rewriting the NLRB's decision without sufficient justification. According to Justice Breyer, the majority "ignored certain evidentiary presumptions.... And it has failed to give the kind of leeway to the Board's fact-finding authority that the Court's precedents mandate."

Although the justices disagreed regarding the outcome in *Allentown Mack*, that case did not purport to alter any of the analysis of *Universal Camera*. Moreover, the Court has not fundamentally altered its understanding of the substantial evidence standard since its *Universal Camera* decision. The fundamental propositions advanced in that case have rarely been questioned. There is, however, some question these days as to whether there is any meaningful difference between the substantial evidence standard and the arbitrary and capricious standard of APA § 706(2)(A) in the context of agency factfinding. That issue is discussed in the following subsection.

[C] The Arbitrary and Capricious Standard

Since agencies use informal adjudication for far more frequently than formal adjudication, it is important to appreciate differences between the two standards. Unfortunately, the case law is not very helpful either in describing the manner in which courts apply the arbitrary and capricious standard to findings of fact or in explaining the difference between the two standards. In fact, several circuit courts have concluded that the two standards are identical in their application to the factual predicates for agency action.

Perhaps the most extensive analysis of the distinction between the arbitrary and capricious standard and the substantial evidence standard is found in an opinion by Justice Antonin Scalia when he was serving as a judge on the United States Court of Appeals for the D.C. Circuit, in *Ass'n of Data Processing Service Organizations, Inc. v. Board of Governors of the Federal Reserve System (ADAPSO)*.[18] Then-judge Scalia was joined on that three-judge panel by future Justice Ruth Bader Ginsburg, also serving on the D.C. Circuit at the time. Other federal circuit courts of appeals have adopted its

17. *Id.* at 372.
18. 745 F.2d 677 (D.C. Cir. 1984).

interpretation of the arbitrary and capricious standard.[19] The Supreme Court has cited *ADAPSO* approvingly, albeit without adopting it outright.[20]

In *ADAPSO*, the D.C. Circuit considered challenges to two separate Federal Reserve Board (FRB) orders. One order was the product of a formal, on-the-record adjudication, approving an application by a subsidiary of Citicorp to offer data processing services. The other "order," notwithstanding that label, was the product of informal, notice-and-comment rulemaking, amending existing FRB regulations regarding the performance of data processing services by banks. The Bank Holding Company Act provided that "[t]he findings of the [FRB] as to the facts, if supported by substantial evidence, shall be conclusive."[21] A question for the court was whether that provision governed only review of factfinding in orders arising from FRB adjudications, or whether it extended also to review of orders arising from FRB informal, notice-and-comment rulemakings—supplanting the APA's arbitrary and capricious standard with respect to the latter. Underlying that question was the assumption of some courts that the arbitrary and capricious standard was more deferential to agencies than the substantial evidence standard.[22]

The court concluded, with little analysis of statutory text, history, or purpose, that the specific statute in question required the substantial evidence standard for both FRB adjudications and FRB rulemakings. That conclusion is the least interesting part of the court's opinion, however, as the court went on to discuss at great length the similarities and differences between the two standards.

As regards the degree of deference to agency findings of fact that the two standards represent, the *ADAPSO* court said that the two standards function more or less the same.

> [I]n their application to the requirement of factual support[,] the substantial evidence test and the arbitrary or capricious test are one and the same....
>
> When the arbitrary or capricious standard is performing that function of assuring factual support, there is no substantive difference between what it requires and what would be required by the substantial evidence test, since it is impossible to conceive of a "nonarbitrary" factual judgment supported only by evidence that is not substantial in the APA sense—*i.e.*, not "enough to justify, if the trial were to a jury, a refusal to direct a verdict when the conclusion sought to be drawn... is one of fact for the jury."
>
> We have noted on several occasions that the distinction between the substantial evidence test and the arbitrary or capricious test is "largely semantic."[23]

In other words, the arbitrary and capricious standard is not more deferential than the substantial evidence standard, or vice versa. In fact, notwithstanding the different

---

19. *See, e.g., Maple Drive Farms LP v. Vilsack*, 781 F.3d 837 (6th Cir. 2015); *Ace Telephone Ass'n v. Koppendrayer*, 432 F.3d 876 (8th Cir. 2005); *Sevoian v. Ashcroft*, 290 F.3d 166 (3d Cir. 2002); *GTE South, Inc. v. Morrison*, 199 F.3d 733 (4th Cir. 1999); *Olenhouse v. Commodity Credit Corp.*, 42 F.3d 1560 (10th Cir. 1994).

20. *Dickinson v. Zurko*, 527 U.S. 190 (1999).

21. 18 U.S.C. § 1848.

22. The assumption was not unfounded. The Supreme Court had suggested on more than one occasion that the arbitrary and capricious standard was less demanding, and thus more deferential, than the substantial evidence standard. *See, e.g., American Paper Institute v. American Electric Power Corp.*, 461 U.S. 402 (1983); *Industrial Union Department, AFL-CIO v. American Petroleum Institute*, 448 U.S. 607 (1980).

23. *ADAPSO*, 745 F.2d at 683–84 (citations omitted).

labels the APA uses for the two standards, the court described the arbitrary and capricious standard as little more than a backstop, "a catchall, picking up administrative misconduct not covered by the other more specific" standards outlined in APA § 706(2).

According to the *ADAPSO* court, treating the arbitrary and capricious standard as more deferential than the substantial evidence standard would be "upside-down."

> If the standards were substantively different, the Citicorp order, authorizing one bank holding company's data processing services, would be subject to more rigorous judicial review of factual support than the Regulation Y order which, due to its general applicability, would affect the operations of every bank holding company in the nation. Or, to put the point another way: If the Board had never issued any Regulation Y,... [the Board's adjudicative] determination, which could be reconsidered and revised in the context of the next adjudication, would require more factual support than the same determination in a rulemaking, which would have immediate nationwide application and, until amended by future rulemaking, would have to be applied to all subsequent applications.[24]

The court's normative conclusion in this regard is not quite so obvious as the court seemed to think. The court was clearly correct that a single regulation typically will affect more parties than a single adjudication, and that an agency can more readily change course from an adjudicative determination than from a regulation. On the other hand, the notice-and-comment rulemaking process ordinarily commands more attention and broader participation from interested parties than an adjudication concerning a single party. As a result, courts often are more concerned about protecting the individualized interests at stake in the adjudication context than they are with respect to rulemaking. For these reasons, courts (and Congress) could reasonably perceive a need for greater scrutiny of agency factfinding in reviewing an adjudication than in reviewing a rulemaking.

Regardless, the *ADAPSO* court did not find the substantial evidence standard and the arbitrary and capricious standard indistinguishable in all respects. Specifically, the court went on to say that the two standards are,

> separately recited in the APA... to emphasize that in the case of formal proceedings the factual support must be found in the closed record as opposed to elsewhere....
>
> The distinctive function of [the APA § 706(2)(E) substantial evidence standard]—what it achieves that [the APA § 706(2)(A) arbitrary and capricious standard] does not—is to require substantial evidence to be found within the record of closed-record proceedings to which it exclusively applied.... It is true that... even informal agency action (not governed by paragraph (E)) must be reviewed only on the basis of the "administrative record already in existence." But that is quite a different and less onerous requirement, meaning only that whether the administrator was arbitrary must be determined on the basis of what he had before him when he acted, and not on the basis of "some new record made initially in the reviewing court." That "administrative record" might well include crucial material that was neither shown to or known by the private parties in the proceeding.... It is true that, in informal rulemaking, at

24. *Id.* at 683.

> least the most critical factual material that is used to support the agency's position on review must have been made public in the proceeding and exposed to refutation. That requirement, however, does not extend to all data, and it only applies in rulemaking and not in other informal agency action....[25]

In other words, the substantial evidence standard and the arbitrary and capricious standard operate differently with respect to which evidence a reviewing court can consider in evaluating the factual support for agency action. Judicial review of agency factfinding under the substantial evidence standard is limited to the closed administrative record. Judicial review of agency factfinding under the arbitrary and capricious standard is not so limited.

§ 13.04 Judicial Review of Agency Interpretations of Statutes

[A] Basic Framework

Statutory interpretation is a difficult and complicated task for courts and for everyone else, including agencies. Agencies routinely interpret statutes in the course of performing their responsibilities. Litigants regularly complain that agencies have based their actions on erroneous interpretations of statutory text, history, and purpose.

Agency statutory interpretation occurs in two principal contexts. The first involves statutes of general applicability—*i.e.*, statutes that no one agency is charged by Congress with implementing and administering, but with which many if not all agencies must engage. For example, the Administrative Procedure Act and the Freedom of Information Act are both statutes of general applicability. Reviewing courts do not confer any special deference on agency interpretations of statutes of general applicability.[26] In other words, courts typically review agency interpretations of these statutes using a de novo review standard.

The other context in which agencies engage in statutory interpretation involves statutes with respect to which they play some administrative role—*i.e.*, statutes over which Congress has given one or more particular administrative agencies some amount of responsibility for implementing and administering statutory programs or requirements.[27] The Supreme Court has long counseled some amount of judicial deference to agency interpretations of statutes in such contexts, but its pronouncements regarding how much deference and under what circumstances such deference is appropriate have varied quite a bit over time.

The Supreme Court has always been highly inconsistent in its approach to evaluating agency interpretations of statutes. The doctrinal standards that the Court has endorsed have changed over time. But even within existing standards, judicial review has been quite variable.

25. *Id.* at 683–85 (citations omitted).

26. *See, e.g., Al-Fayed v. Central Intelligence Agency*, 254 F.3d 300 (D.C. Cir. 2001); *Air North America v. Department of Transportation*, 937 F.2d 1427 (9th Cir. 1991).

27. *See, e.g.*, Chapter 2, § 2.02[F][2], for examples of contemporary delegations of statutory administrative responsibility.

Under the Court's present framework, when a reviewing court is asked to decide whether an agency has erred in interpreting a statute over which the agency possesses some amount of administrative responsibility, the court typically finds itself asking which of two cases—*Skidmore v. Swift & Co.*[28] or *Chevron U.S.A. Inc. v. Natural Resources Defense Council, Inc.*[29]—provides the appropriate evaluative standard. Both of those cases counsel in favor of judicial deference to agency statutory interpretations, but in different ways, under different circumstances, arguably to different degrees, and for different reasons. The principal test for deciding which of the two standards to apply, *Skidmore* or *Chevron*, comes from a later case, *United States v. Mead Corp.*,[30] although the Court has recognized one or two other limitations on the scope of *Chevron* deference in particular circumstances.

Each of *Skidmore*, *Chevron*, and *Mead* is discussed at greater length below. In considering the details of the standards described in each of those three cases, however, it may be helpful to keep in mind the following diagram as one way of thinking about the relationship among those three cases:

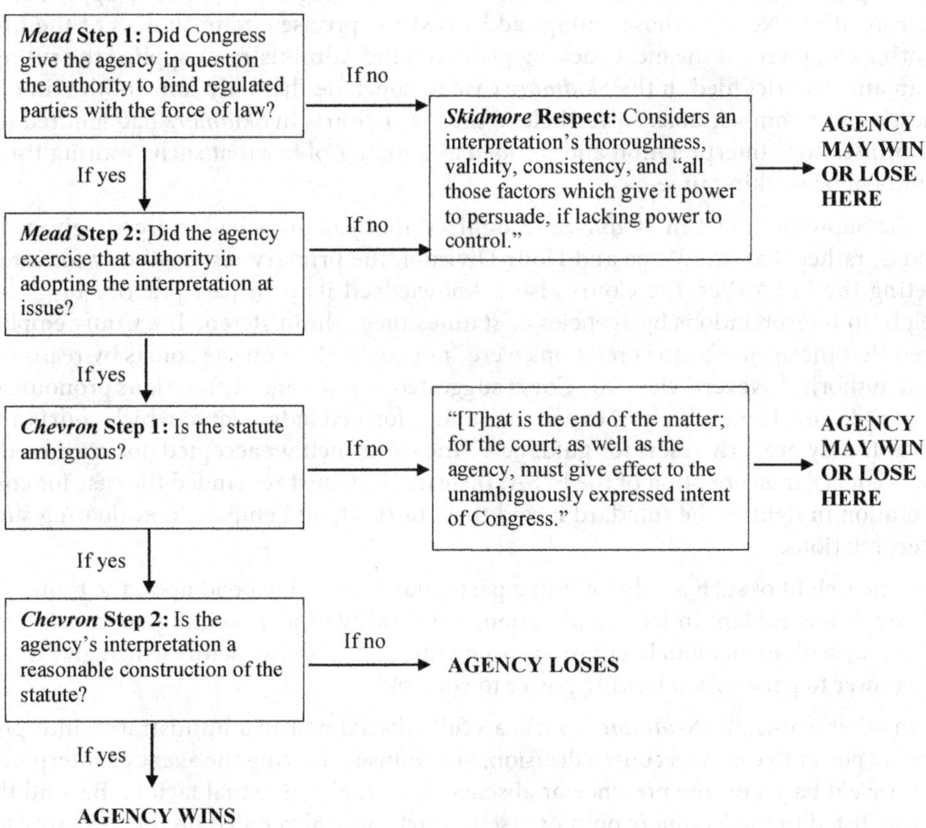

28. 323 U.S. 134 (1944).
29. 467 U.S. 837 (1984).
30. 533 U.S. 218 (2001).

[B] The *Skidmore* Standard

Skidmore v. Swift & Co.[31] involved a challenge to a rule issued by the Department of Labor's Wage and Hour Division. When Congress enacted the Fair Labor Standards Act (FLSA) in 1938, it expressly declined to give the Administrator of the Department of Labor's Wage and Hour Division the power to adopt legally-binding rules and regulations. But Congress assigned the Wage and Hour Division a variety of other administrative powers, functions, and responsibilities, including the authority to bring enforcement actions in court. The performance of those responsibilities gave the Wage and Hour Division extensive expertise respecting matters covered by the FLSA. In exercising its duties, the agency must resolve questions about the FLSA in order to determine how to enforce it.

As a matter of statutory interpretation, the *Skidmore* case itself concerned whether the time that fire-fighting employees of a meat packing plant spent on call for fire alarms constituted "working time" for which the employees were owed overtime pay under the FLSA. The Administrator of the Wage and Hour Division had issued informal rulings applying the statute in various scenarios and advocating a case-by-case approach to interpretation. None of those rulings addressed the precise circumstances of the fire-fighting employees at the meat packing plant, but the Administrator applied the rulings in an amicus brief filed in the *Skidmore* case to conclude that only some of the time in question was compensable. Nevertheless, the lower courts in *Skidmore* had ignored the Administrator's interpretation and decided as a matter of law that such "waiting time" could not be working time.

The Supreme Court in *Skidmore* recognized that Congress had expressly given the courts, rather than the Wage and Hour Division, the primary responsibility for interpreting the FLSA. Yet, the Court also acknowledged its own past practice of giving weight to interpretations by agencies of statutes they administered. The Court emphasized that the agency's interpretations were "not controlling on the courts by reason of their authority." Nevertheless, the Court suggested that the agency's various pronouncements "do constitute a body of experience and informed judgment to which courts and litigants may properly resort for guidance." The Court neither accepted nor rejected the lower courts' interpretation of the FLSA. Instead, the Court remanded the case for consideration in light of the standard it said that courts should employ in evaluating such interpretations:

> The weight of such a judgment in a particular case will depend upon the thoroughness evident in its consideration, the validity of its reasoning, its consistency with earlier and later pronouncements, and all those factors which give it power to persuade, if lacking power to control.[32]

In other words, the *Skidmore* Court carefully disclaimed an administrative interpretation's power to *control* a court's decision, but counseled giving the agency's interpretation *weight* based on the presence or absence of several contextual factors. Beyond the factors listed in the *Skidmore* opinion itself, courts have also relied on the formality (or lack thereof) of the procedures an agency used in adopting a particular interpretation[33]

---

31. 323 U.S. 134 (1944).
32. *Id.* at 140.
33. *See, e.g., United States v. Mead Corp.*, 533 U.S. 218 (2001); *In re Bernard L. Madoff Investment Securities LLC*, 779 F.3d 74 (2d Cir. 2015); *Doe v. Leavitt*, 552 F.3d 75 (1st Cir. 2009); *Tualatin*

and whether the agency's interpretation was longstanding[34] or adopted contemporaneously with the enactment of the statutory text being interpreted.[35] In some cases, courts have considered whether and to what extent the particular agency interpretation at issue really is the product of the agency's core expertise.[36] The Court has never explained, however, how to evaluate each of the factors it identified, what other factors to consider, how the factors relate to one another, or how much weight reviewing courts should accord to each factor.

Another open question regarding *Skidmore* review is whether deference under the *Skidmore* standard requires a threshold finding of statutory ambiguity. As discussed below, the first step of the alternative *Chevron* standard requires a court to evaluate for itself whether the meaning of the statute is clear using traditional tools of statutory interpretation. In describing the *Chevron* standard, the Court has been quite adamant that both agencies and courts are bound to follow the clearly expressed intent of Congress.[37] The same principle would seem to be appropriate in the context of *Skidmore* analysis.

Many federal circuit courts cases have applied the *Skidmore* standard as if it required a finding of statutory ambiguity.[38] Nevertheless, the Court has never expressly required a separate finding of ambiguity before applying *Skidmore*'s contextual factors to determine whether deference is appropriate. In *Catskill Mountains Chapter of Trout Unlimited, Inc. v. U.S. Environmental Protection Agency*,[39] a panel of the United States Court of Appeals for the Second Circuit disagreed over the extent to which *Skidmore* review requires a threshold finding of statutory ambiguity.

The *Catskill Mountains Chapter* case concerned the validity of the EPA's Water Transfer Rule, and both the majority and dissenting opinions agreed that the fact that the agency had promulgated a notice-and-comment regulation meant that *Chevron* rather than *Skidmore* provided the appropriate standard of review. Nevertheless, because the agency's interpretation was a longstanding one, and the court had previously applied the *Skidmore* standard in rejecting the same interpretation when it was expressed in a mere policy statement, both the majority and dissenting opinions discussed the question of whether those earlier decisions implicitly contained a finding of statutory ambiguity. The panel majority said that the court's earlier decisions applying *Skidmore* did not conclusively declare the relevant statutory language to be either ambiguous or unambiguous. Although courts "will defer to the agency's interpretation under the *Skidmore* standard only when the statutory language at issue is ambiguous," the majority said that courts could reject an agency's interpretation under *Skidmore* "without answering this threshold question by considering the statutory text as one of several factors relevant to

Valley Builders Supply, Inc. v. United States, 522 F.3d 937 (9th Cir. 2008); *Structural Industries, Inc. v. United States*, 356 F.3d 1366 (Fed. Cir. 2004); *Ebbett v. DaimlerChrysler Corp.*, 319 F.3d 103 (3d Cir. 2003).

34. *See, e.g., Alaska Department of Environmental Conservation v. Environmental Protection Agency*, 540 U.S. 461 (2004); *Smith v. Aegon Cos. Pension Plan*, 769 F.3d 922 (6th Cir. 2014); *Hagans v. Commissioner of Social Security*, 694 F.3d 287 (3d Cir. 2012).

35. *See, e.g., Hayes v. Harvey*, 903 F.3d 32 (3d Cir. 2018); *Wong v. Doar*, 571 F.3d 247 (2d Cir. 2009); *Cathedral Candle Co. v. U.S. International Trade Comm'n*, 400 F.3d 1352 (Fed. Cir. 2005).

36. *See, e.g., Hall v. Environmental Protection Agency*, 273 F.3d 1146 (9th Cir. 2001).

37. *See Chevron*, 467 U.S. at 842–43.

38. *See* Kristin E. Hickman & Matthew D. Krueger, *In Search of the Modern* Skidmore *Standard*, 107 Colum. L. Rev. 1235 (2007) (making this finding based on a study of *Skidmore* cases).

39. 846 F.3d 492 (2d Cir. 2017).

determining whether the agency interpretation has the 'power to persuade.'" Dissenting, Judge Denny Chin rejected outright the notion that *Skidmore* review includes a threshold finding of statutory ambiguity.

[C] The *Chevron* Standard

In *Chevron U.S.A. Inc. v. Natural Resources Defense Council, Inc.*,[40] the Supreme Court articulated a new two-step standard for courts to apply when evaluating an agency's interpretation of a statute the agency administers:

> When a court reviews an agency's construction of the statute it administers, it is confronted with two questions. First, always, is the question of whether Congress has directly spoken to the precise question at issue. If the intent of Congress is clear, that is the end of the matter; for the court, as well as the agency, must give effect to the unambiguously expressed intent of Congress. If, however, the court determines Congress has not directly addressed the precise question at issue, the court does not simply impose its own construction on the statute, as would be necessary in the absence of an administrative interpretation. Rather, if the statute is silent or ambiguous with respect to the specific issue, the question for the court is whether the agency's answer is based on a permissible construction of the statute.[41]

To break this language down further, the *Chevron* standard requires a reviewing court to ask two questions: first, whether the statute being interpreted clearly and unambiguously resolved the issue; and if not, whether the agency's interpretation of the statute is permissible, or reasonable.

The single issue in *Chevron* was the proper interpretation of the term "stationary source" as that term is used in the Clean Air Act Amendments of 1977.[42] That statute, as amended, required any company that proposes to create a major new source of air pollutants to go through an elaborate new-source review process. The Environmental Protection Agency (EPA) initially defined "source" for this purpose in a way that subjected virtually any significant addition or modification of a plant, such as the addition of a boiler, to the review process. In 1981, the EPA changed its definition of "source" to refer to an entire plant. Under this much broader definition, a company would be required to go through the review process only if the net effect of all additions, deletions, or modifications proposed at a plant would be an increase in emissions above the specified threshold. Thus, a company could avoid the review process by increasing emissions through an addition to a plant while simultaneously reducing emissions by a corresponding amount through other modifications to the same plant. This change in definition of a statutory term was part of EPA's decision to embrace the "bubble concept," which was intended to give company management greater control over specific decisions affecting air quality as long as the total impact of a plant on air quality was not adversely affected by those decisions.

The Natural Resources Defense Council (NRDC) challenged the EPA's new definition of source before the D.C. Circuit Court of Appeals. That court reasoned that the

40. 467 U.S. 837 (1984).

41. *Id.* at 842–43.

42. Pub. L. No. 95-95, 91 Stat. 685 (1977).

language and legislative history did not conclusively resolve what Congress meant by "source," but the court reversed the agency's interpretation anyway on the ground that it was inconsistent with the court's own precedents interpreting the word "source" and evaluating the bubble concept in the context of the Clean Air Act and its goals.[43]

The Supreme Court unanimously reversed the D.C. Circuit and affirmed the EPA's new definition of "source." The Court agreed with the lower court that neither the language nor the legislative history of the Clean Air Act resolved the interpretive question at hand, but said that also meant that Congress did not make the policy decision underlying the choice between the possible meanings of source. Hence, the EPA's choice of definitions reflected a pure policy decision in an area in which Congress delegated to the EPA power to make such policy decisions.

The Supreme Court admonished the D.C. Circuit for attempting to make the policy decision at issue. It emphasized that judges "are not part of either political branch of the Government" and "have no constituency." When Congress has not made a policy decision itself, but has delegated that decision to an agency, that agency can "properly rely upon the incumbent administration's views of wise policy to inform its judgments." In the Court's words,

> While agencies are not directly accountable to the people, the Chief Executive is, and it is entirely appropriate for this political branch of the Government to make such policy choices—resolving the competing interests which Congress itself either inadvertently did not resolve, or intentionally left to be resolved by the agency charged with the administration of the statute in light of everyday realities.[44]

In *Chevron*, the Court also carefully explained its understanding of the relationship between congressional enactment of statutes delegating power to agencies and judicial review of agency policy decisions made through the process of giving meaning to ambiguous language in those statutes.

> The power of an administrative agency to administer a congressionally created ... program necessarily requires the formulation of policy and the making of rules to fill any gap left, implicitly or explicitly, by Congress. If Congress has explicitly left a gap for the agency to fill, there is an express delegation of authority to the agency to elucidate a specific provision of the statute by regulation. Such legislative regulations are given controlling weight unless they are arbitrary, capricious, or manifestly contrary to the statute. Sometimes the legislative delegation to any agency on a particular question is implicit rather than explicit. In such a case, a court may not substitute its own construction of a statutory provision for a reasonable interpretation made by the administrator of an agency.
>
> We have long recognized that considerable weight should be accorded to an executive department's construction of a statutory scheme it is entrusted to administer, and the principle of deference to administrative interpretations has been consistently followed by this Court whenever decision as to the meaning or reach of a statute has involved reconciling conflicting policies, and a full understanding of the force of the statutory policy in the given situation

43. *Natural Resources Defense Council, Inc. v. Gorsuch*, 685 F.2d 781 (D.C. Cir. 1982).

44. *Chevron*, 467 U.S. at 865–66.

has depended upon more than ordinary knowledge respecting the matters subjected to agency regulations.[45]

The Court's analysis in its *Chevron* decision was extensive. Nevertheless, as lower courts started to apply the two-part standard derived from that analysis, many questions emerged regarding its two steps.[46]

[1] *Chevron* Step One

The *Chevron* standard's first step calls upon reviewing courts to evaluate for themselves whether the meaning of the statute is clear or ambiguous regarding the interpretive question. For this purpose, however, how clear is clear enough for a court to resolve statutory meaning at *Chevron* step one? How ambiguous is ambiguous enough to require a court to move on to *Chevron*'s second step? What should the step one inquiry look like?

The *Chevron* opinion itself is far from clear on this point. Initially, the Court described the initial inquiry as "whether Congress has *directly spoken* to the *precise* question at issue." A few sentences later, the Court said that, "[i]f ... the court determines Congress has not *directly* addressed the precise question at issue, the court does not simply impose its own construction on the statute."[47] Taking these two sentences alone would suggest that *Chevron*'s first step is both highly textualist and narrowly tailored, requiring the statute to be quite specific in answering the interpretive question. Yet, few questions of statutory interpretation that rise to the Supreme Court or even a federal circuit court of appeals are likely to be addressed directly and expressly in the statutory text without further inquiry. Consequently, framing *Chevron* step one in this way would result in the vast majority of statutory interpretation cases proceeding rapidly to *Chevron* step two.

In between the two sentences highlighted above, however, the Court said in *Chevron* that, "[i]f *the intent of Congress* is clear, that is the end of the matter; for the court, as well as the agency, must give effect to *the unambiguously expressed intent of Congress*."[48] In interpreting statutes, courts routinely rely on a broad collection of canons and other tools, including legislative history and statutory purpose, to glean congressional intent from facially ambiguous statutory text. In a footnote to this sentence, the Court specified the judiciary as "the final authority on issues of statutory construction" and declared, "[i]f a court, *employing traditional tools* of statutory construction, ascertains that *Congress had an intention* on the precise question at issue, *that intention* is the law and must be given effect."[49] With these words, the *Chevron* Court suggested a substantially more robust, and potentially more purposivist, step one inquiry. Yet, courts often have found themselves disagreeing over whether particular interpretive tools, like legislative

45. *Id.* at 843–44 (ellipses in original, but citations and quotation marks omitted).

46. *See, e.g.*, Nicholas R. Bednar & Kristin E. Hickman, Chevron*'s Inevitability*, 85 Geo. Wash. L. Rev. 1932 (2017); Richard M. Re, *Should* Chevron *Have Two Steps?*, 89 Ind. L.J. 605 (2014); Matthew C. Stephenson & Adrian Vermeule, Chevron *Has Only One Step*, 95 Va. L. Rev. 597 (2009); Gary Lawson, *Outcome, Procedure and Process: Agency Duties of Explanation for Legal Conclusions*, 48 Rutgers L. Rev. 313 (1996); Thomas W. Merrill, *Textualism and the Future of the* Chevron *Doctrine*, 72 Wash. U. L.Q. 351 (1994).

47. *Id.* at 842-43 (emphasis added).

48. *Id.* (emphasis added).

49. *Id.* at 843, n.9 (emphasis added).

history[50] or substantive canons like the rule of lenity[51] or constitutional avoidance,[52] should be taken into account in evaluating statutory clarity at step one.

Finally, at the end of the same paragraph as those other sentences from the *Chevron* opinion, the Court rephrased step one as whether "the statute is *silent or ambiguous* with respect to the specific issue."[53] This language seemed to equate statutory silence regarding a particular interpretive question with statutory ambiguity. Certainly, in some cases, textual silence is indicative of ambiguity.[54] Such was the case in *Chevron* itself, as the Court found ambiguity in the fact that neither the Clean Air Act's text nor its history offered even the merest hint of congressional intent regarding the interpretive question at issue. Yet, although legislatures sometimes will incorporate exceptions from statutory requirements explicitly in statutory text, legislatures do not commonly construct statutes by expressly excluding everything under the sun that is not included. As a result, the post-*Chevron* jurisprudence has seen the emergence of the "elephants in mouseholes" canon: "Congress ... does not alter the fundamental details of a regulatory scheme in vague terms or ancillary provisions—it does not, one might say, hide elephants in mouseholes."[55] Yet, precisely when statutory silence shifts from ambiguity to clarity, or vice versa, remains ill-defined at best.

[2] *Chevron* Step Two

The Supreme Court rarely rejects agency interpretations of statutes at *Chevron* step two, nor has it been very explicit in articulating what the step two inquiry entails. In the *Chevron* opinion itself, the Court first said with respect to step two that "the question for the court is whether the agency's answer is based on a *permissible* construction of the statute." In a footnote to that sentence, the Court elaborated that a reviewing court "need not conclude that the agency construction was the only one it *permissibly* could have adopted to uphold the [agency's] construction." In the next paragraph, however, the Court used slightly different rhetoric to describe the deference owed to "express delegation[s] of authority" versus "implicit" ones. The former are to be "given controlling weight unless they are *arbitrary, capricious, or manifestly contrary to the statute,*" while the latter warrant deference if "*reasonable.*"[56] Is permissible the same as arbitrary

50. Most federal circuit courts will consider legislative history at *Chevron* step one. *See, e.g., Sierra Club v. U.S. Environmental Protection Agency*, 793 F.3d 656 (6th Cir. 2015); *BNSF Railway Co. v. United States*, 775 F.3d 743 (5th Cir. 2015); *Kingdomware Technologies, Inc. v. United States*, 754 F.3d 923 (Fed. Cir. 2014); *Sumpter v. Secretary of Labor*, 763 F.3d 1292 (11th Cir. 2014). But the United States Courts of Appeals for the Third and Seventh Circuits do not. *See, e.g., Coyomani-Cielo v. Holder*, 758 F.3d 908 (7th Cir. 2014); *United States v. Geiser*, 527 F.3d 288 (3d Cir. 2008).

51. *See, e.g., Esquivel-Quintana v. Lynch*, 810 F.3d 1019 (6th Cir. 2016) (Sutton, J., concurring in part and dissenting in part).

52. For example, the majority and dissenting opinions in *Morales-Izquierdo v. Gonzales*, 486 F.3d 484 (9th Cir. 2007) (en banc), debate this question.

53. *Chevron*, 467 U.S. at 843 (emphasis added).

54. *See, e.g., Yellow Transportation, Inc. v. Michigan*, 537 U.S. 36 (2002); *see also* Nathan Alexander Sales & Jonathan H. Adler, *The Rest Is Silence:* Chevron *Deference, Agency Jurisdiction, and Statutory Silences*, 2009 U. Ill. L. Rev. 1497 (identifying cases in which agencies claimed statutory silence gave them the power to regulate).

55. *Whitman v. American Trucking Ass'ns*, 531 U.S. 457 (2001); *see also, e.g., American Bar Ass'n v. Federal Trade Comm'n*, 430 F.3d 457 (D.C. Cir. 2005); Jacob Loshin & Aaron Nielson, *Hiding Nondelegation in Mouseholes*, 62 Admin. L. Rev. 19 (2010).

56. *Chevron*, 467 U.S. at 843-44 (emphasis added).

and capricious or reasonable?[57] What precisely does *Chevron* step two require a reviewing court to do? How should courts apply step two?

To a great extent, one's perception of the scope of *Chevron*'s second step turns on one's view of step one analysis. For example, if a reviewing court pursues a relatively limited inquiry at *Chevron*'s first step and moves on to step two simply because the statutory text on its face does not provide a ready answer to the question at bar, then assessing the reasonableness of the agency's interpretation at step two might entail an evaluation of legislative history and statutory purpose. By contrast, if a court engages in a robust step one inquiry and concludes that the statute is truly ambiguous only after considering all of the statutory text and purpose, legislative history, and the applicability of various canons of construction, then what is left for the court to do at *Chevron* step two?

Some cases seem to suggest that *Chevron* step two refers only to a judicial conclusion that the agency's interpretation of a statute is within the range of meanings the statutory language can support in an abstract, linguistic sense. Sometimes statutory language is sufficiently ambiguous to support many agency interpretations but not the particular agency interpretation at issue. One might describe such an interpretation as an impermissible construction of an ambiguous statute that should be invalidated at *Chevron* step two.

The Supreme Court's decision in *AT&T Corp. v. Iowa Utilities Board*[58] arguably illustrates this approach. The case concerned an effort by the Federal Communications Commission (FCC) to implement the Telecommunications Act of 1996, which sought to facilitate market competition in telephone service by requiring incumbent local service providers to share their networks with potential competitors. The relevant statutory language required FCC to determine which network elements the incumbent providers should make available by evaluating whether access was "necessary" and whether lack of access would "impair" the prospective competitor's ability to provide service. The rule FCC adopted required incumbent providers to make all their network elements available to prospective competitors. A word like "necessary" is obviously open to more than one reasonable interpretation. In evaluating the FCC's rule under the *Chevron* standard, the Court acknowledged that the statutory language was broad enough to allow the FCC to adopt more than one approach to determining network element availability. Nevertheless, the Court concluded that the statute's use of words like "necessary" and "impair" suggested that some limitation on network element availability was necessary, and thus that the FCC's limitless rule was an impermissible interpretation of the statute. "Because the [FCC] has not interpreted the terms of the statute in a reasonable fashion, we must vacate [the rule]."

On the other hand, construing *Chevron* step two as a purely linguistic inquiry that asks only whether an agency's interpretation is within the range of meanings that the statutory language can support arguably renders *Chevron*'s two steps indistinguishable

57. Commentators at times have disagreed over whether these formulations are interchangeable or establish different standards for different types of interpretations. *See, e.g.*, J. Lyn Entrikin Goering, *Tailing Deference to Variety with a Wink and a Nod to* Chevron: *The Roberts Court and the Amorphous Doctrine of Judicial Review of Agency Interpretations of Law*, 36 J. Legis. 18 (2010); Christopher M. Pietruszkiewicz, *Discarded Deference: Judicial Independence in Informal Agency Guidance*, 74 Tenn. L. Rev. 1 (2006).

58. 525 U.S. 366 (1999).

from another. If the agency's interpretation of a statute is clearly wrong, then is the meaning of the statute not clear, at least as regards that particular interpretation?

Another strand of jurisprudence expands the *Chevron* step two inquiry to overlap with the standard for determining whether an agency policy decision is "reasonable," rather than "arbitrary and capricious," stemming from the Supreme Court's decision in *Motor Vehicle Manufacturer's Ass'n v. State Farm Mutual Automobile Insurance Co.*,[59] discussed below in § 13.07 of this Chapter. In the *State Farm* decision, the Supreme Court held that an agency policy decision is reasonable, rather than arbitrary and capricious, if but only if the agency made the decision through a process of *reasoned decisionmaking.*

For many years, scholars and courts have argued that step two of *Chevron* either incorporates or is synonymous with *State Farm* review.[60] Since at least the 1990s, many federal circuit court opinions reflect the approach of blending *Chevron* step two and *State Farm*. More recently, a series of Supreme Court opinions have suggested the same, although without a lot of explanation or elaboration.[61]

[D] *Chevron* "Scope" Issues

Administrative law covers an enormous range of subject matters. Agencies give meaning to ambiguous language in the statutes they administer using a wide variety of procedures and formats. The potential options include, but are not limited to, legislative rules, formal and informal adjudications, interpretative rules, policy statements, enforcement manuals or guidelines, staff instructions, opinion letters, and litigating positions.[62]

Lower courts have often struggled to decide when to apply *Chevron*'s two-step standard.[63] Within a decade of the *Chevron* decision, its two-part standard for evaluating agency interpretations of statutes had begun to dominate judicial decisionmaking in the administrative law space. Consequently, courts and commentators wondered whether and to what extent the new *Chevron* standard had replaced old, pre-*Chevron* standards like *Skidmore*.[64] *Chevron* arose in the context of a legislative rule interpreting the Clean Air Act.[65] To which other agency interpretations should the *Chevron* standard extend?

Several opinions of the Supreme Court have curtailed the scope of *Chevron*'s applicability. Two cases in particular—*Christensen v. Harris County*[66] and *United States v. Mead Corp.*[67]—made clear that many, and perhaps even most, agency statutory interpretations

59. 463 U.S. 29 (1983).

60. *See, e.g.*, Ronald M. Levin, *The Anatomy of* Chevron: *Step Two Reconsidered*, 72 Chi-Kent L. Rev. 1253 (1997); Mark Seidenfeld, *A Syncopated* Chevron: *Emphasizing Reasoned Decisionmaking in Reviewing Agency Interpretations of Statutes*, 73 Tex. L. Rev. 83 (1994).

61. *See Encino Motorcars, LLC v. Navarro*, 579 U.S. 211 (2016); *Michigan v. Environmental Protection Agency*, 576 U.S. 743 (2015); *Judulang v. Holder*, 565 U.S. 42 (2011).

62. The different formats that agencies use are discussed in Chapters 7, 8, and 9.

63. *See, e.g.*, Thomas W. Merrill & Kristin E. Hickman, Chevron*'s Domain*, 89 Geo. L.J. 833 (2001) (documenting more than a dozen different circuit splits and issues confronting lower courts about when to apply the *Chevron* standard).

64. *See, e.g.*, Antonin Scalia, *Judicial Deference to Administrative Interpretations of Law*, 1989 Duke L.J. 511; Peter H. Schuck & E. Donald Elliott, *To the* Chevron *Station: An Empirical Study of Federal Administrative Law*, 1990 Duke L.J. 984.

65. *Chevron U.S.A. Inc. v. Natural Resources Defense Council, Inc.*, 467 U.S. 837 (1984).

66. 529 U.S. 576 (2000).

67. 533 U.S. 218 (2001).

are eligible only for *Skidmore*'s multifactor analysis, rather than *Chevron*'s arguably more deferential standard. Another case, *King v. Burwell*,[68] carved out a class of cases involving major questions that the Court said were beyond the scope of *Chevron*'s applicability. Yet, other cases have expanded *Chevron*'s scope. For example, in *National Cable & Telecommunications Ass'n v. Brand X Internet Services*,[69] the Supreme Court said that, in some instances, an agency's interpretation of an ambiguous statute should receive deference even over a prior court decision interpreting the statute differently. Each of these cases is discussed below.

[1] *Chevron* versus *Skidmore* for Informal Agency Actions

Christensen concerned an interpretation of the Fair Labor Standards Act (FLSA) advanced by the Acting Administrator of the Department of Labor's Wage and Hour Division, first in an opinion letter sent to the respondent and subsequently in an amicus brief to the Court by the Solicitor of Labor. Notably, the *Skidmore* case had concerned the same statute and the same kinds of agency formats, making the case a particularly interesting vehicle for examining the scope of *Chevron*'s applicability and the continued validity of *Skidmore*'s multi-factor standard.

In an opinion written by Justice Clarence Thomas, a five-justice majority stated that *Chevron* deference applies only to "a formal adjudication or notice-and-comment rulemaking" and that "*Chevron*-style deference" is not warranted for statutory interpretations announced in "opinion letters" as well as "policy statements, agency manuals, and enforcement guidelines, all of which lack the force of law." The majority said that interpretations announced in documents of those types are due only a lesser "respect" described in the *Skidmore* decision. Applying *Skidmore*, the majority then rejected the interpretation of the FLSA announced in the Wage and Hour Division's opinion letter and the Labor Solicitor's amicus brief as "unpersuasive."

The *Christensen* decision did not initially garner much attention, maybe because Justice Thomas's opinion represented a mere five-justice majority, or perhaps because the Court quickly signaled its intention to revisit the question of *Chevron*'s scope the following term in the *Mead* case. In *Mead*, with Justice Souter writing for an eight-justice majority, the Court held that tariff classification ruling letters issued by the U.S. Customs Service were eligible only for *Skidmore* review, not *Chevron* deference. In reaching that conclusion, the Court stated its holding broadly:

> We hold that administrative implementation of a particular statutory provision qualifies for *Chevron* deference when it appears that Congress delegated authority to the agency generally to make rules carrying the force of law, and that the agency interpretation claiming deference was promulgated in the exercise of that authority.[70]

In other words, the Court identified two elements that must be satisfied before *Chevron* provides the appropriate standard for evaluating agency interpretations of statutes: first, that Congress gave the agency the authority to act with legal force; and second, that the agency exercised that power in interpreting the statute—*i.e.*, acted with legal force. If

68. 576 U.S. 473 (2015).
69. 545 U.S. 967 (2005).
70. *Mead Corp.*, 533 U.S. at 226–27.

either of these requirements is not met, the Court in *Mead* said that the *Skidmore* standard would apply instead.

Elaborating its holding, the *Mead* Court noted that "the overwhelming number of our cases applying *Chevron* deference have reviewed the fruits of notice-and-comment rulemaking or formal adjudication." It acknowledged, however, the possibility of "some other indication of a comparable congressional intent" to delegate the requisite power to act with legal force, and also that "we have sometimes found reasons for *Chevron* deference even when no such administrative formality was required and none was afforded." For the latter point, the Court cited as an example *NationsBank of North Carolina N.A. v. Variable Annuity Insurance Co.*,[71] in which the Court had extended *Chevron* deference to an informal adjudication by the Comptroller of the Currency interpreting the National Bank Act.

Regardless, the *Mead* Court declined to extend *Chevron* deference to the tariff classification ruling letters at issue in the case before it—also an informal adjudication—for three reasons. First, the Courts found no indication Congress intended to delegate power to the agency to issue classification rulings with the force of law. Second, classification rulings rarely state reasons, have no effect on third parties, and have no precedential effect on the agency. Finally, 46 scattered offices of the U.S. Customs Service issue 10,000 to 15,000 classification rulings per year. Unlike most classification rulings, the ruling at issue had been issued at the highest level of the Customs Service, was accompanied by a statement of reasons, and had precedential effect on the agency. Nevertheless, the Court said "none of the relevant statutes recognizes this category of rulings as separate or different from the others." Instead, the Court analogize the tariff classification ruling letters to "interpretations contained in policy statements, agency manuals, and enforcement guidelines," citing *Christensen*.

Justice Antonin Scalia was the sole dissenter from the Court's decision in *Mead*, and his dissent was scathing. Justice Scalia's view, which he expressed in *Christensen* as well, was that *Chevron* replaced the *Skidmore* standard altogether. He thought that *Chevron* deference should be available to any agency pronouncement, including a Customs Service classification ruling, as long as the agency's interpretation is "authoritative" and reflects the agency's "fair and considered judgment on the issue." He derided *Skidmore* as "th' ol' 'totality of the circumstances' test," "an empty truism," as well as an "anachronism." He predicted that the *Mead* standard would produce confusion in both Supreme Court and lower court decisionmaking, and also "an artificially induced increase in informal decisionmaking," as well as "the ossification of large portions of our statutory law."

Justice Scalia's opinion notwithstanding, post-*Mead* jurisprudence has not been quite so fragmented. Before deciding *Mead*, the Supreme Court deferred to a several agency interpretations of statutes advanced through informal agency formats. Post-*Mead*, except for one highly-formalized but technically informal adjudication,[72] the Court has only applied the *Chevron* standard in evaluating legislative rules adopted through notice-and-comment rulemaking and formal adjudications.[73]

71. 513 U.S. 251 (1995).

72. *United States v. Eurodif S.A.*, 555 U.S. 305 (2009).

73. *See* Kristin E. Hickman & Aaron L. Nielson, *Narrowing* Chevron*'s Domain*, 70 DUKE L.J. 931 (2021).

[2] Major Questions Doctrine

The Supreme Court established another exception from the *Chevron* standard, known as the major questions doctrine, in 2015 in *King v. Burwell*.[74] In *King*, the Court considered an Internal Revenue Service (IRS) interpretation of a Patient Protection and Affordable Care Act (ACA) provision codified into the Internal Revenue Code. The provision in question authorized tax credits for health insurance policies purchased on "an Exchange established by the State," which the IRS interpreted as including health insurance exchanges established by the federal government in addition to exchanges established by state governments.[75] In an opinion authored by Chief Justice John Roberts, the Court agreed with the IRS's interpretation and upheld the regulation advancing it. Yet, the Court rejected arguments claiming the IRS's interpretation was eligible for *Chevron* deference.

In *King*, the Court acknowledged that it usually applies the *Chevron* standard in evaluating an agency's interpretation of a statute that the agency administers. The Court determined, however, that *King* was an "extraordinary case" in which "there may be reason to hesitate before concluding that Congress has intended" to delegate to the agency the authority to resolve the interpretive question as a matter of regulatory policy choice. According to the Court,

> The tax credits are among the Act's key reforms, involving billions of dollars in spending each year and affecting the price of health insurance for millions of people. Whether those credits are available on Federal Exchanges is thus a question of deep economic and political significance that is central to this statutory scheme; had Congress wished to assign that question to an agency, it surely would have done so expressly. It is especially unlikely that Congress would have delegated this decision to the *IRS*, which has no expertise in crafting health policy of this sort. This is not a case for the IRS.[76]

Reviewing the case de novo, the Court acknowledged that the provision in question, when considered alone, was ambiguous. But the Court found that the statute's "broader structure" clarified that ambiguity in favor of the IRS's interpretation.

Justice Antonin Scalia issued a dissenting opinion in *King* in which he described the Court's analysis as "absurd," and accused the Court of rewriting the statute. Notably, however, Justice Scalia never mentioned *Chevron* or questioned the Court's decision not to utilize the *Chevron* standard in evaluating the IRS's interpretation.

Although the major questions doctrine is most closely associated with the *King* decision, the Court's analysis in that case drew inspiration from the opinion for the Court authored by Justice Sandra Day O'Connor several years prior in *Food and Drug Administration v. Brown & Williamson Tobacco Corp.*[77] *Brown & Williamson* concerned whether the Food, Drug, and Cosmetic Act authorized the Food and Drug

---

74. 576 U.S. 473 (2015). For academic analysis of the major questions doctrine, see, *e.g.*, Cass R. Sunstein, *There Are Two "Major Questions" Doctrines*, 73 Admin. L. Rev. 475 (2021); Michael Coenen & Seth Davis, *Minor Courts, Major Questions*, 70 Vand. L. Rev. 777 (2017); Kent Barnett & Christopher J. Walker, *Short-Circuiting the New Major Questions Doctrine*, 70 Vand. L. Rev. En Banc 147 (2017); Kristin E. Hickman, *The (Perhaps) Unintended Consequences of* King v. Burwell, 2015 Pepp. L. Rev. 56.

75. 26 U.S.C. § 36B.

76. *Id.* at 485–86 (emphasis in original; internal quotation marks and citations omitted).

77. 529 U.S. 120 (2000).

Administration (FDA) to regulate tobacco advertising—authority the FDA had denied for decades that it possessed, until reversing course and adopting politically-controversial regulations asserting that nicotine was a "drug" and that cigarettes and smokeless tobacco were "drug delivery devices" as defined in the statute. The Court rejected the FDA's interpretation at *Chevron* step one, concluding that "Congress has directly spoken to the issue here and precluded FDA's jurisdiction to regulate tobacco products" based on statutory context and legislative history. At the end of her opinion for the Court, however, Justice O'Connor offered as a passing final thought that *Chevron* review might not be applicable in some instances.

> Deference under *Chevron* to an agency's construction of a statute that it administers is premised on the theory that a statute's ambiguity constitutes an implicit delegation from Congress to the agency to fill in the statutory gaps. *In extraordinary cases*, however, there may be reason to hesitate before concluding that Congress has intended such an implicit delegation.
>
> This is hardly an ordinary case.[78]

Justice O'Connor went on to suggest that what made *Brown & Williamson* extraordinary was the FDA's several decades of rejecting the very interpretive authority it was then asserting, as well as tobacco's "unique place in American history and society" and "unique political history." Under such circumstances, the Court declared itself "confident that Congress could not have intended to delegate a decision of such economic and political significance to an agency in so cryptic a fashion."

Notwithstanding these decisions, the federal circuit courts have not shown great interest in entertaining arguments that subsequent agency interpretations are similarly extraordinary, and thus ineligible for *Chevron* deference. Most circuit court applications of *King* thus far seem to interpret the Supreme Court's reasoning in that decision merely as a reminder that courts can and should engage in a robust application of traditional tools of statutory interpretation to discern statutory meaning and congressional intent at *Chevron* step one.[79]

In *American Lung Ass'n v. Environmental Protection Agency*,[80] the United States Court of Appeals for the District of Columbia Circuit rejected a creative argument by the Environmental Protection Agency (EPA) that the major questions doctrine justified interpreting the Clean Air Act as limiting its discretion to regulate carbon-dioxide emissions from power plants. The case concerned a challenge to the EPA's Affordable Clean Energy (ACE) rule, adopted during the Trump administration to replace the Obama administration's more robust Clean Power Plan with a more limited approach to regulating the emissions. In litigation, the EPA claimed that the major questions doctrine supported its narrower interpretation of the statute because the Clean Power Plan, by interpreting the EPA's statutory discretion more broadly, "would have had 'billions of dollars of impact on regulated parties and the economy,' would have 'affected every electricity customer,' was 'subject to litigation involving almost every State,' and would have upset the balance of regulatory authority between federal agencies and the states." The court of appeals rejected that argument on the ground that both Congress and judicial precedent had recognized the EPA's broad authority under the Clean Air Act.

---

78. *Id.* at 159 (emphasis added).

79. *See, e.g.*, *Castraneda v. Sousa*, 810 F.3d 15 (1st Cir. 2015) (en banc); *ClearCorrect Operating, LLC v. International Trade Comm'n*, 810 F.3d 1283 (Fed. Cir. 2015).

80. 985 F.3d 914 (D.C. Cir. 2021).

[3] *Brand X* and Stare Decisis

The relationship between *Chevron* deference and stare decisis is important and complicated. For many years after the Supreme Court decided *Chevron*, signals from the courts were mixed regarding the implications for stare decisis in statutory interpretation cases.[81]

In *National Cable & Telecommunications Ass'n v. Brand X Internet Services*,[82] the Supreme Court squarely addressed the stare decisis issue and other, related aspects of *Chevron*'s scope. The question before the Court was whether to uphold a determination by the Federal Communications Commission (FCC), adopted through notice-and-comment rulemaking, that broadband cable internet services were not "telecommunications services" subject to common carrier regulation under the Communications Act, but rather were "information services," which are less regulated. Before the FCC issued its rule, the United States Court of Appeals for the Ninth Circuit had concluded in a different case that the broadband services were telecommunications services. When regulated parties challenged the FCC's rule, the Ninth Circuit rejected the FCC's interpretation on the basis that it was inconsistent with existing circuit precedent. With extensive reasoning, the Supreme Court reversed the Ninth Circuit and extended *Chevron* deference to the FCC's interpretation of the statute.

The Court in *Brand X* announced and applied two important principles in upholding the FCC's rule. First, the Court held that *Chevron* deference trumps stare decisis when an agency-administered statute is ambiguous and the judicial precedent in question merely upholds an agency construction as reasonable or announces a court's preferred construction without consideration of an agency interpretation. Because the Ninth Circuit precedent at issue in this case fell in the latter of those two categories, the Supreme Court held that the court of appeals should have evaluated the FCC's rule using the *Chevron* standard, rather than relying on contrary circuit precedent and stare decisis. According to the Court,

> A court's prior judicial construction of a statute trumps an agency construction otherwise entitled to *Chevron* deference only if the prior court decision holds that its construction follows from the unambiguous terms of the statute and thus leaves no room for agency discretion. This principle follows from *Chevron* itself. *Chevron* established a "presumption that Congress, when it left ambiguity in a statute meant for implementation by an agency, understood that the ambiguity would be resolved, first and foremost, by the agency, and desired the agency (rather than the courts) to possess whatever degree of discretion the ambiguity allows." Yet, allowing a judicial precedent to foreclose an agency from interpreting an ambiguous statute, as the Court of Appeals assumed it could, would allow a court's interpretation to override an agency's. *Chevron*'s premise is that it is for agencies, not courts, to fill statutory gaps. The better rule is to hold judicial interpretations contained in precedents to the same demanding *Chevron* step one standard that applies if the court is reviewing the agency's construction on a blank slate: Only a judicial precedent holding that the statute

---

81. *See, e.g.*, Richard J. Pierce, Jr., *Reconciling* Chevron *and Stare Decisis*, 85 Geo. L.J. 2225 (1997) (documenting early judicial efforts to resolve conflicts between *Chevron* and stare decisis).
82. 545 U.S. 967 (2005).

unambiguously forecloses the agency's interpretation, and therefore, contains no gap for the agency to fill, displaces a conflicting construction.[83]

Second, the Supreme Court in *Brand X* reaffirmed the principle that a court must defer to an agency's reasonable construction of an ambiguous provision of an agency-administered statute even though the agency has adopted inconsistent interpretations over time. As the Court noted in *Brand X*, such was the situation in *Chevron* itself, where the Court deferred to an Environmental Protection Agency regulation that changed the agency's prior interpretation of the term "stationary source" in the Clean Air Act, notwithstanding that the court of appeals had upheld the prior interpretation.[84] As the Court explained in *Brand X*,

> Agency inconsistency is not a basis for declining to analyze the agency's interpretation under the *Chevron* framework. Unexplained inconsistency is, at most, a reason for holding an interpretation to be an arbitrary and capricious change from agency practice under the Administrative Procedure Act.[85]

Justice Stevens wrote a brief concurring opinion in *Brand X* adding the "caveat" that the Court's holding in that case "would not necessarily be applicable to" the Court's own decisions. The issue of the relationship between *Chevron* deference and stare decisis in connection with decisions of the Supreme Court came up subsequently in *United States v. Home Concrete & Supply, LLC*.[86]

The substantive issue in *Home Concrete* was whether a provision of the Internal Revenue Code that extends the period in which the IRS can assess a deficiency from three years to six years when a taxpayer understates his gross income by more than 25 percent applies when the taxpayer overstates his basis in property to such an extent that the overstatement has the same effect as understating his gross income by 25 percent. The four-justice plurality acknowledged that *Chevron* applied but held that the Court's pre-*Chevron* decision in *Colony, Inc. v. Commissioner*[87] had definitively interpreted the provision, thereby ending the *Chevron* inquiry at step one and precluding the Court from applying the reasoning of *Brand X*.

Both before and after the Supreme Court's decision in *Brand X*, the lower courts generally have done a good job of integrating *Chevron* deference and stare decisis. For the most part, they have recognized that careful analysis of a prior judicial opinion can resolve an apparent conflict between that decision and *Chevron* deference.[88]

[E] Looming Doctrinal Change?

After an extended ascendance in which *Chevron* has seemed at times to overshadow almost everything else in administrative law, the twenty-first century has dealt a series of blows both to the scope of *Chevron*'s applicability and, arguably, the Supreme Court's fealty to *Chevron*'s premise.

---

83. *Id.* at 982–83 (citations omitted).

84. The details of the *Chevron* case are discussed above in § 13.04[C].

85. *Brand X*, 545 U.S. at 981 (citing *Motor Vehicle Mfrs. Ass'n of United States, Inc. v. State Farm Mutual Automobile Insurance Co.*, 463 U.S. 29, 46–57 (1983)). *See* § 13.07.

86. 566 U.S. 478 (2012).

87. 357 U.S. 28 (1958).

88. For an especially thorough analysis of circuit precedent in this regard, see *National Labor Relations Board v. Viola Industries–Elevator Division, Inc.*, 979 F.2d 1384 (10th Cir. 1992) (en banc).

One can identify several ways in which the Court arguably has weakened *Chevron* deference in both scope and substance. As described above, with its 2001 decision in *United States v. Mead Corp.*,[89] the Court held that the *Chevron* standard applies only to agency actions carrying the "force of law" pursuant to congressionally-delegated authority, relegating other agency actions like opinion letters, enforcement guidelines, and most informal adjudications to the less deferential *Skidmore* review. In its 2015 decision in *King v. Burwell*, the Court demonstrated its inclination to avoid employing the *Chevron* standard in resolving so-called "major questions."[90]

The Court arguably has exhibited a willingness to apply *Chevron*'s two steps more aggressively as well. For example, the Court has given *Chevron*'s second step greater independent heft by incorporating an expectation of *State Farm*-style reasoned decisionmaking into its assessment of reasonableness into the inquiry.[91]

The Supreme Court's decision in *Perez v. Mortgage Bankers Ass'n*[92] was not a *Chevron* case and did not evaluate the validity of an agency's interpretation of a statute. Nevertheless, writing in concurrence, Justice Antonin Scalia made an interesting statement about the *Chevron* standard and the APA, along with interpretative rules and deference to agency interpretations of regulations under the controlling weight standard of *Bowles v. Seminole Rock & Sand Co.*[93] and *Auer v. Robbins*,[94] discussed below in § 13.05.

> Heedless of the original design of the APA, we have developed an elaborate law of deference to agencies' interpretations of statutes and regulations. Never mentioning [APA] § 706's directive that the "reviewing court... interpret... statutory provisions," we have held that *agencies* may authoritatively resolve ambiguities in statutes. And never mentioning § 706's directive that the "reviewing court... determine the meaning or applicability of the terms of an agency action," we have—relying on a case decided before the APA—held that *agencies* may authoritatively resolve ambiguities in regulations.
>
> The Court's reasons for resisting this obvious point would not withstand a gentle breeze.[95]

Continuing on, however, Justice Scalia stopped far short of counseling reversal of the *Chevron* standard, settling instead for a call to abandon *Seminole Rock*, *Auer*, and the controlling weight standard.[96] Justice Scalia's concerns about *Chevron* may have arisen in part from his disagreement with the Court's decision in the *Mead* case and his dissatisfaction with how other justices and judges have applied the *Chevron* standard.[97]

---

89. 533 U.S. 218 (2001). The *Mead* decision is discussed at length above in § 13.04[D][1].

90. 576 U.S. 473 (2015). The *King* decision is discussed at length above in § 13.04[D][2].

91. *See Motor Vehicle Manufacturers Ass'n of the United States, Inc. v. State Farm Mutual Automobile Insurance Co.*, 463 U.S. 29 (1983). The *State Farm* decision is discussed at length below in § 13.07. *See also, e.g., Encino Motorcars, LLC v. Navarro*, 579 U.S. 211 (2016); *Michigan v. Environmental Protection Agency*, 576 U.S. 743 (2015); *Judulang v. Holder*, 565 U.S. 42 (2011).

92. 575 U.S. 92 (2015).

93. 325 U.S. 410 (1945).

94. 519 U.S. 452 (1997).

95. *Id.* at 109–11 (Scalia, J., concurring) (emphasis and ellipses in original, but citations omitted).

96. The debate over the validity of the controlling weight standard, and the Court's ultimate resolution of that debate in *Kisor v. Wilkie*, 139 S. Ct. 2400 (2019), are discussed below in § 13.05.

97. *See* Nicholas R. Bednar & Kristin E. Hickman, Chevron*'s Inevitability*, 85 GEO. WASH. L. REV. 1392 (2017).

Nevertheless, Justice Scalia had been known as a champion of *Chevron* deference.[98] Given that, his recognition of the somewhat tenuous link between *Chevron* deference and the APA was remarkable.

Regardless, other justices in recent years have questioned whether *Chevron* deference violates separation of powers principles. Justice Clarence Thomas has suggested as much on several occasions.[99] As a judge on the United States Court of Appeals for the Tenth Circuit, Justice Neil Gorsuch advocated abandoning *Chevron*, characterizing it as "permit[ting] all too easy intrusions on the liberty of the people," although he grudgingly conceded that *Chevron* alone is not quite "the very definition of tyranny."[100] Justice Anthony Kennedy has expressed "concern with the way in which the Court's opinion in [*Chevron*] has come to be understood and applied." He suggested that lower courts too often have performed only "cursory analysis" at *Chevron* step one before deferring, which he said was "an abdication of the Judiciary's proper role in interpreting federal statutes."[101] Justice Samuel Alito accused his colleagues of "simply ignoring *Chevron*" when he thought the Court should have applied the doctrine.[102]

Perhaps even more important than statements from individual justices criticizing *Chevron*, the Supreme Court has not actually applied the *Chevron* standard to defer to an agency interpretation of a statute since its 2016 decision in *Cuozzo Speed Technologies, LLC v. Lee*.[103] In several cases since that time, the Court has suggested that *Chevron* might have applied but for the fact that the Court found the meaning of the statute clear.[104] It has been just as common, however, for the Court simply to resolve statutory interpretation cases without invoking deference doctrine at all, even if the agency asserts it.

Considering these decisions collectively, some commentators have suggested that the *Chevron* review standard may be on the wane.[105] This conclusion is premature.[106] *Chevron* has always been controversial, even before its purported decline. Critics have offered all kinds of reasons why *Chevron* is flawed or misguided. Nevertheless, leaving aside stare decisis and whether *Chevron* meets traditional criteria the Supreme Court has applied when overturning precedents, it seems unlikely that either the Court or Congress will do away altogether with *Chevron*-like deference to agency legal interpretations. For one thing, the common narrative of *Chevron*'s revolutionary rise and dominance of judicial review of administrative action is exaggerated. The sheer volume

---

98. *See, e.g.*, Antonin Scalia, *Judicial Deference to Administrative Interpretations of Law*, 1989 Duke L.J. 511.

99. *See Baldwin v. United States*, 140 S. Ct. 690 (2020) (mem.) (Thomas, J., dissenting from the denial of certiorari); *PDR Network, LLC v. Carlton & Harris Chiropractic, Inc.*, 139 S. Ct. 2015 (Thomas, J., concurring in the judgment); *Cuozzo Speed Technologies, LLC v. Lee*, 579 U.S. 261 (2016) (Thomas, J., concurring); *Michigan v. Environmental Protection Agency*, 576 U.S. 743 (2015) (Thomas, J., concurring).

100. *Gutierrez-Brizuela v. Lynch*, 834 F.3d 1142 (10th Cir. 2016) (Gorsuch, J., concurring).

101. *Pereira v. Sessions*, 138 S. Ct. 2105 (2018) (Kennedy, J., concurring).

102. *Id.* at 2121.

103. 579 U.S. 261 (2016).

104. *See, e.g.*, *Johnson v. Guzman Chavez*, 141 S. Ct. 2271 (2021); *Sturgeon v. Frost*, 139 S. Ct. 1066 (2019); *Wisconsin Central Ltd. v. United States*, 138 S. Ct. 2067 (2018).

105. *See, e.g.*, Nathan Richardson, *Deference Is Dead (Long Live* Chevron*)*, 73 Rutgers U. L. Rev. 441 (2021); Lisa Heinzerling, *The Power Canons*, 58 Wm. & Mary L. Rev. 1933 (2017); Michael Herz, Chevron *Is Dead; Long Live* Chevron, 115 Colum. L. Rev. 1867 (2015).

106. *See* Lisa Schultz Bressman & Kevin M. Stack, Chevron *Is a Phoenix*, 74 Vand. L. Rev. 465 (2021); Nicholas R. Bednar & Kristin E. Hickman, Chevron*'s Inevitability*, 85 Geo. Wash. L. Rev. 1392 (2017).

of cases in which courts must consider agency interpretations of statutes means courts inevitably apply *Chevron* a lot. But for all of the hype and attention, *Chevron* is, first and foremost, just one of several standards of review that courts apply in evaluating agency action. And, because the justices have never been able to agree on precisely how *Chevron* review works, predictions of (or hopes for) *Chevron*'s pending demise fail to take into account that *Chevron* deference, or something much like it, is an inevitable corollary to Congress's longstanding and explicit habit of relying on agencies to exercise substantial policymaking discretion to resolve statutory details. As administrative law's best-known doctrine, *Chevron* has become a convenient scapegoat for those who are unhappy with the administrative or judicial review of agency action more generally.

§ 13.05 Judicial Review of Agency Interpretations of Agency Regulations

Just as congressionally-enacted statutes are often ambiguous, so too, agency regulations that attempt to resolve those statutory ambiguities may themselves prove to be unclear. And, just as agencies adopt regulations to resolve ambiguous statutory language and fill statutory gaps, agencies often issue rulings, orders, or other guidance interpreting those regulations. As discussed above, agency interpretations of statutes are eligible for judicial deference. It stands to reason, therefore, that questions have arisen regarding whether agency interpretations of agency regulations should be eligible for judicial deference as well and, if so, under what circumstances such deference might be appropriate.

[A] Evolution of the Controlling Weight Standard

The Supreme Court in 1945 articulated the standard that, for many years, governed judicial review of agency interpretations of agency regulations. In *Bowles v. Seminole Rock & Sand Co.*,[107] the Court considered the substantive validity of an Office of Price Administration bulletin that interpreted an earlier agency regulation promulgated in the course of administering the Emergency Price Control Act of 1942. In evaluating the bulletin, the Court offered the following:

> Since this involves an interpretation of an administrative regulation a court must necessarily look to the administrative construction of the regulation if the meaning of the words used is in doubt. The intention of Congress or the principles of the Constitution in some situations may be relevant in the first instance in choosing between various constructions. But the ultimate criterion is the administrative interpretation, which becomes of *controlling weight unless it is plainly erroneous or inconsistent with the regulation*.[108]

For many years after the Supreme Court issued its decision in *Seminole Rock*, courts did not pay its controlling weight standard much mind, and applications of the standard were relatively modest and restrained. Starting in the 1960s, the courts gravitated

---

107. 325 U.S. 410 (1945).

108. *Id.* at 413–14 (emphasis added).

toward a more expansive and highly deferential approach to the controlling weight standard described in *Seminole Rock*, turning it more into a rebuttable presumption in favor of judicial deference to agency interpretations of their own regulations.[109]

The Supreme Court's *Chevron* decision governing judicial review of agency interpretations of statutes, discussed above in this Chapter at length, initially raised doubts regarding whether *Seminole Rock*'s controlling weight standard remained relevant for judicial review of agency interpretations of regulations.[110] Post-*Chevron* dissenting opinions in *Thomas Jefferson University v. Shalala*[111] and *Shalala v. Guernsey Memorial Hospital*[112] complaining about vague regulations and unreasonable agency interpretations similarly prompted questions regarding the controlling weight standard's continued validity.[113]

The Court put such questions to rest with its 1997 decision in *Auer v. Robbins*.[114] That case concerned an interpretation of Department of Labor regulations setting forth a "salary-basis test" with several criteria for determining whether certain types of employees are exempt from the Fair Labor Standards Act (FLSA). Many years after the regulations were adopted, Congress amended the FLSA to cover public employees as well as private ones. In the context of a private lawsuit regarding the FLSA's applicability to sergeants and a lieutenant employed by the St. Louis Police Department, the Labor Department filed an amicus brief interpreting the salary-basis test as applying to public employees, but also applying that test as exempting the plaintiff employees in question from FLSA coverage. Citing *Seminole Rock* and the controlling weight standard, the Court deferred to the agency's interpretation of its regulations. "Because the salary-basis test is a creature of the Secretary's own regulations, his interpretation of it is, under our jurisprudence, controlling unless plainly erroneous or inconsistent with the regulation." The Court also rejected an argument that the agency's interpretation was undeserving of controlling weight because it had been communicated in the form of an amicus brief. "The Secretary's position is in no sense a post hoc rationalization advanced by an agency seeking to defend past agency action against attack. There is simply no reason to suspect that the interpretation does not reflect the agency's fair and considered judgment on the matter in question."

For many years after its decision in *Auer v. Robbins*, the Supreme Court on many occasions unquestioningly applied a robust version of the controlling weight standard to defer to agency interpretations of agency regulations.[115] Even where the Court chose

---

109. *See* Sanne H. Knudson & Amy J. Wildermuth, *Unearthing the Lost History of* Seminole Rock, 65 EMORY L.J. 47 (2015); Sanne H. Knudson & Amy J. Wildermuth, *Lessons from the Lost History of* Seminole Rock, 22 GEO. MASON L. REV. 647 (2015).

110. *See, e.g.*, Russell L. Weaver & Thomas A. Schweitzer, *Deference to Agency Interpretations of Regulations: A Post-*Chevron *Assessment*, 22 MEM. ST. U. L. REV. 411 (1992).

111. 512 U.S. 504 (1994).

112. 514 U.S. 87 (1995).

113. *See, e.g.*, John F. Manning, *Constitutional Structure and Judicial Deference to Agency Interpretations of Agency Rules*, 96 COLUM. L. REV. 612 (1996).

114. 519 U.S. 492 (1997).

115. *See, e.g.*, *Coeur Alaska, Inc. v. Southeast Alaska Conservation Council*, 557 U.S. 261 (2009); *Federal Express Corp. v. Holowecki*, 552 U.S. 389 (2008); *National Ass'n of Home Builders v. Defenders of Wildlife*, 551 U.S. 644 (2007); *Long Island Care at Home, Ltd. v. Coke*, 551 U.S. 158 (2007); *Washington State Department of Social & Health Services v. Guardianship Estate of Keffeler*, 557 U.S. 371 (2003); *Christensen v. Harris County*, 529 U.S. 576 (2000).

not to defer to the agency's interpretation, it nevertheless continued to recognize the controlling weight standard as appropriate more generally.[116]

Nevertheless, another characteristic of the Court's applications of the controlling weight standard was its occasional identification of the circumstances in which it would not evaluate an agency's interpretation of its regulations under that standard. For example, in *Gonzales v. Oregon*,[117] a majority of the Court declined to apply the controlling weight standard in evaluating an Attorney General interpretation of the Controlled Substances Act on the ground that the regulation in question did "little more than restate the terms of the statute itself." According to the Court, "An agency does not acquire special authority to interpret its own words when, instead of using its expertise and experience to formulate a regulation, it has elected merely to paraphrase the statutory language." Subsequently, in *Christopher v. SmithKline Beecham Corp.*,[118] the Court offered an extensive synthesis and summary of different limiting principles that governed the applicability of the controlling weight standard:

> Although [the controlling weight standard] ordinarily calls for deference to an agency's interpretation of its own ambiguous regulation, ... this general rule does not apply in all cases. Deference is undoubtedly inappropriate, for example, when the agency's interpretation is "plainly erroneous or inconsistent with the regulation." And deference is likewise unwarranted when there is reason to suspect that the agency's interpretation "does not reflect the agency's fair and considered judgment on the matter in question." This might occur when the agency's interpretation conflicts with a prior interpretation, or when it appears that the interpretation is nothing more than a "convenient litigating position," or a "post hoc rationalization" advanced by an agency seeking to defend past agency action against attack.
>
> In this case, there are strong reasons for withholding the deference that [the controlling weight standard] generally requires. Petitioners invoke the [agency's] interpretation of ambiguous regulations to impose potentially massive liability on respondent for conduct that occurred well before the interpretation was announced. To defer to the agency's interpretation in this circumstance would seriously undermine the principle that agencies should provide regulated parties "fair warning of the conduct a regulation prohibits or requires." Indeed, it would result in precisely the kind of "unfair surprise" against which our cases have long warned.[119]

[B] *Kisor v. Wilkie*

In 2011, Justice Antonin Scalia caught many people by surprise when he wrote a concurring opinion in *Talk America, Inc. v. Michigan Bell Telephone Co.*[120] questioning whether the Court should continue to support the controlling weight standard. The case concerned an interpretation by the Federal Communications Commission (FCC) of its own regulations as articulated in an amicus brief filed by the Solicitor General

116. *See Norfolk Southern Railway Co. v. Shanklin*, 529 U.S. 344 (2000).
117. 546 U.S. 243 (2006).
118. 567 U.S. 142 (2012).
119. *Id.* at 155–56.
120. 564 U.S. 50 (2011).

before the Supreme Court. The Court concluded that neither the relevant statute nor any FCC regulation expressly resolved the question at bar. Consistent with its past practice, the Court accepted the FCC's interpretation of its own regulations as advanced in its amicus brief as controlling, noting that it reflected the agency's "fair and considered judgment on the matter in question" and was not "plainly erroneous or inconsistent with the regulations."

Concurring in the Court's *Talk America* decision, Justice Scalia commented that he saw no need to rely on the controlling weight standard at all because he thought the agency's interpretation was "the fairest reading" of its regulations. He added, however, that while he had "in the past uncritically accepted" the controlling weight standard, he had "become increasingly doubtful of its validity."

In questioning the controlling weight standard, Justice Scalia in *Talk America* cited with apparent approval the work of Prof. John Manning. Manning had argued that courts should not defer to agency interpretations of ambiguous agency rules because doing so concentrates the power to create law in the form of legally-binding regulations in the same governmental hands as the power to interpret that same regulatory text. Such concentration, according to Manning, violates separation of powers principles. "[T]he agency lawmaker has effective control of the exposition of the legal text that it has created," with the result that deferring to agency interpretations of agency regulations "leaves in place no independent interpretive check on lawmaking by an administrative agency."[121] In his *Talk America* concurrence, Justice Scalia indicated his agreement with Manning's argument and stated that he "would be receptive to" a request to reconsider *Auer* in an appropriate future case.

Justice Scalia's concurrence in *Talk America* was the first in a series of concurring and dissenting opinions in which several justices indicated their interest in reconsidering whether the Court should continue to apply the controlling weight standard. In *Decker v. Northwest Environmental Defense Center*,[122] Justice Scalia authored an opinion concurring in part and dissenting in part to express frustration that the Court was "giv[ing] effect to a reading of [Environmental Protection Agency] regulations that is not the most natural one, simply because EPA says that it believes the unnatural reading is right." Declaring that "[e]nough is enough," Justice Scalia this time argued outright and at length that the Court should simply overrule its precedents and divest itself of the controlling weight standard. Chief Justice John Roberts and Justice Samuel Alito concurred separately in *Decker* to express support for reconsidering the controlling weight standard, while contending that the arguments for and against that proposition had not been adequately briefed for the Court to resolve the matter in that case. Subsequently, in *Perez v. Mortgage Bankers Ass'n*,[123] Justices Alito, Scalia, and Clarence Thomas all wrote separate concurring opinions urging the Court to take up and reconsider the controlling weight standard.

Finally, in *Kisor v. Wilkie*,[124] the Supreme Court granted certiorari expressly to consider whether to overturn its prior decisions in *Seminole Rock* and *Auer* and repudiate the controlling weight standard. The Court ultimately retained the standard, but with

121. Manning, *supra* note 112, at 639.
122. 568 U.S. 597 (2013).
123. 575 U.S. 92 (2015).
124. 139 S. Ct. 2400 (2019).

reasoning that has fundamentally changed how the courts approach evaluating agency interpretations of agency regulations.

Justice Elena Kagan wrote the opinion of the Court in *Kisor*, but parts of her opinion represented the views of only a plurality of four justices. In a background section, she offered several examples from lower court cases of ambiguous regulations requiring "a choice between (or among) more than one reasonable reading." She defended judicial deference in such circumstances as based on a presumption about congressional intent that agencies be the primary interpreter of their own regulations. That presumption rests on an assessment that (1) the agency that promulgates a regulation can better evaluate its original intentions, (2) choosing among competing interpretations often entails policy choices that agencies are better suited than courts to make, and (3) judicial deference will promote "the well-known benefits of uniformity in interpreting genuinely ambiguous rules."

Purporting to clarify "mixed messages" in the Court's previous jurisprudence regarding the controlling weight standard, Justice Kagan identified and described five conditions that must be satisfied before a reviewing court should defer to an agency's interpretation of its own regulations under *Seminole Rock* and *Auer*:

1. the regulation must be "genuinely ambiguous" after a court "exhaust[s] all the 'traditional tools' of construction";
2. the agency's interpretation of the regulation must be "reasonable";
3. the regulatory interpretation in question must be "the agency's 'authoritative' or 'official position,'" as opposed to a "more ad hoc statement";
4. the regulatory interpretation must implicate the agency's substantive expertise; and
5. the regulatory interpretation must reflect the agency's "fair and considered judgment," meaning that it is not merely a "convenient litigating position" or "post hoc rationalization advanced" to "defend past agency action against attack" and does not "create[] 'unfair surprise' to regulated parties" or disrupt expectations.

With that "background," Justice Kagan addressed arguments that the controlling weight standard is inconsistent with the Administrative Procedure Act (APA) and "meaningful judicial review" and that it violates separation of power principles. Her rejection of those arguments relied extensively on her assumption that the controlling weight standard incorporates the above five conditions. She then asserted stare decisis as an important reason for retaining the controlling weight standard, noting that "[d]eference to reasonable agency interpretations of ambiguous rules pervades the whole corpus of administrative law" and that "abandoning *Auer* deference would cast doubt on many settled constructions of rules." Finally, Justice Kagan noted that Congress has the power to overturn the controlling weight standard if it disagrees with the Court's decision. The Court remanded the case to the lower court for reconsideration, essentially so that it could better explain its thinking regarding the agency interpretation at stake in the case in light of the Court's clarifications of the controlling weight standard's requirements.

Justice Neil Gorsuch wrote a long opinion concurring in the judgment in *Kisor* that was joined in all of its principal parts by Justices Thomas and Brett Kavanaugh and joined to a lesser extent by Justice Alito. Justice Gorsuch outlined the history of the controlling weight standard as "really little more than an accident." He contended that the standard is "incompatible with the APA" and "sits uneasily with" the Constitution's

Article III, §1 Vesting Clause. He countered each of Justice Kagan's policy arguments. And he accused Justice Kagan of only "pretending to bow to stare decisis" while "reshaping [the Court's] precedent in new and experimental ways" with her five conditions for deference.

Chief Justice Roberts concurred in part with Justice Kagan's opinion for the Court, agreeing particularly with her assertion of stare decisis as well as her summary of the limitations and conditions on deference under the controlling weight standard. He wrote separately to suggest that, given all of those limitations and conditions, "the distance between the majority and Justice Gorsuch is not as great as it may initially appear" and that the Court's decision in *Kisor* is "distinct from" and does not "touch upon" questions regarding the validity of the *Chevron* standard of review for agency interpretations of statutes.

Finally, Justice Kavanaugh, joined by Justice Alito, concurred separately to agree with Chief Justice Roberts that the various limitations and conditions on deference imposed by the Court meant that the justices are not practically all that far apart. Justice Kavanaugh contended that requiring courts to exhaust traditional tools of statutory interpretation will deny courts "reason or basis to put a thumb on the scale in favor of" agency interpretations. "Formally rejecting *Auer* would have been a more direct approach," but the majority's method "should lead in most cases to the same general destination."

The Supreme Court's decision in *Kisor* has prompted the circuit courts to approach agency claims to deference under the controlling weight standard with greater skepticism as well as a more robust effort to apply traditional tools of statutory interpretation to resolve regulatory meaning for themselves.[125] Nevertheless, judicial deference to agency interpretations of agency regulations under the controlling weight standard continues to be possible, even under *Kisor*'s more rigorous analytical model.[126]

§ 13.06 Judicial Review of Procedural Challenges

Unlike other types of challenges to agency action, the standards applicable to judicial review of procedural challenges are not complicated. The standard that applies can vary, however, depending upon the source of the challenge.

On some occasions, the procedures that an agency must follow are dictated by the Due Process Clauses of the Fifth and Fourteenth Amendments.[127] Since *Marbury v. Madison*,[128] the Supreme Court has claimed for itself the primary responsibility for interpreting constitutional requirements. Consequently, any claim that an agency's procedures failed to satisfy procedural due process requirements will be reviewed by a court de novo.

---

125. *Callahan v. U.S. Department of Health & Human Services*, 939 F.3d 1251 (9th Cir. 2019); *Romero v. Barr*, 937 F.3d 282 (4th Cir. 2019); *Amazon.com, Inc. v. Commissioner of Internal Revenue*, 934 F.3d 976 (9th Cir. 2019).

126. *See, e.g., Laturner v. United States*, 933 F.3d 1354 (Fed. Cir. 2019) (finding all of *Kisor*'s requirements for *Auer* deference to be satisfied and deferring to the agency).

127. Procedural due process is discussed at length in Chapter 5.

128. 5 U.S. (1 Cranch) 137 (1803).

In many instances, procedural challenges assert that an agency failed to follow procedural requirements outlined in the Administrative Procedure Act (APA)—*e.g.*, what APA § 553(b) specifically requires an agency's notice of proposed rulemaking to include, and whether a particular notice of proposed rulemaking complies with those requirements, as interpreted by the courts.[129] The APA is a statute of general applicability and is not administered by any particular agency. Consequently, courts review claims that agencies have failed to comply with APA procedural requirements de novo as well.[130]

Many procedural requirements derive from an agency's organic statute or from agency regulations. Claims that an agency has failed to follow procedural requirements imposed by a statute that the agency administers may be accorded *Chevron* deference in accordance with the principles described above in § 13.04 of this Chapter.[131] Correspondingly, challenges claiming that an agency has not complied with procedural requirements contained in agency regulations may well be reviewed under the principles of *Kisor v. Wilkie* and the controlling weight standard outlined in § 13.05 of this Chapter.[132]

Litigants seeking to challenge agency actions on procedural grounds thus would be well advised to determine the legal source giving rise to the procedural claim in the first place.

§ 13.07 Judicial Review of Agency Policymaking

Section 706(2)(A) of the Administrative Procedure Act (APA) requires that a reviewing court "hold unlawful and set aside agency action, findings, and conclusions found to be... arbitrary, capricious, an abuse of discretion, or otherwise not in accordance with law."[133] This chapter above addressed the arbitrary and capricious standard in the context of adjudicative fact finding by agencies. Another way that courts consider whether an agency action is arbitrary and capricious is by examining the agency's decisionmaking record and determining whether the agency engaged in reasoned decisionmaking.

The requirement that agencies demonstrate reasoned decisionmaking arises from a fairly basic premise. Agencies are supposed to be experts. Congress relies on their expertise and gives them the authority to adapt and act in response to changing conditions. Nevertheless, fundamental fairness demands that agencies act even-handedly, with deliberation, and in reliance on their expertise, rather than hastily or reflexively in response to political pressure or out of animus for particular parties. Improperly-implemented changes in law and policy can do tremendous damage to regulated parties and undermine public confidence in government institutions.

---

129. The procedural requirements imposed by the APA are discussed at length in Chapters 7, 8, and 9.

130. *See, e.g.*, *American Airlines, Inc. v. Department of Transportation*, 202 F.3d 788 (5th Cir. 2000); *Professional Reactor Operator Society v. U.S. Nuclear Regulatory Comm'n*, 939 F.2d 1047 (D.C. Cir. 1991); *Air North America v. Department of Transportation*, 937 F.2d 1427 (9th Cir. 1991).

131. *See, e.g.*, *Dominion Energy Brayton Point, LLC v. Johnson*, 443 F.3d 12 (1st Cir. 2006); *Chemical Waste Management, Inc. v. Environmental Protection Agency*, 873 F.2d 1477 (1989).

132. *See, e.g.*, *Blackmon-Malloy v. U.S. Capitol Police Board*, 575 F.3d 699 (D.C. Cir. 2009); *Crestview Parke Care Center v. Thompson*, 373 F.3d 743 (6th Cir. 2004).

133. 5 U.S.C. § 706(2)(A).

[A] Pre-APA Cases

Although the Supreme Court has linked the expectation that agencies demonstrate reasoned decisionmaking with the APA §706(2)(A) arbitrary and capricious standard, the requirement predates the APA. Perhaps the first early case to lay out the original arbitrary and capricious standard was *Pacific States Box & Basket Co. v. White.*[134] A California manufacturer challenged the validity of an order issued by the Chief of the Oregon Division of Plant Industry prescribing the type, size, and shape of containers to be used in the sale of raspberries and strawberries in Oregon. The Supreme Court upheld the order solely on the basis that there was a plausible factual relationship between the order's stated purpose of avoiding consumer confusion and the provisions of the order. Describing the standard for reviewing the agency's action, the Court said that, "if any state of facts reasonably can be conceived that would sustain [the order], there is a presumption of the existence of that state of facts, and one who assails [that presumption] must carry the burden of showing... that the action is arbitrary."

Subsequently, in *Securities & Exchange Commission v. Chenery Corp.* in 1943, known as *Chenery I,*[135] the Court further emphasized that the agency's explanation of its action must be expressed at the time of the action itself, not later when that action is challenged in litigation. In *Chenery I,* the Supreme Court overturned an SEC order because the Court found the agency's reasoning flawed, and thus inadequate to support the agency's action. The SEC claimed in the order that its action was supported by case law. The Court disagreed. In litigation, but not in the administrative record, the SEC also asserted statutory authority and specialized expertise as justifications for its order. The Court acknowledged that the agency's statutory powers and expertise were sufficient to support the promulgation of a rule that would accomplish the same outcome as the order. Nevertheless, the SEC had not included that rationale for its action in the administrative record, so the Court refused to consider it. According to the Court,

> The grounds upon which an administrative order must be judged are those upon which the record discloses that its action was based.... [T]he considerations urged here in support of the Commission's order were not those upon which its action was based.... Its action must be measured by what the Commission did, not by what it might have done.[136]

[B] The *State Farm* Decision

In 1983, the Supreme Court linked the APA §706(2)(A) arbitrary and capricious standard with the requirement of reasoned decisionmaking requirement in *Motor Vehicle Manufacturers Ass'n of the United States, Inc. v. State Farm Mutual Automobile Insurance Co.*[137] In this case, the Court reviewed the rescission of a Department of Transportation (DOT) standard requiring the inclusion of passive restraints (automatic seat belts or airbags) in all automobiles.[138] In promulgating the original standard (worked out

134. 296 U.S. 176 (1935).

135. 318 U.S. 80 (1943). The *Chenery* cases, including *Chenery I,* are discussed at length in Chapter 6, §6.04.

136. *Id.* at 87, 92–94.

137. 463 U.S. 29 (1983).

138. For a thorough study and analysis of the DOT's efforts to develop standards providing for passive restraints in automobiles, see JERRY MASHAW & DAVID HARFST, THE STRUGGLE FOR AUTO

during the Ford and Carter administrations), the DOT had determined, among many other things, that many people simply were not fastening their seat belts, and that some kind of passenger safety device that did not require any specific action on the part of a car's occupants would be more effective. The DOT waffled over automatic seat belts versus air bags before adopting, by regulation, Standard 208, which allowed manufacturers to choose between the two, so long as they installed one or the other.

President Ronald Reagan campaigned for the presidency on a platform that included reducing government regulation. Early in the Reagan administration, his Secretary of Transportation prompted a rulemaking to rescind Standard 208. After issuing a notice of proposed rulemaking, considering written comments received, and holding oral hearings, the DOT did just that. A number of insurance companies challenged the rescission in court. After granting certiorari, the Supreme Court looked at the entire history of the proceeding—*i.e.*, both the promulgation of Standard 208 and its rescission—and concluded that, while an agency always has the authority to reconsider its policies, it failed in this instance to adequately explain its reasons for doing so.

The DOT predicated its recission of the rule on three key premises. First, new evidence indicated that automobile manufacturers were likely to comply with Standard 208 almost exclusively by installing automatic seat belts, rather than airbags, which was significantly different from the DOT's previous expectations that manufacturers would use more airbags. Second, the DOT anticipated that automatic seat belts were likely to be used only about five percent more frequently than manual seat belts, because of the ease with which the seat belts could be disconnected. Third, and as a result of the first two points, the agency concluded that Standard 208 was likely to save many fewer lives than anticipated, at a high cost. In other words, based on new evidence, the agency decided that the costs did not justify the benefits of Standard 208.

The Court started its analysis by establishing that the DOT's action was reviewable under the APA §706(2)(A) arbitrary and capricious standard. The Court described the standard as "narrow"—*i.e.*, deferential—and that "a court is not to substitute its judgment for that of the agency." The Court went on, however, to describe at some length the nature of the inquiry in terms that suggest more extensive examination of the administrative record.

> Nevertheless, the agency must examine the relevant data and articulate a satisfactory explanation for its action including a "rational connection between the facts found and the choice made." In reviewing that explanation, we must "consider whether the decision was based on a consideration of the relevant factors and whether there has been a clear error of judgment." Normally, an agency rule would be arbitrary and capricious if the agency has relied on factors which Congress has not intended it to consider, entirely failed to consider an important aspect of the problem, offered an explanation for its decision that runs counter to the evidence before the agency, or is so implausible that it could not be ascribed to a difference in view or the product of agency expertise. The reviewing court should not attempt itself to make up for such deficiencies: "We may not supply a reasoned basis for the agency's action that the agency itself has not given." We will, however, "uphold a decision of less than ideal clarity if the agency's path may reasonably be discerned."[139]

Safety (1990).

139. *State Farm*, 463 U.S. at 43 (internal citations omitted).

The Court identified two particular inadequacies in the DOT's explanation of its action. The Court held unanimously that the agency's explanation of its reasons for rescinding Standard 208 was flawed because the agency had not addressed at all the suggested alternative of amending the standard simply to require airbags. Based on the agency's own findings, that alternative would have saved 12,000 lives per year. The Court stated that the agency might have been able to provide an adequate explanation of its decision to reject that alternative, but the agency could not just ignore such an obvious alternative.

The justices divided five to four, however, with respect to another arguable flaw in the DOT's explanation. In concluding that automatic seat belts were likely to increase the incidence of seat belt use by only five percent, the agency discounted the findings of two studies in the rulemaking record indicating that automatic seat belts would be more effective because people inclined not to buckle their seat belts would be equally disinclined to disconnect automatic seat belts. The agency was of the view that the two studies were unreliable because the automatic seat belts that were the subject of those studies were much more difficult to disconnect than the automatic seat belts required by Standard 208. Five justices concluded that the agency's reasoning was inadequate in light of the studies; four justices dissented on that issue. All nine justices agreed that this issue was close to the line between adequate and inadequate reasoning.

As stated and applied in *State Farm*, the reasoned decisionmaking requirement seems to impose on agencies only a modest burden of explanation. Moreover, imposing such a burden on agencies could have important benefits. It is hard to see how courts could fulfill their responsibility to require agencies to act within statutory boundaries without requiring agencies to explain the relationship between their action, the decisional standards in their statutes, and the data on which they base their predictions concerning the effects of their actions.

State Farm's requirement of reasoned decisionmaking looks different, however, from the perspective of an agency that is considering the issuance of a major rule. The agency knows that it must discuss in some manner all obvious and superficially attractive alternatives, all statutory decisional factors, all important aspects of the problem, all major criticisms offered in comments, and the relationship between its predictions concerning the effects of the rule and the data arguably relevant to those predictions. The agency also knows that its discussion of each of those issues must be "adequate." The agency cannot be certain in advance, however, which alternatives, which aspects of the problem, which criticisms offered, or which data it must discuss, or how much discussion of any alternative, aspect, criticism, or data a reviewing court will consider adequate to satisfy the requirement of reasoned decisionmaking. *State Farm* likely tends to raise the cost, complexity, and difficulty of agency rulemaking.

[C] The Scope of *State Farm* Review

The Supreme Court's *State Farm* decision drew from but nevertheless largely replaced pre-*State Farm* jurisprudence concerning reasoned decisionmaking by agencies. Since deciding *State Farm*, the Court on occasion has explored or addressed questions regarding the meaning and scope of *State Farm*'s interpretation of the arbitrary and capricious standard of APA §706(2)(A). Some of those decisions restricted the kinds of questions or analyses that courts may require agencies to pursue in the name of *State Farm* and the arbitrary and capricious standard. Other decisions speak more expansively about *State Farm* and its expectations.

For example, in *Federal Communications Commission v. Fox Television Stations, Inc.*,[140] the Supreme Court made clear that *State Farm* review does not require agencies to satisfy a "heightened standard" of scrutiny when an agency changes its policy or when an agency's action implicates constitutional liberties. The *Fox Television* case concerned an order issued by the Federal Communications Commission (FCC) finding that several of Fox Television's live broadcasts were actionably indecent. The Communications Act, administered by the FCC, prohibits the broadcasting of "an obscene, indecent, or profane language by means of radio communication."[141] The order reflected a change in FCC's prior policy of allowing a "fleeting use" exception from indecency standards, and imposed penalties upon Fox Television Stations for expletives used by celebrities during a live broadcast that would have passed muster under the old policy.

On behalf of a five-justice majority of the Court, Justice Scalia found the FCC's explanation of its order and its policy change adequate. Explaining why *State Farm* does not require a heightened standard for evaluating agency policy changes, Justice Scalia explained,

> [O]ur opinion in *State Farm* neither held nor implied that every agency action representing a policy change must be justified by reasons more substantial than those required to adopt a policy in the first instance....
>
> To be sure, the requirement that an agency provide reasoned explanation for its action would ordinarily demand that it display awareness that it *is* changing position. An agency may not, for example, depart from a prior policy *sub silentio* or simply disregard rules that are still on the books. And of course the agency must show that there are good reasons for the new policy. But it need not demonstrate to a court's satisfaction that the reasons for the new policy are *better* than the reasons for the old one; it suffices that the new policy is permissive under the statute, that there are good reasons for it, and that the agency *believes* it to be better, which the conscious change of course adequately indicates. This means that the agency need not always provide a more detailed justification than what would suffice for a new policy created on a blank slate. Sometimes it must—when, for example, its new policy rests upon factual findings that contradict those which underlay its prior policy; or when its prior policy has engendered serious reliance interests that must be taken into account. It would be arbitrary and capricious to ignore such matters. In such cases it is not that further justification is demanded by the mere fact of policy change; but that a reasoned explanation is needed for disregarding facts and circumstances that underlay or were engendered by the prior policy.[142]

In addition, Justice Scalia made clear that agencies do not have a heightened duty to explain actions that arguably conflict with the Constitution. The FCC's policies regarding fleeting expletives during live broadcasts arguably raised First Amendment concerns. The Court in *Fox Television* acknowledged that the FCC had predicated its prior policies at least partly on its desire to avoid constitutional doubt. The federal circuit courts had divided over whether and to what extent judicial review for reasoned decisionmaking under *State Farm* and the arbitrary and capricious standard should be more stringent when constitutional liberties were at stake. Justice Scalia disagreed,

140. 556 U.S. 502 (2009).
141. 18 U.S.C. § 1464.
142. 556 U.S. at 514–16 (emphasis in original).

holding in essence that questions of constitutionality are simply separate from whether agencies explain their actions adequately.

> The so-called canon of constitutional avoidance is an interpretive tool, counseling that ambiguous statutory language be construed to avoid serious constitutional doubts. We know of no precedent for applying it to limit the scope of authorized executive action. ... If the Commission's action here was not arbitrary or capricious in the ordinary sense, it satisfies the Administrative Procedure Act's "arbitrary and capricious" standard; its lawfulness under the Constitution is a separate question to be addressed in a constitutional challenge.[143]

Another issue that came before the Supreme Court was how much credence courts should give to the explanations that agencies formally provide in the administrative record, as opposed to unexpressed motives suggested by extraneous sources. In *Department of Commerce v. New York*,[144] the Court considered a challenge to a decision by the Secretary of Commerce to include a citizenship question on the 2020 census questionnaire, contrary to the Census Bureau's recommendation that the government instead rely on administrative records alone or, alternatively, develop a data model based on an alternative survey tool to estimate citizenship across the U.S. population. As the Court noted, censuses prior to 2010 asked at least some households about citizenship. Although the 2010 census did not, the Secretary published a memo explaining his decision to reinstate the citizenship question on the 2020 census. In the memo, he analyzed the strengths and weaknesses of the different alternative approaches to measuring citizenship across the population, and he also stated that he was acting in response to a Department of Justice (DOJ) request for assistance in obtaining better citizenship data to aid in Voting Rights Act enforcement. The administrative record included the DOJ's memorandum to that effect, but also included additional documentation reflecting that the Secretary had considered including the question prior to receiving the DOJ's request, and had inquired of the DOJ whether it would support the question's inclusion in the census. Parties challenging the Secretary's decision as arbitrary and capricious under the APA and *State Farm* argued that the Voting Rights Act justification was pretext for the Secretary's desire to manipulate the census for political purposes.

The Court rejected the Secretary's decision to include the citizenship question on the ground that the expressed justification of responding to the DOJ's request for assistance was "incongruent with what the record reveals about the agency's priorities and decisionmaking process." Considering an expansive administrative record that included not only the above-mentioned documentation but also more than 12,000 pages of internal deliberative materials, the Court concluded that the record "reveal[ed] a significant mismatch between the decision the Secretary made and the rationale he provided" and "tells a story that does not match the explanation the Secretary gave for his decision." Accordingly, the Court said that the Secretary's decision violated *State Farm* by failing to adequately explain the reasons for his action.

Dissenting in part from the Court's decision in *Department of Commerce v. New York*, Justices Thomas, Gorsuch, and Kavanaugh expressed grave concern about the majority's rejection of the Secretary's decision on grounds of pretext. They noted the Court's own conclusion that the administrative record did not support a finding of bad

---

143. *Id.* at 516.
144. 139 S. Ct. 2551 (2019).

faith or improper behavior. They contended as well that the Court had never previously "invalidated an agency action as 'pretextual.'" More ominously, they asserted that, "if taken seriously as a rule of decision, this holding would transform administrative law." The dissent continued,

> It is not difficult for political opponents of executive action to generate controversy with accusations of pretext, deceit, and illicit motives. Significant policy decisions are regularly criticized as products of partisan influence, interest group pressure, corruption, and animus. Crediting these accusations on evidence as thin as the evidence here could lead judicial review of administrative proceedings to devolve into an endless morass of discovery and policy disputes not contemplated by the [APA].[145]

They predicted as well that, "[n]ow that the Court has opened up this avenue of attack, opponents of executive actions have strong incentives to craft narratives that would derail them" and that partisans will "use the courts to harangue executive officers through depositions, discovery, delay, and distraction."

Notwithstanding the concerns raised by the dissenters in *Department of Commerce v. New York*, thus far, the lower courts have not seen an explosion of *State Farm* challenges raising concerns about pretextual agency justifications. However, one decision of the United States Court of Appeals for the Ninth Circuit stands out in this regard. In *Transportation Division of the International Ass'n of Sheet Metal, Air, Rail, & Transportation Workers v. Federal Railroad Administration*,[146] the Ninth Circuit considered a challenge to a Federal Railroad Administration (FRA) Order withdrawing a notice of proposed rulemaking proposing a nationwide requirement that trains be staffed with a maximum crew of one person and purporting to preempt state law. The FRA had initiated the rulemaking after two railroad accidents. The agency held a public hearing and considered nearly 1600 comments, the vast majority of which supported "some kind of multiple crew staffing requirement." Nevertheless, after that process was complete, the FRA's Order withdrew the notice of proposed rulemaking and also "provid[ed] notice of [the agency's] affirmative decision that no regulation of train crew staffing is necessary or appropriate for railroad operations to be conducted safely at this time." In its Order, the FRA addressed the comments received and studies submitted, and the court summarized both arguments raised by the commenters and the FRA's response thereto.

What apparently prompted the Ninth Circuit to contemplate whether the FRA's explanation of its Order was pretextual was the court's assessment that the Order "appear[ed] to adopt a one-person train crew rule and purport[ed] to preempt any state safety laws concerning train crew staffing." The court then interpreted the Supreme Court's decision in *Department of Commerce v. New York* as articulating "four steps for reviewing whether an agency's stated reasons for taking action are pretextual" under *State Farm* and the arbitrary and capricious standard.

> First, in order to permit meaningful judicial review, an agency must disclose the basis of its action. Second, in reviewing agency action, a court is ordinarily limited to evaluating the agency's contemporaneous explanation in light of the existing administrative record. Third, a court may not reject an agency's stated reasons for acting simply because the agency might also have had other unstated reasons. Fourth, the Court recognized a narrow exception to

145. *Id.* at 2576 (Thomas, J., dissenting in part).
146. 988 F.3d 1170 (9th Cir. 2021).

> the general rule against inquiring into the mental processes of administrative decisionmakers where there is a strong showing of bad faith or improper behavior.[147]

Purporting to analyzing the Order in those terms, the Ninth Circuit said that the Order did not merely withdraw the notice of proposed rulemaking, as the FRA claimed. Rather, the Order's "real and intended effect [was] to authorize nationwide one-person train crews and to bar any contrary state regulations."

Despite its claim to reject the FRA's Order as pretextual under the four-step approach it drew from *Department of Commerce v. New York*, however, the Ninth Circuit's analysis did not differ fundamentally from other applications of the *State Farm* standard. For example, the court said that the FRA's claim of a lack of reliable statistical data to support the greater safety of multi-person train crews over one-person train crews also did not support the adoption of a one-person train crew rule. The court accused the FRA of failing to address safety concerns raised by commenters. The court also observed that the agency changed its policy "without fully explaining its reasons for doing so." In short, it is unclear from the Ninth Circuit's analysis precisely what framing the FRA's Order as pretextual or describing *Department of Commerce v. New York* as requiring a special four-step inquiry for determining pretext really accomplished that ordinary *State Farm* analysis would not.

---

147. *Id.* at 1178–79 (internal citations and quotation marks omitted).

Chapter 14

Obtaining Government Information

§ 14.01 Introduction

Chapter 4 discussed the process by which government agencies obtain information from the public and from the entities that they regulate. This chapter discusses the reverse of that proposition: the process by which private citizens obtain information from the federal government. Prior to 1966, there was very little a citizen could do to obtain information from the government. The government could give out information voluntarily, and many agencies did so. But there was little consistency among the agencies in terms of what they might or might not willingly disclose. People who were able to sue the government could sometimes obtain information by using litigation discovery techniques against an agency. Some of this discovery might be available through the agency's own rules of discovery in the context of adjudication within the agency. Some of it might be obtained in civil litigation against the government in federal court.

There were a few devices for obtaining information built into the federal administrative system even before the Administrative Procedure Act (APA) was enacted. The Federal Register Act,[1] enacted in the mid-1930s with additional language codified in 1946 as a component of the APA,[2] required agencies to publish in the *Federal Register* a certain amount of material, usually having something to do with proposed and final agency rules. The impetus for the Federal Register Act arose out of *Panama Refining Co. v. Ryan*,[3] one of the major New Deal decisions in which the Supreme Court struck down a portion of the National Industrial Recovery Act. When the solicitor general and some other government attorneys began to write their Supreme Court brief,[4] they discovered that the underlying National Recovery Administration rules had been amended out of existence by a lapse in regulatory drafting. One of the reasons that the lawyers discovered the error so late in the game was the lack of any statutory requirement that agency rules be published in any generally available format. When the lawyers for the government tried to unravel the agency rules, they found the text of those rules in the desk drawers of agency officials. Only after examining the desk drawer copies of the rules did the lawyers learn that the rules did not actually exist because they had been inadvertently repealed.

One unfortunate result of this inadvertent repeal of the National Recovery Administration's rules was that the Supreme Court held that, because the rules did not exist, the Court could not review them for any substantive or procedural deficiencies. This

1. 44 U.S.C. §§1501 *et seq.*
2. Formerly § 3 of the Administrative Procedure Act, Pub. L. No. 79-404, 60 Stat. 237 (1946).
3. 293 U.S. 388 (1935).
4. The case is discussed in Chapter 2.

conclusion might have had a major impact on the ultimate decision had the Supreme Court taken a different approach to the case, because the government argued, among other things, that the rules promulgated by the NRA were reasonable. However, because the Supreme Court held the underlying statute unconstitutional as a violation of the nondelegation doctrine, the lack of any implementing rules had no effect on the outcome of the case. Nevertheless, the intense embarrassment suffered by the executive branch, along with a subsequent uproar in Congress, led to the enactment of the Federal Register Act and the later incorporation of that legislation's publication requirements in both §§ 552 and 553 of the APA.[5]

In 1966, Congress expanded publication requirements for the executive branch with the Freedom of Information Act and amendments thereto.[6] That legislation was followed by the Privacy Act in 1974,[7] the Government in the Sunshine Act in 1976,[8] and the Electronic Freedom of Information Act Amendments of 1996,[9] among other amendments. All of these pieces of legislation addressed ongoing concerns regarding the disclosure and publication of both private and government-produced information by the federal government agencies. Each is discussed below in this Chapter.

Since the enactment of the Regulatory Flexibility Act[10] in 1980, agencies are also required to publish semi-annual regulatory agendas. An agency's regulatory agenda includes a review of rules published by the agency, the status of ongoing rulemaking proceedings and target dates for the completion of the rulemaking activity. Presently, the *Federal Register* and other agency information required to be published under APA § 552(a) comprises a sizeable compendium of agency data especially useful for lawyers with agency business. This published information is easily accessible by mail, in agency reading rooms, or electronically on agency websites, and is automatically released. Persons seeking this information are not required to invoke the more elaborate procedures necessary to process a request under the Freedom of Information Act, the Government in the Sunshine Act, or the Privacy Act. Lawyers new to the federal administrative process should remember that there is an enormous amount of agency information available on a regular basis. Many administrative law neophytes make unnecessary formal requests for information when the data they need is readily at hand in agency publications. This is terribly inefficient lawyering that often proves costly for the client.

§ 14.02 The Freedom of Information Act

[A] Background

Prior to 1966, the Administrative Procedure Act (APA) merely provided, "Except as otherwise required by statute, matters of official record shall be made available, in

5. This story is entertainingly told in Louis L. Jaffe, *An Essay on Delegation of Legislative Power*, 47 COLUM. L. REV. 561 (1947).

6. Pub. L. No. 89-487, 80 Stat. 250 (1966) (codified as amended at 5 U.S.C. § 552).

7. Pub. L. No. 93-579, 88 Stat. 1896 (1974) (codified as amended at 5 U.S.C. § 552a).

8. Pub. L. No. 94-409, 90 Stat. 1241 (1976) (codified as amended at 5 U.S.C. § 552b).

9. Pub. L. No. 104-231, 110 Stat. 3048 (1996) (codified in scattered subsections of 5 U.S.C. § 552).

10. 5 U.S.C. §§ 601–612. *See also* Michelle Goldberg-Cahn, Note, Associated Fisheries of Maine, Inc. v. Daley: *A Balanced Approach to Judicial Review Under the Regulatory Flexibility Act*, 51 ADMIN. L. REV. 663 (1999).

accordance with published rule, to persons properly and directly concerned, except information held confidential for good cause found."[11] Note the elements of the statute: certain matters must be released *by statute* (essentially those matters required to be published under APA § 552(a); there were a handful of other statutes requiring disclosure, but they did not govern access to the vast bulk of agency information).

The requester of the information had to show that he or she was "properly and directly concerned." An agency could refuse access to information if it concluded that the requester had not shown this requisite concern. Even if a requester were directly concerned, the request could be refused if the agency concluded that there was *good cause* for the refusal. The statute also recognized a *public interest* exception (*i.e.*, information could be withheld if non-disclosure was deemed to be in the public interest) to disclosure that was probably the most frequently invoked reason for withholding information. The cumulative effect of the original version of APA § 552 gave the agencies a virtual *carte blanche* to withhold information from whomever they pleased and to set up what amounted to a *de facto* presumption against disclosure. Agencies read § 552 as permitting them to do almost anything they wanted with their data. In other words, the agencies could release information if they felt like it; otherwise, they could refuse access.

After nearly a decade of debate, Congress enacted the Freedom of Information Act (FOIA), amending APA § 552 to reverse these presumptions against disclosure and to give private persons unprecedented access to government information. FOIA was significantly amended in 1974 to make even more information available, and again in 1996 to require agencies to make more information available electronically. For many reasons, FOIA has been the subject of extensive litigation.

[B] A FOIA Roadmap

FOIA is a long and detailed statute. Someone reading it for the first time can easily become bogged down. Although by no means comprehensive, the following is a basic summary of FOIA's principal elements.

First, FOIA requires agencies to make information available to the public in one of three ways. Section 552(a)(1) requires agencies to publish some types of information in the *Federal Register*, including but not limited to all of the agency's formal and informal procedures, substantive rules, statements of general policy, or interpretations of general applicability. Section 552(a)(2) requires agencies to "make available for public inspection and copying" all final opinions in adjudications, all interpretative rules and policy statements that are not published in the *Federal Register*, and all staff manuals and instructions that affect members of the public. Material required to be published under either of these two provisions cannot be used by the government to affect a member of the public adversely without actual, timely notice.

Section 552(a)(3) contains the third method of publication, for agency records not covered by one of the other two paragraphs. That subsection provides,

> Except with respect to the records made available under paragraphs (1) and (2) of this subsection, each agency, upon request for records which (A) reasonably describes such records and (B) is made in accordance with published rules

11. 5 U.S.C. § 552(d) (repealed 1996).

> stating the time, place, fees (if any), and procedures to be followed, shall make the records promptly available to any person.

This provision of FOIA has accounted for much of the thousands of court opinions resolving FOIA disputes.

All three of the above ways of making information available to the public are subject to nine exemptions specified in § 552(b). Briefly stated, those nine exemptions are as follows:

(1) Matters specifically required by Executive Order to be kept secret in the interest of national defense or foreign policy;

(2) Matters related solely to the internal personnel rules and practices of any agency;

(3) Matters specifically exempted from disclosure by statute;

(4) Trade secrets and commercial or financial information obtained from a person and privileged or confidential;

(5) Inter-agency or intra-agency memoranda or letters which would not be available by law to a private party in litigation with the agency, although this exemption is limited to memoranda that are less than 25 years old;

(6) Personnel and medical files and similar files the disclosure of which would constitute a clearly unwarranted invasion of personal privacy;

(7) Records or information compiled for law enforcement purposes, subject to a number of caveats and limitations;

(8) Information compiled in the process of regulating financial institutions; and

(9) Geological or geophysical information and data, including maps, concerning wells—*i.e.*, oil well data.

The meaning and scope of each of these exemptions has been the subject of litigation as well.

Once you have reviewed the express language of FOIA, the following discussion provides a walk-through of some of the key questions the statute raises. These questions will provide a framework for spotting and resolving FOIA issues.[12]

---

12. The authoritative commercial publication on FOIA is JAMES T. O'REILLY, FEDERAL INFORMATION DISCLOSURE (2021-2), which is updated regularly. There is a mass of law review literature on various aspects of FOIA. In 2018, *Villanova Law Review* convened and published a series of essays commemorating the fiftieth anniversary of FOIA's enactment, including Susan B. Long & Harry Hammitt, *Increased Use of the Freedom of Information Act by the Media: Exploring What Took the Media So Long*, 63 VILL. L. REV. 895 (2018), and Tuan N. Samahon, et al., *The Press, The Academy, and FOIA*, 63 VILL. L. REV. 971 (2018). For other recent examples from the scholarly literature on FOIA, see Margaret B. Kwoka, *FOIA, Inc.*, 65 DUKE L.J. 1361 (2016); Tyler Prime & Joseph Russomanno, *The Future of FOIA: Course Corrections for the Digital Age*, 23 COMM. L. & POL'Y 267 (2018); John C. Brinkerhoff, Jr., *FOIA's Common Law*, 36 YALE J. ON REG. 575 (2019).

§ 14.03 Who May Request Government Information?

[A] Generally

The Freedom of Information Act (FOIA) is clear on this point: *any person* may request information. Note the striking contrast between the unmodified *any person* in FOIA and the much more confined definition (any person *properly and directly concerned*) in the original § 3 of the APA. Even so, there are occasions when *person* must be defined for FOIA purposes. To define *person*, you must leave FOIA itself and go to § 551 of the Administrative Procedure Act (APA) to discover that *person* is "an individual, partnership, corporation, association, or public or private organization *other than an agency* [emphasis supplied]."

Note that this is essentially a residual definition. A *person* appears to be any entity that is capable of making a request and that is not a federal agency. The difficulty with interpreting this term is that it appears in APA § 551, the basic definitional section of the entire APA, rather than as a separate definition in FOIA itself. Nonetheless, there are ways to cope with this problem. Begin with the fundamental purposes of FOIA: to promote as much disclosure of information as possible. Then, recall that FOIA contains a presumption in favor of disclosure. Taken together, the definition of *person* ought to be struck as broadly as possible. Virtually all courts agree, although there is sometimes a question as to whether a foreign government is a person under FOIA. This last issue has been rarely litigated because individuals and law firms are persons within the terms of the Act. A foreign government may simply have its request filed in the name of an entity that is squarely recognized under FOIA.

This broad definition of *person* has other advantages. For law firms, one of the profound benefits of FOIA is that a request may be made in the name of the firm or in the name of an individual employee of a firm. This means that the firm does not have to disclose the identity of the client for whom the request is being made. By contrast, if information were being sought from an agency in the midst of and as part of litigation, the client's name would likely have to be revealed. This is one reason why FOIA has become an important, while confidential, discovery tool for private parties.

[B] Which Agencies Are Subject to FOIA?

Here, as in so many other parts of FOIA, Congress cast as broad a net as possible in favor of disclosure. In contrast to the definition of *person*, FOIA contains its own definition of *agency* that differs in some key respects from the definition of agency in § 551 of the APA. For FOIA purposes, § 552(e) defines *agency* as including independent regulatory commissions, the Executive Office of the President, all other executive departments, all government corporations, and the military. It is now conceded that this definition includes the Central Intelligence Agency (CIA) and the Federal Bureau of Investigation (FBI)—two agencies that now process proportionately more FOIA requests than most other federal agencies. Both of these agencies have asked Congress frequently to create specific exceptions to narrow the range of information that they have to disclose because they deal constantly with highly sensitive national security and criminal material. While the courts have been sympathetic to the special needs of both the CIA and the FBI, Congress has created few special exceptions solely for the benefit of those two agencies. However, merely accepting federal funds does not necessarily convert a private entity into an agency for FOIA purposes.[13] Finally, note that the definition of *agency* includes only entities within the executive branch of government and does not include either Congress or the judiciary.

[C] How and With Whom Do You File a FOIA Request?

No one form exists for making a FOIA request. FOIA requests are generally made in the form of a letter directed to an agency's FOIA officer, although some agencies accept online requests through foiaonline.gov or their own websites. The name of the FOIA officer and the precise address for FOIA requests are published in the *Federal Register* and the *Code of Federal Regulations.* Additional information about making FOIA requests is available online at the government's main FOIA portal, foia.gov.

One of the singular advantages of FOIA is that a requester need give no reasons for making the request. Recall that § 3 of the original APA required an agency to entertain information requests only from a person properly and directly concerned. Prior to FOIA, a requester frequently had to provide a substantial justification for wanting the information. There is no longer such a requirement, and an explanation is no longer necessary. Because no explanation is necessary, many agencies have established Public Information Reading Rooms containing copies of many regularly requested documents that may be read and copied in the reading room. The Electronic Freedom of Information Act Amendments of 1996[14] required agencies to establish *electronic reading rooms* for the same purpose. No formal, written request has to be made to access these documents. If you file a request, you are required, under FOIA, to *reasonably describe* the records sought, and if gathering or photocopying the records takes agency time, you are expected to pay for both copying and search fees.[15]

When FOIA was first passed, it was estimated that the total cost to the Government would be slightly over $150,000 per year, because FOIA is supposed to pay for itself by placing the fee and cost burden on the requesters of information rather than on the agency. It has not worked out that way. Because many agencies waive fees and because fee schedules rarely reflect the actual search and retrieval costs, the costs to many agencies have been far in excess of the original projections. Recent congressional inquiries indicate that FOIA costs agencies millions of dollars each year in processing expenses.

[D] What Documents May Be Requested?

FOIA permits any person to request disclosure of an *agency record.* The term *agency record* is not expressly defined in FOIA or elsewhere in the Administrative Procedure Act. It has fallen to the federal courts to elaborate on what constitutes an agency record.

---

13. *Forsham v. Harris*, 445 U.S. 169, 178–79 (1980).

14. Pub. L. No. 104-231, 110 Stat. 3048 (1996).

15. Congress has issued a handbook on FOIA that contains some sample letters for requesting documents under FOIA: *A Citizen's Guide on Using the Freedom of Information Act and the Privacy Act of 1974 to Request Government Records*, H.R. 109-226 (2005).

The Supreme Court suggested that the term ought to be broadly construed to effectuate the basic purposes of FOIA. In *U.S. Department of Justice v. Tax Analysts*,[16] the Court addressed the question of whether copies of federal district court opinions in the files of the Justice Department constituted agency records that must be disclosed under FOIA. The decisions were sought by the publisher of a tax newsletter; and the Justice Department refused the request on essentially two grounds: (1) that the documents were generated by the courts, and a court is not an *agency* for FOIA purposes; and (2) that the opinions were not initially created by the executive branch, they were not *records* as that term is used in FOIA. Recall that FOIA does not apply to the federal judiciary.

The Supreme Court reviewed its earlier case law and concluded that even court decisions, if they were regularly collected and held by the Justice Department, constituted agency records for FOIA purposes. Among other things, the Court emphasized that an agency resisting disclosure of the records bears the burden of proving that information in its hands is not an agency record. Here, the Justice Department did not meet its burden.

Another issue can arise with regard to the nature of the agency record. Since 1974, FOIA has expressly required that an agency provide a requester with those portions of a record that are not protected from disclosure, even when some other part of the document is protected. In the parlance of FOIA, "[a]ny *reasonably segregable* portion of a record shall be provided ... after deletion of the portions which are [protected]." Eliminating protected data from the entire document is referred to as *redaction* and can be an extremely time consuming and expensive task for the agency. Nonetheless, since 1974, all agencies must redact or must argue that a particular document is not reasonably segregable. Reviewing courts frequently examine documents *in camera* to ascertain whether redaction has been properly carried out.

Yet another problem frequently arises when an agency argues that no part of any of the requested documents may properly be disclosed. Since a 1973 decision by the D.C. Circuit, *Vaughn v. Rosen*,[17] agencies are required to provide a list or an index of the documents (such list is now referred to as a *Vaughn* index) unless the list or index itself may not be disclosed. A *Vaughn* index can be a powerful tool in terms of ascertaining what is in the agency's hands, even if the documents themselves are not disclosable. It has become a principal feature of FOIA activity, particularly in those agencies such as the FBI, CIA and State Department that deal with large amounts of otherwise classified or protected data.

[E] How Long Does an Agency Have to Act on Your Request?

Here we begin to see the teeth Congress put into the Act. Under normal circumstances, until October 1997, an agency had ten days from receipt of an FOIA request to tell the requester (on a *yes* or *no* basis) whether they would honor the request for information. If the answer was no, or only a partial yes, the requester could appeal the denial of access to another level of the agency (the agency's FOIA rules state where and how to take an intra-agency appeal). The agency had twenty days to process the appeal.

16. 492 U.S. 136 (1989).
17. 484 F.2d 820 (D.C. Cir. 1973).

The statutory language was extremely tight, giving the agency very little leeway to avoid compliance with these strict deadlines. If the agency needed extra time to work with field offices or another agency, or if the request was particularly voluminous, the agency could notify the requester in writing that it would pass on her request within an additional ten days beyond the normal ten days for the initial request. The agency, with explanation to the requester, could also obtain a ten-day extension for processing the intra-agency appeal. Given that so many agencies work at a glacial speed in many of their other activities, ten or twenty days for doing anything is not much time. These exceptionally strict time limits showed the seriousness of Congress in enacting FOIA.

If the agency violated any of these deadlines, FOIA expressly provided that the requester was deemed to have exhausted[18] his administrative remedies. The requester could go immediately into federal court to challenge the lack of timely agency action and to pursue the FOIA request directly with the court. The courts were empowered to give the agency more time if the agency could show due diligence and unusual circumstances.

Note that the FOIA provisions establishing time requirements for responding and processing intra-agency appeals applied only to the agency's decision to disclose or to refuse disclosure. These deadlines had nothing to do with how quickly the agency must provide the documents. For most of the lifespan of FOIA, the only provision governing the time in which the agency had to give over the records stated, "[The agency] shall make the records *promptly available*" [emphasis added]. This was a much looser term than the ten- and twenty-day periods specified for passing on requests and, in many cases, had given back to the agency almost everything that was taken away by the ten- and twenty-day deadlines.

In late 1996, Congress finally addressed the problem of delay in the Electronic Freedom of Information Act Amendments (E-FOIA).[19] The E-FOIA amendments permit an agency to handle different FOIA requests on different timetables, rather than merely using a first in/first out schedule. Routine requests may be handled differently from large volume requests. In certain instances, an agency will be required to give expedited processing (defined as processing on an "as soon as practicable" basis) to requests in which the requester makes a showing of compelling need. Of course, if the agency delays excessively, a requester may always seek judicial review for agency action unreasonably delayed, but federal courts are now quite sympathetic to agencies that are heavily burdened with FOIA requests.

[F] How Must a Court Deal with Judicial Review of a Denial?

This is another place where FOIA's pro-disclosure bias is evident. Subject matter jurisdiction is vested in the federal district courts with an exceptionally broad venue provision. Any denial or partial denial of an FOIA request may be taken into a federal district court in the district (1) where the requester resides or has her place of business, or (2) where the records are physically located, or (3) in the District of Columbia. An action is commenced by filing a complaint (often subtitled "Freedom of Information Act Action"). The complaint must be answered within thirty days by the government.

---

18. *See* Chapter 11, § 11.05 for a discussion of exhaustion.

19. Pub. L. No. 104-231, 110 Stat. 3048 (1996) (codified in scattered subsections of 5 U.S.C. § 552).

Recall that the government normally has sixty days to answer a complaint under the *Federal Rules of Civil Procedure.*[20]

To ensure that courts do not delay FOIA cases, FOIA originally provided that FOIA actions were to be given expedited treatment on the court's docket. Of course, this last provision did not work all that well in practice. Many other federal statutes—*e.g.*, some of the civil rights statutes, or the Speedy Trial Act of 1974 (concerning criminal prosecutions)—also require expedited treatment. In 1984, Congress repealed this provision. FOIA lawsuits no longer get expedited treatment.

When an agency denies access to the records or provides only partial release, that denial is to be reviewed by the court on a de novo standard.[21] If the agency contends that the records are protected from disclosure—for example, because the documents contain data involving national security or trade secrets—the court is permitted to examine the documents *in camera* as part of its de novo review. Of course, once again the approach adopted by FOIA sounds better in theory than the *in camera* review process works in practice. Parties are normally not permitted to participate in the *in camera* review; the actual review involves a federal judge sitting in her chambers, without the presence of counsel, and examining the documents. Most federal judges thoroughly detest this burden on their time and avoid *in camera* review whenever possible.

The reviewing court has the power to enjoin the agency from withholding records or to order the production of records properly disclosable under the Act. The court may award attorneys' fees to a private litigant who *substantially prevails* in FOIA litigation, but a request for attorneys' fees must be sought in a separate piece of litigation after the basic FOIA case has been resolved.

[G] What Information Is Protected from Disclosure?

The FOIA case law is voluminous. Most of the reported FOIA cases involve issues of what information is disclosable and what is protected. FOIA itself deals with this aspect of disclosure under the nine separate exemptions summarized above in § 14.02. To reiterate (and shorthand) these exemptions as they are understood in the FOIA case law and among FOIA practitioners, these exemptions cover the following:

1. national security information;
2. internal personnel rules and files;
3. information exempted by separate statute;
4. trade secrets and commercial/financial information;
5. inter-agency and intra-agency memoranda;
6. personnel and medical files, and other files disclosure of which would violate personal privacy;
7. law enforcement and investigation files;

20. *See* Fed. R. Civ. P. 12(b).

21. *See* the scope of review discussion in Chapter 13. In FOIA cases, de novo means that the reviewing court is not bound by any of the assertions or explanations proffered by the agency for refusing disclosure. It may substitute its own judgment as to the propriety of disclosure.

8. data on financial institutions; and
9. oil well data.

In working through these exemptions, the actual language of the statute must be carefully analyzed. Very few types of federal information are categorically protected from disclosure. Many of the exemptions have been amended specifically to overrule court decisions that, in the view of Congress and many commentators, were making it excessively difficult to obtain information.

For example, since 1974, the first exemption protects documents that are, "(A) specifically authorized under criteria established by an Executive Order to be kept secret in the interest of national defense or foreign policy and (B) are in fact properly classified pursuant to such Executive Order." This exemption was rewritten to circumvent some of the more cumbersome aspects of *Environmental Protection Agency v. Mink*,[22] a Supreme Court decision that attempted as a matter of statutory interpretation to create a blanket exemption for all classified documents (*i.e.*, national security materials that bear a classified document stamp) generated and designated as such by the executive branch. This is not to say the Court's interpretation was disingenuous. The original language of FOIA prohibited the disclosure of documents "specifically required by Executive Order to be kept secret in the interest of the national defense or foreign policy." Patsy Mink, a member of Congress, and others asked for agency information on nuclear weapons testing then in the hands of the EPA. The Supreme Court determined that all such documents carried a classified stamp and held that such a stamp ended the court's inquiry. In other words, if a document bore a stamp, the Court held that FOIA allowed it to be kept secret; the Court would not inquire into the propriety of the classification of documents.

Congress reversed the *Mink* decision in 1974 by substantially amending the language of the first FOIA exemption. Note the current language of § 552(b)(1). First, at the time the document is classified, an executive order must exist that provides for classifying national security documents and that specifies the criteria for classifying these documents, for example into categories like *confidential*, *secret*, or *top secret*. Second, the documents in question must have been classified properly according to the substantive criteria established by the executive order, and also must have been classified in a procedurally correct fashion. In other words, a document that is classified only after an FOIA request is received, where the executive order requires classification when the document is created, arguably is not exempt under § 552(b)(1).

A similar analysis must be performed for each of FOIA's exemptions. Congress adopted each exemption for a reason, and each exemption must be given effect consistent with its text, history, and purpose. But simultaneously, the fundamental purpose and presumption of FOIA favor disclosure of information. Recall that the burden of convincing the court that the document should not be disclosed is always on the government.[23] The Supreme Court has stated this requirement by requiring the agency to show that requested records have not been "improperly withheld."[24] The exemptions do overlap. Thus, in defending its decisions not to disclose information, the government frequently invokes more than one exemption because of the stringent burdens on justifying non-disclosure. The agency only has to prevail on one of several exemptions it asserts.

---

22. 410 U.S. 73 (1973).
23. *U.S. Department of Justice v. Tax Analysts*, 492 U.S. 136 (1989).
24. *GTE Sylvania, Inc. v. Consumers Union of the United States*, 445 U.S. 375 (1980).

[H] Some Illustrative FOIA Case Law

[1] Introduction

The federal courts have had a major impact on FOIA. Because Congress adopted the 1974 amendments to FOIA in large part to reverse a number of judicial decisions that Congress regarded as protecting too much information, most FOIA practitioners view pre-1974 cases with caution. Many notable Supreme Court and federal circuit court decisions exist interpreting FOIA. By way of example, three of these cases are described below: *Chrysler Corp. v. Brown*; *National Archives & Records Administration v. Favish*; and *Food Marketing Institute v. Argus Leader Media*.

[2] *Chrysler Corp. v. Brown*[25]

Although perhaps the most obvious users of FOIA requests are litigators, academics, and members of the media, businesses quickly realized that FOIA could provide a gold mine of data on competitors because so many businesses in the United States are subject to comprehensive agency reporting requirements. Because most businesses have no choice in providing information to the government,[26] they would be justifiably concerned that their competitors might use FOIA to obtain access to proprietary information and trade secrets.

On its face, the fourth FOIA exemption, § 552(b)(4), protects from disclosure "trade secrets and commercial or financial information obtained from a person and which is privileged or confidential." Agencies are generally quite sensitive to the release of competitive information. But even if information is protected by one of the FOIA exemptions, agencies may choose not to invoke FOIA. Also, a number of courts have held that if information is disclosed erroneously, it loses its protection under FOIA, even if the disclosure was unintentional.

These problems led a number of companies in the first years of FOIA to bring what came to be known as *reverse-FOIA* lawsuits, by which companies would invoke the jurisdictional provisions of FOIA and ask a federal court to enjoin disclosure of particular information the companies wished to protect. The Supreme Court finally took up the issue in *Chrysler Corp. v. Brown* and decided that, while the issue of industrial espionage was quite sensitive, FOIA does not provide a *jurisdictional* basis for reverse-FOIA litigation.

In reaching its conclusion, the Court took a plain language approach to the statute. Justice Rehnquist, writing for a unanimous Court, determined first that FOIA "is exclusively a disclosure statute." While the Act permits a court to enjoin the withholding of records and to order an agency to make disclosure, nowhere on its face does FOIA give a court express permission to *prohibit* disclosure.

Chrysler argued in the alternative that even if FOIA did not expressly authorize a court to prohibit disclosure, a separate federal statute, the Trade Secrets Act,[27] did provide the courts with the statutory authority to forbid the release of sensitive business information. The Supreme Court disagreed, reasoning that because the Trade Secrets

---

25. 441 U.S 281 (1979).
26. *See* Chapter 4, § 4.05.
27. 18 U.S.C. § 1905.

Act did not create a private right of action, it could not be invoked as a basis for a reverse-FOIA action.[28]

At this point, however, the Court made a minor concession to American business. Even if FOIA or the Trade Secrets Act could not be used as a basis for a reverse-FOIA suit, an agency's act of disclosure was reviewable under § 706 of the Administrative Procedure Act (APA). This conclusion provided the seeds for an alternative route toward halting unauthorized disclosure. If a company is fortunate enough to hear that the agency is about to reveal some of its sensitive data, it is permitted to file a lawsuit challenging the agency decision under some other statute (*e.g.*, the basic federal question jurisdiction provision[29]) and to request, under APA § 702, a stay of agency action pending judicial review.[30] If the stay is issued, and if the company ultimately prevails on its arguments that the disclosure is forbidden under some other statute like the Trade Secrets Act, the documents will not be released. Using the combination of APA §§ 702 and 706 in this way approximates a reverse-FOIA action, even if such a claim cannot be brought under FOIA itself. This alternative necessarily requires continuous monitoring of agency activity to determine whether an agency is considering disclosing a company's sensitive information. Executive branch agencies now also must tell affected companies that information concerning their business practices has become the subject of a FOIA request and permit the affected company to respond before releasing the information.[31]

[3] *National Archives & Records Administration v. Favish*[32]

Favish involves that part of FOIA's seventh exemption, "records or information compiled for law enforcement purposes," and specifically § 552(b)(7)(C), which excuses from disclosure material when disclosure "could reasonably be expected to constitute an unwarranted invasion of personal privacy."[33] In this case, a requester sought records involving the suicide of Vincent Foster, a member of President Clinton's White House staff. Favish was a journalist who sought the release of several color photographs taken at the site of the suicide and including views of Foster's body. The photographs had been taken by the Federal Bureau of Investigation (FBI) as part of its investigation, and the Department of Justice took the position that all FBI criminal investigative sources should be presumed confidential.

On review, the Supreme Court rejected the government's argument, concluding that the proposed presumption of confidentiality would be unduly broad because "[t]he FBI collects information from a variety of individual and institutional sources," and such communications "range from the extremely sensitive to the routine." The Court suggested, however, that it might be receptive to arguments in support of narrower presumptions of confidentiality. "There may well be other generic circumstances in which an implied assurance of confidentiality may be inferred.... We agree that the character of the crime may be relevant.... So too may the source's relation to the crime."

---

28. On the issue of private right of action, the Court worked through the criteria set out in *Cort v. Ash*, 422 U.S. 66 (1975). The Trade Secrets Act, in the Court's judgment, simply did not satisfy the *Cort* criteria.

29. 28 U.S.C. § 1331.

30. *See* the discussion of § 702 in Chapter 10, § 10.04.

31. *See* Exec. Order No. 12,600, 52 Fed. Reg. 23,781 (1987).

32. 541 U.S. 157 (2004).

33. 5 U.S.C. § 552(b)(7)(C).

Regardless, the Court agreed that the photographs in this case were "law enforcement records," having been taken pursuant to an investigation by the FBI. And on the additional question of whether the release of the photos would invade personal privacy, the Court noted that a family such as that of Mr. Foster had a clear interest in protecting itself from "public intrusions long deemed impermissible under the common law and in our cultural traditions." While a family might not necessarily have the same privacy interests as the person whose information is at stake, the family here had a clear interest in protecting the death scene photographs.

As in all other FOIA personal privacy cases, the Court acknowledged the need to balance the privacy issues against the basic presumption in favor of disclosure to conclude that the photos need not be disclosed. In such cases, the requester bears the burden of showing that the public disclosure interests exceed the personal privacy interests. In this case, Favish had not met his burden, and the government was not required to disclose the photos.

[4] *Food Marketing Institute v. Argus Leader Media*[34]

FOIA's fourth exemption, § 552(b)(4), covers "trade secrets and commercial or financial information obtained from a person and privileged or confidential." For several decades, most courts have interpreted the exemption as covering two different but overlapping categories of information: (1) trade secrets, and (2) commercial or financial information obtained from a person and privileged or confidential. If information is not a trade secret, and is not commercial or financial, then it is not exempt from disclosure under this provision.[35] And if information does not fall within the trade secret category, then it must meet all three criteria for inclusion in the commercial or financial category:[36] it must be commercial or financial; it must be obtained from a person (including corporations and foreign governments), as opposed to being generated by the government;[37] and must be within the scope of an evidentiary privilege or confidential.

In *Food Marketing Institute*, the Supreme Court was called upon to resolve a longstanding disagreement over what it meant for commercial or financial information provided to a federal agency to be *confidential*. In its 1974 decision in *National Parks & Conservation Ass'n v. Morton*,[38] the D.C. Circuit had interpreted that term as requiring a demonstration that the persons submitting the information in question would suffer substantial competitive harm if the information were disclosed in response to a FOIA request. Several other circuits followed suit and adopted this requirement as well.

The D.C. Circuit subsequently tried to make a distinction between voluntary and mandatory submissions of allegedly confidential information to an agency, suggesting that information submitted voluntarily would be considered confidential "if it is of a kind that would not customarily be disclosed to the public by the person from whom it

34. 139 S. Ct. 2356 (2019).

35. *See, e.g., Sharyland Water Supply Corp. v. Block*, 755 F.2d 397 (5th Cir. 1985); *Getman v. National Labor Relations Board*, 450 F.2d 670 (D.C. Cir. 1971).

36. *See, e.g., American Airlines, Inc. v. National Mediation Board*, 588 F.2d 863 (2d Cir. 1978); *Brockway v. Department of the Air Force*, 518 F.2d 1184 (8th Cir. 1975); *Washington Research Project, Inc. v. Department of Health, Education & Welfare*, 504 F.2d 238 (D.C. Cir. 1974); *Getman v. National Labor Relations Board*, 450 F.2d 670 (D.C. Cir. 1971).

37. *See, e.g., Stone v. Export-Import Bank of the U.S.*, 552 F.2d 132 (5th Cir. 1977); *Grumman Aircraft Engineering Corp. v. Renegotiation Board*, 425 F.2d 578 (D.C. Cir. 1970).

38. 478 F.2d 705 (D.C. Cir. 1974).

was obtained."[39] The court was concerned that, otherwise, the government might suffer as firms declined to voluntarily disclose information for fear that the information would be released in response to a FOIA request. Critics of this approach argued that the distinction between voluntary and mandatory submissions was illusory because agencies usually have the power to convert voluntary programs into mandatory ones, and also that making such a distinction would encourage agencies to shift to voluntary reporting systems to avoid having to disclose information under FOIA.

The *Food Marketing Institute* case arose when the *Argus Leader*, a newspaper based in South Dakota, filed a FOIA request with the Department of Agriculture seeking the names and addresses of retail stores participating in the Supplemental Nutrition Assistance Program (SNAP), and several years of annual SNAP redemption data on a store-by-store basis. The agency disclosed the requested names and addresses but not the redemption data, contending that the latter was confidential commercial or financial information. At trial, witnesses for the agency offered testimony regarding the competitive harms that would result from disclosure of store-by-store SNAP redemption rates, as the grocery business is highly competitive and actual as opposed to estimated redemption data would enable a store's competitors to refine their sales strategies. The trial court found that disclosure would cause some competitive harm, but not enough harm to be substantial, so ordered disclosure. The circuit court agreed and, moreover, refused the Food Marketing Institute's suggestion that it overturn the substantial competitive harm test.

On review, the Supreme Court unanimously rejected the substantial competitive harm test as contrary to FOIA's text, but the justices disagreed over the proper interpretation of FOIA's fourth exemption. The majority held that information falls within the scope of FOIA exemption four if the information: (1) customarily has been kept private and (2) was provided to the government based on the government's assurance that the information would be kept confidential. The majority concluded that information must satisfy the first of these two conditions, but declined to decide whether the second condition also must be satisfied because the SNAP redemption data in question satisfied both. The concurring justices agreed that requiring proof of *substantial competitive harm* was excessively narrow, but they argued that information should not fall within the scope of exemption four unless its disclosure would "cause *some genuine harm* to an owner's *economic or business interests*."[40] The Court's decision in *Food Marketing Institute* casts doubt on the continuing validity of many of the holdings and the persuasiveness of the reasoning in many past circuit court decisions interpreting FOIA exemption four.

[5] Conclusion

These are not the only important Supreme Court FOIA decisions. They are included here merely as representative examples the Court's consideration of FOIA disputes over time. In general, both the Court and Congress seem to be satisfied with the way FOIA is working. At present, neither the Court nor Congress seems to be of the view that FOIA poses major, unresolvable problems. Undoubtedly changes will come, particularly as the federal government continues its shift from hard copy to electronic data collection

39. *Critical Mass Energy Project v. Nuclear Regulatory Comm'n*, 975 F.2d 871 (D.C. Cir. 1992) (en banc).

40. *Food Marketing Institute*, 139 S. Ct. at 2368 (Breyer, J., concurring in part) (emphasis added).

and recordkeeping. The 1996 enactment of the Electronic Freedom of Information Act Amendments likely were only a first step in that direction. How FOIA will continue to evolve in response to the Internet age remains to be seen.

§ 14.04 The Federal Privacy Act

One reaction to the problems of the Watergate era was the enactment in 1974 of the Privacy Act.[41] The Privacy Act limits agencies' ability to disclose some types of information. It applies only to records regarding individuals, and does not apply to the information of corporations or other organizations. For individuals, the Privacy Act does three things. First, it restricts the manner in which the Government may collect and disseminate personal information. Second, it provides penalties for wrongful disclosure of that information. Third, it gives a person a statutory right to obtain and review information collected on that person and the right for that person to correct, or at least to supplement, information in the file to which the person objects.

The Privacy Act essentially establishes a presumption against disclosure—a policy exactly the opposite of the Freedom of Information Act (FOIA). The Privacy Act also provides exceptions by which certain requesters can obtain data. These exceptions are somewhat like those of FOIA. For example, a system of records can be entered and information retrieved for certain national security and law enforcement purposes. Also, personal data properly redacted may be used for certain statistical and research purposes.

Many sections of the Privacy Act apply only to records maintained as part of a *system of records*, and thus turn on the definition of that term as including only "a group of any records ... from which information is retrieved by the name of the individual or by some identifying number, symbol, or other identifying particular assigned to the individual" like a social security number or tax identification number. While this definition covers a substantial number of government records, it does not reach all personal information in the hands of the federal government. In *McCready v. Nicholson*,[42] the D.C. Circuit held that some provisions of the Privacy Act create a cause of action based on the existence of a record whether or not the record in question is part of a system of records, while other provisions create a cause of action only when a record is kept in a system of records. The court also held that the ability of an outsider to use the search function of an agency's computer records to retrieve information about an individual is irrelevant to a determination that the agency has a system of records—a questionable conclusion, as the search functions of the websites of virtually all agencies now provide each agency with the means to retrieve individual records by name, thereby creating a technological regime in which every agency now has a system of records as the Privacy Act uses that term.

The Privacy Act authorizes both criminal sanctions and civil monetary penalties for violations. Despite this authorization, and notwithstanding the sensitivity of the personal information it addresses, the Privacy Act has not been as heavily litigated as FOIA. In *Doe v. Chao*,[43] the Supreme Court held that an individual can recover damages

41. 5 U.S.C. § 552(a).
42. 465 F.3d 1 (D.C. Cir. 2006).
43. 540 U.S. 614 (2004).

for a violation of the Privacy Act. And in *Federal Aviation Administration v. Cooper*,[44] the Court held that severe emotional distress does not qualify as *actual damages* as the Privacy Act uses that term, so cannot be the basis for a suit for damages under the Privacy Act.

§ 14.05 The Government in the Sunshine Act

In 1976, also in the aftermath of the Watergate scandal, Congress became concerned that too much government decisionmaking was taking place in secret. The Freedom of Information Act (FOIA) requires disclosure of written information held by federal agencies, but no parallel disclosure statute existed requiring agency meetings (where much of the business is transacted orally) to be open to the public. The statute that resulted from this concern, the Government in the Sunshine Act (sometimes also referred to as just the Sunshine Act or the Open Meeting Act),[45] has received a very mixed reception.

Stated briefly, the Sunshine Act requires agencies headed by a collegial body (which includes most major independent agencies) to conduct their meetings in a format that is open to the public. Meeting times and topics are to be published in advance, generally in the *Federal Register.* If the agency wishes to close a meeting, it may do so only by invoking certain specified procedures, and only if that meeting involves a topic that is covered by one of the Sunshine Act's ten exemptions. Many of the Sunshine Act's exemptions are identical to corresponding exemptions from FOIA, although a few are different. For example, the Sunshine Act lacks FOIA's exemption for inter- and intra-agency memoranda and includes an exemption for discussion of matters currently in litigation. Also, the Sunshine Act permits any agency to close a meeting if an open meeting would "be likely to significantly frustrate implementation of a proposed agency action."

The effect of the Sunshine Act's open meeting requirement for agencies headed by multiple members has been significant. By way of example, consider an agency headed by five commissioners. One commissioner stops by the office of another to discuss a difficult issue the agency must address in the near future. If a third commissioner attempts to join the conversation, the three members are in violation of the Sunshine Act, because three or more commissioners can communicate orally only after giving at least one week's public notice of their meeting. Scholars and practitioners alike have lamented that the Sunshine Act's open meeting requirement thus discourages the exchange of ideas among agency members and chills meaningful collective deliberation.[46] Because of the Sunshine Act, agencies headed by multiple members rarely meet and often make important decisions through notational voting with no prior deliberation. Communications at the meetings these agencies do hold are perceived as distorted by the presence of the public, as agency members attempt to disguise their own uncertainty with respect to issues of fact, policy, and law with stilted and contrived discussions. In short, the

---

44. 566 U.S. 284 (2012).

45. 5 U.S.C. § 552b.

46. *See, e.g.*, Randolph May, Recent Development, *Reforming the Sunshine Act*, 49 ADMIN. L. REV. 415 (1997); Ganesh Sitaraman & Ariel Dobkin, *The Choice Between Single Director Agencies and Multimember Commissions*, 71 ADMIN. L. REV. 719 (2019).

idea of open meetings, while healthy in concept, appears to have hindered rather than helped good governance.

The Sunshine Act has seen little significant litigation, even though the statute expressly provides for judicial review. In one important case, *Federal Communications Commission v. ITT World Communications, Inc.*,[47] the Supreme Court clarified the definition of meeting under the Sunshine Act. The statute defines a meeting as "the deliberations of at least the number of individual agency members required to take action on behalf of the agency where such deliberations determine or result in the joint conduct or disposition of official agency business." In this case, three members of the FCC attended "Consultative Process" sessions with their counterparts from Europe and Canada for the purpose of exchanging information on regulatory policies and facilitating joint planning of telecommunications facilities. The FCC has seven members, so the three members who attended the sessions did not represent a quorum. They did, however, represent a quorum of the FCC's Telecommunications Committee. The Court acknowledged that the Sunshine Act can apply to a subdivision of an agency, in addition to the entire agency. As a quorum of the Telecommunications Committee, the three members enjoyed a certain amount of policymaking authority. Nevertheless, the Court found that the Consultative Sessions did not lead to "firm positions on particular matters pending or likely to arise before the [Telecommunications] Committee," but rather merely "provided general background information" for the FCC. Accordingly, the Court held that the Consultative Process sessions were not meetings for purposes of the Sunshine Act.

---

47. 466 U.S. 463 (1984).

Appendix A

Administrative Procedure Act

Title 5, U.S. Code

Chapter 5—Administrative Procedure

Subchapter II—Administrative Procedure

§ 551. Definitions

Freedom of Information Act

§ 552. Public information; agency rules, opinions, orders, records, and proceedings

Privacy Act

§ 552a. Records maintained on individuals

Government in the Sunshine Act

§ 552b. Open meetings

§ 553. Rule making

§ 554. Adjudications

§ 555. Ancillary matters

§ 556. Hearings; presiding employees; powers and duties; burden of proof; evidence; record as basis of decision

§ 557. Initial decisions; conclusiveness; review by agency; submissions by parties; contents of decisions; record

§ 558. Imposition of sanctions; determination of applications for licenses; suspension, revocation, and expiration of licenses

§ 559. Effect on other laws; effect of subsequent statute

Subchapter III—Negotiated Rulemaking Procedure

Negotiated Rulemaking Act

§ 561. Purpose

§ 562. Definitions

§ 563. Determination of need for negotiated rulemaking committee

§ 564. Publication of notice; applications for membership on committees

§ 565. Establishment of committee

§ 566. Conduct of committee activity

§ 567. Termination of committee

§ 568. Services, facilities, and payment of committee member expenses

§ 569. Encouraging negotiated rulemaking

§ 570. Judicial review

§ 570a. Authorization of appropriations

Subchapter IV—Alternative Means of Dispute Resolution in the Administrative Process

Alternative Dispute Resolution Act

§ 571. Definitions

§ 572. General authority

§ 573. Neutrals

§ 574. Confidentiality

§ 575. Authorization of arbitration

§ 576. Enforcement of arbitration agreement

§ 577. Arbitrators

§ 578. Authority of the arbitrator

§ 579. Arbitration proceedings

§ 580. Arbitration awards

§ 581. Judicial review

§ 582. [Repealed]

§ 583. Support services

§ 584. Authorization of appropriations

Chapter 6—The Analysis of Regulatory Functions

§ 601. Definitions

§ 602. Regulatory agenda

§ 603. Initial regulatory flexibility analysis

§ 604. Final regulatory flexibility analysis

§ 605. Avoidance of duplicative or unnecessary analyses

§ 606. Effect on other law

§ 607. Preparation of analyses

§ 608. Procedure for waiver or delay of completion

§ 609. Procedures for gathering comments

Chapter 7—Judicial Review

Chapter 8—Congressional Review of Agency Rulemaking

Other Provisions Pertaining to Administrative Law Judges

Chapter 5—Administrative Procedure

Subchapter II—Administrative Procedure

§ 551. Definitions

For the purpose of this subchapter—

(1) "agency" means each authority of the Government of the United States, whether or not it is within or subject to review by another agency, but does not include—

(A) the Congress;

(B) the courts of the United States;

(C) the governments of the territories or possessions of the United States;

(D) the government of the District of Columbia; or except as to the requirements of section 552 of this title—

(E) agencies composed of representatives of the parties or of representatives of organizations of the parties to the disputes determined by them;

(F) courts martial and military commissions;

(G) military authority exercised in the field in time of war or in occupied territory; or

(H) functions conferred by sections 1738, 1739, 1743, and 1744 of title 12; chapter 2 of title 41; subchapter II of chapter 471 of title 49; or sections 1884, 1891–1902, and former section 1641(b)(2), of title 50, appendix;

(2) "person" includes an individual, partnership, corporation, association, or public or private organization other than an agency;

(3) "party" includes a person or agency named or admitted as a party, or properly seeking and entitled as of right to be admitted as a party, in an agency proceeding, and a person or agency admitted by an agency as a party for limited purposes;

(4) "rule" means the whole or a part of an agency statement of general or particular applicability and future effect designed to implement, interpret, or prescribe law or policy or describing the organization, procedure, or practice requirements of an agency and includes the approval or prescription for the future of rates, wages, corporate or financial structures or reorganizations thereof, prices, facilities, appliances, services or allowances therefor or of valuations, costs, or accounting, or practices bearing on any of the foregoing;

(5) "rule making" means agency process for formulating, amending, or repealing a rule;

(6) "order" means the whole or a part of a final disposition, whether affirmative, negative, injunctive, or declaratory in form, of an agency in a matter other than rule making but including licensing;

(7) "adjudication" means agency process for the formulation of an order;

(8) "license" includes the whole or a part of an agency permit, certificate, approval, registration, charter, membership, statutory exemption or other form of permission;

(9) "licensing" includes agency process respecting the grant, renewal, denial, revocation, suspension, annulment, withdrawal, limitation, amendment, modification, or conditioning of a license;

(10) "sanction" includes the whole or a part of an agency—

(A) prohibition, requirement, limitation, or other condition affecting the freedom of a person;

(B) withholding of relief;

(C) imposition of penalty or fine;

(D) destruction, taking, seizure, or withholding of property;

(E) assessment of damages, reimbursement, restitution, compensation, costs, charges, or fees;

(F) requirement, revocation, or suspension of a license; or

(G) taking other compulsory or restrictive action;

(11) "relief" includes the whole or a part of an agency—

(A) grant of money, assistance, license, authority, exemption, exception, privilege, or remedy;

(B) recognition of a claim, right, immunity, privilege, exemption, or exception; or

(C) taking of other action on the application or petition of, and beneficial to, a person;

(12) "agency proceeding" means an agency process as defined by paragraphs (5), (7), and (9) of this section;

(13) "agency action" includes the whole or a part of an agency rule, order, license, sanction, relief, or the equivalent or denial thereof, or failure to act; and

(14) "ex parte communication" means an oral or written communication not on the public record with respect to which reasonable prior notice to all parties is not given, but it shall not include requests for status reports on any matter or proceeding covered by this subchapter.

Freedom of Information Act

§ 552. Public information; agency rules, opinions, orders, records, and proceedings

(a) Each agency shall make available to the public information as follows:

(1) Each agency shall separately state and currently publish in the Federal Register for the guidance of the public—

(A) descriptions of its central and field organization and the established places at which, the employees (and in the case of a uniformed service, the members) from whom, and the methods whereby, the public may obtain information, make submittals or requests, or obtain decisions;

(B) statements of the general course and method by which its functions are channeled and determined, including the nature and requirements of all formal and informal procedures available;

(C) rules of procedure, descriptions of forms available or the places at which forms may be obtained, and instructions as to the scope and contents of all papers, reports, or examinations;

(D) substantive rules of general applicability adopted as authorized by law, and statements of general policy or interpretations of general applicability formulated and adopted by the agency; and

(E) each amendment, revision, or repeal of the foregoing.

Except to the extent that a person has actual and timely notice of the terms thereof, a person may not in any manner be required to resort to, or be adversely affected by, a matter required to be published in the Federal Register and not so published. For the purpose of this paragraph, matter reasonably available to the class of persons affected thereby is deemed published in the Federal Register when incorporated by reference therein with the approval of the Director of the Federal Register.

(2) Each agency, in accordance with published rules, shall make available for public inspection in an electronic format—

(A) final opinions, including concurring and dissenting opinions, as well as orders, made in the adjudication of cases;

(B) those statements of policy and interpretations which have been adopted by the agency and are not published in the Federal Register;

(C) administrative staff manuals and instructions to staff that affect a member of the public;

(D) copies of all records, regardless of form or format—

(i) that have been released to any person under paragraph (3); and

(ii)

(I) that because of the nature of their subject matter, the agency determines have become or are likely to become the subject of subsequent requests for substantially the same records; or

(II) that have been requested 3 or more times; and

(E) a general index of the records referred to under subparagraph (D);

unless the materials are promptly published and copies offered for sale. For records created on or after November 1, 1996, within one year after such date, each agency shall make such records available, including by computer telecommunications or, if computer telecommunications means have not been established by the agency, by other electronic means. To the extent required to prevent a clearly unwarranted invasion of personal privacy, an agency may delete identifying details when it makes available or publishes an opinion, statement of policy, interpretation, staff manual, instruction, or copies of records referred to in subparagraph (D). However, in each case the justification for the deletion shall be explained fully in writing, and the extent of such deletion shall be indicated on the portion of the record which is made available or published, unless including that indication would harm an interest protected by the exemption in subsection (b) under which the deletion is made. If technically feasible, the extent of the deletion shall be indicated at the place in the record where the deletion was made. Each agency shall also maintain and make available for public inspection and copying current indexes providing identifying information for the public as to any matter issued, adopted, or promulgated after July 4, 1967, and required by this paragraph to be made available or published. Each agency shall promptly publish, quarterly or more frequently, and distribute (by sale or otherwise) copies of each index or supplements thereto unless it determines by order published in the Federal Register that the publication would be unnecessary and impracticable, in which case the agency shall nonetheless provide copies of such index on request at a cost not to exceed the direct cost of duplication. Each agency shall make the index referred to in subparagraph (E) available by computer telecommunications by December 31, 1999. A final order, opinion, statement of policy, interpretation, or staff manual or instruction that affects a member of the public may be relied on, used, or cited as precedent by an agency against a party other than an agency only if—

(i) it has been indexed and either made available or published as provided by this paragraph; or

(ii) the party has actual and timely notice of the terms thereof.

(3)

(A) Except with respect to the records made available under paragraphs (1) and (2) of this subsection, and except as provided in subparagraph (E), each agency, upon any request for records which (i) reasonably describes such records and (ii) is made in accordance with published rules stating the time, place, fees (if any), and procedures to be followed, shall make the records promptly available to any person.

(B) In making any record available to a person under this paragraph, an agency shall provide the record in any form or format requested by the person if the record is readily reproducible by the agency in that form or format. Each agency shall make reasonable efforts to maintain its records in forms or formats that are reproducible for purposes of this section.

(C) In responding under this paragraph to a request for records, an agency shall make reasonable efforts to search for the records in electronic form or format, except when such efforts would significantly interfere with the operation of the agency's automated information system.

(D) For purposes of this paragraph, the term "search" means to review, manually or by automated means, agency records for the purpose of locating those records which are responsive to a request.

(E) An agency, or part of an agency, that is an element of the intelligence community (as that term is defined in section 3(4) of the National Security Act of 1947 (50 U.S.C. 401a(4))[1]) shall not make any record available under this paragraph to—

(i) any government entity, other than a State, territory, commonwealth, or district of the United States, or any subdivision thereof; or

(ii) a representative of a government entity described in clause (i).

(4)

(A)

(i) In order to carry out the provisions of this section, each agency shall promulgate regulations, pursuant to notice and receipt of public comment, specifying the schedule of fees applicable to the processing of requests under this section and establishing procedures and guidelines for determining when such fees should be waived or reduced. Such schedule shall conform to the guidelines which shall be promulgated, pursuant to notice and receipt of public comment, by the

1. Moved to 50 U.S.C. § 3003.

Director of the Office of Management and Budget and which shall provide for a uniform schedule of fees for all agencies.

(ii) Such agency regulations shall provide that—

(I) fees shall be limited to reasonable standard charges for document search, duplication, and review, when records are requested for commercial use;

(II) fees shall be limited to reasonable standard charges for document duplication when records are not sought for commercial use and the request is made by an educational or noncommercial scientific institution, whose purpose is scholarly or scientific research; or a representative of the news media; and

(III) for any request not described in (I) or (II), fees shall be limited to reasonable standard charges for document search and duplication.

In this clause, the term "a representative of the news media" means any person or entity that gathers information of potential interest to a segment of the public, uses its editorial skills to turn the raw materials into a distinct work, and distributes that work to an audience. In this clause, the term "news" means information that is about current events or that would be of current interest to the public. Examples of news-media entities are television or radio stations broadcasting to the public at large and publishers of periodicals (but only if such entities qualify as disseminators of "news") who make their products available for purchase by or subscription by or free distribution to the general public. These examples are not all-inclusive. Moreover, as methods of news delivery evolve (for example, the adoption of the electronic dissemination of newspapers through telecommunications services), such alternative media shall be considered to be news-media entities. A freelance journalist shall be regarded as working for a news-media entity if the journalist can demonstrate a solid basis for expecting publication through that entity, whether or not the journalist is actually employed by the entity. A publication contract would present a solid basis for such an expectation; the Government may also consider the past publication record of the requester in making such a determination.

(iii) Documents shall be furnished without any charge or at a charge reduced below the fees established under clause (ii) if disclosure of the information is in the public interest because it is likely to contribute significantly to public understanding of the operations or activities of the government and is not primarily in the commercial interest of the requester.

(iv) Fee schedules shall provide for the recovery of only the direct costs of search, duplication, or review. Review costs shall include only the direct costs incurred during the initial examination of a document for the purposes of determining whether the documents must be disclosed under this section and for the purposes of withholding any portions exempt from disclosure under this section. Review costs may not include any costs incurred in resolving issues of law or policy that may be raised in the course of processing a request under this section. No fee may be charged by any agency under this section—

(I) if the costs of routine collection and processing of the fee are likely to equal or exceed the amount of the fee; or

(II) for any request described in clause (ii)(II) or (III) of this subparagraph for the first two hours of search time or for the first one hundred pages of duplication.

(v) No agency may require advance payment of any fee unless the requester has previously failed to pay fees in a timely fashion, or the agency has determined that the fee will exceed $250.

(vi) Nothing in this subparagraph shall supersede fees chargeable under a statute specifically providing for setting the level of fees for particular types of records.

(vii) In any action by a requester regarding the waiver of fees under this section, the court shall determine the matter de novo: *Provided*, That the court's review of the matter shall be limited to the record before the agency.

(viii)

(I) Except as provided in subclause (II), an agency shall not assess any search fees (or in the case of a requester described under clause (ii)(II) of this subparagraph, duplication fees) under this subparagraph if the agency has failed to comply with any time limit under paragraph (6).

(II)

(aa) If an agency has determined that unusual circumstances apply (as the term is defined in paragraph (6)(B)) and the agency provided a timely written notice to the requester in accordance with paragraph (6)(B), a failure described in subclause (I) is excused for an additional 10 days. If the agency fails to comply with the extended time limit, the agency may not assess any search fees (or in the case of a requester described under clause (ii)(II) of this subparagraph, duplication fees).

(bb) If an agency has determined that unusual circumstances apply and more than 5,000 pages are necessary to respond to the request, an agency may charge search fees (or in the case of a requester described under clause (ii)(II) of this subparagraph, duplication fees) if the agency has provided a timely written notice to the requester in accordance with paragraph (6)(B) and the agency has discussed with the requester via written mail, electronic mail, or telephone (or made not less than 3 good-faith attempts to do so) how the requester could effectively limit the scope of the request in accordance with paragraph (6)(B)(ii).

(cc) If a court has determined that exceptional circumstances exist (as that term is defined in paragraph (6)(C)), a failure described in subclause (I) shall be excused for the length of time provided by the court order.

(B) On complaint, the district court of the United States in the district in which the complainant resides, or has his principal place of business, or in which the agency records are situated, or in the District of Columbia, has jurisdiction to enjoin the agency from withholding agency records and to order the production of any agency records improperly withheld from the complainant. In such a case the court shall determine the matter de novo, and may examine the contents of such agency records in camera to determine whether such records or any part thereof shall be withheld under any of the exemptions set forth in subsection (b) of this section, and the burden is on the agency to sustain its action. In addition to any other matters to which a court accords substantial weight, a court shall accord substantial weight to an affidavit of an agency concerning the agency's determination as to technical feasibility under paragraph (2)(C) and subsection (b) and reproducibility under paragraph (3)(B).

(C) Notwithstanding any other provision of law, the defendant shall serve an answer or otherwise plead to any complaint made under this subsection within thirty days after service upon the defendant of the pleading in which such complaint is made, unless the court otherwise directs for good cause shown.

(D) [Repealed]

(E)

(i) The court may assess against the United States reasonable attorney fees and other litigation costs reasonably incurred in any case under this section in which the complainant has substantially prevailed.

(ii) For purposes of this subparagraph, a complainant has substantially prevailed if the complainant has obtained relief through either—

(I) a judicial order, or an enforceable written agreement or consent decree; or

(II) a voluntary or unilateral change in position by the agency, if the complainant's claim is not insubstantial.

(F)

(i) Whenever the court orders the production of any agency records improperly withheld from the complainant and assesses against the United States reasonable attorney fees and other litigation costs, and the court additionally issues a written finding that the circumstances surrounding the withholding raise questions whether agency personnel acted arbitrarily or capriciously with respect to the withholding, the Special Counsel shall promptly initiate a proceeding to determine whether disciplinary action is warranted against the officer or employee who was primarily responsible for the withholding. The Special Counsel, after investigation and consideration of the evidence submitted, shall submit his findings and recommendations to the administrative authority of the agency concerned and shall send copies of the findings and recommendations to the officer or employee or his representative. The administrative authority shall take the corrective action that the Special Counsel recommends.

(ii) The Attorney General shall—

(I) notify the Special Counsel of each civil action described under the first sentence of clause (i); and

(II) annually submit a report to Congress on the number of such civil actions in the preceding year.

(iii) The Special Counsel shall annually submit a report to Congress on the actions taken by the Special Counsel under clause (i).

(G) In the event of noncompliance with the order of the court, the district court may punish for contempt the responsible employee, and in the case of a uniformed service, the responsible member.

(5) Each agency having more than one member shall maintain and make available for public inspection a record of the final votes of each member in every agency proceeding.

(6)

(A) Each agency, upon any request for records made under paragraph (1), (2), or (3) of this subsection, shall—

(i) determine within 20 days (excepting Saturdays, Sundays, and legal public holidays) after the receipt of any such request whether to comply with such request and shall immediately notify the person making such request of—

(I) such determination and the reasons therefor;

(II) the right of such person to seek assistance from the FOIA Public Liaison of the agency; and

(III) in the case of an adverse determination—

(aa) the right of such person to appeal to the head of the agency, within a period determined by the head of the agency that is not less than 90 days after the date of such adverse determination; and

(bb) the right of such person to seek dispute resolution services from the FOIA Public Liaison of the agency or the Office of Government Information Services; and

(ii) make a determination with respect to any appeal within twenty days (excepting Saturdays, Sundays, and legal public holidays) after the receipt of such appeal. If on appeal the denial of the request for records is in whole or in part upheld, the agency shall notify the person making such request of the provisions for judicial review of that determination under paragraph (4) of this subsection.

The 20-day period under clause (i) shall commence on the date on which the request is first received by the appropriate component of the agency, but in any event not later than ten days after the request is first received by any component of the agency that is designated in the agency's regulations under this section to receive requests under this section. The 20-day period shall not be tolled by the agency except—

(I) that the agency may make one request to the requester for information and toll the 20-day period while it is awaiting such information that it has reasonably requested from the requester under this section; or

(II) if necessary to clarify with the requester issues regarding fee assessment. In either case, the agency's receipt of the requester's response to the agency's request for information or clarification ends the tolling period.

(B)

(i) In unusual circumstances as specified in this subparagraph, the time limits prescribed in either clause (i) or clause (ii) of subparagraph (A) may be extended by written notice to the person making such request setting forth the unusual circumstances for such extension and the date on which a determination is expected to be dispatched. No such notice shall specify a date that would result in an extension for more than ten working days, except as provided in clause (ii) of this subparagraph.

(ii) With respect to a request for which a written notice under clause (i) extends the time limits prescribed under clause (i) of subparagraph (A), the agency shall notify the person making the request if the request cannot be processed within the time limit specified in that clause and shall provide the person an opportunity to limit the scope of the request so that it may be processed within that time limit or an opportunity to arrange with the agency an alternative time frame for processing the request or a modified request. To aid the requester, each agency shall make available its FOIA Public Liaison, who shall assist in the resolution of any disputes between the requester and the agency, and notify the requester of the right of the requester to seek dispute resolution services from the Office of Government Information Services. Refusal by the person to reasonably modify the request or arrange such an alternative time frame shall be considered as a factor in determining whether exceptional circumstances exist for purposes of subparagraph (C).

(iii) As used in this subparagraph, "unusual circumstances" means, but only to the extent reasonably necessary to the proper processing of the particular requests—

(I) the need to search for and collect the requested records from field facilities or other establishments that are separate from the office processing the request;

(II) the need to search for, collect, and appropriately examine a voluminous amount of separate and distinct records which are demanded in a single request; or

(III) the need for consultation, which shall be conducted with all practicable speed, with another agency having a substantial interest in the determination of the request or among two or more components of the agency having substantial subject-matter interest therein.

(iv) Each agency may promulgate regulations, pursuant to notice and receipt of public comment, providing for the aggregation of certain requests by the same requestor, or by a group of requestors acting in concert, if the agency reasonably believes that such requests actually constitute a single request, which would otherwise satisfy the unusual circumstances specified in this subparagraph, and the requests involve clearly related matters. Multiple requests involving unrelated matters shall not be aggregated.

(C)

(i) Any person making a request to any agency for records under paragraph (1), (2), or (3) of this subsection shall be deemed to have exhausted his administrative remedies with respect to such request if the agency fails to comply with the applicable time limit provisions of this paragraph. If the Government can show exceptional circumstances exist and that the agency is exercising due diligence in responding to the request, the court may retain jurisdiction and allow the agency additional time to complete its review of the records. Upon any determination by an agency to comply with a request for records, the records shall be made promptly available to such person making such request. Any notification of denial of any request for records under this subsection shall set forth the names and titles or positions of each person responsible for the denial of such request.

(ii) For purposes of this subparagraph, the term "exceptional circumstances" does not include a delay that results from a predictable agency workload of requests under this section, unless the agency demonstrates reasonable progress in reducing its backlog of pending requests.

(iii) Refusal by a person to reasonably modify the scope of a request or arrange an alternative time frame for processing a request (or a modified request) under clause (ii) after being given an opportunity to do so by the agency to whom the person made the request shall be considered as a factor in determining whether exceptional circumstances exist for purposes of this subparagraph.

(D)

(i) Each agency may promulgate regulations, pursuant to notice and receipt of public comment, providing for multitrack processing of requests for records based on the amount of work or time (or both) involved in processing requests.

(ii) Regulations under this subparagraph may provide a person making a request that does not qualify for the fastest multitrack processing an opportunity to limit the scope of the request in order to qualify for faster processing.

(iii) This subparagraph shall not be considered to affect the requirement under subparagraph (C) to exercise due diligence.

(E)

(i) Each agency shall promulgate regulations, pursuant to notice and receipt of public comment, providing for expedited processing of requests for records—

(I) in cases in which the person requesting the records demonstrates a compelling need; and

(II) in other cases determined by the agency.

(ii) Notwithstanding clause (i), regulations under this subparagraph must ensure—

(I) that a determination of whether to provide expedited processing shall be made, and notice of the determination shall be provided to the person making the request, within 10 days after the date of the request; and

(II) expeditious consideration of administrative appeals of such determinations of whether to provide expedited processing.

(iii) An agency shall process as soon as practicable any request for records to which the agency has granted expedited processing under this subparagraph. Agency action to deny or affirm denial of a request for expedited processing pursuant to this subparagraph, and failure by an agency to respond in a timely manner to such a request shall be subject to judicial review under paragraph (4), except that the judicial review shall be based on the record before the agency at the time of the determination.

(iv) A district court of the United States shall not have jurisdiction to review an agency denial of expedited processing of a request for records after the agency has provided a complete response to the request.

(v) For purposes of this subparagraph, the term "compelling need" means—

(I) that a failure to obtain requested records on an expedited basis under this paragraph could reasonably be expected to pose an imminent threat to the life or physical safety of an individual; or

(II) with respect to a request made by a person primarily engaged in disseminating information, urgency to inform the public concerning actual or alleged Federal Government activity.

(vi) A demonstration of a compelling need by a person making a request for expedited processing shall be made by a statement certified by such person to be true and correct to the best of such person's knowledge and belief.

(F) In denying a request for records, in whole or in part, an agency shall make a reasonable effort to estimate the volume of any requested matter the provision of which is denied, and shall provide any such estimate to the person making the request, unless providing such estimate would harm an interest protected by the exemption in subsection (b) pursuant to which the denial is made.

(7) Each agency shall—

(A) establish a system to assign an individualized tracking number for each request received that will take longer than ten days to process and provide to each person making a request the tracking number assigned to the request; and

(B) establish a telephone line or Internet service that provides information about the status of a request to the person making the request using the assigned tracking number, including—

(i) the date on which the agency originally received the request; and

(ii) an estimated date on which the agency will complete action on the request.

(8)

(A) An agency shall—

(i) withhold information under this section only if—

(I) the agency reasonably foresees that disclosure would harm an interest protected by an exemption described in subsection (b); or

(II) disclosure is prohibited by law; and

(ii)

(I) consider whether partial disclosure of information is possible whenever the agency determines that a full disclosure of a requested record is not possible; and

(II) take reasonable steps necessary to segregate and release nonexempt information; and

(B) Nothing in this paragraph requires disclosure of information that is otherwise prohibited from disclosure by law, or otherwise exempted from disclosure under subsection (b)(3).

(b) This section does not apply to matters that are—

(1)

(A) specifically authorized under criteria established by an Executive order to be kept secret in the interest of national defense or foreign policy and (B) are in fact properly classified pursuant to such Executive order;

(2) related solely to the internal personnel rules and practices of an agency;

(3) specifically exempted from disclosure by statute (other than section 552b of this title, if that statute—

(A)

(i) requires that the matters be withheld from the public in such a manner as to leave no discretion on the issue; or

(ii) establishes particular criteria for withholding or refers to particular types of matters to be withheld; and

(B) if enacted after the date of enactment of the OPEN FOIA Act of 2009 [enacted Oct. 28, 2009], specifically cites to this paragraph.

(4) trade secrets and commercial or financial information obtained from a person and privileged or confidential;

(5) inter-agency or intra-agency memorandums or letters that would not be available by law to a party other than an agency in litigation with the agency, provided that the deliberative process privilege shall not apply to records created 25 years or more before the date on which the records were requested;

(6) personnel and medical files and similar files the disclosure of which would constitute a clearly unwarranted invasion of personal privacy;

(7) records or information compiled for law enforcement purposes, but only to the extent that the production of such law enforcement records or information (A) could reasonably be expected to interfere with enforcement proceedings,

(B) would deprive a person of a right to a fair trial or an impartial adjudication, (C) could reasonably be expected to constitute an unwarranted invasion of personal privacy, (D) could reasonably be expected to disclose the identity of a confidential source, including a State, local, or foreign agency or authority or any private institution which furnished information on a confidential basis, and, in the case of a record or information compiled by criminal law enforcement authority in the course of a criminal investigation or by an agency conducting a lawful national security intelligence investigation, information furnished by a confidential source, (E) would disclose techniques and procedures for law enforcement investigations or prosecutions, or would disclose guidelines for law enforcement investigations or prosecutions if such disclosure could reasonably be expected to risk circumvention of the law, or (F) could reasonably be expected to endanger the life or physical safety of any individual;

(8) contained in or related to examination, operating, or condition reports prepared by, on behalf of, or for the use of an agency responsible for the regulation or supervision of financial institutions; or

(9) geological or geophysical information and data, including maps, concerning wells. Any reasonably segregable portion of a record shall be provided to any person requesting such record after deletion of the portions which are exempt under this subsection. The amount of information deleted, and the exemption under which the deletion is made, shall be indicated on the released portion of the record, unless including that indication would harm an interest protected by the exemption in this subsection under which the deletion is made. If technically feasible, the amount of the information deleted, and the exemption under which the deletion is made, shall be indicated at the place in the record where such deletion is made.

(c)

(1) Whenever a request is made which involves access to records described in subsection (b)(7)(A) and—

(A) the investigation or proceeding involves a possible violation of criminal law; and

(B) there is reason to believe that (i) the subject of the investigation or proceeding is not aware of its pendency, and (ii) disclosure of the existence of the records could reasonably be expected to interfere with enforcement proceedings,

the agency may, during only such time as that circumstance continues, treat the records as not subject to the requirements of this section.

(2) Whenever informant records maintained by a criminal law enforcement agency under an informant's name or personal identifier are requested by a third party according to the informant's name or personal identifier, the agency may treat the records as not subject to the requirements of this section unless the informant's status as an informant has been officially confirmed.

(3) Whenever a request is made which involves access to records maintained by the Federal Bureau of Investigation pertaining to foreign intelligence or counterintelligence, or international terrorism, and the existence of the records is classified information as provided in subsection (b)(1), the Bureau

may, as long as the existence of the records remains classified information, treat the records as not subject to the requirements of this section.

(d) This section does not authorize withholding of information or limit the availability of records to the public, except as specifically stated in this section. This section is not authority to withhold information from Congress.

(e)

(1) On or before February 1 of each year, each agency shall submit to the Attorney General of the United States and to the Director of the Office of Government Information Services a report which shall cover the preceding fiscal year and which shall include—

(A) the number of determinations made by the agency not to comply with requests for records made to such agency under subsection (a) and the reasons for each such determination;

(B)

(i) the number of appeals made by persons under subsection (a)(6), the result of such appeals, and the reason for the action upon each appeal that results in a denial of information; and

(ii) a complete list of all statutes that the agency relies upon to authorize the agency to withhold information under subsection (b)(3), the number of occasions on which each statute was relied upon, a description of whether a court has upheld the decision of the agency to withhold information under each such statute, and a concise description of the scope of any information withheld;

(C) the number of requests for records pending before the agency as of September 30 of the preceding year, and the median and average number of days that such requests had been pending before the agency as of that date;

(D) the number of requests for records received by the agency and the number of requests which the agency processed;

(E) the median number of days taken by the agency to process different types of requests, based on the date on which the requests were received by the agency;

(F) the average number of days for the agency to respond to a request beginning on the date on which the request was received by the agency, the median number of days for the agency to respond to such requests, and the range in number of days for the agency to respond to such requests;

(G) based on the number of business days that have elapsed since each request was originally received by the agency—

(i) the number of requests for records to which the agency has responded with a determination within a period up to and including 20 days, and in 20-day increments up to and including 200 days;

(ii) the number of requests for records to which the agency has responded with a determination within a period greater than 200 days and less than 301 days;

(iii) the number of requests for records to which the agency has responded with a determination within a period greater than 300 days and less than 401 days; and

(iv) the number of requests for records to which the agency has responded with a determination within a period greater than 400 days;

(H) the average number of days for the agency to provide the granted information beginning on the date on which the request was originally filed, the median number of days for the agency to provide the granted information, and the range in number of days for the agency to provide the granted information;

(I) the median and average number of days for the agency to respond to administrative appeals based on the date on which the appeals originally were received by the agency, the highest number of business days taken by the agency to respond to an administrative appeal, and the lowest number of business days taken by the agency to respond to an administrative appeal;

(J) data on the 10 active requests with the earliest filing dates pending at each agency, including the amount of time that has elapsed since each request was originally received by the agency;

(K) data on the 10 active administrative appeals with the earliest filing dates pending before the agency as of September 30 of the preceding year, including the number of business days that have elapsed since the requests were originally received by the agency;

(L) the number of expedited review requests that are granted and denied, the average and median number of days for adjudicating expedited review requests, and the number adjudicated within the required 10 days;

(M) the number of fee waiver requests that are granted and denied, and the average and median number of days for adjudicating fee waiver determinations;

(N) the total amount of fees collected by the agency for processing requests;

(O) the number of full-time staff of the agency devoted to processing requests for records under this section, and the total amount expended by the agency for processing such requests;

(P) the number of times the agency denied a request for records under subsection (c); and

(Q) the number of records that were made available for public inspection in an electronic format under subsection (a)(2).

(2) Information in each report submitted under paragraph (1) shall be expressed in terms of each principal component of the agency and for the agency overall.

(3) Each agency shall make each such report available for public inspection in an electronic format. In addition, each agency shall make the raw statistical data used in each report available in a timely manner for public inspection in an electronic format, which shall be made available—

(A) without charge, license, or registration requirement;

(B) in an aggregated, searchable format; and

(C) in a format that may be downloaded in bulk.

(4) The Attorney General of the United States shall make each report which has been made available by electronic means available at a single electronic access

point. The Attorney General of the United States shall notify the Chairman and ranking minority member of the Committee on Oversight and Government Reform of the House of Representatives and the Chairman and ranking minority member of the Committees on Homeland Security and Governmental Affairs and the Judiciary of the Senate, no later than March 1 of the year in which each such report is issued, that such reports are available by electronic means.

(5) The Attorney General of the United States, in consultation with the Director of the Office of Management and Budget, shall develop reporting and performance guidelines in connection with reports required by this subsection by October 1, 1997, and may establish additional requirements for such reports as the Attorney General determines may be useful.

(6)

(A) The Attorney General of the United States shall submit to the Committee on Oversight and Government Reform of the House of Representatives, the Committee on the Judiciary of the Senate, and the President a report on or before March 1 of each calendar year, which shall include for the prior calendar year—

(i) a listing of the number of cases arising under this section;

(ii) a listing of—

(I) each subsection, and any exemption, if applicable, involved in each case arising under this section;

(II) the disposition of each case arising under this section; and

(III) the cost, fees, and penalties assessed under subparagraphs (E), (F), and (G) of subsection (a)(4); and

(iii) a description of the efforts undertaken by the Department of Justice to encourage agency compliance with this section.

(B) The Attorney General of the United States shall make—

(i) each report submitted under subparagraph (A) available for public inspection in an electronic format; and

(ii) the raw statistical data used in each report submitted under subparagraph (A) available for public inspection in an electronic format, which shall be made available—

(I) without charge, license, or registration requirement;

(II) in an aggregated, searchable format; and

(III) in a format that may be downloaded in bulk.

(f) For purposes of this section, the term—

(1) "agency" as defined in section 551(1) of this title includes any executive department, military department, Government corporation, Government controlled corporation, or other establishment in the executive branch of the Government (including the Executive Office of the President), or any independent regulatory agency; and

(2) "record" and any other term used in this section in reference to information includes—

(A) any information that would be an agency record subject to the requirements of this section when maintained by an agency in any format, including an electronic format; and

(B) any information described under subparagraph (A) that is maintained for an agency by an entity under Government contract, for the purposes of records management.

(g) The head of each agency shall prepare and make available for public inspection in an electronic format, reference material or a guide for requesting records or information from the agency, subject to the exemptions in subsection (b), including—

(1) an index of all major information systems of the agency;

(2) a description of major information and record locator systems maintained by the agency; and

(3) a handbook for obtaining various types and categories of public information from the agency pursuant to chapter 35 of title 44,[2] and under this section.

(h)

(1) There is established the Office of Government Information Services within the National Archives and Records Administration. The head of the Office shall be the Director of the Office of Government Information Services.

(2) The Office of Government Information Services shall—

(A) review policies and procedures of administrative agencies under this section;

(B) review compliance with this section by administrative agencies; and

(C) identify procedures and methods for improving compliance under this section.

(3) The Office of Government Information Services shall offer mediation services to resolve disputes between persons making requests under this section and administrative agencies as a nonexclusive alternative to litigation and may issue advisory opinions at the discretion of the Office or upon request of any party to a dispute.

(4)

(A) Not less frequently than annually, the Director of the Office of Government Information Services shall submit to the Committee on Oversight and Government Reform of the House of Representatives, the Committee on the Judiciary of the Senate, and the President—

(i) a report on the findings of the information reviewed and identified under paragraph (2);

(ii) a summary of the activities of the Office of Government Information Services under paragraph (3), including—

(I) any advisory opinions issued; and

2. 44 U.S.C. § 3501 *et seq.*

(II) the number of times each agency engaged in dispute resolution with the assistance of the Office of Government Information Services or the FOIA Public Liaison; and

(iii) legislative and regulatory recommendations, if any, to improve the administration of this section.

(B) The Director of the Office of Government Information Services shall make each report submitted under subparagraph (A) available for public inspection in an electronic format.

(C) The Director of the Office of Government Information Services shall not be required to obtain the prior approval, comment, or review of any officer or agency of the United States, including the Department of Justice, the Archivist of the United States, or the Office of Management and Budget before submitting to Congress, or any committee or subcommittee thereof, any reports, recommendations, testimony, or comments, if such submissions include a statement indicating that the views expressed therein are those of the Director and do not necessarily represent the views of the President.

(5) The Director of the Office of Government Information Services may directly submit additional information to Congress and the President as the Director determines to be appropriate.

(6) Not less frequently than annually, the Office of Government Information Services shall conduct a meeting that is open to the public on the review and reports by the Office and shall allow interested persons to appear and present oral or written statements at the meeting.

(i) The Government Accountability Office shall conduct audits of administrative agencies on the implementation of this section and issue reports detailing the results of such audits.

(j)

(1) Each agency shall designate a Chief FOIA Officer who shall be a senior official of such agency (at the Assistant Secretary or equivalent level).

(2) The Chief FOIA Officer of each agency shall, subject to the authority of the head of the agency—

(A) have agency-wide responsibility for efficient and appropriate compliance with this section;

(B) monitor implementation of this section throughout the agency and keep the head of the agency, the chief legal officer of the agency, and the Attorney General appropriately informed of the agency's performance in implementing this section;

(C) recommend to the head of the agency such adjustments to agency practices, policies, personnel, and funding as may be necessary to improve its implementation of this section;

(D) review and report to the Attorney General, through the head of the agency, at such times and in such formats as the Attorney General may direct, on the agency's performance in implementing this section;

(E) facilitate public understanding of the purposes of the statutory exemptions of this section by including concise descriptions of the exemptions in both the agency's handbook issued under subsection (g), and the agency's annual report on this section, and by providing an overview, where appropriate, of certain general categories of agency records to which those exemptions apply;

(F) offer training to agency staff regarding their responsibilities under this section;

(G) serve as the primary agency liaison with the Office of Government Information Services and the Office of Information Policy; and

(H) designate 1 or more FOIA Public Liaisons.

(3) The Chief FOIA Officer of each agency shall review, not less frequently than annually, all aspects of the administration of this section by the agency to ensure compliance with the requirements of this section, including—

(A) agency regulations;

(B) disclosure of records required under paragraphs (2) and (8) of subsection (a);

(C) assessment of fees and determination of eligibility for fee waivers;

(D) the timely processing of requests for information under this section;

(E) the use of exemptions under subsection (b); and

(F) dispute resolution services with the assistance of the Office of Government Information Services or the FOIA Public Liaison.

(k)

(1) There is established in the executive branch the Chief FOIA Officers Council (referred to in this subsection as the "Council").

(2) The Council shall be comprised of the following members:

(A) The Deputy Director for Management of the Office of Management and Budget.

(B) The Director of the Office of Information Policy at the Department of Justice.

(C) The Director of the Office of Government Information Services.

(D) The Chief FOIA Officer of each agency.

(E) Any other officer or employee of the United States as designated by the Co-Chairs.

(3) The Director of the Office of Information Policy at the Department of Justice and the Director of the Office of Government Information Services shall be the Co-Chairs of the Council.

(4) The Administrator of General Services shall provide administrative and other support for the Council.

(5)

(A) The duties of the Council shall include the following:

(i) Develop recommendations for increasing compliance and efficiency under this section.

(ii) Disseminate information about agency experiences, ideas, best practices, and innovative approaches related to this section.

(iii) Identify, develop, and coordinate initiatives to increase transparency and compliance with this section.

(iv) Promote the development and use of common performance measures for agency compliance with this section.

(B) In performing the duties described in subparagraph (A), the Council shall consult on a regular basis with members of the public who make requests under this section.

(6)

(A) The Council shall meet regularly and such meetings shall be open to the public unless the Council determines to close the meeting for reasons of national security or to discuss information exempt under subsection (b).

(B) Not less frequently than annually, the Council shall hold a meeting that shall be open to the public and permit interested persons to appear and present oral and written statements to the Council.

(C) Not later than 10 business days before a meeting of the Council, notice of such meeting shall be published in the Federal Register.

(D) Except as provided in subsection (b), the records, reports, transcripts, minutes, appendices, working papers, drafts, studies, agenda, or other documents that were made available to or prepared for or by the Council shall be made publicly available.

(E) Detailed minutes of each meeting of the Council shall be kept and shall contain a record of the persons present, a complete and accurate description of matters discussed and conclusions reached, and copies of all reports received, issued, or approved by the Council. The minutes shall be redacted as necessary and made publicly available.

(l) FOIA Public Liaisons shall report to the agency Chief FOIA Officer and shall serve as supervisory officials to whom a requester under this section can raise concerns about the service the requester has received from the FOIA Requester Center, following an initial response from the FOIA Requester Center Staff. FOIA Public Liaisons shall be responsible for assisting in reducing delays, increasing transparency and understanding of the status of requests, and assisting in the resolution of disputes.

(m)

(1) The Director of the Office of Management and Budget, in consultation with the Attorney General, shall ensure the operation of a consolidated online request portal that allows a member of the public to submit a request for records under subsection (a) to any agency from a single website. The portal may include any additional tools the Director of the Office of Management and Budget finds will improve the implementation of this section.

(2) This subsection shall not be construed to alter the power of any other agency to create or maintain an independent online portal for the submission of a request for records under this section. The Director of the Office of Management and Budget shall establish standards for interoperability between the portal required under paragraph (1) and other request processing software used by agencies subject to this section.

Privacy Act

§ 552a. Records maintained on individuals

(a) Definitions.—For purposes of this section—

(1) the term "agency" means agency as defined in section 552(e)[3] of this title;

(2) the term "individual" means a citizen of the United States or an alien lawfully admitted for permanent residence;

(3) the term "maintain" includes maintain, collect, use, or disseminate;

(4) the term "record" means any item, collection, or grouping of information about an individual that is maintained by an agency, including, but not limited to, his education, financial transactions, medical history, and criminal or employment history and that contains his name, or the identifying number, symbol, or other identifying particular assigned to the individual, such as a finger or voice print or a photograph;

(5) the term "system of records" means a group of any records under the control of any agency from which information is retrieved by the name of the individual or by some identifying number, symbol, or other identifying particular assigned to the individual;

(6) the term "statistical record" means a record in a system of records maintained for statistical research or reporting purposes only and not used in whole or in part in making any determination about an identifiable individual, except as provided by section 8 of title 13;

(7) the term "routine use" means, with respect to the disclosure of a record, the use of such record for a purpose which is compatible with the purpose for which it was collected; and

(8) the term "matching program"—

(A) means any computerized comparison of—

(i) two or more automated systems of records or a system of records with non-Federal records for the purpose of—

(I) establishing or verifying the eligibility of, or continuing compliance with statutory and regulatory requirements by, applicants for, recipients or beneficiaries of, participants in, or providers of services with respect to, cash or in-kind assistance or payments under Federal benefit programs, or

(II) recouping payments or delinquent debts under such Federal benefit programs, or

(ii) two or more automated Federal personnel or payroll systems of records or a system of Federal personnel or payroll records with non-Federal records,

(B) but does not include—

(i) matches performed to produce aggregate statistical data without any personal identifiers;

3. Section 552(e) of this title was redesignated § 552(f) by § 1802(b) of Pub. L. No. 99-570.

(ii) matches performed to support any research or statistical project, the specific data of which may not be used to make decisions concerning the rights, benefits, or privileges of specific individuals;

(iii) matches performed, by an agency (or component thereof) which performs as its principal function any activity pertaining to the enforcement of criminal laws, subsequent to the initiation of a specific criminal or civil law enforcement investigation of a named person or persons for the purpose of gathering evidence against such person or persons;

(iv) matches of tax information (I) pursuant to section 6103(d) of the Internal Revenue Code of 1986,[4] (II) for purposes of tax administration as defined in section 6103(b)(4) of such Code,[5] (III) for the purpose of intercepting a tax refund due an individual under authority granted by section 404(e), 464, or 1137 of the Social Security Act;[6] or (IV) for the purpose of intercepting a tax refund due an individual under any other tax refund intercept program authorized by statute which has been determined by the Director of the Office of Management and Budget to contain verification, notice, and hearing requirements that are substantially similar to the procedures in section 1137 of the Social Security Act;

(v) matches—

(I) using records predominantly relating to Federal personnel, that are performed for routine administrative purposes (subject to guidance provided by the Director of the Office of Management and Budget pursuant to subsection (v)); or

(II) conducted by an agency using only records from systems of records maintained by that agency;

if the purpose of the match is not to take any adverse financial, personnel, disciplinary, or other adverse action against Federal personnel;

(vi) matches performed for foreign counterintelligence purposes or to produce background checks for security clearances of Federal personnel or Federal contractor personnel;

(vii) matches performed incident to a levy described in section 6103(k)(8) of the Internal Revenue Code of 1986;[7]

(viii) matches performed pursuant to section 202(x)(3) or 1611(e)(1) of the Social Security Act (42 U.S.C. 402(x)(3), 1382(e)(1));

(ix) matches performed by the Secretary of Health and Human Services or the Inspector General of the Department of Health and Human Services with respect to potential fraud, waste, and abuse, including matches of a system of records with non-Federal records; or

4. 26 U.S.C. § 6103(d).
5. 26 U.S.C. § 6103(b)(4).
6. 42 U.S.C. §§ 604(e), 664, 1320b-7.
7. 26 U.S.C. § 6103(k)(8).

(x) matches performed pursuant to section 3(d)(4) of the Achieving a Better Life Experience Act of 2014;

(9) the term "recipient agency" means any agency, or contractor thereof, receiving records contained in a system of records from a source agency for use in a matching program;

(10) the term "non-Federal agency" means any State or local government, or agency thereof, which receives records contained in a system of records from a source agency for use in a matching program;

(11) the term "source agency" means any agency which discloses records contained in a system of records to be used in a matching program, or any State or local government, or agency thereof, which discloses records to be used in a matching program;

(12) the term "Federal benefit program" means any program administered or funded by the Federal Government, or by any agent or State on behalf of the Federal Government, providing cash or in-kind assistance in the form of payments, grants, loans, or loan guarantees to individuals; and

(13) the term "Federal personnel" means officers and employees of the Government of the United States, members of the uniformed services (including members of the Reserve Components), individuals entitled to receive immediate or deferred retirement benefits under any retirement program of the Government of the United States (including survivor benefits).

(b) Conditions of Disclosure.—No agency shall disclose any record which is contained in a system of records by any means of communication to any person, or to another agency, except pursuant to a written request by, or with the prior written consent of, the individual to whom the record pertains, unless disclosure of the record would be—

(1) to those officers and employees of the agency which maintains the record who have a need for the record in the performance of their duties;

(2) required under section 552 of this title;

(3) for a routine use as defined in subsection (a)(7) of this section and described under subsection (e)(4)(D) of this section;

(4) to the Bureau of the Census for purposes of planning or carrying out a census or survey or related activity pursuant to the provisions of title 13;

(5) to a recipient who has provided the agency with advance adequate written assurance that the record will be used solely as a statistical research or reporting record, and the record is to be transferred in a form that is not individually identifiable;

(6) to the National Archives and Records Administration as a record which has sufficient historical or other value to warrant its continued preservation by the United States Government, or for evaluation by the Archivist of the United States or the designee of the Archivist to determine whether the record has such value;

(7) to another agency or to an instrumentality of any governmental jurisdiction within or under the control of the United States for a civil or criminal law enforcement activity if the activity is authorized by law, and if the head of the

agency or instrumentality has made a written request to the agency which maintains the record specifying the particular portion desired and the law enforcement activity for which the record is sought;

(8) to a person pursuant to a showing of compelling circumstances affecting the health or safety of an individual if upon such disclosure notification is transmitted to the last known address of such individual;

(9) to either House of Congress, or, to the extent of matter within its jurisdiction, any committee or subcommittee thereof, any joint committee of Congress or subcommittee of any such joint committee;

(10) to the Comptroller General, or any of his authorized representatives, in the course of the performance of the Office;

(11) pursuant to the order of a court of competent jurisdiction; or

(12) to a consumer reporting agency in accordance with section 3711(e) of title 31.

(c) Accounting of Certain Disclosures.—Each agency, with respect to each system of records under its control, shall—

(1) except for disclosures made under subsections (b)(1) or (b)(2) of this section, keep an accurate accounting of—

(A) the date, nature, and purpose of each disclosure of a record to any person or to another agency made under subsection (b) of this section; and

(B) the name and address of the person or agency to whom the disclosure is made;

(2) retain the accounting made under paragraph (1) of this subsection for at least five years or the life of the record, whichever is longer, after the disclosure for which the accounting is made;

(3) except for disclosures made under subsection (b)(7) of this section, make the accounting made under paragraph (1) of this subsection available to the individual named in the record at his request; and

(4) inform any person or other agency about any correction or notation of dispute made by the agency in accordance with subsection (d) of this section of any record that has been disclosed to the person or agency if an accounting of the disclosure was made.

(d) Access to Records.—Each agency that maintains a system of records shall—

(1) upon request by any individual to gain access to his record or to any information pertaining to him which is contained in the system, permit him and upon his request, a person of his own choosing to accompany him, to review the record and have a copy made of all or any portion thereof in a form comprehensible to him, except that the agency may require the individual to furnish a written statement authorizing discussion of that individual's record in the accompanying person's presence;

(2) permit the individual to request amendment of a record pertaining to him and—

(A) not later than 10 days (excluding Saturdays, Sundays, and legal public holidays) after the date of receipt of such request, acknowledge in writing such receipt; and

(B) promptly, either—

(i) make any correction of any portion thereof which the individual believes is not accurate, relevant, timely, or complete; or

(ii) inform the individual of its refusal to amend the record in accordance with his request, the reason for the refusal, the procedures established by the agency for the individual to request a review of that refusal by the head of the agency or an officer designated by the head of the agency, and the name and business address of that official;

(3) permit the individual who disagrees with the refusal of the agency to amend his record to request a review of such refusal, and not later than 30 days (excluding Saturdays, Sundays, and legal public holidays) from the date on which the individual requests such review, complete such review and make a final determination unless, for good cause shown, the head of the agency extends such 30-day period; and if, after his review, the reviewing official also refuses to amend the record in accordance with the request, permit the individual to file with the agency a concise statement setting forth the reasons for his disagreement with the refusal of the agency, and notify the individual of the provisions for judicial review of the reviewing official's determination under subsection (g)(1)(A) of this section;

(4) in any disclosure, containing information about which the individual has filed a statement of disagreement, occurring after the filing of the statement under paragraph (3) of this subsection, clearly note any portion of the record which is disputed and provide copies of the statement and, if the agency deems it appropriate, copies of a concise statement of the reasons of the agency for not making the amendments requested, to persons or other agencies to whom the disputed record has been disclosed; and

(5) nothing in this section shall allow an individual access to any information compiled in reasonable anticipation of a civil action or proceeding.

(e) Agency Requirements— Each agency that maintains a system of records shall—

(1) maintain in its records only such information about an individual as is relevant and necessary to accomplish a purpose of the agency required to be accomplished by statute or by executive order of the President;

(2) collect information to the greatest extent practicable directly from the subject individual when the information may result in adverse determinations about an individual's rights, benefits, and privileges under Federal programs;

(3) inform each individual whom it asks to supply information, on the form which it uses to collect the information or on a separate form that can be retained by the individual—

(A) the authority (whether granted by statute, or by executive order of the President) which authorizes the solicitation of the information and whether disclosure of such information is mandatory or voluntary;

(B) the principal purpose or purposes for which the information is intended to be used;

(C) the routine uses which may be made of the information, as published pursuant to paragraph (4)(D) of this subsection; and

(D) the effects on him, if any, of not providing all or any part of the requested information;

(4) subject to the provisions of paragraph (11) of this subsection, publish in the Federal Register upon establishment or revision a notice of the existence and character of the system of records, which notice shall include—

(A) the name and location of the system;

(B) the categories of individuals on whom records are maintained in the system;

(C) the categories of records maintained in the system;

(D) each routine use of the records contained in the system, including the categories of users and the purpose of such use;

(E) the policies and practices of the agency regarding storage, retrievability, access controls, retention, and disposal of the records;

(F) the title and business address of the agency official who is responsible for the system of records;

(G) the agency procedures whereby an individual can be notified at his request if the system of records contains a record pertaining to him;

(H) the agency procedures whereby an individual can be notified at his request how he can gain access to any record pertaining to him contained in the system of records, and how he can contest its content; and

(I) the categories of sources or records in the system;

(5) maintain all records which are used by the agency in making any determination about any individual with such accuracy, relevance, timeliness, and completeness as is reasonably necessary to assure fairness to the individual in the determination;

(6) prior to disseminating any record about an individual to any person other than an agency, unless the dissemination is made pursuant to subsection (b)(2) of this section, make reasonable efforts to assure that such records are accurate, complete, timely, and relevant for agency purposes;

(7) maintain no record describing how any individual exercises rights guaranteed by the First Amendment unless expressly authorized by statute or by the individual about whom the record is maintained or unless pertinent to and within the scope of an authorized law enforcement activity;

(8) make reasonable efforts to serve notice on an individual when any record on such individual is made available to any person under compulsory legal process when such process becomes a matter of public record;

(9) establish rules of conduct for persons involved in the design, development, operation, or maintenance of any system of records, or in maintaining any record, and instruct each such person with respect to such rules and the requirements of this section, including any other rules and procedures adopted pursuant to this section and the penalties for noncompliance;

(10) establish appropriate administrative, technical, and physical safeguards to insure the security and confidentiality of records and to protect against any anticipated threats or hazards to their security or integrity which could result

in substantial harm, embarrassment, inconvenience, or unfairness to any individual on whom information is maintained;

(11) at least 30 days prior to publication of information under paragraph (4)(D) of this subsection, publish in the Federal Register notice of any new use or intended use of the information in the system, and provide an opportunity for interested persons to submit written data, views, or arguments to the agency; and

(12) if such agency is a recipient agency or a source agency in a matching program with a non-Federal agency, with respect to any establishment or revision of a matching program, at least 30 days prior to conducting such program, publish in the Federal Register notice of such establishment or revision.

(f) Agency Rules.—In order to carry out the provisions of this section, each agency that maintains a system of records shall promulgate rules, in accordance with the requirements (including general notice) of section 553 of this title, which shall—

(1) establish procedures whereby an individual can be notified in response to his request if any system of records named by the individual contains a record pertaining to him;

(2) define reasonable times, places, and requirements for identifying an individual who requests his record or information pertaining to him before the agency shall make the record or information available to the individual;

(3) establish procedures for the disclosure to an individual upon his request of his record or information pertaining to him, including special procedure, if deemed necessary, for the disclosure to an individual of medical records, including psychological records, pertaining to him;

(4) establish procedures for reviewing a request from an individual concerning the amendment of any record or information pertaining to the individual, for making a determination on the request, for an appeal within the agency of an initial adverse agency determination, and for whatever additional means may be necessary for each individual to be able to exercise fully his rights under this section; and

(5) establish fees to be charged, if any, to any individual for making copies of his record, excluding the cost of any search for and review of the record.

The Office of the Federal Register shall biennially compile and publish the rules promulgated under this subsection and agency notices published under subsection (e)(4) of this section in a form available to the public at low cost.

(g)

(1) Civil remedies.—Whenever any agency

(A) makes a determination under subsection (d)(3) of this section not to amend an individual's record in accordance with his request, or fails to make such review in conformity with that subsection;

(B) refuses to comply with an individual request under subsection (d)(1) of this section;

(C) fails to maintain any record concerning any individual with such accuracy, relevance, timeliness, and completeness as is necessary to assure fairness in any determination relating to the qualifications, character, rights, or opportunities of, or benefits to the individual that may be made on the basis of such record, and consequently a determination is made which is adverse to the individual; or

(D) fails to comply with any other provision of this section, or any rule promulgated thereunder, in such a way as to have an adverse effect on an individual,

the individual may bring a civil action against the agency, and the district courts of the United States shall have jurisdiction in the matters under the provisions of this subsection.

(2)

(A) In any suit brought under the provisions of subsection (g)(1)(A) of this section, the court may order the agency to amend the individual's record in accordance with his request or in such other way as the court may direct. In such a case the court shall determine the matter de novo.

(B) The court may assess against the United States reasonable attorney fees and other litigation costs reasonably incurred in any case under this paragraph in which the complainant has substantially prevailed.

(3)

(A) In any suit brought under the provisions of subsection (g)(1)(B) of this section, the court may enjoin the agency from withholding the records and order the production to the complainant of any agency records improperly withheld from him. In such a case the court shall determine the matter de novo, and may examine the contents of any agency records in camera to determine whether the records or any portion thereof may be withheld under any of the exemptions set forth in subsection (k) of this section, and the burden is on the agency to sustain its action.

(B) The court may assess against the United States reasonable attorney fees and other litigation costs reasonably incurred in any case under this paragraph in which the complainant has substantially prevailed.

(4) In any suit brought under the provisions of subsection (g)(1)(C) or (D) of this section in which the court determines that the agency acted in a manner which was intentional or willful, the United States shall be liable to the individual in an amount equal to the sum of—

(A) actual damages sustained by the individual as a result of the refusal or failure, but in no case shall a person entitled to recovery receive less than the sum of $1,000; and

(B) the costs of the action together with reasonable attorney fees as determined by the court.

(5) An action to enforce any liability created under this section may be brought in the district court of the United States in the district in which the complainant resides, or has his principal place of business, or in which the agency records are situated, or in the District of Columbia, without regard to the amount in controversy, within two years from the date on which the cause of action arises, except that where an agency has materially and willfully misrepresented any information required under this section to be disclosed to an individual and the information so misrepresented is material to establishment of

the liability of the agency to the individual under this section, the action may be brought at any time within two years after discovery by the individual of the misrepresentation. Nothing in this section shall be construed to authorize any civil action by reason of any injury sustained as the result of a disclosure of a record prior to September 27, 1975.

(h) Rights of Legal Guardians.—For the purposes of this section, the parent of any minor, or the legal guardian of any individual who has been declared to be incompetent due to physical or mental incapacity or age by a court of competent jurisdiction, may act on behalf of the individual.

(i)

(1) Criminal penalties.—Any officer or employee of an agency, who by virtue of his employment or official position, has possession of, or access to, agency records which contain individually identifiable information the disclosure of which is prohibited by this section or by rules or regulations established thereunder, and who knowing that disclosure of the specific material is so prohibited, willfully discloses the material in any manner to any person or agency not entitled to receive it, shall be guilty of a misdemeanor and fined not more than $5,000.

(2) Any officer or employee of any agency who willfully maintains a system of records without meeting the notice requirements of subsection (e)(4) of this section shall be guilty of a misdemeanor and fined not more than $5,000.

(3) Any person who knowingly and willfully requests or obtains any record concerning an individual from an agency under false pretenses shall be guilty of a misdemeanor and fined not more than $5,000.

(j) General Exemptions.—The head of any agency may promulgate rules, in accordance with the requirements (including general notice) of sections 553(b)(1), (2), and (3), (c), and (e) of this title, to exempt any system of records within the agency from any part of this section except subsections (b), (c)(1) and (2), (e)(4)(A) through (F), (e)(6), (7), (9), (10), and (11), and (i) if the system of records is—

(1) maintained by the Central Intelligence Agency; or

(2) maintained by an agency or component thereof which performs as its principal function any activity pertaining to the enforcement of criminal laws, including police efforts to prevent, control, or reduce crime or to apprehend criminals, and the activities of prosecutors, courts, correctional, probation, pardon, or parole authorities, and which consists of (A) information compiled for the purpose of identifying individual criminal offenders and alleged offenders and consisting only of identifying data and notations of arrests, the nature and disposition of criminal charges, sentencing, confinement, release, and parole and probation status; (B) information compiled for the purpose of a criminal investigation, including reports of informants and investigators, and associated with an identifiable individual; or (C) reports identifiable to an individual compiled at any stage of the process of enforcement of the criminal laws from arrest or indictment through release from supervision.

At the time rules are adopted under this subsection, the agency shall include in the statement required under section 553(c) of this title, the reasons why the system of records is to be exempted from a provision of this section.

(k) Specific exemptions.—The head of any agency may promulgate rules, in accordance with the requirements (including general notice) of sections 553(b)(1), (2), and (3), (c), and (e) of this title, to exempt any system of records within the agency from subsections (c)(3), (d), (e)(1), (e)(4)(G), (H), and (I) and (f) of this section if the system of records is—

(1) subject to the provisions of section 552(b)(1) of this title;

(2) investigatory material compiled for law enforcement purposes, other than material within the scope of subsection (j)(2) of this section: Provided, however, That if any individual is denied any right, privilege, or benefit that he would otherwise be entitled by Federal law, or for which he would otherwise be eligible, as a result of the maintenance of such material, such material shall be provided to such individual, except to the extent that the disclosure of such material would reveal the identity of a source who furnished information to the Government under an express promise that the identity of the source would be held in confidence, or, prior to the effective date of this section, under an implied promise that the identity of the source would be held in confidence;

(3) maintained in connection with providing protective services to the President of the United States or other individuals pursuant to section 3056 of title 18;

(4) required by statute to be maintained and used solely as statistical records;

(5) investigatory material compiled solely for the purpose of determining suitability, eligibility, or qualifications for Federal civilian employment, military service, Federal contracts, or access to classified information, but only to the extent that the disclosure of such material would reveal the identity of a source who furnished information to the Government under an express promise that the identity of the source would be held in confidence, or, prior to the effective date of this section, under an implied promise that the identity of the source would be held in confidence;

(6) testing or examination material used solely to determine individual qualifications for appointment or promotion in the Federal service the disclosure of which would compromise the objectivity or fairness of the testing or examination process; or

(7) evaluation material used to determine potential for promotion in the armed services, but only to the extent that the disclosure of such material would reveal the identity of a source who furnished information to the Government under an express promise that the identity of the source would be held in confidence, or, prior to the effective date of this section, under an implied promise that the identity of the source would be held in confidence.

At the time rules are adopted under this subsection, the agency shall include in the statement required under section 553(c) of this title, the reasons why the system of records is to be exempted from a provision of this section.

(*l*)

(1) Archival records.—Each agency record which is accepted by the Archivist of the United States for storage, processing, and servicing in accordance with section 3103 of title 44 shall, for the purposes of this section, be considered to be maintained by the agency which deposited the record and shall be subject

to the provisions of this section. The Archivist of the United States shall not disclose the record except to the agency which maintains the record, or under rules established by that agency which are not inconsistent with the provisions of this section.

(2) Each agency record pertaining to an identifiable individual which was transferred to the National Archives of the United States as a record which has sufficient historical or other value to warrant its continued preservation by the United States Government, prior to the effective date of this section, shall, for the purposes of this section, be considered to be maintained by the National Archives and shall not be subject to the provisions of this section, except that a statement generally describing such records (modeled after the requirements relating to records subject to subsections (e)(4)(A) through (G) of this section) shall be published in the Federal Register.

(3) Each agency record pertaining to an identifiable individual which is transferred to the National Archives of the United States as a record which has sufficient historical or other value to warrant its continued preservation by the United States Government, on or after the effective date of this section, shall, for the purposes of this section, be considered to be maintained by the National Archives and shall be exempt from the requirements of this section except subsections (e)(4)(A) through (G) and (e)(9) of this section.

(m)

(1) Government contractors.—When an agency provides by a contract for the operation by or on behalf of the agency of a system of records to accomplish an agency function, the agency shall, consistent with its authority, cause the requirements of this section to be applied to such system. For purposes of subsection (i) of this section any such contractor and any employee of such contractor, if such contract is agreed to on or after the effective date of this section, shall be considered to be an employee of an agency.

(2) A consumer reporting agency to which a record is disclosed under section 3711(e) of title 31 shall not be considered a contractor for the purposes of this section.

(n) Mailing lists.—An individual's name and address may not be sold or rented by an agency unless such action is specifically authorized by law. This provision shall not be construed to require the withholding of names and addresses otherwise permitted to be made public.

(o) Matching agreements.—

(1) No record which is contained in a system of records may be disclosed to a recipient agency or non-Federal agency for use in a computer matching program except pursuant to a written agreement between the source agency and the recipient agency or non-Federal agency specifying—

(A) the purpose and legal authority for conducting the program;

(B) the justification for the program and the anticipated results, including a specific estimate of any savings;

(C) a description of the records that will be matched, including each data element that will be used, the approximate number of records that will be matched, and the projected starting and completion dates of the matching program;

(D) procedures for providing individualized notice at the time of application, and notice periodically thereafter as directed by the Data Integrity Board of such agency (subject to guidance provided by the Director of the Office of Management and Budget pursuant to subsection (v)), to—

(i) applicants for and recipients of financial assistance or payments under Federal benefit programs, and

(ii) applicants for and holders of positions as Federal personnel, that any information provided by such applicants, recipients, holders and individuals may be subject to verification through matching programs;

(E) procedures for verifying information produced in such matching program as required by subsection (p);

(F) procedures for the retention and timely destruction of identifiable records created by a recipient agency or non-Federal agency in such matching program;

(G) procedures for ensuring the administrative, technical, and physical security of the records matched and the results of such programs;

(H) prohibitions on duplication and redisclosure of records provided by the source agency within or outside the recipient agency or the non-Federal agency, except where required by law or essential to the conduct of the matching program;

(I) procedures governing the use by a recipient agency or non-Federal agency of records provided in a matching program by a source agency, including procedures governing return of the records to the source agency or destruction of records used in such program;

(J) information on assessments that have been made on the accuracy of the records that will be used in such matching program; and

(K) that the Comptroller General may have access to all records of a recipient agency or a non-Federal agency that the Comptroller General deems necessary in order to monitor or verify compliance with the agreement.

(2)

(A) A copy of each agreement entered into pursuant to paragraph (1) shall—

(i) be transmitted to the Committee on Governmental Affairs of the Senate and the Committee on Government Operations of the House of Representatives; and

(ii) be available upon request to the public.

(B) No such agreement shall be effective until 30 days after the date on which such a copy is transmitted pursuant to subparagraph (A)(i).

(C) Such an agreement shall remain in effect only for such period, not to exceed 18 months, as the Data Integrity Board of the agency determines is appropriate in light of the purposes, and length of time necessary for the conduct, of the matching program.

(D) Within 3 months prior to the expiration of such an agreement pursuant to subparagraph (C), the Data Integrity Board of the agency may, without additional review, renew the matching agreement for a current, ongoing matching program for not more than one additional year if—

(i) such program will be conducted without any change; and

(ii) each party to the agreement certifies to the Board in writing that the program has been conducted in compliance with the agreement.

(p) Verification and Opportunity to Contest Findings.—

(1) In order to protect any individual whose records are used in a matching program, no recipient agency, non-Federal agency, or source agency may suspend, terminate, reduce, or make a final denial of any financial assistance or payment under a Federal benefit program to such individual, or take other adverse action against such individual, as a result of information produced by such matching program, until—

(A)

(i) the agency has independently verified the information; or

(ii) the Data Integrity Board of the agency, or in the case of a non-Federal agency the Data Integrity Board of the source agency, determines in accordance with guidance issued by the Director of the Office of Management and Budget that—

(I) the information is limited to identification and amount of benefits paid by the source agency under a Federal benefit program; and

(II) there is a high degree of confidence that the information provided to the recipient agency is accurate;

(B) the individual receives a notice from the agency containing a statement of its findings and informing the individual of the opportunity to contest such findings; and

(C)

(i) the expiration of any time period established for the program by statute or regulation for the individual to respond to that notice; or

(ii) in the case of a program for which no such period is established, the end of the 30-day period beginning on the date on which notice under subparagraph (B) is mailed or otherwise provided to the individual.

(2) Independent verification referred to in paragraph (1) requires investigation and confirmation of specific information relating to an individual that is used as a basis for an adverse action against the individual, including where applicable investigation and confirmation of—

(A) the amount of any asset or income involved;

(B) whether such individual actually has or had access to such asset or income for such individual's own use; and

(C) the period or periods when the individual actually had such asset or income.

(3) Notwithstanding paragraph (1), an agency may take any appropriate action otherwise prohibited by such paragraph if the agency determines that the public health or public safety may be adversely affected or significantly threatened during any notice period required by such paragraph.

(q)

(1) Sanctions.—Notwithstanding any other provision of law, no source agency may disclose any record which is contained in a system of records to a

recipient agency or non-Federal agency for a matching program if such source agency has reason to believe that the requirements of subsection (p), or any matching agreement entered into pursuant to subsection (o), or both, are not being met by such recipient agency.

(2) No source agency may renew a matching agreement unless—

(A) the recipient agency or non-Federal agency has certified that it has complied with the provisions of that agreement; and

(B) the source agency has no reason to believe that the certification is inaccurate.

(r) Report on New Systems and Matching Programs.—Each agency that proposes to establish or make a significant change in a system of records or a matching program shall provide adequate advance notice of any such proposal (in duplicate) to the Committee on Government Operations of the House of Representatives, the Committee on Governmental Affairs of the Senate, and the Office of Management and Budget in order to permit an evaluation of the probable or potential effect of such proposal on the privacy or other rights of individuals.

(s) Biennial Report.—The President shall biennially submit to the Speaker of the House of Representatives and the President pro tempore of the Senate a report—

(1) describing the actions of the Director of the Office of Management and Budget pursuant to section 6 of the Privacy Act of 1974 during the preceding 2 years;

(2) describing the exercise of individual rights of access and amendment under this section during such years;

(3) identifying changes in or additions to systems of records;

(4) containing such other information concerning administration of this section as may be necessary or useful to the Congress in reviewing the effectiveness of this section in carrying out the purposes of the Privacy Act of 1974.

(t)

(1) Effect of Other Laws.—No agency shall rely on any exemption contained in section 552 of this title to withhold from an individual any record which is otherwise accessible to such individual under the provisions of this section.

(2) No agency shall rely on any exemption in this section to withhold from an individual any record which is otherwise accessible to such individual under the provisions of section 552 of this title.

(u) Data Integrity Boards.—

(1) Every agency conducting or participating in a matching program shall establish a Data Integrity Board to oversee and coordinate among the various components of such agency the agency's implementation of this section.

(2) Each Data Integrity Board shall consist of senior officials designated by the head of the agency, and shall include any senior official designated by the head of the agency as responsible for implementation of this section, and the inspector general of the agency, if any. The inspector general shall not serve as chairman of the Data Integrity Board.

(3) Each Data Integrity Board.—

(A) shall review, approve, and maintain all written agreements for receipt or disclosure of agency records for matching programs to ensure compliance with subsection (o), and all relevant statutes, regulations, and guidelines;

(B) shall review all matching programs in which the agency has participated during the year, either as a source agency or recipient agency, determine compliance with applicable laws, regulations, guidelines, and agency agreements, and assess the costs and benefits of such programs;

(C) shall review all recurring matching programs in which the agency has participated during the year, either as a source agency or recipient agency, for continued justification for such disclosures;

(D) shall compile an annual report, which shall be submitted to the head of the agency and the Office of Management and Budget and made available to the public on request, describing the matching activities of the agency, including—

(i) matching programs in which the agency has participated as a source agency or recipient agency;

(ii) matching agreements proposed under subsection (o) that were disapproved by the Board;

(iii) any changes in membership or structure of the Board in the preceding year;

(iv) the reasons for any waiver of the requirement in paragraph (4) of this section for completion and submission of a cost-benefit analysis prior to the approval of a matching program;

(v) any violations of matching agreements that have been alleged or identified and any corrective action taken; and

(vi) any other information required by the Director of the Office of Management and Budget to be included in such report;

(E) shall serve as a clearinghouse for receiving and providing information on the accuracy, completeness, and reliability of records used in matching programs;

(F) shall provide interpretation and guidance to agency components and personnel on the requirements of this section for matching programs;

(G) shall review agency recordkeeping and disposal policies and practices for matching programs to assure compliance with this section; and

(H) may review and report on any agency matching activities that are not matching programs.

(4)

(A) Except as provided in subparagraphs (B) and (C), a Data Integrity Board shall not approve any written agreement for a matching program unless the agency has completed and submitted to such Board a cost-benefit analysis of the proposed program and such analysis demonstrates that the program is likely to be cost effective.

(B) The Board may waive the requirements of subparagraph (A) of this paragraph if it determines in writing, in accordance with guidelines prescribed by the Director of the Office of Management and Budget, that a cost-benefit analysis is not required.

(C) A cost-benefit analysis shall not be required under subparagraph (A) prior to the initial approval of a written agreement for a matching program that is specifically required by statute. Any subsequent written agreement for such a program shall not be approved by the Data Integrity Board unless the agency has submitted a cost-benefit analysis of the program as conducted under the preceding approval of such agreement.

(5)

(A) If a matching agreement is disapproved by a Data Integrity Board, any party to such agreement may appeal the disapproval to the Director of the Office of Management and Budget. Timely notice of the filing of such an appeal shall be provided by the Director of the Office of Management and Budget to the Committee on Governmental Affairs of the Senate and the Committee on Government Operations of the House of Representatives.

(B) The Director of the Office of Management and Budget may approve a matching agreement notwithstanding the disapproval of a Data Integrity Board if the Director determines that—

(i) the matching program will be consistent with all applicable legal, regulatory, and policy requirements;

(ii) there is adequate evidence that the matching agreement will be cost-effective; and

(iii) the matching program is in the public interest.

(C) The decision of the Director to approve a matching agreement shall not take effect until 30 days after it is reported to committees described in subparagraph (A).

(D) If the Data Integrity Board and the Director of the Office of Management and Budget disapprove a matching program proposed by the inspector general of an agency, the inspector general may report the disapproval to the head of the agency and to the Congress.

(6) In the reports required by paragraph (3)(D), agency matching activities that are not matching programs may be reported on an aggregate basis, if and to the extent necessary to protect ongoing law enforcement or counterintelligence investigations.

(v) Office of Management and Budget Responsibilities.—The Director of the Office of Management and Budget shall—

(1) develop and, after notice and opportunity for public comment, prescribe guidelines and regulations for the use of agencies in implementing the provisions of this section; and

(2) provide continuing assistance to and oversight of the implementation of this section by agencies.

(w) Applicability to Bureau of Consumer Financial Protection.—Except as provided in the Consumer Financial Protection Act of 2010, this section shall apply with respect to the Bureau of Consumer Financial Protection.

Government in the Sunshine Act

§ 552b. Open meetings

(a) For purposes of this section—

(1) the term "agency" means any agency, as defined in section 552(e) of this title, headed by a collegial body composed of two or more individual members, a majority of whom are appointed to such position by the President with the advice and consent of the Senate, and any subdivision thereof authorized to act on behalf of the agency;

(2) the term "meeting" means the deliberations of at least the number of individual agency members required to take action on behalf of the agency where such deliberations determine or result in the joint conduct or disposition of official agency business, but does not include deliberations required or permitted by subsection (d) or (e); and

(3) the term "member" means an individual who belongs to a collegial body heading an agency.

(b) Members shall not jointly conduct or dispose of agency business other than in accordance with this section. Except as provided in subsection (c), every portion of every meeting of an agency shall be open to public observation.

(c) Except in a case where the agency finds that the public interest requires otherwise, the second sentence of subsection (b) shall not apply to any portion of an agency meeting, and the requirements of subsections (d) and (e) shall not apply to any information pertaining to such meeting otherwise required by this section to be disclosed to the public, where the agency properly determines that such portion or portions of its meeting or the disclosure of such information is likely to—

(1) disclose matters that are (A) specifically authorized under criteria established by an Executive order to be kept secret in the interests of national defense or foreign policy and (B) in fact properly classified pursuant to such Executive order;

(2) relate solely to the internal personnel rules and practices of an agency;

(3) disclose matters specifically exempted from disclosure by statute (other than section 552 of this title), provided that such statute (A) requires that the matters be withheld from the public in such a manner as to leave no discretion on the issue, or (B) establishes particular criteria for withholding or refers to particular types of matters to be withheld;

(4) disclose trade secrets and commercial or financial information obtained from a person and privileged or confidential;

(5) involve accusing any person of a crime, or formally censuring any person;

(6) disclose information of a personal nature where disclosure would constitute a clearly unwarranted invasion of personal privacy;

(7) disclose investigatory records compiled for law enforcement purposes, or information which if written would be contained in such records, but only to the extent that the production of such records or information would (A) interfere with enforcement proceedings, (B) deprive a person of a right to a fair trial or an impartial adjudication, (C) constitute an unwarranted invasion of personal privacy, (D) disclose the identity of a confidential source and, in the case

of a record compiled by a criminal law enforcement authority in the course of a criminal investigation, or by an agency conducting a lawful national security intelligence investigation, confidential information furnished only by the confidential source, (E) disclose investigative techniques and procedures, or (F) endanger the life or physical safety of law enforcement personnel;

(8) disclose information contained in or related to examination, operating, or condition reports prepared by, on behalf of, or for the use of an agency responsible for the regulation or supervision of financial institutions;

(9) disclose information the premature disclosure of which would—

(A) in the case of an agency which regulates currencies, securities, commodities, or financial institutions, be likely to (i) lead to significant financial speculation in currencies, securities, or commodities, or (ii) significantly endanger the stability of any financial institution; or

(B) in the case of any agency, be likely to significantly frustrate implementation of a proposed agency action,

except that subparagraph (B) shall not apply in any instance where the agency has already disclosed to the public the content or nature of its proposed action, or where the agency is required by law to make such disclosure on its own initiative prior to taking final agency action on such proposal; or

(10) specifically concern the agency's issuance of a subpena, or the agency's participation in a civil action or proceeding, an action in a foreign court or international tribunal, or an arbitration, or the initiation, conduct, or disposition by the agency of a particular case of formal agency adjudication pursuant to the procedures in section 554 of this title or otherwise involving a determination on the record after opportunity for a hearing.

(d)

(1) Action under subsection (c) shall be taken only when a majority of the entire membership of the agency (as defined in subsection (a)(1)) votes to take such action. A separate vote of the agency members shall be taken with respect to each agency meeting a portion or portions of which are proposed to be closed to the public pursuant to subsection (c), or with respect to any information which is proposed to be withheld under subsection (c). A single vote may be taken with respect to a series of meetings, a portion or portions of which are proposed to be closed to the public, or with respect to any information concerning such series of meetings, so long as each meeting in such series involves the same particular matters and is scheduled to be held no more than thirty days after the initial meeting in such series. The vote of each agency member participating in such vote shall be recorded and no proxies shall be allowed.

(2) Whenever any person whose interests may be directly affected by a portion of a meeting requests that the agency close such portion to the public for any of the reasons referred to in paragraph (5), (6), or (7) of subsection (c), the agency, upon request of any one of its members, shall vote by recorded vote whether to close such meeting.

(3) Within one day of any vote taken pursuant to paragraph (1) or (2), the agency shall make publicly available a written copy of such vote reflecting the vote

of each member on the question. If a portion of a meeting is to be closed to the public, the agency shall, within one day of the vote taken pursuant to paragraph (1) or (2) of this subsection, make publicly available a full written explanation of its action closing the portion together with a list of all persons expected to attend the meeting and their affiliation.

(4) Any agency, a majority of whose meetings may properly be closed to the public pursuant to paragraph (4), (8), (9)(A), or (10) of subsection (c), or any combination thereof, may provide by regulation for the closing of such meetings or portions thereof in the event that a majority of the members of the agency votes by recorded vote at the beginning of such meeting, or portion thereof, to close the exempt portion or portions of the meeting, and a copy of such vote, reflecting the vote of each member on the question, is made available to the public. The provisions of paragraphs (1), (2), and (3) of this subsection and subsection (e) shall not apply to any portion of a meeting to which such regulations apply: Provided, That the agency shall, except to the extent that such information is exempt from disclosure under the provisions of subsection (c), provide the public with public announcement of the time, place, and subject matter of the meeting and of each portion thereof at the earliest practicable time.

(e)

(1) In the case of each meeting, the agency shall make public announcement, at least one week before the meeting, of the time, place, and subject matter of the meeting, whether it is to be open or closed to the public, and the name and phone number of the official designated by the agency to respond to requests for information about the meeting. Such announcement shall be made unless a majority of the members of the agency determines by a recorded vote that agency business requires that such meeting be called at an earlier date, in which case the agency shall make public announcement of the time, place, and subject matter of such meeting, and whether open or closed to the public, at the earliest practicable time.

(2) The time or place of a meeting may be changed following the public announcement required by paragraph (1) only if the agency publicly announces such change at the earliest practicable time. The subject matter of a meeting, or the determination of the agency to open or close a meeting, or portion of a meeting, to the public, may be changed following the public announcement required by this subsection only if (A) a majority of the entire membership of the agency determines by a recorded vote that agency business so requires and that no earlier announcement of the change was possible, and (B) the agency publicly announces such change and the vote of each member upon such change at the earliest practicable time.

(3) Immediately following each public announcement required by this subsection, notice of the time, place, and subject matter of a meeting, whether the meeting is open or closed, any change in one of the preceding, and the name and phone number of the official designated by the agency to respond to requests for information about the meeting, shall also be submitted for publication in the Federal Register.

(f)

(1) For every meeting closed pursuant to paragraphs (1) through (10) of subsection (c), the General Counsel or chief legal officer of the agency shall publicly

certify that, in his or her opinion, the meeting may be closed to the public and shall state each relevant exemptive provision. A copy of such certification, together with a statement from the presiding officer of the meeting setting forth the time and place of the meeting, and the persons present, shall be retained by the agency. The agency shall maintain a complete transcript or electronic recording adequate to record fully the proceedings of each meeting, or portion of a meeting, closed to the public, except that in the case of a meeting, or portion of a meeting, closed to the public pursuant to paragraph (8), (9)(A), or (10) of subsection (c), the agency shall maintain either such a transcript or recording, or a set of minutes. Such minutes shall fully and clearly describe all matters discussed and shall provide a full and accurate summary of any actions taken, and the reasons therefor, including a description of each of the views expressed on any item and the record of any roll-call vote (reflecting the vote of each member on the question). All documents considered in connection with any action shall be identified in such minutes.

(2) The agency shall make promptly available to the public, in a place easily accessible to the public, the transcript, electronic recording, or minutes (as required by paragraph (1)) of the discussion of any item on the agenda, or of any item of the testimony of any witness received at the meeting, except for such item or items of such discussion or testimony as the agency determines to contain information which may be withheld under subsection (c). Copies of such transcript, or minutes, or a transcription of such recording disclosing the identity of each speaker, shall be furnished to any person at the actual cost of duplication or transcription. The agency shall maintain a complete verbatim copy of the transcript, a complete copy of the minutes, or a complete electronic recording of each meeting, or portion of a meeting, closed to the public, for a period of at least two years after such meeting, or until one year after the conclusion of any agency proceeding with respect to which the meeting or portion was held, whichever occurs later.

(g) Each agency subject to the requirements of this section shall, within 180 days after the date of enactment of this section, following consultation with the Office of the Chairman of the Administrative Conference of the United States and published notice in the Federal Register of at least thirty days and opportunity for written comment by any person, promulgate regulations to implement the requirements of subsections (b) through (f) of this section. Any person may bring a proceeding in the United States District Court for the District of Columbia to require an agency to promulgate such regulations if such agency has not promulgated such regulations within the time period specified herein. Subject to any limitations of time provided by law, any person may bring a proceeding in the United States Court of Appeals for the District of Columbia to set aside agency regulations issued pursuant to this subsection that are not in accord with the requirements of subsections (b) through (f) of this section and to require the promulgation of regulations that are in accord with such subsections.

(h)

(1) The district courts of the United States shall have jurisdiction to enforce the requirements of subsections (b) through (f) of this section by declaratory judgment, injunctive relief, or other relief as may be appropriate. Such actions may be brought by any person against an agency prior to, or within sixty days after, the meeting out of which the violation of this section arises, except

that if public announcement of such meeting is not initially provided by the agency in accordance with the requirements of this section, such action may be instituted pursuant to this section at any time prior to sixty days after any public announcement of such meeting. Such actions may be brought in the district court of the United States for the district in which the agency meeting is held or in which the agency in question has its headquarters, or in the District Court for the District of Columbia. In such actions a defendant shall serve his answer within thirty days after the service of the complaint. The burden is on the defendant to sustain his action. In deciding such cases the court may examine in camera any portion of the transcript, electronic recording, or minutes of a meeting closed to the public, and may take such additional evidence as it deems necessary. The court, having due regard for orderly administration and the public interest, as well as the interests of the parties, may grant such equitable relief as it deems appropriate, including granting an injunction against future violations of this section or ordering the agency to make available to the public such portion of the transcript, recording, or minutes of a meeting as is not authorized to be withheld under subsection (c) of this section.

(2) Any Federal court otherwise authorized by law to review agency action may, at the application of any person properly participating in the proceeding pursuant to other applicable law, inquire into violations by the agency of the requirements of this section and afford such relief as it deems appropriate. Nothing in this section authorizes any Federal court having jurisdiction solely on the basis of paragraph (1) to set aside, enjoin, or invalidate any agency action (other than an action to close a meeting or to withhold information under this section) taken or discussed at any agency meeting out of which the violation of this section arose.

(i) The court may assess against any party reasonable attorney fees and other litigation costs reasonably incurred by any other party who substantially prevails in any action brought in accordance with the provisions of subsection (g) or (h) of this section, except that costs may be assessed against the plaintiff only where the court finds that the suit was initiated by the plaintiff primarily for frivolous or dilatory purposes. In the case of assessment of costs against an agency, the costs may be assessed by the court against the United States.

(j) Each agency subject to the requirements of this section shall annually report to the Congress regarding the following:

(1) The changes in the policies and procedures of the agency under this section that have occurred during the preceding 1-year period.

(2) A tabulation of the number of meetings held, the exemptions applied to close meetings, and the days of public notice provided to close meetings.

(3) A brief description of litigation or formal complaints concerning the implementation of this section by the agency.

(4) A brief explanation of any changes in law that have affected the responsibilities of the agency under this section.

(k) Nothing herein expands or limits the present rights of any person under section 552 of this title, except that the exemptions set forth in subsection (c) of this section shall govern in the case of any request made pursuant to section 552 to copy or inspect the transcripts, recordings, or minutes described in subsection (f) of this section. The requirements of chapter 33 of title 44, United States Code,[8] shall not apply to the transcripts, recordings, and minutes described in subsection (f) of this section.

(l) This section does not constitute authority to withhold any information from Congress, and does not authorize the closing of any agency meeting or portion thereof required by any other provision of law to be open.

(m) Nothing in this section authorizes any agency to withhold from any individual any record, including transcripts, recordings, or minutes required by this section, which is otherwise accessible to such individual under section 552a of this title.

§ 553. Rule making

(a) This section applies, according to the provisions thereof, except to the extent that there is involved—

(1) a military or foreign affairs function of the United States; or

(2) a matter relating to agency management or personnel or to public property, loans, grants, benefits, or contracts.

(b) General notice of proposed rule making shall be published in the Federal Register, unless persons subject thereto are named and either personally served or otherwise have actual notice thereof in accordance with law. The notice shall include—

(1) a statement of the time, place, and nature of public rule making proceedings;

(2) reference to the legal authority under which the rule is proposed; and

(3) either the terms or substance of the proposed rule or a description of the subjects and issues involved.

Except when notice or hearing is required by statute, this subsection does not apply—

(A) to interpretative rules, general statements of policy, or rules of agency organization, procedure, or practice; or

(B) when the agency for good cause finds (and incorporates the finding and a brief statement of reasons therefor in the rules issued) that notice and public procedure thereon are impracticable, unnecessary, or contrary to the public interest.

(c) After notice required by this section, the agency shall give interested persons an opportunity to participate in the rule making through submission of written data, views, or arguments with or without opportunity for oral presentation. After consideration of the relevant matter presented, the agency shall incorporate in the rules adopted a concise general statement of their basis and purpose. When rules are required by statute to be made on the record after opportunity for an agency hearing, sections 556 and 557 of this title apply instead of this subsection.

---

8. 44 U.S.C. §§ 3301 *et seq.*

(d) The required publication or service of a substantive rule shall be made not less than 30 days before its effective date, except—

(1) a substantive rule which grants or recognizes an exemption or relieves a restriction;

(2) interpretative rules and statements of policy; or

(3) as otherwise provided by the agency for good cause found and published with the rule.

(e) Each agency shall give an interested person the right to petition for the issuance, amendment, or repeal of a rule.

§ 554. Adjudications

(a) This section applies, according to the provisions thereof, in every case of adjudication required by statute to be determined on the record after opportunity for an agency hearing, except to the extent that there is involved—

(1) a matter subject to a subsequent trial of the law and the facts de novo in a court;

(2) the selection or tenure of an employee, except a administrative law judge appointed under section 3105 of this title;

(3) proceedings in which decisions rest solely on inspections, tests, or elections;

(4) the conduct of military or foreign affairs functions;

(5) cases in which an agency is acting as an agent for a court; or

(6) the certification of worker representatives.

(b) Persons entitled to notice of an agency hearing shall be timely informed of—

(1) the time, place, and nature of the hearing;

(2) the legal authority and jurisdiction under which the hearing is to be held; and

(3) the matters of fact and law asserted.

When private persons are the moving parties, other parties to the proceeding shall give prompt notice of issues controverted in fact or law; and in other instances agencies may by rule require responsive pleading. In fixing the time and place for hearings, due regard shall be had for the convenience and necessity of the parties or their representatives.

(c) The agency shall give all interested parties opportunity for—

(1) the submission and consideration of facts, arguments, offers of settlement, or proposals of adjustment when time, the nature of the proceeding, and the public interest permit; and

(2) to the extent that the parties are unable so to determine a controversy by consent, hearing and decision on notice and in accordance with sections 556 and 557 of this title.

(d) The employee who presides at the reception of evidence pursuant to section 556 of this title shall make the recommended decision or initial decision required by section 557 of this title, unless he becomes unavailable to the agency. Except to the extent required for the disposition of ex parte matters as authorized by law, such an employee may not—

(1) consult a person or party on a fact in issue, unless on notice and opportunity for all parties to participate; or

(2) be responsible to or subject to the supervision or direction of an employee or agent engaged in the performance of investigative or prosecuting functions for an agency. An employee or agent engaged in the performance of investigative or prosecuting functions for an agency in a case may not, in that or a factually related case, participate or advise in the decision, recommended decision, or agency review pursuant to section 557 of this title, except as witness or counsel in public proceedings. This subsection does not apply—

(A) in determining applications for initial licenses;

(B) to proceedings involving the validity or application of rates, facilities, or practices of public utilities or carriers; or

(C) to the agency or a member or members of the body comprising the agency.

(e) The agency, with like effect as in the case of other orders, and in its sound discretion, may issue a declaratory order to terminate a controversy or remove uncertainty.

§ 555. Ancillary matters

(a) This section applies, according to the provisions thereof, except as otherwise provided by this subchapter.

(b) A person compelled to appear in person before an agency or representative thereof is entitled to be accompanied, represented, and advised by counsel or, if permitted by the agency, by other qualified representative. A party is entitled to appear in person or by or with counsel or other duly qualified representative in an agency proceeding. So far as the orderly conduct of public business permits, an interested person may appear before an agency or its responsible employees for the presentation, adjustment, or determination of an issue, request, or controversy in a proceeding, whether interlocutory, summary, or otherwise, or in connection with an agency function. With due regard for the convenience and necessity of the parties or their representatives and within a reasonable time, each agency shall proceed to conclude a matter presented to it. This subsection does not grant or deny a person who is not a lawyer the right to appear for or represent others before an agency or in an agency proceeding.

(c) Process, requirement of a report, inspection, or other investigative act or demand may not be issued, made, or enforced except as authorized by law. A person compelled to submit data or evidence is entitled to retain or, on payment of lawfully prescribed costs, procure a copy or transcript thereof, except that in a nonpublic investigatory proceeding the witness may for good cause be limited to inspection of the official transcript of his testimony.

(d) Agency subpenas[9] authorized by law shall be issued to a party on request and, when required by rules of procedure, on a statement or showing of general relevance and reasonable scope of the evidence sought. On contest, the court shall sustain the subpena[10] or similar process or demand to the extent that it is found

9. So in original. Probably should be "subpoenas."
10. So in original. Probably should be "subpoena."

to be in accordance with law. In a proceeding for enforcement, the court shall issue an order requiring the appearance of the witness or the production of the evidence or data within a reasonable time under penalty of punishment for contempt in case of contumacious failure to comply.

(e) Prompt notice shall be given of the denial in whole or in part of a written application, petition, or other request of an interested person made in connection with any agency proceeding. Except in affirming a prior denial or when the denial is self-explanatory, the notice shall be accompanied by a brief statement of the grounds for denial.

§ 556. Hearings; presiding employees; powers and duties; burden of proof; evidence; record as basis of decision

(a) This section applies, according to the provisions thereof, to hearings required by section 553 or 554 of this title to be conducted in accordance with this section.

(b) There shall preside at the taking of evidence—

(1) the agency;

(2) one or more members of the body which comprises the agency; or

(3) one or more administrative law judges appointed under section 3105 of this title.

This subchapter does not supersede the conduct of specified classes of proceedings, in whole or in part, by or before boards or other employees specially provided for by or designated under statute. The functions of presiding employees and of employees participating in decisions in accordance with section 557 of this title shall be conducted in an impartial manner. A presiding or participating employee may at any time disqualify himself. On the filing in good faith of a timely and sufficient affidavit of personal bias or other disqualification of a presiding or participating employee, the agency shall determine the matter as a part of the record and decision in the case.

(c) Subject to published rules of the agency and within its powers, employees presiding at hearings may—

(1) administer oaths and affirmations;

(2) issue subpenas[11] authorized by law;

(3) rule on offers of proof and receive relevant evidence;

(4) take depositions or have depositions taken when the ends of justice would be served;

(5) regulate the course of the hearing;

(6) hold conferences for the settlement or simplification of the issues by consent of the parties or by the use of alternative means of dispute resolution as provided in subchapter IV of this chapter;

(7) inform the parties as to the availability of one or more alternative means of dispute resolution, and encourage use of such methods;

11. So in original. Probably should be "subpoenas."

(8) require the attendance at any conference held pursuant to paragraph (6) of at least one representative of each party who has authority to negotiate concerning resolution of issues in controversy;

(9) dispose of procedural requests or similar matters;

(10) make or recommend decisions in accordance with section 557 of this title; and

(11) take other action authorized by agency rule consistent with this subchapter.

(d) Except as otherwise provided by statute, the proponent of a rule or order has the burden of proof. Any oral or documentary evidence may be received, but the agency as a matter of policy shall provide for the exclusion of irrelevant, immaterial, or unduly repetitious evidence. A sanction may not be imposed or rule or order issued except on consideration of the whole record or those parts thereof cited by a party and supported by and in accordance with the reliable, probative, and substantial evidence. The agency may, to the extent consistent with the interests of justice and the policy of the underlying statutes administered by the agency, consider a violation of section 557(d) of this title sufficient grounds for a decision adverse to a party who has knowingly committed such violation or knowingly caused such violation to occur. A party is entitled to present his case or defense by oral or documentary evidence, to submit rebuttal evidence, and to conduct such cross-examination as may be required for a full and true disclosure of the facts. In rule making or determining claims for money or benefits or applications for initial licenses an agency may, when a party will not be prejudiced thereby, adopt procedures for the submission of all or part of the evidence in written form.

(e) The transcript of testimony and exhibits, together with all papers and requests filed in the proceeding, constitutes the exclusive record for decision in accordance with section 557 of this title and, on payment of lawfully prescribed costs, shall be made available to the parties. When an agency decision rests on official notice of a material fact not appearing in the evidence in the record, a party is entitled, on timely request, to an opportunity to show the contrary.

§ 557. Initial decisions; conclusiveness; review by agency; submissions by parties; contents of decisions; record

(a) This section applies, according to the provisions thereof, when a hearing is required to be conducted in accordance with section 556 of this title.

(b) When the agency did not preside at the reception of the evidence, the presiding employee or, in cases not subject to section 554(d) of this title, an employee qualified to preside at hearings pursuant to section 556 of this title, shall initially decide the case unless the agency requires, either in specific cases or by general rule, the entire record to be certified to it for decision. When the presiding employee makes an initial decision, that decision then becomes the decision of the agency without further proceedings unless there is an appeal to, or review on motion of, the agency within time provided by rule. On appeal from or review of the initial decision, the agency has all the powers which it would have in making the initial decision except as it may limit the issues on notice or by rule. When the agency makes the decision without having presided at the reception of the evidence, the presiding employee or an employee qualified to preside at hearings pursuant to section 556 of this title shall first recommend a decision, except that in rule making or determining applications for initial licenses—

(1) instead thereof the agency may issue a tentative decision or one of its responsible employees may recommend a decision; or

(2) this procedure may be omitted in a case in which the agency finds on the record that due and timely execution of its functions imperatively and unavoidably so requires.

(c) Before a recommended, initial, or tentative decision, or a decision on agency review of the decision of subordinate employees, the parties are entitled to a reasonable opportunity to submit for the consideration of the employees participating in the decisions—

(1) proposed findings and conclusions; or

(2) exceptions to the decisions or recommended decisions of subordinate employees or to tentative agency decisions; and

(3) supporting reasons for the exceptions or proposed findings or conclusions.

The record shall show the ruling on each finding, conclusion, or exception presented. All decisions, including initial, recommended, and tentative decisions, are a part of the record and shall include a statement of—

(A) findings and conclusions, and the reasons or basis therefor, on all the material issues of fact, law, or discretion presented on the record; and

(B) the appropriate rule, order, sanction, relief, or denial thereof.

(d)

(1) In any agency proceeding which is subject to subsection (a) of this section, except to the extent required for the disposition of ex parte matters as authorized by law—

(A) no interested person outside the agency shall make or knowingly cause to be made to any member of the body comprising the agency, administrative law judge, or other employee who is or may reasonably be expected to be involved in the decisional process of the proceeding, an ex parte communication relevant to the merits of the proceeding;

(B) no member of the body comprising the agency, administrative law judge, or other employee who is or may reasonably be expected to be involved in the decisional process of the proceeding, shall make or knowingly cause to be made to any interested person outside the agency an ex parte communication relevant to the merits of the proceeding;

(C) a member of the body comprising the agency, administrative law judge, or other employee who is or may reasonably be expected to be involved in the decisional process of such proceeding who receives, or who makes or knowingly causes to be made, a communication prohibited by this subsection shall place on the public record of the proceeding:

(i) all such written communications;

(ii) memoranda stating the substance of all such oral communications; and

(iii) all written responses, and memoranda stating the substance of all oral responses, to the materials described in clauses (i) and (ii) of this subparagraph;

(D) upon receipt of a communication knowingly made or knowingly caused to be made by a party in violation of this subsection, the agency, administrative law judge, or other employee presiding at the hearing may, to the extent consistent with the interests of justice and the policy of the underlying statutes, require the party to show cause why his claim or interest in the proceeding should not be dismissed, denied, disregarded, or otherwise adversely affected on account of such violation; and

(E) the prohibitions of this subsection shall apply beginning at such time as the agency may designate, but in no case shall they begin to apply later than the time at which a proceeding is noticed for hearing unless the person responsible for the communication has knowledge that it will be noticed, in which case the prohibitions shall apply beginning at the time of his acquisition of such knowledge.

(2) This subsection does not constitute authority to withhold information from Congress.

§ 558. Imposition of sanctions; determination of applications for licenses; suspension, revocation, and expiration of licenses

(a) This section applies, according to the provisions thereof, to the exercise of a power or authority.

(b) A sanction may not be imposed or a substantive rule or order issued except within jurisdiction delegated to the agency and as authorized by law.

(c) When application is made for a license required by law, the agency, with due regard for the rights and privileges of all the interested parties or adversely affected persons and within a reasonable time, shall set and complete proceedings required to be conducted in accordance with sections 556 and 557 of this title or other proceedings required by law and shall make its decision. Except in cases of willfulness or those in which public health, interest, or safety requires otherwise, the withdrawal, suspension, revocation, or annulment of a license is lawful only if, before the institution of agency proceedings therefor, the licensee has been given—

(1) notice by the agency in writing of the facts or conduct which may warrant the action; and

(2) opportunity to demonstrate or achieve compliance with all lawful requirements.

When the licensee has made timely and sufficient application for a renewal or a new license in accordance with agency rules, a license with reference to an activity of a continuing nature does not expire until the application has been finally determined by the agency.

§ 559. Effect on other laws; effect of subsequent statute

This subchapter, chapter 7, and sections 1305, 3105, 3344, 4301(2)(E), 5372, and 7521 of this title, and the provisions of section 5335(a)(B) of this title that relate to administrative law judges, do not limit or repeal additional requirements imposed by statute or otherwise recognized by law. Except as otherwise required by law, requirements or privileges relating to evidence or procedure apply equally to agencies and persons. Each agency is granted the authority necessary to comply with the requirements of this subchapter through the issuance of rules or otherwise. Subsequent statute may not be held to supersede or modify this subchapter, chapter 7, sections 1305, 3105, 3344, 4301(2)(E), 5372, or 7521 of this title, or the provisions of section 5335(a)(B) of this title that relate to administrative law judges, except to the extent that it does so expressly.

Subchapter III—Negotiated Rulemaking Procedure

Negotiated Rulemaking Act

§ 561. Purpose

The purpose of this subchapter is to establish a framework for the conduct of negotiated rulemaking, consistent with section 553 of this title, to encourage agencies to use the process when it enhances the informal rulemaking process. Nothing in this subchapter should be construed as an attempt to limit innovation and experimentation with the negotiated rulemaking process or with other innovative rulemaking procedures otherwise authorized by law.

§ 562. Definitions

For the purposes of this subchapter, the term—

(1) "agency" has the same meaning as in section 551(1) of this title;

(2) "consensus" means unanimous concurrence among the interests represented on a negotiated rulemaking committee established under this subchapter, unless such committee—

(A) agrees to define such term to mean a general but not unanimous concurrence; or

(B) agrees upon another specified definition;

(3) "convener" means a person who impartially assists an agency in determining whether establishment of a negotiated rulemaking committee is feasible and appropriate in a particular rulemaking;

(4) "facilitator" means a person who impartially aids in the discussions and negotiations among the members of a negotiated rulemaking committee to develop a proposed rule;

(5) "interest" means, with respect to an issue or matter, multiple parties which have a similar point of view or which are likely to be affected in a similar manner;

(6) "negotiated rulemaking" means rulemaking through the use of a negotiated rulemaking committee;

(7) "negotiated rulemaking committee" or "committee" means an advisory committee established by an agency in accordance with this subchapter and the Federal Advisory Committee Act[12] to consider and discuss issues for the purpose of reaching a consensus in the development of a proposed rule;

(8) "party" has the same meaning as in section 551(3) of this title;

(9) "person" has the same meaning as in section 551(2) of this title;

(10) "rule" has the same meaning as in section 551(4) of this title; and

12. 5 U.S.C. Appx.

(11) "rulemaking" means "rule making" as that term is defined in section 551(5) of this title.

§ 563. Determination of need for negotiated rulemaking committee

(a) Determination of Need by the Agency.—An agency may establish a negotiated rulemaking committee to negotiate and develop a proposed rule, if the head of the agency determines that the use of the negotiated rulemaking procedure is in the public interest. In making such a determination, the head of the agency shall consider whether—

(1) there is a need for a rule;

(2) there are a limited number of identifiable interests that will be significantly affected by the rule;

(3) there is a reasonable likelihood that a committee can be convened with a balanced representation of persons who—

(A) can adequately represent the interests identified under paragraph (2); and

(B) are willing to negotiate in good faith to reach a consensus on the proposed rule;

(4) there is a reasonable likelihood that a committee will reach a consensus on the proposed rule within a fixed period of time;

(5) the negotiated rulemaking procedure will not unreasonably delay the notice of proposed rulemaking and the issuance of the final rule;

(6) the agency has adequate resources and is willing to commit such resources, including technical assistance, to the committee; and

(7) the agency, to the maximum extent possible consistent with the legal obligations of the agency, will use the consensus of the committee with respect to the proposed rule as the basis for the rule proposed by the agency for notice and comment.

(b) Use of Conveners.—

(1) Purposes of conveners.—An agency may use the services of a convener to assist the agency in—

(A) identifying persons who will be significantly affected by a proposed rule, including residents of rural areas; and

(B) conducting discussions with such persons to identify the issues of concern to such persons, and to ascertain whether the establishment of a negotiated rulemaking committee is feasible and appropriate in the particular rulemaking.

(2) Duties of conveners.—The convener shall report findings and may make recommendations to the agency. Upon request of the agency, the convener shall ascertain the names of persons who are willing and qualified to represent interests that will be significantly affected by the proposed rule, including residents of rural areas. The report and any recommendations of the convener shall be made available to the public upon request.

§ 564. Publication of notice; applications for membership on committees

(a) Publication of Notice.—If, after considering the report of a convener or conducting its own assessment, an agency decides to establish a negotiated rulemaking committee, the agency shall publish in the Federal Register and, as appropriate, in trade or other specialized publications, a notice which shall include—

(1) an announcement that the agency intends to establish a negotiated rulemaking committee to negotiate and develop a proposed rule;

(2) a description of the subject and scope of the rule to be developed, and the issues to be considered;

(3) a list of the interests which are likely to be significantly affected by the rule;

(4) a list of the persons proposed to represent such interests and the person or persons proposed to represent the agency;

(5) a proposed agenda and schedule for completing the work of the committee, including a target date for publication by the agency of a proposed rule for notice and comment;

(6) a description of administrative support for the committee to be provided by the agency, including technical assistance;

(7) a solicitation for comments on the proposal to establish the committee, and the proposed membership of the negotiated rulemaking committee; and

(8) an explanation of how a person may apply or nominate another person for membership on the committee, as provided under subsection (b).

(b) Applications for Membership or Committee.—Persons who will be significantly affected by a proposed rule and who believe that their interests will not be adequately represented by any person specified in a notice under subsection (a)(4) may apply for, or nominate another person for, membership on the negotiated rulemaking committee to represent such interests with respect to the proposed rule. Each application or nomination shall include—

(1) the name of the applicant or nominee and a description of the interests such person shall represent;

(2) evidence that the applicant or nominee is authorized to represent parties related to the interests the person proposes to represent;

(3) a written commitment that the applicant or nominee shall actively participate in good faith in the development of the rule under consideration; and

(4) the reasons that the persons specified in the notice under subsection (a)(4) do not adequately represent the interests of the person submitting the application or nomination.

(c) Period for Submission of Comments and Applications.—The agency shall provide for a period of at least 30 calendar days for the submission of comments and applications under this section.

§ 565. Establishment of committee

(a) Establishment.—

(1) Determination to establish committee.—If after considering comments and applications submitted under section 564, the agency determines that a negotiated rulemaking committee can adequately represent the interests that will be significantly affected by a proposed rule and that it is feasible and appropriate in the particular rulemaking, the agency may establish a negotiated

rulemaking committee. In establishing and administering such a committee, the agency shall comply with the Federal Advisory Committee Act[13] with respect to such committee, except as otherwise provided in this subchapter.

(2) Determination not to establish committee.—If after considering such comments and applications, the agency decides not to establish a negotiated rulemaking committee, the agency shall promptly publish notice of such decision and the reasons therefor in the Federal Register and, as appropriate, in trade or other specialized publications, a copy of which shall be sent to any person who applied for, or nominated another person for membership on the negotiating[14] rulemaking committee to represent such interests with respect to the proposed rule.

(b) Membership.—The agency shall limit membership on a negotiated rulemaking committee to 25 members, unless the agency head determines that a greater number of members is necessary for the functioning of the committee or to achieve balanced membership. Each committee shall include at least one person representing the agency.

(c) Administrative support.—The agency shall provide appropriate administrative support to the negotiated rulemaking committee, including technical assistance.

§ 566. Conduct of committee activity

(a) Duties of Committee.—Each negotiated rulemaking committee established under this subchapter shall consider the matter proposed by the agency for consideration and shall attempt to reach a consensus concerning a proposed rule with respect to such matter and any other matter the committee determines is relevant to the proposed rule.

(b) Representatives of Agency on Committee.—The person or persons representing the agency on a negotiated rulemaking committee shall participate in the deliberations and activities of the committee with the same rights and responsibilities as other members of the committee, and shall be authorized to fully represent the agency in the discussions and negotiations of the committee.

(c) Selecting Facilitator.—Notwithstanding section 10(e) of the Federal Advisory Committee Act,[15] an agency may nominate either a person from the Federal Government or a person from outside the Federal Government to serve as a facilitator for the negotiations of the committee, subject to the approval of the committee by consensus. If the committee does not approve the nominee of the agency for facilitator, the agency shall submit a substitute nomination. If a committee does not approve any nominee of the agency for facilitator, the committee shall select by consensus a person to serve as facilitator. A person designated to represent the agency in substantive issues may not serve as facilitator or otherwise chair the committee.

(d) Duties of Facilitator.—A facilitator approved or selected by a negotiated rulemaking committee shall—

---

13. 5 U.S.C. Appx.
14. So in original. Probably should be "negotiated."
15. 5 U.S.C. Appx. § 10(e)

(1) chair the meetings of the committee in an impartial manner;

(2) impartially assist the members of the committee in conducting discussions and negotiations; and

(3) manage the keeping of minutes and records as required under section 10(b) and (c) of the Federal Advisory Committee Act,[16] except that any personal notes and materials of the facilitator or of the members of a committee shall not be subject to section 552 of this title.

(e) Committee Procedures.—A negotiated rulemaking committee established under this subchapter may adopt procedures for the operation of the committee. No provision of section 553 of this title shall apply to the procedures of a negotiated rulemaking committee.

(f) Report of Committee.—If a committee reaches a consensus on a proposed rule, at the conclusion of negotiations the committee shall transmit to the agency that established the committee a report containing the proposed rule. If the committee does not reach a consensus on a proposed rule, the committee may transmit to the agency a report specifying any areas in which the committee reached a consensus. The committee may include in a report any other information, recommendations, or materials that the committee considers appropriate. Any committee member may include as an addendum to the report additional information, recommendations, or materials.

(g) Records of Committee.—In addition to the report required by subsection (f), a committee shall submit to the agency the records required under section 10(b) and (c) of the Federal Advisory Committee Act.[17]

§ 567. Termination of committee

A negotiated rulemaking committee shall terminate upon promulgation of the final rule under consideration, unless the committee's charter contains an earlier termination date or the agency, after consulting the committee, or the committee itself specifies an earlier termination date.

§ 568. Services, facilities, and payment of committee member expenses

(a) Services of Conveners and Facilitators.—

(1) In general.—An agency may employ or enter into contracts for the services of an individual or organization to serve as a convener or facilitator for a negotiated rulemaking committee under this subchapter, or may use the services of a Government employee to act as a convener or a facilitator for such a committee.

(2) Determination of conflicting interests.—An agency shall determine whether a person under consideration to serve as convener or facilitator of a committee under paragraph (1) has any financial or other interest that would preclude such person from serving in an impartial and independent manner.

(b) Services and Facilities of Other Entities.—For purposes of this subchapter, an agency may use the services and facilities of other Federal agencies and public

16. 5 U.S.C. Appx. § 10(b), (c).
17. 5 U.S.C. Appx. § 10(b), (c).

and private agencies and instrumentalities with the consent of such agencies and instrumentalities, and with or without reimbursement to such agencies and instrumentalities, and may accept voluntary and uncompensated services without regard to the provisions of section 1342 of title 31. The Federal Mediation and Conciliation Service may provide services and facilities, with or without reimbursement, to assist agencies under this subchapter, including furnishing conveners, facilitators, and training in negotiated rulemaking.

(c) Expenses of Committee Members.—Members of a negotiated rulemaking committee shall be responsible for their own expenses of participation in such committee, except that an agency may, in accordance with section 7(d) of the Federal Advisory Committee Act,[18] pay for a member's reasonable travel and per diem expenses, expenses to obtain technical assistance, and a reasonable rate of compensation, if—

(1) such member certifies a lack of adequate financial resources to participate in the committee; and

(2) the agency determines that such member's participation in the committee is necessary to assure an adequate representation of the member's interest.

(d) Status of Member as Federal Employee.—A member's receipt of funds under this section or section 569 shall not conclusively determine for purposes of sections 202 through 209 of title 18 whether that member is an employee of the United States Government.

§ 569. Encouraging negotiated rulemaking

(a) The President shall designate an agency or designate or establish an interagency committee to facilitate and encourage agency use of negotiated rulemaking. An agency that is considering, planning, or conducting a negotiated rulemaking may consult with such agency or committee for information and assistance.

(b) To carry out the purposes of this subchapter, an agency planning or conducting a negotiated rulemaking may accept, hold, administer, and utilize gifts, devises, and bequests of property, both real and personal if that agency's acceptance and use of such gifts, devises, or bequests do not create a conflict of interest. Gifts and bequests of money and proceeds from sales of other property received as gifts, devises, or bequests shall be deposited in the Treasury and shall be disbursed upon the order of the head of such agency. Property accepted pursuant to this section, and the proceeds thereof, shall be used as nearly as possible in accordance with the terms of the gifts, devises, or bequests.

§ 570. Judicial review

Any agency action relating to establishing, assisting, or terminating a negotiated rulemaking committee under this subchapter shall not be subject to judicial review. Nothing in this section shall bar judicial review of a rule if such judicial review is otherwise provided by law. A rule which is the product of negotiated rulemaking and is subject to judicial review shall not be accorded any greater deference by a court than a rule which is the product of other rulemaking procedures.

18. 5 U.S.C. Appx. § 7(d).

§ 570a. Authorization of appropriations

There are authorized to be appropriated such sums as may be necessary to carry out the purposes of this subchapter.

Subchapter IV—Alternative Means of Dispute Resolution in the Administrative Process

Alternative Dispute Resolution Act

§ 571. Definitions

For the purposes of this subchapter, the term—

(1) "agency" has the same meaning as in section 551(1) of this title;

(2) "administrative program" includes a Federal function which involves protection of the public interest and the determination of rights, privileges, and obligations of private persons through rule making, adjudication, licensing, or investigation, as those terms are used in subchapter II of this chapter;

(3) "alternative means of dispute resolution" means any procedure that is used to resolve issues in controversy, including, but not limited to, conciliation, facilitation, mediation, factfinding, minitrials, arbitration, and use of ombuds, or any combination thereof;

(4) "award" means any decision by an arbitrator resolving the issues in controversy;

(5) "dispute resolution communication" means any oral or written communication prepared for the purposes of a dispute resolution proceeding, including any memoranda, notes or work product of the neutral, parties or nonparty participant; except that a written agreement to enter into a dispute resolution proceeding, or final written agreement or arbitral award reached as a result of a dispute resolution proceeding, is not a dispute resolution communication;

(6) "dispute resolution proceeding" means any process in which an alternative means of dispute resolution is used to resolve an issue in controversy in which a neutral is appointed and specified parties participate;

(7) "in confidence" means, with respect to information, that the information is provided—

(A) with the expressed intent of the source that it not be disclosed; or

(B) under circumstances that would create the reasonable expectation on behalf of the source that the information will not be disclosed;

(8) "issue in controversy" means an issue which is material to a decision concerning an administrative program of an agency, and with which there is disagreement—

(A) between an agency and persons who would be substantially affected by the decision; or

(B) between persons who would be substantially affected by the decision;

(9) "neutral" means an individual who, with respect to an issue in controversy, functions specifically to aid the parties in resolving the controversy;

(10) "party" means—

(A) for a proceeding with named parties, the same as in section 551(3) of this title; and

(B) for a proceeding without named parties, a person who will be significantly affected by the decision in the proceeding and who participates in the proceeding;

(11) "person" has the same meaning as in section 551(2) of this title; and

(12) "roster" means a list of persons qualified to provide services as neutrals.

§ 572. General authority

(a) An agency may use a dispute resolution proceeding for the resolution of an issue in controversy that relates to an administrative program, if the parties agree to such proceeding.

(b) An agency shall consider not using a dispute resolution proceeding if—

(1) a definitive or authoritative resolution of the matter is required for precedential value, and such a proceeding is not likely to be accepted generally as an authoritative precedent;

(2) the matter involves or may bear upon significant questions of Government policy that require additional procedures before a final resolution may be made, and such a proceeding would not likely serve to develop a recommended policy for the agency;

(3) maintaining established policies is of special importance, so that variations among individual decisions are not increased and such a proceeding would not likely reach consistent results among individual decisions;

(4) the matter significantly affects persons or organizations who are not parties to the proceeding;

(5) a full public record of the proceeding is important, and a dispute resolution proceeding cannot provide such a record; and

(6) the agency must maintain continuing jurisdiction over the matter with authority to alter the disposition of the matter in the light of changed circumstances, and a dispute resolution proceeding would interfere with the agency's fulfilling that requirement.

(c) Alternative means of dispute resolution authorized under this subchapter are voluntary procedures which supplement rather than limit other available agency dispute resolution techniques.

§ 573. Neutrals

(a) A neutral may be a permanent or temporary officer or employee of the Federal Government or any other individual who is acceptable to the parties to a dispute resolution proceeding. A neutral shall have no official, financial, or personal conflict of interest with respect to the issues in controversy, unless such interest is fully disclosed in writing to all parties and all parties agree that the neutral may serve.

(b) A neutral who serves as a conciliator, facilitator, or mediator serves at the will of the parties.

(c) The President shall designate an agency or designate or establish an interagency committee to facilitate and encourage agency use of dispute resolution under this subchapter. Such agency or interagency committee, in consultation with other appropriate Federal agencies and professional organizations experienced in matters concerning dispute resolution, shall—

(1) encourage and facilitate agency use of alternative means of dispute resolution; and

(2) develop procedures that permit agencies to obtain the services of neutrals on an expedited basis.

(d) An agency may use the services of one or more employees of other agencies to serve as neutrals in dispute resolution proceedings. The agencies may enter into an interagency agreement that provides for the reimbursement by the user agency or the parties of the full or partial cost of the services of such an employee.

(e) Any agency may enter into a contract with any person for services as a neutral, or for training in connection with alternative means of dispute resolution. The parties in a dispute resolution proceeding shall agree on compensation for the neutral that is fair and reasonable to the Government.

§ 574. Confidentiality

(a) Except as provided in subsections (d) and (e), a neutral in a dispute resolution proceeding shall not voluntarily disclose or through discovery or compulsory process be required to disclose any dispute resolution communication or any communication provided in confidence to the neutral, unless—

(1) all parties to the dispute resolution proceeding and the neutral consent in writing, and, if the dispute resolution communication was provided by a nonparty participant, that participant also consents in writing;

(2) the dispute resolution communication has already been made public;

(3) the dispute resolution communication is required by statute to be made public, but a neutral should make such communication public only if no other person is reasonably available to disclose the communication; or

(4) a court determines that such testimony or disclosure is necessary to—

(A) prevent a manifest injustice;

(B) help establish a violation of law; or

(C) prevent harm to the public health or safety, of sufficient magnitude in the particular case to outweigh the integrity of dispute resolution proceedings in general by reducing the confidence of parties in future cases that their communications will remain confidential.

(b) A party to a dispute resolution proceeding shall not voluntarily disclose or through discovery or compulsory process be required to disclose any dispute resolution communication, unless—

(1) the communication was prepared by the party seeking disclosure;

(2) all parties to the dispute resolution proceeding consent in writing;

(3) the dispute resolution communication has already been made public;

(4) the dispute resolution communication is required by statute to be made public;

(5) a court determines that such testimony or disclosure is necessary to—

(A) prevent a manifest injustice;

(B) help establish a violation of law; or

(C) prevent harm to the public health and safety,

of sufficient magnitude in the particular case to outweigh the integrity of dispute resolution proceedings in general by reducing the confidence of parties in future cases that their communications will remain confidential;

(6) the dispute resolution communication is relevant to determining the existence or meaning of an agreement or award that resulted from the dispute resolution proceeding or to the enforcement of such an agreement or award; or

(7) except for dispute resolution communications generated by the neutral, the dispute resolution communication was provided to or was available to all parties to the dispute resolution proceeding.

(c) Any dispute resolution communication that is disclosed in violation of subsection (a) or (b), shall not be admissible in any proceeding relating to the issues in controversy with respect to which the communication was made.

(d)

(1) The parties may agree to alternative confidential procedures for disclosures by a neutral. Upon such agreement the parties shall inform the neutral before the commencement of the dispute resolution proceeding of any modifications to the provisions of subsection (a) that will govern the confidentiality of the dispute resolution proceeding. If the parties do not so inform the neutral, subsection (a) shall apply.

(2) To qualify for the exemption established under subsection (j), an alternative confidential procedure under this subsection may not provide for less disclosure than the confidential procedures otherwise provided under this section.

(e) If a demand for disclosure, by way of discovery request or other legal process, is made upon a neutral regarding a dispute resolution communication, the neutral shall make reasonable efforts to notify the parties and any affected nonparty participants of the demand. Any party or affected nonparty participant who receives such notice and within 15 calendar days does not offer to defend a refusal of the neutral to disclose the requested information shall have waived any objection to such disclosure.

(f) Nothing in this section shall prevent the discovery or admissibility of any evidence that is otherwise discoverable, merely because the evidence was presented in the course of a dispute resolution proceeding.

(g) Subsections (a) and (b) shall have no effect on the information and data that are necessary to document an agreement reached or order issued pursuant to a dispute resolution proceeding.

(h) Subsections (a) and (b) shall not prevent the gathering of information for research or educational purposes, in cooperation with other agencies, governmental entities, or dispute resolution programs, so long as the parties and the specific issues in controversy are not identifiable.

(i) Subsections (a) and (b) shall not prevent use of a dispute resolution communication to resolve a dispute between the neutral in a dispute resolution proceeding and a party to or participant in such proceeding, so long as such dispute resolution communication is disclosed only to the extent necessary to resolve such dispute.

(j) A dispute resolution communication which is between a neutral and a party and which may not be disclosed under this section shall also be exempt from disclosure under section 552(b)(3).

§ 575. Authorization of arbitration

(a)

(1) Arbitration may be used as an alternative means of dispute resolution whenever all parties consent. Consent may be obtained either before or after an issue in controversy has arisen. A party may agree to—

(A) submit only certain issues in controversy to arbitration; or

(B) arbitration on the condition that the award must be within a range of possible outcomes.

(2) The arbitration agreement that sets forth the subject matter submitted to the arbitrator shall be in writing. Each such arbitration agreement shall specify a maximum award that may be issued by the arbitrator and may specify other conditions limiting the range of possible outcomes.

(3) An agency may not require any person to consent to arbitration as a condition of entering into a contract or obtaining a benefit.

(b) An officer or employee of an agency shall not offer to use arbitration for the resolution of issues in controversy unless such officer or employee—

(1) would otherwise have authority to enter into a settlement concerning the matter; or

(2) is otherwise specifically authorized by the agency to consent to the use of arbitration.

(c) Prior to using binding arbitration under this subchapter, the head of an agency, in consultation with the Attorney General and after taking into account the factors in section 572(b), shall issue guidance on the appropriate use of binding arbitration and when an officer or employee of the agency has authority to settle an issue in controversy through binding arbitration.

§ 576. Enforcement of arbitration agreements

An agreement to arbitrate a matter to which this subchapter applies is enforceable pursuant to section 4 of title 9, and no action brought to enforce such an agreement shall be dismissed nor shall relief therein be denied on the grounds that it is against the United States or that the United States is an indispensable party.

§ 577. Arbitrators

(a) The parties to an arbitration proceeding shall be entitled to participate in the selection of the arbitrator.

(b) The arbitrator shall be a neutral who meets the criteria of section 573 of this title.

§ 578. Authority of the arbitrator

An arbitrator to whom a dispute is referred under this subchapter may—

(1) regulate the course of and conduct arbitral hearings;

(2) administer oaths and affirmations;

(3) compel the attendance of witnesses and production of evidence at the hearing under the provisions of section 7 of title 9 only to the extent the agency involved is otherwise authorized by law to do so; and

(4) make awards.

§ 579. Arbitration proceedings

(a) The arbitrator shall set a time and place for the hearing on the dispute and shall notify the parties not less than 5 days before the hearing.

(b) Any party wishing a record of the hearing shall—

(1) be responsible for the preparation of such record;

(2) notify the other parties and the arbitrator of the preparation of such record;

(3) furnish copies to all identified parties and the arbitrator; and

(4) pay all costs for such record, unless the parties agree otherwise or the arbitrator determines that the costs should be apportioned.

(c)

(1) The parties to the arbitration are entitled to be heard, to present evidence material to the controversy, and to cross-examine witnesses appearing at the hearing.

(2) The arbitrator may, with the consent of the parties, conduct all or part of the hearing by telephone, television, computer, or other electronic means, if each party has an opportunity to participate.

(3) The hearing shall be conducted expeditiously and in an informal manner.

(4) The arbitrator may receive any oral or documentary evidence, except that irrelevant, immaterial, unduly repetitious, or privileged evidence may be excluded by the arbitrator.

(5) The arbitrator shall interpret and apply relevant statutory and regulatory requirements, legal precedents, and policy directives.

(d) No interested person shall make or knowingly cause to be made to the arbitrator an unauthorized ex parte communication relevant to the merits of the proceeding, unless the parties agree otherwise. If a communication is made in violation of this subsection, the arbitrator shall ensure that a memorandum of the communication is prepared and made a part of the record, and that an opportunity for rebuttal is allowed. Upon receipt of a communication made in violation of this subsection, the arbitrator may, to the extent consistent with the interests of justice and the policies underlying this subchapter, require the offending party to show cause why the claim of such party should not be resolved against such party as a result of the improper conduct.

(e) The arbitrator shall make the award within 30 days after the close of the hearing, or the date of the filing of any briefs authorized by the arbitrator, whichever date is later, unless—

(1) the parties agree to some other time limit; or

(2) the agency provides by rule for some other time limit.

§ 580. Arbitration awards

(a)

(1) Unless the agency provides otherwise by rule, the award in an arbitration proceeding under this subchapter shall include a brief, informal discussion of the factual and legal basis for the award, but formal findings of fact or conclusions of law shall not be required.

(2) The prevailing parties shall file the award with all relevant agencies, along with proof of service on all parties.

(b) The award in an arbitration proceeding shall become final 30 days after it is served on all parties. Any agency that is a party to the proceeding may extend this 30-day period for an additional 30-day period by serving a notice of such extension on all other parties before the end of the first 30-day period.

(c) A final award is binding on the parties to the arbitration proceeding, and may be enforced pursuant to sections 9 through 13 of title 9. No action brought to enforce such an award shall be dismissed nor shall relief therein be denied on the grounds that it is against the United States or that the United States is an indispensable party.

(d) An award entered under this subchapter in an arbitration proceeding may not serve as an estoppel in any other proceeding for any issue that was resolved in the proceeding. Such an award also may not be used as precedent or otherwise be considered in any factually unrelated proceeding, whether conducted under this subchapter, by an agency, or in a court, or in any other arbitration proceeding.

§ 581. Judicial Review

(a) Notwithstanding any other provision of law, any person adversely affected or aggrieved by an award made in an arbitration proceeding conducted under this subchapter may bring an action for review of such award only pursuant to the provisions of sections 9 through 13 of title 9.

(b) A decision by an agency to use or not to use a dispute resolution proceeding under this subchapter shall be committed to the discretion of the agency and shall not be subject to judicial review, except that arbitration shall be subject to judicial review under section 10(b) of title 9.

§ 582. [Repealed]

§ 583. Support services

For the purposes of this subchapter, an agency may use (with or without reimbursement) the services and facilities of other Federal agencies, State, local, and tribal governments, public and private organizations and agencies, and individuals, with the consent of such agencies, organizations, and individuals. An agency may accept voluntary and uncompensated services for purposes of this subchapter without regard to the provisions of section 1342 of title 31.

§ 584. Authorization of appropriations

There are authorized to be appropriated such sums as may be necessary to carry out the purposes of this subchapter.

Chapter 6—The Analysis of Regulatory Functions

§ 601. Definitions

For purposes of this chapter—

(1) the term "agency" means an agency as defined in section 551(1) of this title;

(2) the term "rule" means any rule for which the agency publishes a general notice of proposed rulemaking pursuant to section 553(b) of this title, or any other law, including any rule of general applicability governing Federal grants to State and local governments for which the agency provides an opportunity for notice and public comment, except that the term "rule" does not include a rule of particular applicability relating to rates, wages, corporate or financial structures or reorganizations thereof, prices, facilities, appliances, services, or allowances therefor or to valuations, costs or accounting, or practices relating to such rates, wages, structures, prices, appliances, services, or allowances;

(3) the term "small business" has the same meaning as the term "small business concern" under section 3 of the Small Business Act,[19] unless an agency, after consultation with the Office of Advocacy of the Small Business Administration and after opportunity for public comment, establishes one or more definitions of such term which are appropriate to the activities of the agency and publishes such definition(s) in the Federal Register;

(4) the term "small organization" means any not-for-profit enterprise which is independently owned and operated and is not dominant in its field, unless an agency establishes, after opportunity for public comment, one or more definitions of such term which are appropriate to the activities of the agency and publishes such definition(s) in the Federal Register;

(5) the term "small governmental jurisdiction" means governments of cities, counties, towns, townships, villages, school districts, or special districts, with a population of less than fifty thousand, unless an agency establishes, after opportunity for public comment, one or more definitions of such term which are appropriate to the activities of the agency and which are based on such factors as location in rural or sparsely populated areas or limited revenues due to the population of such jurisdiction, and publishes such definition(s) in the Federal Register;

(6) the term "small entity" shall have the same meaning as the terms "small business", "small organization" and "small governmental jurisdiction" defined in paragraphs (3), (4) and (5) of this section; and

(7) the term "collection of information"—

(A) means the obtaining, causing to be obtained, soliciting, or requiring the disclosure to third parties or the public, of facts or opinions by or for an agency, regardless of form or format, calling for either—

---

19. 15 U.S.C. § 632.

(i) answers to identical questions posed to, or identical reporting or recordkeeping requirements imposed on, 10 or more persons, other than agencies, instrumentalities, or employees of the United States; or

(ii) answers to questions posed to agencies, instrumentalities, or employees of the United States which are to be used for general statistical purposes; and

(B) shall not include a collection of information described under section 3518(c)(1) of title 44, United States Code.

(8) Recordkeeping requirement.—The term "recordkeeping requirement" means a requirement imposed by an agency on persons to maintain specified records.

§ 602. Regulatory agenda

(a) During the months of October and April of each year, each agency shall publish in the Federal Register a regulatory flexibility agenda which shall contain—

(1) a brief description of the subject area of any rule which the agency expects to propose or promulgate which is likely to have a significant economic impact on a substantial number of small entities;

(2) a summary of the nature of any such rule under consideration for each subject area listed in the agenda pursuant to paragraph (1), the objectives and legal basis for the issuance of the rule, and an approximate schedule for completing action on any rule for which the agency has issued a general notice of proposed rulemaking,[20] and

(3) the name and telephone number of an agency official knowledgeable concerning the items listed in paragraph (1).

(b) Each regulatory flexibility agenda shall be transmitted to the Chief Counsel for Advocacy of the Small Business Administration for comment, if any.

(c) Each agency shall endeavor to provide notice of each regulatory flexibility agenda to small entities or their representatives through direct notification or publication of the agenda in publications likely to be obtained by such small entities and shall invite comments upon each subject area on the agenda.

(d) Nothing in this section precludes an agency from considering or acting on any matter not included in a regulatory flexibility agenda, or requires an agency to consider or act on any matter listed in such agenda.

§ 603. Initial regulatory flexibility analysis

(a) Whenever an agency is required by section 553 of this title, or any other law, to publish general notice of proposed rulemaking for any proposed rule, or publishes a notice of proposed rulemaking for an interpretative rule involving the internal revenue laws of the United States, the agency shall prepare and make available for public comment an initial regulatory flexibility analysis. Such analysis shall describe the impact of the proposed rule on small entities. The initial regulatory flexibility analysis or a summary shall be published in the Federal Register at the time of the publication of general notice of proposed rulemaking for the rule. The agency shall transmit a copy of the initial regulatory flexibility analysis to the Chief Counsel for Advocacy of the Small Business Administration. In the

20. So in original. Comma probably should be a semicolon.

case of an interpretative rule involving the internal revenue laws of the United States, this chapter applies to interpretative rules published in the Federal Register for codification in the Code of Federal Regulations, but only to the extent that such interpretative rules impose on small entities a collection of information requirement.

(b) Each initial regulatory flexibility analysis required under this section shall contain—

(1) a description of the reasons why action by the agency is being considered;

(2) a succinct statement of the objectives of, and legal basis for, the proposed rule;

(3) a description of and, where feasible, an estimate of the number of small entities to which the proposed rule will apply;

(4) a description of the projected reporting, recordkeeping and other compliance requirements of the proposed rule, including an estimate of the classes of small entities which will be subject to the requirement and the type of professional skills necessary for preparation of the report or record;

(5) an identification, to the extent practicable, of all relevant Federal rules which may duplicate, overlap or conflict with the proposed rule.

(c) Each initial regulatory flexibility analysis shall also contain a description of any significant alternatives to the proposed rule which accomplish the stated objectives of applicable statutes and which minimize any significant economic impact of the proposed rule on small entities. Consistent with the stated objectives of applicable statutes, the analysis shall discuss significant alternatives such as—

(1) the establishment of differing compliance or reporting requirements or timetables that take into account the resources available to small entities;

(2) the clarification, consolidation, or simplification of compliance and reporting requirements under the rule for such small entities;

(3) the use of performance rather than design standards; and

(4) an exemption from coverage of the rule, or any part thereof, for such small entities.

(d)

(1) For a covered agency, as defined in section 609(d)(2), each initial regulatory flexibility analysis shall include a description of—

(A) any projected increase in the cost of credit for small entities;

(B) any significant alternatives to the proposed rule which accomplish the stated objectives of applicable statutes and which minimize any increase in the cost of credit for small entities; and

(C) advice and recommendations of representatives of small entities relating to issues described in subparagraphs (A) and (B) and subsection (b).

(2) A covered agency, as defined in section 609(d)(2), shall, for purposes of complying with paragraph (1)(C)—

(A) identify representatives of small entities in consultation with the Chief Counsel for Advocacy of the Small Business Administration; and

(B) collect advice and recommendations from the representatives identified under subparagraph (A) relating to issues described in subparagraphs (A) and (B) of paragraph (1) and subsection (b).

§ 604. Final regulatory flexibility analysis

(a) When an agency promulgates a final rule under section 553 of this title, after being required by that section or any other law to publish a general notice of proposed rulemaking, or promulgates a final interpretative rule involving the internal revenue laws of the United States as described in section 603(a), the agency shall prepare a final regulatory flexibility analysis. Each final regulatory flexibility analysis shall contain—

(1) a statement of the need for, and objectives of, the rule;

(2) a statement of the significant issues raised by the public comments in response to the initial regulatory flexibility analysis, a statement of the assessment of the agency of such issues, and a statement of any changes made in the proposed rule as a result of such comments;

(3) the response of the agency to any comments filed by the Chief Counsel for Advocacy of the Small Business Administration in response to the proposed rule, and a detailed statement of any change made to the proposed rule in the final rule as a result of the comments;

(4) a description of and an estimate of the number of small entities to which the rule will apply or an explanation of why no such estimate is available;

(5) a description of the projected reporting, recordkeeping and other compliance requirements of the rule, including an estimate of the classes of small entities which will be subject to the requirement and the type of professional skills necessary for preparation of the report or record;

(6) a description of the steps the agency has taken to minimize the significant economic impact on small entities consistent with the stated objectives of applicable statutes, including a statement of the factual, policy, and legal reasons for selecting the alternative adopted in the final rule and why each one of the other significant alternatives to the rule considered by the agency which affect the impact on small entities was rejected; and

(6)[21] for a covered agency, as defined in section 609(d)(2), a description of the steps the agency has taken to minimize any additional cost of credit for small entities.

(b) The agency shall make copies of the final regulatory flexibility analysis available to members of the public and shall publish in the Federal Register such analysis or a summary thereof.

§ 605. Avoidance of duplicative or unnecessary analyses

(a) Any Federal agency may perform the analyses required by sections 602, 603, and 604 of this title in conjunction with or as a part of any other agenda or analysis required by any other law if such other analysis satisfies the provisions of such sections.

(b) Sections 603 and 604 of this title shall not apply to any proposed or final rule if the head of the agency certifies that the rule will not, if promulgated, have a significant economic impact on a substantial number of small entities. If the head of the agency makes a certification under the preceding sentence, the agency

21. So in original. Two paragraphs (6) have been enacted.

shall publish such certification in the Federal Register at the time of publication of general notice of proposed rulemaking for the rule or at the time of publication of the final rule, along with a statement providing the factual basis for such certification. The agency shall provide such certification and statement to the Chief Counsel for Advocacy of the Small Business Administration.

(c) In order to avoid duplicative action, an agency may consider a series of closely related rules as one rule for the purposes of sections 602, 603, 604 and 610 of this title.

§ 606. Effect on other law

The requirements of sections 603 and 604 of this title do not alter in any manner standards otherwise applicable by law to agency action.

§ 607. Preparation of analyses

In complying with the provisions of sections 603 and 604 of this title, an agency may provide either a quantifiable or numerical description of the effects of a proposed rule or alternatives to the proposed rule, or more general descriptive statements if quantification is not practicable or reliable.

§ 608. Procedure for waiver or delay of completion

(a) An agency head may waive or delay the completion of some or all of the requirements of section 603 of this title by publishing in the Federal Register, not later than the date of publication of the final rule, a written finding, with reasons therefor, that the final rule is being promulgated in response to an emergency that makes compliance or timely compliance with the provisions of section 603 of this title impracticable.

(b) Except as provided in section 605(b), an agency head may not waive the requirements of section 604 of this title. An agency head may delay the completion of the requirements of section 604 of this title for a period of not more than one hundred and eighty days after the date of publication in the Federal Register of a final rule by publishing in the Federal Register, not later than such date of publication, a written finding, with reasons therefor, that the final rule is being promulgated in response to an emergency that makes timely compliance with the provisions of section 604 of this title impracticable. If the agency has not prepared a final regulatory analysis pursuant to section 604 of this title within one hundred and eighty days from the date of publication of the final rule, such rule shall lapse and have no effect. Such rule shall not be repromulgated until a final regulatory flexibility analysis has been completed by the agency.

§ 609. Procedures for gathering comments

(a) When any rule is promulgated which will have a significant economic impact on a substantial number of small entities, the head of the agency promulgating the rule or the official of the agency with statutory responsibility for the promulgation of the rule shall assure that small entities have been given an opportunity to participate in the rulemaking for the rule through the reasonable use of techniques such as—

(1) the inclusion in an advanced notice of proposed rulemaking, if issued, of a statement that the proposed rule may have a significant economic effect on a substantial number of small entities;

(2) the publication of general notice of proposed rulemaking in publications likely to be obtained by small entities;

(3) the direct notification of interested small entities;

(4) the conduct of open conferences or public hearings concerning the rule of small entities including soliciting and receiving comments over computer networks; and

(5) the adoption or modification of agency procedural rules to reduce the cost or complexity of participation in the rulemaking by small entities.

(b) Prior to publication of an initial regulatory flexibility analysis which a covered agency is required to conduct by this chapter—

(1) a covered agency shall notify the Chief Counsel for Advocacy of the Small Business Administration and provide the Chief Counsel with information on the potential impacts of the proposed rule on small entities and the type of small entities that might be affected;

(2) not later than 15 days after the date of receipt of the materials described in paragraph (1), the Chief Counsel shall identify individuals representative of affected small entities for the purpose of obtaining advice and recommendations from those individuals about the potential impacts of the proposed rule;

(3) the agency shall convene a review panel for such rule consisting wholly of full time Federal employees of the office within the agency responsible for carrying out the proposed rule, the Office of Information and Regulatory Affairs within the Office of Management and Budget, and the Chief Counsel;

(4) the panel shall review any material the agency has prepared in connection with this chapter, including any draft proposed rule, collect advice and recommendations of each individual small entity representative identified by the agency after consultation with the Chief Counsel, on issues related to subsections 603(b), paragraphs (3), (4) and (5) and 603(c);

(5) not later than 60 days after the date a covered agency convenes a review panel pursuant to paragraph (3), the review panel shall report on the comments of the small entity representatives and its findings as to issues related to subsections 603(b), paragraphs (3), (4) and (5) and 603(c), provided that such report shall be made public as part of the rulemaking record; and

(6) where appropriate, the agency shall modify the proposed rule, the initial regulatory flexibility analysis or the decision on whether an initial regulatory flexibility analysis is required.

(c) An agency may in its discretion apply subsection (b) to rules that the agency intends to certify under subsection 605(b), but the agency believes may have a greater than de minimis impact on a substantial number of small entities.

(d) For purposes of this section, the term "covered agency" means—

(1) the Environmental Protection Agency;

(2) the Consumer Financial Protection Bureau of the Federal Reserve System; and

(3) the Occupational Safety and Health Administration of the Department of Labor.

(e) The Chief Counsel for Advocacy, in consultation with the individuals identified in subsection (b)(2), and with the Administrator of the Office of Information and Regulatory Affairs within the Office of Management and Budget, may waive the requirements of subsections (b)(3), (b)(4), and (b)(5) by including in the rulemaking record a written finding, with reasons therefor, that those requirements would not advance the effective participation of small entities in the rulemaking process. For purposes of this subsection, the factors to be considered in making such a finding are as follows:

(1) In developing a proposed rule, the extent to which the covered agency consulted with individuals representative of affected small entities with respect to the potential impacts of the rule and took such concerns into consideration.

(2) Special circumstances requiring prompt issuance of the rule.

(3) Whether the requirements of subsection (b) would provide the individuals identified in subsection (b)(2) with a competitive advantage relative to other small entities.

§ 610. Periodic review of rules

(a) Within one hundred and eighty days after the effective date of this chapter, each agency shall publish in the Federal Register a plan for the periodic review of the rules issued by the agency which have or will have a significant economic impact upon a substantial number of small entities. Such plan may be amended by the agency at any time by publishing the revision in the Federal Register. The purpose of the review shall be to determine whether such rules should be continued without change, or should be amended or rescinded, consistent with the stated objectives of applicable statutes, to minimize any significant economic impact of the rules upon a substantial number of such small entities. The plan shall provide for the review of all such agency rules existing on the effective date of this chapter within ten years of that date and for the review of such rules adopted after the effective date of this chapter within ten years of the publication of such rules as the final rule. If the head of the agency determines that completion of the review of existing rules is not feasible by the established date, he shall so certify in a statement published in the Federal Register and may extend the completion date by one year at a time for a total of not more than five years.

(b) In reviewing rules to minimize any significant economic impact of the rule on a substantial number of small entities in a manner consistent with the stated objectives of applicable statutes, the agency shall consider the following factors—

(1) the continued need for the rule;

(2) the nature of complaints or comments received concerning the rule from the public;

(3) the complexity of the rule;

(4) the extent to which the rule overlaps, duplicates or conflicts with other Federal rules, and, to the extent feasible, with State and local governmental rules; and

(5) the length of time since the rule has been evaluated or the degree to which technology, economic conditions, or other factors have changed in the area affected by the rule.

(c) Each year, each agency shall publish in the Federal Register a list of the rules which have a significant economic impact on a substantial number of small entities, which are to be reviewed pursuant to this section during the succeeding twelve months. The list shall include a brief description of each rule and the need for and legal basis of such rule and shall invite public comment upon the rule.

§ 611. Judicial review

(a)

(1) For any rule subject to this chapter, a small entity that is adversely affected or aggrieved by final agency action is entitled to judicial review of agency compliance with the requirements of sections 601, 604, 605(b), 608(b), and 610 in accordance with chapter 7. Agency compliance with sections 607 and 609(a) shall be judicially reviewable in connection with judicial review of section 604.

(2) Each court having jurisdiction to review such rule for compliance with section 553, or under any other provision of law, shall have jurisdiction to review any claims of noncompliance with sections 601, 604, 605(b), 608(b), and 610 in accordance with chapter 7. Agency compliance with sections 607 and 609(a) shall be judicially reviewable in connection with judicial review of section 604.

(3)

(A) A small entity may seek such review during the period beginning on the date of final agency action and ending one year later, except that where a provision of law requires that an action challenging a final agency action be commenced before the expiration of one year, such lesser period shall apply to an action for judicial review under this section.

(B) In the case where an agency delays the issuance of a final regulatory flexibility analysis pursuant to section 608(b) of this chapter, an action for judicial review under this section shall be filed not later than—

(i) one year after the date the analysis is made available to the public, or

(ii) where a provision of law requires that an action challenging a final agency regulation be commenced before the expiration of the 1-year period, the number of days specified in such provision of law that is after the date the analysis is made available to the public.

(4) In granting any relief in an action under this section, the court shall order the agency to take corrective action consistent with this chapter and chapter 7, including, but not limited to—

(A) remanding the rule to the agency, and

(B) deferring the enforcement of the rule against small entities unless the court finds that continued enforcement of the rule is in the public interest.

(5) Nothing in this subsection shall be construed to limit the authority of any court to stay the effective date of any rule or provision thereof under any other provision of law or to grant any other relief in addition to the requirements of this section.

(b) In an action for the judicial review of a rule, the regulatory flexibility analysis for such rule, including an analysis prepared or corrected pursuant to paragraph (a)(4), shall constitute part of the entire record of agency action in connection with such review.

(c) Compliance or noncompliance by an agency with the provisions of this chapter shall be subject to judicial review only in accordance with this section.

(d) Nothing in this section bars judicial review of any other impact statement or similar analysis required by any other law if judicial review of such statement or analysis is otherwise permitted by law.

§ 612. Reports and intervention rights

(a) The Chief Counsel for Advocacy of the Small Business Administration shall monitor agency compliance with this chapter and shall report at least annually thereon to the President and to the Committees on the Judiciary and Small Business of the Senate and House of Representatives.

(b) The Chief Counsel for Advocacy of the Small Business Administration is authorized to appear as amicus curiae in any action brought in a court of the United States to review a rule. In any such action, the Chief Counsel is authorized to present his or her views with respect to compliance with this chapter, the adequacy of the rulemaking record with respect to small entities and the effect of the rule on small entities.

(c) A court of the United States shall grant the application of the Chief Counsel for Advocacy of the Small Business Administration to appear in any such action for the purposes described in subsection (b).

Chapter 7—Judicial Review

§ 701. Application; definitions

(a) This chapter applies, according to the provisions thereof, except to the extent that—

(1) statutes preclude judicial review; or

(2) agency action is committed to agency discretion by law.

(b) For the purpose of this chapter—

(1) "agency" means each authority of the Government of the United States, whether or not it is within or subject to review by another agency, but does not include—

(A) the Congress;

(B) the courts of the United States;

(C) the governments of the territories or possessions of the United States;

(D) the government of the District of Columbia;

(E) agencies composed of representatives of the parties or of representatives of organizations of the parties to the disputes determined by them;

(F) courts martial and military commissions;

(G) military authority exercised in the field in time of war or in occupied territory; or

(H) functions conferred by sections 1738, 1739, 1743, and 1744 of title 12; chapter 2 of title 41; subchapter II of chapter 471 of title 49; or sections 1884, 1891–1902, and former section 1641(b)(2), of title 50, appendix; and

(2) "person", "rule", "order", "license", "sanction", "relief", and "agency action" have the meanings given them by section 551 of this title.

§ 702. Right of review

A person suffering legal wrong because of agency action, or adversely affected or aggrieved by agency action within the meaning of a relevant statute, is entitled to judicial review thereof. An action in a court of the United States seeking relief other than money damages and stating a claim that an agency or an officer or employee thereof acted or failed to act in an official capacity or under color of legal authority shall not be dismissed nor relief therein be denied on the ground that it is against the United States or that the United States is an indispensable party. The United States may be named as a defendant in any such action, and a judgment or decree may be entered against the United States: Provided, That any mandatory or injunctive decree shall specify the Federal officer or officers (by name or by title), and their successors in office, personally responsible for compliance. Nothing herein (1) affects other limitations on judicial review or the power or duty of the court to dismiss any action or deny relief on any other appropriate legal or equitable ground; or (2) confers authority to grant relief if any other statute that grants consent to suit expressly or impliedly forbids the relief which is sought.

§ 703. Form and venue of proceeding

The form of proceeding for judicial review is the special statutory review proceeding relevant to the subject matter in a court specified by statute or, in the absence or inadequacy thereof, any applicable form of legal action, including actions for declaratory judgments or writs of prohibitory or mandatory injunction or habeas corpus, in a court of competent jurisdiction. If no special statutory review proceeding is applicable, the action for judicial review may be brought against the United States, the agency by its official title, or the appropriate officer. Except to the extent that prior, adequate, and exclusive opportunity for judicial review is provided by law, agency action is subject to judicial review in civil or criminal proceedings for judicial enforcement.

§ 704. Actions reviewable

Agency action made reviewable by statute and final agency action for which there is no other adequate remedy in a court are subject to judicial review. A preliminary, procedural, or intermediate agency action or ruling not directly reviewable is subject to review on the review of the final agency action. Except as otherwise expressly required by statute, agency action otherwise final is final for the purposes of this section whether or not there has been presented or determined an application for a declaratory order, for any form of reconsideration, or, unless the agency otherwise requires by rule and provides that the action meanwhile is inoperative, for an appeal to superior agency authority.

§ 705. Relief pending review

When an agency finds that justice so requires, it may postpone the effective date of action taken by it, pending judicial review. On such conditions as may be required and to the extent necessary to prevent irreparable injury, the reviewing court, including the court to which a case may be taken on appeal from or on application for certiorari or other writ to a reviewing court, may issue all necessary and appropriate process to postpone the effective date of an agency action or to preserve status or rights pending conclusion of the review proceedings.

§ 706. Scope of review

To the extent necessary to decision and when presented, the reviewing court shall decide all relevant questions of law, interpret constitutional and statutory provisions, and determine the meaning or applicability of the terms of an agency action. The reviewing court shall—

(1) compel agency action unlawfully withheld or unreasonably delayed; and

(2) hold unlawful and set aside agency action, findings, and conclusions found to be—

(A) arbitrary, capricious, an abuse of discretion, or otherwise not in accordance with law;

(B) contrary to constitutional right, power, privilege, or immunity;

(C) in excess of statutory jurisdiction, authority, or limitations, or short of statutory right;

(D) without observance of procedure required by law;

(E) unsupported by substantial evidence in a case subject to sections 556 and 557 of this title or otherwise reviewed on the record of an agency hearing provided by statute; or

(F) unwarranted by the facts to the extent that the facts are subject to trial de novo by the reviewing court.

In making the foregoing determinations, the court shall review the whole record or those parts of it cited by a party, and due account shall be taken of the rule of prejudicial error.

Chapter 8—Congressional Review of Agency Rulemaking

§ 801. Congressional review

(a)

(1)

(A) Before a rule can take effect, the Federal agency promulgating such rule shall submit to each House of the Congress and to the Comptroller General a report containing—

(i) a copy of the rule;

(ii) a concise general statement relating to the rule, including whether it is a major rule; and

(iii) the proposed effective date of the rule.

(B) On the date of the submission of the report under subparagraph (A), the Federal agency promulgating the rule shall submit to the Comptroller General and make available to each House of Congress—

(i) a complete copy of the cost-benefit analysis of the rule, if any;

(ii) the agency's actions relevant to sections 603, 604, 605, 607, and 609;

(iii) the agency's actions relevant to sections 202, 203, 204, and 205 of the Unfunded Mandates Reform Act of 1995;[22] and

---

22. 2 U.S.C. §§ 1532–35.

(iv) any other relevant information or requirements under any other Act and any relevant Executive orders.

(C) Upon receipt of a report submitted under subparagraph (A), each House shall provide copies of the report to the chairman and ranking member of each standing committee with jurisdiction under the rules of the House of Representatives or the Senate to report a bill to amend the provision of law under which the rule is issued.

(2)

(A) The Comptroller General shall provide a report on each major rule to the committees of jurisdiction in each House of the Congress by the end of 15 calendar days after the submission or publication date as provided in section 802(b)(2). The report of the Comptroller General shall include an assessment of the agency's compliance with procedural steps required by paragraph (1)(B).

(B) Federal agencies shall cooperate with the Comptroller General by providing information relevant to the Comptroller General's report under subparagraph (A).

(3) A major rule relating to a report submitted under paragraph (1) shall take effect on the latest of—

(A) the later of the date occurring 60 days after the date on which—

(i) the Congress receives the report submitted under paragraph (1); or

(ii) the rule is published in the Federal Register, if so published;

(B) if the Congress passes a joint resolution of disapproval described in section 802 relating to the rule, and the President signs a veto of such resolution, the earlier date—

(i) on which either House of Congress votes and fails to override the veto of the President; or

(ii) occurring 30 session days after the date on which the Congress received the veto and objections of the President; or

(C) the date the rule would have otherwise taken effect, if not for this section (unless a joint resolution of disapproval under section 802 is enacted).

(4) Except for a major rule, a rule shall take effect as otherwise provided by law after submission to Congress under paragraph (1).

(5) Notwithstanding paragraph (3), the effective date of a rule shall not be delayed by operation of this chapter beyond the date on which either House of Congress votes to reject a joint resolution of disapproval under section 802.

(b)

(1) A rule shall not take effect (or continue), if the Congress enacts a joint resolution of disapproval, described under section 802, of the rule.

(2) A rule that does not take effect (or does not continue) under paragraph (1) may not be reissued in substantially the same form, and a new rule that is substantially the same as such a rule may not be issued, unless the reissued or new rule is specifically authorized by a law enacted after the date of the joint resolution disapproving the original rule.

(c)

(1) Notwithstanding any other provision of this section (except subject to paragraph (3)), a rule that would not take effect by reason of subsection (a)(3) may take effect, if the President makes a determination under paragraph (2) and submits written notice of such determination to the Congress.

(2) Paragraph (1) applies to a determination made by the President by Executive order that the rule should take effect because such rule is—

(A) necessary because of an imminent threat to health or safety or other emergency;

(B) necessary for the enforcement of criminal laws;

(C) necessary for national security; or

(D) issued pursuant to any statute implementing an international trade agreement.

(3) An exercise by the President of the authority under this subsection shall have no effect on the procedures under section 802 or the effect of a joint resolution of disapproval under this section.

(d)

(1) In addition to the opportunity for review otherwise provided under this chapter, in the case of any rule for which a report was submitted in accordance with subsection (a)(1)(A) during the period beginning on the date occurring—

(A) in the case of the Senate, 60 session days, or

(B) in the case of the House of Representatives, 60 legislative days,

before the date the Congress adjourns a session of Congress through the date on which the same or succeeding Congress first convenes its next session, section 802 shall apply to such rule in the succeeding session of Congress.

(2)

(A) In applying section 802 for purposes of such additional review, a rule described under paragraph (1) shall be treated as though—

(i) such rule were published in the Federal Register (as a rule that shall take effect) on—

(I) in the case of the Senate, the 15th session day, or

(II) in the case of the House of Representatives, the 15th legislative day,

after the succeeding session of Congress first convenes; and

(ii) a report on such rule were submitted to Congress under subsection (a)(1) on such date.

(B) Nothing in this paragraph shall be construed to affect the requirement under subsection (a)(1) that a report shall be submitted to Congress before a rule can take effect.

(3) A rule described under paragraph (1) shall take effect as otherwise provided by law (including other subsections of this section).

(e)

(1) For purposes of this subsection, section 802 shall also apply to any major rule promulgated between March 1, 1996, and the date of the enactment of this chapter.

(2) In applying section 802 for purposes of Congressional review, a rule described under paragraph (1) shall be treated as though—

(A) such rule were published in the Federal Register on the date of enactment of this chapter; and

(B) a report on such rule were submitted to Congress under subsection (a)(1) on such date.

(3) The effectiveness of a rule described under paragraph (1) shall be as otherwise provided by law, unless the rule is made of no force or effect under section 802.

(f) Any rule that takes effect and later is made of no force or effect by enactment of a joint resolution under section 802 shall be treated as though such rule had never taken effect.

(g) If the Congress does not enact a joint resolution of disapproval under section 802 respecting a rule, no court or agency may infer any intent of the Congress from any action or inaction of the Congress with regard to such rule, related statute, or joint resolution of disapproval.

§ 802. Congressional disapproval procedure

(a) For purposes of this section, the term "joint resolution" means only a joint resolution introduced in the period beginning on the date on which the report referred to in section 801(a)(1)(A) is received by Congress and ending 60 days thereafter (excluding days either House of Congress is adjourned for more than 3 days during a session of Congress), the matter after the resolving clause of which is as follows: "That Congress disapproves the rule submitted by the ___ relating to ___, and such rule shall have no force or effect." (The blank spaces being appropriately filled in).

(b)

(1) A joint resolution described in subsection (a) shall be referred to the committees in each House of Congress with jurisdiction.

(2) For purposes of this section, the term "submission or publication date" means the later of the date on which—

(A) the Congress receives the report submitted under section 801(a)(1); or

(B) the rule is published in the Federal Register, if so published.

(c) In the Senate, if the committee to which is referred a joint resolution described in subsection (a) has not reported such joint resolution (or an identical joint resolution) at the end of 20 calendar days after the submission or publication date defined under subsection (b)(2), such committee may be discharged from further consideration of such joint resolution upon a petition supported in writing by 30 Members of the Senate, and such joint resolution shall be placed on the calendar.

(d)

(1) In the Senate, when the committee to which a joint resolution is referred has reported, or when a committee is discharged (under subsection (c)) from

further consideration of a joint resolution described in subsection (a), it is at any time thereafter in order (even though a previous motion to the same effect has been disagreed to) for a motion to proceed to the consideration of the joint resolution, and all points of order against the joint resolution (and against consideration of the joint resolution) are waived. The motion is not subject to amendment, or to a motion to postpone, or to a motion to proceed to the consideration of other business. A motion to reconsider the vote by which the motion is agreed to or disagreed to shall not be in order. If a motion to proceed to the consideration of the joint resolution is agreed to, the joint resolution shall remain the unfinished business of the Senate until disposed of.

(2) In the Senate, debate on the joint resolution, and on all debatable motions and appeals in connection therewith, shall be limited to not more than 10 hours, which shall be divided equally between those favoring and those opposing the joint resolution. A motion further to limit debate is in order and not debatable. An amendment to, or a motion to postpone, or a motion to proceed to the consideration of other business, or a motion to recommit the joint resolution is not in order.

(3) In the Senate, immediately following the conclusion of the debate on a joint resolution described in subsection (a), and a single quorum call at the conclusion of the debate if requested in accordance with the rules of the Senate, the vote on final passage of the joint resolution shall occur.

(4) Appeals from the decisions of the Chair relating to the application of the rules of the Senate to the procedure relating to a joint resolution described in subsection (a) shall be decided without debate.

(e) In the Senate the procedure specified in subsection (c) or (d) shall not apply to the consideration of a joint resolution respecting a rule—

(1) after the expiration of the 60 session days beginning with the applicable submission or publication date, or

(2) if the report under section 801(a)(1)(A) was submitted during the period referred to in section 801(d)(1), after the expiration of the 60 session days beginning on the 15th session day after the succeeding session of Congress first convenes.

(f) If, before the passage by one House of a joint resolution of that House described in subsection (a), that House receives from the other House a joint resolution described in subsection (a), then the following procedures shall apply:

(1) The joint resolution of the other House shall not be referred to a committee.

(2) With respect to a joint resolution described in subsection (a) of the House receiving the joint resolution—

(A) the procedure in that House shall be the same as if no joint resolution had been received from the other House; but

(B) the vote on final passage shall be on the joint resolution of the other House.

(g) This section is enacted by Congress—

(1) as an exercise of the rulemaking power of the Senate and House of Representatives, respectively, and as such it is deemed a part of the rules of each House, respectively, but applicable only with respect to the procedure to be

followed in that House in the case of a joint resolution described in subsection (a), and it supersedes other rules only to the extent that it is inconsistent with such rules; and

(2) with full recognition of the constitutional right of either House to change the rules (so far as relating to the procedure of that House) at any time, in the same manner, and to the same extent as in the case of any other rule of that House.

§ 803. Special rule on statutory, regulatory, and judicial deadlines

(a) In the case of any deadline for, relating to, or involving any rule which does not take effect (or the effectiveness of which is terminated) because of enactment of a joint resolution under section 802, that deadline is extended until the date 1 year after the date of enactment of the joint resolution. Nothing in this subsection shall be construed to affect a deadline merely by reason of the postponement of a rule's effective date under section 801(a).

(b) The term "deadline" means any date certain for fulfilling any obligation or exercising any authority established by or under any Federal statute or regulation, or by or under any court order implementing any Federal statute or regulation.

§ 804. Definitions

For purposes of this chapter—

(1) The term "Federal agency" means any agency as that term is defined in section 551(1).

(2) The term "major rule" means any rule that the Administrator of the Office of Information and Regulatory Affairs of the Office of Management and Budget finds has resulted in or is likely to result in—

(A) an annual effect on the economy of $100,000,000 or more;

(B) a major increase in costs or prices for consumers, individual industries, Federal, State, or local government agencies, or geographic regions; or

(C) significant adverse effects on competition, employment, investment, productivity, innovation, or on the ability of United States-based enterprises to compete with foreign-based enterprises in domestic and export markets.

The term does not include any rule promulgated under the Telecommunications Act of 1996 and the amendments made by that Act.

(3) The term "rule" has the meaning given such term in section 551, except that such term does not include—

(A) any rule of particular applicability, including a rule that approves or prescribes for the future rates, wages, prices, services, or allowances therefor, corporate or financial structures, reorganizations, mergers, or acquisitions thereof, or accounting practices or disclosures bearing on any of the foregoing;

(B) any rule relating to agency management or personnel; or

(C) any rule of agency organization, procedure, or practice that does not substantially affect the rights or obligations of non-agency parties.

§ 805. Judicial review

No determination, finding, action, or omission under this chapter shall be subject to judicial review.

§ 806. Applicability; severability

(a) This chapter shall apply notwithstanding any other provision of law.

(b) If any provision of this chapter or the application of any provision of this chapter to any person or circumstance, is held invalid, the application of such provision to other persons or circumstances, and the remainder of this chapter, shall not be affected thereby.

§ 807. Exemption for monetary policy

Nothing in this chapter shall apply to rules that concern monetary policy proposed or implemented by the Board of Governors of the Federal Reserve System or the Federal Open Market Committee.

§ 808. Effective date of certain rules

Notwithstanding section 801—

(1) any rule that establishes, modifies, opens, closes, or conducts a regulatory program for a commercial, recreational, or subsistence activity related to hunting, fishing, or camping, or

(2) any rule which an agency for good cause finds (and incorporates the finding and a brief statement of reasons therefor in the rule issued) that notice and public procedure thereon are impracticable, unnecessary, or contrary to the public interest,

shall take effect at such time as the Federal agency promulgating the rule determines.

Provisions Pertaining to Administrative Law Judges

Chapter 13—Special Authority

§ 1305. Administrative law judges

For the purpose of sections 3105, 3344, 4301(2)(D), and 5372 of this title and the provisions of section 5335(a)(B) of this title that relate to administrative law judges, the Office of Personnel Management may, and for the purpose of section 7521 of this title, the Merit Systems Protection Board may investigate, prescribe regulations, appoint advisory committees as necessary, recommend legislation, subpena witnesses and records, and pay witness fees as established for the courts of the United States.

Chapter 31—Authority for Employment

Subchapter I—Employment Authorities

§ 3105. Appointment of administrative law judges

Each agency shall appoint as many administrative law judges as are necessary for proceedings required to be conducted in accordance with sections 556 and 557 of this title. Administrative law judges shall be assigned to cases in rotation so far as practicable, and may not perform duties inconsistent with their duties and responsibilities as administrative law judges.

Chapter 33—Examination, Selection, and Placement

Subchapter III—Details, Vacancies, and Appointments

§ 3344. Details; administrative law judges

An agency as defined by section 551 of this title which occasionally or temporarily is insufficiently staffed with administrative law judges appointed under section 3105 of this title may use administrative law judges selected by the Office of Personnel Management from and with the consent of other agencies.

Chapter 53—Pay Rates and Systems

§ 5372. Administrative law judges

(a) For the purposes of this section, the term "administrative law Judge" means an administrative law judge appointed under section 3105.

(b)

(1)

(A) There shall be 3 levels of basic pay for administrative law judges (designated as AL-1, 2, and 3, respectively), and each such judge shall be paid at 1 of those levels, in accordance with the provisions of this section.

(B) Within level AL-3, there shall be 6 rates of basic pay, designated as AL-3, rates A through F, respectively. Level AL-2 and level AL-1 shall each have 1 rate of basic pay.

(C) The rate of basic pay for AL-3, rate A, may not be less than 65 percent of the rate of basic pay for level IV of the Executive Schedule, and the rate of basic pay for AL-1 may not exceed the rate for level IV of the Executive Schedule.

(2) The Office of Personnel Management shall determine, in accordance with procedures which the Office shall by regulation prescribe, the level in which each administrative-law-judge position shall be placed and the qualifications to be required for appointment to each level.

(3)

(A) Upon appointment to a position in AL-3, an administrative law judge shall be paid at rate A of AL-3, and shall be advanced successively to rates B, C, and D of that level at the beginning of the next pay period following completion of 52 weeks of service in the next lower rate, and to rates E and F of that level at the beginning of the next pay period following completion of 104 weeks of service in the next lower rate.

(B) The Office of Personnel Management may provide for appointment of an administrative law judge in AL-3 at an advanced rate under such circumstances as the Office may determine appropriate.

(4) Subject to paragraph (1), effective at the beginning of the first applicable pay period commencing on or after the first day of the month in which an adjustment takes effect under section 5303 in the rates of basic pay under the General Schedule, each rate of basic pay for administrative law judges shall be adjusted by an amount determined by the President to be appropriate.

(c) The Office of Personnel Management shall prescribe regulations necessary to administer this section.

Chapter 75—Adverse Actions

Subchapter III—Administrative Law Judges

§ 7521. Actions against administrative law judges

(a) An action may be taken against an administrative law judge appointed under section 3105 of this title by the agency in which the administrative law judge is employed only for good cause established and determined by the Merit Systems Protection Board on the record after opportunity for hearing before the Board.

(b) The actions covered by this section are—

(1) a removal;

(2) a suspension;

(3) a reduction in grade;

(4) a reduction in pay; and

(5) a furlough of 30 days or less;

but do not include—

(A) a suspension or removal under section 7532 of this title;

(B) a reduction-in-force action under section 3502 of this title; or

(C) any action initiated under section 1215 of this title.

Appendix B

Uniform Law Commissioners' Revised Model State Administrative Procedure Act (2010)

[ARTICLE] 1
GENERAL PROVISIONS

SECTION 101. SHORT TITLE. This [act] may be cited as the [State] Administrative Procedure Act.

SECTION 102. DEFINITIONS. In this [act]:

(1) "Adjudication" means the process for determining facts or applying law pursuant to which an agency formulates and issues an order. "Adjudicate" has a corresponding meaning.

(2) "Adopt", with respect to a rule, includes to adopt a new rule and to amend or repeal an existing rule. "Adoption" has a corresponding meaning.

(3) "Agency" means a state board, authority, commission, institution, department, division, office, officer, or other state entity that is authorized by law of this state to make rules or to adjudicate. The term does not include the Governor, the [Legislature], or the Judiciary.

(4) "Agency action" means:

(A) the whole or part of an order or rule;

(B) the failure to issue an order or rule; or

(C) an agency's performing or failing to perform a duty, function, or activity or to make a determination required by law.

(5) "Agency head" means the individual in whom, or one or more members of the body of individuals in which, the ultimate legal authority of an agency is vested.

(6) "Agency record" means the agency rulemaking record required by Section 302, the hearing record in adjudication required by Section 406, the hearing record in an emergency adjudication under Section 407, or the record for review compiled under Section 507(b).

(7) "Contested case" means an adjudication in which an opportunity for an evidentiary hearing is required by the federal constitution, a federal statute, or the constitution or a statute of this state.

(8) "Electronic" means relating to technology having electrical, digital, magnetic, wireless, optical, electromagnetic, or similar capabilities.

(9) "Electronic record" means a record created, generated, sent, communicated, received, or stored by electronic means.

(10) "Emergency adjudication" means an adjudication in a contested case when the public health, safety, or welfare requires immediate action.

(11) "Evidentiary hearing" means a hearing for the receipt of evidence on issues on which a decision of the presiding officer may be made in a contested case.

(12) "Final order" means the order issued by the agency head sitting as the presiding officer in a contested case, the order issued following the agency head review of a recommended order, the order issued following the agency head review of an initial order, or the order issued by the presiding officer when the presiding officer has been delegated final decisional authority with no subsequent agency head review.

(13) "Final rule" means a rule adopted, amended, or repealed under Sections 304 through 308, an emergency rule adopted under Section 309, or a direct final rule adopted under Section 310.

(14) "Guidance document" means a record of general applicability developed by an agency which lacks the force of law but states the agency's current approach to, or interpretation of, law, or describes how and when the agency will exercise discretionary functions. The term does not include records described in paragraph (30)(A), (B), (C), or (D).

(15) "Index" means a searchable list in a record of subjects and titles with page numbers, hyperlinks, or other connectors that link each index entry to the text to which it refers.

(16) "Initial order" means an order that is issued by a presiding officer with final decisional authority if the order is subject to discretionary review by the agency.

(17) "Internet website" means a website on the Internet or other appropriate technology or successor technology that permits the public to search a database that archives materials required to be published by the [publisher] under this [act].

(18) "Law" means the federal or state constitution, a federal or state statute, a federal or state judicial decision, a federal or state rule of court, or an executive order that rests on statutory or constitutional authority.

(19) "License" means a permit, certificate, approval, registration, charter, or similar form of permission required by law and issued by an agency.

(20) "Licensing" means the grant, denial, renewal, revocation, suspension, annulment, withdrawal, or amendment of a license.

(21) "Notice" means a record containing information required to be sent to a person by this [act].

(22) "Notify" means to take steps reasonably required to inform a person, regardless of whether the person actually comes to know of the information.

(23) "Order" means an agency decision that determines or declares the rights, duties, privileges, immunities, or other interests of a specific person.

(24) "Party" means the agency taking action, the person against which the action is directed, any other person named as a party, or any person permitted to intervene and that does intervene.

(25) "Person" means an individual, corporation, business trust, statutory trust, estate, trust, partnership, limited liability company, association, joint venture,

public corporation, government or governmental subdivision, agency, or instrumentality, or any other legal or commercial entity.

(26) "Presiding officer" means an individual who presides over the evidentiary hearing in a contested case.

(27) "Proceeding" means any type of formal or informal agency process or procedure commenced or conducted by an agency. The term includes adjudication, rulemaking, and investigation.

(28) "Recommended order" means an order issued by a presiding officer if the officer does not have final decisional authority and the order is subject to review by the agency head.

(29) "Record" means information that is inscribed on a tangible medium or that is stored in an electronic or other medium and is retrievable in perceivable form.

(30) "Rule" means the whole or a part of an agency statement of general applicability that implements, interprets, or prescribes law or policy or the organization, procedure, or practice requirements of an agency and has the force of law. The term includes the amendment or repeal of an existing rule. The term does not include:

(A) a statement that concerns only the internal management of an agency and which does not affect private rights or procedures available to the public;

(B) an intergovernmental or interagency memorandum, directive, or communication that does not affect private rights or procedures available to the public;

(C) an opinion of the Attorney General;

(D) a statement that establishes criteria or guidelines to be used by the staff of an agency in performing audits, investigations, or inspections, settling commercial disputes, negotiating commercial arrangements, or defending, prosecuting, or settling cases, if disclosure of the criteria or guidelines would enable persons violating the law to avoid detection, facilitate disregard of requirements imposed by law, or give an improper advantage to persons that are in an adverse position to the state;

(E) a form developed by an agency to implement or interpret agency law or policy; or

(F) a guidance document.

(31) "Rulemaking" means the process for the adoption of a new rule or the amendment or repeal of an existing rule.

(32) "Sign" means, with present intent to authenticate or adopt a record:

(A) to execute or adopt a tangible symbol; or

(B) to attach to or logically associate with the record an electronic symbol, sound, or process.

(33) "Writing" means a record inscribed on a tangible medium. "Written" has a corresponding meaning.

SECTION 103. APPLICABILITY.

(a) This [act] applies to an agency unless the agency is expressly exempted by a statute of this state.

(b) This [act] applies to all agency proceedings and all proceedings for judicial review or civil enforcement of agency action commenced after [the effective date of this [act]]. This [act] does not apply to an adjudication for which notice was given before that date and rulemaking for which notice was given or a petition was filed before that date.

[ARTICLE] 2

PUBLIC ACCESS TO AGENCY LAW AND POLICY

SECTION 201. PUBLICATION, COMPILATION, INDEXING, AND PUBLIC INSPECTION OF RULEMAKING DOCUMENTS.

(a) The [publisher] shall administer this section and other sections of this [act] that require publication. The [publisher] shall publish the [administrative bulletin] and the [administrative code].

(b) The [publisher] shall publish in [electronic and written] [electronic or written] [electronic] [written] format all rulemaking-related documents listed in Section 202(c). The [publisher] shall prescribe a uniform numbering system, form, and style for proposed rules.

(c) The [publisher] shall maintain the official record of a rulemaking, including the text of the rule and any supporting documents, filed with the [publisher] by an agency. An agency engaged in rulemaking shall maintain the rulemaking record required by Section 302(b) for that rule.

(d) The [publisher] shall create and maintain an Internet website. The [publisher] shall make available on the Internet website the [administrative bulletin], the [administrative code], and any guidance document filed with the [publisher] by an agency.

(e) The [publisher] shall publish the [administrative bulletin] at least once [each month].

(f) The [administrative bulletin] must be provided in written form on request, for which the [publisher] may charge a reasonable fee.

(g) The [administrative bulletin] must contain:

(1) notices of proposed rulemaking prepared so that the text of the proposed rule shows the text of any existing rule proposed to be changed and the change proposed;

(2) newly filed final rules prepared so that the text of a newly filed amended rule shows the text of the existing rule and the change that is made;

(3) any other notice and material required to be published in the [administrative bulletin]; and

(4) an index.

(h) The [administrative code] must be compiled, indexed by subject, and published in a format and medium prescribed by the [publisher]. The rules of an agency must be published and indexed in the [administrative code].

(i) The [publisher] shall make the [administrative bulletin] and the [administrative code] available for public inspection and, for a reasonable charge, copying.

(j) The [publisher], with notification to the agency, may make minor nonsubstantive corrections in spelling, grammar, and format in a proposed or final rule. The [publisher] shall make a record of the corrections.

(k) The [publisher] shall make available on the [publisher's] Internet website, at no charge, all the documents provided by an agency under Section 202(c).

Legislative Note: *Throughout this act the drafting committee has used the term [publisher] to describe the official or agency to which substantive publishing functions are assigned. All states have such an official, but their titles vary. Each state using this act should determine what that agency is, then insert its title in place of [publisher] throughout this act. Each state also has an [administrative bulletin] and an [administrative code]. The bulletin is similar to the Federal Register, and the code is similar to the Code of Federal Regulations. The names of the administrative bulletin and the administrative code vary from state to state. Each state should insert the proper title in place of [administrative bulletin], and [administrative code]. The [publisher] has statutory authority under subsections (f) and (i) to provide written materials for a reasonable charge. In many states, [publishers] have statutory authority under a public records act to adopt regulations setting fees for providing written copies of documents under this section.*

SECTION 202. PUBLICATION; AGENCY DUTIES.

(a) Unless the record is exempt from disclosure under law of this state other than this [act], an agency shall publish on its Internet website and, on request and for a reasonable charge, make available through the regular mail:

(1) each notice of a proposed rule under Section 304;

(2) each rule filed under Section 316;

(3) each summary of regulatory analysis required by Section 305;

(4) each declaratory order issued under Section 204;

(5) the index of declaratory orders prepared under Section 204(g);

(6) each guidance document issued under Section 311;

(7) the index of currently effective guidance documents prepared under Section 311(e);

(8) each final order in a contested case issued under Section 413, 414, or 415; and

(9) the index of final orders in contested cases prepared under Section 418(a).

(b) An agency may provide for electronic distribution to a person that requests electronic distribution of notices related to rulemaking or guidance documents. If a notice is distributed electronically, the agency need not transmit the actual notice but must send all the information contained in the notice.

(c) An agency shall file with the [publisher] in an electronic format acceptable to the [publisher]:

(1) notice of the adoption of a final rule;

(2) a summary of the regulatory analysis required by Section 305 for each proposed rule;

(3) each final rule;

(4) an index of currently effective guidance documents under Section 311(f); and

(5) any other notice or matter that an agency is required to publish under this [act].

Legislative Note: *Agencies have statutory authority under subsection (a) to provide written materials for a reasonable charge. In many states, agencies have statutory authority under a public records act to adopt regulations setting reasonable charges for providing written copies of documents under this section.*

SECTION 203. REQUIRED AGENCY PUBLICATION AND RECORDKEEPING.

An agency shall:

(1) publish a description of its organization, stating the general course and method of its operations and the methods by which the public may obtain information or make submissions or requests;

(2) publish a description of all formal and informal procedures available, including a description of all forms and instructions used by the agency;

(3) publish a description of the process for application for a license, available benefits, or other matters for which an application is appropriate, unless the process is prescribed by law other than this [act];

(4) adopt rules for the conduct of public hearings [if the standard procedural rules adopted under Section 205 do not include provisions for the conduct of public hearings];

(5) maintain the agency's current rulemaking docket required by Section 301(b); and

(6) maintain a separate, official, current, and dated index and compilation of all final rules filed with the [publisher], make the index and compilation available for public inspection and, for a reasonable charge, copying at the principal office of the agency [and online on the [publisher]'s Internet website], update the index and compilation at least [monthly], and file the index and the compilation and all changes to both with the [publisher].

SECTION 204. DECLARATORY ORDER.

(a) A person may petition an agency for a declaratory order that interprets or applies a statute administered by the agency or states whether or in what manner a rule, guidance document, or order issued by the agency applies to the petitioner.

(b) An agency shall adopt rules prescribing the form of a petition under subsection (a) and the procedure for its submission, consideration, and prompt disposition. The provisions of this [act] concerning formal, informal, or other applicable hearing procedure do not apply to an agency proceeding for a declaratory order, except to the extent provided in this [article] or to the extent the agency provides by rule or order.

(c) Not later than 60 days [or at the next regularly scheduled meeting of the agency, whichever is later,] after receipt of a petition under subsection (a), an agency shall issue a declaratory order in response to the petition, decline to issue the order, or schedule the matter for further consideration.

(d) If an agency declines to issue a declaratory order requested under subsection (a), it shall notify promptly the petitioner of its decision. The decision must be in a record and must include a brief statement of the reasons for declining. An agency decision to decline to issue a declaratory order is subject to judicial review for abuse of discretion. An agency failure to act within the applicable time under subsection (c) is subject to judicial action under Section 501(d).

(e) If an agency issues a declaratory order, the order must contain the names of all parties to the proceeding, the facts on which it is based, and the reasons for the agency's conclusion. If an agency is authorized not to disclose certain information in its records to protect confidentiality, the agency may redact confidential information in the order. The order has the same status and binding effect as an order issued in an adjudication and is subject to judicial review under Section 501.

(f) An agency shall publish each currently effective declaratory order.

(g) An agency shall maintain an index of all of its currently effective declaratory orders, file the index [annually] with the [publisher], make the index readily available for public inspection, and make available for public inspection and, for a reasonable charge, copying the full text of all declaratory orders to the extent inspection is permitted by law of this state other than this [act].

SECTION 205. STANDARD PROCEDURAL RULES.

(a) The [Governor] [Attorney General] [designated state agency] shall adopt standard procedural rules for use by agencies. The standard rules must provide for the procedural functions and duties of as many agencies as is practicable.

(b) Except as otherwise provided in subsection (c), an agency shall use the standard procedural rules adopted under subsection (a).

(c) An agency may adopt a rule of procedure that differs from the standard procedural rules adopted under subsection (a) if it explains with particularity the reasons for the variation.

[ARTICLE] 3

RULEMAKING; PROCEDURAL REQUIREMENTS AND EFFECTIVENESS OF RULES

SECTION 301. RULEMAKING DOCKET.

(a) In this section, "rule" does not include an emergency rule adopted under Section 309 or a direct final rule adopted under Section 310.

(b) An agency shall maintain a rulemaking docket for all pending rulemaking proceedings that is indexed.

(c) The agency shall maintain a rulemaking docket under subsection (b) that must for each pending rulemaking proceeding state or contain:

(1) the subject matter of the proposed rule;

(2) notices related to the proposed rule;

(3) how comments on the proposed rule may be submitted;

(4) the time within which comments may be submitted;

(5) where comments may be inspected;

(6) requests for a public hearing;

(7) appropriate information concerning a public hearing, if any; and

(8) the timetable for action on the proposed rule.

(d) On request, the agency shall provide, for a reasonable charge, a written rulemaking docket maintained under subsection (c).

SECTION 302. RULEMAKING RECORD.

(a) An agency shall maintain a rulemaking record for each proposed rule. Unless the record and any materials incorporated by reference are privileged or exempt from disclosure under law of this state other than this [act], the record and materials must be readily available for public inspection in the principal office of the agency and available for public display on the Internet website maintained by the [publisher]. If an agency determines that any part of the rulemaking record cannot be displayed practicably or is inappropriate for public display on the Internet website, the agency shall describe the part and note that the part is not displayed.

(b) A rulemaking record must contain:

(1) a copy of all publications in the [administrative bulletin] relating to the rule and the proceeding on which the rule is based;

(2) a copy of any part of the rulemaking docket containing entries relating to the rule and the proceeding on which the rule is based;

(3) a copy and, if prepared, an index, of all factual material, studies, and reports agency personnel relied on or consulted in formulating the proposed or final rule;

(4) any official transcript of oral presentations made in the proceeding on which the rule is based or, if not transcribed, any audio recording or verbatim transcript of the presentations, and any memorandum summarizing the contents of the presentations prepared by the agency official who presided over the hearing;

(5) a copy of all comments received by the agency under Section 306(a) in response to the notice of proposed rulemaking;

(6) a copy of the rule and explanatory statement filed with the [publisher]; and

(7) any petition for agency action on the rule, except a petition governed by Section 204.

SECTION 303. ADVANCE NOTICE OF PROPOSED RULEMAKING; NEGOTIATED RULEMAKING.

(a) An agency may gather information relevant to the subject matter of a potential rulemaking proceeding and may solicit comments and recommendations from the public by publishing an advance notice of proposed rulemaking in the [administrative bulletin] and indicating where, when, and how persons may comment.

(b) An agency may engage in negotiated rulemaking by appointing a committee to comment or make recommendations on the subject matter of a proposed rulemaking under active consideration within the agency. In making appointments to the committee, the agency shall make reasonable efforts to establish a balance in representation among members of the public known to have an interest in the subject matter of the proposed rulemaking. At least annually, the agency shall publish in the [administrative bulletin] a list of all committees with their membership. Notice of a meeting of the committee must be published in the [administrative bulletin] at least [15 days] before the meeting. A meeting of the committee is open to the public.

(c) A committee appointed under subsection (b), in consultation with one or more agency representatives, shall attempt to reach a consensus on the terms or substance of a proposed rule. The committee shall present the consensus recommendation, if any, to the agency.

The agency shall consider whether to use it as the basis for a proposed rule under Section 304, but the agency is not required to propose or adopt the recommendation.

(d) This section does not prohibit an agency from obtaining information and opinions from members of the public on the subject of a proposed rule by any other method or procedure.

SECTION 304. NOTICE OF PROPOSED RULE.

(a) At least [30] days before the adoption of a rule, an agency shall file notice of the proposed rulemaking with the [publisher] for publication in the [administrative bulletin]. The notice must include:

(1) a short explanation of the purpose of the proposed rule;

(2) a citation or reference to the specific legal authority authorizing the proposed rule;

(3) the text of the proposed rule;

(4) how a copy of the full text of any regulatory analysis of the proposed rule may be obtained;

(5) where, when, and how a person may comment on the proposed rule and request a hearing;

(6) a citation to and summary of each scientific or statistical study, report, or analysis that served as a basis for the proposed rule, together with an indication of how the full text of the study, report, or analysis may be obtained; and

(7) any summary of a regulatory analysis prepared under Section 305(d).

(b) Not later than three days after publication of the notice of the proposed rulemaking in the [administrative bulletin], the agency shall mail the notice or send it electronically to each person that has made a timely request to the agency for a mailed or electronic copy of the notice. An agency may charge a reasonable fee for a mailed copy requested by a person.

SECTION 305. REGULATORY ANALYSIS.

(a) An agency shall prepare a regulatory analysis for a proposed rule that has an estimated economic impact of more than $[ ]. The analysis must be completed before notice of the proposed rulemaking is published. The summary of the analysis prepared under subsection (d) must be published with the notice of proposed rulemaking.

(b) If a proposed rule has an economic impact of less than $[ ], the agency shall prepare a statement of minimal estimated economic impact.

(c) A regulatory analysis must contain:

(1) an analysis of the benefits and costs of a reasonable range of regulatory alternatives reflecting the scope of discretion provided by the statute authorizing the proposed rule; and

(2) a determination whether:

(A) the benefits of the proposed rule justify the costs of the proposed rule; and

(B) the proposed rule will achieve the objectives of the authorizing statute in a more cost-effective manner, or with greater net benefits, than other regulatory alternatives.

(d) An agency preparing a regulatory analysis under this section shall prepare a concise summary of the analysis.

(e) An agency preparing a regulatory analysis under this section shall submit the analysis to the [appropriate state agency].

(f) If an agency has made a good faith effort to comply with this section, a rule is not invalid solely because the regulatory analysis for the proposed rule is insufficient or inaccurate.

Legislative Note: *State laws vary as to which state agency or body an agency preparing the regulatory analysis should submit the analysis. In some states, it the department of finance or revenue; in others it is a regulatory review agency or regulatory review committee. The appropriate state agency in each state should be inserted into the brackets.*

SECTION 306. PUBLIC PARTICIPATION.

(a) An agency proposing a rule shall specify a public comment period of at least [30] days after publication of notice of the proposed rulemaking during which a person may submit information and comment on the proposed rule. The information or comment may be submitted in an electronic or written format. The agency shall consider all information and comment on a proposed rule which is submitted pursuant to this subsection within the comment period.

(b) An agency may consider any other information it receives concerning a proposed rule during the rulemaking. Any information considered by the agency must be incorporated into the record under Section 302(b)(3). The information need not be submitted in an electronic or written format. Nothing in this section prohibits an agency from discussing with any person at any time the subject of a proposed rule.

(c) Unless a hearing is required by law of this state other than this [act], an agency is not required to hold a hearing on a proposed rule but may do so. A hearing must be open to the public, recorded, and held at least [10] days before the end of the public comment period.

(d) A hearing on a proposed rule may not be held earlier than [20] days after notice of its location, date, and time is published in the [administrative bulletin].

(e) An agency representative shall preside over a hearing on a proposed rule. If the representative is not the agency head, the representative shall prepare a memorandum summarizing the contents of the presentations made at the hearing for consideration by the agency head.

Legislative Note: *State laws vary on the length of public comment periods and on whether a rulemaking hearing is required. The bracketed number of days in subsections (a) and (d) should be interpreted to require that if a rulemaking hearing is held, it will be held before the end of the public comment period. In that case, the minimum time period would be 50 days rather than 30 days.*

SECTION 307. TIME LIMIT ON ADOPTION OF RULE.

(a) An agency may not adopt a rule until the public comment period has ended.

(b) Not later than [two years] after a notice of proposed rulemaking is published, the agency shall adopt the rule or terminate the rulemaking by publication of a notice of termination in the [administrative bulletin]. [The agency may extend the time for adopting the rule once for an additional [two years] by publishing a statement of good cause for the extension but must provide for additional public participation as provided in Section 306 before adopting the rule.]

(c) An agency shall file an adopted rule with the [publisher] not later than [ ] days after the adoption of the rule.

(d) A rule is void unless it is adopted and filed within the time limits in this section.

SECTION 308. VARIANCE BETWEEN PROPOSED AND FINAL RULE. An agency may not adopt a rule that differs from the rule proposed in the notice of proposed rulemaking unless the final rule is a logical outgrowth of the rule proposed in the notice.

SECTION 309. EMERGENCY RULE. If an agency finds that an imminent peril to the public health, safety, or welfare or the loss of federal funding for an agency program requires the immediate adoption of an emergency rule and publishes in a record its reasons for that finding, the agency, without prior notice or hearing or on any abbreviated notice and hearing that it finds practicable, may adopt an emergency rule without complying with Sections 304 through 307. The emergency rule may be effective for not longer than [180] days [renewable once for no more than [180] days]. The adoption of an emergency rule does not preclude the adoption of a rule under Sections 304 through 307. The agency shall file with the [publisher] a rule adopted under this section as soon as practicable given the nature of the emergency, publish the rule on its Internet website, and notify persons that have requested notice of rules related to that subject matter. This section does not prohibit the adoption of a new emergency rule if, at the end of the effective period of the original emergency rule, the agency finds that the imminent peril to the public health, safety, or welfare or the loss of federal funding for an agency program still exists.

SECTION 310. DIRECT FINAL RULE. If an agency proposes to adopt a rule which is expected to be noncontroversial, it may use direct final rulemaking authorized by this section and must comply with Section 304(a)(1), (2), (3), and (5), Section 304(b), and Section 313(1). The proposed rule must be published in the [administrative bulletin] with a statement by the agency that it does not expect the adoption of the rule to be controversial and that the proposed rule takes effect 30 days after publication if no objection is received. If no objection is received, the rule becomes final under Section 317(e). If an objection to the rule is received from any person not later than [ ] days after publication of the notice of the proposed rule, the proposed rule does not become final. The agency shall file notice of the objection with the [publisher] for publication in the [administrative bulletin], and may proceed with rulemaking under Sections 304 through 307.

SECTION 311. GUIDANCE DOCUMENT.

(a) An agency may issue a guidance document without following the procedures set forth in Sections 304 through 307.

(b) An agency that proposes to rely on a guidance document to the detriment of a person in any administrative proceeding shall afford the person an adequate opportunity to contest the legality or wisdom of a position taken in the document. The agency may not use a guidance document to foreclose consideration of issues raised in the document.

(c) A guidance document may contain binding instructions to agency staff members if, at an appropriate stage in the administrative process, the agency's procedures provide an affected person an adequate opportunity to contest the legality or wisdom of a position taken in the document.

(d) If an agency proposes to act in an adjudication at variance with a position expressed in a guidance document, it shall provide a reasonable explanation for the variance. If an affected person in an adjudication may have relied reasonably on the agency's position, the explanation must include a reasonable justification for the agency's conclusion that the need for the variance outweighs the affected person's reliance interest.

(e) An agency shall maintain an index of all of its effective guidance documents, publish the index on its Internet website, make all guidance documents available to the public, and file the index [annually] with the [publisher]. The agency may not rely on a guidance document, or cite it as precedent against any party to a proceeding, unless the guidance document is published on its Internet website.

(f) A guidance document may be considered by a presiding officer or final decision maker in an agency adjudication, but it does not bind the presiding officer or the final decision maker in the exercise of discretion.

(g) A person may petition an agency under Section 318 to adopt a rule in place of a guidance document.

(h) A person may petition an agency to revise or repeal a guidance document. Not later than [60] days after submission of the petition, the agency shall:

  (1) revise or repeal the guidance document;

  (2) initiate a proceeding to consider a revision or repeal; or

  (3) deny the petition in a record and state its reasons for the denial.

SECTION 312. REQUIRED INFORMATION FOR RULE. A final rule filed by an agency with the [publisher] under Section 316 must contain the text of the rule and be accompanied by a record that contains:

(1) the date the final rule was adopted by the agency;

(2) a reference to the specific statutory or other authority authorizing the rule;

(3) any finding required by law as a prerequisite to adoption or effectiveness of the rule;

(4) the effective date of the rule; and

(5) the concise explanatory statement required by Section 313.

SECTION 313. CONCISE EXPLANATORY STATEMENT. When an agency adopts a final rule, the agency shall issue a concise explanatory statement that contains:

(1) the agency's reasons for adopting the rule, including the agency's reasons for not accepting substantial arguments made in testimony and comments;

(2) subject to Section 308, the reasons for any change between the text of the proposed rule contained in the notice of proposed rulemaking and the text of the final rule; and

(3) the summary of any regulatory analysis prepared under Section 305(d).

SECTION 314. INCORPORATION BY REFERENCE. A rule may incorporate by reference all or any part of a code, standard, or rule that has been adopted by an agency of the United States, this state, or another state, or by a nationally recognized organization or association, if:

(1) repeating verbatim the text of the code, standard, or rule in the rule would be unduly cumbersome, expensive, or otherwise inexpedient;

(2) the reference in the rule fully identifies the incorporated code, standard, or rule by citation, place of inspection, and date[, and states whether the rule includes any later amendments or editions of the incorporated code, standard, or rule];

(3) the code, standard, or rule is readily available to the public in written or electronic form at no charge or for a reasonable charge;

(4) the rule states where copies of the code, standard, or rule are available from the agency adopting the rule for a reasonable charge, if any, or where copies are available from the agency of the United States, this state, another state, or the organization or association originally issuing the code, standard, or rule; and

(5) the agency maintains a copy of the code, standard, or rule readily available for public inspection at the principal office of the agency.

SECTION 315. COMPLIANCE. An action taken under this [article] is not valid unless taken in substantial compliance with this [article].

SECTION 316. FILING OF RULE. An agency shall file in written and electronic form with the [publisher] each final rule. In filing a final rule, an agency shall use a standard form prescribed by the [publisher]. The agency shall file the rule not later than [ ] days after adoption. The [publisher] shall maintain a permanent register of all filed rules and concise explanatory statements for the rules. The [publisher] shall affix to each final rule a certification of the time and date of filing. The [publisher] shall publish the notice of each final rule in the [administrative bulletin].

SECTION 317. EFFECTIVE DATE OF RULE.

(a) Except as otherwise provided in this section, [unless disapproved by the [rules review committee][,] [or] [withdrawn by the agency under Section 703,] a rule becomes effective [30] days after publication of the rule [in the administrative bulletin] [on the [publisher's] Internet website].

(b) A rule may become effective on a date later than that established by subsection (a) if that date is specified in the rule or required by law other than this [act].

(c) A rule becomes effective immediately on its filing with the [publisher] or on any subsequent date earlier than that established by subsection (a) if it is required to be implemented by a certain date by law other than this [act].

(d) An emergency rule under Section 309 becomes effective on adoption by the agency.

(e) A direct final rule under Section 310 to which no objection is made becomes effective [30] days after publication, unless the agency specifies a later effective date.

SECTION 318. PETITION FOR ADOPTION OF RULE. Any person may petition an agency to adopt a rule. An agency shall prescribe by rule the form of the petition and the procedure for its submission, consideration, and disposition. Not later than [60] days after submission of a petition, the agency shall:

(1) deny the petition in a record and state its reasons for the denial; or

(2) initiate rulemaking.

[ARTICLE] 4
ADJUDICATION IN CONTESTED CASE

SECTION 401. CONTESTED CASE. This [article] applies to an adjudication made by an agency in a contested case.

SECTION 402. PRESIDING OFFICER.

(a) A presiding officer must be an administrative law judge assigned in accordance with Section 604(2), the individual who is the agency head, a member of a multimember body of individuals that is the agency head, or, unless prohibited by law of this state other than this [act], an individual designated by the agency head.

(b) An individual who has served as investigator, prosecutor, or advocate at any stage in a contested case or who is subject to the authority, direction, or discretion of an individual who has served as investigator, prosecutor, or advocate at any stage in a contested case may not serve as the presiding officer in the same case. An agency head that has participated in a determination of probable cause or other preliminary determination in an adjudication may serve as the presiding officer or final decision maker in the adjudication unless a party demonstrates grounds for disqualification under subsection (c).

(c) A presiding officer or agency head acting as a final decision maker is subject to disqualification for bias, prejudice, financial interest, ex parte communications as provided in Section 408, or any other factor that would cause a reasonable person to question the impartiality of the presiding officer or agency head. A presiding officer or agency head, after making a reasonable inquiry, shall disclose to the parties any known facts related to grounds for disqualification which are material to the impartiality of the presiding officer or agency head in the proceeding.

(d) A party may petition for the disqualification of a presiding officer or agency head promptly after notice that the person will preside or, if later, promptly on discovering facts establishing a ground for disqualification. The petition must state with particularity the ground on which it is claimed that a fair and impartial hearing cannot be accorded or the applicable rule or canon of practice or ethics that requires disqualification. The petition may be denied if the party fails to exercise due diligence in requesting disqualification after discovering a ground for disqualification.

(e) A presiding officer or agency head whose disqualification is requested shall decide whether to grant the petition and state in a record facts and reasons for the decision. The decision to deny disqualification is not subject to interlocutory judicial review.

(f) If a substitute presiding officer is required, the substitute must be appointed [as required by law, or if no law governs,] by:

(1) the Governor, if the original presiding officer is an elected official; or

(2) the appointing authority, if the original presiding officer is an appointed official.

(g) If participation of the agency head is necessary to enable the agency to take action, the agency head may continue to participate notwithstanding a ground for disqualification or exclusion.

Legislative Note: *The first alternative under subsection (a) would be applicable in states that have adopted central panel hearing offices but would not apply to states that do not have central panel hearing offices. Article 6 governs central panel hearing offices under this act. If a state does not have a central panel hearing agency, presiding officers would include administrative law judges who are employees of the agency with final decision authority. States vary in the terms used to describe agency employees who are presiding officers. The term includes administrative judges, hearing officers, and hearing examiners. Administrative law judges can be employees of the central panel hearing office or of the agency with final decision authority.*

SECTION 403. CONTESTED CASE PROCEDURE.

(a) This section does not apply to an emergency adjudication under Section 407.

(b) An agency shall give notice of the agency decision to a person when the agency takes an action as to which the person has a right to a contested case hearing. The notice must be in writing, set forth the agency action, inform the person of the right, procedure, and time limit to file a contested-case petition, and provide a copy of the agency procedures governing the contested case.

(c) In a contested case, the presiding officer shall give all parties a timely opportunity to file pleadings, motions, and objections. The presiding officer may give all parties the opportunity to file briefs, proposed findings of fact and conclusions of law, and proposed recommended, initial, or final orders. The presiding officer, with the consent of all parties, may refer the parties in a contested case to mediation or other dispute resolution procedure.

(d) In a contested case, to the extent necessary for full disclosure of all relevant facts and issues, the presiding officer shall give all parties the opportunity to respond, present evidence and argument, conduct cross-examination, and submit rebuttal evidence.

(e) Except as otherwise provided by law other than this [act], the presiding officer may conduct all or part of an evidentiary hearing or a prehearing conference by telephone, television, video conference, or other electronic means. The hearing may be conducted by telephone or other method by which the witnesses may not be seen only if all parties consent [or the presiding officer finds that this method will not impair reliable determination of the credibility of testimony]. Each party must be given an opportunity to attend, hear, and be heard at the proceeding as it occurs. This subsection does not prevent an agency from providing by rule for electronic hearings.

(f) Except as otherwise provided in subsection (g), a hearing in a contested case must be open to the public. A hearing conducted by telephone, television, video conference, or other electronic means is open to the public if members of the public have an opportunity to attend the hearing at the place where the presiding officer is located or to hear or see the proceeding as it occurs.

(g) A presiding officer may close a hearing to the public on a ground on which a court of this state may close a judicial proceeding to the public or pursuant to law of this state other than this [act].

(h) Unless prohibited by law of this state other than this [act], a party, at the party's expense, may be represented by counsel or may be advised, accompanied, or represented by another individual.

(i) A presiding officer shall ensure that a hearing record is created that complies with Section 406.

(j) The decision in a contested case must be based on the hearing record and contain a statement of the factual and legal bases of the decision. If a finding of fact is set forth in language of a statute of this state other than this [act], it must be accompanied by a concise and explicit statement of the underlying facts supporting the finding of fact. The decision must be prepared electronically and, on request, made available in writing.

(k) Subject to Section 205, the rules by which an agency conducts a contested case may include provisions more protective than the requirements of this section of the rights of parties other than the agency.

(l) Unless prohibited by law of this state other than this [act], an agency may dispose of a contested case without a hearing by stipulation, agreed settlement, consent order, or default.

SECTION 404. EVIDENCE IN CONTESTED CASE. The following rules apply in a contested case:

(1) Except as otherwise provided in paragraph (2), all relevant evidence is admissible, including hearsay evidence, if it is of a type commonly relied on by a reasonably prudent individual in the conduct of the affairs of the individual.

(2) The presiding officer may exclude evidence in the absence of an objection if the evidence is irrelevant, immaterial, unduly repetitious, or excludable on constitutional or statutory grounds or on the basis of an evidentiary privilege recognized in the courts of this state. The presiding officer shall exclude the evidence if objection is made at the time the evidence is offered.

(3) If the presiding officer excludes evidence with or without objection, the offering party may make an offer of proof before further evidence is presented or at a later time determined by the presiding officer.

(4) Evidence may be received in a record if doing so will expedite the hearing without substantial prejudice to a party. Documentary evidence may be received in the form of a copy if the original is not readily available or by incorporation by reference. On request, parties must be given an opportunity to compare the copy with the original.

(5) Testimony must be made under oath or affirmation.

(6) Evidence must be made part of the hearing record of the case. Information or evidence may not be considered in determining the case unless it is part of the hearing record. If the hearing record contains information that is confidential, the presiding officer may conduct a closed hearing to discuss the information, issue necessary protective orders, and seal all or part of the hearing record.

(7) The presiding officer may take official notice of all facts of which judicial notice may be taken and of scientific, technical, or other facts within the specialized knowledge of the agency. A party must be notified at the earliest practicable time of the facts proposed to be noticed and their source, including any staff memoranda or data. The party must be afforded an opportunity to contest any officially noticed fact before the decision becomes final.

(8) The experience, technical competence, and specialized knowledge of the presiding officer or members of an agency head that is a multi-member body that is hearing the case may be used in evaluating the evidence in the hearing record.

SECTION 405. NOTICE IN CONTESTED CASE.

(a) Except as otherwise provided in an emergency adjudication under Section 407, an agency shall give notice in a contested case that complies with this section.

(b) In a contested case initiated by a person other than an agency, not later than [five] days after filing, the agency shall give notice to all parties that the case has been commenced. The notice must contain:

(1) the official file or other reference number, the name of the proceeding, and a general description of the subject matter;

(2) contact information for communicating with the agency, including the agency mailing address[, electronic mail address,] [facsimile number,] and telephone number;

(3) a statement of the date, time, place, and nature of the prehearing conference or hearing, if any;

(4) the name, official title, mailing address, [electronic mail address,] [facsimile number,] and telephone number of any attorney or employee who has been designated to represent the agency; and

(5) the names and last known addresses of all parties and other persons to which notice is being given by the agency.

(c) In a contested case initiated by an agency, the agency shall give notice to the party against which the action is brought. The notice must contain:

(1) a statement that a case that may result in an order has been commenced against the party;

(2) a short and plain statement of the matters asserted, including the issues involved;

(3) a statement of the legal authority under which the hearing will be held citing the statutes and any rules involved;

(4) the official file or other reference number and the name of the proceeding;

(5) the name, official title, mailing address, [and] [electronic mail address,] [and] [facsimile number,] [and] [telephone number] of the presiding officer and the name, official title, mailing address, [electronic mail address,] [facsimile number,] and telephone number of the agency's representative;

(6) a statement that a party that fails to attend or participate in any subsequent proceeding in the case may be held in default;

(7) a statement that the party served may request a hearing and includes instructions in plain English about how to request a hearing; and

(8) the names and last known addresses of all parties and other persons to which notice is being given by the agency.

(d) When a hearing or a prehearing conference is scheduled, the agency shall give parties notice that contains the information required by subsection (c) at least [30] days before the hearing or prehearing conference.

(e) A notice under this section may include other matters that the presiding officer considers desirable to expedite the proceedings.

SECTION 406. HEARING RECORD IN CONTESTED CASE.

(a) An agency shall maintain the hearing record created under Section 403(i) in each contested case.

(b) The hearing record must contain:

(1) a recording of each proceeding;

(2) notice of each proceeding;

(3) any prehearing order;

(4) any motion, pleading, brief, petition, request, and intermediate ruling;

(5) evidence admitted;

(6) a statement of any matter officially noticed;

(7) any proffer of proof and objection and ruling thereon;

(8) any proposed finding, requested order, and exception;

(9) any transcript of the proceeding prepared at the direction of the agency;

(10) any recommended order, final order, or order on reconsideration; and

(11) any matter placed on the record after an ex parte communication under Section 408(f).

(c) The hearing record constitutes the exclusive basis for agency action in a contested case.

SECTION 407. EMERGENCY ADJUDICATION PROCEDURE.

(a) Unless prohibited by law of this state other than this [act], an agency may conduct an emergency adjudication in a contested case under this section.

(b) An agency may take action and issue an order under this section only to deal with an imminent peril to the public health, safety, or welfare.

(c) Before issuing an order under this section, an agency, if practicable, shall give notice and an opportunity to be heard to the person to which the agency action is directed. The notice of the hearing and the hearing may be oral or written and may be by telephone, facsimile, or other electronic means.

(d) An order issued under this section must briefly explain the factual and legal reasons for using emergency adjudication procedures.

(e) To the extent practicable, an agency shall give notice to the person to which the agency action is directed that an order has been issued. The order is effective when signed by the agency head or the designee of the agency head.

(f) After issuing an order pursuant to this section, an agency shall proceed as soon as practicable to provide notice and an opportunity for a hearing following the procedure under Section 403 to determine the issues underlying the order.

(g) An order issued under this section may be effective for not longer than [180] days or until the effective date of any order issued under subsection (f), whichever is shorter.

SECTION 408. EX PARTE COMMUNICATIONS.

(a) In this section, "final decision maker" means the person with the power to issue a final order in a contested case.

(b) Except as otherwise provided in subsection (c), (d), (e), or (h), while a contested case is pending, the presiding officer and the final decision maker may not make to or receive from any person any communication concerning the case without notice and opportunity for all parties to participate in the communication. For the purpose of this section, a contested case is pending from the issuance of the agency's pleading or from an application for an agency decision, whichever is earlier.

(c) A presiding officer or final decision maker may communicate about a pending contested case with any person if the communication is required for the disposition of ex parte matters authorized by statute or concerns an uncontested procedural issue.

(d) A presiding officer or final decision maker may communicate about a pending contested case with an individual authorized by law to provide legal advice to the presiding officer or final decision maker and may communicate on ministerial matters with an individual who serves on the [administrative] [personal] staff of the presiding officer or final decision maker if the individual providing legal advice or ministerial information has not served as investigator, prosecutor, or advocate at any stage of the case, and if the communication does not augment, diminish, or modify the evidence in the record.

(e) An agency head that is the presiding officer or final decision maker in a pending contested case may communicate about that case with an employee or representative of the agency if:

(1) the employee or representative:

(A) has not served as investigator, prosecutor, or advocate at any stage of the case;

(B) has not otherwise had a communication with any person about the case other than a communication a presiding officer or final decision maker is permitted to make or receive under subsection (c) or (d) or a communication permitted by paragraph (2); and

(2) the communication does not augment, diminish, or modify the evidence in the agency hearing record and is:

(A) an explanation of the technical or scientific basis of, or technical or scientific terms in, the evidence in the agency hearing record;

(B) an explanation of the precedent, policies, or procedures of the agency; or

(C) any other communication that does not address the quality or sufficiency of, or the weight that should be given to, evidence in the agency hearing record or the credibility of witnesses.

(f) If a presiding officer or final decision maker makes or receives a communication in violation of this section, the presiding officer or final decision maker:

(1) if the communication is in a record, shall make the record of the communication a part of the hearing record and prepare and make part of the hearing record a memorandum that contains the response of the presiding officer or final decision maker to the communication and the identity of the person that communicated; or

(2) if the communication is oral, shall prepare a memorandum that contains the substance of the verbal communication, the response of the presiding officer or final decision maker to the communication, and the identity of the person that communicated.

(g) If a communication prohibited by this section is made, the presiding officer or final decision maker shall notify all parties of the prohibited communication and permit parties to respond in a record not later than 15 days after the notice is given. For good cause, the presiding officer or final decision maker may permit additional testimony in response to the prohibited communication.

(h) If a presiding officer is a member of a multi-member body of individuals that is the agency head, the presiding officer may communicate with the other members of the body when sitting as the presiding officer and final decision maker. Otherwise, while a contested case is pending, no communication, direct or indirect, regarding any issue in the case may be made between the presiding officer and the final decision maker. Notwithstanding any provision of [state open meetings law], a communication permitted by this subsection is not a meeting.

(i) If necessary to eliminate the effect of a communication received in violation of this section, a presiding officer or final decision maker may be disqualified under Section 402(d) and (e), the parts of the record pertaining to the communication may be sealed by protective order, or other appropriate relief may be granted, including an adverse ruling on the merits of the case or dismissal of the application.

SECTION 409. INTERVENTION.

(a) A presiding officer shall grant a timely petition for intervention in a contested case, with notice to all parties, if:

(1) the petitioner has a statutory right under law of this state other than this [act] to initiate or to intervene in the case; or

(2) the petitioner has an interest that may be adversely affected by the outcome of the case and that interest is not adequately represented by existing parties.

(b) A presiding officer may grant a timely petition for intervention in a contested case, with notice to all parties, if the petitioner has a permissive statutory right to intervene under law of this state other than this [act] or if the petitioner's claim or defense is based on the same transaction or occurrence as the case.

(c) A presiding officer may impose conditions at any time on an intervener's participation in the contested case.

(d) A presiding officer may permit intervention provisionally and, at any time later in the contested case or at the end of the case, may revoke the provisional intervention.

(e) On request by the petitioners or a party or by action of the presiding officer, the presiding officer may hold a hearing on the intervention petition.

(f) A presiding officer shall promptly give notice of an order granting, denying, or revoking intervention to the petitioner for intervention and to the parties. The notice must allow parties a reasonable time to prepare for the hearing on the merits.

SECTION 410. SUBPOENAS.

(a) On a request in a record by a party in a contested case, the presiding officer or any other officer to whom the power to issue a subpoena is delegated pursuant to law, on a showing of general relevance and reasonable scope of the evidence sought for use at the hearing, shall issue a subpoena for the attendance of a witness and the production of books, records, and other evidence.

(b) Unless otherwise provided by law or agency rule, a subpoena issued under subsection (a) shall be served and, on application to the court by a party or the agency, enforced in the manner provided by law for the service and enforcement of a subpoena in a civil action.

(c) Witness fees shall be paid by the party requesting a subpoena in the manner provided by law for witness fees in a civil action.

SECTION 411. DISCOVERY.

(a) In this section, "statement" includes a record of a person's written statement signed by the person and a record that summarizes an oral statement made by the person.

(b) Except in an emergency hearing under Section 407, a party, on written notice to another party at least [30] days before an evidentiary hearing, unless otherwise provided by agency rule under subsection (g), may:

(1) obtain the names and addresses of witnesses the other party will present at the hearing to the extent known to the other party; and

(2) inspect and copy any of the following material in the possession, custody, or control of the other party:

(A) statements of parties and witnesses proposed to be called by the other party;

(B) all records, including reports of mental, physical, and blood examinations, and other evidence the other party proposes to offer;

(C) investigative reports made by or on behalf of the agency or other party pertaining to the subject matter of the adjudication;

(D) statements of expert witnesses proposed to be called by the other party;

(E) any exculpatory material in the possession of the agency; and

(F) other materials for good cause.

(c) Parties to a contested case have a duty to supplement responses provided under subsection (b) to include information thereafter acquired, to the extent that the information will be relied on in the hearing.

(d) On petition, the presiding officer may issue a protective order for any material for which discovery is sought under this section which is exempt, privileged, or otherwise made confidential or protected from disclosure by law of this state other than this [act] and material the disclosure of which would result in annoyance, embarrassment, oppression, or undue burden or expense to any person.

(e) On petition, the presiding officer shall issue an order compelling discovery for refusal to comply with a discovery request unless good cause exists for refusal. Failure to comply with the order may be enforced according to the rules of civil procedure.

(f) On petition and for good cause, the presiding officer shall issue an order authorizing discovery in accordance with the rules of civil procedure.

(g) An agency may provide by rule that some or all discovery procedures under this section do not apply to a specified program or category of cases if it finds that:

(1) the availability of discovery would unduly complicate or interfere with the hearing process in the program or cases, because of the volume of the applicable caseload and the need for expedition and informality in that process; and

(2) alternative procedures for the sharing of relevant information are sufficient to ensure the fundamental fairness of the proceedings.

SECTION 412. DEFAULT.

(a) Unless otherwise provided by law of this state other than this [act], if a party without good cause fails to attend or participate in a prehearing conference or hearing in a contested case, the presiding officer may issue a default order.

(b) If a default order is issued, the presiding officer may conduct any further proceedings necessary to complete the adjudication without the defaulting party and shall determine all issues in the adjudication, including those affecting the defaulting party.

(c) A recommended, initial, or final order issued against a defaulting party may be based on the defaulting party's admissions or other evidence that may be used without notice to the defaulting party. If the burden of proof is on the defaulting party to establish that the party is entitled to the agency action sought, the presiding officer may issue a recommended, initial, or final order without taking evidence.

(d) Not later than [15] days after notice to a party subject to a default order that a recommended, initial, or final order has been rendered against the party, the party may petition the presiding officer to vacate the recommended, initial, or final order. If good cause is shown for the party's failure to appear, the presiding officer shall vacate the decision and, after proper service of notice, conduct another evidentiary hearing. If good cause is not shown for the party's failure to appear, the presiding officer shall deny the motion to vacate.

SECTION 413. ORDERS: RECOMMENDED, INITIAL, OR FINAL.

(a) If the presiding officer is the agency head, the presiding officer shall issue a final order.

(b) Except as otherwise provided by law of this state other than this [act], if the presiding officer is not the agency head and has not been delegated final decisional authority, the presiding officer shall issue a recommended order. If the presiding officer is not the agency head and has been delegated final decisional authority, the presiding officer shall issue an initial order that becomes a final order [30] days after issuance, unless reviewed by the agency head on its own initiative or on petition of a party.

(c) A recommended, initial, or final order must be served in a record on each party and the agency head not later than [90] days after the hearing ends, the record closes, or memoranda, briefs, or proposed findings are submitted, whichever is latest. The presiding officer may extend the time by stipulation, waiver, or for good cause.

(d) A recommended, initial, or final order must separately state findings of fact and conclusions of law on all material issues of fact, law, or discretion, the remedy prescribed, and, if applicable, the action taken on a petition for a stay. The presiding officer may permit a party to submit proposed findings of fact and conclusions of law. The order must state the available procedures and time limits for seeking reconsideration or other administrative relief and must state the time limits for seeking judicial review of the agency order. A recommended or initial order must state any circumstances under which the order, without further notice, may become a final order.

(e) Findings of fact must be based exclusively on the evidence and matters officially noticed in the hearing record in the contested case.

Alternative A

(f) Hearsay evidence may be used to supplement or explain other evidence, but on timely objection, is not sufficient by itself to support a finding of fact unless it would be admissible over objection in a civil action.

Alternative B

(f) Hearsay evidence is sufficient to support a finding of fact if it constitutes reliable, probative, and substantial evidence.

End of Alternatives

(g) An order is issued under this section when it is signed by the agency head, presiding officer, or an individual authorized by law of this state other than this [act] to sign the order.

(h) A final order is effective [30] days after all parties are notified of the order unless reconsideration is granted under Section 416 or a stay is granted under Section 417.

SECTION 414. AGENCY REVIEW OF INITIAL ORDER.

(a) An agency head may review an initial order on its own initiative.

(b) A party may petition an agency head to review an initial order. On petition by a party, the agency head may review an initial order.

(c) A petition for review of an initial order must be filed with the agency head or with any person designated for this purpose by agency rule not later than [15] days after notice to the parties of the order. If the agency head decides to review an initial order on its own initiative, the agency head shall give notice in a record to the parties that it intends to review the order. The notice must be given not later than [15] days after the parties are notified of the order. If a petition for review is not filed or the agency head does not elect to review the initial order within the prescribed time limit, the initial order becomes a final order.

(d) The period in subsection (c) for a party to file a petition or for the agency head to notify the parties of its intention to review an initial order is tolled by the submission of a timely petition under Section 416 for reconsideration of the order. A new [15]-day period begins on disposition of the petition for reconsideration. If an order is subject both to a timely petition for reconsideration and a petition for review by the agency head, the petition for reconsideration must be disposed of first, unless the agency head determines that action on the petition for reconsideration has been unreasonably delayed.

(e) When reviewing an initial order, the agency head shall exercise the decision-making power that the agency head would have had if the agency head had conducted the hearing that produced the order, except to the extent that the issues subject to review are limited by law of this state other than this [act] or by order of the agency head on notice to the parties. In reviewing findings of fact in an initial order, the agency head shall consider the presiding officer's opportunity to observe the witnesses and to determine the credibility of witnesses. The agency head shall consider the hearing record or parts of the record designated by the parties.

(f) If an agency head reviews an initial order, the agency head shall issue a final order disposing of the proceeding not later than 120 days after the decision to review the initial order or remand the matter for further proceedings with instructions to the presiding officer who issued the initial order. On remanding a matter, the agency head may order such temporary relief as is authorized and appropriate.

(g) A final order or an order remanding the matter for further proceedings must identify any difference between the order and the initial order and must state the facts of record that support any difference in findings of fact, the law that supports any difference in legal conclusions, and the policy reasons that support any difference in the exercise of discretion. Findings of fact must be based exclusively on the evidence and matters officially noticed in the hearing record in the contested case. A final order under this section must include, or incorporate by express reference to the initial order, the matters required by Section 413(d). The agency head shall deliver the order to the presiding officer and notify the parties of the order.

SECTION 415. AGENCY REVIEW OF RECOMMENDED ORDER.

(a) An agency head shall review a recommended order pursuant to this section.

(b) When reviewing a recommended order, the agency head shall exercise the decision-making power that the agency head would have had if the agency head had conducted the hearing that produced the order, except to the extent that the issues subject to review are limited by law of this state other than this [act] or by order of the agency head on notice to the parties. In reviewing findings of fact in a recommended order, the agency head shall consider the presiding officer's opportunity to observe the witnesses and to determine the credibility of witnesses. The agency head shall consider the hearing record or parts that are designated by the parties.

(c) An agency head may render a final order disposing of the proceeding or remand the matter for further proceedings with instructions to the presiding officer who rendered the recommended order. On remanding a matter, the agency head may order such temporary relief as is authorized and appropriate.

(d) A final order or an order remanding the matter for further proceedings must identify any difference between the order and the recommended order and must state the facts of record that support any difference in findings of fact, the law that supports any difference in legal conclusions, and the policy reasons that support any difference in the exercise of discretion. Findings of fact must be based exclusively on the evidence and matters officially noticed in the hearing record in the contested case. A final order under this section must include, or incorporate by express reference to the recommended order, the matters required by Section 413(d). The agency head shall deliver the order to the presiding officer and notify the parties of the order.

SECTION 416. RECONSIDERATION.

(a) A party, not later than [15] days after notice to the parties that a final order has been issued, may file a petition for reconsideration that states the specific grounds on which relief is requested. The place of filing and other procedures, if any, must be specified by agency rule and must be stated in the final order.

(b) If a petition for reconsideration is timely filed, and if the petitioner has complied with the agency's procedural rules for reconsideration, if any, the time for filing a petition for judicial review does not begin until the agency disposes of the petition for reconsideration as provided in Section 503(d).

(c) Not later than [20] days after a petition is filed under subsection (a), the decision maker shall issue a written order denying the petition, granting the petition and dissolving or modifying the final order, or granting the petition and setting the matter for further proceedings. If the decision maker fails to respond to the petition not later than [30] days after filing, or a longer period agreed to by the parties, the petition is deemed denied. The petition may be granted only if the decision maker states findings of facts, conclusions of law, and the reasons for granting the petition.

SECTION 417. STAY. Except as otherwise provided by law of this state other than this [act], a party, not later than [seven] days after the parties are notified of the order, may request the agency to stay a final order pending judicial review. The agency may grant the request for a stay pending judicial review if the agency finds that justice requires. The agency may grant or deny the request for stay of the order before, on, or after the effective date of the order.

SECTION 418. AVAILABILITY OF ORDERS; INDEX.

(a) Except as otherwise provided in subsections (b) and (c), an agency shall create an index of all final orders in contested cases and make the index and all final orders available for public inspection and copying, at cost, in its principal offices.

(b) Except as otherwise provided in subsection (c), final orders that are exempt, privileged, or otherwise made confidential or protected from disclosure by [the public records law of this state] are not public records and may not be indexed. The final order may be excluded from an index and disclosed only by order of the presiding officer with a written statement of reasons attached to the order.

(c) If the presiding officer determines it is possible to redact a final order that is exempt, privileged, or otherwise made confidential or protected from disclosure by law of this state other than this [act] so that it complies with the requirements of that law, the redacted order may be placed in the index and published.

(d) An agency may not rely on a final order adverse to a party other than the agency as precedent in future adjudications unless the agency designates the order as a precedent, and the order has been published, placed in an index, and made available for public inspection.

SECTION 419. LICENSES.

(a) If a licensee has made timely and sufficient application for the renewal of a license or a new license for any activity of a continuing nature, the existing license does not expire until the agency takes final action on the application and, if the application is denied or the terms of the new license are limited, until the last day for seeking review of the agency order or a later date fixed by the reviewing court.

(b) A revocation, suspension, annulment, or withdrawal of a license is not lawful unless, before the institution of agency proceedings, the agency notifies the licensee of facts or conduct that warrants the intended action, and the licensee is given an opportunity to show compliance with all lawful requirements for the retention of the license. If the agency finds that imminent peril to public health, safety, or welfare requires emergency action and incorporates a finding to that effect in its order, summary suspension of a license may be ordered pending proceedings for revocation or other action. These proceedings must be promptly instituted and concluded.

[ARTICLE] 5

JUDICIAL REVIEW

SECTION 501. RIGHT TO JUDICIAL REVIEW; FINAL AGENCY ACTION REVIEWABLE.

(a) In this [article], "final agency action" means an act of an agency which imposes an obligation, grants or denies a right, confers a benefit, or determines a legal relationship as a result of an administrative proceeding. The term does not include agency action that is a failure to act.

(b) Except to the extent that a statute of this state other than this [act] limits or precludes judicial review, a person that meets the requirements of this [article] is entitled to judicial review of a final agency action.

(c) A person entitled to judicial review under subsection (b) of a final agency action is entitled to judicial review of an agency action that is not final if postponement of judicial review would result in an inadequate remedy or irreparable harm that outweighs the public benefit derived from postponing judicial review.

(d) A court may compel an agency to take action that is unlawfully withheld or unreasonably delayed.

SECTION 502. RELATION TO OTHER JUDICIAL REVIEW LAW AND RULES.

(a) Except as otherwise provided by law of this state other than this [act], judicial review of final agency action may be taken only as provided by rules of [appellate] [civil] procedure [of this state]. The court may grant any type of legal and equitable remedies that are appropriate.

(b) This [article] does not limit use of or the scope of judicial review available under other means of review, redress, relief, or trial de novo provided by law of this state other than this [act]. Except to the extent that prior, adequate, and exclusive opportunity for judicial review is available under this [article] or under law of this state other than this [act], final agency action is subject to judicial review in civil or criminal proceedings for judicial enforcement.

SECTION 503. TIME TO SEEK JUDICIAL REVIEW OF AGENCY ACTION; LIMITATIONS.

(a) Judicial review of a rule on the ground of noncompliance with the procedural requirements of this [act] must be commenced not later than [two] years after the effective date of the rule. Judicial review of a rule or guidance document on other grounds may be sought at any time.

(b) Judicial review of an order or other final agency action other than a rule or guidance document must be commenced not later than [30] days after the date the parties are notified of the order or other agency action.

(c) The time for seeking judicial review under this section is tolled during any time a party pursues an administrative remedy before the agency which must be exhausted as a condition of judicial review.

(d) A party may not petition for judicial review while seeking reconsideration under Section 416. During the time a petition for reconsideration is pending before an agency, the time for seeking judicial review in subsection (b) is tolled.

SECTION 504. STAYS PENDING APPEAL. A petition for judicial review does not automatically stay an agency decision. A challenging party may request the reviewing court for a stay on the same basis as stays are granted under the rules of [appellate] [civil] procedure [of this state], and the reviewing court may grant a stay regardless of whether the challenging party first sought a stay from the agency.

SECTION 505. STANDING. The following persons have standing to obtain judicial review of a final agency action:

(1) a person aggrieved or adversely affected by the agency action; and

(2) a person that has standing under law of this state other than this [act].

SECTION 506. EXHAUSTION OF ADMINISTRATIVE REMEDIES.

(a) Subject to subsection (d) or law of this state other than this [act] which provides that a person need not exhaust administrative remedies, a person may file a petition for judicial review under this [act] only after exhausting all administrative remedies available within the agency the action of which is being challenged and within any other agency authorized to exercise administrative review.

(b) Filing a petition for reconsideration or a stay of proceedings is not a prerequisite for seeking judicial review.

(c) A petitioner for judicial review of a rule need not have participated in the rule-making proceeding on which the rule is based or have filed a petition to adopt a rule under Section 318.

(d) The court may relieve a petitioner of the requirement to exhaust any or all administrative remedies to the extent the administrative remedies are inadequate or the requirement would result in irreparable harm.

SECTION 507. AGENCY RECORD ON JUDICIAL REVIEW; EXCEPTIONS.

(a) If an agency was required by [Article] 3 or 4, or by law of this state other than this [act], to maintain an agency record during the proceeding that gave rise to the action under review, the court review is confined to that record and to matters arising from that record.

(b) In any case to which subsection (a) does not apply, the record for review consists of the unprivileged materials that agency decision makers directly or indirectly considered, or which were submitted for consideration by any person, in connection with the action under review, including information that is adverse to the agency's position. If the agency action was ministerial or was taken on the basis of a minimal or no administrative record, the court may receive evidence relating to the agency's basis for taking the action.

(c) The court may supervise an agency's compilation of the agency record. If a challenging party makes a substantial showing of need, the court may allow discovery or other evidentiary proceedings and consider evidence outside the agency record to:

(1) ensure that the agency record is complete as required by this [act] and other applicable law;

(2) adjudicate allegations of procedural error not disclosed by the record; or

(3) prevent manifest injustice.

SECTION 508. SCOPE OF REVIEW.

(a) Except as provided by law of this state other than this [act], in judicial review of an agency action, the following rules apply:

(1) The burden of demonstrating the invalidity of agency action is on the party asserting invalidity.

(2) The court shall make a ruling on each material issue on which the court's decision is based.

(3) The court may grant relief only if it determines that a person seeking judicial review has been prejudiced by one or more of the following:

(A) the agency erroneously interpreted the law;

(B) the agency committed an error of procedure;

(C) the agency action is arbitrary, capricious, an abuse of discretion, or otherwise not in accordance with law;

(D) an agency determination of fact in a contested case is not supported by substantial evidence in the record as a whole; or

(E) to the extent that the facts are subject to a trial de novo by the reviewing court, the action was unwarranted by the facts.

(b) In making a determination under this section, the court shall review the agency record or the parts designated by the parties and shall apply the rule of harmless error.

[ARTICLE] 6

OFFICE OF ADMINISTRATIVE HEARINGS

SECTION 601. CREATION OF OFFICE OF ADMINISTRATIVE HEARINGS.

(a) In this [article], "office" means the [Office of Administrative Hearings].

(b) The [Office of Administrative Hearings] is created in the executive branch of state government [within the [ ] agency].

SECTION 602. CHIEF ADMINISTRATIVE LAW JUDGE; APPOINTMENT; QUALIFICATIONS; TERM; REMOVAL.

(a) The office is headed by a chief administrative law judge appointed by [the Governor] [with the advice and consent of the Senate].

(b) A chief administrative law judge serves a term of [five] years and until a successor is appointed and qualifies for office, is entitled to the salary provided by law, and may be reappointed.

(c) At the time of appointment, the chief administrative law judge must have been admitted to the practice of law in this state for at least five years and have substantial experience in administrative law.

(d) A chief administrative law judge:

(1) must take the oath of office required by law before beginning the duties of the office;

(2) shall devote full time to the duties of the office and may not engage in the private practice of law; and

(3) is subject to the code of conduct for administrative law judges adopted pursuant to Section 604(7).

(e) A chief administrative law judge may be removed from office only for cause and only after notice and an opportunity for a contested case hearing.

SECTION 603. ADMININSTRATIVE LAW JUDGES; APPOINTMENT; QUALIFICATIONS; DISCIPLINE.

(a) The chief administrative law judge shall appoint administrative law judges pursuant to the [state merit system].

(b) In addition to meeting other requirements of the [state merit system], to be eligible for appointment as an administrative law judge, an individual must have been admitted to the practice of law in this state for at least [three] years.

(c) An administrative law judge:

(1) shall take the oath of office required by law before beginning duties as an administrative law judge;

(2) is subject to the code of conduct for administrative law judges adopted pursuant to Section 604(7);

(3) is entitled to the compensation provided by law; and

(4) may not perform any act inconsistent with the duties and responsibilities of an administrative law judge.

(d) An administrative law judge:

(1) is subject to the administrative supervision of the chief administrative law judge;

(2) may be disciplined pursuant to the [state merit system law];

(3) except as otherwise provided in paragraph (4), may be removed from office only for cause and only after notice and an opportunity for a contested case hearing; and

(4) is subject to a reduction in force in accordance with the [state merit system law].

(e) On [the effective date of this [act]], administrative law judges employed by agencies to which this [article] applies are transferred to the office and, regardless of the minimum qualifications imposed by this [article], are administrative law judges in the office.

SECTION 604.CHIEF ADMINISTRATIVE LAW JUDGE; POWERS; DUTIES.

The chief administrative law judge has the powers and duties specified in this section. The chief administrative law judge:

(1) shall supervise and manage the office;

(2) shall assign administrative law judges in a case referred to the office;

(3) shall assure the decisional independence of each administrative law judge;

(4) shall establish and implement standards for equipment, supplies, and technology for administrative law judges;

(5) shall provide and coordinate continuing education programs and services for administrative law judges and advise them of changes in the law concerning their duties;

(6) shall adopt rules pursuant to this [act] to implement [Article] 4 and this [article];

(7) shall adopt a code of conduct for administrative law judges;

(8) shall monitor the quality of adjudications conducted by administrative law judges;

(9) shall discipline [pursuant to the state merit system law] administrative law judges who do not meet appropriate standards of conduct and competence;

(10) may accept grants and gifts for the benefit of the office; and

(11) may contract with other public agencies for services provided by the office.

SECTION 605. COOPERATION OF AGENCIES.

(a) Every agency shall cooperate with the chief administrative law judge in the discharge of the duties of the office.

(b) Subject to Section 402, an agency may not reject a particular administrative law judge for a particular hearing.

SECTION 606. ADMINISTRATIVE LAW JUDGES; POWERS; DUTIES; DECISION MAKING AUTHORITY.

(a) In a contested case, unless the hearing is conducted by a presiding officer assigned under Section 402(a) other than an administrative law judge, an administrative law judge must be assigned to be the presiding officer. If the administrative law judge is delegated final decisional authority, the administrative law judge shall issue a final order. If the administrative law judge is not delegated final decisional authority, the administrative law judge shall issue to the agency head a recommended order in the contested case.

(b) Except as otherwise provided by law of this state other than this [act], if a contested case is referred to the office by an agency, the agency may not take further action with respect to the proceeding, except as a party, until a recommended, initial, or final order is issued. [This subsection does not prevent an appropriate interlocutory review by the agency or an appropriate termination or modification of the proceeding by the agency when authorized by law of this state other than this [act].]

(c) In addition to acting as the presiding officer in contested cases under this [act], subject to the direction of the chief administrative law judge, an administrative law judge may perform duties authorized by law of this state other than this [act].

SECTION 607. AGENCIES EXCLUDED. [This [article] does not apply to the following agencies: [list agencies exempted]].

[ARTICLE] 7
RULES REVIEW

SECTION 701. [LEGISLATIVE RULES REVIEW COMMITTEE]. There is created a standing committee of the [Legislature] designated the [rules review committee].

Legislative Note: *States that have existing rules review committees can incorporate the provisions of Sections 701 and 702, using the existing number of members of their current rules review committee. Because state practice varies as to how these committees are structured, and how many members of the legislative body serve on this committee, as well as how they are selected, the act does not specify the details of the legislative review committee selection process. Details of the committee staff and adoption of rules to govern the rules review committee staff and organization are governed by law other than this act including the existing law in each state.*

SECTION 702. REVIEW BY [RULES REVIEW COMMITTEE].

(a) An agency shall file a copy of an adopted rule with the [rules review committee] at the same time it is filed with the [publisher]. An agency is not required to file an emergency rule adopted under Section 309 with the [rules review committee].

(b) The [rules review committee] may examine each rule in effect and each newly adopted rule to determine whether the:

(1) rule is a valid exercise of delegated legislative authority;

(2) statutory authority for the rule has expired or been repealed;

(3) rule is necessary to accomplish the apparent or expressed intent of the specific statute that the rule implements;

(4) rule is a reasonable implementation of the law as it applies to any affected class of persons; and

(5) agency complied with the regulatory analysis requirements of Section 305 and the analysis properly reflects the effect of the rule.

(c) The [rules review committee] may request from an agency information necessary to exercise its powers under subsection (b). The [rules review committee] shall consult with standing committees of the [Legislature] with subject matter jurisdiction over the subjects of the rule under examination.

(d) The [rules review committee] shall:

(1) maintain oversight over agency rulemaking; and

(2) exercise other duties assigned to it under this [article].

SECTION 703. [RULES REVIEW COMMITTEE] PROCEDURE AND POWERS.

(a) Not later than [30] days after receiving a copy of an adopted rule from an agency under Section 702, the [rules review committee] may:

(1) approve the adopted rule;

(2) disapprove the rule and propose an amendment to the adopted rule; or

(3) disapprove the adopted rule.

(b) If the [rules review committee] approves an adopted rule or does not disapprove and propose an amendment under subsection (a)(2) or disapprove under subsection (a)(3), the adopted rule becomes effective on the date specified in Section 317.

(c) If the [rules review committee] proposes an amendment to an adopted rule under subsection (a)(2), the agency may make the amendment and resubmit the rule, as amended, to the [rules review committee]. The amended rule must be one that the agency could have adopted on the basis of the record in the rulemaking proceeding and the legal authority granted to the agency. The agency shall provide an explanation for the amended rule as provided in Section 313. An agency is not required to hold a hearing on an amendment made under this subsection. If the agency makes the amendment, it shall give notice to the [publisher] for publication of the rule, as amended, in the [administrative bulletin]. The notice must include the text of the rule as amended. If the [rules review committee] does not disapprove the rule, as amended, or propose a further amendment, the rule becomes effective on the date specified under Section 317.

(d) If the [rules review committee] disapproves the adoption of a rule under subsection (a)(3), the adopted rule becomes effective on adjournment of the next regular session of the [Legislature] unless before adjournment the [Legislature] [adopts a [joint] [concurrent] resolution] [enacts a bill] sustaining the action of the committee.

(e) Before the effective date specified in Section 317, the agency may withdraw the adoption of a rule by giving notice of the withdrawal to the [rules review committee] and to the [publisher] for publication in the [administrative bulletin]. A withdrawal under this subsection terminates the rulemaking with respect to the adoption but does not prevent the agency from initiating new rulemaking for the same or substantially similar adoption.]

Legislative Note: *The 30-day time period in subsection (a) is the same as the 30-day period in Section 317. State constitutions vary as to whether or not a joint resolution is a valid way of disapproving an agency rule. In some states, the Legislature must use the bill process with approval by the Governor. In other states, the joint resolution process is proper. States should use the alternative that complies with their state constitution. State constitutions vary on the federal constitutional issue decided by the U.S. Supreme Court in I.N.S. v. Chadha (1983) 462 U.S. 919, 103 S. Ct. 2764. The U.S. Supreme Court held that the one house legislative veto provided for in Section 244(c)(2) violated the Article I requirement that legislative action requires passage of a law by both Houses of Congress (bicameralism) and presentation to the President for signing or veto (presentation requirement). Those state constitutions that require presentation to the Governor need an additional step, presentation of the joint resolution to the Governor for approval or disapproval. With state constitutions that do not require presentation of a resolution to the Governor, the rules review process can be completed with legislative adoption of a joint resolution.*

[ARTICLE] 8
MISCELLANEOUS PROVISIONS

SECTION 801. RELATION TO ELECTRONIC SIGNATURES IN GLOBAL AND NATIONAL COMMERCE ACT. This [act] modifies, limits, and supersedes the Electronic Signatures in Global and National Commerce Act, 15 U.S.C. Section 7001 et seq., but does not modify, limit, or supersede Section 101(c) of that act, 15 U.S.C. Section 7001(c), or authorize electronic delivery of any of the notices described in Section 103(b) of that act, 15 U.S.C. Section 7003(b).

SECTION 802. REPEALS. [The State Administrative Procedure Act] is repealed.

SECTION 803. EFFECTIVE DATE. This [act] takes effect [ ]....

Table of Cases

Index

[References are to sections.]